Awakening China

D1300172

AWAKENING CHINA

Politics, Culture, and Class in
the Nationalist Revolution

John Fitzgerald

Stanford University Press

Stanford, California

Stanford University Press
Stanford, California
©1996 by the Board of Trustees of the
Leland Stanford Junior University
Printed in the United States of America

CIP data appear at the end of the book

To Antonia and Daniel

PREFACE

Now even the children are old enough to ask when the book will be finished. I would like to think that Siobhan, Therese, Genevieve, and Bernard have been partly responsible for the delay, but in fact they have been endlessly patient sources of inspiration, not of enervation. The reason lies elsewhere.

My interest in the idea of national "awakening" goes back beyond graduate research on the Chinese Nationalist Propaganda Bureau, completed in 1983, to the days of the Vietnam War, when undergraduate inklings of personal and cultural liberation seemed to resonate with the national liberation struggle in Vietnam and with resounding calls for a New Society echoing over the short-wave transmissions of The Voice of China. Since then I have been puzzled by the subterranean link between the personal awakenings many of us seemed to undergo in those heady days (not always prompted by revolution) and the rhetoric of national liberation and social reconstruction coming out of China and Vietnam. This book is an attempt to trace that link. Parts of three chapters—Chapters 5, 6, and 7—have their roots in the dissertation. The rest of the book is an expanded footnote on the lived and recorded history of the idea of personal and national awakening, and it has taken a long time to expand.

For a start, I had no idea how many fine scholars in China and abroad had gone over this ground before me, and I have learned enough from them in the interim to satisfy much of my early curiosity. In place of adding to this body of scholarship I have settled for an exercise in translation. Personal awakenings and national awakening came as a pair in China, too. The aim of the book is to reproduce the language and debates of a select group of people in China who first made the connection between the personal and the national earlier this century, partly to highlight the ways in which some connections came to seem more plausible than others, but chiefly to show how a "politics of awakening" came to be institutionalized in a mass revolutionary movement. Basically, the book traces the history of a single metaphor from its roots in imperial Chinese

and European Enlightenment thought to its flowering in China's modern state-
and nation-building.

In China's own histories, the term "awakening" appears as if its meaning and significance had little need of clarification. Women, youth, particular
social classes, and the nation are all said to awaken, alone or in tandem, and to
discover in their awakening a way out of the morass of feudal superstition and
imperialist oppression. Perhaps this is because contemporary historians encounter this idea whenever they consult the speeches and writings of China's
nationalists themselves. In Western scholarship, the word appears more often in
titles than in texts.[1] Books such as *The Awakening of Modern China*, *The Dragon
Awakes*, or *China Wakes Up* occupy half a shelf in any reasonable library. These
titles also pay homage to historical precedent, although in this case a European
one. "Behold the Chinese Empire," Napoleon is reported to have warned. "Let
it sleep, for when this dragon wakes the world will tremble."[2] Certainly the
words people use to describe themselves and their predicament at any point in
history are worth taking seriously, as are the ways others see them. The absence
of the word "awakening" from any index or concordance to China's nationalist
movements is an omission worth correcting here. But we can, I think, go further. The idea of China's awakening is so central to the cultural and political reconstruction of the nation this century that it offers a useful point of entry into
a reflective history of modern China and for an inquiry into the dialogue that
took place, at every stage, between Chinese reformers and foreign observers.[3]

The design of this book warrants caution on a number of counts. Fiction and
fashion, architecture and autobiography, take their places alongside politics and
history, and the reader is asked to move about among writers, artists, philosophers, ethnographers, revolutionaries, and soldiers who have little in common
apart from their appearance in the book itself. Rumor is sometimes taken as
seriously as truth, novels are consulted as frequently as documents, and dreams
are given a prominence normally reserved for facts in the writing of history.

The book is, all the same, a work of history, although not as far removed
from fiction as I had imagined when starting out. This has costs as well as
benefits. Authors of fiction are at liberty to hover over their texts and comment
from an Olympian height on the foibles of their characters without worrying
unduly if they fail to profit from their experience. For the historian this can be
risky: life may not always be stranger than fiction, but it is usually a little more
complicated. Certainly no work of history can tell the whole story, and I do
not presume to do so here. And when historians are outsiders (as in this case),
they run the additional risk of presumption in commenting at all on their cast.
Fortunately, imaginative fiction writers and essayists of the period reflected
more often and more deeply on the world about them than did their political
contemporaries, certainly a good deal more than a foreign observer writing in

the late twentieth century could possibly hope to do. So I have had recourse to fiction not just to identify and illustrate my themes, but to offer contemporary reflections on them as well.

In fiction, too, authors are free to create characters suited to their purpose. Historians are duty-bound to select their cast from life. What are the grounds for selection in this case? I have chosen my voices to a purpose, to show that the evolution of thinking about nation, state, and class in the Nationalist Revolution proceeded along lines established in more general debate about the identity of China in ethics, ethnography, literature, journalism, and history. These voices mark the boundaries of the greater discursive field in which political theorists and activists formulated their ideas, and in which others made sense of their demands to "wake up" and save China.

Historians, needless to say, must show as well not only that the story has some basis in fact, but also that at no point does it depart from the facts as these can be reconstructed from the record. Fortunate are the historians who stumble upon an exemplary individual or group whose experiences faithfully trace the pattern of the story they hope to tell and whose diaries, correspondence, and publications enable them to reconstruct reactions to events in ways that help readers make sense of the story. How far I deviate from the record or whether I make sense at all is for others to judge. But I do count myself very fortunate to have profited from the tireless work of librarians, archivists, and historians in the People's Republic of China, Taiwan, the United States, Australia, Europe, and Japan who have not only preserved many of the historical records of the period but in many cases have collated and published them as well. To them I owe an enormous debt of gratitude. Where such sources have been translated into English, I refer to the translations, to aid the English reader.

The two most valuable library collections consulted in the course of this research are located in Canberra. Y. S. Chan at the Australian National University Library and Sidney Wong at the National Library of Australia helped to uncover all the relevant materials they had in store and to acquire a good deal more that they did not. Lily Hu and Bick-har Yeung at the University of Melbourne Library, Eugene Wu at the Harvard-Yenching Library, and Chester Wang at the library of the University of Wisconsin-Madison offered similar assistance. I particularly appreciate Eugene Wu extending his hand across the Pacific to pass on valuable materials long after my return to Australia. Chen Dingyan (Leslie Chen) kindly made available an invaluable collection of materials about his father, Chen Jiongming. To all I express my heartfelt appreciation.

In China, Zhang Xianwen, Cai Shaoqing, and Yang Zhenya went out of their way to secure obscure sources for me and to point me in useful directions. It came as no surprise to learn that the History Department of Nanjing University is now rated the best in the country. Also in Nanjing, the Second Historical

Archives generously opened its files. To the directors and staff I offer my sincere thanks. Above all, this project could not have been completed without the assistance of the administrators and staff of the Historical Archives Commission of the Kuomintang in Taipei. I especially wish to thank Lü Fangshang and Li Yunhan, whose help and scholarship has added immeasurably to my understanding of the Nationalist Revolution.

Professor Wang Gungwu supervised my doctoral dissertation. In completing the present book I have frequently heard distant echoes of his advice and have tried to follow it a little more closely. I have also learned much over the years from staff and fellow students at the Australian National University, whose help has been as bountiful as their friendship, especially John Fincher, Beverley Hooper, Pauline Keating, Brian Martin, Warren Sun, Ken Wells, and Tim Wright. My education started all over again when I began teaching at the University of Melbourne and, later, at La Trobe University, where colleagues and students suggested that I look beyond China and rediscover America, Europe, and the Pacific. Space prevents my listing all who pointed the way, but I must expressly thank Judith Brett, Ian Britain, Dipesh Chakrabarty, Greg Dening, Rhys Isaacs, Jack Gregory, Robin Jeffrey, Janet McCalman, Angus McIntyre, Stuart Macintyre, Anne MacLaren, Donna Merwick, Paul Rule, and Sanjay Seth. Gabrielle Finnane highlighted the importance of theory.

Maurice Meisner disguised his dismay when I showed up with a family of four young children at his doorstep on a fellowship from Australia. The quiet encouragement he gave in his graduate seminars is deeply appreciated. Nor shall we forget the kindness extended to us in Madison by Jackie and Jim Meuhl, Lynda and Jim Ray, and Dick and Nancy Shultz. Research in the United States was also aided by generous hosts at the universities of Illinois-Urbana, Columbia, Princeton, Harvard, St. John's, Indiana-Bloomington, and Duke. I particularly value the help of Prasenjit Duara, Arthur Waldron, Brantly Womack, Philip Kuhn, Martin Wilbur, and Lloyd Eastman. My debt to Arif Dirlik is clear in the notes, where his citations rival those of Sun Yatsen. But the notes give little indication of debts to other pioneering scholars of modern China to whom I have deferred at every stage but who receive little mention in the finished work. The longest missing footnotes belong to Joseph Levenson, Harold Isaacs, and C. Martin Wilbur. In addition, Stuart Schram offered helpful criticisms of key parts of the dissertation incorporated here. Readers and editors at Stanford University Press have saved me from making egregious errors, for which I wish to thank Muriel Bell. The title of the book pays homage to Lynn Hunt, whose *Politics, Culture, and Class in the French Revolution* first alerted me to the riches that lie at the crossroads where politics and culture meet.

Antonia Finnane has been my guide for so long now that I can no longer tell whether the words I write are hers or my own. I am not sure, either, whether I should thank Antonia for producing her parents or Patricia and Peter Finnane for producing Antonia. Either way I have much to be thankful for. My mother and father are no longer around to accept my love and thanks, but if faith makes angels, they are sure to be busy playing guardians to their grandchildren.

Research toward this book has been assisted by funding from the Fulbright Foundation, the Australian Research Council, the Victorian Vice-Chancellors' Committee, the Department of Pacific and Asian History at the Australian National University, the Faculty of Humanities at the University of Melbourne, and the School of Social Sciences at La Trobe University.

Some of the ideas canvassed here were first raised in my earlier publications: "The Misconceived Revolution: State and Society in China's Nationalist Revolution, 1923–1926," *The Journal of Asian Studies* 49, no.2 (May 1990): 323–43, reprinted with the permission of the Association for Asian Studies, Inc.; "The Invention of the Modern Chinese Self," from *Modernization of the Chinese Past*, edited by Mabel Lee and A. D. Syrokomla-Stefanowska, 1993, reprinted with permission of Wild Peony Press; and "The Stars on China's Flag: Appropriating the Universe for the Nation," from *The State in Transition: Reimagining Political Space*, edited by Joseph A. Camilleri, Anthony P. Jarvis, and Albert J. Paolini, copyright © 1995 by Lynne Reinner Publishers, Inc., used with permission of the publisher.

J.F.

CONTENTS

(Six pages of illustrations follow p. 260)

Awakening China

—

A remarkable circumstance, not easily to be accounted for, occurred in opening a cask of Birmingham hardware. Everyone knows the necessity of excluding the sea-air as much as possible from highly-polished articles of iron and steel, and accordingly all such articles intended to be sent abroad are packed with the greatest care. The casks, or cases, are made as tight as possible, and covered with pitched canvas. Such was the cask in question. Yet, when the head was taken off, and a few of the packages removed, an enormous large scorpion was found in the midst of the cask, nearly in a torpid state, but it quickly recovered on exposure to the warm air.

> John Barrow, Beijing, on unpacking gifts brought from London by Lord Macartney for the Qianlong Emperor in 1793; Barrow 1806: 114

INTRODUCTION

Awakening the Beast

> The first way to revive our nationalism is to awaken our four hundred
> million people. . . . We must first make our four hundred millions know
> that their death hour is at hand, then the beast will turn and fight.
>
> Sun Yatsen, 1924[1]

> It sometimes happens that the masses objectively need some reform
> but are not yet subjectively awakened to it and willing or determined
> to bring it into effect. In that case, we should wait patiently and intro-
> duce the reform only when, through our work, the great majority of
> the masses have become awakened to the need and are willing and
> determined to start it.
>
> Mao Zedong, 1944[2]

Shortly after news of Sun Yatsen's death reached Guangzhou on 12 March 1925,
the Nationalist administration of the city embarked on construction of a memorial in his honor. A brilliant young American-trained architect, Lü Yanzhi, won
a competition for the design of the building, and the artist Gao Qifeng earned
a commission to paint three scrolls for the entrance hall: one of an eagle, one
of a horse, and one of a lion. Architect and artist both put their hearts into their
work. While busy designing the Guangzhou memorial, Lü Yanzhi was awarded
a commission for the Sun Yatsen Tomb in Nanjing, and he devoted himself so
completely to the two projects that he died of exhaustion. Lü passed away in
1929, at the age of 35 years, before either building was completed. The artist
Gao Qifeng also "worked furiously" on his commission, his biographer tells
us, and "soon became a household name in Guangdong."

Lü's Memorial Hall and Gao's paintings are fair samples of the energy,
the brilliance, and the personal sacrifices of the Nationalist Revolution of the
1920s. Their sense of urgency was widely shared, and Lü's sacrifice was repeated many times over by peasants and workers, revolutionary cadre and
soldiers as well the artists and writers of the Nationalist movement. The
Sun Yatsen Memorial Hall in Guangzhou stands as a monument not only to
Sun Yatsen but also to those who shared his vision that the Chinese nation

was awakening from a deep, deep slumber.[3] "Since our subjugation by the Manchus," Sun counseled the year before his death, "our four hundred millions have been asleep, our ancient morality has been asleep, our ancient learning has been asleep." [4] Sun's Nationalist Revolution marked the awakening of modern China.

Still, there is something sleepy about the Memorial Hall today. Its well-tended grounds delight the eye of overseas Chinese visitors and compatriates from Taiwan, but the dank and dusty hall no longer hosts ceremonies to commemorate the awakening of modern China. There was a time not long ago when the hall was still in frequent use. During the Cultural Revolution, "Nationalist traitors" and "capitalist roaders" were led into the auditorium by Red Guards before being paraded before angry crowds and taken off to internment or execution. Red Guard factions armed with pikes and bottles occasionally broke into the hall to disrupt meetings of other factions. Many were injured in the ensuing scuffles.[5] Certainly Sun Yatsen never intended such an outcome from his revolution. There is nevertheless a connection between the culture and the politics of the Nationalist Revolution that stormed Guangzhou and Guangdong in the 1920s and the later mass politics of the People's Republic. This thread of continuity can be traced in the history of the politics of mass "awakening" from the turn of the century to the Maoist era. If the hall appears sedate and solemn today, it is not because Sun Yatsen is dead, but because Mao Zedong has joined him.

The Memorial Hall in Guangzhou is an appealing blend of traditional aesthetics and modern engineering brought together in such a way that they seem both distinctively Chinese and yet unabashedly modern. Here the architect Lü Yanzhi excelled. Gao Qifeng's three paintings, too, count among the finest examples of a new and yet self-consciously Chinese style of painting that came of age in the Nationalist Revolution. Of Gao's three paintings in the Memorial Hall, it was his lion that earned him the greatest fame. Lions were still a good deal rarer than eagles or horses in the repertoire of the Chinese painter, but they were rising to prominence in the revolutionary iconography of Nationalist China. They came into their own over the year following Sun Yatsen's death. The only known painting of a lion by another noted painter, Chen Shuren, dates from the same year, when Chen worked closely with the Nationalists and divided his time and talents between art and propaganda. Another prominent Nationalist party member and women's movement activist, He Xiangning, turned her hand to lion paintings in the wake of Sun's death as well.[6] Yet even after roaring lions came into vogue in 1925 and 1926, Gao Qifeng's lion stood out from the pride.

What set Gao's lion apart was not its subject but the way in which the lion was presented. Gao's was a lion observing, not a lion observed. It peered out at the artist and at the mourners in the Sun Yatsen Memorial Hall, alert, and on the point of pouncing. Its bold and confident gaze announced that this was a lion awakened. Sun and China were both represented in the design and decorations of the Guangzhou Memorial Hall as he would have wished them to be remembered: as modern, as distinctly Chinese, and as "awakened."

Awakening is a nebulous concept, poised somewhere between the transitive and the intransitive, and referring to nothing in particular apart from a transition in a state of consciousness from sleep to wakefulness. In Chinese, the word usually takes the intransitive forms *jue*, *juewu*, *xing*, or *juexing*, meaning "to undergo an awakening." In mass politics it also takes the transitive form of awakening others (*huanqi*, *huanxing*), or may take the imperative mood, "Wake up!" (*xing! juewu!*). In the general context of the nationalist movement, the term was understood to mean that the people of China were awakening to their nationhood in a gradual process involving changes in popular fashion and taste, a growing curiosity about personal identity and the meaning of life, a disturbing engagement with the judgments of colonial racism, and the cumulative effects of accelerating commercialization and industrialization. Nationalists, however, were reluctant to let the nation awaken of its own accord. The country cried out to be "awakened" by reformers and revolutionaries possessing an intense sense of purpose, a keen commitment to the dictates of reason, and a formidable capacity for political organization and discipline.

This conjunction of passive and active forces is common to nation-building movements in colonial states, where, in the words of Benedict Anderson, "one sees both a genuine, popular nationalist enthusiasm, and a systematic, even Machiavellian, instilling of nationalist ideology through the mass media, the educational system, administrative regulations." [7] Both senses of the term "awakening," the intransitive and the transitive, must be retained to remain faithful to the language of China's national awakening. At the same time, each needs to be distinguished from the other in order to distinguish the evolutionary from the revolutionary aspects of China's national revolution. The problem, then, is to explain the transition from one sense of awakening to another, from the intransitive to the transitive, and to trace the institutionalization of the idea of a national awakening from an inchoate aspiration into a distinctive style of disciplined mass politics under the supervision of a highly disciplined, pedagogical state.

The motif of an awakening complicates any attempt to isolate the systematic and public efforts of political activists from the more personal and less deliberate awakenings of ordinary people. It was ubiquitous. Although the term makes no appearance in any concordance to Chinese nationalism, any survey of the culture of the period would show that it was one of the most common expressions to make an appearance in the diaries and autobiographies, the art and

literature, the ethics and education, the history and archaeology, the science
and medicine, the geography and ethnography, and, of course, the politics of
the day. Its ubiquity helps to explain the convergence of a nationally oriented
cultural movement with a movement to build an independent and sovereign
nation-state. That is to say, the idea of a national awakening helped to link a
variety of distinctive cultural fields with one another and with the world of
political action. It was sufficiently universal to cross discursive boundaries and
make room for nationalist politics in science, philosophy, and literature, and it
was sufficiently agile to draw political activists to the worlds of science, philosophy, and literature in an effort to conscript intellectuals to the service of
the revolutionary state.

The moment of convergence was the Nationalist Revolution of the 1920s.
Literature and ethics had been at the center of a cultural storm that emanated
from Beijing in 1915 and made its way down the coast and inland over the following decade. The New Culture movement began, as one participant recalled,
as an "awakening of individuality" among youths and intellectuals.[8] By 1919 it
had come to embrace an awakening of the nation, as well, when students, merchants, and workers protested the transfer of German concessions in Shandong
to Japan at the Versailles Conference. But even after the protests of 1919, the
movement essentially eschewed politics. The champions of the New Culture
movement imagined that China would be revived through cultural reconstruction. This is where Sun Yatsen and his Nationalist Revolution came in.

Literature, ethics, and mass education never quite converged with politics before the Nationalist Revolution, and it was Sun, more than anyone, who
helped bring them together. The historian Fu Sinian recalled the point of connection in 1935:

Beijing was of course at the forefront of the new current when the thinking of the Chinese people took a turn to the left, criticizing traditional literature and casting doubt
on traditional ethics, but when Sun Yatsen founded *Reconstruction* (*Jianshe*) magazine
in Shanghai he really gave the movement a hefty push in the direction of politics. We
can see clearly from the comments he made at the time that [Sun] believed cultural
reform alone was not enough and that new life had also to be injected into politics before China would be able to stand on its own two feet; there had to be a new political
program before China could be turned around.[9]

Within a short space of time after the founding of *Reconstruction* in 1919,
writers and artists were as committed as revolutionaries to a "political program." Gao Qifeng's painting shows that art and politics were heroically
matched in the image of the one who brought them together around the motif
of the awakened nation.

Though there were historical antecedents for the terms "awakening" and
"to awaken" in orthodox ethics and popular religious practice, the awakening

of modern China was not a product of inherited vocabulary or traditional practices alone. The ideal of a national awakening is coeval with nationalism itself.
Napoleon, we are told, awoke the nations of Europe from their sleep and foresaw the same fate for China if he were to head its way: "Behold the Chinese
Empire. Let it sleep, for when this dragon wakes the world will tremble." [10] In
fact, China was not the first among the states of Asia to shock the world, nor
was it the only one to lay claim to a national awakening. In the mid-twentieth
century, the Imperial Army of Japan did for Asia what Napoleon's armies had
done for Europe a century before, stimulating mass movements and armed resistance against monarchical and colonial rule. Indonesia's national day is now
known as the Day of National Awakening.

In recent times, the idea of national awakening has largely been displaced
by the idea of national "development" among postcolonial states. China, we
noted, has also discarded the turbulent politics of mass awakening in favor of
the gradualist politics of national development. Yet the development of the
postcolonial state has its own antecedent in the awakening of the colonial one.
"Although the figure of speech at the time was of China's 'awakening' (not 'developing')," Lucian Pye acutely observes, "the country was in a sense the first
of the newly emerging nations." [11] Napoleon's famous warning was a prediction
of what might lie in store for the world should China "awaken," and at the same
time was a challenge to elites within China to awaken their nation and make the
world take notice. The self-conscious, purposeful, and at times feverish young
cadre of the Nationalist Revolution was determined to do for China what Napoleon is said to have advised Europe *not* to do: to awaken the sleeping dragon.

The idea of an awakening was also common to the European Enlightenment, although in this case in the form of an awakening to reason and to
universal human values. To this day the concept has remained a fundamental
component of all the emancipatory systems of knowledge ushered in by the
French Revolution, from Saint-Simon's science of society to Hegelian meta-
physics, Marxism, Freudian psychoanalysis, and Critical Theory in our own
time.[12] Not only nations but social classes, women, youth, and individuals are
promised freedom if they awaken to the true nature of their predicament and
discover, in their awakening, the key to their emancipation. In China, too, the
promise of awakening was held out not just to the nation but to the many communities that constituted it.

Discovering what the term meant in China, to whom and by whom it was
applied, how it may have affected the form and style of democratic politics, and
why it has been so ubiquitous in the rhetoric of modern Chinese nationalism
calls for a voyage of exploration beyond the fields of philology and national
history to seek sources often overlooked in the literature of national development. The present study is organized around the categories of cultural history

(Chapter 1), ethics (Chapter 2), ethnography (Chapter 3), and statecraft (Chapter 4), and around the construction of political institutions (Chapter 5), and the disciplining (Chapter 6), organization (Chapter 7), and rhetoric (Conclusion) of national awakening over the first three decades of this century. To highlight the symmetry between the evolutionary and revolutionary aspects of China's awakening, developments in each of these categories are illustrated through contemporary developments in the fields of art and architecture, museums and medicine, fiction and essays, journalism and propaganda, political institutions and mass organization.

There is little to unite these broad and separate fields apart from the motif of awakening itself. But the theme of an awakening does more than link them together. In fact, there was a consistent narrowing of focus on the awakening subject and a corresponding reduction in the fields to which the term was applied over the period under review. The earliest of China's modern awakenings were awakenings to selfhood and individuality in relation to a rational and material universe. The "self" awoke, awestruck and alone, and looked to the stars for its inspiration. The awakening of this universal self was soon displaced by the awakening of a distinctly Chinese self that preferred to commune with its nation. Defining the particularity of this nation invited reflection, in turn, on the ideal form of a state charged with the responsibility of awakening the people as "self-conscious" citizens. And a determination to "awaken the people" prompted those first awakened (*xian juezhe*) to develop organizations, technologies, and procedures for awakening the people to citizenship and nationhood. As these procedures evolved into a system for manufacturing a New People, the system itself came to bear many of the hallmarks of the totalitarian state.[13] But it was not simply totalitarian; it was *nationalist*. These were Chinese New People. The narrowing of focus in the politics of awakening was effected through the exercise of political power in pursuit of a nationalist end: the unity and sovereignty of the nation-state. Ultimately, the sun and the stars were ushered down from the heavens and woven into the fabric of the flags of the Nationalist and Communist party-states of New China.

The book is structured to trace the transition from the "spontaneous" awakening of the self to the "Machiavellian" awakening of the nation through a number of distinct phases. First, it traces the outline of the intellectual milieu of the late nineteenth and early twentieth centuries, specifically those aspects which nurtured faith in the ideas of progress, enlightenment, and "awakening" to a new world order. It then follows the development of the idea of awakening from an awakening to a universal order of "One World" (*datong*) to an ideal of a single national people. From the ideal of one nation, we move to the idea of a united and powerful state, from the idea of one state to the ideal of one party, and from the ideal of one party to the emergence of the single, definitive voice of the awakened leader. At no point do we lose sight of the exercise of power. We begin, then, with the awakening of the modern self, and end with the achievements of a revolutionary movement in Guangdong Province in the 1920s, the Nationalist Revolution.

I hope to show that the significance of this historical journey reaches well beyond Guangdong and beyond the second and third decades of this century. The awakened leader to whom I refer was Sun Yatsen, and the director of awakenings in the revolution was Mao Zedong, head of the propaganda bureau of the Nationalist party at a critical moment in 1925 and 1926. In fact, what we are tracing is the birth of one of the most effective elements of Chinese Communist organization this century, its propaganda apparatus, and two of its most distinctive forms of action, organized mass movements and purges. The organization of the study may test the patience of some readers and stretch the credulity of others. Certainly the world could be spared another account of the awakening of modern China. But if we take the awakening of China to be a historical problem rather than a historical narrative—a series of questions provoking a series of more and less authoritative answers—then the story of China's awakening becomes, I think, a very interesting one indeed.

The Sun Yatsen Memorial Hall is a useful point of entry into the central themes of this book. Faint traces of the ethics, the ethnography, and the centralism, statism, socialism, and mass propaganda of the Chinese revolution cluster around the hall to this day, sometimes in monumental and sometimes in incidental ways. Over the entrance to the hall, for example, some distance above the atrium that once housed the awakened lion, still hangs a large sign in the style of Sun Yatsen's own calligraphy. The sign reads, "All Under Heaven Belongs to All" (*tianxia wei gong*).

This old saying, one of very few with a secure place in Sun's limited classical vocabulary, is an ethical statement. It first appeared in a couplet from the Han dynasty *Book of Rites* (*Liji*) and gained wide currency in later Confucian commentaries and popular literature. In its earliest usage, the expression "Belongs to All" evoked the idea of common interest, or of public association outside the sphere of government, and established an ethical framework governing relations between individuals and society.[14] When Sun made use of the term "Belongs to All" (*wei gong*), it had not yet lost this sense of collective ownership. In the Republic, the word for "all" (*gong*) was frequently used to denote organizations or functions poised, as it were, between the personal sphere and the state. A number of the new historical and natural science museums founded in the Republic were established as local community institutions (*gongli*), as distinct from others set up under the auspices of the state at various levels (*shili, shengli, guoli*).[15]

Yet community ownership was not quite what Sun had in mind when he used the term "Belongs to All." He was making a competing claim on the term that conflated the concepts of government and public in the idea of a "world in which the people would rule," or a democratic state. In Sun Yatsen's calligraphy, the sign "All Under Heaven Belongs to All" is a statement merging ethics with statecraft and conflating the relationship between individuals and communities with that between citizens and the national state. No Chinese person who strolled by this sign would fail to recognize that it speaks not only of ethics but also of government.

Sun himself spelled out what he meant in a series of lectures on his Three Principles of the People (*Sanmin zhuyi*) delivered just a year before his death. He quoted the expression "All Under Heaven Belongs to All" in his inaugural lecture on democracy where the point of the citation was to establish an authentic Chinese antecedent for the principle of democratic rule. In the language of the time, the Chinese nation was asleep and in desperate need of awakening. Yet the yearning for democracy was said to have a historical pedigree as impressive as the people, the morality, and the learning of ancient China. Confucius was a democrat at heart:

Confucius said, "When the Way prevails, All under Heaven Belongs to All." He was pleading for a free and fraternal world in which the people would rule. . . . Thus China more than two millennia ago had already considered the idea of democracy, but at the time could not put it into effect. This democracy was what foreigners call a Utopia, an ideal which could not be immediately realized.[16]

In speaking of the national awakening, Sun celebrated the liberation of the individual and the national people from the absolutism of the imperial state, and at the same time reclaimed this awakening for the modern state. He dismissed history as a sleepy utopia while reclaiming all that was progressive about it.

The identification of the awakened self with the awakened state was effected gradually over the first quarter of this century. Sun's citation was a classical allusion, but it alluded as well to a recent textual tradition concerned with the immediate problem of defining the self in relation to its community at a time when old forms of community were rapidly collapsing. The nation was being mooted as a new kind of community to take their place. Yet the awakened self had an independent history, and its struggle for autonomy was not initially identified with the freedom of the nation. The history of the awakened self was etched in ethics. It was only when ethics were conflated with statecraft that the awakening of the individual merged with the awakening of the nation.

The Sun Yatsen Memorial Hall offers a clue to the identity of the awakened self. Not far from the doorway hangs another sign, a smaller one, but as fitting a memorial to Sun Yatsen as the immense calligraphy over the entrance. The sign reads "Please do not spit on the ground." On 2 March 1924, not far from the site where the Memorial Hall now stands, Sun interrupted the last of his public lectures on the Three Principles of the People to counsel his audience against spitting and burping in public and to urge the practice of a new kind of personal culture that would give form to Nationalist ideals in the practice of everyday life. Sun wished to forge a new China by remaking the "Chinaman." Ethics merged with etiquette around an ethos of personal deportment that was to make the nation as self-disciplined as the selves that constituted it.[17]

In this respect, at least, the colonial critique of John Chinaman was a formative element of modern Chinese nationalism. Sun Yatsen paid colonial racism an indirect tribute when he unveiled the keystone of Nationalist party ideology over a series of weekly lectures from January through August 1924. The Three Principles of the People—nationalism, democracy, and people's livelihood— were presented as the ideological armory of the revolution, and each principle was framed to correspond with a specific aim of the revolutionary movement: nationalism with the elimination of foreign imperialism, democracy with the overthrow of warlords (and later "feudalism"), and people's livelihood with the improvement of the living and working conditions of the common people. These were the three aims of the Nationalist Revolution of the 1920s.[18] The repetitive, convoluted, and even misleading arguments of the lectures have invited apologies from his supporters and scorn from historians because they offer little guidance for a systematic reading of Nationalist ideology. Sun Yatsen pointed out, in his defense, that he would have made a better job of the lectures if his warlord ally Chen Jiongming had not "unexpectedly revolted" two years beforehand, on 16 June 1922:

My notes and manuscripts which represented the mental labor of years and hundreds of foreign books which I had collected for reference were all destroyed by fire. . . . In these lectures I do not have the time necessary for careful preparation nor the books necessary for reference. I can only mount the platform and speak extemporaneously.[19]

The improvised nature of the lectures precluded the systematic analysis of the rationale and strategy of the revolution that Sun had in mind. Still, extemporaneity is not always a bad thing. The lectures remain lively and insightful, and they are revealing to the point where they invite an *unsystematic* reading of Nationalist ideology starting from the extemporanous motifs and working back to the rationale and strategy of the revolution. One of these motifs was the colonial critique of John Chinaman. In his lectures, Sun engaged Western racists in a dialogue on the character of the Chinese race.

In his six lectures on nationalism, Sun focused on the political and economic domination of China by foreign imperialism, specifically the historical "decline" of China's population, the relative weakness of the Chinese state, and the imminent demise of race and state unless the Chinese people "awoke," as he put it, to the dangers of imperialism.[20] But in his final lecture he qualified his political critique by asking what it was that made his compatriots no match for the foreigners in governing their country. The answer, he felt, was their want of "personal virtue":

Government is progressing in every other country today; in China, it is going backward. Why? Because we are under the political and economic domination of foreign nations, yes; but if we search for the *fundamental reason* we will find it in the Chinese failure to cultivate personal virtue.[21]

By personal virtue Sun seems to have meant not ethics alone but attention to hygiene and personal deportment. He recounted a conversation with the captain of an American steamer who once told him, with barely disguised disgust, that a minister of the Chinese government had blown his nose and spat all over his ship's costly carpets. How, the captain implied, could an ill-mannered official so patently incapable of controlling his olfactory organs be expected to manage a whole country?[22]

In fact, the history of spitting is as long as the history of modern contact between China and the West. In 1793 England's first ambassador to the court at Beijing, Lord Macartney, registered disgust at the "foul" behavior of Chinese Mandarins: "They seldom have recourse to pocket handkerchiefs, but spit about the rooms without mercy, blow their noses in their fingers, and wipe them with their sleeves, or upon anything near them."[23] Macartney's comptroller, John Barrow, was a comparative ethnographer who thought Chinese officials as ill-mannered as the French: "Many are not so cleanly, but spit about the rooms, or against the walls like the French, and they wipe their dirty hands on the sleeves of their gowns."[24] In 1793 the Mandarins of Beijing do not seem to have taken note of their guests' heightened sensibilities. By the 1920s, after a century and more of repeated demonstrations of Western military superiority along the coast of China, the casual remarks of a foreign sea captain could stir deep embarrassment in the soul of a revolutionary nationalist. Sun Yatsen could only agree.

Another point of contact between East and West that brought a blush to Chinese reformers was the dining table. Lord Macartney's comments on Chinese table manners were as harsh as those on hygiene. Yet within a hundred years or so Chinese revolutionaries were offering timely personal advice on how to improve their compatriots' conduct at dinner. One disconsolate young modernist turned to the anarchist Wu Zhihui for advice in 1908 after discovering that foreign women consistently turned down his invitations to dinner. Wu counseled that closer attention to hygiene and manners would probably do the trick. As an anarchist, Wu believed that the need for a state would be obviated if everyone practiced personal self-government (*zizhi*).[25] But Sun Yatsen was no anarchist. He drew a more explicit connection between governing the self and governing the state. In his lectures on the Three Principles in 1924, Sun Yatsen told two stories about the reaction of foreigners to Chinese table manners. The first was set abroad:

It was just at the dinner hour; ladies and gentlemen of refinement were thronging the dining room and enjoying themselves, when suddenly a Chinese present noisily let off some gas. The foreigners scattered with exclamations of disgust, while the proprietor put the Chinese out. Since that experience no other Chinese has been allowed to eat in the dining room.

The second took place in Shanghai:

Once, in Shanghai, a big Chinese merchant invited some foreigners to a feast and passed gas right at the table until the foreigners' faces were red with embarrassment. He not only did not check himself but even stood up and slapped his clothes, loudly saying, "Ee-s-ko-s-me." Such behaviour is uncivilized and vulgar in the extreme, yet even scholars and students are constantly guilty of it and reform is certainly difficult.

Sun catalogued a number of other faults in the personal grooming of the Chinaman that were in need of reform, including the venerable custom of growing fingernails to an unseemly length and ("another great defect in the care of the person") failure to brush the teeth.[26] The point of the fable was to reclaim the respect of the foreign observers from Lord Macartney to the more recent observations of H. G. W. Woodhead and Rodney Gilbert, who felt that Chinese were incompetent administrators because they could not even care for themselves:[27]

All these bad habits can be regulated by simple, everyday personal culture, yet Chinese do not seem to care. As a result . . . as soon as foreigners meet us they say that we are barbaric. . . . If everyone would devote some systematic effort to the cultivation of his person, "let the character within be manifested without," pay attention to even the smallest matters of conduct, on meeting foreigners not rudely trespass on their freedom, then foreigners would certainly respect the Chinese.[28]

Reclaiming the respect of foreigners was a condition for reclaiming the right to govern China: "Why can we not govern China? What reveals the fact to foreigners? In my personal opinion, foreigners have no way of observing whether we rule our families well or not, but they can see that we are very much lacking in personal culture." [29] Sun was, as always, highly perceptive. From classical Rome to the age of modernity, the high culture of Europe counted competent governance of the body's natural functions and preternatural desires as a necessary condition for competent government of the city.[30] The private and the public converged around a code of decorous conduct that applied equally to the body, to the family, and to the state. By the time Sun addressed his audience in Guangzhou, foreigners had long been pointing to an indissoluble connection between the state of personal ethics, hygiene, and deportment among the Chinese people and the deficiencies of Chinese social organization and imperial administration. Sun himself had traveled widely abroad and had become acutely sensitive to the reactions of foreigners to the Chinese people he met along the way. In time he came to regard his own countrymen much as Lord Macartney had done. The sight of "yellow or black teeth," the scrape of a long fingernail, or the sound of a hearty expectoration sickened him and dampened his expectations of a national revival. So in addition to reorganizing the party, cementing new international alliances, and building up his military forces, Sun took time out to advise the people of China that they should take note of what foreigners said about them, and change their ways.

Sun was not alone in this conviction. Over the years he built up a staff of loyal deputies who were equally committed to a new style of personal self-management that would reflect well on the country's capacity for self-government. In 1923 the municipal administration of Guangzhou installed new public toilets throughout the city when there was no demand for them at all. It did not *matter* that there was no demand. The public had yet to be shown how to keep itself tidy—indeed, shown how to act as a "public" capable of making orderly public demands.[31] Nationalist observations on spitting, burping, and personal grooming were not frivolous digressions but indications of their determination to remake the Chinaman and remake the state together. When they spoke of the need for the people to wake up, or become "self-conscious" (*zijue*), this is generally what they meant.

The most striking thing about the Guangzhou Memorial Hall is not the paintings and signs that adorn it but the fate of the hall itself. The hall was rapidly superseded by another, far grander memorial built in Nanjing after the Nationalists left Guangzhou on the Northern Expedition (1926–28) and succeeded in establishing their central government in Nanjing. Both were designed by the same architect. But the Nationalists had abandoned the one for the other even before Lü's untimely death. The Guangzhou Hall looks modest and neglected alongside the massive and austere Tomb of Sun Yatsen, which nestles in the hills outside Nanjing. More particularly, the Guangzhou memorial is parochial and hollow by comparison, bereft of a body and irredeemably "local" (*bendi, difang*) in its relation to the new central monument where Sun's body was finally laid to rest.[32]

The hierarchical relationship between the central and national monuments highlights another aspect of the national awakening. The Nationalist Revolution was, among other things, a struggle to define the significance of the "local" within the national polity and to establish a political framework for managing central-local relations. The contest within nationalist thought between the idea of local and national communities, periphery and center, was contested in a variety of symbolic arenas, including public monuments, art, literature, and language.

There was more to language reform, for example, than merely forging a medium of mass instruction. By facilitating education and expanding literacy, the language-reform movement helped to create a community of nationals. Indeed, the nation was invented in literature and manufactured in the movement for language reform. But it was writers, not readers, who were to decide what form the national polity should take. They argued fiercely over the merits of uniform or local phonetic scripts for attaining national unity, much as they did over the advantages of centralized and federal systems of government for achieving state unification. The new language and literature, art and architecture were not merely instruments for achieving state unification but were formative elements prescribing the limits of tolerable diversity within the nation.[33]

All the modern nations of Europe were initially "the creations of writers," in A. J. P. Taylor's memorable phrase, and "existed only in imagination; they were nations in which there were more writers than readers."[34] The nation of the Chinese nationalist movement was no exception. There were almost as many writers as readers in the New Culture and May Fourth movements: 700 new journals were issued over the eight or nine years to 1923, and the total number of scribes came close to matching the largest subscription lists.[35] Still, few nationalists either in Europe or in China anticipated that their nations would be confined to paper or that the nation of their dreams would remain an exclusive club of writers. If nothing else, this would threaten the nation's survival. As a concerned Czech nationalist remarked to a gathering of his peers: "If the ceiling were to fall on us now, that would be the end of the national revival."[36]

Chinese nationalists were prone to similar fears because they shared the conceit that the history and the future of the nation rested in their hands. "If our nation's antiquity and our people's historical record come to an end in my hands," wrote Zhang Binglin with genuine trepidation, "and China's broad and magnificent scholarship should ultimately find its continuance severed, this will be my crime to bear."[37] Sun Yatsen spoke for his Nationalist movement: "If China perishes the guilt will be on our own heads and we shall be the world's great sinners."[38] For all their conceit, nationalists such as Zhang Binglin and Sun Yatsen were genuinely concerned to ensure that the nation extended beyond the walls of their studios or the purview of their committees. Zhang worked to dispel his own fears with imagination and enthusiasm, inventing a phonetic alphabet for the Chinese language and actively promoting popular literacy. Sun set out to awaken the nation politically. In time, the literacy movement in China developed into a movement to create a community of readers commensurate with the nation imagined in writing—a nation that was massive in size, united by its written language, and able to satisfy the literary function of *being* awakened.

The problems that divided language reformers, however, were among the most intractable problems besetting the country as a whole. The majority of the people of China were illiterate, and together they spoke hundreds of distinct languages and dialects. Language activists and literary reformers, then, faced a common dilemma in attempting to promote popular literacy within particular language groups while retaining the universal legibility of the written language. This contradiction was symptomatic of a more general tension within nationalist thought between the ideal of a strong central state that placed severe limits on local autonomy and the competing idea of a national state that was little more than the sum of its regional parts.

Here missionaries and Chinese Christians played key roles in the national awakening through education, medical practice, and other interventions in civic life, and indirectly by the example they set in seeking to convert people to their cause. Missionaries sought to win converts to the Kingdom of God without risking the integrity of the nation.[39] Frederick Lee noted the intimacy of the connection between the work of the heavenly and temporal missions in his description of a church school in Shanghai in the period of the Nationalist Revolution:

These boys and girls come from fifteen provinces, each province representing a different class of people, each with its prejudices and provincial jealousies. While they are all people of one country, yet judging from their clannish feelings towards the boys and girls of their own province, one would think they were from so many different countries. . . . But the process of education goes on, here a little leveling of the hills of separation, and there a little broadening of the sympathies to include others than those of one's own clan. Boys and girls return home with extended vision, and greater appreciation for those of other places. There is nothing like this intercourse in school to unite the church in China.[40]

The secular nationalist movement was no more willing than the Reverend Lee to concede that China was made up of "so many different countries." But, unfortunately for the Reverend Lee, it was intolerant of imported religions. Nationalist revolutionaries turned their fury on Christian "cultural imperialism" on the one hand, while targeting the "clannish feelings" of local communities on the other. Foreign imperialism was one enemy. Other enemies were identified by their attachment to a particular locale: local patois (*tuhua*), local bullies (*tuhao*), regionalism (*difang zhuyi/guandian*) and clanism (*jiazu sixiang*).[41]

Although dedicated to Sun Yatsen, the Memorial Hall in Guangzhou actually stands as testimony to the strength of parochial sentiment in Guangdong. Funding for the hall ceased after the revolutionary army left the city in 1926.

The memorial was then completed under the supervision of the Guangdong warlord, Chen Jitang, with the aid of subscriptions from overseas Chinese of Guangdong descent. Typically, however, localist sentiment was neither un-patriotic nor even anti-Nationalist. Provincial sentiment commemorated Sun as a national hero who happened to hail from Guangdong Province. It just happened that the nationalism of provincial warlords was not consistent with the centralist brand of nationalism proclaimed by the Nationalist movement.

This revolution was nationalist in the sense of subordinating all ancillary aspects of culture and society that were not easily accommodated under the rubric of a unified national state. Revolutionaries mounted an assault upon cus-tomary language and culture, upon affective bonds of family and locality, and upon patterns of social organization and authority resistant to the inroads of an intrusive, centralizing national state. Indeed, so intent were they on displacing old forms of social organization with a new kind of state structure that the revolution, which began as a political revolution, ended up a social one.

This brings us to another theme of the book. The onset of social revolution, or "class struggle," in the Nationalist Revolution of the 1920s marked a part-ing of the ways for the Nationalists and Communists and served to distinguish their rhetoric and practice in the ensuing competition to unify and liberate the country. Some Nationalists, following Sun Yatsen, declared that class struggle had no part in national revolution. Others responded that class struggle had a role so long as it promoted national revolution. Insofar as this debate on the sa-lience of "class struggle" in national revolution revolved around strictly politi-cal imperatives, it foreshadowed the language, the argument, and the style of the mass politics of the People's Republic.

It would be overstating the case to suggest that the class struggle of the Nationalist Revolution was of the same order as the class struggle that charac-terized post-Liberation politics, or more particularly, the struggles of the Cul-tural Revolution, which spilled over into the Memorial Hall in Guangzhou. The relationship between society and the state had changed beyond measure over the intervening decades, to the point where state organization after Liberation effectively substituted for the social networks that confronted the Nationalists in the 1920s.[42] In the earlier period, moreover, there were sufficient grounds and ample opportunities for tensions between tenant farmers and their land-lords or between factory workers and their employers to erupt in conflicts of a kind made redundant (if not illegal) in the People's Republic. The coinci-dence of rhetorical style between the revolutionary politics of pre- and post-Liberation China is elegantly explained by dismissing the Cultural Revolution as a bizarre shadow play of the "real" class struggle that took place in the social revolution preceding Liberation. If the Cultural Revolution imitated the tragedy of China's national revolution, it did so as farce.

There was, for all that, an element of farce in the original script of the Chinese revolution. When the term "class struggle" made its appearance in the Nationalist Revolution, it was generally applied to political conflict within the revolutionary movement itself, or to confrontation between the revolutionaries and agents of social resistance, and only metaphorically to struggle within society. Indeed, the presence of "class struggle" within society was incidental to its function in politics. The political was identified implicitly with the social through a realist aesthetic that linked conflict at the level of the state to class struggle in the socioeconomic base and to national struggle among the peoples of the world. Factional disputes were then readily interpreted as allegories of a greater confrontation between elemental forces of history, which all competing parties and factions were determined to "represent" and to command. In representing the forces of class and nation, revolutionaries conceived of their violent conflicts with agents of social and political resistance—chiefly local elites—as marking a confrontation within society itself. So although there were certainly social classes, social contradictions, and social interests in the revolutionary period, the class struggle of the national revolution was not quite the straightforward drama its leading actors made it out to be.

Class struggle arose in the Nationalist Revolution less from conflict within society than from the form of the state and the style of politics embraced by the Nationalist revolutionaries. Sun Yatsen showed his distaste for the cut-and-thrust of liberal politics soon after the founding of the Republic in 1912, and in the following decade announced he would be content with nothing less than a state founded on the model of his highly disciplined and centralized revolutionary party: in short, a Leninist party-state. In the Nationalist Revolution, Sun and the Communists were partners in establishing China's first party-state in Guangdong Province. They were also pioneers in devising procedures for achieving ideological uniformity and political centralization through mass propaganda and revolutionary discipline. In this respect, the most telling point of similarity between the class struggle of the Nationalist Revolution and that of the Cultural Revolution is the part played by Mao Zedong in both. Mao was director of the Nationalist Propaganda Bureau when he agitated for "class struggle" in the Nationalist Revolution, and it was his determination to wrest control of propaganda organs from his political competitors that launched him on the path to the Cultural Revolution. The rhetoric of class struggle was, from the beginning to the end of Mao's political career, a measure of his commitment to the realist, representative politics of mass awakenings.

In fairness to Sun Yatsen, we must acknowledge that there never was a "Sun's China" to match "Mao's China." If anything, Sun's death in 1925 highlighted the contrast between his dream of national unity and the brutish fact of China's territorial, social, cultural, and political "disunity." Amidst the chorus of eulogies in his honor, cynics could be heard muttering that he was just "a madman spouting dreams" (*chi ren shuo meng*).[43] But even cynicism helped to confirm the identification of Sun and his Nationalist party with China itself. Sun Yatsen died a romantic dreamer because his China was still only a dream.[44] Nevertheless, his strategy for bringing New China into being was anything but a comedy of reconciliation.

Sun believed that the liberal polity of the Republic was ill-suited to the task of "awakening" the nation. This called for a new kind of politics. In a farewell message to the Huangpu Military Academy on 3 November 1924, he made an important statement on the meaning of politics. "A revolution," Sun announced, "is a joint effort by everybody to reform public (*gonggong*) affairs. So I say that revolution is a political affair." Sun then explained what he meant by politics, merging the idea of the crowd with the idea of the state:

Everyone knows that revolution is basically a political transformation, but what does politics itself actually do? If we take the two syllables of the word "politics" (*zheng-zhi*), the first refers to the affairs of a crowd of people and the second to managing the affairs of a crowd of people, so the management of the affairs of a crowd of people is "politics" — or to put it another way, managing the affairs of a crowd of people is managing the affairs of state.

Here Sun was instructing military trainees, who professed "not to understand politics," that the realm of the state was not some exotic place far removed from the drill ground of their daily concerns. Politics was as much a part of the human condition as eating and sleeping, and everybody who ate and slept was implicated in "affairs of state":

Eating, dressing, and sleeping are all part and parcel of what it means to be human, and everyone should be familiar with them. I ask you, can anybody fail to know these everyday aspects of being a person? Whoever you are, you should all know what it takes to be a person from day to day. And everybody is capable of knowing that politics, too, is an everyday aspect of being human. When all are able to come together publicly (*gonggong*), as persons (*ren*), then they become a people (*renmin*) with political capacity.

As politics was not out of place in the everyday world, so the world needed to make room for politics every day. There was little doubt in Sun's mind that this would restrict the exercise of everyday liberties. He told the cadets that alien "European and American" ideals of liberty and equality had long outlived their usefulness. What China needed from a nationalist revolution was not personal freedom but "corporate (*tuanti*) freedom and equality." Sun went on:

Political organizations such as states and political parties . . . should all enjoy freedom and equality in their dealings, whether in struggles between one country and another or struggles between one party and another. But this is not to say that in our party or our state everyone should have freedom and equality.[45]

The requirements of corporate freedom, needless to say, placed severe limits on individual freedom of action. In another of his formal lectures on the Three Principles, delivered on 26 April, Sun predicted that the Nationalist Revolution would need to produce a state capable of exercising far greater authority in China than liberal democracies exercised in the West, and at the same time tried to allay fears that this might place government beyond the control of the people by highlighting the new constitutional arrangements he had devised for China. "After China secures a powerful government we must not be afraid, as Western peoples are, that the government will become too strong and get from under our control." [46] His followers later buttressed the restrictive practices of the Nationalist state by claiming that the Chinese people had been spoiled by the excessive liberties of the old imperial state, which had allowed them "to live and die as they pleased." [47] Corporatist politics was a technique for realizing the unity, sovereignty, and freedom of action of the state. To clinch his argument, and incidentally to establish his own place in the genealogy of traditional statecraft, Sun concluded with the remark that "the state is the Essence (*ti*) and politics is the Means (*yong*)." [48] When supreme value resided in the state, it followed that all other values, including individual, social, and community liberties, were not inalienable rights but privileges granted by the state in pursuit of its own higher interest.

Sun proposed to set up a party-state that would institutionalize a new style of mass-democratic politics, a politics of mass "conversion" (*ganhua*). Nationalist and Communist revolutionaries often complained that the people of China were misguided in what they thought about their communities and their country, and just as often consoled themselves that the people could be improved through mass indoctrination. Here they found some justification in the classics. The principle that human nature was basically good and could be perfected through ethical cultivation was a foundation of the Mencian school of Confucian ethics. Perhaps the clearest expression of the principle is found in the opening line of a children's catechism known as the Three Character Classic (*Sanzijing*). In reciting the principle that they were perfectable, students perfected themselves: "People at birth are naturally good; their natures are much the same, but their habits differ widely. If, unfortunately, they are not taught then their natures will deteriorate." [49] Self-cultivation was linked with an imperative for popular instruction in the opening lines of the orthodox Confucian canon, *The Great Learning* (*Daxue*): "What the Great Learning teaches, is— to illustrate illustrious virtue, to renovate the people; and to rest in the highest excellence." [50] Renovating the people did not, however, require that those renovated believe everything that they were taught. What mattered in Confucian lore was ritual practice rather than professed belief. It was enough for the purpose to "illustrate" virtue and quite unnecessary to brand uniform belief upon every living soul.[51]

Illustrating virtue was not quite what the revolutionaries had in mind when they thought of revolutionary propaganda. They intended to make everyone as "conscious" or awake as they were. Nationalists and Communists imagined that the nation was a clean sheet of paper and that the shape of the people and the color of popular belief could develop in any of a thousand different ways depending upon who wielded the brush. Dai Jitao, a leading anti-Communist theorist in the Nationalist movement, pronounced China a "blank sheet" in 1925, three decades before Mao Zedong made his famous remark that China's people are "poor and blank" (*yi kong er bai*).[52] "China is really a blank sheet of paper," Dai announced; "color it green, and it is green; color it yellow and it is yellow." By inferring that the people were not just "good" but in fact blank, Dai Jitao and Mao Zedong turned an ethical imperative for renovating the people into a political maxim for mass indoctrination of a particular color. Both felt that what people believed would be determined, in the last instance, by the outcome of political struggle among revolutionaries, reactionaries, and counterrevolutionaries for control of the brush.

"A clean sheet of paper has no blotches and so the newest and most beautiful words can be written on it," Mao wrote in April 1958, "the newest and most beautiful pictures can be painted on it." [53] Reference to the people as a clean sheet of paper was not intended to be taken literally, but there were plenty of sheets of paper in circulation nevertheless. Mao revived the image of the blank sheet in launching the first issue of a new mass-circulation propaganda journal, *Red Flag*, and within a matter of months warehouses of paper had been filled with his beautiful words and pictures. So it was with Dai Jitao. When Dai wrote of China as a clean sheet of paper, he had not long before stepped down from the position of director of propaganda for the Nationalist party and was hurriedly proofing copy for a new party magazine to issue from his home office in Shanghai.[54] Dai was eventually succeeded as director of Nationalist propaganda by Mao himself in the autumn of 1925. The two men competed for access to brush and paper and eventually fell to blows, not over the question of whether the Nationalist party should paint the nation after its own colors, but over the claims of particular factions to command the brush. Each had good reason to believe that China was a clean sheet, because Sun Yatsen had already succeeded in clearing the ground for the first party-state in China and had already set about "converting" and "partifying" (*danghua*) the country. The epic struggle between Dai and Mao in the Nationalist Revolution, and between the Nationalists and Communists more generally in a later phase of the revolution, took place in an arena staked out by Sun Yatsen's earlier achievements.

The relationship between the conversion and "partification" of China was an elliptical one. As a style of politics, the new mass pedagogy was to succeed not when it had remade the people of China but as soon as it had established beyond doubt that they were in need of remaking, that is, as soon as it was generally conceded that China was a blank sheet open to instrumental reconstruction. Sun Yatsen spoke frequently of the need to convert the "entire country" to the cause, and his speeches were often enlivened by images of China's "four hundred million" awakening to his vision and pouncing upon his enemies like an awakened lion. But even for Sun, what mattered was how successfully the party could establish its credentials for delivering the right kind of awakening. This was a key function of the awakening trope in revolutionary rhetoric.[55] When people conceded their need to *be* awakened, the rest would follow. That is to say, the end of pedagogical politics was not simply the awakening of the people but the erection of a pedagogical state structure that would relate to its citizens as a teacher might relate to a pupil, or, as Sun liked to think, as the imperial tutor once instructed the emperor.[56] Pedagogy was a style of politics as much as it was a goal of political action, and it was a style first instituted under the aegis of the Nationalist state in the 1920s. In establishing the party-state, in centralizing authority over its operations, in extending its authority over the community at large, and in promoting tighter discipline within the party and society, Sun Yatsen was tutor to Mao Zedong.

Yet neither the Communists nor the Nationalists imposed their will from outside, so to speak, upon a captive people. The subsequent "partification" of culture, society, and government would have been all but impossible were it not for the cooperation of the artists and intellectuals, the social institutions and the government scribes who went along with it all. In fairness to those concerned, we might turn this observation the other way around. Chinese nationalism has never been the preserve of a particular political party or movement and has always presented itself as more than an "ideological apparatus of state power." [57] Parallel developments in ethics, culture, and the social movement anticipated the politicization of nationalism and its partification under the Nationalists and Communists. Though the parties certainly authorized and propagated the icons and rituals of the nation, their authority was built on a repertoire of symbols, concepts, and ideals that had already undergone a long period of gestation in nationalist thought. It was nonparty intellectuals who first imagined that discipline might be a condition of freedom, who argued passionately that the awakened self was but an aspect of the state, and who predicted that the emancipation of the self awaited the liberation of the nation. It did not take much for a political party to turn these ethical and literary insights to partisan political advantage.

Carol Gluck, a historian of Japanese nationalism, has advised taking the multiple and often conflicting channels of nationalist ideology in their entirety in order to "avoid the pitfall of taking any particular ideological source at its totalizing word." Certainly the background white noise generated by multiple channels of nationalist debate in China supplied the symbols and master narratives upon which political activists were to draw in staking their particular claims to represent the nation. This broader field also marked out space for the popular reception of party ideology. In Republican China, as in Meiji Japan, nonparty sources of ideas and values helped to locate party sources in a larger context, which sometimes reinforced and sometimes conflicted with their orthodoxies.[58] Even in focusing on particular ideological sources, such as the Nationalist movement, Gluck's advice offers wise counsel. The Nationalist party was far from homogeneous. Its various propaganda arms in the armed forces, in government, and in different sections of the party spoke for themselves as well as for the organization as a whole, and their differences frequently reflected disputes within the wider domain of nationalism. The establishment of a new orthodoxy within the party is best illustrated by working horizontally across the broader field of Chinese nationalism to show linkages that may only be hinted at in Nationalist party orthodoxy itself. And foremost among these linkages, I believe, is the motif of an awakening to national unity.

It goes without saying that an ideal of national unity extended well beyond the Nationalist party's political movement. In order to trace the range of variations within this ideal and explain why some variations came to appear more authoritative than others, we need to follow the precedent of the revolutionaries themselves in linking the world of letters to the world of political institutions. "Everything must be changed," Mao Zedong announced in 1919, "from thought and literature to politics, religion and art." Despite the broad range of their reformist impulses, writers and activists strove for the creation of a unified intellectual field that would draw on common assumptions and values. They sought to create and popularize a common language and culture capable of unifying the nation, and they struggled to find a common purpose around which they could awaken the people in a unified political movement. Without a disciplined sense of purpose, it was felt, all of these efforts were doomed to fail. Certainly this was Mao Zedong's impression at the height of the New Culture movement. "An examination of the reasons why the new studies have not taken hold," he wrote, "would show that this results entirely from the fact that the new studies have never had a well-established central core of thought." [59]

The quest for a "central core of thought" was analogous with political unification in the Nationalist Revolution.

The idealization of unity in turn buttressed the authority of disciplined revolutionary parties over the awakening enterprise. When the propaganda apparatus of the Nationalist and Communist parties took hold of the generic icons of nationalism—the awakened lions and dragons, the figures of the New Citizen and the New Woman, the signatures of modernity, historical progress, and scientific rationality—it rapidly converted them into instruments for policing the cultural fields in which they had first been cultivated. This process of exchange, disarmament, and surrender between intellectuals and the revolutionary state is just as important to an understanding of the roots of party-state nationalism in China as the establishment of the state apparatus itself. Artists and intellectuals entered into the exchange with enthusiasm. Gao Qifeng, after all, first earned his reputation as a painter while working on a scroll of an awakened lion for the Guangzhou Memorial Hall. Lü Yanzhi died at his drafting board while trying to immortalize his hero, Sun Yatsen.

1

Awakening and Being Awakened

In the past clothing was uniformly made in the old "large lapel" style. The new style of center-cut [shirts and jackets] coincided with the introduction of new-style education. In 1918 or 1919, this style gradually began to be worn by more and more people. But even last year, if we speak of the population of all of Xunwu County, most people still wore old-style clothing. Wearers of new-style clothing were in a minority. But in the past two years, particularly after the victory of the land revolution, the wearing of new-style clothing has increased daily, especially among the young people. . . . Cadres in the Red Guard and soviet not only, without exception, wear new-style clothing and new-style shoes, but also want to use electric flashlights and wear scarves. Some want to wear pants padded with down.

Mao Zedong, 1930[1]

Along with the other achievements of the Nationalist Revolution of the 1920s came a revolution in fashion. Late in the decade, men throughout the country took to wearing the "Sun Yatsen suit" (*Zhongshan zhuang*), a style of dress distinguished by the severity of its cut, the placement of conspicuous pockets on either side, and a single row of prominent buttons down the middle—not unlike the Mao jacket of a later generation. The spread of this new style of dress generally passed unremarked alongside the military and political reunification of the country. Still, the adoption of a new civic uniform signaled unification of a different but no less important kind, in the coming together of a new national community around symbols of its own choosing. In this case, the symbol happened to reflect the new Nationalist state. The nation was awakening to consciousness of itself in its public performances, at a pace to match the awakening being urged upon it by its political leaders.

The neat correspondence between political reunification under the Nationalist state and cultural unification around a Nationalist style of dress highlights the relationship between the dictates of popular taste and the *dictat* of the state. Men's fashion settled on a partisan insignia in the Sun Yatsen suit and converted it into a national symbol without direct state intervention. There was a half-hearted attempt to codify the new fashion according to the ideology and symbols of the Nationalist movement. One zealous citizen presented a petition to the central government in Nanjing to the effect that "All men should wear uniform, with three pockets representing the three principles of Sanmin Doctrine, and five buttons representing the Five Powers of the Constitution."[2] The petition was rejected. The number of buttons and pockets on a Sun Yatsen suit was never to supply an accurate measure of ideological commitment. Nationalists and Communists alike laid claim to the Sun Yatsen jacket, and tolerance in the selection of pockets and buttons was a fair measure of political license in either camp.

In any case, strict codification of dress was not really necessary, since the appeal and authority of the suit were grounded not in law, but in example, and in the market for fashion. The role of the state was an indirect one. The "first-awakened" (*xianjue*) cadre of the Nationalist movement, who advertised the suits in the course of their daily routines, conferred on the suit an authority that was readily conveyed to all who awoke after them. In a broader sense, the market for fashion marked the passage of the community through progressive time. The Sun Yatsen suit advertised that the wearer was keeping up with a conspicuously Chinese kind of time, and this was enough to ensure the place of the style in popular fashion in a community awakening to its identity as a nation.

The petition of the overzealous citizen does, nevertheless, remind us of the critical or analytical distinction between "genuine, popular nationalist enthusiasm" and the "systematic, even Machiavellian, instilling of nationalist ideology" that Ben Anderson says characterizes nationalist movements in general.[3] The Sun suit managed to negotiate the transition from the Machiavellian to the popular with ease. As a symbol of the national awakening, it linked individual choice to community taste and merged the fate of the nation with the fate of the Nationalist movement. But how did it manage to do so? How are we to characterize the link between a popular awakening to nationalism and modernity, and the systematic awakening of the people by a partisan nationalist movement?

Awakening and Politics

The advent of fashion—any fashion—suggests that the distinction between awakening and *being* awakened may not be as clear as it appears. The line needs to be drawn cautiously because nationalist ideologies are themselves subject to fashion, and because partisan ideologies compete with one another in the wider arena of nationalism. The birth of modern Chinese nationalism entailed an awakening not only to the nation but to the universal ideals of enlightenment, progress, and science, to the autonomy of the individual and "self-realization," and to the claims of mass communities for a place in the polity and the claims of the polity itself for unity and sovereign independence. The rise of fashion in the Republic was a signature of progress in this general sense: fashion was a medium through which people kept in touch with mass communities of their choice as they moved together through time. The spread of fashion followed the contours of other signs of progress in literature and art, in a new history, and in public museums and monuments. Fashion linked the personal and the public through an ideal of community that was not just imagined but in fact was closely observed going about its business, in more and less tasteful ways, and that constantly renewed itself by redefining its preferences.

At the same time, partisan politics was fashion-conscious. Sun Yatsen did not invent the suit that came to bear his name. He adapted a style of dress already popular among students in Tokyo and Beijing, known generically as the "Student suit" (*xuesheng zhuang*), which covered a range of different styles for both men and women. Sun attached his name to one version of the suit, and this went out bearing a Nationalist label. The Communists did the same at a later date, adapting the Sun suit to a poorer grade of cloth and launching a style that eventually found its way into the world market as the Mao jacket. In each case the partisan movement adapted an existing style, appended its own imprimatur, and launched a fashion revolution. And in each case the new fashion could only take root in ground that had already been harrowed with the ideas of progress and new forms of mass community. Any request for codification of the approved style quite missed the point. The state needed the suit no less than the suit needed the state, and the march of progress could only be prescribed at the greater risk of a particular state going out of fashion.

Nationalism came to China in characteristically hybrid form, blending the universal claims of progress and civilization with the particular claims of nations.[4] There were few boundaries that were not blurred: the ideal of the nation was nested in a cluster of ethical communities, some underpinned with universal sciences, others overlaid with cosmopolitan ideals, and all finding their way into Nationalist practice at some point or another. Typically, China's reformers and revolutionaries were part-time political activists. The bulk of their energy was consumed studying and practicing the medical, agricultural, and social sciences, inventing new histories, composing new literature, writing a new kind of philosophy, and engaging readers in the new field of journalism. Others pulled down city walls to make way for urban ring-roads and installed public toilets and sewage systems, set up hospitals and libraries, opened public schools and museums, published journals and newspapers, and organized reading groups, antifootbinding leagues, women's cooperatives, and other mass organizations. China's "awakening" helped to make sense of politics. It signaled the birth of a new common sense within which people made sense of nationalism and nationalists alike. The national awakening was forging ahead at such a rapid pace that full-time, partisan revolutionaries had to work furiously to ensure that they were not left behind.

Alongside the military contests of the Nationalist Revolution there was in fact another equally important political competition to make and possess the new icons of the Chinese nation. In this Sun Yatsen was singularly successful: he started life as an iconographer and died an icon. Sun was thought an ignorant if not crazy zealot when he staged his first insurrection in 1895, but when he passed away, 30 years later, he was widely celebrated as a prescient nationalist leader. Certainly the transition did not come easily. As late as 1924, when Reuter's news agency issued a mistaken report of his death, the news that Sun had passed away was greeted with relief throughout North China in the expectation that the country might at last enjoy political unity.[5] Sun took delight in strolling through Guangzhou to show that reports of his death were greatly exaggerated. Yet his status was even less secure in Guangzhou. The Guangdong provincial administration was under attack from local warlords, while the municipal government in Guangzhou faced a strike and insurrection by shopkeepers and street peddlers who were angered by Sun's exorbitant rates of taxation. Elsewhere, his party faithful were harboring doubts about his leadership. Some old comrades in North China were still furious with Sun for entering into an agreement with members of the Chinese Communist party and for forging close ties with the socialist government of Soviet Russia. In Shanghai, party members were voicing doubts about Sun's choice of comrades to sit on the Central Executive Committee.[6] Sun Yatsen was trying to escape conflict in the party and escalating problems in Guangdong when he set out on the fatal visit to Beijing over the winter of 1924–25 that converted him, in death, into a symbol of national unity.

Much had happened over the final months of Sun's life to raise his standing as a national figure. In the winter of 1924–25 he traced a pilgrimage of Republican shrines in his journey, his death, and his burial. Setting out from his remote southern base in Guangdong for the great commercial center of Shanghai, Sun made national headlines with his strident call for the abrogation of the Unequal Treaties and an end to all foreign privilege in China. He moved on from Shanghai to Japan, and thence to the national capital of Beijing, where he was involved in unsuccessful negotiations for the restoration of constitutional government. He was finally buried at the original site of the Republican capital, Nanjing, by a Nationalist government that was gradually extending its authority over the country. This national and international pilgrimage "would lift him out of the sphere of provincial politics," in the words of a contemporary observer, and turn him into a "national hero."[7] By the time of his death, Sun had come to remind people from many different regions of the old empire that they were all supposed to be compatriots and that he himself, for all his faults, had selflessly devoted his life to making them so. For a brief moment, their many differences were shelved as people contemplated the fragile dream of a united, harmonious, and independent nation, which was the only legacy Sun Yatsen bequeathed them.[8] Sun's dream was theirs as well.

Sun Yatsen's reputation and standing grew further over the period between his death in Beijing and his internment in Nanjing in 1929. As the *Peking Leader* was moved to note, this period

[has] seen Sun Yat-sen transformed from a starkly determined but fallible revolutionary leader into the all-wise founder and guiding spirit of the Revolution, before whom all should bow and to whom all should turn for guidance and inspiration. . . . It is no small gain to China that it should have acquired such a symbol, to which all eyes can turn, as the transformed Sun Yat-sen has become. Through the centuries, the visible symbol of the throne served as the focal point for governmental activities and for such sense of national unity as existed. With the establishment of a Republic this symbol disappeared and there was nothing to take its place. . . . In these four years since he died, Dr. Sun has come in no small measure to supply that lack.[9]

Over these four years Sun's portrait came to be imprinted on every dollar bill in circulation around the country, on packets of cigarettes, and on the backs of watch cases. His picture was framed in the halls and classrooms where students and government employees met and paid their respects each Monday morning. It hung in shop windows where picture-framers mounted his portrait in the finest frames on display. Sun's words decorated the streets and numerous public monuments, and 365 of his sayings adorned the pages of the standard Chinese desk calendar.[10]

Some of this was clearly orchestrated by the state. By the mid-thirties, particular commemorative ceremonies that had first been pioneered in party and government agencies a decade or more before were extended to weddings and other civic occasions. At a mass wedding ceremony held before the mayor of Shanghai in the Shanghai Civic Center on 3 April 1935,

brides filed from the west of the building, grooms from the east, marched around the circular driveway, and up the white stone steps into the great hall. Here on a stage, decorated in scarlet and gold, where stood two immense red candles embossed with Chinese characters reading "Harmony for one hundred years," waited the witnesses. Two brides and two grooms at a time, coming from left and right simultaneously, mounted the stage, stood before a bas-relief of Doctor Sun Yat-sen, over which the Kuomintang and National flags were crossed, and awaited directions. The announcer indicated that they bow: three times to the flag and the portrait of Doctor Sun, twice to each other, and once to the witnesses.[11]

This had no precedent in Sun's lifetime. In fact, public adulation of Sun Yatsen awaited the establishment of the Nationalist state.

Sun Yatsen was as much an artist, in his own way, as the architect Lü Yanzhi and the lion painter Gao Qifeng, who designed and decorated the mag-

nificent Sun Yatsen Memorial Hall in Guangzhou. Sun's art lay in devising and
appropriating the techniques and symbols for "awakening" the nation. Looking back over his revolutionary career from his deathbed in Beijing in March
1925, Sun reflected:

I, Sun Wen, have promoted the cause of the People's Revolution for 40 years in order
to achieve freedom and equality for China. These 40 years have impressed upon me
the fact that before reaching this goal I must awaken (*huanqi*) the masses.[12]

For 40 years inside and outside China, in office and out, in disguise and in
his own name, as captive and as escapee, solvent and bankrupt, Sun had tried
everything in his power to "awaken" China, and through the worst of times
had continued to insist not only that it could be awakened but also that, when
it finally stirred, its roar would strike terror into the hearts of its enemies.

The artifice that went into the merger of politics and art in Gao Qifeng's
painting of the awakened lion was generally overlooked by visitors to the
Memorial Hall who filed past in silent contemplation. This was as Sun would
have intended. The dream of China's awakening required technique as well as
imagination, and the best technique is the one that passes unremarked. Chinese
Nationalists needed to convince their spectators and their audience that the
nation was neither a dream nor a rumor but was really out there, in the historic
past and imminent future, pining for release through a heroic act of emancipation. In their eyes, China had had a dormant "national spirit" long before it
became a modern nation-state. Sun Yatsen put it nicely when he inverted the
metaphor of the dream to show that it was not he who was dreaming but the
nation itself. "Our old national spirit is asleep," he was fond of saying; "we
must awaken it and then it will begin to revive." The deep sleep into which
the nation had fallen reduced the country to impotence; hence a national revival was dependent on the "revival" of nationalism. "When our nationalism
is revived, we can go a step further and study how to restore our national standing." [13] Sun Yatsen and his Nationalist party set out to manufacture the nation
of their dreams while insisting that they were merely stirring the beast from
its sleep.

It was not just his technique that made Sun a great artist but the keenness
of his vision and the tenacity with which he clung to it. He gave the distinct
impression that he could see into the heart of the Chinese people, that he could
make out the shape of a lion within it, and that he could entice this lion into
the clearing by the force of his conviction. There were certainly more gifted
writers in the Nationalist movement in the early Republic, but few had the conviction to match Sun Yatsen. Ye Chucang, for example, wrote many pungent
editorials for the party's *Republican Daily* when he was director of propaganda
in 1923, but his editorials were often tinged with a debilitating irony that was

quite alien to Sun Yatsen. In an editorial, "China the Sleeping Lion," published on 6 November 1923, Ye recalled how the "sleeping lion" awoke in the Republican Revolution:

When the provisional government of the Republic of China was set up in Nanjing the whole country shouted its rejoicing; its spirit could have been no bolder. Then it was truly like an awakened lion.

But the lion was not up and about for long:

Then the provisional government was abolished, the power of state passed from the hands of the revolutionary party to the old bureaucrats. So it was as if the sleeping lion simply gave a yawn, stretched a little, and then fell back into a sound sleep.

Events over the decade that had elapsed since the lion "fell back into a sound sleep" gave Ye cause to wonder whether the sleeping beast was really a lion at all, and not perhaps some more timid creature:

Is it really sound asleep? And is the sleeping creature really a lion? From that moment . . . the sleeping lion turned into a sleeping mouse.[14]

Ye Chucang may have been a fine polemicist, but he had little of Sun Yatsen's revolutionary faith.[15] In fact, for a director of propaganda, Ye placed very little faith in words, and at times showed less than complete loyalty to his party leader. In November 1923 he wrote an editorial lambasting Sun's high-sounding proposals to disarm the Nationalist movement and "turn soldiers into workers" (hua bing wei gong) with the comment that "empty words just will not do." Ye continued:

"Disbanding armies" is certainly a thorough proposal. After the awakening of the whole of humankind there may well come such a day, indeed there must be such a day, but right now it is out of the question. . . . Sun Yatsen is proposing to "turn soldiers into workers," but why not have "worker-soldiers" and turn all the workers of the country into soldiers instead?[16]

Sun Yatsen would never admit that his words were "empty" or that he should await the "awakening of the whole of humankind" before he set foot out the door. Self-doubt was a stranger to him. Where Ye Chucang thought he saw a mouse, Sun dreamed he saw a lion. He removed Ye Chucang from directorship of the propaganda bureau to signal his disapproval of Ye's loss of vision.[17]

Sun's conviction that the Chinese nation was a powerful and right royal lion worked to his advantage in the Nationalist movement. Indeed, his more faithful publicists argued that only Sun Yatsen's capacity for dreaming stood between China the lion and China the mouse. This was brilliantly captured in a cartoon neither of a lion nor of a mouse but of the cognate pairing of a tiger and a dog.

The cartoon appeared in 1912, in a magazine that counted among its contributors the noted lion artist Gao Qifeng. Ralph Croizier has described it for us:

In the first panel ("Past"), Sun Yat-sen in artist's garb measures a picture of a majestic tiger preparatory to starting on a blank canvas. In the second panel ("Present"), Yuan Shikai takes over as the artist to the consternation of a group of onlookers in semi-modernized apparel. In the third panel ("Future"), onlookers and artists alike are dumbfounded when the copied picture turns out to be a mangy dog instead of a tiger.[18]

Here the newspaper artist clearly recognized a kindred spirit in Sun Yatsen and was sympathetic to the artifice as well as the imagination behind Sun's engagement with the Chinese nation. At the same time, the cartoon evaluated political figures on the strength of their artistry: its satire was directed squarely against Yuan Shikai for the poverty of his vision, a poverty that reaffirmed the value of the original vision and, in turn, the majesty of its creator. Sun Yatsen was converted into an icon of the Chinese nation because, it appeared, he alone could paint the tiger.

The cartoonist was a political artist as well, to the extent that he could paint Sun Yatsen as leader of the nation. But political artists did not advertise their craft. They wished to be identified by their paintings rather than by their brushstrokes, with the images they promoted rather than with their technical expertise in promoting them. The political artist, like the state, was to be made invisible. The state would ultimately achieve invisibility in its perfection: "There is no empire when the empire is in perfect peace," went an old saying, and "no state when the state is perfectly governed."[19] Until the Nationalist state had been perfected, however, it was to be rendered invisible to itself and to its citizens through an ideology linking the Nationalist party with the state and an iconography identifying the state with the nation. New China was to be identified with the central state, and the state with the Chinese Nationalist party. This was the task of the political artist: to paint China as if it were awakening under Nationalist instruction.

It was a formidable task. Sun Yatsen had many rivals, and his party held no patent on the trope of awakening. Interest groups, study societies, and political factions of many different persuasions impressed the word "awakening" on their mastheads. They also employed images of lions and tigers, in many cases in settings hostile to the Nationalist movement. The Chinese Youth party (*Zhongguo qingnian dang*) began publishing the *Awakened Lion* (*Xingshi*) in October 1924 as a vehicle for attacking the Nationalist and Communist parties over the period of the Nationalist Revolution. The revolutionaries responded through their more prosaically titled *Chinese Youth* (*Zhongguo qingnian*).[20] Similarly, the *Tiger Weekly* (*Jiayin zhoukan*) was published by Zhang Shizhao in 1925 on behalf of the conservative northern government of Duan

Qirui, which was then locked in combat with the Nationalists in the south.[21] The lion was a symbol of contestation within the leadership of the Nationalist movement as well. Qiu Jin, a prominent member of the early revolutionary movement, turned the awakened lion to the service of the women's movement. Launching a new women's paper in 1906, she complained bitterly after the fashion of the day of the "darkness" into which the country had descended and of the "drunken stupor" of the Chinese people. With her *Chinese Women's Paper* (*Zhongguo nübao*), Qiu Jin proposed to shine the "clear light of dawn" on her sleeping gender, to arouse them with the "first movement of the sunrise bell." Once awakened, women were expected to fight for their rightful place at the head of the revolution "as leaders, awakened lions." [22] The *Chinese Women's Paper* did not survive beyond the first few issues, but the "awakening" of women was stimulated by Qiu Jin's personal example. She was executed for her revolutionary activity in July of the following year.

In 1920 the Women's Patriotic Comrades of Tianjin published a new serial, *The Awakening World* (*Xingshi zhoukan*), and over the years a variety of Dawn Bells, Morning Tocsins, Crowing Cocks, and Dawn Societies competed for space in the literary supplements of the great metropolitan dailies.[23] Some were devoted to science. In 1920, students of Tongji Medical and Engineering College in Shanghai put out *Self-Awakening Monthly* (*Zijue yuekan*) with the aim of promoting a spirit of scientific inquiry, and staff of the Agricultural College of Beijing founded the journal *The Awakened Peasant* (*Xingnong*) to "awaken the peasants" and "improve agriculture." Others were devoted to social movements: an entirely different model of peasant awakening served as the inspiration for a journal issued by the farmers' cooperative of Pingyuan County in Guangdong in 1923, which circulated under the identical title of *The Awakened Peasant* (*Xingnong*).[24] The term "awakening" featured prominently in the struggles between mass nationalists and liberals within the Nationalist party as well. *Popular Awakening* (*Minjue*) was published by constitutional lawyers and assemblymen of the Guangzhou rump parliament in competition with radical Nationalists associated with the Shanghai party journal, *Awaken* (*Juewu*).[25] Young Communists were as keen on the motif as the Nationalists, and contributed significantly to making *Awaken* one of the most influential of all May Fourth journals. One young Bolshevist, Zhou Enlai, earned the distinction of contributing to two different "awakening" journals in succession: the Tianjin *Awakening* (*Juewu*) in 1920, and *The Awakening Mail* (*Jueyou*) in 1923.[26] So long as colonial writers and artists continued to portray Britain as an awakened lion, pouncing upon "Bolshevist Propaganda" in China, the many awakened beasts of the Nationalist imagination still had something in common. A nation clasped in the claws of the British lion had little choice but to wake up and bite back.[27]

Where Sun Yatsen spoke of the awakening nation, and Qiu Jin of women, others counseled awakenings to science and democracy, to humanist ethics and literature, to cosmopolitanism and class consciousness, and they celebrated the awakening of youth, workers, and peasants. China was awakening altogether too rapidly and rather too broadly for many in the Nationalist party, who had their work cut out for them ensuring that their awakening took precedence over all others. It was essential that Gao Qifeng's painting of the lion should speak eloquently and forcefully of the preeminent claim of Sun Yatsen and the Nationalist movement to lead the national awakening, and that its roar should silence the rivals as well as the internal critics of the leading faction of the Nationalist movement. The one overriding condition that Sun and his successors set upon the liberation of China was that the party and the people should be organized and disciplined as they had never been before. The elevation of the awakened lion above the Memorial Hall in Guangzhou was a fitting symbol of this determination.

Sun Yatsen is remembered among Chinese communities around the world as the champion of a nation rather than as the leader of a partisan political movement. There was in fact no place for political division in Sun's dream of China. New China was in need of a new state because, as Ernest Gellner has observed, nation and state always appear destined for each other in the nationalist imagination.[28] There was, however, no place for partisan politicians in China's state. The ideal political activist was not a politician at all, but a statesman who eschewed the politics of self-interest and sectional representation, who elevated the nation to the supreme political value, and who worked tirelessly for the welfare of the people. The Nationalist party conceived of itself not as a partisan institution within a national state structure, but as a national institution embracing the "common good."[29] Sun Yatsen cultivated mercenary warlords but was never included in their notorious fraternity; he worked with parliamentary assemblies and elected delegates but never stood for public election himself; and he hosted delegates from the Communist International and the Soviet government in Moscow without ever suggesting that he was an international socialist. Yet there was a bit of the warlord, the representative, and the socialist in Sun Yatsen: like China itself, he was all of these things and yet none of them. At the time of his death, the dream of a united China and the ideal of the transcendent statesman merged in the person of Sun Yatsen. In this he achieved something few of his contemporaries could match: a political career that helped to establish the meaning of politics and yet was never tainted by the opprobrium that attached to the political.

In accounting for the Nationalists' success in identifying Sun Yatsen with the nation, distinguishing between manifest signs of "popular nationalist enthusiasm" and the systematic projection of Nationalist ideology on the part of his movement is a formidable task.[30] The awakened lion was as much an effect as a cause of this identification. Indeed, Nationalist party attempts to capitalize on Sun's death through a massive nationwide propaganda campaign backfired rather badly in 1925, and earned the party little but derision.[31] The public status of Sun Yatsen was not the result of popular enthusiasm alone, nor was it simply the product of "the acumen and energy of the Kuomintang politicians and Intellectuals," who "imposed a cult of Sun Yat-sen" upon the people. It was a little of both.[32] Nationalist propagandists were as energetic and able as this claim would suggest, but their efforts would have been in vain had not the cultivation of Sun Yatsen made sense in a public arena of which the party was only a *part*. Indeed, the party ran the risk of revealing its own partisan character in claiming Sun for itself. He was showered with honors because people could make sense of him in their own way, and they made sense of him in a way that his own party, as a partisan institution, could not.

For much the same reason, the story of Sun Yatsen the dreamer and the history of China, the dream, are not easily separated. Sun's biography has become both part and analogue of the history of the nation. He was born on 12 November 1866 in Xiangshan County in Guangdong, to a peasant family that was ill-equipped to provide a classical education but sufficiently well-connected through the overseas Chinese network to provide a modern-school education in Hawaii and subsequent medical training in Hong Kong. Sun's common background and limited acquaintance with the Confucian canon and classical literature, his foreign associations, and his close acquaintance with Western learning were all barriers to a bureaucratic career and to orthodox political activity at the turn of the century. But by the time of Sun's death in 1925, they had turned to his advantage. Textual exegesis of the Confucian canon had yielded to scientific discourse in elite culture, with a new foundation in Western learning, and the common people from among whom Sun had sprung were learning that sovereignty was vested in themselves as equal citizens (*guomin*) in a democratic state. It was not Sun Yatsen who had changed but the world about him. The new values were conveyed implicitly in the ideology of the Nationalist party and explicitly in Sun's own words. But political activists were overshadowed by novelists and storytellers, artists and artisans, architects and engineers, historians, philosophers and journalists, musicians and fashion-designers, all of whom were helping to place the nation at the center of the new common sense that came to permeate everyday life in the second and third decades of this century. The people of China themselves created the symbols of national awakening that converted a patriotic, forward-looking commoner into an icon of the nation. These symbols, in turn, urged the people of China to *be* awakened by their icon.

Awakening and Tutelage

In scholarship, the idea of an awakening was not easily separated from the idea of being awakened by others. The disciple is invariably awakened by the master, the pupil by the teacher. In Chan or Zen Buddhism, "awareness" was counted the "gateway to all mysteries," and attainment of awareness typically came in the form of a sudden awakening to the light, or a blow to the head delivered by a master.[33] These ethical and religious motifs recur in the memoirs of modern nationalists to characterize the relationship between a mentor and his disciple. Kang Youwei recorded in his autobiography that his experience of apprenticeship under the Guangdong scholar Zhu Ciqi was like "a blind man seeing the light." Liang Qichao recalled of his own studies under Kang, in turn, that he was awoken by the clarity of the master's words as if he had been struck by "a blow on the head."[34] In later decades the motif was preserved among readers of the New Literature to describe their own awakenings under the prompting of radical journalists. An older subscriber to *New Youth* magazine wrote of his astonishment on first reading the journal:

This spring I read your magazine for the first time. As if woken by a blow on the head, I suddenly realized the value of youth. . . . Although at present I am not what you might describe as a new youth, I am sure that I can sweep from my mind all the old thoughts from the past.[35]

In broaching their new communities of youth, women, class, and nation, twentieth-century writers never quite escaped "all the old thoughts from the past" that they professed to disown.[36] They derived from ethics a compulsion to engage in social and political action, and they confronted in ethics a choice of strategies for action that was effectively limited to varieties of individual and mass awakening. The awakened citizen of twentieth-century China was heir to a literary tradition that remained vital to the extent that it obliged the awakened self to acknowledge its debt to its master and its duty to "awaken" the world.

The moral compulsion to awaken others was set down in the earliest of Confucian canons in the ideal of the "superior man" (*junzi*), whose cultivation of personal virtue served as a paradigm for ordering the affairs of the family and arranging the affairs of state.[37] The Confucian ethic was reinvigorated in the late eighteenth century in debate between the schools of Song Learning and Han Learning, which was partly resolved in the syncretic School of Han-Song Learning, and which remained vital to the end of the Confucian world-order in lively controversies over rival New and Old texts of the Confucian classics.[38] Differences within late Confucian scholarship emerged as differences of emphasis within an overarching moral-political order. That is to say, they arose out of a common concern for establishing the ethical foundations for personal virtue, they centered on a common affirmation of the integrity of the cultivated self and its moral community, and they were each directed toward the common end of identifying the proper relationship between moral perfection, social organization, and management of affairs of state.[39]

The partiality of reformers and revolutionaries for counting themselves awakened, and for conceiving of cultural, social, and political action in terms of mass awakenings, sat easily alongside developments in Confucian thought over the last century of Qing rule.[40] Kang Youwei made a number of radical innovations in Confucian thought but retained a commitment to the orthodox teaching of Mencius: the "first awakened" (*xianjue*) among the people were burdened by that awakening with the additional responsibility of saving the people (*jiumin*) by awakening them (*juemin*).[41] The burden was not lifted from the cultural, social, and political activists of the Republic when they cast aside all that was "old," "feudal," and "Confucian," and it was urged upon Nationalist party propagandists by Sun Yatsen in words all but identical to those of Kang Youwei.[42]

Similarly, a revolutionary emphasis on "practice" had direct antecedents in the scholarship of the late empire.[43] Consistent stress upon the practical dimensions of ethical reflection, in the judgment of the historian Hao Chang, "separated the Confucian thought of the nineteenth century from that of the preceding century." [44] Moral and political philosophy converged on the motif of action. Ethical philosophers stressed self-awareness and self-cultivation, yet at the same time counseled active engagement with the life of the moral community. And statecraft scholarship, although wedded to practical affairs, remained grounded in a Confucian moral order.[45] This marriage of ethics and action survived the collapse of Confucianism in the twentieth century. Where the moral community was conceived as a paradigm of the cultivated self in imperial scholarship, the national community was conceived as an extension of the awakened self in nationalist thought. Self-cultivation yielded to self-awareness (*zijue*), or self-awakening, and the cultivation of the superior man gave way to the awakening of the citizen. Awakened Nationalists ushered their compatriots into a refurbished theater of moral politics, where they directed them to occupy the seats once reserved for gentry-scholars.

For the Nationalist party, the idea of action embraced military affairs, constitutional politics, and mass organization. Action also meant issuing propaganda to awaken the people. Sun Yatsen cited the example of the imperial tutor guiding the young Shang emperor, Dai Jia, to illustrate the relationship between his party and the Chinese people.[46] The emperor was sovereign under the empire, as citizens were sovereign in a republic. Where the sovereign needed his tutor, the citizen required a tutelary state. Sun had plotted armed putsches early in his revolutionary career, and he retained a keen interest in constitutional politics to the end. But he had, Sun confessed, grown tired of fighting and politicking after the founding of the Republic. By 1924 he proposed replacing the old emphasis on "guns and cannon" with an "awakening of the mind." For this he favored mass propaganda:

If we were to compare the struggles in which we used guns and cannon with those in which we used our tongues and our pens, then clearly in times past we resorted to armed struggle above all. We long ago eliminated the government of the Manchu Qing dynasty with rifle and cannon fire. Yet although that government has now been out of action for thirteen years, the revolution has not been carried through to completion. Why do we have nothing to show for it? Put simply, it is because we have expended too little effort on the propaganda struggle.

The sorry history of the revolution, Sun counseled, confirmed the old saying that "it is important to attack their hearts before attacking the walls of their city" (*gongxin wei shang, gongcheng wei xia*).[47] His choice of words is revealing. The citadel to be breached in this new round of political warfare was not the imperialist metropole. Certainly the belligerent attitude of the Western powers, their continued occupation of China's territory, and their insistence upon retaining authority over their own nationals were all thorns in the side of the Nationalist movement. But even when his hostility toward imperialism boiled over into invective in the winter of 1923, Sun refrained from urging any attack against the foreign powers directly. Instead, he chose to overcome the indifference of the Chinese people to imperialism. It was the hearts of the people of China that Sun proposed to target in the Nationalist Revolution, in the hope of "awakening" them to the evils of imperialism.

The imperialists themselves provided his first lesson. Sun noted in his lectures on the Three Principles of the People that China possessed the largest population of any country on earth, yet in the same breath he cautioned against complacency on this account. In the first place, he argued, the race was in decline and would soon be outstripped by its rivals unless more care were taken with medicine and hygiene. More importantly, he felt that in China's case there was no direct correlation between the size and health of the race and the wealth and power of the nation. China's masses, for all their size, are "born in a stupor and die in a dream." [48] China's size could be turned to advantage only by awakening the masses from their slumber. Sun then looked to the example of Western missionaries to master the arts of public hygiene *and* mass propaganda.

Western missionaries pioneered the way in public campaigns for health reform, initially through small-group agitation against footbinding, and eventually through the first of the mass campaigns of twentieth-century China, focusing on public-health issues. In 1915, missionary health workers were drawing crowds of 7,000 in Hangzhou, 10,000 in Changsha, and around 20,000 in Shanghai to attend public-education meetings designed to eradicate tuberculosis.[49] Missionaries also showed a single-minded devotion to the task of winning converts to Christ. Traditional methods of indoctrination, Andrew Nathan has noted in a seminal study of democracy in China, "sought to train but not to mobilize people; to maintain but not to remake society." [50] These older techniques were directed to communities as groups rather than as collections of individuals. Missionaries, by contrast, aspired to awaken the individual conscience on a massive scale.

Mass campaigns promoting public health, popular education, and the rights of women were not directly related to the mission of winning converts to Christ. But nor were they entirely incidental. Civilization and Christianity marched hand in hand across Africa, India, Oceania, and China. Certainly for the missionary in early twentieth-century China, Christianity was the religion of the civilized person.[51] But the relationship between Christian proselytization and the promotion of civilization was a contingent one easily severed by China's nationalists. The "Great Awakening," which sent missionaries across the Pacific to China, was a religious event.[52] The Chinese awakening was, in the main, a secular one. In this respect, missionaries and nationalists were competing for the same congregation and seeking to gain from them something that had no place in the work of the Confucian functionary: the awakening of the individual soul.

Missionaries also pioneered journalism. In 1815 William Milne published the first civic periodical to circulate in China, the *General Monthly Record*. Hundreds of other magazines followed, some in European languages and others in Chinese, and although few won converts to Christianity, many of these missionary journals garnered enthusiastic converts to the profession of journalism itself, particularly among those who recognized the potential of magazines and newspapers for promoting secular values in addition to religious ones. Extant Chinese newspapers (which confined their coverage to commercial and government information) were merely aids to "falling asleep," Liang Qichao acidly observed. Following China's defeat by Japan in 1895, Liang pioneered a new kind of political journal for the express purpose of awakening the people. Liang's *Chinese and Foreign News* seems to have had the desired effect—or at least to have popularized the idea that the people of China needed to be shaken from their sleep. One subscriber likened the appearance of *Chinese and Foreign News* to "the explosion of a large bomb, which awoke many people from their dreams." [53]

Their comparable ambitions need not have made competitors of the missionary and Nationalist movements had their enterprises not been competitive in other respects as well. Nationalists bore witness to an immense range of missionary initiatives in fields they wished to reserve for themselves: in promoting public health and hygiene, in championing language reform and popular education, in emancipating women, and in caring for the socially disadvantaged. Missionary demands for better urban planning, more reliable fresh water supplies, improved sanitation and waste disposal systems, more public schools, and modern hospitals also anticipated, in the aggregate, a new and expanded role for the state, which came to be spelled out in Nationalist ideology. The state summoned up by these expectations was nationalist, and hence jealous of its own autonomy, and so thoroughly rational that it could hardly countenance "superstition" of the kind that Christian missionaries professed. So although missionaries supplied some of the vision, much of the science, and many of the techniques employed by national revolutionaries, they also supplied many of their easiest targets.[54] Their tragedy was an indirect tribute to the success of the missionaries themselves.

Sun Yatsen was himself a convert, but his religious belief was not the source of his admiration for foreign missionaries. Their Christianity was incidental. He admired their daring, their dedication, and their success in the act of conversion itself. Sun argued without fear of contradiction that missionary propaganda differed little from the practices of the Chinese sages, and that the example of Confucius, "roaming the various states . . . propagating the Way of Yao, Shun, Yu, Tang, Wen, Wu, and the Duke of Zhou," was an indigenous precedent for the work of the modern missionary or political propagandist.[55] When he elaborated upon the Confucian adage "To win over their minds is to win over their people, and to win over their people is to gain hold of their state" (de qi xin zhe, de qi min, de qi min zhe, de qi guo), he paid indirect homage to missionary practices of conversion.[56] The object of the Nationalist Revolution was, as the saying went, to "gain hold of their state," but the strategy was no longer simply a matter of winning hearts and minds. It was to "convert" (ganhua) the people of China. Conversion entailed a transformation of the mind. "If we want to change [minds] thoroughly," said Sun in 1923, "then we must think of ways to convert them. Conversion is propaganda." [57]

In counseling propaganda for conversion, Sun deferred explicitly to the example of missionary workers. Introducing a new program for political propaganda on 25 November 1923, he reflected on the success of missionaries in instilling ideals and faith in their converts:

The reason religion can convert people is because [missionaries] have a set of principles that people can believe in. If ordinary people have faith in the principles, the principles enter deep within their bones and they can lay down their lives for their principles.[58]

The prospect of embedding principles "deep within their bones" held some appeal in 1923, at a time when his followers were showing little inclination to lay down their lives for Sun's principles. But it was not only his followers Sun had in mind. He was proposing to convert the entire country on the missionary model.[59] This called for additional precedents to show that a foreign model of mass conversion was both consistent with China's traditional culture and well suited to the Nationalists' revolutionary aspirations. Sun then turned to the example of the Bolshevik Revolution in Russia, leavened with Confucian precedent:

The sole reason for the success of the revolution in Russia is that their revolutionary party [members] are all true believers and converted the entire country to their principles, with the result that they were able to reform their government from its foundations without resorting to arms. When Confucius roamed the various states in his final years, what was he trying to do? Nothing but propagate his principles.[60]

Sun advised his followers that the Nationalist Revolution would achieve the required rate of "conversion" only if all party members dutifully followed his example:

One party member who works hard propagating principles on behalf of our party can convert a thousand and more people, and if this thousand and more people also work hard propagating principles on behalf of our party they can convert several hundred thousand or even a few million more. If we continue in this fashion then our party's principles should become universal among the people of the entire country of their own accord.[61]

In fact, people were already awakening "of their own accord," although not to the party's principles. In speaking of conversion to partisan belief, Sun was proposing to take advantage of a greater process of conversion launched by missionaries in the nineteenth century and followed by his predecessors in the nationalist movement. The creation of a nonpartisan community of *nationals* preceded partisan nationalism. So Sun had to appeal to reason, to science, and to the universal principles of the Enlightenment if he wished to "convert" the country to the principles of his party.

Awakening and Enlightenment

Ernest Gellner has hinted at the technical function of the awakening trope in the self-projection of modern nationalism: "Nationalism is not the *awakening* of nations to self-consciousness; it invents nations where they do not exist." [62] The nation establishes its pedigree in a greater enlightenment enterprise that pictures the nation as a hidden or sleeping element of a universal order that happens to predate the appearance of merely ephemeral nationalist movements. Whereas Enlightenment *philosophes* looked to the texts and traditions of the scholar-bureaucracy of China for inspiration, Chinese social and political activists of the twentieth century turned to the European Enlightenment for guidance themselves, indirectly recovering elements of an indigenous ethics that they now declined to take seriously at home. Where an earlier generation had sought native roots for foreign ideas, twentieth-century nationalists looked less to their own traditions than to those of Europe and America in seeking precedents for their invention.[63] But neither generation drifted far from its historical roots in ethics and statecraft. The rhetorical awakening from "feudal" superstition to reason and modernity, for example, was conducted in the language of Leninism but mediated by long acquaintance with the contest between feudal particularism and bureaucratic rationalism in the earlier statecraft tradition.[64]

For all its resonance with native ethics and statecraft, however, the idea of a national awakening was a borrowed one. It is said that Napoleon uttered his famous warning that China would awaken and shake the world after reading an account of Lord Macartney's mission to the court of Beijing. In fact, he could have been referring to any kingdom or empire. Reference to a sleeping people was a universal code for the monarchical states that had encountered Napoleon's armies and for the native communities of Asia, Africa, and the Americas, which were being colonized by the newly emerging national empires. Whether an existing state was counted asleep or awake ultimately depended on its capacity to resist the modern conscript army or to mobilize mass armies of its own. There was no hope of escaping the iron grip of the metaphor any more than there was reasonable prospect of avoiding the armies of France or Russia, or forestalling the arrival of the British or Japanese navies.

Even if a people were counted "awake" in all other respects, their inability to defend their sovereignty sufficed to rank them among the sleeping peoples of the world. So J. A. Hobson, in his pioneering book *Imperialism: A Study* (1902), acknowledged a "genius of the Chinese peoples" in life and letters that qualified them to be counted among the awakened peoples of the world. But, he added, China needed to bestir itself from its tranquility to face the armies that were rapidly approaching it. "Unless China can be roused quickly from the sleep of countless centuries of peace and can transform herself into a powerful military nation, she cannot escape the pressure of the external powers." [65] China, like other states confronting the expanding nationalist empires, had either to awaken its people to stage effective resistance or to suffer the rude awakening that came in train of the defeat and collapse of the monarchical state. The country would awaken because Europe supplied it with the incentive, the technologies, and the metaphors to do so.

An awakening of the martial spirit was not the only awakening in store for

China. Few Chinese nationalists shared Hobson's naive conviction that China had known "countless centuries of peace," and some were especially wary of arousing the more bellicose spirit of either the rebel or the imperial tradition. Sun Yatsen was astonished when the British consul called on him in his capacity as commander in chief of the southern government in 1917, to request that he send troops to assist in the Great War. Sun rejected the offer outright with the advice that an invitation to send troops to Europe was in effect an invitation to stage an "awakening of the martial spirit," which could as well be turned upon British interests in Hong Kong as against the Axis powers in Europe. This had never been his intention in awakening the sleeping lion.[66]

The more comprehensive idea of national awakening embraced by Sun Yatsen had different European precedents. "It was the foreigners who used to describe China as a sleeping lion," recalled the Nationalist director of propaganda, Ye Chucang, in a characteristically intemperate editorial in November 1923. Ye was more ambivalent about the national awakening than was Sun Yatsen, partly because Ye recognized the foreign source of the metaphor and partly because he thought it failed to capture the complexity of the situation in which China found itself. Yet even Ye's cynicism was derivative. He insisted that China was more like a sleeping mouse than a sleeping lion because foreigners thought so too: "This is not my observation. It is the feeling of most foreigners." [67] The foreigners to whom Ye Chucang deferred were on the whole less generous than Hobson, acknowledging little genius among the people of China and employing the motifs of sleep and dreaming in ways that did not flatter China at all. Ye had good cause for skepticism.

Indeed, sleeping and dreaming were associated not only with peace and tranquility but also with the irrational and the primitive. European thought staked its claim to be rational and empirical along a notional boundary separating reason from dreaming, and the change of phase between dream and wakefulness was associated with an evolutionary or historical transition from the irrational to the rational, first among animals and humans and then among races of people. In early Enlightenment science, the line between dreams and the real helped to distinguish animals from humans. Thus Buffon in 1812: "The only difference between us and the brutes is that we can distinguish dreams from ideas or real sensations." Later in the nineteenth century, a comparable line was drawn in the ethnographic sciences between races or "breeds" of people in place of the earlier distinction between "us and the brutes." Dreaming was now a mark not of beasts but of primitive peoples. The German anthropologist Adolf Bastian noted of the tribal groups he was studying: "For them, hallucinations and illusions maintain a half-conscious oscillation between dreaming and waking as a normal condition." As Patrick Wolfe has noted, the advent of Darwinism in the mid-nineteenth century, in the interval between Buffon and Bastian, "relativized Buffon's hiatus and enabled the opening up of comparable divisions within *genus homo*." Darwin's own role was more than just inspirational. In an attempt to capture the consciousness of the aboriginal Australians, Darwin himself employed the metaphor of a sleeping dog, twitching in its dreams.[68]

The motif of awakening had assimilated the idea of the primitive to the brute fact of colonial conquest well before the advent of the Enlightenment, in the literature and art of the age of discovery. Perhaps the earliest representation of the European awakening of a sleeping people is Theodor Galle's engraving of Amerigo Vespucci's "rediscovery" of America, based on a drawing by Jan van der Straet and published around 1580. The upright figure of Vespucci, bearing a sword and armed with the tokens of Christian faith and scientific learning, gazes down upon a naked woman in a hammock who has been awakened from her sleep, and who holds forth her arm in a gesture of supplication. The caption reads: "America rediscovers America; he called her once and thenceforth she was ever awakened."

What Amerigo Vespucci awoke by compass, sword, and cross, the engraver Galle conquered with his pen. In *The Writing of History*, Michel de Certeau connects the promethean, masculine spirit of European conquest over the sleeping female native with the later practices of historical representation, tracing their conjunction to the publication of Galle's engraving. "This erotic and warlike scene has an almost mythic value," he writes. "It represents the beginning of a new function of writing in the West. . . . This is *writing that conquers*. It will use the New World as if it were a blank, 'savage' page on which Western desire will be written." A later evocation of the blank page (*tabula rasa*) in Enlightenment philosophy merged Western desire and human reason in a self-consciously universal enterprise that all but disguised its origins in the awakening of sleeping peoples by European conquest.[69] Similarly, on the Chinese continent, the page pronounced blank by China's own conquerors—Dai Jitao for the Nationalists and Mao Zedong for the Communists—was scrubbed clean not by enlightened reason alone but by the desire to discover and awaken a distinctively *Chinese* people.

European historians and philosophers applied the metaphor to the clash of nations. The awakening of civilizations beyond Europe was thought to await the arrival of Europeans. In the monumental histories of civilizations emanating from the German universities, early in the nineteenth century, sleep and wakefulness served to distinguish among nations. Georg Hegel explicitly counterpointed dreaming with rationality in his contemplation of Indian civilization. The "generic principle of the Hindoo Nature," he announced, was "Spirit in a state of Dream." Hegel's description of the dreaming Indian, in contrast to the awakened self of Europe, deserves to be counted among the classics of the trope:

In a dream the individual ceases to be conscious of self *as such*, in contradistinction from objective existences. When awake, I exist for myself, and the rest of creation is an external, fixed objectivity, as I myself am for it. As external, the rest of existence expands itself to a rationally connected whole; a system of relations, in which my individual being is itself a member—an individual being united with that totality. This is the sphere of *Understanding*. In the state of dreaming, on the contrary, this separation is suspended. Spirit has ceased to exist for itself in contrast with alien existence, and thus the separation of the external and individual dissolves before its universality— its *essence*. The dreaming Indian is therefore all that we call finite and individual; and, at the same time—as infinitely universal and unlimited—a something intrinsically divine. . . . This gives us a general idea of the Indian view of the universe. *Things* are as much stripped of rationality, of finite consistent stability of cause and effect, as *man* is of the steadfastness of free individuality, of personality, and freedom.[70]

The awakened European of Hegel's imagination was an awakened self, individual, personal, and free, at once separated from things and reunited with them by Understanding. Understanding, for Hegel, entailed a good deal more than rationality. It embraced the relationship between the self and the world, or more specifically, between consciousness of individuality and freedom in relation to a rational and material world.

The awakened self was born and raised in the Europe of the Enlightenment at a time when the quest for rationality, autonomy, and progress, in all spheres of life, sired an ideal of a self-conscious human subject who would discover freedom in mastering the laws of nature and mastering the world. The alternative—submission to nature or to fate—entailed a conscious, or perhaps repressed and hence unconscious, ignorance of the laws that governed historical development. Awakening to reason entailed self-knowledge of a kind that stripped away layers of received tradition and surface appearances to reveal the historical laws that animated the whole. Here, in the language of enlightenment, lay the seeds of the depth metaphor and of the realist aesthetic of the modern age, which account in equal measure for the Sleeping Hindoo of Hegel, for "false consciousness" in Marxist social critique, and, perhaps, for the Unconscious in Freudian psychoanalysis.[71]

The Enlightenment was concerned with the destiny of the entire world and the civilizations that constituted it. But it was partial in its judgments. Indeed, it is hard to read the indictment of the sleeping "Hindoo" as anything but an indictment of one civilization by another in a contest among civilizations for mastery of the world. The Hindoo was sleeping because he was oblivious of the freedom that the awakening of the Enlightenment afforded the peoples of

France, Britain, and Prussia. There was little prospect of the awakening of the individual Hindoo short of being awoken from his sleep by the arrival of Europeans. The idea of an awakened Europe, then, helped to explain and to justify the advance of European civilization across the globe, and to disarm its most trenchant critics. It was in this spirit that Marx composed his famous dictum on the effects of "English steam and English free trade" on the "semi-barbarian, semi-civilized communities" of village India. "We must not forget," Marx reminded his readers, that these villages

subjugated man to external circumstances instead of elevating man to be the sovereign of circumstances, that they transformed a self-developing social state into never-changing natural destiny, and thus brought about a brutalizing worship of nature. . . . England, it is true, in causing a social revolution in Hindustan, was actuated only by the vilest interests, and was stupid in her manner of enforcing them. But that is not the question. The question is, can mankind fulfil its destiny without a fundamental revolution in the social state of Asia?[72]

The awakening of Europe and the pursuit of its "vile interests" demonstrated that it was pointless to think otherwise. India and China had to be awoken by Europe for the fulfillment, not of their own, but of human destiny.

The idea that human destiny would be fulfilled by the awakening of the nations of Asia was embraced by China's Nationalists. In the Hegelian system, China, in contrast to India, boasted at least one site of freedom and one awakened individual in the person of the emperor. For Hegel, this signaled no more than the primitive state of development of civil society in China relative to India, and offered further cause to reflect on the backwardness of the empire.[73] Hegel knew little of China and rather underestimated the incidence of "voluntary association" in Oriental societies, much as Marx was to do in deriving his model of the Asiatic Mode of Production.[74] Yet at the same time, Hegel was prescient in attributing wakefulness to none but the sovereign in China. Chinese Nationalists were inclined to do the same. The historical continuity of the central imperial state supplied China's revolutionaries with an ideal of political autonomy within a unified state system within which the "people" would now play the part of emperor. Hegel's attribution of understanding and freedom to the sovereign anticipated the attribution of freedom to the awakened citizen in Chinese Nationalist thought, which tended to conceive of freedom not in terms of civil society but in relation to political sovereignty.

This was certainly the case among leaders of the Chinese Nationalist party. For Sun Yatsen, the revolution would make kings of the people:

Political sovereignty used to be entirely in the hands of the emperor and had nothing to do with the people. Today we who advocate democracy want to put political sovereignty into the hands of the people. What, then, will the people become? Since China has had a revolution and has adopted a democratic form of government, the people should rule in all matters. The government now may be called popular government; in other words, under a republic we make the people king.[75]

Sun was not unduly perturbed by the want of civil society in China. He was frequently irritated by the emergence of public associations outside the framework of his own party.[76] Far more frustrating for Sun was the apparent failure of the people to awaken to their *political* autonomy: "Although autocracy is overthrown, a republic is established, and we are apparently free, yet the people have not gotten rid of their idea of autocracy." [77] He applied the metaphors of enlightenment exclusively to political agents capable of awakening the people from their slumber, and proposed that state sovereignty be transferred to a few "gifted specialists" possessing superior "understanding." [78] In his fifth lecture on democracy, Sun described people of superior understanding as "those who awaken first" (*xian juezhe*), and he conceived of their awakening in universal terms, as

people of superior wisdom who take one look at a thing and see numerous principles involved, who hear one word and immediately perform great deeds, whose insights into the future and whose achievements make the world advance and give mankind its civilization.[79]

The awakened sovereign of Hegel's imagination was converted into the awakened functionary of the Nationalist party.

Even for Sun, the trope of awakening tied the quickening of self and nation to intellectual movements claiming universal validity. When reformers and scholars spoke of a national awakening in China, they generally meant national development in its broadest sense, broaching every subject of the Enlightenment, from the natural sciences to high art, and virtually every project of post-Enlightenment modernity, from modern communications to high fashion. Still, there is a significant difference between the trope of an awakening nation and the idea of a developing one. Awakening counsels action, whereas development implies passive submission to historical process. The code of the developing nation had not yet been invented when Chinese nationalists first proposed awakening China. It is doubtful, nevertheless, that an appeal for national development would have captured the mood of the young patriots who were calling on their countrymen to wake up. An awakening promises instantaneous relief, a "blow on the head," in contrast to the gradual and incremental change that accompanies development, and patience was a rare virtue—indeed, it was rarely *counted* a virtue—among nationalists in China. The trope of awakening made virtues of passion and haste.

Development is also a comparative concept. It asks nationalists to wait their turn in history. This was not a very appealing option to Sun Yatsen or his Nationalist party when it seemed that other nations less deserving than China were already far ahead in the queue. Sun's call for a national awakening was intended to show people outside of China how far China had already advanced beyond them. "Our civilization has already advanced two thousand years beyond yours," Sun informed the British consul in Guangzhou. "We are willing to wait for you to progress and catch up with us." [80] The idea of a national awakening was satisfying because it appealed to a sense of history that flattered China, and gratifying because it was available to each and every nation with the good sense to will itself "awake."

The motif of an awakening worked in the other direction as well, to merge the universal aspects of the Enlightenment with the singular claims of nation-states. The Enlightenment claimed universal validity, but from the moment of the French Revolution it in fact sired particular nations. "Far from spreading liberty in the world," writes Connor Cruise O'Brien, "the French Revolutionary expansion strengthened reaction by ensuring resistance . . . would be associated with nationalism in other countries." [81] The universal claims of European science inspired resistance as well. In preparing for his mission to China in 1793, the British emissary Lord Macartney requisitioned a hot-air balloon to take to Beijing as a tangible sign of British achievement. Balloons had become a paramount symbol of the Enlightenment since the Montgolfier brothers first paraded their invention of glue and paper over the streets of Paris in 1783, and one of the first Englishmen to make the ascent, John (later Sir John) Barrow, appears to have taken to the air shortly before accompanying Lord Macartney on his mission to China.[82] Macartney then had cause for regret when He Shen, grand secretary under Emperor Gao Zong, refused permission to inflate the balloon in Beijing. "Had a hot-air balloon risen over Peking," Macartney's biographer observes, "all China would have known of Western superiority." [83]

Macartney, a brilliant but arrogant diplomat, was eager to deal a blow to the Court of Beijing as rude as any that had been delivered to a Zen disciple by his master. Over a dozen missions had made their way to Beijing since the founding of the Qing dynasty in 1644, but none had set out so deliberately to shake the court from its "vain and arrogant sentiments" about its place in the world. Macartney's refusal to kowtow on the occasion of the emperor's birthday, noted Barrow, "mortified, and perplexed, and alarmed" the Department of Ceremonies in Beijing.[84] In fact, Macartney did not propose to follow precedent in anything but the exchange of gifts — and even here there was a difference. He came to barter science and progress in exchange for greater trade and influence. Macartney brought news of the scientific revolution in Europe and proposed to discover China, for Europe, in the new categories of scientific thought. Among his complement were an artist, a draftsman, a metallurgist, a general scientist, a botanist, a medical doctor, and John Barrow himself. Macartney and his train traveled through the empire inquiring into all manner of local customs, languages, and beliefs, capturing some of the architectural achievements of the country in their draftsmanship, catching the mood of the country in their etchings, and collecting samples of plant life to take back to London.[85]

Barrow, Macartney's comptroller, was a scientist and adventurer with a special interest in mathematics and geography. His subsequent career traced a pattern common to his time: the young man's enthusiasm for exploration and ballooning, his fertile imagination, and his scientific training were all turned in maturity to the service of the Crown. Barrow eventually rose to greater heights as permanent undersecretary at the Admiralty, from which position he oversaw an immense naval exercise to chart all of the world's coasts and oceans. With Barrow's active encouragement, the Royal Navy brought back to England specimens of rock strata, fossils, and exotic flora and fauna to satisfy the curiosity of the Royal Society (and Charles Darwin), and it established new naval bases wherever the opportunity was afforded.[86] The Colonial Office was a little more cautious than Barrow and indirectly rebuked Sir John for his overwheening imperial ambition. Barrow, however, was proud to be counted an imperialist.[87] He sought without apology to extend science and civilization throughout all of the newly charted lands of Asia and Africa under the exclusive dominion of the Union Jack. He shared Macartney's disdain, in particular, for the personal habits and the administrative style of China's imperial officials—so "ill agreeing with the feeling of Englishmen"—and he did his personal best to bring the empire down.[88] Barrow advised his own government through the decades of tense contestation between Britain and the imperial government of China over his term of office in the Admiralty from 1804 to 1845, which culminated in British victory in the First Opium War.

Awakening and History

The history of China from the Opium Wars to the mid-twentieth century has been told and retold as the "awakening" of modern China from the illusions and lethargy of empire. This kind of historical memory is largely silent about daily life under the old empire; some of its shortcomings as a framework for historical analysis have been noted elsewhere as well.[89] The idea of China's awakening has a certain tenacity all the same, because it is deeply embedded in that country's own history. China's awakening represents a historical event as well as a historical framework, because the idea of an awakening relegated the humiliations of the past to the world of dreams among China's most tenacious dreamers—its political reformers and revolutionaries.

There were certainly sufficient humiliations to encourage wakeful opti-

mism. The empire's defeat at the hands of the British in the Opium War was
followed closely by humiliation at the hands of combined forces in 1860, by
a French victory in 1884, and by Japanese victory in 1894. As each defeat invited close reflection on the incapacity of the old order to defend the realm,
the idea of a national awakening promised a day of historical redemption when
the country would finally shake off the shackles of foreign imperialism and
domestic feudalism and stand wealthy, strong, and proud as an independent
state.[90] It was not historians but China's reformers and revolutionaries who
first telescoped the history of national defeat and progressive reform into a
simple schema of historical progress punctuated by awakenings of one kind
and another.

Toward the end of his career, the reformer Liang Qichao noted the dialectical movement between progress and historical consciousness when he
observed that "during the last fifty years the Chinese have gradually realised
their own insufficiency. This little consciousness, on the one hand, is the cause
of the progress of learning; and, on the other, it may be counted as the result of progress of learning."[91] Liang defined progress as a series of national
awakenings in response to foreign intervention, and in his reflections on the
history of reform and revolution he anticipated that future progress would take
the form of new and even better "awakenings." Looking back over the past
half century in 1922, Liang noted that the first lesson came with the realization
that China's "mechanical articles" were inadequate to the task of repelling the
foreign invaders, following defeat in the Opium Wars. This awakening corresponded with the period of the Tongzhi Restoration (1861–74). Defeat in the
Sino-Japanese War in 1894 prompted a second awakening that struck like "a
thunderbolt in a dream." In this phase, a few people "with good minds" came
to recognize that not only the weapons of war but also the political and administrative institutions of the empire were inadequate to the task demanded of
them. They proposed far-reaching political reforms. The third and most recent
awakening dawned shortly before Liang spoke, when the combined effects of
the New Culture and May Fourth movements cast a harsh light on traditional
culture and society and demanded a "reawakening of the whole psychology."[92]
This final phase entailed in addition a political awakening on the part of the
common people to their rightful place in government, accompanied by demands for a government that was more responsive. Attainment of national
self-government was the ultimate awakening. All of China's greatest accomplishments in recent history, Liang concluded, were "achieved by the fundamental awakening of the people," and this "awakening of our citizens towards
government is the general source of political progress."[93]

Liang's lecture repeated the emphatic rhetoric of popular awakening that
permeated literature in the early 1920s.[94] His reasoning offered an operational

explanation for this reawakening as well, anticipating that future progress would take the form of additional awakenings under the prompting of nationalists like himself. In time, Sun Yatsen picked up the model where Liang left off, partly to explain his own revolutionary progress and setbacks and partly to justify a new and even more progressive kind of Nationalist politics: the politics of "mass awakening."

Sun adopted the schematic flow of Liang Qichao's progressive teleology, beginning with the military sciences and ending with popular awakening, although at first he applied it to his own revolutionary movement in its struggle against the Qing, rather than to the conflict between the Qing dynasty and the foreign powers. By the 1920s, however, he had come to believe that China's awakening should take the form of an anti-imperialist movement. "The foreign powers' attitude was formerly something like this," he wrote. "Since China would never awaken and could not govern itself, they would occupy points along the coast like Dalian, Weihaiwei and Kowloon as bases for 'slicing up' China." Sun was determined that China should "awaken" not only to prove the powers wrong but also to compel them to return China's lost territory.[95]

The idea of successive awakenings, each marking an advance from the preceding one, was of course grounded in a much broader idea of historical progress. This was perhaps the most innovative aspect of the national awakening, that it was imagined as progressive. A new generation of historians felt that the country's past weighed like a nightmare on the brain of the living, and they set out to reconstruct China's history as a sequence of successive improvements, in the belief that the country needed to awaken from its illusion of timeless grandeur before it could possibly shake off the foreigners. And well before these new historians set pen to paper, public-minded citizens had already begun to reorganize their histories in local museums, where they placed specimens of scientific, ethnological, and political interest in progressive sequence. Time itself was taking on a different inflection in everyday life as many of China's citizens now wished to claim a little progress for themselves. The community was awakening, in Benedict Anderson's suggestive phrase, to a "secular, historically-clocked, imagined community" with a distinctly Chinese character.[96]

This new sense of time marked a change from the sense conveyed by the built environment of China's cities, gardens, and terraces. The past certainly impressed itself upon city-dwellers in the empire, but architecturally, "the present was never strikingly new or different," and the habits and values of any one generation of sojourners did not impress themselves so indelibly on the buildings, monuments, and public roads as to mark them off from the efforts of generations preceding them.[97] Beyond the high walls of the merchant villas, private gardens invited contemplation of time and space, civilization and nature, around a simultaneous moral order expressed as fate.[98] A little wine and poetry was not out of place here, for the submission of the visitor to the pleasures of a highly cultivated society had its counterpoint in the submission of nature to the artful design of the gardener. Designers arranged the features of each garden in such a way as to make human society and the built environment appear natural in contrast to the artful contrivance of cultivated plants and arresting rocks. Passing seasons added a cyclical dimension to this design, as patterns of death and rebirth shared sacred time with the vicissitudes of human history.[99] Elsewhere, portrait galleries worked a similar magic by displaying mortals and immortals drawn from a gallery of the ages to demonstrate a simultaneous order of merit: the faces of Confucius, Mencius, and their disciples were ranged alongside portraits of legendary kings, mortal emperors, and lesser officials to illustrate a sacred line of succession that served to legitimate imperial rule in an ethical community of sages. The universe of sacred time and ethics was advertised widely throughout the empire in China's cities, galleries, and gardens.[100]

European contact undermined the line of sacred succession in symbolic ways as well as material ones. The process began in daily life. The languid pace of theatrical shows or storytellers' tales and the endless courses and conversations associated with banquets encouraged European expatriates to write disparagingly of the "Oriental sense of time." Occidental time was much too valuable to waste: the discomfort of Old China hands seems to have derived from an eagerness to get things done, rather than from acute consciousness of an epic confrontation between modern progress and a premodern sense of fate. When Arthur Smith wrote of John Chinaman's "disregard for time"—his lack of punctuality for social engagements and his want of diligence or urgency when asked to do a job of work—he was referring chiefly to its impact on the foreigners' business schedules. But he clearly meant to imply something more.[101]

Isolating two different senses of time in this way is misleading when it essentializes a timeless Orient and a progressive Occident, as members of the Treaty Port community were inclined to do. It is well to remember that Hong Kong Chinese have been prone to make similar comments about the leisurely pace of life and work in the People's Republic in recent years.[102] In comparing the imagined community of the nation with earlier forms of community, Benedict Anderson has drawn a historical distinction rather than a cultural one, which applies equally to Europe in the age of monarchy and to China under the emperors. This historical distinction is one between consciousness of a moral order outside of progressive time and consciousness of movement in history. In Europe, the transition from one to the other marked a watershed in the development of a distinctively modern consciousness, "which, more than anything else, made it possible to 'think' the nation." [103] In China, this transition from an ethical to a progressive historical consciousness can be traced through the gradual displacement of the garden by scientific and historical museums. Museums began to proliferate over the first decades of the twentieth century as gardens went out of fashion, and as museum patrons "awoke" to progressive history.

The first museum organized on new principles was the Zhendan Museum, established in 1868 by a French Catholic missionary, Monsignor Pierre Heude, in the Xujiawei district of Shanghai. The next was established by the North China branch of the Royal Asiatic Society, also based in Shanghai, in 1872. Zhang Jian opened the first Chinese museum in 1905 on his model estate in Nantong. The precursor of the monumental state museums of modern China was founded in 1912 to mark the downfall of the Manchu dynasty.[104] In welcoming ordinary citizens over their thresholds, quite often in vast numbers, these museums played a major part in dismantling the old ethical order and replacing it with a historically progressive one. The visitor to the museum was still invited to look downstream, as in the garden, but the museum relegated the past to history and, unlike the garden, hinted at what the future held in store beyond the rocks and terraces. The museum promised progressive awakenings.

Museums had another important mission deriving from their origins in the schemes of missionaries who wished to mark an insuperable divide between the timeless Orient and the progressive Occident. They became sites of nationalist contestation. Early missionary museums were set up with the express purpose of correcting Chinese misapprehensions about Western civilization. The immediate impulse for setting up a missionary museum at Qingzhou, in Shandong—as the Reverend J. S. Whitewright explained to delegates attending the Shanghai conference of the Educational Association of China in April 1893— was to show that foreigners were not quite as silly as they looked. "It may be well to remind ourselves at the outset that the Chinese look down on us as foreigners with profound contempt, that they regard us as people entirely destitute of learning and culture of any kind, and the idea that we come to China with anything to teach them is to them utterly absurd." Whitewright opened his museum (much as Lord Macartney tried to launch his hot-air balloon) to correct any misapprehension about the inferiority of the West. The purpose of the museum attached to the Qingzhou mission was "to seek to enlighten the people in the district by shewing something of the superiority of Western civilization, science and invention." [105]

The number of inquisitive visitors who flocked to the museum more than justified the Reverend Whitewright's confidence. He welcomed around 350,000 visitors over the threshold in the first three or four years of operation, at an average of 100,000 people each year, and at a rate that encouraged the mission to anticipate a million visitors before the decade was out. Most highly prized among the visitors to the museum were the elite students from neighboring districts who regularly boarded in Qingzhou for the prefectural examinations.

"The importance of influencing this class can hardly be overestimated," White-wright remarked, "as it is from it that the future rulers, leaders and teachers of China will come." The museum was equipped for this task by the addition of a small lecture theater. As many as 20,000 students crossed its threshold in any given examination period to inquire about the electrical gadgetry, model trains, and scale dredges on display and to marvel at the ornithological, veteri-nary, astronomical, and geological exhibits set out in scientific array.[106]

Their scientific education was, however, counted incidental to the real work of conversion. "None of us imagines," cautioned the Reverend White-wright, "that he has done his work should he succeed in enlightening men on the value of foreign science." The real work was done in the chapel, which complemented the museum's mission to "open the blind eyes and unstop the deaf ears . . . to open men's minds so that they may be able to perceive and understand the truth." For those with eyes to see, the truth was on display in a separate glass case housing copies of the Bible, in a variety of languages.[107]

The unparalleled success of the little museum in Qingzhou in demonstrat-ing the superiority of Western civilization before an immense number of people commended it to foreigners and Chinese alike. After a day spent observing Chinese specimens as they passed through the Qingzhou museum, the Rev-erend V. F. Partch decided to build a similar museum in Jinan, where his mis-sion had experienced problems similar to Whitewright's in persuading people that they should take Christianity seriously. Partch was deeply impressed by what he had seen. "Many, if not most of these people, had been taught to de-spise us. This display of science and invention enforced respect." [108]

The lesson was not lost on Chinese visitors, either, who returned home and set up museums of their own to rival those of Shanghai, Qingzhou, and Jinan. This was not a simple case of emulation. Local curators competed for access to the same historical treasures, and tried to achieve for the home civili-zation what the missionary institutions were doing for the West. For a century and more, foreigners had acquired the habit of carrying Chinese artifacts out of the country to demonstrate to the people of Britain, France, or Canada the timelessness of the East, instead of placing them on display in their country of origin and showing how far China had itself progressed beyond timelessness. An eagerness to display China's cultural and material civilization was matched by a growing concern to preserve the store of national treasures before they were all smuggled out of the country, or had made an irremediable impression of China's rarified stagnancy on Western museum-goers.[109] But it was an un-equal contest. The museum would not allow Chinese civilization to speak on its own terms because it adjudicated among the contestants according to the principles of scientific classification and historical evolution that underpinned modern European culture.

The state itself came to assume major responsibility for establishing museums after the founding of the Republic. The first Chinese museum, we noted, was founded by the philanthropist Zhang Jian, but the next significant museum to open was sponsored by the Republican government within months of coming to office. Its purpose was to display the treasures of the fallen Qing dynasty. These were housed in June 1912 at the old imperial university and subsequently displayed in two minor palaces in Beijing before being transferred to the imperial palace in 1925, once the royal family had finally been forced to evacuate the premises. The Imperial Palace Museum was opened to the public on the fourteenth anniversary of the Wuchang uprising, on 10 October 1925, in a celebration befitting the relegation of the empire to history.[110]

Significantly, the next spurt in the creation of museums occurred over the period of the Nationalist Revolution. In the first decade of the Republic, some thirteen museums were registered in the country—including Zhang Jian's private museum in Nantong, two missionary establishments, four museums attached to local or provincial libraries, and three national museums (two in Beijing and one in Nanjing). In the second decade, to 1929, the number had almost trebled, to 34. The rate of growth accelerated further once the Nationalists came to office. By 1933 there were 64 museums, and by 1934, 72. The proliferation of museums does not appear to have devalued the currency of public interest. Over a four-week period in 1926, 185,000 people visited a single display in Beijing of artwork and manuscripts from the Datong region.[111]

One reason for the dominance of the state over the private development of museums was, of course, that the skills and resources available to individuals and civic associations were dwarfed by those of provincial and central governments. Another was the part museums were expected to play in forging a sense of national civic community in Nationalist China. As set out in the charter of the National Central Museum (*Guoli zhongyang bowuyuan*) in April 1933, the aim of the modern museum was "to promote scientific research and assist in mass education." The national museum was located, appropriately, within the Ministry of Education. Its responsibilities were defined as "researching, collecting, preserving, displaying and explaining all materials and items in the natural, human and industrial sciences." [112] An evolutionary method of explanation was set out in the museum's technical statement—"the method should be to set out, systematically, the processes of historical evolution"—and reiterated in its system of classification "by scientific method . . . so as to be able to show, horizontally, the classifications within a system and, vertically, their historical evolution." [113]

The relationship between the province, the nation, and the world was also reflected in the classification of the new state museums. The universe of the provincial museum was the nation. In 1930 the provincial government of Henan described the functions of a new provincial museum established under the provincial education department: "First, to extol national culture; second, to promote scholarly research; third, to expand the knowledge of the masses; and fourth to raise civic consciousness." The world beyond the nation barely featured at all. The focus of the national museum was more ambitious. It embraced ethnology (with a particular emphasis on the study of border peoples) and biological evolution with the aim of demonstrating that human life originated in China. But the workings of historical evolution were nowhere better illustrated than in the establishment of the national museum itself, which marked the culmination of a contest between the Occident and the Orient first launched by Christian missionaries in the nineteenth century, subsequently developed by public-minded citizens early in the twentieth century, and completed when the nation found the will and the resources to set up a museum that would affirm the nation's rightful place in the history of the world. The relationship between province and center in the new polity was then reflected in the functions and classifications of state museums. The National Central Museum was, as its name implied, a national and central one. Its establishment spelled out for museums all over the country a lesson that had already been spelled out for provincial governments by the Nationalist state: local and provincial institutions were incomplete without their central counterpart.[114]

Historical study was itself a "province," in the phrase of historian Fu Sinian, of "national studies." [115] While local communities were rearranging old and familiar artifacts in their museums, a younger generation of historians was beginning to rearrange China's textual history in an order that demonstrated that the past was a bad dream from which the future marked a glorious awakening. The aim of the new historians was to show that the sacred tradition was founded on a hoax. To this end, Gu Jiegang attacked the three foundations of traditional historical scholarship: sacred origins, continuity of transmission through approved Confucian texts, and the concept of historical regression from a Golden Age in high antiquity. His techniques were scientific, but the central principle underlying Gu's commitment of progressive history was to establish what was "relevant to the needs of the modern nation." "We have been as though in a dream in regard to our past," wrote Gu in 1936. It was time to wake up.[116]

Museum curators formed a united front with historians in their assault on the old order. Both groups were keen to demonstrate the progressive order of history and eager to identify outmoded customs and beliefs that seemed to persist in defiance of the laws of progress. In this respect, the museum was an invaluable aid to the historian. In classifying and preserving its range of objects, the museum symbolically confined them to the past. So when Gu Jiegang resolved to undermine "men of antiquity," he assigned a key role to the museum: "What we propose to do with history," he announced in 1930, is a great act of destruction, but without it our nation will not find a viable path. Our acts of destruction are not cruel activities; we are only restoring these various things to their historical position . . . in sum we are sending them to the museum.

The destruction of the past, concluded Gu, "is limited to classifying and arranging within the museum." [117]

In theory, nothing that occupies a historical position, in Gu Jiegang's sense of the term, needs to be destroyed. It is already dead and buried. In practice, however, the "museumification" of China was a new kind of historical procedure. Gu Jiegang was intent on killing a culture that was, in many respects, still vital, by making history of it.[118] This was a mammoth undertaking calling for the will and the energy to purge society, culture, and the polity of everything that could conceivably be counted a survival of a decrepit and now fraudulent tradition. The task certainly could not be entrusted to historians and archivists alone. Indeed, Gu was voicing a conviction common to many young people of his day, who spread their efforts widely over the fields of publishing, education, and the literary and performing arts, and through a variety of social and political movements dedicated to New China. While they were busy destroying stubborn remnants of Old China, the champions of New China were anxious to show that they belonged to a more vital and vibrant community, a community of the here and now that could be readily distinguished from the "dead" culture in which they happened to be living. Although the old culture remained vibrant and alive, it could not renew itself in the sense the citizens of New China had in mind. That is, it could not become fashionable. Awakened citizens distinguished themselves from their sleeping countrymen by staying abreast of new trends in ideas and keeping pace with fashion in hairstyles, dress, and manners. They discarded their long gowns and braids in favor of suits and bobtails, and entered the museum as patrons, not as exhibits.

This returns us to fashion. Fashion, we noted, is at once a personal statement about keeping up with the times and a mass medium for conveying the idea that there are times with which everybody should be keeping up. Dress and hairstyle had not been uniform under the empire, but they varied with place rather than with time. Variety of local custom was celebrated in imperial times in the popular saying "Every thousand miles a different atmosphere (*feng*), every hundred miles a different set of tastes (*su*)." [119] When customs and tastes moved from one place to another, they seem to have moved at the rate of continental drift, and then to have settled into place with the full weight of empire. The practice of binding women's feet, rumored to have started in the eleventh century, had become the norm throughout most of northern and central China by the nineteenth century, but even then footbinding was not universally practiced throughout southern China. Footbinding was not a fashion in the present sense of the word. The progress of the custom followed the spread of elite Han culture from the north to the south of the continent, and its endurance over many centuries suggests that it helped to distinguish between civilization and barbarity rather than between progressive and outmoded taste.

Fads traveled faster under the Republic and faded with greater rapidity because they marked the passage of time itself. For the people of China, the most spectacular sign of transition from the empire to the Republic was the cutting of men's queues, which was enforced by law throughout the territories of the old empire.[120] But the elimination of the queue would have marked little other than a change of dynasty were it not accompanied by more widespread and frequent changes in the hairstyles that replaced the queue, and by constant and rapid change in the dress accompanying each new hairstyle. The speed with which each new fashion displaced the old shows how changes in the political order were accompanied by changes of a very different order in the everyday lives of citizens of the Republic. Modern fashion declared to the world that the past, even the very recent past, was passé. And the curiously ephemeral quality of fashion enabled the most progressive members of the elite to identify through clothing and hairstyle with others of like mind across the country, while it enticed people of all classes and regions who came into contact with them to aspire to keep up.

The urge to keep up was conveyed with each new trend as fads made their way through a developing national marketing network.[121] Over the last decades of the Qing, marketing networks underwent a realignment from their origins in the old imperial and provincial capitals toward new sources along the metropolitan sea-coast. Shanghai and Shantou, Hong Kong and Amoy began setting the trends; Beijing, Nanjing, Changsha, and, in their turn, the myriad inland market towns all followed suit. The transformation began, appropriately, in the imperial capital itself. The wraparound silk gowns favored by examination candidates in Beijing lost their appeal after 1905, when the imperial examination system was abolished. With the introduction of new-style education, based on Western curricula, long silk gowns were rapidly replaced by new styles of student dress that featured shorter jackets opening down the center after the Western fashion. This was an early prototype of the severe style of dress that eventually evolved into the national costume of the People's Republic. But it was also Beijing's last major contribution to the development of the modern Student suit. The new fashion spread rapidly from Beijing to the rest of the country before giving way, in the Republic, to variations introduced from the burgeoning coastal cities.

In 1929, Mao Zedong took note of the introduction and effect of fashions among the people of Xunwu County in a fairly remote part of southern Jiangxi Province. In imperial times, the Xunwu city market had serviced eastern Guangdong with native goods and silks from the inland provinces.[122] Early in the Republic, the direction of trade altered when residents of Xunwu began to purchase their textiles and clothing from the coast. Xunwu natives adapted readily to the new center-cut jackets, and continued to adapt when fashions emanating from outside Xunwu began to dictate variations in the new jacket every few years. The most favored jacket in Xunwu in 1920 was cut to the "Shanghai style," with characteristic cloth buttons and embroidery. This gave way in 1923 to a square-bottomed style, which yielded in turn to the "Canton style" in 1929.[123] Men's hairstyles followed a similar pattern. They were modeled in the first instance on the styles in fashion on the coast. No sooner had the men of Xunwu lost their queues in 1911 than they adopted the Monk style in 1912, followed in 1913 by the Japanese style, in 1917 and 1918 by the crew cut and army cut, in 1921 by the "Ph.D." style, and later in the decade by a new Japanese style and a variety of Southeast Asian styles imported through Mei County in Guangdong.[124]

Through the medium of fashion, the market also helped to break down barriers separating local communities and brought with it ideas of national revolution. Like the "fake foreign devil" who led the revolution in Lu Xun's "The True Story of Ah Q," the local trendsetters in Xunwu were the leaders of the local revolutionary movement: it was the students at the fore of the revolution who introduced the crew cut and army styles that eventually claimed the scalp of every able male in Xunwu.[125] Within a few years after students had adopted short jackets, the majority of young peasants and workers were wearing them too. But peasants and workers could never quite keep up. By the time they had adapted to short jackets, the revolutionary students in Xunwu had moved on to new-style shoes and "wanted to use electric flashlights." [126] By introducing the latest trends from the coast, and alerting their communities to what was happening in the rest of the country, educated young men and women of Xunwu County represented the nation to their locale. Yet they continued to distinguish themselves from their slower kin and their backward neighbors by their mastery of style and gadgetry. That is to say, the styles that held the widest appeal confirmed their positions of authority within their communities. Their short hair indicated they meant business, their simple suits showed a stern but stable demeanor, and their flashlights told, as words could never do, that they were ready for any emergency. Early in the 1920s, in Guangdong, the peasant movement activist Peng Pai added a final touch to the uniform that was soon to spread like a prairie fire through the cadre of the revolution: an imported fountain pen.[127]

Awakening and Dream Fiction

The new literature favored by the youths of Xunwu played a role comparable to that of fashion in helping to foster a sense of progressive national community in the act of "waking up." Traditional popular fiction, after the fashion of the earlier histories, represented time through the episodic unfolding and recounting of a range of morality plays. In contrast, the new literature of the late Qing and early Republic was a literature of the progressive unfolding of plot. In this it marked a transition similar to one in European literature, from the older epic form to the classic modern novel, noted by Gabriel Josipovici:

> The classic novel exists in time in ways in which even the longest [traditional] epic cannot be said to do. That is, it both takes time to read and it is concerned with the passing of time. . . . Perhaps we should say that in the classic novel time exists as a beneficient deity, one who will bring forth whatever is in her womb. Its other name is plot.[128]

The significance of narrative for the plotting of national revolution is a subject of the following chapter. Here we need only note how literature combined forces with science in dream fiction to popularize the idea that time is a beneficient deity responsive to human invocation.

Western science brought to China a profound conviction that progress was ready to bestow its gifts on anyone prepared to "awaken" to the promise of the future. Faith in science was faith in progress. "In general," proclaimed Wu Zhihui in his manifesto on the "scientific approach to life" (1923), "the ancients are inferior to the moderns and the moderns are inferior to the men of the future." [129] A new wave of utopian fiction gave form to this idea. Chinese students in London, Paris, and New York encountered a growing body of utopian works in the fiction of William Morris, Edward Carpenter, Charles Fourier, Antole France, and Jules Verne.[130] When utopia was transferred from "no place" to the future in euchronian fiction, it conveyed the idea that the future would be better than the present and that the present, for all its faults, was a marked improvement on the past. Euchronian fiction was a partner to science in promoting this idea.

One of the favorite narrative devices of euchronian fiction is the inaugural motif of a protagonist falling into a deep sleep and then awakening, after a suitable interval, to discover that the world has been transformed.[131] The pioneer for the awakenings of utopian fiction was Louis-Sebastien Mercier's novel *The Year 2440* (*L'An 2440*), published in 1771, in which the narrator awakens (as an old man) in the year 2440 to discover that his world has been transformed.[132] Mercier's vision of the ideal society was orthodox for his day, but he broke new ground in projecting his sleeping figure into the future; that is, Mercier transferred the idea of progressive time from Enlightenment philosophy into the otherwise timeless canon of traditional utopian literature.[133] *The Year 2440* inspired many imitators, among them Washington Irving's figure of Rip Van Winkle in *The Sketch Book* (1819). But the most influential literary awakening of the nineteenth century, and the first of the genre to make a significant impact upon Chinese readers, was Edward Bellamy's *Looking Backward* (1888).[134]

The narrator of *Looking Backward* is neither a foreigner nor a graybeard, but a young man named Julian West who awakens in the year 2000 after a sleep of 113 years, which he accidentally induced by taking a sleeping draught. The world that young West discovers on awakening is a pastiche of the youthful ideals of social, political, and technological progress of the late nineteenth century: a world governed by reason, made prosperous by industry, established on collectivist principles, and centered on the nation-state. The vision appealed to the world that sired it, and within the space of a decade *Looking Backward* was translated into all major languages and inspired an organized popular movement espousing progressive state socialism.[135] Equally powerful was the dystopian reaction it inspired among other writers, who shared many aspects of Bellamy's forward-looking vision but rejected his uncomplicated optimism. William Morris offered his critique in *News from Nowhere*, written in 1889. H. G. Wells presented a pessimistic reading of Bellamy's awakening in *When the Sleeper Wakes* (1898–99; republished 1910 as *The Sleeper Wakes*).[136]

Looking Backward was published serially in Chinese three years after its first appearance in English. From December 1891 to April of the following year, the American missionaries Allen J. Young and Timothy Richard published an abridged translation of the text in their journal *Review of the Times* (*Wanguo gongbao*). It made a wide and deep impression. The subscription list of *Review of the Times* was impressive, with a claimed circulation of over 39,000 copies each issue at its height, and an audience (magazines were often read aloud in tea shops and by the village bulletin board) of many times that number.[137] Coincidentally, the reach of the journal matched the patronage of the small missionary museum in Qingzhou, which opened for visitors around the time that the serialized version of *Looking Backward* went to press. The magazine, like the museum, reached the class of scholars from which "the future rulers, leaders and teachers of China will come." [138] Among those who followed the installments of Bellamy's book as they appeared in print were influential officials of the court of Beijing and a party of reformers who rose to prominence in the ill-fated Reform movement of 1898, including Tan Sitong, Liang Qichao, and Kang Youwei (Kang had been a regular subscriber to *Review of the Times* for eight years).[139] *Looking Backward* came to the attention of a younger generation of Chinese students in Japan in 1903 and 1904, when the novel was translated into Japanese, and was available in French translation to Chinese students living in France under the work-study program.[140]

The appeal of the book lay partly in its resonance with the rational utopia of the classical tradition, and partly in its projection of this ideal world into the imminent future. This conjunction was not novel in itself. The Taiping rebellion had only recently professed to herald the arrival of the Confucian era of "Great Peace" (*Taiping*), and even classical scholars had begun to lend a forward momentum to the cyclical or regressive "ages" of the Confucian canon.

Looking Backward nevertheless propelled the trend toward a unilinear view of historical progress.[141] In his *Exposition of Benevolence* (*Renxue*; 1896), Tan Sitong turned to the Confucian and Buddhist classics in an effort to establish the claims of China's ethical tradition among scholars grappling with the problem of accommodating the nation-state in a universal world order. "The earth must be governed in such a way that there is only one world," Tan declared, "but no states." He then fused the *Book of Rites* and *Looking Backward* into the vision of a world where "there were no states, [where] there would not be any boundaries, wars, suspicion, jealousy, power-struggles, distinction between the self and others, and equality would emerge." Tan was fully conscious of his two sources of inspiration. "It would be like the man mentioned in a western story book," he wrote, "who wakes up after dreaming for a hundred years, and finds that the atmosphere of One World is almost like that described in the chapter on the 'Evolution of Rites' in the *Book of Rites*." [142] Bellamy, needless to say, never mentioned the *Book of Rites*. It was Chinese reformers who awoke to see their own literary traditions in a new light.

The literary tradition had long embraced dreams and awakenings of its own. These served a didactic function: in the fiction and drama of high empire, dreams of love and riches warned of the vanity of human desire, and nightmares told of the punishments that would befall immoral folk should they fail to mend their ways. In fiction, dream adventures typically carried the hero from the lower realm of the quotidian world to a higher life of romance and success, where the hero wins a beautiful maiden, sires numerous progeny, enjoys great wealth and social standing, and perhaps even comes to exercise influence at court. The awakening of the plot, however, generally returns the dreamer to his pot of thin gruel; it offers a useful lesson in the futility of dreaming.[143] In epic fiction, dreams also served as a medium for conveying messages from the netherworld and for announcing the incontrovertible Will of Heaven. Dreams of heaven's will feature throughout the standard editions of the greenwood epic *Water Margin* (*Shuihu zhuan*). Jin Shengtan's truncated edition of the epic concludes with a dream of the heroic outlaws summoned to execution for transgressing heaven's will.[144] In either case, whether the hero awakens from futile dreams of personal self-aggrandizement or from dreams conveying messages from heaven, the awakening enlightens the hero to the preordained order of things. In traditional fiction, an awakening to the reality of the daylight world was an awakening to a universal moral order from which there was, in effect, no "way out."

This changed in the twentieth century. Among the works of fiction published after the turn of the century were a number of awakening narratives that predicted the future that lay in store for the nation as a whole. The futures they envisaged were different from Edward Bellamy's comforting predictions for

Boston, and yet only vaguely reminiscent of the dream narratives of tradition. Two of the most highly acclaimed novels of the turn of the century were narratives of dreams and awakening that conveyed, most significantly, discovery of a "way out." Liu E's popular novel *The Travels of Lao Can* (*Lao Can Youji*), published serially between 1903 and 1907, was prefaced by a dream sequence from which the hero awakens to a vision of impending doom. Lao Can dreams that a ship is in danger of sinking, along with its passengers and crew, and he awakens to a sense of mission to right the vessel. His awakening propels Lao Can to plot a program of national regeneration. In Zeng Pu's equally popular *Flower in an Ocean of Sin* (*Niehai hua*; 1905), readers are presented with an allegory of lotus eaters who awaken to discover that their island is sinking into the sea. The islanders' awakening is a moment of revelation of the fate that lies in store for China should the social and political problems exposed in the narrative pass unnoticed or go unrectified.[145]

The motif found its way into short stories as well. In 1904 Cai Yuanpei, then a prominent educationalist, employed the awakening device in a well-known short story entitled "New Year's Dream" (*Xinnian meng*). In this case the story carried an ironic twist of a kind that only a readership well versed in the conventions of the awakening narrative was likely to understand. The story projects the time-traveling narrator backward into the past so that his dreams of the future mature in the real time of the story itself. The dawn of the new world is scheduled to begin with New Year's Day in 1904 (the year the story went to press). After reliving the hopes of his youth in his dream, the narrator awakens, in a deft inversion of the new conventions of the awakening narrative, to discover that *nothing has changed*.[146] By the turn of the twentieth century, the old awakening motif, that of a preordained fate from which there is no escape, presented the most terrifying prospect of all.

There was obviously more at work here than the evocation of a literary tradition of dream narratives or the celebration of progress. Progressive evolution had already begun to find its way into an evolutionary cosmology in late Qing philosophy without generating the same sense of alarm, and the transformation envisioned in Bellamy's *Looking Backward* was not only progressive but beneficent.[147] The awakenings of modern Chinese fiction, on the other hand, were stories of regressive devolution: they foretold not the glory but the shame in store for their readers if they postponed their awakenings to some date in the future instead of waking up in real-time *now*. The awakenings portrayed by Liu E, Zeng Pu, and Cai Yuanpei were each moments of revelation in which the true features of the characters, the nature of their present situations, and the character of the social and political forces working upon them were laid bare for all to see. Their climactic awakenings served the dual purpose of casting the familiar world in an entirely new light and conferring upon the protagonists a capacity to liberate themselves from the bonds that restrained them by waking up in the act of reading itself.

Even so, a literary awakening was not held to be sufficient. The story of China's national awakening was neither a morality play about the futility of dreaming nor a narrative carried along by the momentum of plot alone. Neither the past nor the future offered any comfort of its own accord. The emancipation envisioned in the new fictional awakenings was the work of human agency. The awakenings of fiction called on people to cast the book aside, to seize the time, and to engage the world. They served as literary archetypes for the later narratives of personal, class, gender, and national awakening, which foretold that people would awaken to the possibilities inherent in their own situations, and would discover in this awakening the will to make a future of their choice. In the plot of the Nationalist Revolution, the sleeping nation was invited, like the lotus eaters in *Flower in an Ocean of Sin* or the ship of fools in *The Travels of Lao Can*, to awaken to the nature and causes of its captivity and to discover, in revolution, a "way out."

Napoleon and the Awakening of the Dragon

In all likelihood, Napoleon never uttered the words that legend now attributes to him about China, the "sleeping dragon." There is no reference to a sleeping dragon in his recorded speeches or writings and no mention of the terrible fate in store for the world should China suddenly "wake up." The saying is part of an oral legend that blossomed around the figure of Napoleon in the early nineteenth century, recounting the strengths and the limits of his accomplishments. Europe had awakened under his sway, the legend implied, but not remote Cathay. For the moment, China was an oriental screen onto which the European imagination projected the hopes and fears of its own self-awakening. Nevertheless, the legend predicted that even China would eventually awaken, because the vision Napoleon portrayed and the forces he helped to unleash were not parochial European ones. The awakening of modern Europe foretold the awakening of the world. If Napoleon did not say as much himself, then someone had to say it for him.

For China, the legend also suggested that the nation's destiny lay in *being* awakened by a hero of Napoleonic vision and stature—perhaps by a Chinese Napoleon. The mass politics of progressive nationalism is best captured at that moment when a historical community stands transfixed in the figure of its heroic leader. Hegel tried to capture such a moment in a letter to his publisher in 1803, when he recorded his impression of Napoleon passing through the town of Jenna on horseback:

The emperor—this world soul—I saw riding through the city to a review of his troops; it is indeed a wonderful feeling to see such an individual who, here concentrated in a single point, sitting on a horse, reaches out over the world and dominates it.[148]

It was the concentration of history in a single point that gave the world its progressive momentum. But the real hero was the people. In filling the role of hero, it was to Napoleon's advantage that his birth, his physique, and his education were commonplace, because he was the point at which the commonplace exercised influence over its own destiny. Napoleon was, in other words, a heroic and *representative* figure.[149] The figure of Napoleon dissolved the tension between a people awakening and a people being awakened: the great leader was at once a representative of the people and a remote figure whose heroic stature compelled him to awaken those whom he represented. In being awakened by Napoleon, the people awoke themselves.

Such, at least, was the significance of the Napoleonic figure in China's national revolution. In an article intended to shore up his leadership of the revolutionary party at a critical moment in 1918, Sun Yatsen observed:

The course taken by a nation is determined by the psychology of the multitude; if the direction is set then it certainly cannot be altered by the intelligence of one or two persons who have risen to leadership through force of circumstance. Neither Washington nor Napoleon was an initiator of the American or French Revolution.[150]

In July of the following year, the young Mao Zedong made a remarkably similar observation about the place of the kaiser in Germany: "We do not see the bellicose spirit of Germany as having been unleashed by one man, the Kaiser. The Kaiser is the crystallization of the German people. Because there is a German people, there is a Kaiser." [151] Mao also regarded Napoleon as a paramount symbol of the great popular leader, as did Kang Youwei, Liang Qichao, and Chiang Kaishek, along with many of their supporters and their critics.[152] They judged themselves as they judged Napoleon, not as the moving forces of the revolution but as historical beneficiaries of the "psychology of the multitude" that thrust them to national prominence. Sun, Chiang, and Mao were, in their own estimations, as *insignificant* as a Napoleon, a Washington, or a kaiser. They were representative figures of the awakened nation.

They profited, too, from an ideal of a heroic leader that developed independently in late Qing thought. The New Text school of the nineteenth century portrayed Confucius as a sage king who imposed ideal political institutions by the force of moral suasion—in contrast to an earlier Neo-Confucian tendency to stress exemplary inner self-cultivation. The Old Text school, in turn, developed the projection of Confucius as a kingly sage into a hero more closely approximating the Napoleonic model. This was a hero responsive to the times, blessed with the vision to see what needed to be done, and possessing the courage to do it without regard for the trappings of tradition.[153] In the early Republic, the appeal of the hero transgressed the borders dividing constitutional reformers and Republican revolutionaries and found expression in essays, stories, and songs celebrating the achievements of heroic figures drawn from the civic pantheon of European history. Napoleon and Washington were inserted into the Song of the Republic, which beseeched these "two sons of Liberty" to become "incarnated in the people" of China.[154]

Though aspiring Napoleons and Cromwells were to be spotted many times and in many guises in twentieth-century China, early reformers could find little evidence of a Napoleonic figure in China's recorded history. Liang Qichao, a student of the Old Text school, drew up an inventory of "adventurist and heroic men" in European history to demonstrate that heroes were the personification of a heroic spirit embedded in national cultures. When he ransacked Chinese history for telltale signs of a Napoleon, a Wellington, or a Washington, he came away disappointed. China's old culture, he concluded, was incapable of siring heroes, and this was a grievous form of impotency in a world embracing many heroic peoples. When races were competing against one another for survival, a nation without the spirit of Napoleon was sure to disappear: "With it, people live; without it they die. With it countries prosper; without it they perish." [155] Liang failed to uncover any historical figures of Napoleonic stature in China chiefly because the elite histories he consulted made little provision for them. Napoleon was out of place in a world that made no provision for progress, and which attributed historical process to fate rather than to willful human agency. In order to wake up, as the Napoleonic legend had predicted, the people of China needed to reconstitute themselves as a nation and make room for a Napoleon of their own.

Self-styled awakenings in literature and fashion, history and popular storytelling each anticipated the Machiavellian intervention of political leaders such as Sun Yatsen or Mao Zedong, whose claims on the nation made sense because they parasitized metaphors and motifs that circulated quite independently of themselves. Sun may have come dressed in a fashionable jacket and called on his countrymen to awaken to a glorious future, but the Nationalists controlled fashion no more than they did rumors, and a place had already been carved out for dreams and dreamers in a litany of inspirational writings that anticipated the Nationalist Revolution.

"What we dream about . . . is a guide to what we actually will do when we enter the ideal or future world," Liang Qichao advised at the turn of the century. Over the decades leading up to the Nationalist Revolution, Liang composed numerous maxims and proverbs to encourage a more ambitious kind of dreaming among his countrymen: "Dream is the mother of reality," he advised, "and the future is an offspring of the present"; and "The more one dreams about the greater one's hopes will be." It was Liang who said that only visionaries like Napoleon could ever conquer the world.[156] Liang Qichao, Zeng Pu, Liu E, and their generation of awakened authors imagined a dreamer and dreamed of a dream; and along came Sun Yatsen with a cadre of visionaries to lead and point the way.

In time, Lenin came to displace Napoleon as the representative hero of the age. From 1923, Sun Yatsen began speaking of Lenin with even greater reverence than he did of Napoleon. Now he referred to Lenin when reflecting on his own leadership of the Nationalist movement. "The reason they have achieved such complete success," Sun remarked of the Bolsheviks in 1924, "is that Russia brought forth a revolutionary sage (*geming shengren*), a sage we all know as Lenin; and they formed a revolutionary party and advocated that it is the revolutionary party which should exercise freedom, and not individual party members." In 1924 Sun deployed the figure of Lenin, just as he had done Napoleon six years before, to bolster an appeal for absolute loyalty to his own person and total commitment to his party.[157] Lenin's distinctive style of party organization supplied the model for the Nationalist Revolution of the 1920s, and his style of leadership made him a rightful successor to Napoleon in the eyes of China's Nationalists. If the dragon were to awaken, as predicted, now China needed to find its own Lenin.

The last word on the place of the Napoleonic hero in the awakening of modern China should be reserved for the most astute observer of the Nationalist Revolution, the essayist Lu Xun. At one point Lu Xun had contemplated studying medicine, as Sun Yatsen had done, but he turned instead to literature in an effort to cure the nation of its cultural delusions. One of these delusions was the tenacious legend of Napoleon. In an essay on Napoleon and Jenner written in 1934, Lu Xun complained:

I know a doctor who works hard yet is often attacked by his patients, and once he consoled himself by saying "If a man wants praise, he had better take to killing. Just compare Napoleon with Jenner." I believe he is right. What have Napoleon's military achievements to do with us? Yet we still admire him as a hero. . . . Since the practice of vaccination, countless children's lives have been saved throughout the world—though some when they grow up still have to serve as cannon fodder for heroes—yet who remembers the name of Jenner, the discoverer? The murderers are destroying the world, the saviours are restoring it; but all the gentlemen eligible to be cannon fodder insist on praising the murderers.[158]

In condemning the "murderers" who passed as Napoleons in China, Lu Xun was referring in characteristically guarded prose to Chiang Kaishek and the

Nationalists. But he was not, in this case at least, content to score a political point. Lu Xun was more deeply concerned about the gentlemen who insisted on praising the murderers than he was about the murderers themselves. What most worried him was that the source of Napoleon's authority derived not from his will, nor even from his military prowess, but from common consent, that is, from his status as a representative figure. In asking what Napoleon's achievements had to do with "us," the civic community of China, Lu Xun was asking neither about Napoleon nor about Chiang Kaishek, but about the community more generally, and about the bonds that cemented the people to their rulers. This question could not be answered by reference to armies and politicians alone. It was a question of ethics.

2

ONE WORLD, ONE CHINA
From Ethical Awakening to National Emancipation

Today, if we appeal to the hearts of all under heaven on the basis of
great ultimate principles, can any of them fail to be moved? And if
all the hearts in the realm are moved, is there anything which cannot
be achieved? And if the affairs of the realm can be dealt with, how,
then, can the state fail to be rich, powerful and happy? . . . In today's
world there should be broad minded people who will begin with philosophy and ethics to reform philosophy, reform ethics, and change
fundamentally the mentality of the whole country.

Mao Zedong, 1917[1]

Happy are those ages when the starry sky is the map of all possible
paths—ages whose paths are illuminated by the light of the stars.
Everything in such ages is new and yet familiar, full of adventure and
yet their own. The world is wide and yet is like a home, for the fire that
burns in the soul is of the same essential nature as the stars.

Gyorgy Lukács, 1920[2]

The nervous breakdown of an eremitic scholar is never likely to be celebrated
in the songs of Chinese nationalism or the rituals of China's national day. Yet
Kang Youwei's collapse on learning of the death of his grandfather in 1877
brought with it a sudden personal awakening that would serve as an analogue
for the awakening of modern China. Kang himself was not the first among
China's modern philosophers to grapple with the country's predicament, and
the solutions he came up with were in many cases derivative. Nor, of course,
is a nation simply something dreamed up by philosophers. But Kang was the
first of the Confucian philosophers to undergo a nervous collapse on a scale to
match the collapse of an entire civilization and to live to tell the tale. The hyperrational reconstruction of Kang Youwei's self, on awakening, supplied a model
for the rational reconstitution of China as an "awakened" nation.[3] The awakening of the self logically and historically preceded the awakening of the nation.

    The modern self was discovered in Europe, Thomas Nipperday has re-
marked, from amidst the rubble of a collapsing civilization that at once freed
it from a "concrete and vivid presence of tradition" and yet left it feeling un-

anchored and alone. The European literature of self-discovery reveals two sides to this epiphany: a euphoric experience of personal emancipation offset by a hellish revelation of individual alienation.[4] The collapse of the established order in imperial China launched literati on comparable voyages of self-discovery. These were, for the most part, solo voyages, which heightened the intensity of the revelation and intensified the pain of alienation. Lyrical elements of the literary tradition encouraged China's literary travelers to interpret their alienation as the "awakening of the individual soul."[5] At the same time, the awakening of the self fostered cravings for new forms of community (which were yet to "awaken") and stimulated reconsideration of the relationship between self and community in exemplary works of ethics.

Ethics is to be understood here to mean establishing the grounds for human community and the moral principles for guiding behavior in a universal order linking the self to the stars. Autobiographical ethics traces a story of self-awakening and of the rational reconstitution of new ethical communities — a story that anticipates, in broad outline, the idea that a Chinese nation also awaited its awakening and liberation. Rational nationalism, for want of a better term, was grounded in a utopian vision.[6]

Kang was just twenty years old when his grandfather died in 1877. Over the following two years he alternately locked himself at home, shunning his friends, or retreated to the Xiqiao hills in Guangdong to meditate. For Kang it was a time of revelation: "A light dawned within me, and believing that I was a sage, I would be happy and laugh . . . then I would be sad and cry." To others it was a spell of madness. His schoolmates, "hearing me laugh and weep so irrationally, thought that I was mad and were much concerned about me." Kang learned to master his madness, and eventually came down from the hills determined to rid the world of suffering and carrying with him the germ of his major tome, *One World Philosophy (Datongshu)*.[7]

For Kang, the completion of *One World Philosophy* in 1902 marked the culmination of two decades of reflection, study, and writing, interrupted over the last seven years by frenzied bouts of political activity. He had been at the fore of the first student demonstration to take place in Beijing, in 1895, when scholars visiting the capital to sit for the imperial examinations protested the terms of the Treaty of Shimonoseki under which Taiwan, the Liaodong Peninsula, and the Pescadores were ceded to Japan.[8] Kang, then age 37, also took advantage of the occasion to present a memorial to court. The memorial never reached the emperor, but news of Kang's proposals for reform and of his growing reputation among younger scholars could not be kept from the inner sanctum for long. Within three years Kang was invited to assist Emperor Guangxu in a wide-ranging reform movement launched from within the court itself. The reforms were blocked, with tragic consequences, and Kang was forced to flee the country in September 1898 to escape the fury of the conservatives who had seized power at court. It was a poignant moment for Kang, who lost his brother Guangren to the court executioner, and for the dynasty itself, which forfeited the prospect of reforming itself from within on its own terms. By the 1890s revolutionaries no longer counted themselves Confucian at all. Henceforth they targeted the Confucian imperial system as well as the Manchu Qing dynasty.[9]

Kang had been invited to assist the emperor because he was *not* a revolutionary. He was a radical Confucian, whose writings reflected many of the concerns of Confucian scholars of his day. Kang acquired the syncretic methodology of Guangdong Learning (*Yuexue*) from his teacher, Zhu Ciqi, and drew on the rival traditions of Song Learning (*Songxue*) and Han Learning (*Hanxue*) while acquainting himself with the debates within Han Learning between New Text and Old Text adherents. He borrowed from Mahayana Buddhism and from the less orthodox schools of classical philosophy (*zhuzixue*), which were undergoing a contemporary revival. Throughout his studies Kang managed to maintain a balance between the universal concerns that animated Confucianism and Buddhism and an incongruously "particularistic" concern for his country.[10] From the time of his earliest reflections, the idea of One World made at least as much sense to Kang as the idea of China did. It took a further twenty years for him to light upon a method for inserting the particular, China, into a universal One World Philosophy.

The most radical propositions in Kang's early essays, as the historian Hao Chang has noted, arose from a consistent elevation of the Confucian concept of sympathy, or human-heartedness (*ren*), and from Kang's habit of severing this ideal from the cognate ideals of righteousness (*yi*) and propriety (*li*). Dong Zhongshu, a leading scholar of the New Text school to whom Kang frequently deferred, elevated human-heartedness to a high order in his own philosophy but had not thought to pluck it from its niche in the greater cluster of Confucian values, which mediated compassion through recognition of social hierarchy and limited its application through the exercise of social constraint. Dong Zhongshu's concept of human-heartedness, however elevated, still accommodated the hierarchical order of the family and the parallel hierarchy of the imperial state: the heart doled out its love in portions, to each as was his due.

Kang's compassion, however, knew no bounds. In the language of Confucian scholarship, he collapsed the standard five relationships and the three bonds into the ideals of human-heartedness and sincerity (*cheng*), and reduced the four virtues of Mencius to human-heartedness alone.[11] The family and the monarchical state were both at risk in this reformulation. Kang was writing within a venerable ethical tradition, but he was also self-consciously introducing to the tradition a radically different way of envisioning the world in which it found itself. A Buddhist ideal of undifferentiated compassion, a Mohist concept of universal love (*jianai, boai*), and an Enlightenment concept of universal citizenship came together in the language of Confucius.

Kang Youwei's undifferentiated self was not initially identified with the nation. The identification of self and nation was effected gradually over the first quarter of this century, when the self awoke to learn that it was not only human but also a citizen of modern China. The literary tradition into which the self was born, the world to which it awoke, and the identities that the text and the world imposed upon the awakened self all worked to press the self into public service and to harness ethics to nation-building and state-building. By the 1920s, young people who underwent a "self-awakening" encountered a distinctly Chinese self that related to its community around an ideal of the nation-state.

This was neither accidental nor inevitable. As the awakened self had an ethical history, so, too, did New China. Here we shall trace the discursive history of the self from Kang Youwei's discovery of his "body," naked under the starry sky, to the awakening of the citizen and the patriot in the Nationalist Revolution, and trace in the history of the self an outline of the history of modern China as an ethical community. This was a time when artists painted their lions awakened, when writers turned their hand to propaganda, and when philosophers distributed pamphlets in the streets. The literature of self-awakening in ethics and fiction dressed the self in the garb of citizenship and draped it with the flag of patriotism. By the 1920s the self could still shrug off its dress and "awaken," but it could no longer discover its nakedness with the same astonishment that struck Kang Youwei in the mists of the Xiqiao hills.

The Function of Ethics

The prominence of ethics in Chinese nationalism is easily illustrated in the writings of early twentieth-century nationalists, but an explanation for its prominence is not to be found within ethics itself. Part of the explanation is historical. The removal of scriptural Confucianism from the educational system in 1905 and its banishment from the secular rituals of the Republican state in 1912 heralded an age of "chaos" (*luan*) in the early Republic. One way or another, Confucian ethics was held to be responsible: responsible by default, because it had been undermined by reformers and revolutionaries, or alternately responsible because it had not been banished effectively enough and continued to cast its shadow over New China like an ancient family curse. Either way, ethics remained at the center of controversy throughout the early years of the Republic. And insofar as the awakening of the New Culture movement was an awakening from an outmoded ethical system, it entailed an awakening to a new one. An ethical awakening, as one founder of the movement remarked in 1916, was "the final awakening of final awakenings." [12]

A further clue to the prominence of ethics in Chinese nationalism is to be found in the unifying imperative common to ethics and nationalism alike. The historian Qian Mu noted with a wistful backward glance toward the empire that it was only ethics that had ever held China together. Chinese "culture" was unlike any other because it was not a culture at all, in the Western sense, but an ethical system. As Qian Mu explained in conversation with Gerry Dennerline, "For a westerner, culture is bound to place, so that local customs and language serve to distinguish cultures. For a Chinese, culture is universal, so that languages and local customs only serve to distinguish place." The culture that was distinctively Chinese was divorced from the particularisms of custom, language, and place and associated instead with a universal ethical principle, *li*.

Qian Mu held that there are no Western-language equivalents for the word *li*. It is a general concept that applies to standards of customary behavior throughout the Chinese world and distinguishes Chinese culture from all others. As Qian Mu explained:

Because Western cultures have no *li*, you distinguish among them by measuring the differences between *fengsu*, "local customs," as if a culture were the sum total of the customs practiced within its area of influence. If you set out to observe local customs in China, you will find that they vary greatly from place to place. Even within Wuxi county, the fengsu of Dangkou, where I grew up, and those of Rongxiang, where I taught after the war, are different. The differences from one end of the country to the other are much greater. But the *li* are the same. By the same token, the *li* that are standards for the family—its internal relations, its external relations, birth, marriage, death—are equivalent to the *li* that are standards for the workings of government and state ceremonies—internal relations, relations between state and society, recruitment, treaties, successions. This is the only way to understand Chinese culture.[13]

Li was an early casualty of Kang Youwei's purge of the ethical tradition, and it came under attack again in the New Culture movement. But in each case the unifying imperative of ethics was left intact. Local atmosphere and taste helped to differentiate people within China, but they did little to distinguish them *as* Chinese, and this was the level of identification that concerned China's nationalists. Natives of Wuxi County might call Dangkou or perhaps Rongxiang home, but as Chinese they required a new and distinctive ethical system that made a home of China.

In the ethical, geographic, and demographic spectrum of the nationalist imagination, the landscape and the social communities of China possessed one feature in common: they had too many divisive barriers (*jie*). Even the landscape appeared set on resisting its national destiny by raising giant mountain ranges and spilling out wide, turbulent, and impassable rivers. Like the people, the land asked to be brought to a realization of its own unity. While people were to be awakened through instruction, the landscape was to be awakened with saws and dredges, picks and hammers, road rollers and steam trains, to the rhythms of "construction" (*jianshe*). Sun Yatsen compiled elaborate plans to bring the country together by constructing tunnels and highways, huge canals and deep-sea ports. He did not consider it a demotion when he moved across to the Ministry of Railways after ceding the presidency to Yuan Shikai in 1912. Sun's longest, most finely detailed, and in many ways most consistent writings of the Republican period were plans for the infrastructural development of ports and harbors, canals and roads, railways and bridges.[14]

The cultural landscape presented obstacles, and emblems of unity, of a different kind. The literature of nationalism aspired to the general and the typical. It craved standardization even when it celebrated differences among languages, styles of dress, standards of behavior, and the scenic backgrounds of its stories. Natural features of the landscape that were depicted in the poetry and prose of the new fiction tended to eschew local characteristics, or at best to convert particularity into a metaphor for a landscape that had no room for particularity at all except as a universal feature of the *idea* of place. This, too, had its roots. The elite culture of empire had represented the empirium in its paintings and its poetry as a series of key geographical features encountered from one generation to the next along the bureau-tracks of the empire: sacred mountains, lakes, craggy rocks, particular species of tree and varieties of flower, the particularity of which was mediated by standardization of vocabulary and style. The landscape of the nation traced similar lines around the religious and cultural monuments identified by imperial state functionaries en route from one job of work to another. Modern citizens democratized the same sites. From the 1920s, ordinary citizens began to make the pilgrimage to the Nine Sacred Mountains or journeyed to Guilin and the West Lake for a holiday. In the 1930s they began to pose for photographs before carved inscriptions dating from the Tang and the Song dynasties.

In literature, the particularities of landscape and local culture were abstracted from place and presented as emblematic features of the nation. In the 1920s, the everyday poetry of the great metropolitan newspapers referred constantly to sky, clouds, mountains, and flowers—chiefly chrysanthemums—and to the seasons and their effects. But only rarely were these natural features named or grounded in identifiable places. In fiction this tendency toward abstraction left an impression of "abstract formalism" on a later generation of readers, and prompted a realist reaction that emphasized "local color" over the following decade.[15] Even then, local particularity served chiefly to highlight the universal features of a new fictional subject, the masses. Attachment to locality was counted a typical feature of China's peasants. Writers aiming to reproduce the typical peasant in their fiction were obliged to pay "painstaking attention to the unique cultural and linguistic traits" of their characters in order to make them, not particular, but universal.[16] Particularity finally found a place in generalizations about the Chinese people.

Differences separating the people themselves, however, were to be bridged with ethics. Given the variety of local languages and customs, and the potential of these to foster "particularist" loyalties, there was a general reluctance to abandon the idea of a universal ethical principle altogether. So the old ethics was the common point of rendezvous for search parties that set off in pursuit of the new ethics. The immediate inspiration often came from extratextual events: from war and disease, from the opaque and irresistible desires of the body, from spontaneous encounters with the self, and from an intense desire to assign the awakened self a place in the world. These events found purpose in the universal principles derived from them. As Kang recalled of his self-awakening in 1884, "from these thoughts I endeavoured to find my place in society and my purpose in life." [17] Kang inserted his newly discovered self into an ethical system that gave not just meaning but a framework for purposeful action to his discovery. Kang recovered the ideal of One World from utopian thought and recast it in a new role, in progressive programmatic reasoning.

Community, Reason, and "Consciousness"

One World Philosophy commences with the kind of autobiographical preface that literati customarily attached to books of personal importance.[18] It is here that Kang explains the origins of his One World: he was a grieving witness to the suffering about him. "Master K'ang," he wrote of himself, "was grieved and distressed, sighing and sobbing for days and months, ceaselessly." [19] The involuntary reactions of his body prompted Kang to explore the problem highlighted by his solitude, specifically the nature of the bonds of sympathy tying the solitary figure of Mr. Kang to the world. "I myself am a body. Another body suffers; it has no connection with me, and yet I sympathise very minutely." Kang derived a need for community from reflection on his own body and its involuntary reactions to the suffering about him, and he identified his community as one for which he was capable of feeling pain.[20]

For all his intensity of feeling, Kang defined this community in rationally ordered stages. He first traced an ascending hierarchy of subjects from the individual Mr. Kang to his family, then to his country and to planet Earth and out into the solar system and beyond—to "the fixed stars, the numerousness of the galactic clusters, the nebulae and the globular clusters, the aspect of all the heavens"—before returning in reverse order and arriving back at his individual self in its most familiar and most loved setting. He was, after all, a "gentleman from a family with a tradition of literary studies for thirteen generations" in "a country with several thousand years of civilization." On his journey through the universe and back, Kang established new ethical ground for a community of rational Chinese thinkers. And yet, for Kang, the desired community was a grouping of rational thinkers generally and not just Chinese ones. China itself was a category of inefficiency, an obstruction in the way of clear thinking about the proper course of history and the management of the universal state. Even for Kang, however, programmatic reasoning dictated that the centralization of the authority of the Chinese state was an appropriate intermediate stage along the route to One World. The nation-state would ultimately be subsumed into One World, but, for the moment, One World resided in the nation-state itself.

Kang was keen to show that the ideas he derived from his utopian visions were not unrealistic. He thought himself a pragmatist. Kang tried as best he could to identify a terminal community for the awakened self, and then to conceive how this ideal community might be brought into being in a new ethical and political order.[21] Though the concept of One World was free-floating, the actual identity of One World was tethered to the goal of practical attainment: it was a maximum *realizable* community.[22] Here he was comforted by the idea of historical progress. In traditional usage, One World referred to an age in the past from which the present fell away with every passing year. But in Kang's usage, One World was located at a time in the future from which the present was an unfortunate, but now remediable, deviation. Kang introduced the notion of beneficent historical progress to endorse his claim that utopian thought was not incommensurable with praxis.[23] Vision, reason, progress, and programmatic planning could together convert a utopian One World into a historical or euchronian one.

Kang's thinking was historical in another sense shared by his successors. Identifying the historically contingent ethical community meant identifying the transcendental subject of history. When Kang's awakened self first merged with the universe, he imagined that he spoke on behalf of a collective subject that impelled him to rail against the boundaries that made it plural. History was the "work" of this collective subject. But what was the subject? Practical philosophers after Kang Youwei tended to narrow their ethical communities in the first instance from the planet Earth to the nation, or to the laboring masses of China.[24] The views of his students and successors, then, differed from those of Kang not as utopia differs from actuality, or idealism from pragmatism, but in their competing assessments of which ideal community was most likely to be realized through historical action; that is, they differed chiefly in their identifications of the acting subject of history. Inevitably, identification of the historical subject cast given identities and primordial attachments into doubt.

If history was the realization of a collective subject, then the identity of the individual self was bound up with the historical designs of the greater subject. After Kang Youwei, self-awakening could only properly take the form of an awakening to the identity of this historical subject and hence to the contours of history's design.[25]

Kang's One World was utopian all the same, in its uncompromising commitment to reason. In Kang's world there was little place for historical accidents and no patience for particularities that appeared to be given in the world rather than arranged on its behalf. His ideals were utopian in the sense that they were "systems of prearranged harmony" and practical in the sense that someone had to *do* all the prearranging and the harmonizing.[26] His practice was a form of praxis. Praxis need not yield the desired effect to be counted "practical," because action that ends in failure is not discredited when the world is inherently unreasonable. Utopia and praxis come as a pair.

Concern with practice, we noted, was one of the distinguishing features of late Confucian scholarship.[27] Kang succeeded in retrieving and reworking key concepts from the literary tradition to serve as a bridge linking patently Chinese visions of a utopia of practical reason (which had only faint echoes in the tradition itself) with the rational utopias springing from Europe and America around the turn of the century. Edward Bellamy in the United States and H. G. Wells in Britain arrived independently at similar visions of rational utopias that, although differing in their details, envisioned societies motivated by faith in progress, united by solidary national or human "consciousness," ruled by reason, and governed by technocratic elites, from which factional politics and divisive capitalism were banished forever.[28] More particularly, in the case of China, Kang helped to remove the last of the obstacles impeding reception of the rational utopias of applied science, of Saint-Simon and Comte, of applied history, of Marx and Engels, and of the rational utopias of applied politics of anarchism and Leninism.

What brought Kang Youwei and the anarchists and Leninists of China's Nationalist Revolution together was their compulsive rationality. One World was an ideal not of natural harmony but of prearranged harmony. Affective or sentimental bonds such as those normally associated with family, native place, and nation counted for little to the awakened self in its contemplation of the good life. Kang Youwei, for example, listed the family among the obstacles to the realization of One World. The anarchists Liu Shipei and He Zhen called for a "family revolution" to remove children from the care of their parents and liberate women from the home.[29] Others were concerned with the effacement of all particularity. In Cai Yuanpei's short story "New Year's Dream" (1904), the world was populated by people without qualities. Not only were there no designations for ruler and minister, for husband and wife, or for parent and child, there were no designations at all that might hint at any relationship of inequality. Instead, everyone was "identified by number." [30] The limits of revolutionary tolerance for social and cultural difference were placed on display at the anarchist Labor University in Shanghai, one of the few colleges in China to offer classes in Esperanto and the only one to make Esperanto mandatory in degree courses. Anarchism was to the world of politics what Esperanto was to culture and language: a rational politics without irrational "boundaries," to match a universal language destined for a more rational world than the one in which it happened to find itself. [31]

Kang also shared with China's anarchists a curiously statist notion of society. In his study of Chinese anarchism, Peter Zarrow makes the astute observation that the terms in which anarchists discussed society were remarkably similar to those in which the state had been discussed in traditional scholarship—notably in their tone of serious decorum, their affirmation of the benevolence of the ruling agent (emperor or people), and their disdain for personal or sectional gain. [32] Anarchists shared with China's Leninists a belief that they were not just enemies of the state but self-confessed enemies of society as it was presently constituted. All social and cultural markers were to go, including the Chinese nation itself, because (as Kang Youwei had noted) such markers set up irrational sentimental boundaries between people, and sentimental boundaries were the source of the problems afflicting China and the world. [33] With its rational-statist conception of society, Chinese anarchism helped to link the hyperrational ethics of Kang Youwei with statist revolutionary movements modeled after Lenin's party-state, which ultimately conceived of state organization as an effective *substitute* for society. [34]

Lenin's only substantial piece of theoretical writing on the state, *The State and Revolution* (1917), was condemned by supporters and critics alike as "utopian," "a straightforward profession of anarchism," and "utopian anarchism." [35] Anarchists might wish to dispute the point in view of Lenin's insistence on maintaining a new kind of state in the postrevolutionary period and his triumphalist justification of the "dicatorship of the proletariat," and because they have always come out worse in their confrontations with Leninists. What created an impression of anarchism in Lenin's theoretical writing on the state, nevertheless, was his attempt to remove all of the barriers separating the economic, social, and political spheres and hence to make the state appear *invisible*. Lenin's treatise on the state puts forward a vision of a self-governing society in which proletarian councils and the bureaucracy are both reduced to technical functions of a self-governing society. Insofar as there is no differentiation between ordinary workers going about their business and the functionaries and delegates who are "self-governing" them, there is little room within the thesis itself for a critique of politics that makes sense of the state *qua* state. [36]

The ideal of self-government espoused by China's anarchists and Leninists derived from a rational-bureaucatic vision of the world that professed to do away with state bureaucracy while retaining all the compulsions of its rationality. In a world of sentimental people, however, there can be no rationality without bureaucrats, or at least without a quasi-bureaucracy of teachers and tutors. In promoting a statist notion of society as a rational aggregation of awakened selves, early utopian theorists helped to establish one of the ground rules of revolutionary politics in China: that ordinary, sentimental people who fail to match up to the ideal of the New People, the citizen, the patriot, the proletarian, or the People have to be taught to make up the difference through instruction by a caste of vanguard tutors.

There was considerable agreement among Chinese radical philosophies on the need for mass political action and, in a very general sense, on the forms that this should take. Typically, mass politics has taken as its problem the gap between an ideal of the historical subject (citizen, nation, class) and the irrefutable fact that in the actual world, ordinary people do not quite match up to the ideal. It finds its solution to this paradox in mass education (for anarchists), mass "tutelage" (for Nationalists), the "mass line" (for Communists), and other pedagogical strategies intended to bring the slumbering masses more closely into conformity with the universal code of the awakened self and its appropriate ethical community. Each solution entailed awakening the people of China.

The historical transition between ethical reflection and revolutionary propaganda was not, in fact, a difficult one. Modern forms of propaganda are generally associated with partisan political institutions and with their particular struggles. But it was not politics or state-building that brought ethics and propaganda together in the Chinese revolution. Propaganda was an imperative of rationalist ethics. Ethical philosophers distinguish three aspects of ethics that frequently overlap in social and cultural movements: interpretative ethics (establishing the grounds of an ethical system, or why people should do what they should), normative ethics (specifying the values of an ethical system, or what people should do), and educational ethics (promoting the values of an ethical system, or motivating people to act as they should).[37] The three have rarely been separated in the history of the Chinese revolution.

The connection between ethical reflection and mass propaganda is laid out neatly in the writings of China's anarchists. Anarchists were the least inclined to speak of state-building among China's modern revolutionaries, and were extremely shy of partisan politics. Yet they placed the highest value on propaganda to "awaken" the people. Anarchists stressed the ethical relationships binding individuals within communities because they allowed no place for the state in mediating relations within society. Where there is no state, or for that

matter no other permissible agency of compulsion, social behavior is condi-
tioned and regulated by ethical norms alone. So anarchists were among the
pioneers of "educational ethics" in China.

"The essence of anarchism," wrote Wu Zhihui in 1908, "is arousing the
civic virtue of the people, attending to the relationship between the individual
and society." [38] Arousing the civic virtue of the people was the task of education. "Revolution," Wu continued, "is nothing more than what happens when
education is widespread, when everyone has abandoned their old customs and
created a new life." The education Wu had in mind was an education in science and ethics, and ethics of a kind consistent with scientific skepticism, and
that encouraged the abandonment of "old customs." In writing of customs,
Wu was referring to the Confucian practices that served to maintain the time-
honored moral and social hierarchies that he found objectionable. Anarchist
ethics was an ethics of social egalitarianism, expressed as an antinomy between selfish interests (*si*) and the public interest (*gong*). Revolution entailed
a process of mass conversion from an old ethical system to a new one, sub-
suming consciousness of selfish interest under a higher consciousness of the
public good, as Confucian ethics had done, but redefining the public good so
that it embraced revolutionary egalitarian ideals. In a (regrettably) Confucian
society, this called for "propaganda." The anarchist conception of revolution,
concludes Peter Zarrow in his study of Chinese anarchism, was "one of the
word: written and spoken propaganda, of careful explanation to the people of
where truth lay." [39]

Needless to say, propaganda was crucial to national and state-building
movements as well. National awakenings required instructors in nationalism.
In the Constitutional movement of the late Qing, reformers anticipated a new
role for "public opinion" and debated how it might be directed into appropriate channels. Liang Qichao defined popular constitutional government as
"government by public opinion," and then qualified his remark with the warning that public opinion should be shaped by newspapers and other institutions
on the public's behalf.[40] State functionaries had a part to play in this exercise
as well. When he proposed converting people into citizens through a program
of ethical self-cultivation, Liang went out of his way to specify the Chinese
state as the proper object of worship.[41] In the late teens and early twenties, New
Culture activists sought to transform the nation through public enlightenment,
and after them Communists and Nationalists. These groups favored mass politics over liberal democracy and, in place of Liang's citizens, hoped to awaken
youth, women, workers, or the nation. But arguments over the structure of representative institutions and competing ideals of community were set aside on
one point at least: in each case there appeared to be a chasm between the actual

and the ideal community, into which awakened individuals and enlightened institutions should step and awaken the people.

The idea of mass awakenings—to nation, youth, class, and gender—supplied the rationale for an even more intensive style of mass pedagogy in the Nationalist Revolution. Gone were the well-meaning and bumbling mass tutors of the anarchist model. In their place, Nationalist revolutionaries established a pedagogical polity in which the ethical community was defined not by its awakening but in the act of *being* awakened: political instructors were entitled to rule the country and discipline the people until the community had reached an approved level of self-consciousness. The relationship between a conscious state and an unconscious community was installed in the ideology and programs of both parties to the Nationalist Revolution. National consciousness was located in the leadership of the Nationalist party under a tutelary (*xunzheng*) state, which was legitimated by its role in teaching people how to be Chinese citizens. The vanguard party of the Chinese working class developed its own pedagogical strategies.[42] The respective nations of the Nationalists and the Communists were to be counted self-conscious not when all nationals had awakened under their instruction, but when all *obstacles* to political instruction had been removed—that is, when the pedagogical state could say whatever it liked, wherever it chose, without fear of contradiction. At this point the myth of national or class consciousness would cease to be mythical, for community consciousness extended as far as the reach of the state, into the heart of society and to the outermost borders of the land.

The privilege accorded to the awakened functionary presented challenges as well as opportunities to the Nationalist movement. The notion that communities were not given but made eased the introduction of new mass communities of nation and of social class into ethical thought. Yet if the ideal community was born in ethical reflection, rather than in the organic development of communities themselves, what was it about the nation or a particular social class that gave it precedence over other forms of community? And how did the particular community relate to the universal one? China's Nationalists gave these questions due attention, as had Hegel and Marx before them.

Hegel and Marx both posited ideal communities that logically preceded the attainment of self-consciousness on the part of their members. For Hegel this was the Prussian, or more generally the national, state. For Marx it was class position in the relations of production. Not unnaturally, the question arose whether a social class could be said to exist if the objective conditions for its existence appeared to be satisfied but its members were not yet aware of their common identity. Marx supplied his answer in *The Eighteenth Brumaire of Louis Bonaparte*:

In so far as millions of families live under economic conditions of existence that separate their mode of life, their interests and their culture from those of other classes, and put them in hostile opposition to the latter, they form a class. In so far as there is merely a local interconnection among (them) and the identity of their interests begets no community, no national bond, and no political organization among them, they do not form a class.

In the absence of appropriate bonds and organization, people "do not form a class." Yet even when the "identity of their interests begets no community," class remains a category of ethical reflection. In this abstract form, class belongs to a higher category of existence than class consciousness, to the extent that a peasant class may have interests that it does not recognize of its own accord. In pursuing these interests, in Marx's famous phrase, they "must be represented" by others.[43] There seem to be sufficient grounds in Marx's reflections on the nature of class consciousness for later social theorists to dismiss the idea of class out of hand, or alternatively to develop this distinction into a criterion for distinguishing between "true" and "false" consciousness. True consciousness is manifest identification with a social class and recognition of its ascribed class interests. Consciousness of other forms of community that diminish class consciousness—such as religious communities, ethnic groups, or nation-states—are deemed "false." [44]

Hegel assigned a different content to false (or what he called "defective") consciousness. Consciousness of a community beyond the nation was misplaced if it threatened loyalty to the nation-state. In the face of the nation, consciousness of a higher claim on loyalty to "manhood" or humanity would be "defective," a form of "cosmopolitanism in opposition to the concrete life of the state." [45] Cosmopolitanism was, needless to say, a positive force for Marx where it set social classes in opposition to the concrete life of the national state. But this is a relatively minor quibble for the Marxist and the Nationalist revolutionary pedagogue. The fact that both Hegel and Marx agreed on the categorical existence of ideal communities, and of states of consciousness corresponding to these ideal communities that bore no necessary relation to existing forms of consciousness, outweighed their differences. Strategically at least, each raised a common problem for the political activist: how to bridge the gap between actual and ideal social consciousness and so bring the ideal community into "concrete" existence.[46] A Chinese political activist schooled in national revolution to bring a nation into being needed little retraining to do the same for a social class. These were parallel pedagogical projects, turning on different definitions of the ideal community and corresponding states of consciousness. In the Chinese revolution, both were thought to require the services of the awakened functionary.[47]

The Rational Nation

Whereas the transition from ethical reflection to mass propaganda seems to have run an easy course, the discovery of China as a *particular* ethical community followed a more tortuous route. One signpost along the way, we have seen, was a statist conception of society found in the ethical reasoning of Kang Youwei and China's anarchists. Kang placed little importance in the national state as an institution in its own right, and China's anarchists, it goes without saying, were professed enemies of the state. Among those who glorified the national state, on the other hand, the state was rarely celebrated *as* a state (*guo*). The romances, the polemic, the anthems, and the constitutions of Chinese nationalism have invariably celebrated the historical subject whom the *guo* is thought to "represent" (*daibiao*) rather than the *guo* itself, and then to invest this represented sample (the nation) with the particular qualities of the state.

A second sign marking the way from universal to more particular models of community lay in a paradox at the heart of rationalist ethics itself. National boundaries were anathema in the universal utopia of Kang Youwei; families and social classes annoyed anarchists; and factional, local, and all other varieties of "particularist" boundaries were eschewed in the communities dreamed up by Leninist and Nationalist revolutionaries. Institutions policing these boundaries (the patriarch, civic associations, the nation-state) were counted obstructions to clear thinking and obstacles to rational social and political reconstruction. Yet the strategies designed to bring the ideal community into the world called for the creation of particular institutions on their own account, including political parties, armies, and "representative" bodies of distinct social groups that were to act as midwives at the birth of the community. In this lower realm of instrumental reason, well below the stars, boundaries and their institutions were transformed from impediments to One World into agencies for its realization. Parties and armies were, after all, only partisan institutions so long as they were alienated from the state. The paradox was resolved among state-oriented political movements by the imperative to seize state power within the nation-state. A particular institution would cease to appear particular once the nation had been made identical to the institution that governed in its name.

The chief reason for the ethical reduction of the universal community to the nation-state was a historical one. An earthbound One World seemed well out of reach by the time of the Nationalist Revolution. Indeed, it was beyond reach even as Kang wrote. It was his student, Liang Qichao, who selected the nation as the proper ethical community for the awakened self. Liang retained his master's interest in the relationship between self and community and, in common with many of his contemporaries, focused upon the place of the "mass" (*qun*) in his ethical system. Maintaining the identity and coherence of the "mass" was the central thematic of his ethics. Liang hoped dearly for the emergence of a universal mass, but by the time he sat down to write *The New Citizen* (*Xinminshuo*) in 1902, it had become clear that its boundaries ran parallel to the borders of the nation-state.[48]

Liang's reasoning was, after the fashion of his master, eminently rational. Kang Youwei had already devised the first minimum program of the revolution. The ideal community for Kang's awakened self embraced the "living creatures on Mars, Saturn, Jupiter, Uranus and Neptune" as well as those on Earth. In more sanguine moments, Kang had even hoped to put an end to intergalactic warfare: "I have pondered deeply how to rid all the stars and all the heavens of war, but could not [resolve it]." Out of concern that his One World be realized, however, he chose to limit his community to the planet Earth and to the creatures inhabiting it: "I am only going to consider how to do away with the calamity of war in the world in which I was born." In a significant gesture to practice, Kang settled for the first minimum program of the revolution, embracing peace on earth.

Liang Qichao carried Kang's line of reasoning a step further and concluded that present historical circumstances placed the ideal of a world community out of the question for the time being.[49] For Kang, the logical outcome of his thinking was a One World state; for Liang, it was a Chinese nation-state. This difference in the site of the state marked a dispute over the boundaries of the ethical community, or over the practical limits of instrumental reason, and not a disagreement over the preeminence of reason in the contemplation of public affairs. When Liang argued for the elimination of parochialism and particularism within the national territory, for example, he merely echoed Kang's call for the elimination of national, racial, and gender boundaries in the world as a whole. And when Liang tried to standardize Chinese identity in the *New Citizen*, he was only seeking for the nation-state what Kang set out to achieve for the world: the elimination of all prior claims on the identity of the self.

The earliest of Nationalist revolutionaries made similar choices. In fact, the nation was selected as a *rational* community long before it had become an affective one. Some nationalists resented the compulsion to compromise with the irrational and the accidental that the idea of the nation seemed to impose. Zhang Binglin is remembered as the "father of racial consciousness" among China's nationalists. Like Kang Youwei, Zhang cried out against the "boundaries" that divided the world and trained his fury upon races and nations as among the worst offenders. They were too arbitrary and accidental: "Now, in this multitudinous universe, the earth is but a small grain of rice in a vast granary, yet today [we] who live on it have divided it up into territories, we protect what is ours and call it a 'nation.' Then we established institutions, divided [ourselves] into various classes, and called it 'government.' " Nations had no rationale for being other than their historical emergence as categories for orga- nizing the affairs of men.[50] In fact, Zhang had little choice at all in settling on the "race" as his ethical community. Given China's present predicament, the nation was a rational community before it was an affective one, and it was his duty to give effect to the rational. Zhang became the founding father of mod- ern Chinese racism because it was the rational thing to do.[51]

The convergence of statist nationalism with antistatist revolutionary phi- losophies in the Nationalist Revolution was long prefigured by Kang Youwei and Zhang Binglin. At the turn of the century, Zhang wrote of the nation-state as "lack[ing] authentic existence" because it resulted from historical accidence rather than reasoned deliberation. Its claims over the lives of citizens and sub- jects were devalued accordingly.[52] But calculation about the status and function of the nation-state led in more statist directions when combined with a rational concept of the awakened self and its reconstituted community. Kang Youwei wrote of the state as if it were no more than a desideratum of existing commu- nities, and yet his calculations on the function and duty of the state were no less chilling on this account. In Kang's view, the state was not itself a boundary but an institution for maintaining boundaries. So the source of the suffering that had so shaken him on the mountaintop was not the state but the boundaries that the state was duty-bound to police; the real culprits were the boundaries of particularity that each community imposed upon itself. The fewer the bound- aries, the fewer the states, by this reasoning; and the sum of human suffering would decrease as smaller communities were incorporated into larger commu- nities and smaller states fell to more powerful ones. Kang proposed a number of rational improvements in the provenance and organization of the state de- signed to reduce suffering in the community. And he put forward an ultimate ideal of the state that corresponded to his ideal community: a One World state, policing a boundary drawn by the physical limits of the planet itself. With chilling reason, albeit some regret, he concluded that the achievement of a world state justified the "grinding down of bodies" because it eliminated the intermediate boundaries marking community differences, which were the true sources of suffering.[53]

On praxis, too, Kang set the pace when he questioned whether it was realistic to hope for an end to intergalactic warfare in his lifetime. His succes- sors were more skeptical and asked instead whether they might put an end to international or civil war, or perhaps eliminate differences among classes and between men and women, and if not, then what they might settle for in the in- terim. Internationalists, nationalists, socialists, and anarchists were all idealists, yet all were deeply concerned with *practice*. Whether the ethical community was made up of all creatures on earth or merely humans, all humans or merely Chinese ones, all Chinese or only some of them defined by class, ethnicity, or gender, were questions best answered by reference to how readily such a community could be summoned into existence through programmatic planning and political intervention. The quality of the relationship between self and community remained one of "sympathy," but in time the community itself was defined with ever greater precision until it had reached a level consonant with the assertion of its own autonomy as a historical subject. The ideal community for the alienated body, Kang had noted, was nothing less than the universe itself. Everything else was a practical and, in the last instance, a political compromise to arrive at a realizable historical subject through political action.

The particular and historically contingent community for the awakened self was to be decided in the realm of politics. "Reality" (*shishi*) and "real force" (*shili*) were code words for political and armed struggle, conceived within a framework of the international state system and acknowledging the implications of this system for the effective autonomy of the self and its community in old imperial states such as China. The state featured in the new ethics from the start. History was moving in the direction of fewer and more highly centralized states, Kang argued, and "that to which the general state of affairs tends will eventually be reached." [54] If the source of his suffering was not the state, but rather the boundaries that the state was duty-bound to police, then the real culprit was the artificial limit to the ethical community imposed by particularist sentiment—in effect, the *limited* authority of the state.[55] Ultimately it was the historical process of securing the territory and people of China within the international state system that brought the nation to China. The Chinese nation was an imagined compromise, and nationalism was a rational strategy for bringing it into being.[56]

The ideal nation-state shared the qualities of the particular and the universal because it was poised, as it were, between the village and the universe. The existence of a central imperial state governing a more-or-less stable territory in the Qing dynasty had set a clear precedent for the establishment of a national state in twentieth-century China. But how the new state would negotiate its way into a position of authority, how it would represent the village to the world, and even who would make up the nation, were all questions for rational deliberation and political struggle. The sides taken in struggle and debate often reflected different approaches to the two tasks facing nationalist reformers in China. With one hand they needed to raise the myths and symbols of national consciousness to bridge particularist divisions of "clan" and "native place," and with the other they felt compelled to sever new bridges linking the emancipated self to universal or cosmopolitan communities whose time was yet to come.

Sun Yatsen was not persuaded that primordial communities of family and native place were insurmountable barriers to nation-building, nor that they necessarily limited the fostering of wider human values. In contrast to Kang Youwei and the anarchists, Sun proposed that national sentiment take priority over all others; but in contrast to Liang Qichao, he believed that links of lineage and locality could be turned to the service of the nation. All the same, Sun shared with Kang Youwei and Liang Qichao a concern to overcome the boundaries dividing kin and regions from one another. One question that divided them was precisely *how* this was to be done.

"On the surface the government seems to be a centralized one," complained Liang. "However, the country is actually divided into innumerable small units and groups on the basis of either territory or biological relatedness or occupation." Liang Qichao put forward a model of the New Citizen with the aim of dissolving groups bounded by locality, family, and occupation into individual, awakened citizens who would relate directly to the national state without the aid of intermediary agencies in society.[57] There were two rival schools of nationalist thought that argued otherwise. In an early attempt to reconcile loyalties of family and locality with national ones, He Qi (Ho Kai) and Hu Liyuan argued that there was little need to quash attachment to family and locality in the name of the nation: "If members of a certain family are encouraged in their attachment to their own family, and if people of a local area have a particular concern for their own area, then the people may well value their own country more than any other." [58] Sun Yatsen, on the other hand, was determined to ensure that family, clan, and native-place sentiments were self-consciously elevated to the level of the nation by "awakening" the people to the organic connections among their communities. Like Liang, Sun was concerned that particularist sentiment appeared to diminish "national sentiment" and hence limited the nation's capacity to defend itself:

Foreign observers say that the Chinese are like a loose sheet of sand. Why? Simply because our people have shown loyalty to family and clan but not to the nation—there has been no nationalism. The family and clan have been powerful unifying forces; again and again the Chinese have sacrificed themselves, their families, their lives in defense of their clans. . . . But for the nation there has never been an instance of the supreme spirit of sacrifice. The unity of the Chinese people has stopped short at the clan and has not extended to the nation.[59]

In a later lecture, Sun added that the "native-place sentiment of the Chinese is very deep-rooted too; it is especially easy to unite those who are from the same province, prefecture or village." Sun proposed reorienting local and family sentiment upward, to the nation-state. "In the relation between the citizens of China and their state," Sun proclaimed in 1924, "there must first be family loyalty, then clan loyalty, and finally national loyalty." [60]

And there it was to stop. Sun's nation was counterposed not only to the family and to the village below, but to higher forms of community claiming universal membership above. "A new theory is emerging in England and Russia, proposed by intellectuals, which opposes nationalism on the ground that it is narrow and illiberal," Sun Yatsen warned in 1924. This trend was "simply a doctrine of cosmopolitanism." It was indistinguishable on the one hand from the universal claims of the Chinese empire, and on the other, from the false doctrines of British imperialism.[61] Sun was not opposed to cosmopolitanism in principle. The particularism of the race was grounded in universal scientific principles, and his nationalism aspired to universal human values. But he was reluctant to welcome "cosmopolitanism" before its time had come. Cosmopolitanism may well be "hidden in the heart of nationalism," he conceded, but it had no business emerging before nationalism had run its course in China:[62]

Those young students who prate about the new Culture and espouse cosmopolitanism, saying that nationalism is out of date, might have some ground if they spoke for England or America or even for our forefathers, but if they think they are speaking for Chinese today, we have no place for them.[63]

The day of cosmopolitanism would dawn when China had earned a rightful place as a full and equal member of an international community of nations. "We must talk nationalism first," Sun concluded, "if we want to talk cosmopolitanism. . . . Let us revive our lost nationalism and make it shine with greater splendour, then we will have some ground for discussing internationalism." [64]

The differences that divided early nationalists were not, however, simply differences of method. In reflecting on how people who were divided by ties of blood and native place should be brought together in the nation, Sun Yatsen and Liang Qichao revealed different conceptions of the nation itself. After settling upon the nation as his ethical community, Liang Qichao employed the latest tools of history and science to probe its identity. He was prepared to concede that "race" was an irreducible unit of natural selection and went so far as to trace a "natural" history of the world in the rise and fall of racial empires. Echoing Hegel, he declared the winners to be "historical peoples" (*you lishi de renzhong*) and the losers "unhistorical peoples" (*fei lishi de renzhong*).[65] British imperialism, then, offered a scientific demonstration of the "inescapable working of the law of natural evolution." If the Chinese were to remain a historical people in the face of imperialism, they would need to harness the same natural laws by crafting their own society and state on the model of Britain, and become corporate, democratic, and strong. In short, China needed to develop an ethics of "nationalism." [66]

But Liang was emphatically not a racial nationalist. Historically, he noted, a single state might house many ethnic nations and a single race might well be

scattered over numerous states, so there was no general law governing the relationship between ethnicity and statehood. An ethnic definition of the nation-
state might even prove a barrier to state-building in a multiethnic community
such as China, where nationalism needed to sever all connections between
ethnic identity and patriotism in order to maintain the territorial integrity of the
empire and the centrality of the state. Liang invented the term "broad nationalism" (*da minzu zhuyi*) to distinguish his ideal of corporate national identity—
focusing on the nation-state—from ethnic identity, which focused on ethnicity
or race. Liang's nationalist ethics was at base an ethics of citizenship, linking self and community in a relationship revolving about the national state.[67]
So he defined ethnic identity using customary distinctions of common territory, ancestry, language, religion, and custom, while identifying the citizenry
subjectively as a group whose consciousness of their corporate identity bestowed upon them individual identities as citizens. Ethnicity was a birthmark
people carried in their sleep; citizenship was a graduate diploma from the state
granted to those who had "awakened" as citizens. In time Liang came to use
the terms *citizen* and *state* interchangeably and to press for their simultaneous
awakening.[68] The national awakening was coterminous with the manufacture
of an awakened citizenry, and the nation with the state.

Sun Yatsen, on the other hand, identified nation and state indelibly with the
idea of a distinctly Chinese race. Sun's own self-awakening in Hawaii and Hong
Kong seems to have entailed an acute consciousness of his skin color and facial
features, and in his adult life he was more sensitive to etiquette than to ethics.[69]
And, significantly, his recognition of race as the foundation of the nation seems
to have brought with it a wider tolerance of other forms of primordial community—including the immediate family and the local lineage—and to have
mitigated the rationalist impulse to reconstitute existing communities *ab initio*.
He certainly disparaged the limitations of family and clan loyalty, but promised
to redeem them by redirecting them toward the national state. In this respect
he specifically repudiated what he termed the "Western" model (favored by
Liang Qichao), in which isolated citizens related directly to the national state.[70]

Sun's views on the place of the nation in the world also marked him off
from a later generation of nationalists. The New Culture movement embraced
a host of communities in addition to the nation, and it did not always place the
nation first among them. It championed the inherent value of the individual, the
universal principles of science and democracy, and the universal communities
of youth, gender, and class. Sun dismissed these trends as "cosmopolitanism"
in the belief that awakened youth were mistaking Western values for universal
ones, or were substituting alien values for more familiar Chinese ones.[71] When
the May Fourth movement eventually channeled the energies of young cos-
mopolitans into a movement to save the nation, Sun counseled young people

about the dangers of cosmopolitanism and encouraged his comrades Hu Han-min, Liao Zhongkai, and Wang Jingwei to direct the youth movement toward the Nationalist party.[72]

For this, at least, Liang Qichao gave him credit. Despite their differences over the identity of the nation, Sun and Liang both believed the nation should take priority over all other forms of ethical community. Looking back in 1922 over the preceding decade, Liang could see a "dark and colourless period." But things had improved in recent years because the "former leaders seem to have reawakened, caught their breath and renewed their struggle." In the twi-light of his career, Liang could reflect with equanimity on the achievements of a revolution that had not always been to his liking, and he could share the satisfaction of Nationalist party members in observing that another awaken-ing was under way. He signaled his approval with a characteristic sally into the meaning of self-awakening. "To what do we awaken," he asked, "when we attain self-awakening? . . . First we awaken [to the fact] that all who are not Chinese lack the right to control Chinese affairs. Secondly, we awaken [to the fact] that all Chinese have the right to control Chinese affairs." [73] In awakening as a Chinese citizen in the 1920s, the self awoke at once to citizenship and to patriotism. Liang and Sun were both determined that patriotism not yield to cosmopolitanism among the generations that followed them.

The Self as Citizen and Patriot

Once self-awakening had been defined as an awakening to membership in the nation-state, the relationship between self and community could be more readily explored in discussion of the relationship between citizen and state. Talk of citizenship had never veered far from the claims of the state upon the citizen. Twenty years earlier, when Liang Qichao first concluded that the awak-ened self should be a self-conscious citizen, he chose to evaluate the citizen according to the principle of Reason of State. By this he meant the subordi-nation of citizen to state in a relationship that ensured the survival of the state at any cost. Kang Youwei, it is true, had preferred to speak of Citizens of Heaven (*tianmin*) rather than of national citizens, but his heavenly citizens de-rived little advantage from their elevation. Citizens of any dimension could be sacrificed if they stood in the way of the perfection of the state. Liang argued that the citizen should be forfeited to the nation-state when the interests of the state demanded it, and Kang Youwei expressed few qualms about "grinding down bodies" in the interest of achieving his One World state.[74] Once self-awakening had been conceived as consciousness of the relationship between the self and the state, custodians of the state felt obliged to supervise and to direct the awakening of the self more generally.

Nevertheless, disillusion with the early Republican state had prompted an additional question that had not troubled Sun Yatsen or Liang Qichao. Were citizens obliged to honor and obey a democratic national state if they did not approve of it? Or could they reserve the exercise of their obligations pending the arrival of an ideal state? The subject of an ideal state arose in 1915, after three years of Republican government, in a celebrated dispute over the relationship between the self and the state that involved the two cofounders of the Chinese Communist party, Chen Duxiu and Li Dazhao.[75] The self in Chen Duxiu's article "Patriotism and Consciousness of Self" was the now-familiar "awakened" self, which awoke as a fully-constructed citizen. Self-awakening was neither more nor less than an awareness of the relationship between self and state: "To what does one awaken in awakening to selfhood? One awakens to the aims of the state and the situation in which this state finds itself." Chen also wrote of the sympathy that bound the self to its community and, like Kang Youwei before him, inquired into the foundation and character of this emotion. But where Kang's sympathy extended to the universe, Chen's emotion was directed unequivocally to the nation-state. It aspired no higher than "patriotism" (*aiguozhuyi*).

Yet patriotism was not greatly in evidence in the first years of the Republic. Chen naturally (given his understanding of "awakening to selfhood") traced the omission of patriotism to an "absence of self-awakening":

In present day China . . . public security, or a common threat, seems to have no bearing on the happiness or misfortune of individuals because they have no emotional [ties]. This I call lack of patriotism. It is due to lack of knowledge that one understands neither others nor oneself. This I call the absence of self-awakening. If citizens lack patriotism, their states should normally perish; but if citizens fail to awaken to themselves, their state is equally jeopardized.

Though he could find little evidence of patriotism or self-consciousness among his compatriots, Chen could not bring himself to blame them on this account. The fault lay with the state, he argued, which was endangered by its own incompetence. The state and its functionaries were duty-bound to generate emotion and self-awareness among the national community. The self awoke in the early Republic as a disappointed citizen, pining for a state worthy of its own self-awakening.

The awakened self, in other words, was not just a citizen in search of a state but a potential patriot who craved an ideal state capable of firing its emotion. A state that failed to inspire patriotism was more deserving of criticism than a citizen who felt none, for the self could only awaken to consciousness within a state deserving of its love and sacrifice, and capable of inspiring love of nation. This was the case in Europe and America, argued Chen, where the state was "an organization whose members cooperate in the search for the security and happiness of the citizens" and for which all citizens felt corresponding love and respect. Such a state had never been known in China, which consequently boasted few patriots. Or, as Chen put it, since there had been no patriots, there has been no *state*:

Once the meaning of the state has been cleared up, one is able to say that we Chinese are not patriots. One can even say that there have never been as yet any patriots among us; one can even go so far as to say that we Chinese have never as yet set up a state.

A state that did not inspire patriotism failed to qualify as a state at all, for a true state was one that manufactured an awakened citizenry by virtue of its own perfection. From these reflections, Chen Duxiu derived the radical conclusion that the collapse of the Republican state, as it was presently constituted, would be a matter of little moment to the awakened self. Where a state does not "defend the rights of the people" nor "increase the happiness of the people . . . it is neither glorious to maintain one's state nor regrettable to lose it." [76]

Li Dazhao was scandalized by Chen's claim that the present state was not worth saving. He conceded that the Republican state had brought considerable suffering on the people and was in all respects far from perfect. But, Li argued, it was at least a Chinese one: "The sufferings which result from a bad state are only a temporary phenomenon. It is not a calamity comparable to the loss of one's state, which cannot be repaired for all eternity." [77] Fear that the state would disappear was expressed in the phrase "death of the state" (*wangguo*), which seems to have recurred as frequently in nightmares as it did in print in the early Republic. Sun Yatsen touched on the theme in his lectures on the Three Principles of the People when he equated the loss of the state with the disappearance of the race. The fate in store for China was far worse than that endured by the Koreans and Vietnamese, he counseled, who were already "slaves who had lost their states" (*wangguonu*).[78] The people of China would not even be preserved as slaves, for in China the loss of state threatened the "destruction of our race." [79] Sun drew a connection between the death of the state and the destruction of the race by invoking the laws of nature. The race was threatened by "forces of natural selection" operating through "foreign economic and political domination" that threatened "the death of the state." [80]

Li Dazhao had only recently expressed his dread of the death of the state when Chen Duxiu's article went to press. He all but despaired to find his fears foreshadowed and dismissed in Chen's casual disregard for the survival of an identifiably Chinese state. Even if the prospect of losing the state did not threaten racial genocide, in Li Dazhao's calculations, it certainly involved a grave risk of China losing its territory and its political identity. Whether it was thought to entail loss of race, territory, or political identity, the death of the state was counted the greatest loss of all. In earlier usage, the term *wangguo* had referred to the downfall of a dynasty, and as one dynasty was generally replaced by another in a dynastic cycle, the term had implied little more than a historical transition between ruling houses. Once history shifted from a cyclical to a secular route, however, the idea of death of state posed a threat of graver proportions. The progressive history of the nation-state offered little reassurance, on its relentless forward march, that the collapse of a recognizably Chinese state would yield another in its place.[81] Li Dazhao identified the idea of a historically continuous state with the continued existence of China, such that the term "death of the state" implied the death of China.

Li then attempted to resolve the contradiction that Chen Duxiu had identified by qualifying his definition of self-awakening, as a static relationship between self and state, through the addition of *will*, or a commitment to improving the state. Creating an ideal state was an obligation imposed on the conscious self by the universe to which it awoke:

It is not fitting to renounce one's state and not love it because it is not worthy of being loved. Still less is it advisable, because our people have not yet benefited from a state worthy of being loved, to neglect the one we have, thus finding ourselves in the position of a people without a state and putting ourselves in the position of those who are incapable of creating a state worthy of being loved. For it is men who create the state; we are the ones who dominate the immensity of the universe; the universe allows us to exist, we people of the same species, and admits that we may be capable of creating a state . . . we have only to rely on the strength of our consciousness of self and to advance with all our might toward the goal defined by our will.[82]

Chen Duxiu certainly acknowledged the value of the citizen and the patriot, and had talked at length of reason and emotion, but he had neglected to mention will—specifically the will "to create the state," which was a gift that the heavens bestowed on the awakened self. The citizen without a state and the patriot without a country could each complete itself, with heaven's blessing, by creating a state worthy of itself. When the citizen was at one with the state, the self was finally at one with the "immensity of the universe." [83]

It was not just fear of death of the state that fueled the dispute between Chen Duxiu and Li Dazhao in 1915. Both men were keen to explain the weakness of patriotic sentiment among the people of China. For Chen this was proof that China had no state; for Li it was persuasive argument that China ought to acquire a better one. Others were equally puzzled. Sun Yatsen frequently complained that there was little sign of patriotism among his compatriots, in the belief that love between patriot and *patria* was ordained by the stars. "Heaven has placed great responsibility upon us Chinese," he noted in his lectures on the Three Principles; "if we do not love ourselves we are rebels against Heaven." [84]

Sun's appeal to the stars was understandable, but perhaps misdirected. The appropriate model for love of country was not the relationship between the awakened self and the heavens nor the contract between citizen and state. Though these were certainly expected to displace the sentimental bonds of family and native place, neither could inspire passion of its own accord. The inspiration for patriotism was to be found elsewhere: in the search for individual freedom and in the quest for romantic love. Individual freedom needed to be thought conditional on collective freedom, and the moon had to gaze down upon star-crossed lovers in Shanghai and Beijing, Changsha and Guangzhou, before Heaven could really expect Chinese to love one another as compatriots.

Patriotism was born in the self-awakenings chronicled in romantic fiction. The discovery of the personal self and of the heroic nation took place successively in modern fiction in an extraordinary phenomenon known as the "literary revolution" of modern China. Two thousand years of literary history was ruptured in the space of a generation.[85] The new literature started out on its pathfinding journey from the same point of departure Kang Youwei had taken; that is, from a moment of ecstatic self-awakening accompanied by an excruciating sense of loss.

Over the decade from 1915, every youth who could pick up a pen seems to have undergone an awakening. "I often say that I am a product of May Fourth," recalled the novelist Ba Jin in his essay "Awakening and Action." "The May Fourth Movement awoke me from my sleepy dreams like a clap of spring thunder. I opened my eyes and beheld a new world." [86] The awakening came as a shock as well as a revelation as the discovery of the self coincided with a woeful melancholia in the literary imagination. In the stories of Yu Dafu and Bing Xin, the awakened self wanders dark and deserted streets contemplating suicide or traces footsteps in the sand wrapped in melancholy.[87] But because fiction also placed the awakened self in a social setting—of unawakened others—it offered scope for exploring narrative solutions to the problem of alienation by awakening the society of the novel on the one hand, and awakening the community of readers on the other.[88]

This is not to say that self-awakening in fiction was subsumed within the national awakening. It was a very personal affair. In the view of Yu Dafu, an ardent celebrant of self-discovery, "the greatest success of the May Fourth Movement lay, first of all, in the discovery of individual personality." [89] Poets celebrated the discovery with paeans to the first-person pronoun. Fiction writers explored, often in excruciating detail, what the self could get up to once it had awoken from a slumber of centuries induced by old familial, ethical, and political communities. The line between fiction and autobiography had blurred. Yu Dafu's own fiction was autobiographical in the simplest and most direct sense of the word because, as Yu explained, "all literary work is nothing but the author's autobiography." It seemed an act of bad faith to pretend otherwise.[90] The preoccupation with the self left its mark on literary artifacts as well: in the production of diaries and autobiographies and in the exchange of personal letters, which came to be incorporated into the repertoire of literature as fictional devices for exploring themes of alienation and love, captivity and emancipation.[91] The collective counterpart of this discovery of the individual was not the nation but the universe or the world in general. "The development of new theories in history, anthropology and psychology," Bonnie McDougall observes, "all tended to encourage the conviction, common among Western intellectuals in the twenties and reflected in China, that identification with mankind as a whole was a more progressive and enlightened way of thinking than identification with any particular race or nation." [92]

All the same, in broaching questions of self and community, the new fiction inevitably explored the community of the nation. Although awakened youth may have imagined they were writing for the world, few outside China knew of their efforts, and fewer cared. The horizons of fiction, history, and journalism were clearly etched in form and language to mark out a national community of characters and a national community of readers.[93] Indeed, the New Culture and May Fourth movements are remembered today not for the emergence of a new world order but for the disappointment of such expectations at Versailles, and for the awakening of the nation at home. To Liang Qichao, we have seen, these two movements signaled the awakening of citizenship and patriotism. Despite his ambivalence about "cosmopolitanism," Sun Yatsen appreciated the nationwide political ramifications of the May Fourth movement.[94] And Mao Zedong conceded that the "whole of the Chinese revolutionary movement found its origin in the action of young students and intellectuals who had been awakened" in the May Fourth movement of 1919.[95]

Mao's appreciation of its national revolutionary significance highlights the dual character of the movement. Over the years preceding May Fourth, awakened youths were chiefly concerned with individuality and self-realization. Mao himself was no exception. The awakening of the individual clearly came before the awakening of the nation, both historically and logically, in the development of Mao's own philosophy. "The value of the individual is greater than that of the universe," he had written in 1918. "Thus there is no greater crime than to suppress the individual or to violate particularity. . . . The group itself has no meaning, it only has meaning as a collection of individuals." [96] Yet the student demonstrations that began in May 1919 rapidly expanded into a collective movement of students, workers, and merchants intent on embarrassing the Beijing government and dealing a blow to Japanese trade in China.[97] The experience at Versailles suggested that their personal bondage—the liberation of the individual from "feudalism" — was bound up with a collective struggle — the liberation of the nation from "imperialism" — and hence that the attainment of individual freedom was a collective enterprise. In time, self and nation were both thought to be chained by the same alliance of forces in feudalism and imperialism. Hence from May Fourth, in 1919, a particular national identity was imprinted on the awakened self, that of an individual and a people in chains. The awakening of the individual to its place in the universe anticipated the awakening of the nation to its place in the international state system, but the emancipation of the individual would now have to await the emancipation of the nation.

Alongside these political negotiations came a literary reworking of self and nation in the literature of the movement. First, the freedom and autonomy of the awakened self served as a model for the liberation and independence of the nation. Individual freedom was conceived as a negative freedom, as freedom *from* something rather than freedom *for* something. The emancipated individual, often imagined as a sleeper awakening from sleep, escaped from the bonds of family and tradition in the act of awakening. Similarly, national liberation was conceived as an act of emancipation from foreign imperialism rather than as a set of practices relating to civic freedoms.[98]

Second, even at its most self-indulgent, the new literature of May Fourth helped to give shape to the awakening nation by confronting issues of self-consciousness and alienation and by exploring themes of bondage, emancipation, and romantic love. It publicized themes first expounded in the new ethics to a readership that might well have turned its back on more weighty philosophical tomes. The fiction of the early twenties spoke of romance and excitement, promised freedom and adventure, and educated its readers in the arts of love. Before the decade was out, these early experiments in the literature of self-indulgence, love, and freedom had found their way into the propaganda of the Nationalist Revolution.

Some artists of the New Culture movement understood the call for "free love" in the sense the term connotes today — of libertarian sexual practice — but to most young men, at least, free love meant freedom from family coercion in choosing a marriage partner or freedom to enter into companionate marriage. In this respect it marked an attack on the patriarchal father figure without undermining the patriarchal institution of marriage itself. Permissive sex was at any rate commonplace among male heads of families and posed little threat to the patriarchal family. Companionate marriage was far more subversive. It limited the capacity of the lineage to reproduce itself, and it asked young lovers to enter into a freely chosen contract with one another, and then to adhere to the contract through thick and thin. This commitment was not unlike the one that nationalists asked of their compatriots.

A further point of affinity between romantic love and nationalism was the vision of affective community conveyed in romance, as distinct from older communities of lineage and locality. Part of the attraction of romantic fiction lay in the prospect that anyone might be singled out as a partner for the lover. All that was required was a skip of the heart. The archetypical lover of the New Fiction severed all sentimental links with family, custom, and place to embrace a community of potential lovers that overlapped with the young nation itself. In this way, the nation was put forward as an object not just of loyalty but of affection. The extensive, varied, and finely nuanced treatment of romantic love in fiction, then, helped to craft and popularize a model of the relationship between self and community that supplied a model for love of nation, or patriotism.

In the 1920s, writers were able to draw on an extensive repertoire of techniques and motifs that had been developed over a decade of writing about the awakening of the self and the discovery of romantic love, and apply them to love of the nation. In *The Romantic Generation of Chinese Writers*, Leo Lee has noted the ease and frequency with which authors of fictional romance turned their pens to the service of revolution. Romantic love and revolutionary patriotism came as a pair. One of the better-known authors of romance, Jiang Guangci, noted the connection quite explicitly:

Romantic? I myself am romantic. All revolutionaries are romantic. Without being romantic, who would come to start a revolution? . . . Idealism, passion, discontent with the status quo and a desire to create something better—here you have the spirit of romanticism. A romantic is one possessed of such a spirit.[99]

In 1930 Jiang published a "romantic" novel on the Nationalist Revolution, *Chongchu yunwei de yueliang* (The moon breaking out from behind the clouds), which went through many editions. The heroine, Wang Manying, runs off with her boyfriend to join the revolution but is forced to flee when the revolution turns sour. She resorts to prostitution by way of compensation, selecting her clients with an eye to infecting the counterrevolutionary bourgeoisie with venereal disease and exacting revolutionary vengeance. Love and revolution finally converge when Manying meets a young revolutionary, Li Shangzhi, whose faith has not failed him. Her disease disappears without trace.[100]

Revolutionary romantics scoffed at Jiang Guangci's contrived sentimentality but shared his determination to explore the themes of love and patriotism in their fiction. Guo Moruo and Yu Dafu set off together for Guangzhou in March 1926 to join the Nationalist propaganda service. Earlier in the same year, the novelist Shen Yanbing (Mao Dun) took up a position as deputy director of the same bureau under the direction of Mao Zedong. Guo, Yu, and Shen were among the most prolific of the romantic writers of the 1920s. They were also pioneers in the new genre of historical realism around the turn of the decade.

Mao Dun's massive trilogy, *The Canker* (*Shi*), has been described as "the first major written work after the May Fourth Movement of 1919 which gives a coherent picture of a whole historical period." [101] In the first volume, published in 1927, Mao Dun reflects on the Nationalist Revolution through the story of a young woman's juvenile sexuality. It is a tale of self-awakening and disappointed expectations. The title, *Disillusion* (*Huanmie*), refers specifically to the heroine's responses to her first sexual experience. Early in the story Miss Jing learns about sex from an old friend, Miss Hui, who has already "awakened to the arts of social behaviour." Miss Jing's sexual encounter is fortuitously delayed until the first anniversary of the revolutionary May Thirtieth Incident, on 30 May 1926. So her unprepossessing young lover, Baosu, boasts of his dalliance with Jing as his very own "May Thirtieth Incident." But that Incident is as disappointing for Jing as the original May Thirtieth Incident was for the author, Mao Dun.

Upon awakening the following morning, on 1 June, Jing realizes that her dreams of the past and her hopes for the future have both been punctured by her experience. "Last night," Jing reflects, "she had done without thinking things which she was generally afraid even to contemplate." She was glad that the Incident was behind her but could not help grieving over her loss of innocence, "like a young child who has just got what it wants only to find that 'this is all there is to it.' " [102] These words possibly echo the thoughts of many young women, but they also recall the author's personal experience of the Nationalist Revolution. In an essay on the revolution published in 1928, Mao Dun used an almost identical expression to describe his reaction as a Nationalist propaganda officer to the disappointment he experienced at the barricades: "It was like this all along." [103] Mao Dun and Miss Jing both awoke to find that nothing had changed but themselves.

The peripatetic Yu Dafu was not long in the service of the revolution, but he was there long enough to discover the connection between passion and patriotism. Yu made the additional discovery that the source of revolutionary hatred was to be found in sexual passion as well:

The emergence of a revolutionary career is possible only for that little passion, the cultivation of which is inseparable from the tender and pure love of a woman. That passion, if extended, is ardent enought to burn down the palaces of despots and powerful enough to destroy the Bastille.[104]

Yu Dafu left Shanghai in March 1926, to "plunge myself into the revolution with all my ardour and sincerity, grief and indignation." His experience of the tawdry factional politics of Guangzhou did not live up to his heightened expectations.[105] Yu returned to Shanghai and worked his ardor and his grief into his fiction instead.

Romantic love and revolutionary hatred merge in his terrible but revealing story of the Nationalist Revolution, "Flight" (1935), which recounts the fall and redemption of Qian Shiying, a director of propaganda in the Nationalist movement over the period of the Northern Expedition, from 1926 to 1927. Qian is entrapped by one of his propaganda officers, a "healthy specimen of the opposite sex," who entices him to sacrifice his revolutionary principles for a baser kind of love. He marries the subordinate, Dong Wanzhen, and moves to Lanxi in Zhejiang Province to take advantage of her family's wealth and privilege in the local community. Overcome with self-loathing for compromising his principles, Qian resolves to beat a retreat to Shanghai. The story ends with Qian picking up a newspaper in a dingy Shanghai hotel room and learning that a fire that he had lit before leaving home had set the entire house alight: "When he saw in a column of news from the provinces that a fire breakout in Lanxi had burned an entire family to death, a frank, unaffected smile dawned on his face." [106] The ardor of Qian's longing and self-loathing was converted, with no loss of intensity, into a revolutionary hatred for the object of his passion, the hapless "specimen" Dong Wanzhen, whose charms had beguiled him to the point of betrayal.

Passionate anger propelled China's national revolution. In Lucian Pye's judgment, anger took precedence over love in China's revolutionary politics:

The emotional basis of all movements that have been relatively popular has been the explicit appeal to anger and national humiliation . . . those who could display passion, anger, and a sense of national humiliation were quickly identified as the politically awakened, while those who might be rationally concerned with solving China's problems were seen as less nationalistic.[107]

It is difficult, however, to fault the *rational* foundations of passionate love of country or to condemn revolutionary hatred on the ground that it is irrational. Revolutionary hatred was the more powerful for its uncomprising rationality.[108] The rational self-awakenings of ethics reinforced the convergence of love and hatred in the personal awakenings of romantic fiction, and both reinforced the idea that only the "politically awakened" deserved to command the revolution. When the object of love was transferred from the beloved to the nation, fictional romance helped to prosecute a revolutionary war of hatred, humiliation, and remembered grievance.

The novels of the Nationalist Revolution were not counted romantic in their day, but "realistic." The focus of new fiction had shifted from personal awakenings to the awakening of the nation. This transition has been characterized by Marston Anderson as "a battle of pronouns, as a contest between the romanticist *wo/women* (I/we) and the realist *ta/tamen* (he/they)." [109] The flight from the first-person pronoun was not, however, a flight from the self entirely, for the victory of realism introduced a more inclusive definition of the self that embraced "they" and "them." It took as its subject the awakening and emancipation of the crowd (*qunzhong*), on the model of the awakening of the individual self.

The evolution of the subject in historical scholarship followed a similar trajectory from the singular to the plural, and from the first person to the third. The generation of historians that came of age in the 1920s was trained in Western critical method and wedded to a progressive teleology of history.[110] At first the new historians showed as keen an interest in the historical role of the individual as did the fiction writers of their day. The biographical subjects of history were treated in the early twenties "after a romantic fashion, as unique struggling individuals—moral men in an amoral society." [111] Within the space of a few years, however, the individual subject began to make its appearance in historical scholarship as the representative of a larger community—generally a community of scholar-officials—which in turn appeared as part of a greater national community. In his *Autobiography* (1926), the historian Gu Jiegang confessed his melancholia in an exemplary romance of the awakened self. Within a few years, however, his biography could no longer be read as a simple account of a unique, struggling individual. Gu's suffering and melancholy, one reader remarked, represented "the suffering of the whole class." [112] Gu Jiegang and his circle of nationalist historians pressed the limits of historical scholarship further over the period of the Nationalist Revolution to forge a new kind of relationship between intellectuals and commoners. Gu introduced the masses into elite scholarship in the form of the Chinese people. "The 'people' of this new history," Laurence Schneider explains, "were considered by this group to be the great unwashed and untutored (but vital and spontaneously creative) body of the new nation." [113]

For historians, philosophers, and fiction writers, the significance of their discovery of the crowd lay not in its coincidence but in its implications for the practice of their craft. It called their arts to the service of the nation. To the historian Gu Jiegang, the discovery of the crowd meant that research and investigation needed to be tailored "to the needs of the modern nation." For writers of the new fiction, it entailed a transition from literary revolution to revolutionary literature. In each case, the relationship forged between intellectuals and the common people was one in which intellectuals tutored the crowd. There was certainly little sympathy for the people in their untutored state. As Gu Jiegang observed in a candid moment, mass culture could only be put to good use by "studying the people in order to reform them." [114] For all their effort to democratize their practice, writers were distanced from their spectral subject (the masses) by their positions as authors of the story of national emancipation.

One of the most common story lines of the day was the emancipation narrative recounting the captivity, the sudden awakening, and the subsequent escape of the hero. The emancipation narrative has a finite number of plots, and its range of strategies and outcomes is effectively limited by the initial conditions of the plot. These include an imprisoned (or sleeping) self, an imprisoning (or sleep-inducing) other, and a self-awakening that reveals a means of escape.[115] While the plot itself is more or less predictable, the identities of the captive and the captor, the form of the awakening, and the means of escape are all open to creative interpretation.

The range of possible variations is illustrated in the local reception to a European classic of self-awakening and emancipation, *The Doll's House*. Ibsen's play was first translated in 1918 and continued to exercise a mesmeric effect in China well into the following decade. Ibsen ranked alongside Karl Marx in contemporary debate. "Marx," remarked Liang Qichao in 1922, "is more or less competing for the seat of honour with Confucius, and Ibsen is set to overthrow Qu Yuan." [116] The plot of *The Doll's House* suggests why Marx and Ibsen should have been ranked as equals. In the language of the day, Nora, the hero of the play, awakens from a naive belief in the loyalty of her husband and in the benevolence of society to a proper appreciation of the way these impinge on her personal autonomy. Her awakening is central to reception of the plot. Had she not awoken to her situation, Nora might have gone quite happily about her business. Once awakened, however, she has only two choices: to surrender herself knowingly to the forces constraining her, or to escape. She chooses to escape. Nora closes the door on her husband and children and abandons forever the security of a comfortable position in society in favor of a more heroic if less certain future of personal freedom.[117]

The conjunction of awakening and emancipation from social constraint seems to have been the source of the play's appeal in China, but it was also the source of controversy surrounding *The Doll's House*. Few doubted that Nora should awaken and in awakening find her "way out." The controversy focused on the questions of whom Nora represented in her captivity and what it was that confined her—and hence the nature of her awakening.[118] When Hu Shi introduced the work in a special issue of the New Culture magazine *New Youth (Xin qingnian)* in June 1918, he was particularly impressed by the bold strokes of Ibsen's pen in exposing the "actual conditions of society and the family" that surrounded and suffocated Nora.[119] Few took issue with this claim. There seems to have been an unspoken consensus among commentators that, for all their disagreement over the definition of self and community in contemporary Chinese society, both were captive and both were struggling to be free. It was, rather, Hu Shi's emphasis on Nora as an *individual* that was disputed in a lengthy debate that ranged over the definition of the captive self, the causes of Nora's oppression, and the appropriate literary mode for encoding a story of emancipation.

Although a woman, Nora was considered a representative individual in Hu Shi's analysis. His definition of Nora effectively defined the forces that constrained her. In Nora, the individual confronted and overcame the family, law, accepted moral norms, and all of the social and cultural forces that buttressed a repressive and undemocratic state. As discussion proceeded, however, other contributors presented Nora as a woman rather than as an individual, or rather as the representative of a community of women who confronted in their families the larger social forces of patriarchy. The critic and author Ding Ling, who started out from a position of "complete individualism" (as Hu Shi's position came to be known) in her assessment of Nora's predicament, came in time to develop a feminist critique that identified Nora not just with individuals striving for their freedom, but with her gender as well. Nora's emancipation, it seemed, was conditional on the liberation of the class of women.[120] Mao Dun went a step further, linking the fate of women with that of all oppressed social classes and declaring individual emancipation and women's liberation conditional on the liberation of the proletariat and the nation. In this extended reading, the laboring poor were oppressed by the property owners of China, and the autonomy of China itself was constrained by the international capitalist system. If they wish to attain their freedom, China's Noras should awaken to the class nature of their oppression and join the social revolution as soon as they step out the door.[121]

The emancipation narrative began to lose its innocence with each redefinition of the captive subject and each new consideration of the forces constraining Nora. In the New Culture movement, radical intellectuals had anticipated little conflict between the wider demands of nation-building and their own demands for individual freedom. They anticipated that the nation-state would liberate the individual from all forms of social and political oppression.[122] But the extension of the idea of the captive self from the individual to mass communities raised a further question about the relationship between individual and national emancipation: did individual freedom require collective solidarity? In writing of Nora's emancipation as an individual, Hu Shi had recognized the wider social context of her dilemma. His perspective was a liberal one: "Once you have independent men and women you will naturally create a good society." [123] Neither society nor the nation was in any sense a collective self in Hu Shi's estimation, so neither was an appropriate subject for awakening or emancipation. As a liberal, Hu Shi believed that identification of the awakened self with a greater social self (or with the nation) was inimical to freedom because it turned a narrative of individual emancipation into one of collective bondage.[124] But the story of Nora's emancipation could also be read to show that collective discipline is a condition of individual freedom. Definitions of the self that extended from the individual to women, to the proletariat, and to the nation were by no means incommensurable, but they served to subordinate the lesser self under different disciplinary regimes, each premising the emancipation of the individual on the prior emancipation of its ethical community.

The personal fate of Ding Ling illustrates the procedure at work.[125] After abandoning individualism for gender solidarity, Ding Ling moved to embrace national and class liberation in the mid-1920s. She was seized in a Nationalist police raid on her apartment in Shanghai in May 1933, shortly after joining the Communist party. In September 1936, she managed to escape from custody and make her way to the Communist headquarters in Baoan before proceeding to Yenan, where she was asked to supervise political education on behalf of the Communist party. There she turned to composing poetry, prose, scripts, and literary criticism with an enthusiasm befitting the "paradise" (as she called Yenan) in which she had finally found her own freedom. But Ding Ling never abandoned her commitment to her gender, and by 1940 began to hint in her writing of a contradiction between the liberation of women and the discipline of the party.

In a daring reflection on the meaning of International Women's Day, written in March 1942, Ding Ling reversed pious party pronouncements on the significance of the occasion in a bitter denunciation of the deprivation, drudgery, and social constraints endured by women in the revolutionary base area. When they staged resistance, she noted, women were counted undisciplined. Yet when they submitted, women were disparaged as "Noras who came home." Though she dutifully policed the borders of the women's movement for telltale signs of errant individualism, Ding Ling failed to take note of others who were policing the boundaries of class solidarity for signs of indifference to proletarian discipline. Once again, in 1942, her critical stance brought down on her head the full weight of party-state discipline, although this time from the Communist quarter. She lost her position editing *The Liberation Daily* (*Jiefang ribao*) and was "integrated" with the masses over a long spell of internal exile. Yet Ding Ling seems to have accepted her fate with resignation. In the party's reading of the emancipation narrative, imprisonment of wayward individuals was a sign of collective freedom.[126]

Ding Ling's expulsion from Yenan, Jonathan Spence has noted, offers an ironic counterfoil to Nora's triumphal departure from home in *The Doll's House*. The play is a classic romance in which the hero presumably triumphs over her adversaries. An audience well acquainted with the conventions of romance would probably not speculate on Nora's fate beyond the closure of the play. Still, it is not expected that she would end up imprisoned by the very forces that champion her emancipation as an individual and as a woman. Not surprisingly, Chinese devotees of *The Doll's House* were tantalized by the question "What happens after Nora leaves home?"

In his reflections on *The Doll's House*, Lu Xun cast a jaundiced eye over the whole enterprise of awakening and emancipation—for men and women, for the individual and for the nation. His suspicions were partly grounded in belief that youthful innocence is perennially vulnerable to romantic fakery. In a story intended as a tragic postscript to *The Doll's House*, entitled "*Shangshi*"

(Regret for the past), Lu Xun wrote of a young man who spends many hours in his hotel room regaling his young beloved with accounts of Nora's flight from patriarchy. She duly runs away from home to join him. A year or so later, when their romance has worn too thin to disguise the poverty and drudgery of their companionship, the young man urges his lover to imitate Nora once again, although this time to close the door on himself and leave him to get on with his own life unencumbered. The advice can no longer be uttered with the innocence of awakened youth:

All this had been said the previous year in the shabby room in the hostel, but now it rang hollow. As the words left my mouth I could not free myself from the suspicion that an unseen urchin behind me was maliciously parroting everything I said.[127]

The young women, Zijun, returns home in disgrace and dies of grief. Lu Xun's commentary on the romantic conclusion of *The Doll's House* hints at an awakening that offers no emancipation at all — or at best, an emancipation that offers no redemption. Lofty appeals to high sentiment are all too readily turned to the advantage of the "unseen urchin" of experience, who parrots talk of truth and freedom at terrible cost to genuine innocence.

In his essay "What Happens After Nora Leaves Home?" Lu Xun qualifies this tragic vision with irony. In fact, he is not content to let the question rest with a simple inquiry into Nora's fate but raises a further question that has no place on any revolutionary agenda. If an awakening offers no "way out," after all, of what use is awakening?

Since Nora has awakened it is hard for her to return to the dream world; hence all she can do is to leave. After leaving, though, she can hardly avoid going to the bad or returning. Otherwise the question arises: What has she taken away with her apart from her awakened heart?

Lu Xun's rhetorical question invites the answer that an awakening brings no freedom, which in turn challenges the desirability of an awakening in the first place. "If no way out can be seen, the important thing is not to awaken the sleepers." [128] This would not do, however, for Young China. Nora might return home rather than go to the bad, but there was no turning back for the awakened nationalist.

The awakening of self and nation plotted in China's Nationalist Revolution was a romance of captivity, self-awakening, and emancipation that was to end with the closure of the curtain. Few revolutionaries were prepared to peek beyond the veil to see what lay in store. Perhaps no revolutionary faction could afford to abandon the quest to discover a "way out" without yielding its claim to leading the revolution. At any rate, there always seemed to be another and greater awakening waiting in the wings.[129]

3

ONE CHINA, ONE NATION
The Unequal Treatise of Ethnography

"Mrs Wendell peered at Mr Ma and his son from beneath her eyebrows. What she saw was two Chinamen who were nothing like as ugly as film Chinamen. She couldn't avoid feeling a little suspicious. Perhaps they were not authentic Chinamen."

Lao She, *Ma and Son*, 1929[1]

Nationalist ethics and fiction favored a particular narrative form in China, climaxing at the moment the people awaken to the nature of their captivity and discover a "way out." Having awoken, as Lu Xun cautioned, they could never be quite the same again. To less reflective nationalists, the emancipated nation could not possibly be the same as the one held captive anyway, because a nation capable of freeing itself would never have been captured in the first place. New China needed a new people. So what remained of "Old China" had to be cut and buffetted, squeezed and shoved until it was lean enough to fit through the approved "way out." In the Nationalist Revolution, this way out was marked "Overthrow Warlords" (*dadao junfa*) and "Overthrow Imperialism" (*dadao diguozhuyi*). The struggle between the Nationalists and the warlords gave a definitive shape to their state.[2] The struggle with imperialism gave shape to the people of New China.

The ways and habits of the New People (*xin min*), as they came to be known, bore a striking resemblance to those of the foreigners who were the targets of the anti-imperialist movement. Similarly, the habits and vices that revolutionary nationalists asked the New People to discard were, in the main, those associated with old John Chinaman in Treaty Port literature. Here New China was not alone. Postcolonial nationalism, in the evocative phrase of Partha Chatterjee, is a "derivative discourse" of colonial Orientalism. It accepts the essentialist premises of Orientalism in order to turn them back on colonialism itself:

The problematic in nationalist thought is exactly the reverse of that of Orientalism. That is to say, the "object" in nationalist thought is still the Oriental, who retains the essentialist character depicted in Orientalist discourse. Only he is not passive, nonparticipating. He is seen to possess a "subjectivity" which he himself can "make."[3]

There was no John Chinaman in China before he was identified in European letters. Yet only by engaging with European representations of John Chinaman could Chinese nationalists begin to reclaim their nation for themselves and discover their own "way out."

Needless to say, no one aspect of the colonial presence in China can fully account for the tide of anti-imperialist sentiment that arose in the Nationalist Revolution. The intensity of Nationalist opposition to imperialism seems to have been quite out of proportion to the size of the foreign sector of the economy. The Christian community targeted in the movement against "cultural imperialism" was quite insignificant, and popular resentment aroused by the presence of colonial police was unrelated to their number and influence.[4] No matter what measure of foreign influence we might employ or how many instances of oppression we might enumerate, the intensity of Nationalist resistance in the Nationalist Revolution is difficult to account for on a simple balance sheet of opposing forces in the economy, polity, and popular culture. But the economy of Chinese nationalism never lent itself to simple accounting procedures. Any attempt to devise an accurate measure of foreign economic or political influence in China in an attempt to explain or justify the strength of anti-imperialist sentiment is likely to be misplaced.

One explanation, favored by the colonial Treaty Port community in the 1920s, was that anti-imperialist sentiment was whipped up by the "Reds" in order to seize control of the country on behalf of Marx and Moscow. The evidence for this is rather thin. It attributes to the "Reds" a capacity beyond their number and powers of persuasion—certainly there were no more "Reds" than foreign colonials in China—and whatever their number, they could hardly stir up antiforeign sentiment that was not in some sense already there. An alternative explanation is to be found in colonial *racism* and the reaction it incited among a people already quite familiar with a racism of their own. The cumulative impact of European racism, over a century of dialogue between colonial ethnography and nationalist reflection on the nature of the Chinese people, contributed to a new kind of racial sensibility that sought desperately to find a "way out" of its predicament. Foreign colonials pointed out what was wrong with John Chinaman, explained how he could rectify his faults, and then promised that if he made the necessary improvements he could have his country back. Overthrowing imperialism was part of the contract with imperialism itself. In the Nationalist Revolution, overthrowing imperialism made as much sense as good *manners*.

In his final lectures on the Three Principles of the People, Sun Yatsen heaped scorn on the manners and habits of the audience assembled in the National University lecture hall, advising them to avoid the vices of spitting and burping in public and to practice the virtues of brushing the teeth and trimming the fingernails. Here he was echoing the clichés of foreign visitors. Paradoxically, both his scorn and his advice were motivated by an intense urge to awaken his countrymen to drive the foreigners, or "imperialists" as he called them, from China's soil. So long as the imperialists were under the impression that "China would never awaken and could not govern herself," he said, they would continue to cast their "greedy eyes" on China. "Why can we not govern China?" he asked. "What reveals the fact to foreigners?" Sun answered on behalf of his audience: "They can see that we are very much lacking in personal culture." [5]

Ten years later, in 1934, Chiang Kaishek launched his New Life movement with the similar objective of improving public etiquette. Chiang reiterated Sun's advice, but with a military precision befitting his standing as commmander-in-chief he codified his program for the New Life movement into 96 rules governing personal hygiene, punctuality, and pests. Chiang decided to launch the New Life movement after he came across an unkempt student lolling about in the streets of Nanchang and, in the words of the *North China Herald*, "thought he perceived one of the main causes why some foreigners appear to despise the Chinese people." [6] Chiang, like Sun Yatsen, despised the Chinese people because foreigners did, and, like Sun, he was determined to improve his people in order to prove the foreigners wrong. One measure of the success of this later Nationalist enterprise is to be found in the transformation of the meaning of the word *zijue* ("self-awakening," or "self-awareness") over the course of the twentieth century. By the mid-twentieth century it no longer referred to an ethical self-awakening but to consciousness of what *others* might think of one's behavior—in dress, in personal hygiene, and in table manners. Liang Qichao's ethics became Sun Yatsen's etiquette: in the Nationalist Revolution, it seemed, China would awaken when its people paid as much attention to etiquette as they did to ethics.

To the extent that modern Chinese etiquette has its origins in the wider Nationalist movement, it was an act of political resistance. For Sun and Chiang, the others for whom one ought to be "self-conscious" were foreigners.[7] Yet it is sobering to reflect that the advice on personal virtue that Sun Yatsen and Chiang Kaishek dispensed to their countrymen was intended to contest the hold of imperialism over China, for it paid homage to colonial racism. Indeed, their redemptive vision of a better kind of Chinese person illustrates, in its deference to European racist representations of the faults of the Chinese, a paradox at the heart of modern Chinese nationalism. The New People were a mirror image of John Chinaman.

Nationalism rarely acknowledges its origins. Unlike some compatriots who advocated the "Westernization" of the Chinese person, Sun Yatsen was loathe to convert Chinese into foreigners.[8] He wanted to produce a better kind of *Chi-*

nese person, and nationalism was his instrument for manufacturing it. "Suppose," he asked rhetorically, "that England should subjugate China and our people become English—would that be good for us?" Clearly not. "Just as the scholar uses the pen in his hand as an instrument of livelihood, so the human family employs nationalism as a means of its subsistence."[9] The Chinese had to mend their ways not so that they might become English but so that they might become more authentically Chinese.

But what was an authentic Chinese? The derivative character of Chinese nationalism is clearly revealed in a dialogue between colonial commentators and nationalist reformers and revolutionaries when they tried to define and classify the Chinese people—or, in the language of the day, when they probed the "character" (*xingge*) and "characteristics" (*tedian*) of the Chinese "race" (*minzu*). This was a genuine dialogue. Neither side wrote in ignorance of the other, and each responded to new depositions from the other side in an effort to identify the "real" Chinaman and hence locate China in a competitive order of national peoples. It was, however, an unequal dialogue. In colonial critiques of John Chinaman, Chinese nationalists confronted a kind of knowledge about themselves that they could never quite repudiate without calling their own awakenings into question. It was, above all, an important dialogue. Debate over the character of John Chinaman proceeded at a pace to match the formal negotiations between the governments of Beijing and representatives of the Great Powers in Versailles and Washington over the status of the Unequal Treaties. Success in the ethnographic reclamation of the "Chinaman" was a condition for the success of China's Nationalists in reclaiming the right to negotiate treaties with foreign powers on an equal footing.

Captive China

Those who plotted China's awakening and emancipation presumed, as a matter of course, that the country and its people were held captive by foreigners. But what exactly was captured? The Unequal Treaties of the nineteenth century continued to limit state authority over foreign nationals in the early Republic, to restrict the scope of state autonomy over customs, tariffs, and state monopolies, and to impose a range of punitive indemnities from which the state could not escape without abrogating all existing treaties and repudiating the sum of inherited debt.[10] Yet the people of China enjoyed greater freedoms than they had under the empire. They were free to travel abroad, at liberty to trade wherever markets led them, entitled to write and speak with limited but nevertheless unprecedented license in the foreign concessions, and relatively free to band together in social and political organizations.

The people were held captive in a sense quite different from the captivity of the state. When the Chinese state was held for ransom by the Western powers in the eighteenth and nineteenth centuries, the self-image of the Chinese people was taken captive as well. European visitors painted word portraits, made etchings, took photographs of the people and landscape of China, and captured numerous specimens of the "Chinaman" to pin down in their ethnographic scrapbooks and parade around Europe.[11] Enterprising Chinese artists and entrepreneurs prepared picturesque scrolls and willow-pattern crockery to cash in on the boom in Europe and the Americas. But when Chinese nationalists came across these caricatures of John Chinaman late in the nineteenth century in their reading and their travels, though they found his features vaguely recognizable, they strongly resented the mockery and derision that the caricature now engendered in European society. They vowed to set free not just their country but the Chinaman of the European imagination.

The attempt by colonials and nationalists to define and characterize the people of China was an elementary exercise in ethnography, understood around the turn of this century as "the scientific description of nations or races of men, with their customs, habits, and points of difference."[12] The practice of ethnography, even when not notably scientific, played an important part in the manufacture of its objects of study, that is, in fabricating and disseminating the idea of "nations or races of men" and in essentializing their "customs, habits, and points of difference." When Chinese nationalists began to explore the character of the Chinese people around the turn of this century, they did so in full consciousness of competing European claims to define the characteristics of their people. In the main, nationalist ethnography came to bear an uncanny resemblance to essentialist, racist European writings on the curious habits, customs, and morals of the Chinaman of the European imagination, because only by engaging with European representations of John Chinaman could nationalists begin to reclaim the Chinese people for themselves. Nationalists asserted the authority to define and describe the people of China in a popular ethnography of their own as a first step toward the liberation of the nation. They would decide, after all, what the authentic Chinese were really like and, equally importantly, who would qualify to be counted among them.

This competition to assign national characteristics was by no means divorced from the larger contest between the states of Europe and China. It was part of the struggle. Foreign visitors, for their part, insisted on assigning China a "point of rank . . . in the scale of civilized nations," and their rankings invariably coincided with the country's ability to defend its territory and preserve its sovereignty as a state.[13] Within China, competition between states came to be understood as a free-for-all among races, nations, and cultures for a place in history, and not a contest between armies or states alone. Liang Qichao made the connection explicitly: "Officials come, after all, from among the people," he wrote; "they are not members of a separate race. . . . The fruit of a tree is only as good as its roots."[14] Viewed in this light, national states represented, however unwittingly, bodies of people possessing unique national cultures, each of which could be reduced to a set of finite and quantifiable characteristics. "A nation," Liang noted on another occasion, " . . . must have some peculiar characteristics on the part of its nationals." Every national culture, in turn, could be evaluated by the relative success of its national state in trade, diplomacy, and war because each culture was thought to endow its state with the capacity to win or to lose in international competition. Hence the national "characteristics" of a people—which to Liang Qichao's way of thinking included everything "from morals and laws down to customs, habits, literature, and fine arts"—were all thought to contribute to the capacity of the state to defend its territory, uphold its sovereignty, and establish its autonomy in the international state system.[15]

Even among members of the old scholar elite, who showed little sympathy for evolutionary theory and placed less faith in progress, the defeat of the Chinese empire at the hands of European and Japanese imperialism was experienced as the humiliation of a civilization. Loss in war raised a momentous question about China's civilization and culture that to this day encapsulates the elite's experience of its own history: "What is wrong with China?" Similar problems had arisen in other colonial nationalist movements, but in China this was much more than a problem.[16] It was the central problematic, generating a hundred different questions that covered every aspect of life and letters from Confucian ethics to popular sanitary habits. For Chinese nationalists, something was wrong with China because something was amiss with the Chinese people themselves. The emperor of China was no match for the king of England because John Chinaman was no match for John Bull.

By the advent of the Nationalist Revolution, only eccentrics were bold enough to claim that national self-recrimination, or a scientific probe of the faults of the Chinaman, might possibly be misdirected. Gu Hunming insisted publicly that little was amiss with China or the Chinaman. But he also persisted in wearing a queue to the day he died. Gu's reflections do nevertheless offer an instructive counterfoil to the prevailing mood among his contemporaries. He loved the "real Chinaman" and loathed the young students who attacked China's traditional culture and society in the hope of reforming them and restoring national pride. China, in his view, had nothing of which it should be ashamed. "Why does the white man despise the yellow?" he asked W. Somerset Maugham. "Shall I tell you? Because he has invented the machine-gun. That is your superiority." If nothing was wrong with China, it followed that little was wrong with the Chinaman: "The real, the most valuable asset of civilization in the world is the unspoilt real Chinaman; and the real unspoilt Chinaman is an asset of civilization, because he is a person who costs the world little or nothing to keep him in order." [17] Gu's reference to order betrayed his fear of the power of the modern nation-state. He did not want China to become the kind of state that possessed the capacity to keep its people in order. For Gu, nothing was wrong with China apart from the nationalist insistence that something *was* wrong with it. The problem lay in the problematic of nationalism itself: Gu was impatient with the breast-beating of Chinese nationalists and with their constant harping on the faults of the Chinaman, but his impatience was as eccentric as his queue. To the despair of Gu Hunming, Chinese nationalists echoed the complaints of foreign commentators, who never hesitated to venture an opinion on the faults of the Chinese or to suggest remedies for their general improvement.

In view of the close relationship between Chinese nationalist and European colonial thinking on the faults of the Chinaman, it is well to remember that representations of the Chinese in European letters were not always unsympathetic to the Chinese "character," and to recall when and why they changed so markedly for the worse. Europe discovered a Kingdom of Reason in Cathay in the seventeenth and eighteenth centuries, more on account of its own battles with privilege and tyranny than through any close acquaintance with China. It was enough that the scholar-bureaucrats of imperial China seemed to offer an improvement on the courts of Europe. Nevertheless, when Enlightenment thinkers appropriated selective features of the Chinese imperial system to make their case for political reforms at home, they also went on to draw other, and often quite generous, conclusions about the character of the Chinese. "If a wise man were to be appointed judge . . . of the goodness of peoples," in the famous judgment of the German philosopher Leibniz (1646–1716), "he would award the golden apple to the Chinese." [18] When the Chinese state proved less amenable to the case for political reform at home in Europe, the golden apple soured on the tongue. Harsh observations on the character of the Chinese state were then accompanied by equally harsh judgments on the morality and personal habits of the Chinese people. The mask gradually slipped from the Oriental sage to reveal the face of John Chinaman.

The revelation of the authentic Chinaman in the second half of the eighteenth century came about through closer acquaintance with China, but it was acquaintance of a particular kind. It came about through the capture of China. Chinese officials were not keen to admit foreign visitors and at first tried to impose the customary tributary framework upon official embassies from Europe while confining trade to the coastal port of Guangzhou. Neither ruse worked for long. Once ships of His Majesty's Navy took to sinking the junks of the Chinese navy and foreign marines had shown how readily they could rout contingents of the banner armies on Chinese territory, visitors could enter the country a little more freely. They then came to know the country and its people in much the same way that a hunter comes to understand its prey or a captor to appreciate its captives. Among the more obvious marks of this unequal relationship were the imposition of "Unequal Treaties" and huge financial indemnities upon the Chinese state, and the stationing of foreign troops and creation of foreign settlements on Chinese soil. But the foreign visitors were not just interested in acquiring power and wealth; they also wanted to know about China and the Chinese, and to know about them with greater accuracy and in greater detail than ever before. In captivity, China's people became the object of another people's scrutiny and gradually lost the confidence to make bold claims about themselves.

The expansion of the modern empires of Europe was driven by a thirst for knowledge no less than by competition for wealth and influence. Napoleon's venture into Egypt might well be counted a failure as a military expedition, but its achievements in recording the history, customs, and languages of the Orient were without precedent.[19] On the British side, the hard-nosed British East India Company set aside funds for commissioning ethnographic and cultural studies of the Indies, establishing exemplary botanical gardens in Sibpur, Samalkot, and Sharanpur, setting up zoological parks for the study of exotic fauna, and supplying specimens for the Royal Botanical Gardens back home in London. Under John Barrow's direction, the Royal Navy was obliged to transport scientific specimens without charge and to ensure that they reached the home ports in good condition. The individual renegades and eccentrics of the British empire were just as addicted to the knowledge game. Braving East India Company indifference, Thomas Raffles ventured out in 1891 to transform the old city of Singapura into a modern port. From the start he envisioned the city not just as a free port for commercial trade but as an entrepôt for the export of scientific knowledge and specimens from Asia to Europe and for the importation of European science, ethics, and law into East and Southeast Asia. Raffles spent much of his time traveling along the coast, studying the customs of the native peoples and collecting specimens of local flora and fauna for cataloguing and dispatch to England. The East India Company repaid his enthusiasm by fining him for exceeding his expenditure allowance.[20]

The civilizing mission of colonialism was taken very seriously before the expansion of empire was held accountable to a balance sheet—before "imperialism in the age of capital," as it came to be known.[21] Old imperialists feared that the crass pursuit of wealth would diminish the imperial aura in the eyes of colonial subjects. There was, at any rate, no simple correspondence between the quest for knowledge and the cruder business of empire. The two enterprises frequently worked at odds with one another, as Raffles discovered to his cost. The great traders were the first of the economic reductionists and were roundly condemned on this account for failing to acknowledge the relationship between "knowledge and power." "There are too many in the world," complained W. C. Taylor in 1834, ". . . who desire much to see the power [of empire] increased and perpetuated, but neglect the knowledge which is its first element." [22] In his address to the Royal Asiatic Society, Taylor dwelt at length on the relationship between commerce and learning in an extended reflection on the fate of successive empires over the past two millennia. Empires might be founded on "the golden bonds of commercial intercourse," he noted, but these bonds were destined to rupture unless reinforced with the study of the "social condition." The Greeks, Romans, Parthians, and Persians had failed to acknowledge the connection between commerce and learning, and their empires had suffered accordingly. The oversight was partially rectified in the Middle Ages, when Christianity finally "awakened attention to the religion and philosophy of the Asiatic nations." But it was still not fully absorbed in the age of Reformation. Nor could it be, for the true dawn of Oriental Studies was heralded not by religious intercourse but by the rise of a new empire "more glorious than that of which Rome was the mistress." In the British empire, knowledge finally found its home: the last and greatest of empires was an empire of reason. Its sole foundation was the good opinion of its subjects, and "its maintenance must consequently depend upon its continued accommodation to the opinions of its subjects." [23]

The acquisition of India demanded intensive inquiry into the nature of the colonial subject over a far wider range of disciplines than had ever before been undertaken, in order to embrace all of the elements that made up the "national character" of the Indian. Similarly, relations with China "demand a most extensive and accurate knowledge of customs and institutions peculiar to the Chinese." If the empire restored Oriental Studies to its rightful place, Taylor assured his detractors, then students of the Orient would serve the empire well from the Mediterranean to China:

The ROYAL ASIATIC SOCIETY is designed to be the great storehouse of intelligence for all who desire information respecting the present state of trade and capabilities of all the countries between the eastern Mediterranean and the Chinese seas. . . . In nothing more than in trade, and in no branches of trade more than in those between England and eastern countries, has the truth of the aphorism been demonstrated, that "KNOWLEDGE IS POWER." [24]

The knowledge so acquired would play an instrumental role in managing the empire; but more importantly, it would serve to impress upon the natives the foundation of British superiority in knowledge itself. "The foundation of our empire in the East," Taylor concluded, "is the opinion entertained of our intellectual superiority." [25]

The relationship between knowledge and power was not unfamiliar to Chinese nationalists. By the 1920s, Chinese intellectuals had begun to suspect that

foreigners knew more about them and their country than they did about themselves—or at least knew about China in a more authoritative way than they did.
So the struggle to reclaim China's territory, sovereignty, and political unity
was matched by a struggle to reclaim knowledge of China *for* China. Imperialism had taught this much at least. "Imperialism overlooks nothing," observed
the novelist Lao She after accidentally stumbling across the Oriental corner of
the Royal Botanical Gardens in London, sometime in the mid-1920s:

> It doesn't confine itself to usurping a people's land and destroying a people's coun-
> try. It really does take away all people possess for investigation—animals, plants,
> language, customs, geography—all are investigated. This is the terrible part of im-
> perialism. Imperialists are not only specialists in military tyranny. Their knowledge
> is overwhelming too! Knowledge and military power![26]

Authentic knowledge about the "real character" of John Chinaman filtered
back to Europe, along with plant specimens, stuffed animals, and the skele-
tal remains of bound feet from the middle of the eighteenth century. Between
1740 and 1744 Captain George (later Admiral Sir George) Anson undertook the
second English circumnavigation of the globe with explicit authorization from
His Majesty to "return home by the way of China" if the opportunity arose.[27]
Anson's destination was the South Seas. He set sail on a course already notorious for the deeds of "terrible and brutal" English buccaneers at a time when
empire-building was all but indistinguishable from piracy.[28] After three years
of raiding merchant vessels, kidnapping men of high birth, taking women and
children for ransom, ransacking ports, setting fire to settlements (and losing
two-thirds of his men to scurvy), Anson finally steered his vessel H.M.S. Centurion into Guangzhou Harbor for repairs and replenishment in 1743. On meeting resistance to his demands, he decided to call the bluff of local officials and
demanded entry to the port on threat of destroying the Chinese fleet stationed
in the harbor. He had tried the same with a Spanish settlement in the Pacific
not long before and summarily razed it when he failed to get his way. Officials
in Guangzhou yielded.[29]

Their actions may have saved the city, but the compliant response of local
officials tarnished the reputation of the Chinese as a people. Unbeknownst to
themselves, the behavior of the imperial authorities fell into a pattern of native
submission to European bullying that had begun with the Spanish conquest of
Mexico early in the sixteenth century, and which Captain Anson was eager
to emulate in his attacks on Spanish settlements en route to China. The tale
of Hernando Cortés' encounters with Montezuma, Inga Clendinnen observes,
provided "the first great paradigm for European encounters with an organized
native state; a paradigm that quickly took on the potency and the accommodating flexibility of myth." Although the myth began in the 1540s, it continued

to flourish well into the nineteenth century in W. H. Prescott's *History of the Conquest of Mexico* and other specialist studies of encounters between Europeans and native states in Asia, Africa, the Americas, and the Pacific. At the heart of the myth lay a conviction that Europeans triumphed over their enemies because of "cultural superiority, manifesting itself visibly in equipment but residing much more powerfully in mental and moral qualities." [30] Its effect was to associate falling states with fallen peoples.

No sooner had Anson succeeded in gaining his forced entry to Guangzhou than the picturesque edifice of earlier Western representation of China came tumbling down.[31] Writing in 1838, Anson's biographer, Sir John Barrow, noted the procedure whereby Anson's bold actions had uncovered the "real character" of the Chinese people:

By the novelty of a British ship-of-war, by the firmness of her captain, by a judicious display of her power, mixed occasionally with a few threats of the probable necessity of having recourse to the use of it, and moreover by an early insight into the real character of the people, Anson succeeded.

Barrow went on to note Anson's pioneering achievement in exposing the "falsehood, the duplicity and knavery, of the Chinese, which not only pervaded every department of the government, but also, naturally enough, affected the people generally." [32] Anson's memoirs convey with precision the significance of the Chinese surrender for the fate of the stereotypical Chinaman. By failing to put up effective resistance, the Chinese exposed the "timidity, dissimulation and dishonesty" that underlay their cultivated appearance of civility and wisdom.[33] China's officials, "notwithstanding the fustian eulogiums bestowed upon them by the Catholic missionaries and their European copiers . . . [were] composed of the same materials with the rest of mankind." [34]

More particularly, in Barrow's view, the submission of the officials in Guangzhou revealed a distinct want of character at a time when "firmness" of character was coming to be counted a virtue among Englishmen. So Anson deserved credit for his "early insight into the real character of the people"; this was not, in Barrow's words, "so generally known [then] as now." [35]

In fact, over the century that had lapsed between Anson's triumphal return to Portsmouth and Barrow's writing, the English buccaneer's revelations about the "real character" of the Chinese had been promoted to the ranks of common sense. Daniel Defoe recorded Robinson Crusoe's fleeting impressions of China as the solitary sailor passed through Guangzhou on his way home to England, as if these were the impressions of any honest observer in the wake of Anson's single-handed victory:

What are their ports, supplied with a few junks and barks, to our navigation, our merchant fleets, our large and powerful navies? Our city of London has more trade than all their mighty empire. One English, or Dutch, or French man-of-war of eighty guns would fight and destroy all the shipping of China.

Not only cities and ports were held up to ridicule after Anson's fateful visit. So were the Chinese people. Robinson Crusoe appears to have taken a schoolboy's delight in the power of a single man-of-war to expose an entire civilization to the harsh light of critical judgment. It was an affront to common sense to count China powerful, rich, or glorious when the whole empire could not resist an 80-gunner vessel; clearly the Chinese people were "a barbarous nation of pagans, little better than savages." [36] More products of the English public-school system were to visit China over the course of the following century, including Anson's biographer John Barrow in the company of Lord Macartney's embassy from 1793 to 1794, and another embassy under Lord Amherst from 1816 to 1817, before the outbreak of the Opium War in 1842. Macartney and Amherst showed their "firmness" of disposition by refusing to kowtow before the emperor, and they brought back to England the same message of corruption, cowardice, and dissimulation on the part of the officials and people of China.[37]

Many more sat in judgment by the fireside at home, and their estimation of the Chinese people fell a little lower with each new display of British courage and, in time, each British naval triumph.[38] John Chinaman's flaws were first exposed in his submission to Captain Anson in Guangzhou, but this was only an initial and partial exposure. The century between Anson's raid on Guangzhou and the Opium Wars, in the words of one armchair observer, entailed "all that has ever been done by war or negotiation to bring down upon their knees this ultra-gasconading, but also ultra-pusillanimous, nation." A distressing catalogue of faults was uncovered in "war and negotiation," trade and commerce, and in the day-to-day encounters that were the fruits of British victory. These encounters came to inform English relations with the Chinese, which were dictated, in Thomas de Quincey's judgment, "by our improved knowledge of the case, and by that larger experience of Chinese character which has been acquired since our last treaty with their treacherous executive." Anson's mission had been intended to teach the Chinese a lesson about John Bull. "The first person who taught the astonished Chinese what difference might happen to lurk between nation and nation was Lord Anson," remarked de Quincey. One lesson was clearly not enough. Representations of the English in "Chinese ethnography" — de Quincey's phrase — failed to take sufficient account of Britain's "national grandeur." The unaccountable failure of Chinese ethnographers in recognizing the Englishman for what he was worth was the ultimate proof of Chinese folly. China's nationalists were determined to correct the shortcomings of Chinese ethnography.[39]

By the turn of the twentieth century, the gilded image of Enlightenment

China was visible only in its inversions. Even the "splendid vices" of the
philosopher-kings now showed up as "debilitating virtues" in John Chinaman.[40] Familiarity frequently bred contempt, particularly among Anson's fellow countrymen. "A real mutual understanding between individuals," wrote
the British expatriate Rodney Gilbert from Shanghai in 1926, ". . . leads just
as often to mutual dislike, suspicion, contempt, antagonism or real hatred, as it
does to sweet sympathy and love." British pundits competed with one another
over the length and intimacy of their encounters with China and its people to
establish their qualifications for pronouncing on the character of the race. Not
all, by any means, declared the Chinaman an unworthy member of the human
race. An established tradition of popular ethnographic literature in the English
language painted a sympathetic portrait of the Chinese and their "characteristics." From the mid-nineteenth century, however, even sympathetic authors
felt obliged to adopt a defensive tone. They had critics of their own. "A great
many books," scorned Gilbert, "have been written in English about Oriental
countries . . . with the pious hope that they will promote to some degree that
mutual understanding which leads to mutual sympathy." But their efforts were
misdirected, because real understanding could only breed contempt. Writings
favorably disposed toward the Chinese, in the view of English cynics, arose
from their authors' limited acquaintance with "real" China or from some selfish or ulterior motive bearing on trade or Christianity.[41] In the view of the missionary community, however, charity obliged a more generous estimate: "The
higher the personal character of the critic," remarked Edwin Joshua Dukes,
"the more favourable is his estimate." Dukes and his missionary brethren
rallied to the defense of John Chinaman because John Bull was on the attack.
"John Bull," concluded Dukes, "has recently adopted Bret Harte's ballad on
Ah Sin of San Francisco." To the cry "For ways that are dark, and for tricks
that are vain, the heathen Chinee is peculiar," Dukes replied that there was
little darkness or treachery in the peculiarity of the Chinese people.[42]

As the twentieth century dawned, even well-intentioned English authors
could draw upon an established liturgy of Chinese vices. Isabella Bird wrote
at length of the virtues of the Chinese people before concluding that it was
"needless to run through the established formula of their vices." At the time of
her writing, in 1899, the Chinaman's vices were sufficiently well established to
require little further elaboration. In fact, English authors tended to agree on the
nature of the Chinese vices and to differ chiefly in the degree to which they pronounced them remediable or, at least, offset by compensating virtues. Gilbert
and Bird could both recite the "established formula" of Chinese vices, but
where Gilbert believed that these shortcomings prepared the Chinese people
for perpetual servitude, Bird conceded virtues as well and imagined that "it
may be possible that an empire genuinely Christianized . . . may yet be the

dominant power in Eastern Asia." Christianity held out hope for the fallen much as the ideology of progress held promise for the backward. For a country as backward as China, and a people who had stooped to unspeakable vices, there was hope yet.[43]

Such observations were not confined to the English. Captain Anson's success inspired imitators among other European states, and his observations forced Enlightenment thinkers to concede that the renowned wisdom of the Chinese was of little value if it could not serve the defense of the realm. Rousseau, writing shortly after Anson's mission, echoed the naval commander's sentiments:

If neither the ability of its ministers, nor the alleged wisdom of its laws, nor even the numberless multitudes of its inhabitants, has been able to protect the realm against subjection by ignorant and rude barbarians, of what service have been all its wise men?[44]

Rousseau, with Gallic charm, reserved the term "barbarians" for the English. Even so, his argument implied that if a civilization could not hold out against barbarity, it was as good as barbarous itself. Either way, China was captured, and with it the reputation of John Chinaman. If the Chinaman could not stand up to foreign attack, he was neither worth emulating nor worth adulating; he was a subject for diagnosis and treatment.

When China's failure as a state exposed failings among its subjects, it summoned up the specter of a civilizing mission to remedy them. A casual glimpse through an open doorway, the whiff of odors drifting up from a creek, the din of raucous voices, the clickety-clack of mah-jongg echoing down the lanes of the Chinese quarter all worked to confirm an impression among European visitors of disorder, filth, docility, and fatalism that needed to be rooted out from the Chinese breed. A determination to intervene in affairs of state was then matched by a consuming interest in the moral improvement of the Chinese people. Only the crudest of colonial expatriates felt this should be effected through direct intervention.[45] Among missionaries and other, more hopeful, observers, salvation appeared to lie in convincing the Chinese that they could not *remain* themselves and expect to find a place in the new world order—and that it would be best for all concerned if they would take this burden upon themselves. "Nobody wanted to conquer China," recalled one sympathetic foreigner in 1923, "but everybody wanted China to conquer herself." [46] On this point the civilizing mission of European imperialism found common cause from Beijing to Delhi and wherever else the natives could be persuaded to embrace "the new forms of a civilized and rational order": this was the order of the modern, self-governing nation-state.[47]

What's Wrong with the Chinese?

Sun Yatsen and Chiang Kaishek were not the first nationalists to probe the faults of the Chinaman. Liang Qichao was equally well acquainted with foreigners' opinions of China and the Chinese and had begun to compile a catalogue of local vices decades before Sun and Chiang launched their moral crusades. He also prescribed a set of remedial exercises for correcting them.

Characteristically, Liang began his inquiry into the faults of the Chinese people from first principles, in the belief that there could be no real Chinese person if there were in fact no real China. Was there a real "China"? Among the many faults Liang discovered among his countrymen, the one he found "most astonishing" was their inability to put a name to their country. "Hundreds of millions of people have maintained this country in the world for several thousand years," he noted in his essay "On China's Weakness," "and yet to this day they have not got a name for their country." Liang repeated this claim in several of his essays and always in the same tone of astonishment.[48] China had, it was true, been given a name in recent times, but not by the Chinese themselves. Even the word "China" (*zhongguo*) "is what people of other races call us. It is not a name the people of this country have selected for ourselves." [49] The custom of referring to the historical community by dynasty (*chaodai*) rather than by country (*guojia*) implied that there was in fact no Chinese nation at all. In Liang's view, the want of a name was not so much an indication of the want of a country as an indictment of the cultural and intellectual immaturity of the Chinese people. Indeed, it was the first of the flaws in the national character. There was a nation, he asserted, and the want of a name for it was no more than a "conceptual" error "lodged in every [Chinese] person's brain." Liang planned to launch the national awakening by alerting the Chinese people to their own egregious errors.[50]

National weakness was the second great flaw of the nation. Liang opened his two seminal essays, "On Adventure" and "On China's Weakness," with an expression of shame and regret at China's current "weakness." [51] His sense of shame served as a benchmark for his exploration of Chinese characteristics. In "On Adventure," Liang framed the question "What's wrong with China?" by comparing Chinese vices with the virtues of the "European race" (*Ouzhou minzu*). The assumption of national weakness was also embedded in the second essay, "On China's Weakness," but buried so deeply that few explicit comparisons with Europe were required. The evidence for China's weakness lay outside the text, in warfare and diplomacy; passing reference to bloodshed or humiliation sufficed to justify Liang's enquiries into the shortcomings of his people.

In his essay "On China's Weakness," Liang classified the symptoms of

China's "illness" under four headings: Concepts, Customs, Political Arts, and Recent Events. Under "Concepts" he wrote of the lack of conceptual clarity in traditional thinking on the world, the state, the country, and the people of China (and on the want of a name for China itself). Liang was at his most brilliant in identifying and clarifying these conceptual distinctions. But it was under the heading "Customs" that he touched most directly on the characteristics of the Chinese as a people, illustrating how these contributed to the national malaise. The first characteristic was a "slavish mentality" (*nuxing*) that permeated personal relations, education, and government. Slavishness rendered the Chinese people unfit for self-government and incapable of staging effective resistance to oppression by "alien races." The second national characteristic was "stupidity" (*yumei*), which Liang thought everywhere apparent in the illiteracy and want of common sense among ordinary people. The stupidity of the people had great bearing on the well-being of the state. States had brains, much as individual people did, so if the State Brain (*guonao*) were to function as the collective brain of the citizenry (*guomin*), it followed that there was little hope of creating an intelligent state with stupid citizens. Liang estimated that in a country of 400 million people, there were no more than a few million who could qualify as informed citizens, and fewer than 200 truly enlightened people who were fully capable of promoting the well-being of their country.

Selfishness (*weiwo*) was a third characteristic of the Chinese that prevented the attainment of national strength and unity. "Our four hundred million people have turned into four hundred million separate states," Liang complained. Curing the people would thus unify the state. A fourth characteristic was mendacity (*hao wei*), or habituated deceit. Here Liang took his cue directly from foreign observers: "Our mendacity has reached such extremes that today the Chinese are renowned throughout the world [for it]." [52] John Chinaman's reputation for deceit and corruption had sparked similar comments among other Chinese reformers acquainted with the colonial critique of the Chinese. Most were inclined to accept the slur rather than to rebut it. "The Chinese people are inherently corrupt," wrote Wu Zhihui in 1908. "The whole world knows this." Wu, like Liang, turned his observation into an admonition for improvement of the national character.[53] The fifth fault that Liang identified was timidity (*qienuo*), or cowardice, which ill befitted a national people living in a world of ferocious tigers and fearsome devils. Finally, Liang condemned the passivity and inaction (*wudong*) of the Chinese people, who seemed to be growing more passive with every new action taken against them by "foreign forces." Liang then proceeded to show how each flaw in the makeup of the people was rooted in a range of popular sayings and attitudes that exasperated him at every turn.[54]

In another essay, Liang lamented the fact that popular folk-sayings abounded in advice for avoiding shame, and rarely counseled daring or adventure. High culture was little better. The works of Confucius and his disciples encouraged caution in place of boldness, fate over intervention, passivity over activity, and silence over outspokenness. As these formed the ethical foundations of the national culture, it did not surprise Liang that the people of China should be servile, timid, passive, unambitious, and cowardly. When in its long history could China lay claim to a single hero comparable to Luther, Lincoln, or Columbus? Three times Liang answered: "We have none." China had been beset with a terrible affliction in this dearth of heroes for "several thousand years," with the result that today the Chinese people "are all sick in body and soul." This popular malaise threatened the survival of China as a state. Liang concluded his analysis with a cry of despair: "I cannot imagine how our state can survive." [55] Liang was certainly exaggerating, if not in the extent of his disappointment, then at least in the depth of his despair.[56] A capacity for hope was the redeeming feature of the Chinese people, in Liang's view, and held out promise for their improvement.

Liang Qichao did not have the resources to convert his observations into anything approaching a mass movement. In calling for the application of Neo-Confucian techniques of self-cultivation to his new ethical system, he certainly had in mind something on the scale of Chiang Kaishek's New Life movement, or the morning exercises orchestrated to the sounds of wired radio in Mao's China, but he wrote without the authority of the state behind him. Radio, at any rate, was still some way off. The ideals of forthrightness and bravery expounded in his new ethics were nevertheless disseminated widely in the Treaty Ports and abroad. Liang's appeal for the systematic conversion of the subjects of empire into citizens of a modern nation-state were echoed daily in chatter among the colonials about the faults of John Chinaman and reinforced in the reactions of Chinese people to the evidence of European revulsion at the sight of them.

Things were changing even as Liang was writing. Until the turn of the century, few Chinese residents in Shanghai appear to have noticed, let alone to have taken offense at, the now infamous sign forbidding entry to dogs and Chinese at the entrance to a park in the International Settlement. The association of Chinese and dogs was not at all clear, in part because the sign failed to make the comparison explicit, but also because the comparison made little sense to Chinese passing by. It was more readily understood on the colonial side, where the British and French communities cultivated a united front of civility against an imagined enemy of vermin, spitting, and public squalor. As Lin Yutang observed of the colonial expatriate in Republican Shanghai:

He drinks Lipton's tea and reads the *North China Daily News*, and his spirit revolts against the morning reports of banditry and kidnapping and recurrent civil wars, which spoil his breakfast for him. He is well shaved and dresses more neatly than his Chinese associates, and his boots are better shined than they would be in England.[57]

European expatriates kept up their appearance in the great demoralization of the land, after the manner of the chief accountant in Conrad's *Heart of Darkness*, whose "starched collars and got-up shirt fronts were achievements of character," in face of the terror lurking beyond the compound.[58] Beasts, and Chinese, had to be kept out.

The colonial community of Shanghai had good reason to worry about bandits and kidnapping after the Lincheng Outrage of May 1923.[59] Until then, however, it worried unduly about keeping its chins shaven, its collars starched, and its shoes shiny. The natives were not generally hostile. For over 50 years, Chinese residents of Shanghai had taken weekend excursions to watch and to ride the new steam train running between Shanghai and Wusong, had gathered around the race track to observe the Europeans at play, and had queued for rides on the roller coaster in the amusement park.[60] So long as the Chinese community of Shanghai thought of itself as part of the spectacle, not apart from it, the only dogs in the city went about on four legs.

The curious legends that built up around the notorious sign in the park barring Chinese and dogs signify how rapidly these perceptions began to change, starting around the turn of the century. In fact, there may not even have been a sign prohibiting "Chinese and dogs" at all. In a style characteristic of British municipal administration the world over, the sign appears to have listed a number of regulations governing use of the park, including one concerning the entry of dogs and another dealing with the admission of local Chinese (and permitting entry by Chinese servants of Europeans).[61] The intervening regulations needed to be elided with an editorial stroke of the nationalist imagination to arrive at the condensed statement that dogs and Chinese were forbidden.

The people of Shanghai had to learn that their daily routines and personal habits were linked to the welfare of the nation before the sign barring "Chinese and dogs" could reveal itself with such elegant simplicity. Around the turn of the century, we have seen, Liang Qichao all but despaired at the want of resistance to the popular surrender of customs, culture, land, wealth, and sovereignty. To Sun Yatsen it seemed that the incapacity of his countrymen to think of themselves as a race was one of their most debilitating features *as* a race. For hundreds of years their racial "ignorance" had blinded the people of China to the humiliation of their subjection to the alien Manchu. In the early revolutionary period, "the majority of the Chinese people still did not realize that they were conquered by the alien Manchus, so they lived in a stupor and died dreaming." [62] In the period of the Nationalist Revolution, Sun declared, the people would once again surrender their birthright without a murmur unless racial feeling could be aroused among them.[63] The people had to learn that their daily encounters with Europeans were historic moments in an epic encounter between races engaged in a struggle for survival.

Han Chinese had long distinguished "barbarians" (*yi*) from themselves by outward signs of skin color, odor, body hair, gait, and manners. The written script accommodated these racial distinctions by adding an animal radical to written characters referring to people from outlying border regions. A dog radical was incorporated into the character for the *Di* people of the north, a sheep radical for the *Qiang*, and reptiles for the *Man* and *Min* of the south to indicate their various bestial origins.[64] In more recent times, similar images had been turned against Christian missionaries in the Boxer Uprising and against the Manchu Qing dynasty in the racist propaganda of the Republican revolutionaries, when such slurs were used to good effect in targeting the Manchus as members of an inferior race that had occupied the country and usurped the throne. The Manchus were derided as dogs. The revolutionary anarchist Wu Zhihui, who felt little remorse upon learning of the deaths of the empress dowager and the Guangxu emperor in 1908, recorded their passing as "Manchu Dogs, one male and one female . . . nothing but a bunch of dog slaves making up lies." In the same essay Wu referred to the Tongzhi emperor as a "piglet." [65]

Gratuitous insults did not, however, make for racial feeling of the kind Sun Yatsen had in mind. Earlier references to barbarians as degenerate animals had been framed within an ethical hierarchy rather than a "scientific" racial one and had usually counseled that the Han might well degenerate to the level of beasts and barbarians if they dropped their guard. Wang Yangming, writing in the Ming, conceived of Han history as a moral fable in which, at one early stage, "people degenerated to the status of birds, beasts and barbarians" because they failed to cultivate virtue.[66] The moral order also redeemed barbarity: the empire held out the prospect of incorporating border peoples into Greater Han civilization if they adopted appropriate standards of belief and behavior. This did not, of course, inhibit the Han from finding Manchus or Europeans funny and repulsive in the nineteenth century. But conceiving of relations among peoples as a struggle between races and nations for a place in history was something else again. For this, the Chinese people needed to be awoken from their "stupor" to something approaching modern racism.[67]

The earliest of the nationalist revolutionaries who cultivated racism never discarded their ethical roots entirely. Even Zhang Binglin, widely proclaimed as the father of modern racism in China (*minzuzhuyi zhi fu*), harbored the old fear that the people of China could well degenerate to the level of "barbarians" if they failed to cultivate the appropriate virtues—although with a new twist. For Zhang, the first of the virtues was not the Confucian dyad of filiality and loyalty but knowledge of racial history. He advised that in the event the Han lost an appreciation of their national history, "the essence of the people will perish, the people will lose their foundations, sink into ruination, and become barbarians." [68] Zhang's new historical conception of the race was quite distinct from the earlier moral histories of civilization and barbarity. His was a history of a national people rising and falling to the rhythm of the natural laws that governed the animal kingdom.

As long as the revolutionary movement focused its racial enmity on the Manchu Qing dynasty, the term "Han" sufficed to identify the Chinese race. In the Nationalist Revolution, however, the word "Han" failed to accommodate the variety of ethnic communities now thought to comprise the "race." Sun Yatsen insisted that the Chinese people were racially distinct from all other peoples of the world but would allow no distinctions to be drawn within China itself. He drew the boundaries of the Chinese race along the borders of the old imperial state.[69] Chiang Kaishek presented a similar argument in *China's Destiny* (1943), the better to illustrate his point that the Chinese people "constitute not only one nation, but one race." Minority peoples were asked to adjust their belief and behavior accordingly if they wished to be counted among the "Chinese people." Sun and Chiang favored policies of ethnic "amalgamation" and interpreted lingering signs of ethnic diversity within China to mean that the procedures of assimilation were not yet quite complete. China was a "melting pot," Chiang observed, whose historical function was to assimilate all differences into one national culture. The five "stocks" that made up the race were not to be confused with ethnic or racial groups, for their identities were formed by environmental conditioning and belief:

The fact that [China] comprises five stocks is due not to diversity in race or blood but to dissimilarity in creed and geographical environment. In a word, the distinction between the five stocks is territorial as well as religious, but not *ethnological*. This is something that our people must thoroughly comprehend.[70]

In his *International Development of China*, Sun Yatsen anticipated further Han colonization of Manchuria, Mongolia, Xinjiang, and Tibet. The Nationalist government implemented his program under an elaborate cultural regimen intended to assist the indigenous people of these regions to achieve a thorough comprehension of their common racial identity—and, not incidentally, to recover their sentiment of "central loyalty" toward the Nationalist state.[71] In time the word "Han" gave way to a new term, "Chinese race" (*zhonghua minzu*), and the old bestial lexicon referring to border peoples was abandoned. Significantly, the custom of affixing animal prefixes to words referring to the border peoples of China came under concerted attack in the 1930s, at the very moment that the state celebrated the historical unity of the newly amalgamated "race." [72]

Growing Han sensitivity to bestial imagery contributed to this process of domestic racial accommodation. For all their foreboding that they might sink to the level of the beasts and barbarians, Han Chinese were not generally accustomed to thinking of themselves as dogs and pigs. It came as a rude shock to find that foreigners treated them with the derision they themselves reserved for minority peoples. In earlier decades, the national "stupor," as Sun Yatsen called it, had delayed close reading of the sign in the Shanghai municipal park. But once it was read and understood in the light of Han sensitivity to bestial imagery, the sign prohibiting Chinese and dogs was rapidly converted into a potent symbol of Han subjection. The slurs of European, American, and Japanese racists were digested in the form of self-loathing that reflected back upon the Han themselves the scorn once reserved for barbarians. The novelist Yu Dafu noted with barely disguised contempt for his own people, "The Japanese look down upon Chinese just as we look down upon pigs and dogs." [73] But self-loathing also offered inspiration: procedures of racist representation were accepted in order to be reversed, in an organized movement to remake the people of China so that they would no longer *resemble* dogs.

The sign in the park in the International Settlement started on its path to notoriety when local residents began to share the sense of urgency felt by Liang Qichao. In 1907, Li Weiqing wrote of the park:

On the banks of the Huangpu river the foreigners have set up a garden where the green grass is like carpet and the flowers like silks and satins. People from all countries of the world are admitted, even Indians who have lost their country, indeed even the dogs of foreigners are admitted. Only Chinese are not allowed to go there. Foreigners despise us so much, they regard us as more base than slaves, horses and dogs. . . . So it can be seen that in the modern world only power counts. We should exert ourselves to obliterate this disgraceful humiliation.[74]

The details of the regulations were unimportant. In this case, it seems, dogs *were* permitted but not Chinese. In fact, many different versions of the story circulated in nationalist literature before a definitive version of a sign explicitly forbidding entry to "Chinese and dogs" eclipsed the rest. What counted was not the sign itself but the connection that came to be drawn among Chinese residents of Shanghai between a race of people and dogs, and, in turn, the associated compulsion to "obliterate this disgraceful humiliation." By 1920 it was no longer possible for a Chinese person to stroll past the park without reflecting on what it meant to be "Chinese *and* dogs."

This sentiment had become pervasive by the end of the decade. Ba Jin's short story "The Dog" (*gou*) is one of many accounts of "self-awakening" to appear in the texts of the New Literature movement, and one of a number featuring dogs.[75] In this case, however, the troubled narrator awakens to learn that he *is* a dog. The revelation comes as a surprise. And yet the surprise brings relief to the tormented soul of the narrator, whose humanity never quite made sense anyway.

In the story, Ba Jin dwells on this species metamorphosis in a tone of morbid fascination. He begins by identifying the physical features distinguishing

Chinese from Europeans before touching on the relations of power between them, which stamped Chinese physical traits as a trademark of racial inferiority:

I have yellow skin, black hair, black eyes, a tiny nose, and a short, slight frame. But there are in this world others with white skins, yellow hair, blue eyes, long noses, and tall big frames. They walk on the road and on the pavement with great strides, one, two, or three of them, raising their heads haughtily to take in all around them, singing at will, shouting at random and laughing without control as if they are the only three people on the pavement. Other people walk past them nervously, or timidly keep their distance.

Ba Jin was an anarchist at the time of writing, committed to the humanist ideals of individual equality and the fraternity of humankind. Yet the first discovery to dawn on our narrator is that the ideal of common humanity is a fraud. There are no such things as human beings (*ren*), but instead two distinct classifications of beings resembling people: "I have made a new discovery. So-called 'people' are in fact divided into different ranks. Above the kind of people I usually mix with there is another and far greater order of people." The line between "the kind of people I usually mix with" and the "greater order of people" is drawn satirically around the habits and manners of Treaty Port colonials. The author invites reflection on what it is that makes the "greater" people so great. It is certainly not their morals:

I have often seen these greater people on the streets. They are always smiling, singing and shouting, or beating people with wine bottles or pawing the faces of women. At times I have even seen them sitting in rickshaws with a pair of those lovable pink legs sitting on their laps.

The narrator's disdain for the crude behavior he observes can hardly disguise his own longing for a pair of "lovable pink legs" draped across his own lap. The dog imagery of Chinese nationalist texts, Rey Chow has observed, is both a metaphor for the subject nation and a sign of male impotence, here expressed in masturbatory fantasies.[76] The narrator's own people keep a watchful distance, yet derive a vicarious pleasure from what they see. In this sense, the observed colonial is a gendered model to which the male nationalist cannot help but aspire:

People avoid them out of respect, and I am even less inclined to come close to them because they are far too great. I just watch them from a safe distance and admire and congratulate them in secret. I feel that it is cause to rejoice when there are such people in this world. I even manage to forget my own suffering. I secretly admire them and congratulate them.

In the last analysis, it is only fear that commands respect:

I often remind myself that I should not get too close to them for fear of showing disrespect. But on one occasion I did in fact get close. One evening, when I was again so cold and tired that I could not even move, I sat on a wall by the roadside to rub my bloodied, mud-stained feet. Hunger pierced my heart. My eyes went dim and I could not see anything about me at all, not even one great man as he walked over toward me. When I finally spotted him and took to flight it was already to late. My left shoulder felt the kick of an extraordinarily sharp foot, as if my arm and hand had been cut off with a knife, and I fell to the ground rolling with pain.

The narrator's weakness needs only to be named, and the "great man" obliges him by calling him a dog. It is a moment of revelation for our narrator, who savors the word and embraces it as his own:

"Dog!" I clearly heard the great man spit the word from his mouth. As my hand rubbed the wound, my mouth kept repeating the word: "Dog." I finally returned to the run-down temple. Ignoring the pain, I crawled along the ground wagging my head, wiggling my bottom and barking. I felt I was a dog. I was light of heart. I smiled and cried tears of joy. I understood that at last I was indeed a dog.[77]

Ba Jin's disingenuous tone and rather heavy irony betray an underlying determination to stir his readers to throw off the racist slurs of the Europeans. Still, his keen eye for the detail of his own skin and hair, his eyes, his nose, his frame and bearing, and his acknowledgment of sexual impotence in contrast to the "greater order of people" from abroad, betray an intimate personal knowledge of the shame of a subject people that has been exposed to racism and that has been taught to associate its subjectivity with its physical traits. The author's irony reinforces a racist critique of the Chinese people in the process of exposing and resisting it.

Other writers preferred exhortation to irony. In a novel published two years earlier, *Ma and Son (Er Ma,* 1929), Lao She drew upon his personal observations in England to recount the hilarious cross-cultural encounters of a Chinese family running a store in London. Lao She also dwelt on the racist association of Chinese and dogs in a passage that bears a striking resemblance to Li Weiqing's stern reaction to the sign in the Shanghai park:

In the twentieth century attitudes towards "people" and "country" are alike. Citizens of a strong country are people, but citizens of a weak nation? Dogs! China is a weak country, and the Chinese? Right! People of China! You must open your eyes and look around. The time for opening your eyes has come! You must straighten your backs. The time for straightening your backs has come unless you are willing to be regarded as dogs forever![78]

There was, however, a significant difference between Lao She's command to "straighten your backs" and Li Weiqing's call to "obliterate this disgraceful humiliation" enunciated two decades earlier. Li had not been prepared to accept that Chinese *were* dogs. In 1929, Lao She conceded the aptness of the comparison before turning it back upon his countrymen in an exhortation to self-improvement so that they would not remain "dogs forever."

Lao She touched succinctly on Ba Jin's dilemma. In trying to represent his fellow countrymen in literature, each writer felt obliged to accept the foreigners' curse on the Chinese as dogs in order to bestir them to become "people." Lao She was bitterly conscious of the stock Chinese of the popular English cinema, who, he recalled, "would smoke opium, smuggle munitions, mutilate dead men and conceal their heads under beds, rape women whether old or young . . . the Chinese have been transformed into the most sinister, filthy, repulsive debased creatures on two legs in the whole world!" [79] Until they reclaimed the right to say who they were and discovered the will to say it forcefully on their own two feet, Chinese would remain dogs. Meanwhile, those aspects of the national character which prevented Chinese from standing on their own two feet were to be identified and eliminated. Lao She and Ba Jin wanted to awaken the dog. This was irony of a different order, not easily captured in avowedly nationalist literature. As Lu Xun pointed out in another context, even an awakened wolf is still, after all, a dog.[80]

Over the period of the Nationalist Revolution, the call for a new ethics and for new citizens echoed an equally resounding call for a new kind of Chinese person who could not possibly be confused with a dog. Nationalists first began to dissociate themselves from dogs by denouncing any Chinese who associated with foreigners as "running dogs," a phrase that made its appearance in the armory of revolutionary slogans quite early in the Nationalist Revolution. In August 1923, peasant-movement proclamations were to be found ending with the injunction "Overthrow the running dogs of imperialism—the warlords and servants of the foreigners!" [81] Chinese were no longer servile dogs on their own account but were made so ("running dogs") by their association with foreigners. Authentic Chinese were to be found inland, in the unexplored reaches of China's vast hinterland, where few foreigners or dogs ever ventured.

Nationalist Exploration and Discovery

Responsibility for exploring China's hinterland and discovering an authentic Chinese people fell to China's nationalists.[82] Young students set off on foot into the hinterland. Scholars, at their desks, launched expeditions into China's history with hopes and aspirations similar to those of European explorers setting off to discover the New World. Columbus, not surprisingly, was one of the heroes of the age, and the discovery of the "common people" (*pingmin*) with their alternative cultures and histories led to flights of the imagination that echoed Europe's acclaim for Amerigo Vespucci's "rediscovery of America." [83]

The rediscovery of China was not, of course, as literal a discovery as the achievements of Vespucci and Columbus—even conceding that the Americas were already familiar to their native inhabitants. Their explorations were voyages of discovery only in the sense that Columbus and Vespucci appropriated knowledge about the Americas for Europe.[84] Still, it was all pretty new to the explorers themselves. But China's young explorers had a fair idea of what they would discover even before they set out.[85] They were trained in what to expect by the categories of the modern social sciences.

The sciences of society supplied navigational aids for nationalist movements around the globe in the twentieth century. In 1945, Jawaharlal Nehru chose to call the personal memoir of his involvement in the nationalist movement *The Discovery of India*. Nehru had little doubt of what he would find when he commenced his explorations of the heritage and the "essence" of India. Nevertheless, he discovered the Indian people in a way that they had never known themselves, that is, through the eyes of rational scientific thought. Nehru approached India, he recalled, "almost as an alien critic. . . . To some extent I came to her via the West, and looked at her as a friendly Westerner might have done." [86] Like China's young Nationalists, Nehru wanted to know about an old and familiar country in a new and less familiar way. His life was a voyage of exploration and discovery.

The discovery of China was not, however, entirely metaphorical, because the geography of the country was still much a mystery to reformers and revolutionaries. Until the last decade of the Qing, access to official maps was limited on a need-to-know basis to senior-ranking officials, a practice that irked those who found themselves excluded. "No one below the rank of a mandarin of the seventh rank," complained Sun Yatsen to his English mentor, Dr. James Cantlie, "is allowed to read Chinese geography." [87] In fact, the problem was not confined to maps of China. Few maps of any kind were available over the counter.[88] When Kang Youwei went looking for a decent map of the world in 1895, he could find none for sale in the bookstore district of Beijing. He asked a friend to send one up from Shanghai.[89] Sun Yatsen made up for the omission in his own education by getting hold of maps from abroad. But these were too fragmented for his liking. So he traced firm red lines up, down, and across the landscape to signify railway lines and highways stretching from one end of the country to the other in the belief that communication networks would give the country a unity that it did not yet possess. Sun elevated his aspirations for a united China to a new law of economics: "Economists have always spoken of three necessities of life—food, clothing and shelter. My study leads me to add a fourth necessity: means of travel." [90]

Mapping the country was no more than an incidental aid toward the main work of discovery in the 1920s—exploring the people, the customs, and the culture of the land. This was undertaken with the enthusiasm of Columbus but with a Nehruvian sense of purpose. Scientific ethnographers set off on expeditions to remote towns and villages to record the customs, songs, and histories of the real people of China. Literary delegations from the cities traveled the country "going among the people" and writing up their impressions in stories and travel diaries for prompt dispatch back to the metropole. Like Columbus, China's young explorers came across lands that were already inhabited but whose inhabitants had never quite known about themselves in a way that really counted. Like Nehru with the people of India, these explorers were determined to teach the people of China what it meant to be Chinese. And their civilizing mission had something of the flavor of a colonial enterprise. In fact, Sun Yatsen himself cited the U.S. colonial administration in the Philippines as a good illustration of the kind of tutelage he had in mind for the common people of China.[91]

This nationalist discovery of China mimicked the explorations of European adventurers because it was part of the dialogue with the civilizing mission of European imperialism. Pearl Buck observed the dialogue at work among young intellectuals of her own acquaintance. "One of the most important movements in China today," she observed, "is the discovery of their own country by young Chinese intellectuals." Buck's remark on the discovery of China appeared in an introduction to the most eloquent and forceful challenge to the colonial specimen of John Chinaman ever to appear in English, Lin Yutang's *My Country and My People*. Lin, Buck rightly observed, needed to discover his country and his people before he could mount a defense of them in the language of reason, democracy, and progress. Lin Yutang and his fellow explorers approached their task like visitors from an alien land bringing with them a little of science, of Christianity, of atheism, of free love, of communism, of Western philosophy, of modern militarism, "something, in fact, of everything" except a sense of belonging organically to the communities they discovered.[92] All the same, they were determined to defend their country. Lin himself was conscious at every turn of the scribblings of Rodney Gilbert and H. G. W. Woodhead, whose unflattering remarks on "Chinese characteristics" seemed to misrepresent what he himself had discovered. John Chinaman had become a grotesque caricature of the ordinary Chinese—a "stage fiction," Lin called it—with characteristics sometimes counted as virtues and sometimes as vices but that, in either case, could only be redeemed by rubbing them out and starting all over again. Like Nehru in India, Lin went looking for authentic Chinese among the great mass of "common people." With the aid of an intellectual compass pointing unerringly in the direction of the new sciences, he knew where to find the real China, how to interpret what he found, and (when he found them) how to defend his country and his people against the scandalous, racist representations of Treaty Port colonials.[93]

By the 1920s, the local response to popular Western ethnography had developed into an industry. Knowledge of nineteenth-century ethnographic studies such as Arthur Smith's *Chinese Characteristics* and the Reverend Doolittle's *Social Life of the Chinese* inspired journalists to capture local custom and national character for a readership that was growing inquisitive about its characteristics and was keen to discover what was distinctive about it as a society.[94] Hu Puan, an editor of the Nationalist party newspaper, the *Shanghai Republican Daily*, published a gazetteer of local customs in 1922.[95] Hu's *Gazetteer* was compiled from the Local Customs section of district gazettes of the Ming and Qing dynasties, supplemented by miscellaneous entries from published travel diaries and newspaper articles. The scope of Hu's work was far more ambitious than that of the popular ethnography of the newspapers, and its purpose was quite different from that of his classical sources. The imperial library and repositories of local gazetteers held, among them, comprehensive surveys of the beliefs, habits, and customs of local communities along with summaries of the administrative history, virtuous women, philanthropic enterprises, and public works of districts from every corner of the empire. Had they wished, ethnologists could have extracted a great deal of information from the imperial library. But the isolation of local custom from its immediate context in imperial administration and its incorporation into a single volume was more than an instrumental aid to ethnology. This was an ethnographic text of a new variety that marked the transition from empire to nation.

The purpose and significance of Hu's innovations were pointed out in the preface by Zhang Shizhang:

Foreigners scoff at us, saying China is not a country and that the Chinese people are not a national people. I feel truly ashamed at this and yet I cannot deny it. Why? The founding premise of all nationalisms is to know others and to know oneself. To put it another way, one must know about the world as well as one's own country before patriotic sentiment can be cultivated, and I know very little about either.

Chinese students seemed to be familiar with the latest customs circulating in Paris and London, Zhang lamented, and could recite passages from ancient Latin and Greek, but the history and customs of their own country were foreign to them. Hu Puan had found the answer. With his easy style and his eye for detail, Zhang explained, Hu captured "all the flavour of a tour of London and Paris" in his voyages through China, with the result that his readers "come to understand the thoughts and feelings of our ancestors in a natural way." [96] In his postscript, Hu passed over the metaphor of the tourist, but he was not happy with the idea that China was a foreign country. He was especially alarmed at the prospect that his choice of illustrations of local custom drawn from various parts of the country might imply that China's localities were "like different countries" themselves. The book was designed to counter this impression. After combing the local gazetteers for evidence of local customs, Hu bound them together again under one cover. The empire was well represented in a library, but the nation was best brought together in a single volume.[97]

Ethnography took new forms in Chinese fiction as well. National self-portraiture generally operates on the principle, identified by Zhang Shizhang in his preface, that to know one's self one must know others. Nationalist fiction took its cue from the Occidental critique of the Chinaman in that it was chiefly concerned with identifying the essential characteristics that served to distinguish the Oriental from the Occidental. In the event, Chinese self-portraiture in the fiction of the late nineteenth and early twentieth centuries had much in common with European fiction of the age of discovery. When knowledge of other lands first turned great civilizations into national cultures in the seventeenth and eighteenth centuries, European artists developed the literary convention of the Oriental traveler who roamed the Occident bestowing pearls of wisdom on European culture and convention.[98] Similar conventions evolved in China's age of self-discovery, when the Oriental traveler brought back news from Europe offering new perspectives on the customs of the Chinese, and when the Occidental traveler showed up in China as an authority on Oriental customs and habits.

One of the favorite devices of Chinese authors for establishing a critical distance from the Orient was the voyage of discovery to a distant land. Li Ruzhen sent his hero on a voyage of discovery to 33 countries in his novel *Flowers in the Mirror* (*Jinghua yuan*; 1828), the better to engage in a series of reflections on Chinese custom and belief in a manner resembling Swift's *Gulliver's Travels*. Although apparently unacquainted with Swift's work, Li was more acutely aware than most of his contemporaries of the significance of recent Chinese contacts with Europe.[99] Li Ruzhen's achievement lay in turning a venerable Chinese literary tradition of travelers' tales to new effect: the traveler brought back news of China as it might be seen from outside China itself. A related device was to depict China as a foreign land onto which the narrator happens to stumble. Zeng Pu employed both devices in his *Niehai hua* (Flower in the ocean of sin; 1905), in which China is first associated with an alien land—the Island of Enslaved Happiness—before the protagonist, Jin Wenqing, is dispatched to Europe and Russia on an exploratory mission that turns out to be a voyage of self-reflection and discovery.[100]

Lao She's novel *City of Cats* (*Maocheng ji*; 1933) is the *locus classicus* of the alien-land device in vernacular fiction of the twentieth century. It merges the genre of the voyage of discovery with the animal metaphors of racist self-deprecation. Lao She was well acquainted with English fiction and film, but his own fiction was inspired less by European precedent than by a personal sense of mission to explain the cross-cultural aspects of his literary excursions and his travels abroad. Certainly Lao She's work reveals a critical dimension that is generally lacking in English literature on John Chinaman and, for that matter, largely missing from English literature on John Bull as well. By the time Lao She came onto the scene, the Oriental had already been well and truly captured in English letters. Lao She had to account for the Chinaman of English letters before he could reclaim him for China. To complicate matters further, the critical distance of the rational narrator of modern fiction located the author in a European discourse on the Orient that alienated him from his own compatriots. Lao She showed sensitive awareness of the first problem in *Ma and Son* when he presented "a Chinese view of the English view of the Chinese." [101] When he rocketed his first-person narrator to a land of cats in *City of Cats*, he revealed an awareness of the second problem. Lao She was the rational observer, and China a land of beasts.

In *City of Cats*, real people appear, by definition, to be Occidental, and with the exception of the narrator, the Chinese are depicted throughout the book as creatures of another species. Their continued existence as a distinct civilization seems to place the Chinese in perpetual and flagrant violation of reality, which is located across the sea in Europe.[102] But the solution to their alienation is also to be found in Europe, or at least in the voice of a Chinese narrator, who speaks from a critical distance that is located, so to speak, across the seas. Lao She then explores the faults of the Chinese in an effort to remedy them. His intention is clearest in the detailed descriptions of the flaws of the cats, which are pictured quite as opiated, cruel, superstitious, corrupt, selfish, and irresponsible as the film Chinamen of the English cinema. It is no coincidence that the narrator is a Chinese person. Lao She takes on the perspective and characteristics of a rational Chinese narrator in order to identify the faults of his fellow countrymen in the name of China. The irony of *City of Cats* is the irony of Chinese nationalism itself: the novel is a parable, in its inversions, of the nationalist reclamation of the nation.

The irony of fictional ethnography is most readily apparent where it draws directly on European conventions. Shen Congwen wrote his short novel *Alice in China* in 1928, shortly after reading a translation of Lewis Carroll's original.[103] Once again, however, the established tradition of European ethnography of China complicates the transference of Alice as an innocent alien traveler into the Chinese idiom. Here she appears as something more than an Occidental traveler through whom a Chinese readership might reflect upon itself. Alice discovers a land where the power of cultural representation has already been appropriated by foreigners. Her first acquaintance with the characteristics of the Chinese is a guidebook to China written by an Englishman, which prepares her for the encounter by detailing the dirty habits and grasping demeanor of the

Chinese. Alice tests these prejudices against her personal experiences in the company of the White Rabbit. In Shen's hands, Alice is converted into a device for exploring the ways in which the Chinese have come to be represented by the Occident and for measuring the accuracy of these representations — and, ultimately, for ironic reflection on the fact that Shen's own exploration of Chinese characteristics has to take serious account of the observations of a young English girl and a foreign rabbit.

The many faults and rather modest virtues of the Chinese were treated with less irony in the ethnography of political nationalism. A more serious sense of purpose is evident in writings on the position of women in traditional society and on the role of the "people" in national revival. There was no room for joking in revolutionary politics. The term "New People" (xin min, or xin shidai de ren) embraced renovated women (xin funu) as well as new men. Yet even here, the most racist of European observers anticipated Chinese nationalists in regarding the position of women as the source of China's shame and in anticipating that the common people might yet prove to be the country's salvation. Only fiction writers could appreciate the irony.

The female condition served as an indisputable sign of the unredeemed barbarity of the people of Asia. "That no Asiatic state has debarbarized itself," Thomas de Quincey pronounced in 1857, "is evident from the condition of WOMAN at this hour all over Asia." [104] De Quincey was one of the most intemperate critics of Chinese culture in his day, yet his views on women were widely shared and frequently reiterated by more sober critics. This was partly the result of recent developments in Europe itself, where women had begun making inroads into previously male-dominated preserves of literature, science, and public life. Reflecting in 1753 on the recent upsurge in women's literature and in scientific research, Samuel Johnson remarked that "the revolution of years has now produced a generation of Amazons of the pen, who with the spirit of their [Amazonian] predecessors, have set masculine tyranny at defiance, asserted their claim to the regions of sciences, and seem resolved to contest the usurpations of virility." [105] When defiance failed, masculine tyranny made a virtue of necessity and counted the liberalization of its own attitudes toward women the latest benchmark of progressive civilization.

A man's stand on the women question rapidly became a mark of character. When women began to play a prominent role in the physical sciences, Sir Humphrey Davey remarked that the "standard of the consideration and importance of females in a society is I believe likewise the standard of civilization." [106] The Davey standard was soon applied to the civilizations of Asia, and then began to acquire a racial inflection. It was helped on its way by the women's suffragette movement in the United States. In 1869, Elizabeth Stanton called upon American women "of refinement" to join her in rejecting extension of the suffrage to the "lower orders of the Chinese, Africans, Germans and Irish, with their low ideas of womanhood." Anglo-Saxon men were difficult enough to live with. The prospect of heeding the word of "Patrick and Sambo and Hans and Yung Tung" was too much to expect.[107]

The Davey standard was applied with particularly telling effect to the Yung Tungs of China. "It may, perhaps, be laid down as an invariable maxim, that the condition of the female part of society in any nation will furnish a tolerable just criterion of the degree of civilization to which that nation has arrived," remarked John Barrow in the memoirs of his travels with the Macartney mission. He then applied the criterion to China. "The Chinese . . . have imposed on their women a greater degree of humility and restraint than the Greeks of old, or the Europeans in the Dark Ages."[108] Barrow's comments were picked up by de Quincey in his remarks on Asian barbarity, and subsequently incorporated into the ethnographic archive on China. In 1906 the former United States minister to China, Charles Denby, commented that "if the civilization of a country be tested, as has been said, by the condition of its women, a low place in the order of rank must be assigned to China."[109] The standard was applied again in the Republican period, although by this time the emergence of assertive antiforeign nationalism required some modification to the general sentiment. The irrepressible Rodney Gilbert, writing in Shanghai in 1926 at a time when the Nationalists were placing the colonial community on notice of eviction, derived comfort from the observation that a man who could not protect his woman could not be expected to defend his country. The Chinaman's attitude to his womenfolk now cast a slight on the nation's manhood as well as its civilization: "The Chinese put a lower rating on women than we do, but a lower rating of women implies a lower standard of manhood." The venerable practice of chivalry toward women in the West, in contrast to China, served as "a testimony to the existence of courage and fighting capacity in the breed." In Gilbert's rather crude estimation of manhood—chiefly as the ability to put up a good fight—it was clear that the West would win in China.[110] The challenge this posed for the nationalist was to acknowledge that China could redeem itself neither as a civilization nor as a virile young nation until it had addressed the "women problem."

Reference to the mistreatment of women in Asia, as Partha Chatterjee has observed, was one of the foundations upon which the "entire edifice of colonialist discourse was fundamentally constituted."[111] Chinese nationalists could ill afford to ignore the complaint. In late imperial times, members of the Chinese literati had condemned cruel practices affecting women with little concern for their manhood and no external prompting.[112] Their complaints failed to assume the dimension of a popular movement, however, until the fighting capacity of the breed and the survival of the nation appeared to be at issue. Arguments for the liberation of women in the twentieth century, then, rested less on premises of right and justice than on the assertion that the nation could not be liberated until women were.

This was Liang Qichao's point of entry into the women question in his essay "On the Education of Women" (1897). The custom of footbinding had mutilated women and made them subservient to men, Liang observed. But it was not concern for the well-being of women that prompted him to take up their case. Footbinding, he noted, was "mocked by foreign races" and brought irreparable harm to the reputation of the nation. Footbinding also placed an un-necessary burden on the nation's productive capacity by withholding women from the workforce: "Our two hundred million females are consumers but none are producers, and as they cannot support themselves they must be supported by others." A battery of "stale old concepts" denied women equal access to education and so limited the nation's capacity for self-strengthening as well. "In my opinion the basic reason for our country's weakness arises from the fact that women have not been educated." Only when women were unbound, educated, employed, and treated as men's equals would China become a match for the foreigners. Other reformers neglected the women question, Liang con-cluded, only because they failed to appreciate the connection between liberat-ing women and liberating the country:

Today people who devote themselves to propaganda and discuss ways of strength-ening our country have been so shaken by the foreigners that they model their ideas on the strengths of the foreigners, and yet they focus on nothing more than powerful ships, effective weapons, fast rail links and flourishing mines. As these things are all beyond the capacity of women, so our policy makers say that the education of women is not a matter of urgency. Little do they know that [female education] is the great strength of the Westerners.[113]

Not long after Liang had concluded his essay, the "women question" made its way into the mainstream of nationalist debate.[114]

Along with women came the common people. Racism and nationalism are instinctively democratic. Liang Qichao felt that the failings of the ruling elite were necessarily those of the common people because all belonged to the one national culture: the slavish mentality, stupidity, selfishness, mendacity, timidity, and passivity of the officials were all rooted in popular culture.[115] This echoed the white supremacist argument to a degree. But Rodney Gilbert saw a different connection between the flawed national character and the *demos*. Gilbert was inclined to excuse the flaws in John Chinaman by blaming them on the literate elite. "The Chinese *literati*," he explained, "always are and always have been a cautious, timid, evasive cult of physical weaklings, with passive rather than active—defensive rather than aggressive—minds." Commoners were tainted with the affliction through historical contact with the literati, who "conveyed" their attitude to the people.[116] Left to themselves, it seemed, the people might have developed all of the qualities that Gilbert and Liang Qichao so admired among Europeans. But the people of China had not been left alone. So thoroughly had they been contaminated by the literati that they retained their pristine manliness only in remote pockets of the country far from the reach of effete high culture. China's redemption, then, lay in tapping the resourcefulness of its untainted common people. "Among the Chinese," Gilbert announced on behalf of the white community of China,

we like the rough mountaineers and the border folk better than the more highly culti-vated natives of supposedly pure breed; we like the primitive and uncouth countrymen better than the effete town-dwellers, and we like the illiterate better than the cultured. The ruffian from the "back blocks" in China is the less essentially Chinese and there-fore the fellow with whom we savages from the West, we conquerors and exploiters of the world, with our delight in virility and fair play, find most in common.[117]

Chinese nationalists shared Gilbert's preference for the common folk. The pioneers of nationalist ethnography in China confidently announced their intention to go hunting for authentic Chinese culture and tradition in the high-lands and the backwoods, where they expected to find, intact, whole commu-nities of people who had escaped the baneful influence of city life and Con-fucianism. The historian and ethnographer Gu Jiegang discovered a "natural genius" in remote mountain villagers. To his added delight and that of his col-leagues, Gu also discovered that remote countryfolk possessed the qualities that colonial racism ascribed to "primitive and uncouth countrymen" and that nationalism prescribed for the New People: spontaneity, anonymity, freshness, imagination, even a capacity to absorb "new things and foreign influences." [118] But Gu was not a revolutionary, at least in the sense that he never imagined that he could transform the people he discovered into something more closely approximating his ideal. He was a scholar, and a quietist nationalist in com-parison with many of his contemporaries. Gu's optimistic expectations of the villagers' innate capacity to adapt to "foreign influence" sufficed to distinguish his nationalism from Gilbert's racism.[119]

Their shared interest in the commoner was, however, offset by disagree-ment between white racial supremacists and Chinese nationalists over who, among the people of China, were the "real" Chinese. Nationalism and colonial racism shared a concern to identify the essential Chinaman but parted ways, as a rule, when it came to awarding the title of authenticity to the effete city-dwellers or to uncouth countryfolk. Both generally favored the coarse peasant to the civilized burgher. But before the Nationalist Revolution, few foreign visi-tors conceded that peasants were real Chinese. The "hasty West," J. C. Keyte observed at the height of the peasant movement in 1925, generally mistook the "coast-spoiled scum" of China's great cities for the "real Chinese type." Rodney Gilbert was no exception.[120]

Gilbert's favorable judgment on China's peasants was intended to offer little comfort to the Nationalists, because peasants were not "essentially Chinese" at all. He was, nevertheless, prepared to concede that the best hope for China's national survival lay in tapping this "less essentially Chinese" tradition of outlaw culture with its "thrilling novels," its "clever patter" of vernacular theater, its folk stories, theatrical songs, and folk ballads. In this he echoed the refrain of China's Nationalists themselves. But Gilbert was not at all sanguine about the prospects of a national revival if it were undertaken by the effete "essential Chinese" who filled the ranks of the Nationalist movement.[121]

The Chinese peasant movement was founded on a similar contrast drawn within nationalist thought itself, between coast and hinterland or city and countryside. This was not simply a reaction to colonial racism. It was born in an ethical critique of bourgeois life that equated the city with false values and the countryside with an elemental native purity, and it harked back to the pastoral imagery of an earlier Chinese literary tradition. The nationalist celebration of the common people nevertheless reversed colonial racism in its essentialist reading of where the "real" Chinese were to be found: the ruffian from the black blocks was not less but *more* essentially Chinese than the "coast-spoiled scum" of the cities. Thus Li Dazhao, tutor to Mao Zedong, compared city life to the life of "ghosts" and equated country life with that of the "people" in an influential article published in 1919:

My young friends drifting about in the cities! You should know that the cities are full of crime, and that great contentment is to be found in the villages; that life in the city is more or less the life of a ghost, but that the work going on in the villages is the work of people; that the air in the city is foul and the air in the villages is pure. Why don't you just pack up your things, settle your travel expenses and go back to your home towns?

The countryside was an Arcadian site of reconciliation and joy, with plenty of time for joking and ethical contemplation after the day's work was done:

It does not matter whether you work with your hands or with your mind, whether you grow vegetables or plough the fields, or perhaps become a primary-school teacher, so long as you do eight hours work each day that will profit others as well as yourselves. And with the rest of your time, do something to develop the village or to improve the livelihood of the peasants. This way you will be working yourselves, and working alongside others, with whom you can share a joke or talk about the principles for bettering human existence.[122]

Li's call to youth was echoed over the next few years in the manifestos and publications of New Culture activists and by champions of the ethnographic movement, who exhorted youth to "Go among the People!" and to "Head inland!" It was also taken up by the peasant-movement cadre of the Nationalist Revolution.[123]

The Nationalist Revolution, however, was more than a cultural renovation movement or an inland ethnographic expedition. It combined "principles for bettering human existence" with nationalist ethnography and married romantic expectation with Leninist party strategy in a mass movement for political and social revolution. And yet even at its height, the peasant movement verged on a rustic pageant. In a revolutionary reenactment of the New Year festival in 1927, "those who used to rank lowest now rank above everybody else," Mao Zedong reported, and are "turning things upside-down." Revolution was not, as Mao observed in the same report, a "dinner party." But it was a party all the same. Peasants took to crowning captive landlords with peaked caps and parading them through the streets while village riffraff "lolled for a minute or two on the ivory-inlaid beds" belonging to the young ladies of the household. Crowds raided landlord houses, slaughtered their pigs, and consumed their grain in riotous abandon. "There was a case recently," Mao continued with evident glee, "where a crowd of fifteen thousand peasants went to the houses of six of the evil gentry and demonstrated; the whole affair lasted four days during which more than 130 pigs were killed and eaten." Revolution was not a dinner party, it was a rustic feast.[124]

From the mid-1920s, the peasant movement was also endorsed by sympathetic foreigners who found delight and humor, inspiration and "reality" in the Chinese countryside. Now sympathetic foreigners could be distinguished from hostile ones by the degree to which they acknowledged that uncouth peasants were the real Chinese after all. Pearl Buck, reflecting on the achievements of the revolutionary movement a decade after Gilbert, was moved to make a similar judgment on China's peasants but to give her judgment an entirely different inflection:

The young intellectuals . . . are beginning to find that life in the countryside, in small towns and villages, is the real and native life of China, fortunately fairly untouched with the mixed modernism which has made their own lives unhealthy. They are beginning to feel themselves happy that there is this great solid foundation in their nation, and to turn to it eagerly for fresh inspiration. It is new to them, it is delightful, it is humorous, it is worth having, and above all, it is purely Chinese.[125]

Buck's discovery of delight and humor in the countryside and her evident discomfort with the "mixed modernism" of city life were shared by China's Nationalists, even though they were responsible to some degree for concocting the mixture of the modern and the traditional that both found so disconcerting. The New Culture movement and the Nationalist Revolution promoted "progressive" culture in place of the old "feudal" one, but neither movement quite managed to establish the New People as a credibly "Chinese" substitute for those they replaced. The faults attributed to the old culture in the 1910s and 1920s amounted to little more than an addendum to Liang Qichao's earlier essays on the passivity and inertia, conservatism and inequality, bad temper and pessimism of the people of China. These faults were giving way, at last, to youth and vigor, science and utility. But the achievements of the New Culture movement were decidedly "mixed."

This paradox at the heart of Chinese nationalism was never far from the minds of reflective Chinese writers. The old civilization that they condemned had equipped them more than adequately to make sense of what was going on about them. Gu Hunming flung back his queue and scoffed at it all. Ba Jin, Shen Congwen, and Lao She resorted to a heavy-handed irony in explaining an awkward national predicament. They could never quite urge their compatriots to change their ways without at the same time showing a taint of regret. Yet even their regret was tinged with irony. Shen Congwen hinted at his bitterness over the fate of a people who had to be turned into Europeans in order to save their culture, their territory, and their state from the Europeans. In the opening scene of *Alice in China*, set in the mid-twenties, Alice is advised to hasten to China before the mysterious wonderland of the old culture should disappear under the assault of the new:

We know there is a revolution is the south of the country at the moment, and that whenever a revolutionary government is in place it is bound to launch an energetic assault on every kind of custom. No evil system can survive under the new dispensation: all the most curious customs will disappear and all of the people will be turned into New Age People (*xin shidai de ren*).

Shen was writing in 1928, when New Age People had come to bear too close a resemblance to foreigners to be counted truly authentic. "New Age People," Alice is informed by her Chinese adviser, "are much the same as Europeans. Their clothes are made of the same coarse wool and their collars are stiff and white; they walk with their waists and shoulders disjointed, and they talk bluntly." The joke was at the expense of the visitors if China was forced to shed its exotic charm to cope with uninvited Europeans. It was no loss to China, however, which could happily dispense with the sickly exotica that substituted for China in the European imagination:

The gentry scholars in their melon-skin caps will not be seen again, nor the beautiful maidens now wasting away with consumption. All the color of the East will go with them. Nothing of interest to the visitor will be left in China in a year or two.[126]

Yet little of interest remained for the nationalist, either, when New People could no longer be distinguished from Europeans. The gap that opened up between the consumptive culture of the old elite on the one hand and the effete, Westernized urban elite on the other was filled in the nationalist imagination by an idealized popular rural culture. Admittedly, the common folk of the villages were not yet New People. But faith in the transformative capacity of the revolution held out hope that China's peasants could be persuaded to make the necessary transition once they had been awakened to its urgency.

At this point the irony stopped. Revolutionaries wanted not only to discover the authentic Chinese of the villages—ethnographers had already done as much—but to remake them. They turned to the countryside in the Nationalist Revolution to find the raw material for an authentically Chinese people who could be made new in the act of revolution. The director of the Nationalist Peasant Bureau, the Communist Luo Qiyuan, placed little value on peasant culture or consciousness in its untutored state and encouraged his cadre to instruct peasants in the class nature of their grievances. As we shall see, Luo's strategy for awakening the peasants was subsequently developed into the "mass line" by Mao Zedong.[127] Later still, when Mao reflected on the source of his optimism that China would emerge victorious from the war against Japan, he was not content to note that peasants were spontaneous, bold, and imaginative. Peasant bravado was no match for an invading foreign army. Mao recalled Sun Yatsen's morbid fear that China might lose its state (*wangguo*) to a foreign power and perhaps fall into a state of decline comparable to colonial India if the people did not awaken to the dangers confronting them. But China's political, military, and social development over the intervening years offered new grounds for hope. The Communists had turned peasants into New People:

If, a few decades ago, China had been conquered militarily by a great imperialist country, as England conquered India, then we could hardly have avoided losing our state. But today things are different. Today, in particular, China has progressed: there are new political parties, new armies and a new type of people, and this is the basic force for defeating the enemy.[128]

Pearl Buck, writing some years before Mao, noted that the discovery of the "purely Chinese" peasant was a fitting conclusion to an extended historical dialogue between Western critiques of China and the haunted deliberations of Chinese nationalists over the death of their state. Modern theories of proletarian revolution, she wrote, had inspired New China "to discover the extraordinary quality of her country people, maintaining their life pure and incredibly undisturbed by the world's confusion." [129] When this discovery had been turned into a revolutionary program for remaking the people, the dialogue between Western racism and Chinese nationalism took a sharp turn.

The Nationalist Capture of the Colonial

Colonial apologists were confronted by a new and more militant nationalism in the mid-1920s, partly as a consequence of the general trends we have been following in journalism and literature, ethics and ethnography, and partly as a result of the emergence of an organized Nationalist movement over the decade. The two trends came together quite accidentally in 1923, with the appearance of a new and more terrifying kind of bandit. Roving bandits were the first Chinese to disturb the colonial Englishman (as Lin Yutang acidly observed) over his breakfast of marmalade and tea.[130] The effect of this development was to compel a reassessment of the revolutionary potential of peasant bandits among China's Nationalists and, on the colonial side, to force a reevaluation of the Chinese character in a desperate attempt to reclaim the initiative for English letters. The foreigners' efforts were ultimately in vain. The Nationalist movement succeeded not only in mobilizing people in the villages and in the cities but in reversing the fundamental procedures of captivity on which the entire edifice of colonial ethnography had been founded.[131]

Rodney Gilbert's confidently racist work *What's Wrong with China?* was published at the height of the Nationalist Revolution in 1926. It was not appreciably more defamatory than Liang Qichao's essays; indeed, were it written in Chinese, many sections could be mistaken for a work by a nationalist critic of Old China.[132] Gilbert's book was not, however, intended to pay homage to the nationalist movement. Its argument differed crucially from those of nationalists in denying the Chinese people any hope of attaining the virtues that Europeans claimed for themselves. *What's Wrong with China?* was intended to show that Liang Qichao and Sun Yatsen were part of the problem.

Gilbert drew freely from contemporary pseudoscientific theories of inherited racial characteristics, evolutionary theory, and "Nietzschean militarism" to expose the "real problem of China" for the consideration of the English-reading public. "What is really wrong with China and will continue to be wrong with her," pronounced Gilbert, "is that the Chinese are children, that their world is a world of child's make-believe."[133] Yet the nationalist movement found its strength in dreams. In Gilbert's considered view, China's problems could only be overcome with the aid of "a commission of biologists and ethnologists."[134] In fact, China's own ethnologists had been working on the patient for a century and more and had come up with a cure in nationalism itself. What Gilbert would not allow, in simple terms, was that there was any hope of China recovering its sovereignty, because he saw little prospect of renovating the Chinese as a people. Yet hope was the virtue most cherished by China's nationalists.[135] Hope held out promise of a cure for the mental and physical illnesses that European racists and Chinese nationalists both ascribed to the Chinese people.

In writing of bandits, even Gilbert was prepared to make a notable exception to his blanket condemnation of the Chinese character. Their vision, virility, bravery, and chivalry distinguished bandits from city scum.[136] Lin Yutang conceded some ground to Gilbert on this point in *My Country and My People*, a work otherwise devoted to correcting Gilbert's malicious slanders. "Chinese robbers and bandits," Lin wrote, "who do not depend upon legal protection, do not develop . . . indifference, but are the most chivalrous and public-spirited class of people we know in China today." [137] Certainly there was little cause for colonial expatriates to fear bandits before the 1920s because they were known to show sensible discrimination in their choice of prey; that is, they used to allow foreigners to pass unmolested through their territories. From 1923 this was no longer the case.

In May 1923, the French consul-general in Shanghai, M. Wilden, presented a lecture on the moral decline of the Chinese outlaw at a meeting of the local Rotarians. Never in all his travels through Sichuan, Yunnan, Gansu, and Tibet had Wilden ever encountered trouble with the many bandits he met along the way, "for in those times . . . robbers belonged to the old type who used to consider the foreigner as a guest." The new breed of bandit showed no greater courtesy for the foreigner than for the native. The result, Wilden concluded, was that China's present situation had reached its most critical level since the Boxer Uprising of 1900.[138] Not long before Wilden's address, in October 1922, the foreign community had been shaken by the capture of ten foreigners from a missionary compound (along with several hundred Chinese) in Henan Province.[139] But no earlier kidnapping quite matched the "Lincheng Outrage" — the subject of Wilden's address—in concentrating the attention of the foreign community in China. It was a significant moment in the transformation of John Bull and John Chinaman in Chinese and Western eyes.

The holdup and kidnapping of foreign and Chinese train-travelers at Lincheng in Shandong Province in May 1923 was carried out with such extraordinary daring and skill that it appeared to mark the coming of age of the Chinese outlaw. The Lincheng bandits derailed the most modern train in service in China, an all-steel express reputed to be "the very last word in Occidental Railway efficiency and luxury." [140] The party of captives was well acquainted with luxury: it included Miss Lucy Aldrich (sister-in-law of John D. Rockefeller Jr.), two U.S. Army officers, several French, Italian, and American businessmen, a honeymooning couple from Mexico, and one of the more unsavory millionaires from the Shanghai International Settlement, "Commendatore" G. D. Musso.[141] The Lincheng kidnappings were counted an outrage against foreign privilege and property without precedent since the turn of the century.

Paradoxically, the incident inspired foreign writers to treat the Lincheng bandits more respectfully than they did the roving bands who made a habit of capturing missionaries. The skill and daring of the Lincheng outlaws made honorary Occidentals of them. "It is with Oriental bandits that our Occidental folk find more in common than with the staid and respectable townsmen," proclaimed Rodney Gilbert, "as the testimony of every one of the little party held by the notorious Lincheng outlaws will confirm." [142] The *North China Daily News* carried an interview with the bandit chief, Sun Meiyao, dutifully reporting his testimony that the honorable band was motivated solely by a desire to achieve political reform in China. Sympathy for the bandits in English-language newspapers almost drowned out the cries of the foreign captives themselves, who found the pastoral or "Greenwood" flavor of the stories surrounding Sun Meiyao and his gang difficult to credit in view of the terror, suffering, and discomfort they were experiencing in captivity. One captive managed to smuggle a message to the *North China Herald* urging it to halt the "fairy tales" from Lincheng. "Make them cut out the fancy stuff in the newspapers and let the public know the real truth about what we are going through." Another columnist tried to restore sense to the debate "in view of all that has been written about the good times the captives at Lincheng were having as guests of the bandits." He concluded with an apposite reference to the Robin Hood legend: "One begins to sympathize with the portly Prior of Jorvaulx in his treatment of Robin Hood." [143] On the example of the portly prior, those responsible had to be trapped and dealt with.

But who was responsible? Sun Meiyao and his gang were clearly at fault, but the Outrage was more widely understood within the foreign community as a sign of the collapse of civil government in China. By their action, the Lincheng outlaws upheld the foreigners' complaint that the government was failing to maintain law and order and, further, confirmed their argument that the Chinese were incapable of governing themselves. Indeed, one reason the bandits found favor with sections of the foreign press was their success in humiliating the national government. On 12 May, the Shanghai *Weekly Review* pointed to the shameful implications of the incident for the government of China:

Failure of the government to check banditry has made possible an occurrence which cannot but cause a feeling of deep humiliation to the people of a government that has a shadow of self-respect. That which is called a government in China has proved itself woefully lacking; it has not and is not functioning in a manner and to a degree worthy of the name.[144]

Responsibility was then transferred from the bandits to the government of President Cao Kun. Foreign organizations in China pressed their governments and their diplomatic representatives to lodge formal protests with Cao Kun's government and to intervene politically and militarily to protect foreign life and property. The Tianjin General Chamber of Commerce called on the diplomatic body to take immediate action. The China Association cabled its headquarters in London to pressure Western governments to disband the Chinese army and to police its national railway system.[145] Others urged retaliation in kind. The proper remedy for the capture of the Blue Express, in the views of the most influential English newspapers in the country, was to capture the man chiefly responsible for the Outrage, the president himself. An editorial in the *North China Daily News* ventured:

To urge once more that the only effective way of striking terror into the official heart, is to strike at the biggest men in sight, the men who are verily guilty of this as of countless other outrages. Arrest [President] Tsao Kun and two or three other leading men. Make them pay out of their own pockets and then dismiss them forever from public service.[146]

The *North China Herald* echoed these sentiments:

If some concrete punitive action is not taken now, preferably directed personally against one or more conspicuous Chinese officials, the Lincheng affair will end in the worst disaster for foreign prestige in China that will ever have happened.[147]

In view of the overriding concern to preserve the reputation of the Occidental in China, the capture and exemplary punishment of Cao Kun would have been an appropriate course of action. When the reputation of a civilization rests on a simple gesture of captivity, it must find a "way out" or remain captive forever.

In fact, the foreign community was far more deeply humiliated by the affair than were members of the Chinese government. Brigadier-general C. D. Bruce commented in a letter to *The Times* of London that the worst aspect of the Lincheng affair was the challenge it presented to the prestige of Europeans in China. Bruce was in a position to know, having served as commissioner of the International Police in Shanghai from 1907 to 1914. This was not, he argued, simply a case of bandits capturing a trainload of innocent victims but a direct challenge by "the Oriental to the Occidental." If either the government or the bandits were allowed to get away unscathed, then heaven alone knew what might follow. The Occident, and all that it had come to represent in China, would be held in contempt by the Orientals. To the dismay of Bruce and Gilbert, the foreign powers not only declined to "arrest" President Cao Kun but offered to recognize his bribed election to the presidency in 1923 on the condition that he resolve the Lincheng affair.[148]

As the foreign community feared, the Lincheng Outrage was followed closely by a Chinese newspaper readership that was eager to absorb every installment of the thriller as it unfolded before its eyes. This was a tale of captivity with a difference: it was not China that was held against its will but uninvited Westerners. When a succession of similar incidents occurred over succeeding months, a distinct sound of cheering could be heard emanating from the Chinese quarter. Toward the end of the year, a British subject, Mr. A. J. Campbell, was assaulted on a section of the Beijing city wall within the foreign-controlled Legation Quarter, and his assailant, Private Li, was hailed as a national hero in the Chinese press. In February of the new year, an Australian rail-traffic manager by the name of Bessell was beaten up by a Chinese military officer while Bessell was supervising the foreign management of the Beijing-Tianjin line. When the Chinese officer, Captain Chen, showed up in disguise at his trial, Bessell failed to recognize him as the assailant, and was held to ridicule in the Chinese newspapers for his naivety.[149] The Occidental was becoming a target of open mockery. And yet, it must be said in Bessell's defense, John Chinaman was becoming much more difficult to recognize.

Rodney Gilbert could see where this was heading and warned of the "general hostility of the whole Chinese public, growing in courage of expression" as each new incident revealed the weakness of the Occidental in China.[150] Worse was in store. On 30 May 1925, Gilbert's worst fears were realized in a momentous clash between Chinese and foreigners in Shanghai—the May Thirtieth movement—which so overshadowed the Lincheng Outrage that the railway bandits are all but forgotten today.[151] Gilbert noted how the two events were related and recognized their cumulative effects on the prestige of the white race in Asia:

Problems are being formulated by two-thirds of humanity which the Anglo-Saxon, or more properly the Anglo-Germanic peoples, will be called upon to solve. Failure to solve these problems may mean the swamping of Occidental culture and the loss of the white race's identity. It will at least spell world-war on an enormous scale in which a mere handful of Anglo-Germanic superiors, with no preparation and no binding organization among themselves, will be called upon to revert completely to Nietzschean militarism and subdue, exterminate or enslave all the inferior peoples of the earth, organized into a vast rebellion of the unfit, or go under.[152]

Gilbert was explicitly racist in an age when racism required little apology, and his alarm was symptomatic of a more general concern within the Treaty Port communities. In the mid-1920s the question "What's wrong with China?" could no longer be answered with the simple catalogue of vices that had sufficed in earlier years. The unequal dialogue had turned. In ripping up a length of railway track and leading a small party of influential foreign captives to a remote and impregnable mountain lair, the Lincheng bandits had begun to reverse the progressive capture of China and the Chinaman that had been taking place since Captain Anson first paid his fateful visit to Guangzhou in 1743. Anson's entry into Guangzhou Harbor had been equally disproportionate to its effects in undermining the prestige of the old empire. All that was required was a simple and incontestable act of captivity.[153]

By the mid-1920s, however, it was not only foreigners who were falling captive to the resurgent nationalist movement. So were the people of China.

Nationalists wished to discover who the Chinese really were in order to identify whom, exactly, they were destined to liberate. Their enthusiasm for discovering the authentic people of China rested on assumptions about the essential characteristics of the nation that differed little from Rodney Gilbert's racist remarks about effete town-dwellers, or from Pearl Buck's more generous judgments of China's peasants. Within China itself, their conclusions had much in common with those of their opponents. When the antiquarian Gu Hunming spoke out in defense of the "real Chinaman" of old, he was engaging in invention no less than sympathetic foreign observers or the reformers and revolutionaries who spoke in defense of New China and the New People. In each case, the credibility of the call to preserve or to transform China rested on a static and ideal presumption of what the Chinese were really like. These essentialist premises rested, in turn, upon a new realist aesthetic intrinsic to the literary forms in which historical, ethnographic, literary, and political debates were conducted.[154] China had first to be captured in letters before it could be either preserved or transformed, and the customs of its people needed to be set in aspic for scientific inspection before they could be diagnosed or cured.

What if "real" China was a living and evolving creature rather than a captive object of scientific scrutiny? This seems to have been the question on Lu Xun's mind over the last months of his life, in 1936, when he remarked with an irony that had grown so tired that it had become barely detectable:

I am still looking forward to the time when Smith's *Chinese Characteristics* will be translated into Chinese. We should read this, reflect and analyse ourselves to see whether he has said anything correctly or not, then make reforms, struggle and change ourselves without asking others for their forgiveness or praise. So we shall prove what the Chinese are *really* like.[155]

Lu Xun's comment on what the Chinese were "*really* like" was prompted by the recent arrival of Hollywood director Josef Von Sternberg in Shanghai. Some years earlier, in 1932, Von Sternberg had made a film loosely based on the capture of the train at Lincheng in 1923, but with a number of significant amendments. In the film version it was not bandits who held up the train, but revolutionaries, and the kidnapped party consisted of powerless foreigners and hapless Chinese who conspire in the end to kill the revolutionary leader and secure their freedom. Von Sternberg succeeded where Rodney Gilbert had failed in converting a historical incident revealing colonial weakness and Chinese resilience into a more familiar story of righteous foreign vengeance vented against native Chinese cunning—although this time *revolutionary* cunning. Henceforth bandits and revolutionaries were conflated in Western representations of China.[156]

The film raised such a storm of protest when it was first screened in Shanghai that the distributors were forced to withdraw it from circulation. Von Stern-berg could not understand all the fuss and, on his visit to Shanghai in 1936, persisted in expressing open contempt for what he saw of China and its people. Lu Xun understood the fuss and, with the irony that had become his trade-mark, professed his admiration for Von Sternberg's forthrightness.[157] Lu Xun had followed the story of the Lincheng Outrage and the course of the National-ist Revolution in his travels from Beijing to Amoy, Guangzhou, and Shanghai, and had grieved at the opportunities that bandits and revolutionaries had fore-gone to show what the Chinese were "*really* like" over the preceding decade. It had seemed that real China would reveal itself in the act of its own revolu-tionary transformation. Lu Xun then laid down his pen and left the field to the revolutionaries. "During a great revolution," he explained in 1927, "literature disappears and there is silence."[158] Only after the guns had fallen silent did he resume writing, and look forward to reading Smith's *Chinese Characteristics* in the hope of fathoming the secret of Hollywood's contempt.

4

ONE NATION, ONE STATE
"Feudalism" and Social Revolution

> After the revolution of 1911, [Chen Jiongming] was constantly telling
> people of a dream he used to have in his youth in which he grasped the
> sun with one hand and the moon with the other. On one of his poems
> there was this line, "Failing to grasp the Sun and moon I have been
> untrue to my youth."
>
> Sun Yatsen, 1924[1]

In January 1921, Major John Magruder left the headquarters of Guangdong
Provincial Governor Chen Jiongming believing that he had just met a most
unusual Chinaman. "He is very intelligent looking, has the most benign and
kindly eyes I've seen in a Chinaman. He is particularly good looking, nerve
very calm and deliberate but alert." [2] Magruder was assistant military attaché
to the United States legation in Beijing. Although only 34 years of age, he had
already encountered a good many "visionaries and dreamers," as he called
them, on his tour of duty in China. He was not, on the whole, impressed.[3]
Some years later he grew so exercised over the national genius for dreaming
that he sent an official dispatch to the War Department to complain of a local
preference for "make believe" over "cold facts." [4] Governor Chen Jiongming
was certainly a dreamer, and his expression was a little too benign to suggest
strength of character. "I should not call him a strong looking character—perhaps because he has such a kindly expression." [5] But for all his dreaminess
there was something about the eyes and the expression of Chen Jiongming that
inspired confidence in a hardened realist.

Some years earlier Sun Yatsen had made an equally deep impression on an
Englishman, Dr. James Cantlie. Cantlie met Sun Yatsen in 1887 when Sun enrolled in the College of Medicine in Hong Kong, and later came to Sun's aid in
London in 1896, to help secure his release from the Chinese legation.[6] The two
men formed a close and enduring friendship that lasted well into the Republic. Over this time, Cantlie recalled, he had come to appreciate Sun's "strength
of character, his earnestness of purpose, his modesty of mind, and to understand the secret of his power." [7] Strength of character was not bought at the
expense of "courtesy and kindliness." Where Magruder had found Governor

Chen Jiongming an exemplary "Chinaman," Cantlie thought Sun a model for
the whole world to emulate: "If I were asked to name the most perfect character I ever knew, I would unhesitatingly say Sun Yatsen." Governor Chen
represented his province before the nation; Sun was a patriot who carried the
reputation of his country to the world. "No one who has come in close touch
with Sun Yatsen but has felt the magic of his presence," Cantlie confessed.
"Honesty and patriotism endowed him with an 'atmosphere' that convinces
his opponents to his views and serves to turn aside the assassin's knife and the
betrayer's purpose." [8] Cantlie was right, with one exception. Governor Chen
Jiongming betrayed Sun Yatsen.

Behind the "courtesy and kindliness" of Sun Yatsen and the "benign and
kindly" expression of Chen Jiongming lay two fiercely irreconcilable dreams
of China that collided in June 1922 in the most notorious personal betrayal of
the Nationalist Revolution. It was deeply felt because it was quite unexpected.
Governor Chen was a talented lawyer and a loyal military officer with a substantial personal following in his native East River region of Guangdong. Born
into an established gentry family of Hakka descent, Chen first came to public
notice at the age of 29, when he led a public campaign to impeach the imperial
prefect of Huizhou. Two years later, in 1909, he joined the Revolutionary Alliance (*Tongmenghui*), in which he allied himself with Sun Yatsen's faction. In
1911 he was instrumental in capturing Guangdong for the revolutionary forces
and, at the turn of the year, was honored with the position of acting governor of the province. Chen remained loyal to Sun Yatsen when President Yuan
Shikai broke with the revolutionary forces in 1913—despite generous offers to
join Yuan's side—and over the first decade of the Republic he worked tirelessly
in support of Sun's constitutional and military maneuvers and in promoting
educational and social reforms in areas under his control. In fact, it was Chen
who secured a home base for the expansion of Sun Yatsen's Nationalist movement in Guangdong in the early 1920s. There was, however, a side to Chen
Jiongming that sat uneasily alongside his loyalty to Sun Yatsen. Chen was a
consistent champion of local self-government. The two men finally came to
blows when he refused to subsidize Sun's latest military campaign for national
reunification from the local treasury.

On 16 June 1922, Chen ordered an attack on Sun Yatsen's headquarters in
Guangzhou City. Sun escaped to the warship Yongfeng, on which he spent
seven stifling weeks moored in the Pearl River, just beyond the city, awaiting
the arrival of reinforcements. They never came. On 9 August, Sun was spirited
out of Guangzhou under humiliating circumstances aboard a British gunboat
bound for Hong Kong. Sun looked back on Chen's betrayal as the greatest disappointment in a life made memorable by disappointments. Neither Sun nor
his successors ever forgot it.

By nature, as Dr. Cantlie observed, Sun Yatsen was a genial man inclined to forgive those who crossed him. The most brilliant of Sun's early revolutionary comrades, Zhang Binglin, brought shame on him in 1909 by accusing Sun of squandering funds earmarked for the revolution, yet Sun invited Zhang to join his Guangzhou military government in 1917. Sun delivered a glowing eulogy at the funeral of another comrade who had crossed him at a critical moment in the revolution, Huang Xing.[9] But Sun could not bring himself to forgive Chen Jiongming. The sound of Chen's name transformed Sun Yatsen's kindly expression to a murderous glare, and he had to be restrained from lunging at the throat of any who came to Chen's defense. Sun was at his Guangxi forward post of Wuzhou when he received news that Chen Jiongming would not be supporting him on the expedition. One of Sun's advisers in Wuzhou, Lai Shihuang, asked him to show clemency despite Chen's "betrayal." Sun turned to Lai in fury: "Are you one of his party? Are you?" and, motioning to his guards, ordered "Kill him! Kill him! Kill him!" Lai was reportedly saved by the intervention of another adviser, Jiang Baiqi.[10] The Nationalists never quite managed to catch Chen Jiongming, but shortly after Sun died they chased him from Guangdong and hounded him to an early death in Hong Kong. Nationalist historians vilify him to this day.[11] The Communists followed suit, adding the suffix "traitor" (*pantu*) to Chen Jiongming's name. Chen was a "traitor to the democratic revolution," wrote Communist propaganda officer Cai Hesen shortly after the Communists had come out on the side of Sun Yatsen in 1922. "The footsteps of his betrayal are clear for all to see and everyone has spat him aside." [12]

Nevertheless, Major Magruder and Dr. Cantlie were quite right in their estimations of the characters of Chen Jiongming and Sun Yatsen. Sun died a man of modest means. He dedicated his life to the service of China without regard for his personal fortune or the wealth of his family. Despite managing large sums of money on behalf of the revolution, Sun left only a house, his books, and some clothing to his wife Song Qingling.[13] In spite of his easy access to the Guangdong provincial treasury, Chen Jiongming also died in poverty — unlike his more worldly successor in Guangdong, Chen Jitang.[14] But the personal characters of Sun and Chen were not at issue in this dispute. Sun harbored a fierce hatred for Chen Jiongming not because he was so very different from himself but because he pursued a different dream of national reunification with the same selfless vigor.

Communist and Nationalist accounts of Chen Jiongming's "betrayal" have preserved Sun Yatsen's preeminent claim as the authentic dreamer of modern China. Yet Sun's dream of a sovereign nation united under a powerful centralized state was not the only dream nursed by China's nationalists. Chen Jiongming harbored a dream of a different kind. Although a regional warlord, Chen cherished ambitions that reached beyond the provincial borders. In the first of his lectures on democracy, Sun counseled those who felt that Chen Jiongming was just another provincial satrap with the warning that he was far more dangerous than he appeared. Chen, said Sun, would never be content to gain control of the regional base of Guangdong and Guangxi and ignore the rest of China. Sun cited a dream that he attributed to Chen Jiongming to show that Chen "coveted the throne." [15] In truth, Chen's dream of China was not one in which he would be crowned king, but it was dangerous all the same. Chen envisioned a federation of self-governing provinces, enjoying a high degree of regional autonomy, and a correspondingly diminished role for the central state—in short, a federal system of government. Certainly the country had neither a strong central state nor a viable federal system when the alliance between Chen and Sun broke down in June 1922. But well before Chen's betrayal, the political struggle between Sun Yatsen and Chen Jiongming had already revealed a clash between two dreams of what the nation might look like if only each of the dreamers could grasp the sun, or the moon, in his hands.

Local Self-Government and "Feudalism"

Local self-government ranked high in the order of Chen Jiongming's aspirations for China. Sun was known to favor "party rule in Guangdong" (*dang ren zhi Yue*), whereas Chen was widely associated with the motto "The people of Guangdong rule Guangdong" (*Yue ren zhi Yue*). The distinction, as far as Sun was concerned, was one between rule by a political faction with particular party loyalties and rule by elites with particularist local ones. It was becoming clear over the months leading to Chen's "betrayal" which of the two principles was the more popular among local elites in Guangdong. Chen suggested putting the matter to a vote. The opportunity arose in 1921 and 1922, when Chen proposed that county heads and assemblymen should be selected and appointed through popular election. Sun was quite upset. He felt that the people of Guangdong had not yet reached a standard of political consciousness commensurate with party rule and would, in any event, probably vote against his favored candidates.[16] Chen went ahead with the elections anyway. By year's end, voting for local-representative assemblies and county heads had been completed in all 92 counties, and elections were under way for urban municipal councils.

In discussions leading up to the elections, Chen conceded ground on an important issue concerning the election of county heads. In the absence of candidates to rival incumbent political leaders in the province, Chen felt that local elections would be likely to return incumbents to office. So for the inaugural election, his provincial government reserved the right to appoint county heads from among the three candidates who polled highest in each county.[17] It was probably just as well, for the chief problem with the elections was not voter consciousness but electoral administration. Technical irregularities attending the election were commonplace and, in the estimation of one foreign observer, approached the "farcical." Ballot tickets were distributed to village elders and militia chiefs according to the size of each village, and in some cases the elders and militia proceeded to fill in the ballots themselves in favor of their patrons. Not surprisingly, incumbent magistrates received the highest number of votes in many counties. By reserving the right to appoint county heads from among elected candidates, the provincial government compensated for the shortcomings of its own electoral procedures.[18] But even this procedure did not prevent wily candidates from pooling their resources in an effort to ensure that at least three of their number would top the local lists, and hence that one of the three would be certain to be appointed county head. All three, under this ruse, would agree to divide the proceeds of office among themselves. There was little Chen Jiongming could do to circumvent this problem, although he did make allowance for legal challenges against allegedly corrupt practices.

In the main, Chen Jiongming exercised discretion in his selection of candidates. In the vicinity of Shantou he appointed four county heads from among the candidates who had received the highest number of votes, five from among those who had received the second highest count, and two who ranked third in the local elections.[19] As a further corrective, the provincial government resolved in December to send inspection teams to all counties over the new year to evaluate the performance of county heads.[20] Chen promised to keep a watchful eye on them. "County heads should establish the closest of contact with the people," he reminded his new appointees. "When I was in Changchow (Changzhou) I used to keep a record of the administration of county heads. I wish to do the same with the county heads of this province again." [21] Elections went more smoothly in the city of Shantou, where around 20,000 registered voters were enrolled to elect six councillors. Another six were elected by public associations, including two by the chamber of commerce and one each from among labor unions and local educational, medical, and legal associations. A further six councillors were directly appointed by Governor Chen, making eighteen municipal councillors in total.[22]

Governor Chen was held to account for his commitment to self-government in Guangzhou, where he proposed a more gradual procedure for introducing direct elections in the provincial capital. He proposed to appoint one-third of all councillors in the first year and to reduce his appointments over a five-year period, after which he would relinquish the right to make further appointments.[23] Chen also proposed to appoint a provisional mayor of the city for the intervening period. When the draft plan for local self-government was made public in Guangzhou, it attracted criticism from the provincial assembly on both counts. How was it, the assemblymen asked, that rural counties were entitled to elect their own local assemblies (although not county heads) directly, whereas the governor reserved the right to appoint councillors and the mayor for Guangzhou? Chen's reluctance to concede further ground on these points was taken as a slight on the "political awareness" of the "people of Guangzhou."[24] Shanghai Nationalist party headquarters was rather more generous. The *Shanghai Republican Daily* conceded that, for all their limitations, the elections "were not only a breakthrough in Guangdong but unprecedented in the history of democracy in China."[25] In fact, as the historian Winston Hsieh observes, they were "unprecedented in Chinese history."[26]

Chen's problems with the voters of Guangzhou paled alongside the friction with Sun Yatsen that resulted from his persistence in staging elections at all. The dispute over the merits of local or party rule in Guangdong in 1921 was one of the factors that precipitated the split between Chen Jiongming and Sun Yatsen. Sun decided to launch his Northern Expedition. For Sun, toppling the national government in Beijing was more straightforward than dealing with the intricacies of local politics and elections in Guangdong, and was also more in keeping with his commitment to reunifying the country. For his part, Chen Jiongming feared that the Nationalist leader would try to impose party rule on the province from a secure position in the national capital in order to compensate for his failure to impose it on Guangdong from within the province.[27] Chen's fear was well placed but misdirected. Sun did not gain control of Beijing, but he did descend on Guangdong within a year of the local elections, bringing armies recruited from outside the province. He then chased Chen from Guangzhou and established a new party-state within Guangdong itself. Under Sun's new administration, established with the aid of Soviet advisers and the assistance of the Chinese Communist party, local officials were no longer elected but were appointed from among candidates known to be hostile to the "feudal forces" that had won the electoral contests.

It was not Sun himself but the Communists who first equated Chen Jiongming's model of local self-government with "feudalism" (*fengjianzhuyi*). By June 1922, the federalist movement had gained considerable support from leading liberal intellectuals, including Hu Shi, and had received additional momentum from provincial military and political leaders in Hunan, Yunnan, and Guangdong.[28] When support for federalism began to assume the dimensions of a national movement, leading members of the Communist party mounted the public platform to debate the merits of federal and centralist models of state organization. Initial Communist hostility toward federalism was based not on principle but on contingency. "I am not fundamentally opposed to federal self-government nor to the system of federation itself," explained Party General Secretary Chen Duxiu in September 1922. Chen Duxiu built his case against federalism on certain "facts" that he thought beyond dispute. One was his claim that current political problems in China could all be traced to competition among rival warlord factions and hence that anything that encouraged their separatist tendencies would only make things worse. "The source of chaos in China's present political situation," complained Chen, "is militarist separatism."²⁹ A week later Cai Hesen resorted to almost identical words when he followed Chen Duxiu in attacking the movement for federal self-government: "The source of chaos in Chinese politics is, of course, the warlords."³⁰

The perfidy of warlords became an article of faith in Communist and Nationalist circles in the aftermath of Chen Jiongming's "betrayal," when the move for federal self-government was said to have originated among regional warlords as a concerted attempt to secure *de iure* recognition for *de facto* autonomy. The simplest way to slander the federalist movement was to show that warlords like Chen Jiongming were keen on it. "Recent talk of federal self-government arises not from the needs of the people but from the leadership of the warlords of Hunan, Guangdong and Yunnan Provinces."³¹ But even this was not enough for the Communists. Principle merged with contingency when the term "feudalism" was introduced to explain the perfidious relationship between warlords and the federalist movement. Federalism was now said to be tainted by association with "the persistence of the old forces of feudalism."³² If feudalism was the basic problem, it followed that federalism under warlord sponsorship was just one more enemy to be overcome along with all other vestiges of "the old forces of feudalism" in the Nationalist Revolution.

It is not hard to appreciate why warlords should have been counted frontline targets of a national revolution. Their apparent role in fracturing the polity and "cooperating" with imperialism corresponded neatly with the twin targets of the Nationalist Revolution of securing national reunification and independence. But it is a little more difficult to explain why this tendency on the part of warlords should have been counted feudal with such alacrity. Some warlords certainly owned estates, but none kept serfs in bondage, and all were determined to present themselves as the most forward-thinking provincial rulers in China's long history. They thought of themselves as representing progressive federal forces, not ancient feudal ones. For the Communists, however, the relative merits of a federalist or centralist system of rule were evaluated entirely within the framework of lingering "feudal forces."

Perhaps the most important contribution of the Nationalist Revolution to the greater revolution in China this century was its way with words. At the time Chen Jiongming broke with Sun Yatsen over the issue of adopting a central or federal state structure, the revolutionaries were busy inventing a new language to redescribe the predicament and prospects facing the nation. The language of Confucianism had been repudiated in the New Culture and May Fourth movements, when activists substituted the vocabulary of progressive liberalism. A number of different countries, including the United States and Japan, had earlier been targeted in nationalist boycotts, and the disappointing outcome at Versailles in 1919 extended patriotic outrage against all the victors of the Great War. In the May Fourth movement, the categories of liberal thought still required that these countries be separated discretely into countries, or "Great Powers" (*lieguo*), each with its own national history, characteristics, and unique blend of interests and policies bearing on China. Though warlords were targeted by liberals, socialists, and anarchists alike, all critics were inclined to discriminate among warlords and to make due allowance for the more progressive ones. Warlords and Great Powers were not uniformly counted friends of the national revolution, nor were they all counted among its enemies. In fact, before June 1922, Chen Jiongming was counted the most progressive warlord of them all. Yet when he broke with Sun Yatsen he was no longer regarded as merely a warlord, nor even as a traitor serving British interests in Hong Kong. In the space of a few years, the language in which his crimes could be comprehended had changed dramatically. Chen was a "feudal warlord" and the Hong Kong interests he was alleged to have served were no longer those of Great Britain, or even of a Great Power, but were the interests of "British imperialism." By 1922, neither liberalism nor Confucianism sufficed to explain New China's predicament as elegantly as Leninism.

The Language of Politics and the Politics of Language

The salience of this revolutionary redescription of the early 1920s is best understood in light of Richard Rorty's observation in *Contingency, Irony and Solidarity* that "revolutionary achievements in the arts, in the sciences, and in moral and political thought typically occur when somebody realizes that two or more of our vocabularies are interfering with each other, and proceeds to invent a new vocabulary to replace both." The appearance of the terms "imperialism" and "feudalism" in the linguistic armory of the revolution offered a new way of apprehending the world, and supplied new foundations for political action that retained their relevance and vitality long after the Nationalist Revolution of the 1920s had drawn to a close. More importantly, the new vocabulary transformed the object of the quest itself. The China that was saved from feudalism and imperialism would not be the same China as one rescued from the clutches of warlords and Great Powers, nor for that matter from Western learning and barbarians. The revolutionary thinker "is typically unable to make clear what it is he wants to do before developing the language in which he succeeds in doing it. His new vocabulary makes possible, for the first time, a formulation of its own purpose." [33] The failure of liberal and Confucian language to offer a simple answer to the question "What's wrong with China" certainly made selection of a new conceptual language more urgent. Still, the language of the Nationalist Revolution enabled the revolutionaries to conceive of their purpose, of saving China (*jiuguo*), in ways that were to transform, in radical ways, the nation they set out to save.

Language itself was at issue in the revolution. The form of the Chinese nation-state was under negotiation in a concurrent movement for language reform. There was indeed a clear isomorphism between political competition over the shape of the Chinese state among centralists and federalists on the one side, and contestation in the language-reform movement between champions of uniform and variable scripts on the other. The domains of language and politics were quite distinct, but political nationalists tended to press for a degree of variety or uniformity in language and script befitting the kind of unity they had in mind for the nation. The Nationalist party's position was captured in a combative remark by the powerful Nationalist official Chen Guofu, on completion of the Nationalist Revolution: "China's ability to achieve unity is entirely dependent on having a unified written language." [34] Language federalists also framed their arguments in the rhetoric of national unity but conceived of unity as an aggregation of distinct local communities, grounded in existing conditions rather than in an abstractly reconstituted nation: "The unity which we need is neither abstract, illusory or artificial, but one derived from real life." Federalists also advocated universal literacy but believed that literacy was best promoted through a system of writing capable of accommodating local variation sufficient to "enable the masses within a region to communicate with each other internally." [35] Language centralists, on the other hand, wanted people to communicate locally through a national language. What was at issue in the movement for language reform, at least as it bore on politics, was not national unity, but the relationship between local communities and the center in a unified national polity. As John de Francis concludes in his masterful survey of the Chinese language-reform movement, "The problem of the Chinese script reduces itself at almost every point to some aspect or other of Chinese nationalism itself." [36]

The nation of the centralizing language-reform movement shared a family resemblance to the rational-bureaucratic self that Kang Youwei discovered on returning to his studio after touring the stars. Kang broached the question of language and nationalism directly in his One World philosophy. He was certainly not a national-language chauvinist. Kang confidently predicted the demise of all national languages and, if we are to take him on his word, was quite prepared to help his own beloved Chinese language on its way if this should hasten the universal acceptance of a common script. To all appearances, nothing could be more hostile to the claims of nationalism. Yet Kang's arguments for One World echoed the intolerance of cultural difference that later emerged in the rhetoric of triumphant nationalism. His advocacy of a universal language at the expense of a specifically Chinese language anticipated the call within China to standardize a national language at the expense of regional language-families and local dialects. When Kang declared that "national languages must be abolished as being one of the major barriers which perpetuates disunity in the world," he prefigured Chen Guofu's claim on behalf of the Nationalists that local dialects perpetuated disunity within the nation itself.[37] Both hankered after maximal rationality, the one for the world and the other for the nation.

Kang's disciple, Liang Qichao, shared his concern for efficiency and order, although applied to the nation-state rather than to the universe. Kang experimented with an international phonetic system, whereas Liang developed a keen interest in phonetic systems for the exclusive use of Chinese-language speakers.[38] Supporters of a unified national language also invoked Kang's historical law of unification and centralization that was pushing events in the direction of a One World state. But nationalists who wished to move on from the empire to a universal world order felt obliged to stop over at the level of the nation-state, as history was not yet ready to proceed to the higher stage of One World.

In the 1920s, reference to "feudalism" helped to explain their predicament. The Marxist Zhang Tingfei, for example, proposed moving on from the "feudal" or highly differentiated culture of the old empire to a universal world order, and like Kang and Liang he was prepared to settle in the interim for unification at the level of the nation-state:

Modern Chinese history is in the process of moving from feudalism to capitalism. It is still in the stage of nationalism. Hence Chinese characters are still suited to this stage. The special characteristics of this stage are economic, cultural and political unification. Only that which unifies is progressive; division means reaction.

Zhang's equation of feudalism with division and, in turn, of division with reaction signals the strength of the revolutionary reaction against feudalism in all its guises—in language, culture, social organization, and political administration. In the case of language, Chinese characters were well suited to China at the moment in question—poised between a disunity imagined as feudal and a confederation imagined as international—because they were sufficiently inclusive to overcome differences within China and yet exclusive enough to give those using them a common identity in the present world order of nation-states. Zhang, like Kang Youwei and Liang Qichao, wanted more. He wished first to replace local languages with a standardized national one, and then to supply the standard language with a uniform phonetic alphabet in order to hasten "the internationalization of Chinese writing, so that in the future it can proceed to the stage of world language." [39]

This argument was, of course, a restatement of the Marxist-Leninist paradigm of world history in the sphere of language. But it was also consistent with centralizing nationalism. Even Sun Yatsen counted nationalism an intermediate stage on the road to a universal order; indeed, it was this universal order that made nationalism imperative. "We must understand that cosmopolitanism grows out of nationalism," Sun counseled; "if we want to extend cosmopolitanism we must first establish strongly our own nationalism." [40] Revolutionaries who resented the boundaries dividing a world that they believed to be destined for ultimate unification saw everything short of One World as irrational and inefficient. Local languages, like warlords, were reactionary because they perpetuated division and postponed the attainment of "cosmopolitanism." The level of language standardization and political centralization was fixed, appropriately, at the highest attainable level in the present historical moment. For language centralists, this meant a uniform national language. For political centralists, it meant a uniform system of centralized administration.

The target of centralist fury was the "feudal" patois of local communities resistant to the centralizing nation-state. Historically, national language-reform movements tend to launch attacks against enemies on both sides of the national border: against local vernacular and foreign influence.[41] In China, however, the emphasis was all but exclusively on the enemy within. Latinization of the script and new-style punctuation were both branded as foreign and criticized on this account. Yet what actually mattered was the part foreign borrowings could play in achieving national unity, that is, in hastening or retarding the development of a standardized national script. Even foreign punctuation was tolerated insofar as it aided standardization. This emphasis on protecting the national language against impurities from within, rather than from without, led to a number of anomolies in Nationalist party propaganda. Sun Yatsen opposed the use of Western-style punctuation in Chinese texts, yet Nationalist party journals were among the first publications to adopt the new system of punctuation in 1919. In 1924, at the height of his party authority, Sun could not persuade party members to act on a memo from the Nationalist director of propaganda forbidding the use of question marks and other foreign imports in Nationalist publications.[42] This was a futile gesture. Nationalist propagandists generally targeted language reform to eliminate local produce, not foreign imports. On the whole, national revolutionaries were less concerned with imperialist influence on the national language than with overcoming the stubborn resistance of "feudal" particularism.

The traditional script taught centralizing Nationalists the advantages of a standardized system of writing for holding the country together, and they planned to surrender none of them. Their stress upon unity-through-uniformity spotlighted the route by which they proposed to lead unawakened subjects to their destination as awakened citizens. This was a route signposted by the ideographic print-language of the old empire. The traditional script traced a pattern of songlines back and forth across the empire, in a language of state coextensive with the territorial reach of the state and yielding a sense of community among its functionaries that was as extensive (and limited) as literacy itself.[43] Imperial functionaries were replaced by citizens in the Republic, and the old language of state gave way to a new national language more appropriate to a democratic state structure. That is, it conformed more closely to everyday speech. But the match was not exact: although the national vernacular language (*baihua*) was based on Beijing dialect, its nearest spoken equivalent was not the northern vernacular at all but the "official speech" of the mandarin court. It was aptly termed "official speech" (*guanhua*) when first mooted in the halls of government, and only renamed "national language" (*guoyu*) or "vernacular language" (*baihua*) to correct the misleading impression that it was intended exclusively for official communication. Hardy advocates of the term "official speech" insisted, nevertheless, that the terms "official" (*guan*) and "public" (*gong*) were interchangeable in a democracy, and hence that "official speech" meant "public speech" in a republic.[44] By adhering to their local dialects, people might still speak or write as members of social communities, but they could only qualify as citizens once they had acquired fluency and literacy in the code of the central bureaucracy.

In Guangdong the isomorphism between national political reform and national language reform was complicated by attempts to build a distinctively provincial identity consonant with the federalist ambitions of provincial warlords. In view of their own language differences, however, few Guangdong natives favored elevating particular local dialects to the status of a national language, or at least not to the degree that they might compete with the national language based on the official language of Beijing. Speakers of Guangzhou dialect looked down their noses at fellow provincials mouthing the rustic dialects of Seeyup (*Siyi*), while speakers of Chaomei dialect in the vicinity of Shantou tried valiantly to preserve their own tongue against the inroads of Guangzhou dialect. But as the most prominent local warlords in Guangdong, Chen Jiongming and Chen Jitang, both hailed from outside the provincial capital, their attempts to forge a distinctly provincial identity rarely favored Guangzhou at the expense of more outlying districts, except, significantly, in the development of major urban infrastructure.[45] At any rate, the record of ethnic conflict in the province meant that for all practical purposes, Guangdong provincialism could not settle easily into a form of ethnic identity.[46] The people of Guangdong were, first and foremost, people of China. So students of Guangdong Senior Teachers College petitioned their lecturers in December 1920 to use the new standard national language in class, and cited Chen Jiongming's enlightened educational policies in support of their case.[47] The preservation of local dialect was not to be at the expense of the national language, even under a federal arrangement.

Instead, the claim to a distinctly provincial identity took the form of the historical argument that Guangdong dialects were not local languages at all, as the pronunciation preserved in Guangdong dialects was more faithful to the spoken languages of central China at the height of imperial glory. The people of Guangdong "came down from the central plains," one local patriot announced in 1933, and as direct descendants of the soldiers and officials of the Southern Song dynasty, their languages "are based on the correct pronunciation of the central regions. They cannot be compared with local languages." [48] It was people born outside Guangdong who spoke "local languages." Claims made on behalf of particular Guangdong dialects against others in the same province also eschewed the word "local" because it shared the opprobrium that attached to the word "feudal." Even champions of local dialects of the Guangdong language preferred to compete for national ascendency. "In ancient times there was no such term as 'local language,' " wrote Dong Ziguang in his introduction to the history of the Chaomei dialect. Bearing in mind the argument that Guangdong languages were not to be counted local, he maintained that the Chaozhou dialect was the least local of all: "The sounds of the people of high antiquity are chiefly preserved in Chaozhou, in Guangdong." [49] Claims about the historical vintage of the languages of Guangdong were not inconsistent with the assertion of political autonomy for the province. The demand for provincial autonomy was grounded in a vision of the Chinese nation that encouraged localities and provinces to mount competitive claims to national ascendency and not, as their detractors claimed, to an alternative national identity.

"Feudalism" and the Ideal of the Central State

Reluctance to champion local languages *as* local languages offered an indirect tribute to the success of the Nationalist Revolution. One final contribution of the revolution to the manufacture of a national language was its recovery and reworking of the word "feudal" itself. The word *fengjian* had long been elaborated as a strain of anticentralist thought in debate on imperial statecraft. It was reworked in the 1920s to the point where it acquired its present-day connotation of backwardness, patriarchy, and superstition.[50] Between its recovery and its reworking, the term retained some of the earlier sense of decentralized administration (counterposed to centralized bureaucratic administration), particularly when applied as a term of abuse to advocates of provincial autonomy and champions of local self-government under a federal system. Local languages, like warlords and federalism, were feudal in this inherited sense because they threatened a new ideal of a national reunification under a strong central state. Local languages and customs, provincial warlords, and political federalism all appeared irremediably backward to centralists because they were all irrecoverably *local*.

Feudal "disunity" was first associated with backwardness in the May Fourth movement, when the term *fengjian* was employed to condemn arranged marriages, widow suicides, and other practices offensive to progressive thinkers, and when discussion of the feudal polity was subsumed into political arguments about the responsibility befalling the modern state to correct such practices.[51] Chen Duxiu and Qu Qiubai brandished the term "feudalism" liberally to condemn feudal patriarchy, and they referred to the cellular structure of China's economy and society in tracing the historical roots of feudal social practices.[52] The two primary meanings of *fengjian* were subsequently conflated in the rhetoric of the Nationalist Revolution, when the term was incorporated into the historicist argument that the feudal system was an early stage in the march of history toward modernity. There is little hint in Chen Duxiu's musings that earlier advocates of the feudal model had been imaginative scholars and iconoclastic reformers who found fault with the workings of the imperial system.[53] In fact, the enemies of feudalism in the Nationalist Revolution were more faithful to the great tradition than were the federalists, whom they condemned as remnants of imperial rule. The irony was lost in revolution. Henceforth no movement proclaiming nationalist ideals could look to a decentralized model of political organization and still claim to be modern without fear of self-contradiction.

Similarly, arguments for and against federalism were each founded on particular readings of China's history as a nation, and on different understandings of the larger historical forces at work within the nation. One measure of these different perspectives is to be found in debate within the Communist party itself, notably between the two cofounders of the party, Li Dazhao and Chen Duxiu, in 1923. Li mounted an aggressive historical defense of federalism in January. Those who argued that federalism would "split the country," he counseled, "fail to appreciate what federalism is all about." To the contrary, federalism would bring the country together. Li was acutely conscious of social and ethnic differentiation not just in the world at large but within China itself. He was also a progressive humanist. Progress, he counseled, was propelling peoples and states in the direction of One World (*shijie datong*)—"a world through which the common spirit of humanity flows, like blood through a single vein"—and federalism was an ideal system for bringing different communities together because it was uniquely suited to resolving the paradox of "particularity" and "commonality" in the transition to One World:

On the one hand [federalism] marks the liberation of particularity (*gexing*), and on the other the coming together of One World . . . localities, countries, races, and social units each have their own particularity, just as individual people do, and federalism enables them to preserve their particularities while preventing the encroachment of others. There are also points in common between each locality, country, race, and social unit, just as there are among individual people, and federalism enables them to realize their commonalities as well by combining different levels of organization and affirming each of their particular positions, in principle, and so achieving the goal of mutual assistance. The boundary between the freedom of the particular, and the mutual benefit of the wider community, is determined in each case by the requirements of life itself.[54]

In the case of China, Li concluded, political divisions between the rival national governments in Beijing and Guangzou, and between provinces and the center, were best resolved by adopting a federal model of government.

Chen Duxiu, on the other hand, resorted to an alternative reading of the historical foundations of national unity, denying that there were significant categories of difference dividing the country. Appropriately, he identified different historical forces threatening the nation. Chen isolated for criticism all emblems of cultural, social, and economic particularity that threatened to divide the country, and argued that there would be little scope for introducing federalism in China even if there were no warlords at all. Federalism, he asserted, was best suited to countries with regionally differentiated economies, languages, religions, and cultures. This was not the case with China. China was one country housing a single "Chinese people" (*Zhonghua minzu*) within a uniform socioeconomic system. As China's economy was subject to the universal laws of history, the nation's million-strong industrial proletariat would supply the historical fixative to bond their 400 million compatriots into one. "The economic situation of the people of China has uniformly and gradually moved from the stage of agriculture and handicraft industry to that of industrial production," he announced in September 1922. "There is little difference between north and south." [55]

Chen's claim that emergent social classes supplied a new force for national unity was developed further by Cai Hesen, his propaganda assistant at Shanghai party headquarters. Cai argued that the political division between the northern and southern governments was, at base, a political manifestation of class struggle. Hence "class warfare" (*jieji zhanzheng*) would ultimately supply a force for unity sufficient to overcome regional differences:

The domestic chaos and fighting of the last decade is not a struggle for territory between "North" and "South," nor a struggle over "Protecting the Constitution" or

"Breaking the Constitution," nor even a struggle between "Unity" and "Division." It is a struggle between the old dominant feudal class and the newly arisen revolutionary class: a kind of class warfare.[56]

Though Chen and Cai could hardly deny that there were significant differences of custom, language, and religious belief among the people of China, they were inclined to downplay their significance in light of the emergence of national social classes. Other kinds of difference, Chen argued, offered little comfort to advocates of local self-government under a federal system:

Although there is some slight difference in pronunciation in the native language, the written script and structure of the language are identical. And although there are religious distinctions among Buddhism, Daoism, Christianity and Islam in no case do these correspond with places of dwelling.[57]

These comments are best read as statements of "make-believe" or intention rather than of "cold fact." Chen could claim with confidence that there was little correspondence between religious belief and geography because Tibet, Xinjiang, and Mongolia were not at issue among his partisan readers. But nor were they at issue among federalist dreamers. Proponents of a federal system did not base their case for provincial self-government on the kinds of argument Chen Duxiu and Cai Hesen set out to demolish in their characterization of the Chinese nation. Even distinctive local languages and customs did not feature prominently in the arguments of federalists, who mounted their case not as an alternative to the ideal of a unified Chinese nation but as an alternative reading of national unity. Provincial autonomy with a federal system was conceived not as an end in itself but as a prelude to "the independence of all China."[58] Nevertheless, fear of national disintegration under a federal system inspired a new rationale for class struggle in the Nationalist Revolution: class struggle would *unite* a country that was otherwise threatened with divisions perhaps greater in their magnitude. Class struggle was conceived as a nation-building enterprise on a *centralist* model of the state.

The political target of self-government movements in Guangdong and Hunan was neither the unified nation nor, initially, an interventionist central state. In Guangdong, the federalist slogan "The people of Guangdong rule Guangdong" was directed against the officials, officers, and soldiers of the occupying forces of General Lu Rongting from neighboring Guangxi, whereas in Hunan, Zhao Hengti's provincial movement targeted rival warlords as the chief enemies of provincial self-government.[59] Occasional expressions of provincial patriotism among the communities of each province also took the form of preferences for local warlords over alien ones.[60] Collaboration with out-of-town warlords occasionally met with punishments that in other times and places might have been meted out for crimes of treason. On resuming control of Guangdong in October 1920, Chen Jiongming confiscated the property of local people who had assisted Lu Rongting and the Guangxi warlords in running the province over the preceding five years.[61] But even here, in its starkest form, the assertion of provincial loyalty was conceived in relation to other localities and not in relation to China itself.[62] The fury of Zhao Hengti and Chen Jiongming was reserved for provincial outsiders (and their local collaborators) who dared to control a province other than their native one.

Over the long term, however, proponents of a powerful central state proved more potent enemies of provincial self-government than did warlords from neighboring provinces. The Nationalist movement conceived of national unification in terms of the expansion of the central state and the penetration of local society. Sun Yatsen made frequent reference to a saying (attributed to colonial expatriates) that the Chinese people resembled a "loose sheet of sand." By this he meant that his compatriots lacked social cohesion beyond the level of the extended family, and lacked the capacity for political organization beyond that which a centralizing nationalist movement would supply. Sun proposed an unprecedented reorientation of state activity toward every grain of sand, to infuse the cement that he thought lacking in the old imperial state and from contemporary society.

The state was to expand its reach at the expense of local autonomy, customary liberties, and new political freedoms. Europeans rightly struggled for liberty, claimed Sun, because they had "suffered so bitterly from despotism." But as the Chinese people "have not suffered such despotism," they had less cause to strive for freedom from the state. In fact, the Chinese people suffered from a surfeit of freedom: "If Chinese are like loose sand, [it is because] they already have complete freedom." It was not freedom but rather discipline that the people required: "Being like loose sand is not a good thing, we ought to add cement and water as quickly as possible, consolidate into rock, and become a firm body." In place of liberty, the Nationalist Revolution would strive for unity: "We must use revolutionary methods to weld our state into firm unity." [63] And in place of the federalist ideal of local self-government, Sun substituted a model of unified central administration. In the event, Chen Jiongming's nemesis was not his rival from Guangxi, Lu Rongting, but his old partner within the Nationalist movement, Sun Yatsen.

Sun's sandstone model of the nation was clearly intended to displace the aggregate model of the federal self-government movement, which pictured substantial provincial units each practicing local "self-government" and aggregating in a national federation.[64] This confederal model of self-government, put forward in the 1920s, was to be distinguished from an earlier model of a federal "state union" on the one hand, and from alternative ideas of federation and self-government circulating within the Nationalist movement on the other.[65] Sun Yatsen and his party occasionally employed the terms "federalism" and "self-government" to describe their own platform, but in this case the intention was to bypass the province as a significant political unit and to limit self-government to local party institutions. At one stage Sun himself had promoted what he called a "federal" model, linking a confederation of counties to a strong central state and all but eliminating the province from the political geography of the country.[66] Chen Jiongming, on the other hand, envisioned a national confederation of self-governing *provinces*.

The Nationalists employed the term "self-government" to refer to local party rule. On proclaiming its commitment to local self-government in July 1925, the Nationalist government in Guangzhou proceeded to call for the replacement of local civic associations and self-defense leagues with more compliant party-affiliated peasant associations and self-defense armies. Even the county heads responsible for implementing "self-government" were appointed directly by the Nationalist government from among candidates who could demonstrate loyalty to the Nationalist party and familiarity with the Three Principles of the People, that is, from among those who could be said to have undergone an appropriate form of "self-awakening" (*zijue*).[67]

The contrasting attitudes of Chen and the Nationalists toward federation and self-government highlight two of the most contentious issues of the Nationalist Revolution: the place of the province in the polity and the role of the gentry in local government. Disagreement over the political status of the province in the 1920s arose partly from tensions inherited from the old imperial administrative system and partly from the democratic reform movement of the late empire. In the earlier democratic movement, the political unit of self-government was neither the nation nor a particular social constituency but a geographical unit corresponding to county, department, prefecture, and province. These units marked the internal borders of the administrative system of the empire and had been kept under close surveillance by imperial officials determined to prevent the development of affinity between local administration and local interest. The same units were patrolled by champions of "feudal" autonomy who looked upon the local administrative unit as a bulwark against the arbitrary authority of an absolute monarchy. In debate between these rival schools of statecraft, the idea of local self-rule was presented as an alternative system of imperial administration rather than of self-government. Supporters of "feudalism," in particular, defended self-rule as a novel administrative device for transmitting information and instructions up and down the imperial network with greater efficiency and effect than the centralized bureaucratic system.[68] In consequence, few political theorists working within the feudal framework seem to have worried unduly whether local elites were recruited or delegated, dragooned or elected into imperial administration, so long as they were local and so long as they worked effectively.

In time, however, the campaign for administrative reform at the local level spilled over into a wider campaign for more fundamental democratic reforms among local elites themselves. As Min Tu-ki, a historian of the *fengjian* system, has observed: "The initial proposal of having native people deal with the affairs of their own provinces gradually developed into an argument for local self-government, centering around the local parliaments, with the gentry class as the core." [69] The gentry had long dealt with local affairs, but its contribution to the welfare of communities and to the stability of the imperial state was neither formalized in statute nor given institutional acknowledgment. In the late empire, the prospect of local self-government offered the gentry a place in the formal apparatus of state and a measure of the recognition and rewards that its members felt they deserved and that, toward the end of the nineteenth century, they began to demand with increasing boldness.

The province emerged as the significant domain of the gentry over the last decade of imperial rule. The provincial gentry was the beneficiary of two distinct but related processes, one of political devolution and the other of political evolution. The late Qing reforms devolved power from the center to the province and at the same time assisted in centralizing power from the locality to the province. This provincial nexus was strengthened in the wake of the 1911 revolution, when newly established provincial institutions grew increasingly jealous of their autonomy from the center and yet refused to fall captive to local power structures. Similar developments were taking place among local civic associations. Though provincial political institutions and civic associations cultivated allegiance to the province as a community—and at a higher level of abstraction than village or lineage—they directed loyalties higher still, to the national polity. Regional associations of merchants (*huiguan*), of fellow townspeople and provincials (*tongxianghui*), of itinerant workers, and of students were as likely to heighten consciousness of the national community as of distinctly provincial ones. The first provincial study associations were set up in the imperial capital itself in the 1890s, to take advantage of parochial networks among senior officials in Beijing, and the many provincial associations that sprang up over the following decades were generally committed to the defense of the realm.[70] The provincialization of social and political life was not antithetical to nationalism, in John Fincher's estimation, but "transitional" to its development.[71]

Friction between federalists and centralists in the Nationalist Revolution represented competing attempts to promote this transition from regional institutions to national ones. Circumstances had changed in the interim. Warlords sought national unity as earnestly as national revolutionaries did, but the slow pace of integration of county, provincial, and national political institutions over the period tested the patience of many Nationalists. Warlord politics lent weight to the claim that the province had become more an impediment than an aid to the development of a unified national polity. To the federalist argument that provincial autonomy was a first step toward the independence of the country, the Nationalists replied that national unity was a precondition for provincial autonomy. Such was their position at the outset of the Nationalist Revolution: "No single province can maintain true freedom and independence," announced the First Congress of the Nationalist party in 1924, "so long as the whole nation is not yet free and independent." [72]

In the 1920s, the province earned additional authority as a site of democratic agitation, because only provincial governments could raise armies on a scale to resist the inroads of a central government such as the Nationalists had in mind. Warlord armies supplied federalists with their most potent arguments for retaining provincial autonomy and offered Nationalist revolutionaries the most cogent of reasons for downgrading the province in the hierarchy of political places. There was more at stake here than provincial chauvinism and national self-aggrandizement. Chen Jiongming's armies formed a bold line around Guangdong, setting up a barrier against the incorporation of smaller local units into a centralizing administrative system. Chen wished to defend the principle of local self-government against the inroads of the central administrative state by defending his province, while at the same time demonstrating his commitment to local self-government by conducting the most successful local elections to have been held in any part of the country to that time.

As a consequence of local elite interest in self-government, the conflict between the Nationalists and Chen Jiongming rapidly developed into a conflict between an expanding centralist state and local elite resistance. The Nationalist Revolution made powerful social enemies. Indeed, one source of "class struggle" lay in this conflict between a centralizing state and local resistance. On the Nationalist side, the intensification of political struggle with entrenched social elites was illustrated over the course of the revolution in subtle changes that found their way into the definition of the enemy in official party documents. The word "class," for example, was used to identify the enemy in the declarations issued at the close of both the First and the Second Nationalist Party Congress in January 1924 and 1926, but with significantly different inflections. The first declaration defined the enemy as warlords and imperialists, which it termed "special classes harmful to farmers and labourers." The second declaration expanded the "class" of warlords and imperialists to embrace "bureaucrats," "local bullies," and the "comprador class." [73] This elaboration on the social character of the enemy came about not through Communist infiltration of the movement (which undoubtedly occurred) but chiefly through the intensification of political struggle consequent on the growing reach of the Nationalist state. Urban compradors were defined as agents of imperialism despite their prominent role in the early nationalist movement because they led the defense of urban civic associations against the demands of the Nationalist state. The rural gentry was counted feudal despite its pioneering role in promoting democratic "self-government" because feudalism was equated with the assertion of local autonomy from the Nationalist state.[74]

In time, the term "self-government" was abandoned in favor of "local administration" in Nationalist publications. By the early 1920s, federalists were framing their arguments in the rhetoric of popular sovereignty, and centralists in the language of unified national administration.[75] But the two terms were not mutually exclusive. The Nationalist party continued to use the term "self-government" to refer to local party appointees and party-affiliated mass associations in the Nationalist Revolution. In 1926, however, the Nationalist government finally abandoned the term "self-government" in favor of local administration when the Guangdong provincial government announced plans to open the Personnel Training Institute for Local Administration in Guangdong. It then dissolved the existing Self-Government Personnel Training Institute on the pretext that the two schools were "the same in nature." [76] The choice of title for the college was, however, no trifling matter. Local administration and self-government only became the "same in nature" once the tension between the two—which had characterized the democratic movement from its inception in the late Qing—had been overcome. That is to say, local self-government finally yielded to local administration when the function of local elites was reduced to administering the national state rather than participating in government. The Nationalist Revolution of the 1920s started out as a political revolution against imperialism and feudalism, but ended up a social revolution directed against the social foundations of the movement for local autonomy.

From Political to Social Revolution

The pattern of this development seems to have come as a surprise to many of the revolutionaries, not least to the Communists, who put a great deal of effort into planning a limited political revolution. The term "Nationalist Revolution" (*Guomin geming*) was coined by Comintern agent Henk Sneevliet and adopted by the Chinese Communist party in September 1922 as a gesture of solidarity with the Nationalist party, well in advance of the Nationalists' own use of the term.[77] The Communists were also the first to define the aims of the revolution: first, to "eliminate internal disorder, overthrow warlords and establish peace throughout the country," and second, to "reverse the oppression of international imperialism and achieve the complete independence of the Chinese race." [78] For all their astuteness and initiative, the Communists could not, however, plot the course of the revolution. Their enemies turned out to be more elusive than either the Communists or the Nationalists had anticipated. The revolution was carried along by its own political momentum and ended up confronting not the enemies of the nation but the enemies of the revolutionaries.

The first contingent of enemies was discovered within the ranks of the revolution itself, which set a precedent for identifying allies and enemies in the nation at large. Generally speaking, the criteria for identifying the enemy varied with the development of internal party struggle. In April 1924, Communist Secretary-General Chen Duxiu distinguished radical from conservative factions within the Nationalist party by the simple expedient of identifying party members' attitudes toward warlords and imperialism. Their class origins, or at least their attitudes toward the role of various social classes in the revolution, were declared irrelevant.[79] Chen's limited definition of radicals and conservatives was nevertheless quite explosive, for within the parameters of an "all-class" national revolution there were still plenty of Nationalists who objected to the blanket condemnation of warlords (for fear that it would alienate the party's warlord allies), and many others who feared that the militant tone of anti-imperialist rhetoric would make life difficult for the conduct of party work in China's foreign concessions and in the overseas colonies of the metropolitan powers.[80] Some Nationalists were uneasy about admitting Communists into their party; others were embarrassed by their party's close association with the Soviet Union; and within the Chinese Communist party, disputes erupted over the details of its cooperation with the Nationalists and over the high-handed attitude of the Communist International and its advisers in China. The rationale and conduct of the alliance was a source of controversy in Moscow as well, both within the Soviet Russian leadership and among the major institutions that claimed a legitimate interest in the matter, including the Comintern, Narkomindel, and Profintern.[81] Such misgivings and disputes were initially arbitrated around a common agreement on the goals of the Nationalist Revolution: to "eliminate internal disorder" and "reverse the oppression of international imperialism," or simply to "overthrow warlords and imperialism." It was only when these goals proved elusive that conflict within the movement was said to have its roots in social conflict within society at large—or in "class struggle."

Even the choice of imperialism and warlords as generic targets did not come easily. Both parties initially focused their attention exclusively on domestic political reunification, reflecting their antipathy to autonomous sources of local authority. As late as June 1922, the Communist party isolated internal enemies in the "feudal ruling class" of warlords and paid little heed to "imperialism." In fact, party documents all but ignored foreign imperialism until the party was prompted to take the sword against international capital by the

Communist International. This followed closely on reports from Moscow that the struggle against international imperialism was to take priority in bourgeois democratic revolutions in the colonial world. As a consequence, from mid-1922, the Communists began to rank imperialism alongside warlords as a separate and equal target of national revolution in China.[82] On the Nationalist side, warlords were counted responsible for overthrowing legitimately constituted party authority from the time of Yuan Shikai's presidency in 1913 to the rebellion of Chen Jiongming in 1922, so there was little difficulty accommodating the Communist slogan to "overthrow warlords" in Nationalist strategy. Yet in 1923, the Nationalist leader was reluctant to concede Communist claims that warlords maintained a *system* of rule facilitating imperialist penetration.

Opposition to imperialism made its way into the Nationalist movement over concerted opposition from within the party. The Nationalists were deeply divided on the issue. Some prominent members, including the theorist Dai Jitao, wrote passionately of the dangers of imperialism, and welcomed signs of public outrage over foreign intervention in China.[83] Overseas party members, however, were sensitive to the implications of such a policy for their position in the colonies and metropolitan centers targeted by the anti-imperialist movement, rightly fearing that they might become targets of imperialist reaction, or even victims of indigenous anti-Chinese pogroms in Indochina and Southeast Asia, where Comintern agents were stirring native opposition to foreign imperialism with equal vigor.[84] Overseas chapters of the party objected to the insertion of an anti-imperialist clause in the revised party program; the Guangdong branch of the party argued that if the clause were inserted "our party will never again win international sympathy, nor will Overseas Chinese party members be left with any place they can call their own." [85] In discussion leading up to the First Nationalist Party Congress in January 1924, Hu Hanmin proposed an amended resolution in which the party would announce its opposition to imperialism but refrain from specifying concrete demands or detailing measures for achieving them.[86] Despite pleas from overseas Chinese, Sun Yatsen would not bend. The loyalty of overseas members was jolted when Sun not only cast the colonial powers as enemies of the nation but began to cast doubt on the patriotism of overseas members themselves.[87] They returned his contempt by declining to reregister for membership in the reformed party and withholding their financial support for the party.[88]

The hope that Sun Yatsen might modify his position under pressure was not groundless. He had never denounced imperialism with the fervor of some of his comrades. In fact, Sun favored a policy of international assistance for China's national development and had spent much time in recent years corresponding with foreign friends and dignitaries in the hope of securing their support and assistance for his ambitious plans.[89] His language was less inflamma-

tory as well. Sun preferred the term "Great Powers" to "imperialism" because
it made allowance for discrimination among friendly and unfriendly powers.
Generally speaking, Sun rejected crude antiforeign sentiment and reserved his
strongest condemnation for domestic enemies, whom he held responsible for
foreign intervention in China's affairs.[90] In August 1923, he took exception to a
slogan raised at a radical students' congress that read "Resist the Great Powers
abroad and overthrow the warlords at home!" arguing that "in my view these
two problems cannot be discussed in the same breath . . . for if the home government is good then foreign relations present no problem." [91] To Sun's mind,
warlords and Great Powers were related only in the sense that warlords were
not up to the difficult task of handling complex foreign relations. Good government meant benign international relations.

To the chagrin of overseas Chinese activists, Sun abruptly changed his
mind in the autumn of 1923. The issue was already in balance when Sun opened
a dialogue with Soviet Russia while keeping open his options for securing
help from Britain, Germany, and the United States. He was partly persuaded to
throw in his lot with the Russians when the British, Germans, and Americans
turned down his appeal.[92] But it was the Customs Surplus Affair that finally
convinced him of the need to "overthrow imperialism." The Affair began
with a formal note from Sun to the diplomatic corps in Beijing on 5 September 1923, requesting a share of the revenue collected by the foreign-controlled
Maritime Customs Service. Sun's intention was to deprive the Beijing government of a portion of the customs revenue and divert it to his use in Guangzhou.
The request was not unreasonable in light of the Great Powers' claim that the
revenue was collected on behalf of the legitimate government of China. In
fact, E. H. Carr, then third secretary of the Far Eastern department of the Foreign Office, conceded that it was "outrageous that all the revenues collected
under foreign control should go to the unrepresentative and worthless Peking
government." There was, Carr minuted, "a certain basis of justification for
the Canton claim." [93] Whitehall was not persuaded and refused to comply with
Sun's request. Sun then addressed a note of demand announcing his intention
to seize the Canton customs by force "if necessary." The diplomatic corps responded with an impressive demonstration of naval power in Guangzhou Harbor that succeeded in deterring the immediate threat at the cost of incurring
an even greater one.[94] The battle lost, Sun retired to prepare for a protracted
war against "imperialism" and turned to Russian advisers for moral support.
Mikhail Borodin, chief of the Soviet Russian delegation in Guangzhou, drafted
a political program committing the Nationalist party to "overthrow imperialism and overthrow warlords," which was subsequently incorporated into the
declaration of the First National Party Congress in January 1924, with Sun
Yatsen's assent.[95]

Moscow Communists were also instrumental in drawing the connection between warlord-based regionalism on the one hand and feudalism as a social formation on the other. Early Chinese Marxists, we noted, focused chiefly on the regional political aspects of warlord rule in their analysis of Chinese feudalism.[96] The idea that feudalism was also an extensive social formation was introduced through Lenin and the Communist International—first in the form of Lenin's theses on the national and colonial questions, and later in successive manifestos and strategic blueprints issuing from Comintern headquarters between 1922 and 1927. Precisely what constituted this feudal social order was a matter of dispute. One aspect of this dispute long recognized in studies of China's revolution was the identity and relationship among the social agents who were to come together in the alliance for national liberation. For many contemporaries, a more pressing problem than locating friends for the revolution was ensuring that one was not branded an enemy, or target, of the revolution. Given the flexibility of Lenin's vision, this was not an easy task.

In Comintern thinking, the native social target of a national bourgeois-democratic revolution was the social order of "feudal forces." Lenin declined to identify the feudal enemies of national revolutions in every particular case, but he did enunciate a few general principles. In the 1920 theses on the colonial and agrarian questions, he located the social base of feudalism among agrarian landlords, particularly among the owners of large estates, or Junkers.[97] The greater struggle to emancipate peasants from landlord oppression was not to be confused with the struggle against feudalism in this sense, understood as a limited struggle against the owners of feudal estates. Lenin was proposing only that a minority of large landlords were "feudal remnants" and should be singled out for attack and expropriation. As his health declined following a series of crippling strokes in mid-1922, it fell to others to interpret his theses.

The Comintern attempted to relate the socioeconomic features of feudalism to the political situation in each national case. In China, few feudal lords still ruled over their domains, serfs and slaves were historical anomalies, and there was a healthy tradition of private ownership and trade in land. Lenin's concept of feudalism was then stripped of much of its descriptive power when reference to feudatories, lords, serfs, and inalienable rights in property were diluted in Comintern debate and revision on China. To retain its analytical utility, the model of the feudal social order was modified to embrace virtually all precapitalist (and premodern) forms of landlord-peasant social and economic systems in states, such as China, held to be ripe for national revolution. The criterion for identifying feudal forces was then reduced to a simple evaluation of social groups and individuals who opposed national revolution *itself*.

The Comintern was sufficiently flexible to concede that raw class status was an inadequate criterion for distinguishing friends and enemies in national

revolutions. At its Fourth Congress in November 1922, the Comintern attempted to apply Lenin's general pronouncements on the social enemies of
national liberation struggles. The "Directives on the Application of the 1920
Agrarian Theses" had already set an important precedent for flexible interpretation of agrarian feudalism by noting that whether or not a landlord class
should be singled out for struggle in the national phase of revolution depended
upon the position landlords adopted toward imperialism.[98] Here the Comintern
established the cardinal principle that the political attitudes of people toward
a national enemy counted more in national revolution than positions in relations of production. Another criterion for identifying friends and enemies was
Lenin's remark on the ownership of large estates. In its 1922 "Theses on the
Eastern Question," the Comintern identified the domestic enemy of national
revolution as feudal large landowners, and confirmed Lenin's call for the expropriation of their properties. These twin criteria—political attitudes and
ownership of "estates"—were considered closely related in practice because
"alien imperialism" makes the "feudal" elite an "instrument of its rule." [99]
The Comintern explicitly identified the feudal class in native Chinese society
as the "Tuchuns," or warlords, and equated them with the Junkers of the German states, thus elevating them to the status of a social class. This perfunctory
accreditation of class status to a political and military target—the warlords
of China—was initially held to satisfy and to exhaust the category of social
enemy of China's national revolution. Even then, warlords were enemies only
incidentally on account of their positions in the relations of production, and
chiefly because they opposed a national revolutionary movement of the kind
the Comintern had in mind for China.

   Within China, it took some time before the star-spangled military officers
in command of warlord armies could plausibly be counted representatives of a
greater social order. Few made such connections before the Nationalist Revolution got under way. Even so, warlords were targeted at the outset not for
their part in suppressing peasants but because they committed treason against
the state by carving it up among themselves. If they represented anything at all
(apart from self-interest), it was thought to be the alien force of foreign capital
in its highest stage of imperialism.[100] Their role in "representing" the landlord
class, retarding the growth of the bourgeoisie, and hindering the operation of
liberal democratic institutions came some way down the list of warlord crimes.
It was enough that they seemed to be dividing the national cake and surrendering it, on a platter, to foreigners.

   So in June 1922, some months before the Comintern deliberated on the
Eastern question at its Fourth Congress, the Chinese Communists defined the
social character of the national revolution in their "First Manifesto on the Current Situation" as "a struggle of the bourgeoisie against feudal lords and the

system of feudal economy." They forswore the opportunity to elaborate on the character of the feudal economy and proceeded instead to limit the task of the revolutionary "bourgeoisie" to "an active struggle against feudalism in the form of the military." [101] In fact, the party leadership chose to equate the social with the military struggle and to identify feudalism explicitly with warlords. Foreshadowing the Comintern's elevation of warlords to the status of a social class, Chinese Communists presumed that an attack upon warlords was an attack upon the *social* foundations of Chinese feudalism. Over the following year, the party interpreted the Comintern Executive Committee's "Instructions to the Third Congress of the Chinese Communist Party" to mean that it should push ahead with the "agrarian revolution of the peasantry against the survivals of feudalism" and proceed with the "confiscation of land" as an instruction to confiscate warlord property.[102] China's Communists, like the Comintern, were too impatient to get on with the job of dealing the final death blow to "warlords and imperialism" in Asia to do justice to their principled belief in the social character of political revolutions.

The maxim that warlords and imperialism were enemies of the nation was sufficiently flexible to accommodate wider social enemies as the revolution progressed. As we have seen, the attack on feudalism entailed uprooting everything that smacked of locality, tradition, and superstition, while their opposition to imperialism threatened foreign ties in business, religion, education, public health, journalism, and communications, which had come to be counted part of everyday life among wide sections of the Chinese community by the 1920s. The Nationalists announced at their First Congress that they would spare no sympathy for people who stood between the revolutionaries and their warlord and imperialist enemies. "Those who betray the nation, those who give their loyalty to the imperialists or to the warlords, will be permitted neither freedom nor rights." [103] In effect, any institution or group of people that was reluctant to take up the invitation to attack "feudalism and imperialism," or was bold enough to challenge the right of the revolutionaries to decide the friends and enemies of the nation on its behalf, could conceivably be counted an ancilliary of feudal interests or a lackey of imperialist ones. In cases where groups were organized around social interests, such interests could be evaluated by political criteria as well. Chambers of commerce, craft unions, local benevolent societies, church and community groups not only would forfeit their "freedoms and rights" if they failed to support the revolution but would tarnish as well the social interests they were held to "represent."

At this point the Communists and Nationalists parted company. The Communists were prepared to target social interest in the name of class struggle, but the Nationalists preferred to "represent" and to discipline social interest through the party's internal structures. Sun Yatsen, we have noted, frequently bemoaned the failure of Chinese society to organize itself around national goals, and from the 1920s his propaganda advisers began promoting the idea of "partifying the masses" as an alternative to independent social organization. The party itself had a particular interest in this proposal. In February 1920, the editor of the *Shanghai Republican Daily*, Ye Chucang, foresaw that a revolutionary movement that lurched from issue to issue without disciplined organization or clear goals could achieve neither the mass nor the movement required of a political revolution. The chief fault of "mass politics," Ye argued, was the absence of a "clear and universal ideology" such as the Three Principles of the People. Ideology needed to be installed in disciplined sectoral institutions before it could possibly take effect.[104] The party journal *Awaken* continued the theme in its New Year's issue in January 1922, with publication of Li Hanwei's article "Why Do the Chinese People Lack the Capacity to Organize?" Li echoed Sun Yatsen's refrain that the people of China were a "loose sheet of sand." [105] By 1923, Ye Chucang had announced confidently that the Nationalists had at last begun to supply the kind of mass organization that the nation required. In "The Massification of the Nationalist Party and the Nationalist Partification of the Masses," written to commemorate the third anniversary of Sun Yatsen's accession to the extraordinary presidency in 1920, Ye boasted of Nationalist achievements in "partifying the masses." Education alone could not lay an adequate foundation for building a new China, he argued. Nationalist party initiatives in mass organization, on the other hand, were yielding results because they tailored political education to mass organization. The party was building New China not by educating it but by "partifying" it, that is, by educating people through directed participation in mass party organizations.[106]

The sympathy for mass organization shown by Ye Chucang was widely shared in Nationalist propaganda circles. When propaganda officer Shao Yuanchong set out the reasons for the failure of intellectuals to "awaken" the masses in January 1923, he could not bring himself to blame the students or their patrons in the party, whose planning and reasoning he considered beyond reproach. The failure to awaken the masses was attributed instead to the shortcomings of the people themselves, who were counted conservative, indolent, shortsighted, indecisive, unreliable, and incapable of distinguishing right from wrong. When "planning for the happiness of the great majority of the masses," concluded Shao, the Nationalist party should compensate for the glaring deficiencies in "mass psychology" by herding the people into mass organizations. At the outset of the Nationalist Revolution, party planners were already contemplating a corporatist strategy that would displace community organization in civil society with more compliant mass organizations under Nationalist party supervision, the better to awaken the people.[107]

Although the Nationalists acknowledged differences among social inter-

ests, they were reluctant—unlike the Communists—to admit to potentially antagonistic contradictions between social interests and the national interest.[108]
A national revolution was a patriotic cause, Sun announced, and as all Chinese
were patriots (or at least would become so when they had finally awakened
under Nationalist tutelage), the only domestic enemies of the revolution were
likely to be found among disgruntled militarists and bureaucrats left over from
the Qing.[109] No identifiable sector of Chinese society would be found con-
sorting with them. Ideally, sectional interests would correspond with peoples'
interests as citizens, or the national interest, and if these happened to conflict, then sectoral interest would willingly yield to the national interest. Sun
and his followers proposed that the Chinese people should be taught to act as
"national citizens" (*guomin*)—a term enshrined in the name of the party (*Guomindang*)—before acting as self-interested parties.[110]

Party discipline and mass organization were intended to defuse conflict
among social interests and at the same time to prevent tension between sectional interests and the state from erupting in open confrontation. That is to
say, mass organization and mass mobilization were intended to dispel rather
than to generate social conflict. Groups with distinct social interests were to
lend uniform support to the revolution in the form of "mass power" (*qunli*).[111]
Sun claimed without a hint of irony that he had learned this lesson from the
October Revolution in Russia. His discovery of the Russian revolution was a
discovery not of the revolutionary potential of class struggle but of the cohesive potential of disciplined mass power. Only enemies of the nation needed
to fear the masses, he argued, and as the nation was the mass of the Chinese
"race" (*minzu*), no sector of society need fear the Nationalist movement. Sun
fully expected that the entire country would rise up, as one, and carry the
Nationalists to power.[112] People were to be segregated and organized into distinct social categories of workers, peasants, merchants, women, and youth, and
taught to reconcile their differences and sublimate their sectional interests to
those of the revolutionary government, which claimed to be above "special"
interest.[113] The party's social movements were organized in order *not* to function in pursuit of sectoral interest.[114]

Still, the differences between the Communists and Nationalists are easily
exaggerated. In putting forward his ideological and tactical resolutions to a
problem that might have led to conflict between social interests and the state,
Sun Yatsen drew comfort from Lenin, from the Communist International, and
from the Chinese Communist party. There had long been a tendency in Chinese radical circles to downplay the potential for social conflict in assessments
of China's national revolution. In 1920 Li Dazhao put forward a theory of China
as a "proletarian nation" in a world dominated by capitalist imperialism. The
corollary to Li's argument was that the people of China—with the exception

of a few warlords, their bureaucratic staff, and the comprador agents of imperialism — all stood on the side of national revolution. Once Comintern agent Henk Sneevliet had presented the Comintern position regarding the bourgeois-democratic nature of the Chinese revolution to the Communist party in August 1922, Li Dazhao's thinking on the all-class nature of the revolution made him one of the most enthusiastic supporters of the Comintern line among Chinese Communists.[115] There seems at the outset to have been very little disagreement between the Nationalists and the Communists on the likely extent of mass support for their revolution.

To be sure, the Communists considered national revolution a partial revolution, on completion of which they would launch a new struggle for proletarian socialist revolution. They took on faith the class nature of all revolutions and interpreted this general principle in the case of China's national revolution to mean a struggle of the bourgeoisie and the proletarian masses against the feudal social order. But, we have seen, their actual identification of the feudal social order was so narrow at the outset that it excluded all of Chinese society proper from among the targets of the revolution. The only domestic enemies of the revolution appeared to be warlords, who were duly assigned a feudal class status of their very own.

Nor did the Communists' belief that this was to be a partial revolution undermine their determination to see it through to completion. Debate within the Communist party over whether or not to enter into a united front with the Nationalists revolved not around questions of the possibility of a socially cohesive national revolution but around the advisability of Communist participation and the form that it should take. Secretary-General Chen Duxiu went so far as to suggest that an "all-class" revolution was the *only* kind of revolution possible in China at this time.[116] Chen did not query the likely involvement of the bourgeoisie, and even landlords, in a national drive against warlords and imperialists. In fact, this was one consideration that made the prospect of a united front so unattractive to many of his comrades, for it ill fitted a party claiming to champion the cause of the oppressed to be seen allying with wealthy bankers and rural landlords.

As with the Nationalists, there was also a firm conviction among the Communists and their Comintern advisers that if social interest conflicted with national interest, meaning the progress of the revolution itself, then the social must yield to the national. This was an axiom of the revolution, a parameter that set the limits for debate within the Communist party and with its advisers. There was some division over how it should be interpreted, but very little dispute about the principle itself. Even in the case of social classes for which the Communist party had little sympathy, it was hoped that class members would act as national citizens and not as social actors on behalf of sectional interests.

Yun Daiying, a Communist who never sang the virtues of the Chinese bourgeoisie, learned to confine his criticism of that class to its behavior as a body of *citizens*. Merchants would declare themselves counterrevolutionary not by oppressing the working class but by ignoring the interests of their fellow citizens, that is, the interests of the nation as defined by the state.

Merchants grow rich by assisting foreign capitalists to oppress other Chinese citizens (*guomin*). But in the Nationalist Revolution it is of course to be hoped that their consciences will awaken to the need to sacrifice their own narrow, immediate personal interests and consider the welfare of all Chinese citizens—even if there is little prospect of this.[117]

Yun's expectations that the bourgeoisie would abandon its "narrow, immediate personal interests" and act as national citizens for the sake of the Nationalist Revolution were not, admittedly, very sanguine. Yet the revolution was launched into the world with high expectations precisely because its advocates insisted that national unity *could* be achieved without generating significant tension between bourgeois interests and the national good. No eggs were to be broken for this omelet. The revolutionaries' relationship with various sectors in society was nevertheless qualified by their intention to expand state capacity, to work toward specific political goals, and to use mass mobilization to achieve them. Friends and enemies of the revolution would declare themselves by the sides they elected to take in the contest for state power between the revolutionaries (representing the nation), the feudal warlords, and imperialism.[118] The definition of the national interest could, then, plausibly exclude sections of society that did not happen to share the same view of state goals from citizenship, and from membership in the nation.

Communist assessments of rural society followed a similar trajectory. In 1923 the Communist party overlooked the significance of the land revolution in a movement to overthrow the feudal social order, and instead mooted the idea of organizing and mobilizing peasants to consolidate the mass base of the revolution.[119] Here they echoed Sun Yatsen's understanding of the role of peasants in mass revolution; at first, neither party integrated the "interests" of the peasant class into a political strategy for targeting the landlord class as an enemy of the nation. The excessive rents, abuse of customary rights, and unbridled local authority of the landlord class counted far less in early Communist strategic thinking than did the potential value of landlords in an alliance with their tenants against warlords.

The first call for peasant participation in the antifeudal struggle through land reform was issued after the arrival of Soviet emissary Mikhail Borodin in Guangzhou toward the end of 1923. Even then, the incentive for land reform was to rally popular defenses against the "feudal" class enemy besieging the gates of the city, the federalist dreamer Chen Jiongming.[120] Eight months later, Communist publicists in Shanghai were still eager to dispute the claim that warlords could possibly enjoy a measure of support in their local communities. In June 1924, a propagandist writing for *The Guide Weekly* challenged the truth of reports that a local warlord had recently received widespread popular acclaim as he passed through his territories in Anhui. Others trumpeted the potential of landlord popular militia (*mintuan*) to defend their communities from warlord aggression.[121] In the case of local resistance in Hunan against intrusion by a warlord from Shaanxi Province, prominence was given to the role of landlord popular militia in leading resistance to the Shaanxi army units. At this stage of the revolution, there seems to have been little hesitation in concluding that "we should recognize the importance of [landlord] popular militia in the movement to overthrow warlords." [122]

The role of the popular militia and of landlords in general was soon to undergo drastic revision. In June 1924, a peasant-movement activist working in the East River region of Guangdong penned a brief letter to *The Guide* to make a simple but telling point. Peng Pai cited a candid comment from the lips of Chen Jiongming: "The gentry and I still depend on one another for our survival." [123] Some sections of society, it seemed, *did* cheer warlords in the streets, and local militia were often in cahoots with warlords to suppress the mass movement. So, it seemed, Chen Jiongming could not be removed from Guangdong without confronting entrenched local interests. The Nationalists undertook two expeditions against Chen in 1925 before finally routing him in November. Observers noted with alarm that, between the two campaigns, gentry militia acted in concert with Chen to claw back much of the authority transferred by the Nationalist Revolutionary Army to peasant associations and local governing bodies, and landlords turned their militia to Chen's use to preserve the authority they had enjoyed under him.[124] Such behavior appeared to confirm an emerging left-wing consensus that the gentry formed the social base of warlord power. Warlords were now held to "represent" entrenched social interests.

Events were to show that this was an oversimplification of the relationship between warlords and local elites. When the revolutionary army turned south, it encountered a very different situation in the counties where Chen Jiongming's warlord ally, Deng Benyin, was feared and despised by local elites no less than by merchants and peasants. Southern civic associations had petitioned Chen Jiongming to remove Deng in 1923, but to their annoyance Chen ignored their request and petitioned the Beijing government to confirm Deng's appointment.[125] So in the southern counties, prominent local landlords, peasants, and merchants all came to the Nationalists' assistance in 1925 and 1926 to chase Deng from southern Guangdong. Merchants refused to pay his taxes, peasants pursued his troops into the marshes, and landlords set their militia against him on Hainan Island.[126] On this campaign, unlike the Eastern Expeditions, elite behavior appeared to confirm Sun Yatsen's prediction that warlords could be displaced by concerted action on the part of citizens without regard to the social problems that might otherwise have divided them. But the lesson came too late.

Even where the behavior of local elites suggested they did not form the social base of warlord power, state expansion now justified concerted action against them. As had often been noted by Sun Yatsen, defeating warlords on the field of battle was only half the struggle. Not until the people liberated from warlord control came to welcome Nationalist intervention in their communities would the revolution be considered complete.[127] On this point, southern elites were no more cooperative than their eastern counterparts: they resisted the imposition of an alien Nationalist administration in the region following the military campaigns.[128] The difference between elite attitudes toward the antiwarlord struggle in eastern and southern Guangdong was at base a tactical one, for in both cases attitudes were shaped by a concern to preserve local autonomy from outside interference, whether this took the form of warlord or Nationalist authority. By resisting Nationalist state expansion, they showed they were as counterrevolutionary as warlords and, at least for the purpose of revolutionary mobilization, that they should be lumped together with them. In confronting a social elite, along with a dreaming warlord, the revolutionaries confronted the limits of Sun Yatsen's dream of cohesive nation-building.

The assumption that social and national interests were reconcilable in the city and in the countryside was seriously challenged when the revolutionaries traveled south to Guangdong in 1923 and 1924 to set up a new kind of revolutionary state. A social revolution against feudalism then emerged as an offshoot of the political revolution against warlord power, as a desideratum of state and party-building in Guangdong on completion of the Southern and Eastern expeditions. Class struggle served as a potent rationale for restructuring local administration under a new party-state rather than reforming it under a federal and liberal democratic one. Social revolution, in other words, entered China's national revolution at the invitation of a centralizing party-state. This was not as Sun Yatsen had intended. But when he deflated Chen Jiongming's dream of a federation of self-governing provinces, Sun eased the way for others to puncture his own dream of a unified, sovereign, and socially united national state.

5

ONE STATE, ONE PARTY
Liberal Politics and the Party-State

> Do you know out of what the German Empire arose? Out of dreams,
> songs, fantasies and black-red-gold [flags]. . . . Bismarck merely shook
> the tree that fantasies had planted.
>
> Theodor Herzl, 1895[1]

> You all know that our [parliamentary] representatives have all become
> mere "swine."
>
> Sun Yatsen, 1924[2]

One day in August 1924, a day not commemorated on any calendar, Sun Yatsen
ordered that the five-bar flag of the Republic of China be lowered from the flag-
poles and mastheads of all units under his command in southern China. Within
weeks the Republican flag was lowered from party and government offices in
Guangzhou, and on New Year's Day 1925, the municipal chief of police began
issuing fines to private citizens who persisted in flying the Republican colors.[3]
In place of the Republican flag, Sun Yatsen raised a bright red one, bearing in
its top inner corner the distinctive Nationalist motif of a white sun against a
blue sky that was known colloquially as the "Blue Sky and White Sun" (*qing-
tian bairi*). This change of flags marked neither a change of government nor a
change of leadership in the Nationalist movement, but it signaled a sea change
in the history of the Republic of China. It foreshadowed the disappearance of
the five-bar national flag of the liberal Republic at all public ceremonies in
China and its replacement by two national flags, each identified exclusively
with a particular political party.

The five colors of the original Republican flag, layered in horizontal stripes
of identical width, represented the five major nationalities that its designers
imagined made up the citizens of the Republic: red for the Han, yellow for the
Manchurian, blue for the Mongolian, white for the Tibetan, and black for the
Moslem community of China.[4] It was certainly not the only flag or pennant
draped from poles and podiums over the first decade of the Republic. Long before the Nationalist Revolution got under way, Sun Yatsen's parties identified
themselves by unfurling a partisan flag alongside the Republican flag at party

gatherings. Lu Haodong, a member of the Revive China Society (*Xingzhong-hui*), had laid out the design for the Blue Sky and White Sun (although without the red backing that distinguished the Nationalists' national flag) shortly before surrendering his life to the revolution in an abortive uprising in Guangzhou in 1895. Sun Yatsen adopted the symbol for his party as a mark of respect for Lu. Still, the five-bar flag was recognized as the only national flag. Before 1924, all parties and factions flew their partisan banners as pennants accompanying the five-bar flag to signal their loyalty to the liberal Republic.

Nor was Sun's pennant the only one to fly alongside the Republican one. Many groups that had participated in the 1911 revolution (and some that had not) sought to claim credit for the achievement by aligning their own pennants with the national flag. Another that often accompanied the five-bar flag de-picted nine stars surrounding a circle and enfolding the traditional symbols for yin and yang.[5] This nine-star insignia was unfurled on 10 October 1911 by mili-tary units involved in the Wuchang Uprising, and later resurfaced among the insignia of the Central China revolutionary faction when that faction waved the pennant in competition with the Blue Sky and White Sun of Sun Yatsen. Huang Xing initially favored a flag bearing the symbol of the mythical "well-field" system of village agriculture. When his design failed to win support, he coupled the five-bar flag of the Republic with the nine-star flag of Wuchang (in preference to the Blue Sky and White Sun) to mobilize resistance against Presi-dent Yuan Shikai in the Second Revolution of 1913.[6] Another pennant often used by army units in the early Republic depicted eighteen stars for the eigh-teen provinces arranged in two concentric circles. It flew alongside the Blue and White at the tenth anniversary celebrations of the Republic in Guangzhou, when both were flanked by a grand pair of Republican flags.[7] The pennant favored by Chen Jiongming before he broke away from the Nationalist gov-ernment in Guangzhou pictured a well-field grid similar to that used by Huang Xing.[8] There were many partisan pennants, always distinctive and invariably mattering a great deal to the partisans who gathered beneath them, even when it was not entirely clear what they were meant to signify.[9]

The fate of each flag served as a kind of talisman of the fortunes of each party in the heated politics of the early Republic. Sun Yatsen attributed partisan magnetism to the Blue Sky and White Sun. When the first Republican admin-istration assigned partisan insignia to units of the armed forces in recognition of the contributions of political associations and military units to the revolu-tion, Sun sought appropriate recognition of his own party flag. It was assigned by the Senate to the Republican Navy. This gesture, Sun felt, accounted for the exceptional loyalty that the navy displayed toward him in the civil wars that followed. Sun secured the support of the navy, under Chen Biguang, in July 1917, when he attempted to establish a national government in Guangzhou to rival that of Duan Qirui in Beijing. The navy escorted Sun's retinue to Guang-zhou.[10] But apart from the Blue Sky and White Sun flag of Sun's faction, none of the other approved partisan insignia was seriously put forward as a substitute for the national flag.

Many of Sun's colleagues remained loyal to the Republican flag. In February 1912 the Republican flag flew over the Provisional Senate Building in Nanjing where the Senate sat and deliberated on the constitution. Between 1913 and 1916, when Yuan Shikai outlawed the parliamentary Nationalist party (as distinct from Sun Yatsen's Chinese Nationalist party, which dates from 1919), the Republican flag served as the insignia for Yuan's government on the one side and for Huang Xing's Counter-Yuan Army on the other. After President Yuan Shikai died in 1916, President Duan Qirui reinstated liberal representative government under the Republican constitution, but then barred the entrance to the National Assembly in Beijing with armed guards standing beneath massive Republican flags. Angered by Duan's imperious behavior, the leaders of rival parliamentary factions retreated to Guangzhou, where they joined Sun Yatsen in setting up an alternative national government under the same flag that had barred them from meeting in Beijing. In 1919 the five-barred flag adorned the hall in Shanghai where peace talks were conducted between the rival northern and southern governments. And out on the streets of Shanghai, students marched under the five-bar flag of the Republic to declare their loyalty to "science" and "democracy" in the May Fourth movement.[11]

Sun himself was more equivocal. He passed the years 1918 and 1919 in Shanghai, writing and consulting with comrades at his home in the French concession. When he returned to Guangzhou in triumphal procession in November 1920, he was carried along streets decked out with the five-bar flag of the Republic and, in the course of the following year, rode at the head of an armed column from Guangdong to Guangxi Province under the Republican flag.[12] Significantly, Sun was mustering forces for an attack on the national capital under his alternative national flag when he was unseated by Chen Jiongming and forced to flee Guangzhou in the summer of 1922.[13] He then employed mercenaries from Guangxi and Yunnan to defeat Chen Jiongming, and returned to enjoy his last great triumph in Guangzhou in January 1923. This was the last time he paraded under the Republican banner. Although the Nationalists had argued and fought under the five-bar flag of the Republic of China for over a decade, Sun was determined that he would meet his enemies under his own flag after the betrayal of Chen Jiongming.

In fact, Sun had never sat comfortably under the multiracial Republican flag. He made no contribution to the design of the flag before the revolution, when he consistently promoted monoracial unity, and in candid moments after the revolution he professed an intense distaste for it.[14] He believed that his Blue

Sky and White Sun—"drenched," as he put it, "by the blood of martyrs from the revolutionary party"—was far and away the best choice for a national flag. If the navy had steered a loyal course because it sailed under his colors, Sun reasoned in 1919, so the rest of the country had drifted off course because it had opted for the wrong flag.[15] Sun felt that the Republican flag betrayed the most fundamental principle of the revolution: racial unity. He never wavered from the conviction that in the 1911 revolution "the whole country finally awoke" to the "tyranny of an alien race." In the revolution of 1911, he told a public gathering in December 1921, "the authority to rule China was placed back in the hands of Han people and China's territories were all bestowed on the Han race."[16] As the revolution was a victory by one race over another, he mused in 1918, why did the victors celebrate the vanquished race among the stripes of their triumphal flag? The Republican flag obscured the overwhelming achievement of the Han race in overthrowing the "alien" Manchus:

When the Han race overthrew the political power of the Manchu Qing dynasty and the people of our country escaped the bondage of that alien race, the goal of nationalism was achieved at last. But then the strangest thing happened: just as the revolution succeeded, some bureaucrats took hold of the idea of a republic of five races made up of the Han, the Manchus, the Mongolians, the Moslems, and the Tibetans, and selected a five-color flag [devised by] some Qing general as the national flag of the Chinese Republic, with the five colors representing the Han, the Manchus, the Mongolians, the Moslems, and the Tibetans. Members of the revolutionary party took little notice and made use of this decrepit bureaucratic flag, abandoning the national flag of the Republic of China with its Blue Sky and White Sun designed by the first martyr of the Republic, Lu Haodong.[17]

Sun was convinced that he was steering the revolution back to its proper course in the autumn of 1924, when he lowered the "decrepit" five-bar flag of the Republic in Guangzhou and substituted the partisan flag of the Nationalist movement.

Coincidentally, the raising of the Blue and White in Guangzhou on 1 January 1925 signaled the onset of a concerted pogrom against descendants of the original Manchu Banners, who had been sent south to pacify Guangdong in the mid-seventeenth century. The Guangzhou Bannermen had lost their official positions with the fall of the empire, and the pension entitlements that had been extended by the Republican government lapsed long before the Nationalists came to power in the city. By the 1920s the local Manchu community was heavily dependent on small property inheritances. The authorities in Guangzhou isolated these properties in January 1925, for a program of property reregistration, punitive levies, and confiscations directed against the local Manchu community. Guangzhou Manchus were given until the end of January to pay a special levy of ¥25 per 100 square feet of property; on 12 February, 197

Manchu families received notices of eviction for failure to pay the tax.[18] By March, 3,000 Manchu holdings had been confiscated.[19]

Sun Yatsen was not keen on the Republican national anthem either.[20] "You might say it is the national anthem," he told a student audience in August 1923, "but I know it was promulgated by some bureaucrat or other. What meaning does it have [for us]?" [21] In fact, there were few precedents for "bureaucrats" to build upon. A few lines from poetry of the Warring States period show hints of patriotism—in relation to the state of Chu (Hunan)—and a couple of Tang poems touch marginally on national character. But there is nothing to match the nostalgic references to "national life" found in European and American anthems.[22] It was the Nationalist Revolution of the 1920s, not the Republican Revolution of 1911, that should determine the shape of the flag and the lyrics of the anthem. "Now is still a time of struggle. Let us not use the worthless national flag and anthem. Once peace has returned we can decide on them together, with all the worthy people of the country." [23] It was not, in the event, the people of China who decided the matter. On 24 January 1924, delegates to the First Nationalist Party Congress endorsed a motion for a new party anthem, on the model of the party flag, "which will one day serve as the national anthem of China." [24] The Republican national anthem was duly replaced with another that professed loyalty to a particular political party:

> The Three Principles of the People our party reveres,
> To found a republic, to advance to One World.
> Lead on comrades, as vanguards of the people,
> Don't bend to the elements, hold fast to your principles.
> Be earnest and brave, your country to save,
> Be faithful and loyal,
> One heart, one soul,
> One mind, one goal.[25]

Although discussion surrounding the flag and anthem was conducted on questions of principle, it touched intimately on Sun's personal standing in the party and the polity. Sun had tried on an earlier occcasion, in 1914, to replace the five-bar flag with the Nationalist flag in the insignia of the Chinese Revolutionary party (*Zhonghua gemingdang*).[26] This signaled much more than a change of livery for his party. In 1914, the new flag accompanied a new ritual for entry into the party that required all recruits to swear an oath of loyalty to Sun Yatsen in person. A number of his former colleagues declined.[27] Their distaste for the oath of personal loyalty was matched by a general reluctance to wave Sun's alternative national flag in China, where it was outlawed, or even abroad, where it was not.

Sun was reluctant to concede that the appeal of the five-bar flag to various factions and governments in the Republic demonstrated its resilience as a national symbol. This was, rather, proof of its weakness. The flag was tainted by association with the imperious style of President Yuan Shikai, and later through a series of notorious political deals that culminated in open bribery in the national elections of 1923. All the same, the Republican flag still represented in 1924 the liberal values expressed in the Provisional Constitution of 1912. But Sun was no longer interested in the redemptive powers of liberal politics. The flag was not, in his view, redeemed by those who died fighting Yuan Shikai under its colors, nor by any of the movements to protect the liberal constitution and promote the values of science, democracy, and individual liberties that had been proclaimed under it. As far as Sun was concerned, their allegiance to the five-bar flag condemned all of these movements to failure. In raising the flag and anthem of the partisan Nationalist movement to the status of national symbols, he declared his allegiance first to himself and second to a new kind of revolutionary politics. The distinctive flag of Nationalist China announced the arrival of a single-party state.

The Birth of the Party-State

Sun was initially quite discreet about his dislike for the Republican flag and went public only after his party's stake in liberal constitutional politics had fallen to its lowest ebb. Early in 1923 Sun began to distinguish clearly between "political" activity, in the liberal sense, and what he termed "party activity," which he thought aloof from politics. "Political activity is unreliable," he announced, "only party activity promises certain returns." [28] There is no denying that the year 1923 marked the nadir of liberal politics in the Republic.[29] When Sun spoke again of "party activity" toward the end of the year, he did not even bother to grace the liberal alternative with a mention—he spoke then of party activity and of military activity, but made no mention of political activity at all.[30] Months later, when he raised his Blue and White flag in place of the Republican one, Sun signaled an end to compromise with all political groups that were still happy to work within the framework of a liberal democratic polity. The party flag was to be converted into a national one by making the Nationalist party identical with the national state. The only scope for compromise or cooperation lay in others joining his party and helping it expand to the point where it was identical with the state, and where its membership was coextensive with the nation.

Sun had long proposed to "to govern the state through the party" (*yi dang zhi guo*), but now he was proposing rather more.[31] In his opening address to the First Nationalist Party Congress in January 1924, Sun explained that he no longer proposed to "govern" but to "build" the state through the party (*yi dang jian guo*):

At this point the state is in great disarray and society has regressed, so the responsibility of the revolutionary party at present must be first to establish the state. [We have] still not reached the point of governing the state. . . . At this moment the state foundations of the republic have yet to be consolidated. We must carry out more work and build the country once again before the state foundations of a republic can be consolidated.[32]

At a later session of the congress, Sun spoke in favor of founding a Nationalist government (*Goumin zhengfu*) in place of the Republican one, and employed the new term "build the state through the party" once again to clarify his position. The party was to duplicate the organization of the government and oversee its operations at every level.[33]

The assembled delegates to the congress were alert to the implication of Sun's attack on the Republic in this call for a new Nationalist state. Not all were persuaded by his arguments. Immediately after Sun had finished explaining why China needed a new Nationalist government, a delegate named Li Zirong rose to ask whether such a government should ever be allowed to see the light of day:

The first question to be resolved in relation to this proposal is whether or not a Nationalist government should be organized at all. . . . This question has very important implications. As I see it, if a government is to be organized it should be organized as the formal government of the Republic of China (*Zhonghua minguo*).[34]

Sun's loyal associate Liao Zhongkai intervened to point out that doubts of this magnitude were off the agenda. Still the doubters persisted. Delegates arose in succession to suggest that the word "Nationalist" be dropped from the title of any new government, until Mao Zedong, clearly impatient with his querulous new comrades in the Nationalist party, motioned to set the discussion in order and to bring the matter to a vote. The chairman called for a show of hands, the assembled delegates voted to combine the words "Nationalist" and "government," and the majority of delegates toasted the marriage of the party and the state over dinner that evening.[35]

Feelings were running high on a number of closely related issues. Some delegates felt that the more controversial decisions of the congress did not reflect the view of rank-and-file members. On the penultimate day of the congress a delegate from North America, Huang Jilu, proposed adopting a system of proportional representation to give voice to dissident opinion at the highest levels of the party. Huang was unhappy with many of the new directions in party policy arising out of the congress, but on this issue his argument went beyond particular questions of policy. Huang was concerned that rank-and-file opinion should find formal representation in the party organization. His reasoning challenged the rationale underlying the reorganization of the party along

Leninist lines and questioned the validity of Sun Yatsen's appeal in his opening speech for all party members to surrender their freedom to the party.[36] Where the party had gone wrong in the past, Sun had explained, was that it had allowed members to operate freely and develop strengths and abilities in excess of the party itself. Huang Jilu came close to arguing the contrary in proposing a motion for proportional representation:

A proportional electoral system would eliminate the recurrent faults afflicting elections today, because under the current electoral system the majority dominates the minority, while under the proportional electoral system each can develop according to its strength.

Huang, like Sun, was troubled by the prospect of internal disunity and its potential for sapping the strength of the party. But he could see "no room for conflict" in a party that made constitutional allowance for differences of view. Instead, he argued, liberalism would prove a new source of strength. Huang noted that significant divisions had already formed around the issue of Communist admission to the party, and he concluded that the best way to ensure party unity was to make constitutional provision for the expression of different points of view. This, he argued, was the case in the "democratic countries of Europe which all uphold the principle of protecting the minority."

Comparison with the states of Europe revealed another side to Huang's argument. Like Sun, Huang spoke of the party as an analogue of the national state. But each seems to have had a different kind of state in mind. Huang saw the party as a preparatory school for the national state and believed that procedures adopted in the party would establish precedents for the national polity as a whole. The system of proportional representation was well suited to the party because it was well suited to a liberal state: "This system can be adopted [in the party] as a form of training, in preparation for that time in the future when it might be put into universal practice in the administration of the nation as a whole." What Huang Jilu was proposing in this brief intervention in the final days of the congress was a liberal model of party organization and state-building in place of the highly disciplined party-state proposed by Sun Yatsen. Sun wanted nothing less than a "revolutionary autocracy." [37]

Other delegates saw in Huang's last-minute motion some prospect of retrieving the Republic from the dustbin into which Sun Yatsen had discarded it on the opening day of the congress. There was little need to replace the Republic with a Nationalist government if the introduction of a more liberal electoral system could "sweep away in one stroke all of the faults afflicting provincial and national elections." Even Sun's close associate Dai Jitao suggested that in view of the motion's "extraordinary importance" it should be held over for discussion at the next national congress. But another delegate from North

America, Lu Liuyin, disagreed. It had to be decided now. At this point Mao Zedong stepped in again:

At the present time the proportional electoral system is the fruit of agitation on the part of minority parties. Ours is a revolutionary party. Whatever confers advantage on the revolution should be adopted and whatever brings harm to the revolution should be discarded. The proportional system is harmful to the revolutionary party because when a minority is elected and acquires some strength it can destroy the revolutionary enterprise. It offers opportunities to the minority faction.

When another Communist, Xuan Zhonghua, described proportional representation as "a device of the capitalist class for deceiving people," Huang Jilu rose to his feet once more. Proportional representation was neither capitalist chicanery nor harmful to the revolution, Huang responded, but a democratic political procedure for ensuring "government by all the people."

With these remarks Huang once again turned attention from internal party procedure to the greater issue of the organization of the state itself. Mao Zedong and Xuan Zhonghua had something to say on this matter as well. Xuan could think of no more damning indictment of the motion at hand than Sun Yatsen's proposal to found a party-state. He cited Sun to condemn Huang, noting that the Nationalist party "proposes 'to build the state through the party' and to seize government through the party. The system of proportional elections is fundamentally incompatible with these objectives." Mao went a little further in spelling out the larger implications for a single party-state once the Nationalist party had seized state power. "This system is most harmful to the very idea of revolution. If freedom were granted to an opposing party the revolutionary enterprise would be placed in extreme jeopardy." [38]

Mao's concern for the internal procedures of the Nationalist party reflected a greater concern to eliminate all political rivals to the revolutionary movement in a single-party state. In fact, both sides clearly acknowledged that the constitution of the party had a profound bearing on the ultimate shape of the state, and each expressed its concerns for the ultimate shape of the polity in debate over the party constitution. For the opponents of Sun, Mao, and Xuan—chiefly the North American delegates Huang Jilu and Liu Liuyin—the ideal polity was a liberal-democratic one that reserved a place for minority voices. The party should do likewise.

Huang and Liu were at a distinct disadvantage. They were arguing not only against members of the Communist party but against Sun Yatsen's doctrine of party rule. It was quite in order for Xuan Zhonghua to cite Sun in attacking Huang and the liberal-democratic system. The party was a paradigm of the national state, and Sun had already made quite clear the kind of state he had in mind. He soon put his teaching into practice. Within two months of the close of the party conference, the Central Executive Committee sacked the president of the Judicial Yuan (*Daliyuan*) for insisting that party rule should not override the principle of rule of law. Zhao Shibei, an eminent liberal jurist, had been appointed by Sun only a year before to head the Judicial Yuan. Zhao was a graduate of Columbia University and had served as senator in the Provisional Senate of 1912 before holding a number of key positions in law and administration under the Republican administration.[39] But on 31 March 1924, he was dismissed for expressing the view that "the law is above parties" (*sifa wudang*). He was evidently wrong. There was to be no law outside of "the principle of party rule and the system of party government."[40] Xuan Zhonghua and Mao Zedong had mounted the first successful defense of party rule, but Sun Yatsen was the first to put the principle into effect.

Sun's new notion of "party activity" also brought him into closer contact with the Communists generally. The first indication of his resolve never again to cooperate with another political party came a year earlier in negotiations over the shape of an alliance with the Chinese Communists. Sun steadfastly refused to enter into any form of cooperative arrangement with the Communist party. Instead, he insisted that Communists should enter the Nationalist party as individuals, that they should work toward expanding the size and influence of the Nationalist party, and that they should remain subject to its discipline. Sun's terms were accepted by Henk Sneevliet for the Comintern, and by Chen Duxiu and the Communist party at its controversial Hangzhou Plenum in August 1922. This was not simply a clever ruse to keep the Communists in check, but a clear sign of his conviction that the scope of the revolution was to be confined to Nationalist "party activity."

A number of Communists dissented from the initial decision on the ground that it limited their capacity for independent action. By January of 1924, however, none disputed Sun Yatsen's refusal to participate in the liberal-democratic process. The Communist party itself had worked with parliamentarians for a brief spell in 1922 to secure influence in the Beijing government. But by the close of the following year they had come to share Sun Yatsen's disdain for parliament and rallied round the new Nationalist flag when it was unfurled in Guangzhou. The Communists then began to attach pennants of their own to the Nationalist flag, much as Republican factions had once attached their insignia to the five-bar flag of the Republic. One, depicting a plow beneath the Blue Sky and White Sun, was designed for the party's peasant movement; another flag was assigned to the labor movement.[41] The Communists popularized these flags throughout China and waved them in the face of political parties and factions that still professed loyalty to the liberal constitution. The mass movement of their united front was an aspect of the party-state that owed no loyalty to the Republic.

Mao Zedong lent his approval to the change in revolutionary insignia in his capacity as acting director of propaganda for the Nationalist party. On 29 November 1925, the *Shanghai Times* (*Shishi xinbao*) carried a report of a demonstration in Beijing in which "the students bore aloft a Guangzhou flag, the workers carried a red flag and the national flag was nowhere to be seen." The report appeared under the headline "A Terrifying Demonstration." Mao noted the signs of discomfort in Beijing with relish:

> If a real "Nationalist government" (*guomin zhengfu*) is set up some time in the future and the "Guangzhou flag" should fly high from the roof of government house, then surely there will be "chaos" on the scale of the chaos in Guangzhou as well. Better still, perhaps this "chaos" will extend throughout the whole country and things will be done the same everywhere. The majority will then seize their "freedom" and the minority will have their freedom taken from them.[42]

Sun Yatsen never explicitly advocated seizing the freedom of the minority and, unlike Mao, used words such as "chaos" with caution. He was conscious of his earlier reputation for destruction (*pohai*). From the time of the May Fourth movement Sun spoke instead of reconstruction (*jianshe*). Still, in raising his distinctly Nationalist flag from the roof of the government house in Guangzhou, Sun sent out a message that could be seized upon by Mao Zedong and the Communist party of China. The Nationalist Revolution would brook no compromise in remaking the state after the fashion of a particular party and in asserting the party's exclusive authority to speak on behalf of the nation.

The Purge of Liberalism Within the Nationalist Movement

Although the Communists were on his side, Sun Yatsen still had to confront members of his own party before he could wave the Blue Sky and White Sun over the government house without fear of open contradiction. He had, in effect, to disown the Nationalist party's own long heritage of engagement with liberal politics in the Republic. His associates in the Nationalist party had helped to create the Republic in 1912, and they had contested and won the first national elections in 1913. For much of the following decade, many of his most faithful comrades had valiantly defended the Republican constitution against those who would subvert it. Sun could not erase this impressive historical record without striking resistance from veteran party members. In the lead-in to the Nationalist Revolution, conflict erupted in Nationalist ranks over which of the flags should command the allegiance of party members and, in effect, determine the color of the state.

Conflict arose over the character and the form of the Nationalist party itself. When Sun returned to Shanghai from his enforced exile in Japan in April 1916, he found the party structure in disarray. He soon learned that its program and policies were irrelevant to the new cultural and social movements unfolding in China's coastal cities. At first he repaid this indifference in kind, and gave the New Culture movement little heed in attempting to resuscitate the moribund Chinese Revolutionary party. At this stage Sun was still keen to work with the Nationalist parliamentarians who had gathered in Guangzhou to "Protect the Constitution." Many parliamentarians had dissociated themselves from Sun's Chinese Revolutionary party in 1914, and they continued to raise objections to proposals for a new party structure that Sun had put forward in the interim. By 1917 "party affairs had ground to a halt." [43] Sun Yatsen's efforts to reorganize the party came to little until the New Culture movement spilled over into violent and direct political action in the May Fourth movement of 1919.

When students, teachers, and workers took to the streets of Beijing in May 1919 to protest the imminent surrender of former German concessions in Shandong Province to Japan, they managed to gather a sizable public following by circumventing parliamentary procedures in favor of mass agitation and direct action. Although no fan of the wider New Culture movement, which precipitated the May Fourth movement, Sun was impressed by the patriotism of the activists and by their considerable political achievement. In a letter sent to overseas party branches in January 1920, he described the New Culture movement as "a great movement indeed, unprecedented in intellectual circles in our time." [44] Toward the end of the year he resolved to tap the patriotic sentiment of the movement and recruit a new generation of activists into his own party through another party reorganization.

May Fourth activists touted a model of enlightened democracy that echoed Sun Yatsen's thinking on "political tutelage." They tended to be even more skeptical than Sun about the prospects for liberal democracy in China. And when they classified the enemies of democracy, May Fourth activists failed to discriminate between the superstition and autocracy of the old society and the more fragile symbols of the new liberal Republic. One leading activist, Qu Qiubai, recalled:

The three years from my arrival in Peking to the eve of the May Fourth Movement were the most solitary in my life. I had then no friends. The new bureaucrats in the capital, with their "republican" way of living, disturbed me as a source of painful irritation. . . . The taste of colonialism, in its full bitterness, had never come home to the Chinese until [1919], even though we had already had the experience of several decades of foreign exploitation behind us. The sharp pain of imperialistic oppression then reached to the marrow of our bones and it awakened us from the nightmares of impractical democratic reforms.[45]

Republican politicians and officials had appeared unheroic and self-interested for the better part of the decade, but treachery was added to the list of grievances against them in 1919 when they failed to resist Japanese demands for

Chinese territory in Shandong. It was then that Qu Qiubai "awakened" from the nightmare of liberal democracy. His youthful anxieties and the fury of his fellow demonstrators were subsequently directed against the new symbols of the liberal Republic as well as the "feudal" customs of the old society.[46] Qu left for Russia the following year, and was elected to the Central Committee of the Chinese Communist party on his return to China in 1923. He rose to become secretary-general in August 1927.[47]

Yet liberal democracy was undergoing a significant revival in the Nationalist party at large. Nationalist parliamentarians felt that Qu Qiubai's nightmares were still distant and unrealized dreams—although in a rhetorical inversion common to political rhetoric of the day, they argued that it was the people of China who were dreaming. Wu Tingfang, a respected foreign minister in successive Republican administrations, wrote on behalf of his parliamentary colleagues in February 1920:

As the theory of democracy has prospered, the trend of world affairs has been towards national self-determination. Esteemed members of the National Assembly grieve over their countrymen who are lost in cavernous dreams, who behave as if they are under hypnosis and who fail to meet the needs of our time.[48]

The May Fourth movement seems to have inspired intense efforts among Nationalist parliamentarians to awaken citizens to distinctly liberal dreams of "self-enlightenment," "self-determination," and "self-government."

Wu Tingfang published his lament for the "cavernous dreams" of his countrymen in a new journal issued in the May Fourth period by a body of parliamentarians and Republican officials associated with the Constitution Protection movement in Guangzhou. According to the explanation offered in the inaugural issue, the title of the assemblymen's journal, *Popular Awakening* (*Minjue*), drew upon the populist language of the May Fourth movement but carried a distinctive emphasis. In this case the word "Popular" (*min*) in the title referred neither to the crowd (*minzhong*) nor to the common people (*pingmin*) of May Fourth literature but to citizens (*guomin*). The adjunct, "Awakening" (*jue*), implied not mass awakening (*minzhong juewu*) but individual awareness of the self (*zijue*) as a citizen (*guomin*). The self-awakening alluded to here was of a particular kind: the stated purpose of the journal was to promote "self-awareness on the part of citizens" (*guomin de zijue*). Self-awakening meant awakening to an identity as a citizen of a liberal republic.[49]

Contributors to *Popular Awakening* showed a strong preference for directed enlightenment, channeled toward the ideal of "self-determination" (*zijue*). Nationalist party veteran Lin Sen announced his position in a scanned couplet: "Enlighten the world and awaken the people to go out and seek self-government (*zizhi*)." [50] As if to stress the self-directed nature of the exercise, other contributors played with the homonyms "self-awareness" (*zijue*) and "self-determination" (*zijue*):

Self-determination (*zijue*) is but the effect; self-awareness (*zijue*) is the cause. To achieve self-determination we must first achieve self-awareness, for without genuine self-awareness it is pointless to speak of self-determination.[51]

Consistent emphasis on the individual self, on self-awareness, and on self-determination was clearly intended to counter the claims of two perceived enemies of liberal democracy in 1920. One was the corrupt and autocratic practice of Yuan Shikai and his successors in Beijing—of which Nationalist parliamentarians were only too well aware. The other was the specter of social revolution that had recently appeared in the literature of the May Fourth movement. Zhang Qiubai, another prominent Nationalist party parliamentarian, declared that only by carrying out a "revolution of the self" could citizens ensure there would be no return to the autocratic practices of the past. But Zhang seems to have been even more concerned by the prospect of social revolution in the foreseeable future:

Revolutionaries must first carry out revolutions on themselves before they contemplate carrying out a revolution in society. If all can truly carry out a revolution on themselves, then each of the four characters that make up the terrifying words "social revolution" (*shehui geming*) can be broken up and thrown one by one into the depths of the Pacific, the Atlantic, the Arctic, and the Antarctic oceans. . . . Never again would we need to raise the specter of "social revolution." [52]

It is not entirely clear what Zhang Qiubai meant in writing of social revolution, although its "specter" seemed to promise an end to everything Zhang and his fellow parliamentarians had been striving for over the past decade. Certainly some liberal democrats shared the disdain of May Fourth activists for the social and political order of the Confucian tradition. "For several thousand years," ran one of the prefaces, "our minds have been steeped in autocratic thinking in this country." [53] But liberals imagined that the symbols and institutions of the Republic were less likely to revive traditions of autocratic thinking than the terrifying words issuing from the mouths of May Fourth activists.

The achievements and the promise of the 1911 revolution were quite revolutionary enough for the liberals. The queue had been eliminated as a sign of vassalage among Han men. The advent of the Republic had hastened the decline of footbinding among women and had introduced a simplified language of state along with new symbols of political authority, a legitimating rhetoric of popular sovereignty, reformed schools and higher institutes of education, currency reforms, new public rituals, a reformed calendar, a modest repertoire of nationalist songs and literature, and, not least in the calculation of Guangzhou assemblymen, a set of political institutions through which they could speak and act on behalf of New China. The symbols of the Republican state may have been desecrated by Yuan Shikai and his successors, but only the iconoclasts and social revolutionaries of the May Fourth movement could actually destroy them. This, it seems, is what the liberals feared most of all. The aim of parliamentarians in the Nationalist movement was not to destroy the symbols of the Republic but to restore their sheen.

The New Culture movement's enthusiasm for founding literary clubs, opening reading rooms, and launching journals in the comfort and security of Shanghai seems to have held little appeal for Sun Yatsen. Sun hankered after something grander and at once more concrete. In April 1920, he was relieved to return to a more familiar brand of politics when the circulation of a number of Nationalist party journals—including *Weekly Commentary (Xingqi pinglun)*— was restricted by a series of prohibitive regulations.[54] Sun had seen this before. He reacted preemptively, closing down *Weekly Commentary* and forcing his flagship magazine, *Reconstruction*, to cease publication. The third major party organ in Shanghai, *Awaken*, was exempted because it operated as part of the general commercial operations of the *Shanghai Republican Daily*.

Sun's closest colleagues kept their feelings to themselves, but others were highly critical of the closures. On 7 June, an editor of *Awaken* questioned the stated reasons for the closure of the journals and frankly suggested that the real reason lay in a determination to return to "real politics."[55] This was not far from the truth. Just a few days before *Reconstruction* ceased publication, on 3 June, Sun joined Wu Tingfang, Tang Shaoyi, and Tang Jiyao in announcing the formal dissolution of the Guangzhou military government. This announcement signaled the start of a new campaign to unseat the incumbent government in Guangdong and marked the end of Sun's brief alliance with the enlightenment enterprise in Shanghai.

The suggestion that Sun Yatsen was engaging in "real politics" in Guangdong would not have troubled Sun himself. It was commonplace for Sun and the Nationalists to counsel that the best way to achieve results in mass propaganda was to practice principles rather then preach them.[56] And practicing principles was what Sun had in mind when he stemmed the flow of funds for the party magazines. He now proposed that a propaganda of "practical reconstruction" should replace the recent propaganda of "empty words":

To unite China by conversion (*ganhua*), through the civilian arts (*wenzhi*), one has to rely on propaganda. Yet a propaganda of "hollow words" has no force at all. We must now genuinely reconstruct Guangdong into a model province where reformers from every province can learn by experience, and where even die-hard conservatives might be inspired to reform. Practical reconstruction of this kind will provide immense cultural propaganda.[57]

All the thinking that needed doing had been done; the summer of 1920 was a time for action. Sun put forward his person and his party in place of the "empty words" of Shanghai journalism and set out to awaken the people of China by the force of his example. And as a parting gesture to the May Fourth movement, he offered to create a first-class publishing house for party propaganda, also in Shanghai, on the model of the "enlightened" publishers of the New Culture movement.

The history of "Popular Wisdom Press," as it was called, does little to allay the suggestion that Sun's real interests lay outside the cultural politics of Shanghai. The press did little more than assimilate the pedagogical style of the May Fourth movement to the demands of realpolitik in the south. After Sun wrote to all branches abroad soliciting funds for the press, party members in the United States remitted around US$100,000 to Shanghai party headquarters. The American party network accounted for around 60 percent of all revenue from abroad at the time, so it can reasonably be assumed that another US$60,000 was solicited from branches elsewhere. What actually happened to this fortune is a mystery: by my estimates no more than $32,000 was actually invested in Popular Wisdom Press. It seems the missing money went to buying the warlord allies who dispatched Chen Jiongming from Guangzhou in 1922 and 1923; at any rate, the press remained an insignificant publisher until the close of the decade.[58]

In another parting gesture, Sun also decided to revise the party constitution before he departed Shanghai for Guangzhou in December 1920. His revised constitution encountered almost as many problems as Popular Wisdom Press. In one respect the draft issued on 9 November was indebted to the style of politics ushered in by the May Fourth movement as well: Sun decided, for the first time, to set up a propaganda bureau (*xuanchuan bu*) at party headquarters in Shanghai. But the overriding concern of the first draft of the new party constitution was to create a revolutionary party loyal to Sun's person. In the debate that ensued, Nationalist party elders, parliamentarians, and Sun Yatsen resurrected a host of old grievances about the merits of constitutional liberalism and the role of Sun Yatsen in the party structure.

Although Sun turned away from the "hollow words" of May Fourth activism in the winter of 1920, he had no intention of embracing parliamentary politics in its place. What he wanted was "government":

The responsibility of the military government on its return to Guangzhou is now, as before, to continue to "Protect the Constitution." But protecting the constitution cannot, as I understand the general situation, resolve the fundamental problem. From this day onward we must set a clear direction, launch a new era, make solid the foundations of the Republic of China, and bring an end to chaos. What is this direction? Toward establishing a formal government.[59]

Only by establishing a formal government could Sun hope to exercise a propaganda of "practical reconstruction." Still, he shared an interest in "Protecting the Constitution" with his parliamentary colleagues because parliaments were part of the paraphernalia of government in a democratic polity. They also conferred advantage. It was far less taxing to maintain a presence in the Beijing or Guangzhou assembly than on the field of battle, and when Sun was forced to wage war to secure government, his parliamentary connections conferred an aura of legitimacy over his murky warlord alliances.

These alliances were very costly. In the preceding year, while the passions of May Fourth were still running high, Sun had unveiled the first of his revived party constitutions to capitalize on the momentum of the movement and to raise funds for a military expedition to recover Guangdong. By reviving the overseas chapters of the defunct Chinese Revolutionary party, he hoped to establish a line of credit with the party's mercenary allies.[60] But the 1919 party constitution made little or no allowance for participation by party parliamentarians on higher party councils. In fact, the reorganization of the continental party structure was delayed for a further thirteen months, until Sun prepared to leave Shanghai for Guangzhou. His imminent departure brought to a head the question of the place of parliamentarians in the Nationalist movement.

His colleagues subjected Sun's draft constitution to close scrutiny early in November 1920. At the heart of a controversy that preceded the publication of a revised version of the party constitution ten days later, on 19 November, lay questions about the nature of the party and the quality of Sun Yatsen's leadership.[61] The interests of parliamentarians found expression in slight but significant alterations in the phrasing of the two documents.[62] First, Sun included an oath of personal loyalty in the sixth clause of the draft constitution unveiled on 9 November. After some discussion, delegates to the party reorganization in Shanghai forced a change in the draft: the third clause of the revised text issued on 19 November altered the original wording from "must take an oath" to the more precise "must swear *to the party*." [63] A second point at issue was government by tutelage (*xunzheng*). In Sun Yatsen's earliest strategic formula, tutelage was to be the second of three proposed stages in a revolutionary process beginning with military victory and ending in the proclamation of representative government. In the interim, the Chinese people were to be tutored in the operation of republican government by a Nationalist party-state.[64] Although it had found mention in slightly different form in a manifesto of the Revolutionary Alliance, published in 1905, the tutelage phase of this three-stage proposal had never found favor among liberal democrats.[65] Critics of Sun's Chinese Revolutionary party hinted that government by tutelage was little more than an excuse for Sun Yatsen to rule in place of duly elected representatives and without reference to due process.[66] The fate of tutelage in debate over the party constitution in November 1920 shows that this source of tension had not abated over the intervening decade. On proclamation of the first draft, Sun lectured his comrades on the need to include party tutelage as one phase in the three-stage periodization of the revolutionary movement.[67] Even before the draft of 9 November had been released, party elder Hu Hanmin anticipated liberal objections with a compromise proposal that was agreeable to Sun and effectively removed tutelage from practical consideration. Hu's suggestion, incorporated into the third clause of the first draft, was that tutelage be undertaken during the period of military offensive, rather than after it. Victory on the field of battle would then immediately herald a period of constitutional republican government.[68] Yet even this diluted version of Sun's concept of tutelage was deleted from the final version of the text published ten days later. Tutelage failed to gain mention at all.[69] Sun's views on the issue, expressed forcefully in his speech of 9 November, carried little weight against the concerted opposition of liberal parliamentarians, who made up the core of the new party.

A final point of controversy was the status of Sun Yatsen as leader. A reference to Sun Yatsen's leadership found in the ninth and tenth clauses of the first draft was watered down in the twelfth clause of the final version. In defense of his draft, Sun lectured his comrades on the necessity for strong personal leadership in the party, arguing that although the state might be based upon law, a party needs to be founded upon an individual.[70] Party politicians found these sentiments no more palatable in 1920 than they had in 1914. The first draft was subsequently amended. The initial reading, "Party Centre comprises one president . . . who holds absolute power to direct all party affairs," was changed in the later document to read "The party has one president who, *as representative of the party*, directs party affairs." [71] Once again, Sun was forced to concede the point to his liberal colleagues. Although he lost the battle, Sun never admitted defeat. "The Chinese Nationalist Party," he observed a few months later, "is in fact just the Chinese Revolutionary Party." [72] He could not claim final victory until the great party reorganization of 1924.

Nationalist Propaganda and the Liberal Reaction

Nationalist parliamentarians were not inclined to give up without a struggle. After securing a place for themselves in the new party, parliamentary liberals strove to ensure that the party would still speak on their behalf. Disagreement over the shape of the party then came to be refracted from 1920 to 1924 in a number of separate maneuvers by parliamentary representatives to gain hold of the symbols and the bullhorns of the party, which were stored for safekeeping in the propaganda institutions of Shanghai, Guangzhou, and Beijing. The opening of a new propaganda bureau at party headquarters (*benbu*) in Shanghai was delayed by the departure of party officers and parliamentarians for Guangzhou on completion of the 1920 reorganization. The Shanghai bureau carried on as before, chiefly disseminating propaganda abroad to raise funds for party activities at home.

Responsibility for domestic propaganda followed Sun Yatsen and the parliamentarians south to Guangzhou, where the pioneers of the new party structure descended in November and December 1920. Little time was wasted in establishing a special Guangdong office of Party Center (*benbu zhu yue teshe banshichu*) on 3 January 1921, to serve as a de facto propaganda bureau.[73] The Special Office was intended to operate, in Sun's words, as "a general headquarters for the marshalling of propaganda." [74] So 38 of the total complement of 84 staff members were employed in the propaganda division of the Special Office, and nine of these were dispatched to Guangxi, three to Hubei, and one to Hunan. As the Guangzhou office extended its authority as far as Shanghai, the opening of a new propaganda bureau at Shanghai Party Center was postponed indefinitely.[75]

The appointment of senior staff to the propaganda division of the Special Office confirmed the hold of parliamentarians over the party's new propaganda apparatus in southern China. Deng Jiayan, who had recently returned from negotiations with the Beijing government on Sun's behalf, was appointed director of the propaganda division.[76] Deng shared with his deputy in the division, Wang Hongtu, and with the chief officer of the Special Office, Zhang Ji, the distinction of having served as elected delegate to the Extraordinary Parliament of 1917.[77] Constitutional issues featured prominently in the propaganda emanating from the office. The parliamentarians published some of Sun's better-known works on parliamentary democracy, including *The Five Power Constitution* and an early version of his *Three Principles of the People*, through the new Guangzhou propaganda facility.[78]

Events in Guangdong conspired to revive Sun's own interest in parliamentary politics. Early in 1921, shortly after he had returned to Guangzhou, one of his critics condemned Sun's new administration for implementing "Party rule in Guangdong" (*dang ren zhi Yue*). Sun rather relished the accusation. He was, nevertheless, committed to the reconstituted Extraordinary Parliament in Guangzhou and felt obliged to work closely with the warlord Chen Jiongming, at whose invitation he had returned to the province. The problem for Sun was that Chen Jiongming had for some time touted a rival slogan — "The people of Guangdong rule in Guangdong" — and had begun to develop marked liberal tendencies in relation to his own province. Chen insisted on undertaking experiments in local democracy.

In 1921, we have seen, Chen Jiongming favored the popular election of county magistrates without prior Nationalist party tutelage. Sun recognized that Chen Jiongming's proposals for local democratic rule posed a threat to party rule in the province. Yet he was obliged to acknowledge that a movement espousing democracy among its Three Principles could hardly object to rule by popular election, even if the people had not yet reached the "standard" of political consciousness required of them. "Permit me to ask," he inquired of the Guangzhou Special Office,

have the people of Guangdong reached [an appropriate] standard? Some among us fear that they have not reached this standard. But surely it will invite chaos if they have not reached this standard and yet we carry out [local elections]? And yet as Democracy is a founding principle of our party, we simply cannot admit of any doubts.

Sun was caught in a quandary. His doubts were momentarily allayed by the prospect of a remedial course of propaganda to raise voter consciousness to the required level. He asked the Special Office to consider what kind of propaganda might prepare voters to exercise their democratic rights in favor of the Nationalist party:

How can county heads be elected by popular vote? We must think how to avoid spoiling things in the future, and this can only be done through intensive drilling in the Three Principles of the People, and [achieving] "Party rule in Guangdong." [79]

Sun did not yet command a party capable of launching "intensive drilling" in party doctrine of the kind he had in mind for every county, village, and hamlet in the province. This was to come later, when he teamed up with the Chinese Communist party. For the moment, Sun decided that the best way out of the dilemma was to remove himself as far as possible from local politics. He embarked on a series of deals with other warlords culminating in a military expedition designed to topple the national government in Beijing.

His own propaganda train then followed the direction of Sun's political and military strategy, pulling out from Guangzhou for his forward military stations in Guangdong and Guangxi. The Guangzhou Special Office continued in operation throughout 1921 with a change in directorship. Its chief officer, Zhang Ji, was replaced by another prominent Nationalist parliamentarian, Tian Tong, in October, but the life of the Special Office was cut short when Sun went off to do battle. Once Chen Jiongming had routed Lu Rongting from the neighboring province of Guangxi, Sun proceeded to Guilin to establish the forward headquarters for a military expedition into southern Hunan.[80] Party propaganda operations then followed Sun to Guilin, where a propaganda office was set up on 16 January 1922.[81] Tian Tong was immediately transferred from the Guangzhou Special Office to help run the Guilin propaganda office.[82] Sun urged the "one or two hundred" party members in Guangxi to undertake widespread propaganda on the Three Principles of the People, to match the "intensive drilling" he had urged on his comrades in Guangdong.[83] In light of the weakness of the local party organization, there was even less prospect of success in Guangxi than in Guangdong. Sun's new priorities were set out in his instruction to "propagate the Three Principles of the People and the Outline for National Reconstruction to the troops and to the people." [84] Converting the people was subordinate to ensuring the loyalty of the troops. Indeed, Sun's most memorable speech over this period was "The Spiritual Education of Soldiers" (*junren jingshen jiaoyu*), delivered on 10 December 1921.[85]

His attention was also diverted to a more distant audience in the United States and Japan, where journalists were keen to learn of his reactions to an international conference then under way in Washington. The Washington Conference concluded in February 1922 with an agreement to limit Japanese naval power in the Pacific and to respect China's sovereignty and territorial integrity. Sun was not impressed. The government in Beijing—the focus of the Washington Conference—was not the legitimate government of China but a tool of the Japanese, he argued, so Americans should not expect the conference to have any appreciable influence over his own actions. The aim of his expedition, Sun informed a visiting correspondent for the *Washington Post*, was to recover China for the Chinese and to establish the rightful claim of his southern government to international recognition. "The aim of the Guangdong legitimate government in undertaking a northern expedition has nothing to do with [attacking] the people of North China," he announced, "and all to do with [attacking] Japan and the Northern Court, which acts as a client government for Japan." [86] Mass politics and parliamentary politics were both put on hold pending the outcome of the expedition.

Party parliamentarians, however, found new publicity outlets of their own after Zhang Ji surrendered his directorship of the Guangzhou Special Office to Tian Tong. Zhang Ji made his way to Shanghai, where he finally opened the party's first central propaganda bureau.[87] On 4 October he was concurrently appointed to head the Beijing party branch. Zhang Ji used his two positions to good effect, straddling both cities to attune the new Shanghai propaganda office to the constitutional arguments under way in Beijing.[88] With his return, Shanghai Party Center also began to assert more authority over the Guangzhou and Guangxi party apparatus. By February 1922, Party Center had appointed three new propaganda officers and unveiled plans for an expanded propaganda committee.[89] On 11 April, regulations governing the propaganda committee were ratified at a joint meeting of bureaus at Party Center, and two days later 27 prospective committee members were notified by mail of their selection. The choice of personnel for the committee suggests the strength of the parliamentary lobby and gives some idea of the role it was expected to play in national politics. At least fifteen members of the propaganda committee had served as elected representatives in one or more of the provincial and "national" parliaments convened since 1913. Two others had held formal office in the southern administration.[90] Many could also claim a measure of propaganda experience. Eight had worked previously as newspaper journalists or had been involved in the propaganda activities of the Guangdong Special Office, and a further three committee members were drawn from among the staff of the *Shanghai Republican Daily*.[91]

The range of the committee's contacts within newspaper circles was not confined to Shanghai and Guangzhou. One of its members, Hang Xinzhai, had founded newspapers in Beijing and in his native province of Zhejiang before joining the committee. Following his appointment he worked for the Beijing paper *Guofeng ribao* (National currents daily). Tan Zhen managed a daily paper in Changsha, Hunan. Wang Leping worked as a journalist in Shandong, and Guan Peng established *Minzhi bao* (The democrat) in Anhui Province shortly after his selection.[92] The career profiles of committee members also reveal the pattern of their propaganda activity: the committee renewed contacts with established newspapers throughout the country and created new publicity organs where required, chiefly to launch attacks upon the "unconstitutional" Beijing government and to promote the rival claims of the Nationalist party and its elected representatives. This pattern was poignantly revealed in the arrest and imprisonment of Guan Peng's brother, Guan Shudong, for his part in *The Democrat's* relentless criticism of the Cao Kun government in Beijing.[93]

For five years Sun and his parliamentary colleagues had sounded the refrain "Protect the Constitution" to explain their opposition to the government in Beijing and at the same time to justify the expense and suffering entailed in the conquest, consolidation, and expansion of their territorial base in the south. By mid-1922 this motif had come to be so closely associated with the Nationalist party that it could be turned effectively against Sun himself.[94] When Sun Yatsen set out on his last military expedition under the standard of Constitution Protection in the winter of 1921, events in North China contrived to rob the term of its eloquence and distinctiveness. In October and November, the Beijing prime minister Jin Yunpeng and the most powerful military leader in North China, Wu Peifu, both found cause to revitalize their own claims to constitutional legitimacy. The politics of the Constitution Protection movement were further complicated when Zhang Zuolin, a leader of the rival Fengtian Clique, took issue with Wu Peifu, cemented a military alliance with Sun Yatsen in February of 1922, and then announced that he supported Sun's claims to constitutional legitimacy. Constitution Protection no longer served to differentiate the southern from the northern government but became instead an issue in dispute among factions contesting control of North China.

On 15 May, Sun Chuanfang, commander-in-chief of a contingent of the

Zhili forces, issued a telegram that confidently addressed Sun Yatsen on his own terms. The Zhili general proposed a restoration of the original constitution along lines similar to the constitutional formula that had been championed by the southern government. Wu Peifu made a conciliatory gesture to Nationalist parliamentarians by intimating that the interests of the Zhili Clique would not be damaged by a restoration of the original constitution, even though the Clique had fought the southern government on this very issue. Wu wished it to be understood that the Zhili Clique was making a magnanimous gesture for national reunification. All the same, the advantages of the change of policy for the Zhili Clique were spelled out in the conclusion to Sun Chuangfang's telegram, which indicated that there was now "no reason for the southern government to continue in existence." [95]

It was a brilliant maneuver. Newspaper approval for the Zhili proposal was overwhelming, and before public acclaim subsided Sun Chuanfang followed his first telegram with another that extended the logic of the Zhili argument. The presidents of North and South China were both urged to resign. President Xu Shichang was in no position to resist his patrons, and on 31 May vacated the presidential palace in Beijing.[96] But Sun Yatsen would not budge. He called a press conference in Guangzhou on 8 June in a desperate attempt to earn by persuasion the allegiance that his arms could no longer compel. The appeal was muted and, in any case, seems to have fallen on deaf ears. A subordinate of Chen Jiongming, Ye Ju, placed Sun and his retinue under siege before presenting him with a "request," on 15 June, to follow the example of President Xu Shichang in Beijing and resign from office. The ultimatum was couched in terms of popular aspirations for national reunification through a return to constitutional legitimacy, playing upon public sympathies that had been nurtured by Sun Yatsen's own publicity on Constitution Protection over the preceding five years and that had risen to a crescendo in public telegrams and declarations over the second quarter of 1922.[97] While he was esconced as titular head of a southern government, Sun could ignore rival claims to constitutional legitimacy, but he was at something of a disadvantage when his lack of authority among his own allies lay exposed for all to see. As Sun tried to forestall Chen Jiongming's maneuvers in Guangzhou, his enemies in Beijing trained the spotlight of his party's own constitutional propaganda down upon him.

Sun's refusal to comply with the request for his resignation supplied the pretext for Chen Jiongming to order an attack upon his Guangzhou headquarters on 16 June. Sun made a furtive escape in August, and left behind not just his armed forces but all the precious books and manuscripts with which he had been preparing a revised version of his Three Principles of the People. All were lost when his presidential offices in Guangzhou were ransacked. But Sun would have had to revise the manuscripts anyway. When he stepped onto the docks in Shanghai, a forlorn figure, he had already begun to rethink his commitment to liberal constitutional politics and to reconsider his loyalty to the flag of the Republic. Henceforth he would work more closely with Soviet Russia, with Chinese Communists, and with the organized "masses," and lead a revolutionary movement of a kind he had never managed to mobilize before. The Three Principles of the People had to be written all over again, and, with them, Sun's contract with the liberal-parliamentary wing.

When Sun Yatsen reached Shanghai in August 1922, members of the Guangzhou Extraordinary Parliament came as well, just as they had in 1918 and 1920. Now, however, they shared Sun's humiliation, and humored his attempts to negotiate with the Comintern and the Chinese Communist party. On 4 September 1922, a body of prominent Nationalist party members held a party summit in Shanghai under the informal leadership of Zhang Ji to discuss and confirm this new turn in party affairs. By far the largest groups in attendance at the reorganization conference were parliamentarians and former government officials with an immense store of experience in representative politics and government administration among them. No less than 25 of the delegates had held seats in one of the chambers of national parliament in Beijing, in Guangzhou, or in both. Another three had been closely associated with constitutional politics over the previous five years. A few Communist party members also participated.[98] One result of their deliberations was a vote of "unanimous approval" for a party reorganization that would allow Communists to enlist as Nationalist party members, as Sun Yatsen proposed. The group's support for a style of mass political activity potentially antagonistic to its own was to have ramifications for party cohesion and party policy for decades after the closure of the 1922 reorganization conference. In ensuing years, some of the most outspoken critics of Communist activity within the Nationalist party were drawn from its ranks.[99]

Nationalist parliamentarians were partly distracted by events in Beijing. Before the conference got under way, a committee of nine party members charged with drafting the platform for the 1922 reorganization lost half its number to Beijing, where negotiations over the reconvening of the national parliament were taking place.[100] It seems others hoped that forging a closer relationship between the two parties would hasten their return to Beijing. In August and September, Soviet Russian delegates and local labor-movement activists were promoting an entente between Sun Yatsen and the Beijing government of Wu Peifu, and as the new parliament was to be convened under Wu's aegis, parliamentarians involved in the reorganization saw in the Communists' proposal a chance to advance their claims to representation.[101]

The views of Nationalist parliamentarians and Communist party members also converged on the issue of parliamentary representation itself. Over the months leading up to the reorganization conference, the Communist party had adopted a conciliatory attitude toward parliamentary politics in line with a call from the Third International for Communists to work through established parliaments in pursuit of revolutionary goals. At its Second National Congress in July 1922, the Communist party resolved to organize sympathetic members of parliament into a "democratic alliance" to help press their claims and disseminate their propaganda.[102] Nationalist parliamentarians seem to have believed that they were the most likely candidates for a "democratic alliance" with the Communist party.[103] So when Sun Yatsen proposed (for reasons of his own) that Communists should be admitted into his party, parliamentarians were happy to oblige. Zhang Ji stepped forward and offered to sponsor Li Dazhao as the first Communist to gain entry into the Nationalist party.[104]

It was a fatal move. Certainly parliamentarians retained considerable authority within the reconstituted Shanghai Party Center and continued to enjoy access to party propaganda institutions.[105] A new panel of 21 advisers attached to Party Center included fourteen members who might, in better times, have claimed seats in the national parliament.[106] They were less well represented within working bureaus, although one of their number was appointed to the influential post of deputy head of the propaganda bureau.[107] Advisers and senior bureau officers were entitled to sit on the Central Cadre Council, the highest policy-formulating body of the party under the revised party constitution, and parliamentarians appear to have made up an absolute majority on the council.[108] And the Central Propaganda Bureau kept constitutional issues alive. In November its deputy head, the parliamentarian Mao Zuquan, summoned around 150 parliamentarians temporarily resident in Shanghai to form a new association, the Reconstruction Discussion Society. Provision was made within the society for a propaganda section, for which Mao recruited the parliamentarians Zhang Ji and Chen Baixu.[109] In fact, the Reconstruction Discussion Society was a reconstituted version of the parliamentary liaison office established by Nationalist parliamentarians in Beijing over the final months of 1922, when Zhang Ji was assigned to manage the propaganda activities of the Beijing liaison office. His new appointment in Shanghai, after the collapse of talks in Beijing, ensured his tenure in office under a new title.[110]

The dogged determination of parliamentarians to keep their foot in the door of Nationalist party headquarters presented serious problems for the developing relationship between the Nationalist and Communist parties. The dominance of the parliamentary wing of the party among the policy and propaganda organs of Party Center limited its capacity to respond effectively on matters of concern to the new mass movement. It was silent, for example, on a bloody incident in Changsha that incited popular indignation against Japanese interests in the city. On 1 June, a Japanese naval vessel berthed in Changsha and offloaded a party of sailors, who subsequently shot and killed a worker and a teacher. The military governor of Hunan, Zhao Hengti, was keen to placate Japanese interests in the city. He arrested local demonstrators and outlawed mass activity in Changsha.[111] Other organizations in Beijing and Shanghai recognized the significance of the incident and gave it appropriate publicity, but not the propaganda officers of Shanghai Party Center. Their attention was focused exclusively on Beijing.[112] Nor, to its cost, did Shanghai Party Center pay sufficient attention to developments under way in Guangzhou, where Sun Yatsen was ruminating on another party reorganization that was destined to rob Shanghai of its historical position as the site of the central party headquarters and deprive it of its more recent role as a haven for liberal democrats. The staff at Shanghai Party Center did not have an inkling of what lay in store.[113]

It was, however, the Communists who first professed dismay at the behavior of their "democratic allies" in parliament. Their change of heart was largely due to changes in Communist party strategy. Shortly after the reorganization conference had endorsed the admission of Communists into the Nationalist party, the Communists began to have misgivings about their dealings with the northern government of Wu Peifu. More particularly, Wu Peifu's forces crushed a miners' strike in Tangshan with considerable bloodshed in February 1923. Before the ink had dried on Li Dazhao's membership, he was obliged to withdraw his support for the "able men" cabinet that had given him entré into the Nationalist party.[114] The Communists then turned on Nationalist parliamentarians with a vengeance they should perhaps have reserved for Wu Peifu.

Writing under a Chinese pseudonym, Comintern agent Henk Sneevliet announced that China's national parliament was too blunt an instrument for national revolution. He singled parliamentarians out for scathing public criticism in November 1922.[115] Parliamentarians elected in 1917 under the "illegitimate" constitution had, by this time, all but eliminated Nationalist parliamentarians from contention in the battle for control of the Beijing assembly. The Chinese Communist Zhang Guotao then poured salt upon their wounds by advocating recognition of the "illegitimate" 1917 elements. Zhang argued that the national parliament was by its very nature a counterrevolutionary institution, and hence that denying recognition to the 1917 faction robbed the revolutionaries of a tangible enemy. They might be ignored if they did not wield power, "but before the successful completion of the revolution we must acknowledge the existence of warlords and bureaucrats." [116] Six weeks later, Communist Secretary-General Chen Duxiu lumped Nationalist delegates in with the rest. Within the Chinese parliamentary system, he asserted, "of all political organizations there is not one which is not comprised of classless, displaced persons who have gathered together purely for the pursuit of personal advantage." Chen's remedy envisaged a completely new panel of representatives appointed through selection procedures representing organized sectoral interests.[117] Fittingly, Henk Sneevliet rounded off the attack in July 1923, by once again berating Sun Yatsen's dependence upon "shiftless politicians and parliamentarians" in his party.[118]

Sun Yatsen was not slow to join the chorus of critics. His own hopes for a constitutional settlement had yielded to despair.[119] In January 1923 he finally announced a shift in emphasis from the constitutional issues occupying "many persons in Beijing" to "party rule" in Guangdong. Party rule he defined as mass propaganda, or "assaulting the heart . . . in order to entice the hearts of China's four hundred million people into favouring our party." [120] Communist critics of the party's involvement in constitutional politics also put forward a new style of mass pedagogy as an appropriate alternative to parliamentary liberalism.[121] Only through mass propaganda, declared Sneevliet in May, could the Nationalist party aspire to lead a national revolution. The party's attention had been focused too narrowly on the "secret schemes of politicians and parliamentarians" and should be refocused on a "forceful and systematic propaganda venture." [122] Mass pedagogy was no longer posited as an alternative to other forms of propaganda. It was now an alternative to liberal constitutional politics itself: a disciplined mass party was to substitute for an unruly liberal state.

Liberal Politics, Mass Politics, and "Public Opinion"

The reorientation of party policy, from liberal to mass politics, entailed a systematic downgrading of "public opinion" (*yulun*) in social organizations and state institutions. Early experiments in liberal representative government had been closely associated with developments in urban society, at a time when civic identity was taking shape in an expanding urban culture situated at the junction between the private world of the household and the lineage, and the public world of the imperial state. It was here, in the public sphere at local and provincial levels, that the imperial state built upon existing institutions of public opinion to conduct China's earliest experiments in representative government.[123]

The institution of public opinion had a longer history still in the administration of the empire. William Rowe has suggested that the origins of public opinion are to be found in the administrative practice of local officials consulting with local notables before implementing imperial policy.[124] This argument is confirmed by a contemporary observer, Naitō Konan, who commented on the development of provincial assemblies in the late Qing: "Contrary to what one might expect, China is first and foremost a nation of public opinion." [125] Naitō traced the strength of the institutions of public opinion to the common practice of imperial regents in making and confirming the appointment of local officials:

"Public opinion" is an expression of Chinese origin, and in China emphasis is placed upon one's reputation among the masses. When the emperor would question the quality of the local officialdom, he would first listen to whether their reputation was regarded as good or bad. He did not care much whether or not an official had accomplished anything. There was nothing a local Chinese official was likely to be able to accomplish in three or four years at a post, and in any case the emphasis was placed on one's reputation. If someone were said to be "shengming hao," it meant that he was a good official.

On the basis of hardy indigenous precedent, Naitō concluded, China was ripe for representative constitutional government.[126]

By 1924, the Nationalist party begged to differ. The late imperial and early Republican states had attempted to co-opt local public opinion through an articulated system of representative assemblies, reaching from county level to the province and, ultimately, to the national state. Now the Nationalists proposed to replace these assemblies with party institutions, to reconstruct local communities *ab initio*, and to ensure that unwieldy institutions of public opinion no longer featured prominently in the public life of the nation.

The party's new resolve reflected more recent developments in the cities, notably the urban youth movements of 1919 and 1920, in which youthful activists were persuaded to "go among the people" and transform the patriarchal "feudal" culture of Old China. Among the feudal targets of the movement was the venerable institution of public opinion. May Fourth magazines held the "common people" (*pingmin*) and the "masses" (*qunzhong*) in high esteem but counted public opinion an enemy of New Culture, a domain of prejudice and superstition, and a cover for sectional interests seeking hegemony over the direction of public life.[127] Their contemptuous attitude contrasts strikingly with the more cautious judgment of parliamentary factions and broadsheet newspapers of the period, which rarely exalted the masses but took public opinion very seriously.

"Constitutional government," wrote Liang Qichao in 1910, "is in essence government by public opinion." [128] Newspapers had been agents and beneficiaries of the greater prominence of public opinion in the late Qing and early Republic, when national and provincial governments conceded a legitimate role for the press, for chambers of commerce, and for philanthropic associations in public life. Journalists themselves believed the press to be "a central institution in the functioning of a democratic polity," and their newspapers reflected the variety of "public opinion" they professed to represent.[129]

The formats of newspapers manifested variety of a different kind. In addition to editorials, newspapers carried columns on local, regional, and national news, timetables of shipping movements, columns of commercial news, fashion pages, weather reports, advertisements for traditional and modern products, and a variety of weekly supplements on art, literature, and social issues. They operated in an open commercial environment that offered wide customer choice, and over which no single newspaper could acquire a monopoly. In contrast, the small magazines that proliferated after the onset of the May Fourth movement tended to carry essays in place of news, and spirited editorial commentaries that reflected the concerns of the special-purpose societies (*she*) that published them. They strove, above all, for uniformity of opinion. Whereas newspapers were varied in content, open in format, big and often cumbersome to hold in the hand, the little magazines were easier to grasp in every sense, more brazen in their professions of belief and more highly disciplined in their formulation of principles, strategies, and policies.

As the decade progressed, newspapers and magazines sat uneasily alongside one another in the Nationalist propaganda stable. The party subsidized major newspapers in Shanghai and Guangzhou as well as dozens of little magazines throughout the country. Its *Shanghai Republican Daily* was one of the great newspapers of the period. The party also published three of the most influential magazines of the May Fourth movement: *Reconstruction (Jianshe)*, *Weekly Commentary (Xingqi pinglun)*, and *Awaken (Juewu)*.

From its foundation in 1915, the *Shanghai Republican Daily* served as a mouthpiece for the parliamentary factions associated with the Nationalist movement. This frequently involved coalition-building. Its chief editor, Ye Chucang, formed close personal ties with journalists working for the Political Study Group's *China News (Zhonghua xinbao)*, and, in 1917, formalized his relations with other factions by founding the Shanghai Journalists Club.[130] The Shanghai club served the party well in promoting the common interests of allied factions, and several times deflected attempts by hostile political groups to take advantage of differences among factions within the club itself.[131] In fact, the club proved such a success that within two years Ye Chucang proposed expanding it into a national newspaper association. Favorable responses from journalists in Guangzhou, Changsha, Hankou, Kunming, and Tianjin encouraged him to summon representatives of over 50 provincial newspapers into a National Newspaper Union, which was inaugurated on 15 April 1919. In time, the national union expanded the network of contacts linking the *Shanghai Republican Daily* with other newspapers to around 80 in all.[132]

The shadowy links between newspapers and partisan factions were frequently subject to ridicule, often for good reason. By the 1920s, only newspapers that managed to steer clear of politics entirely could expect to preserve their reputations. Lin Yutang wryly observed that the highly regarded newspaper *Shenbao* secured its reputation by confining its coverage to foreign issues, distant news, and general subjects such as "The Importance of Diligence" or "The Value of Truth." [133] Such caution was alien to Nationalist journalists. They acknowledged and welcomed the dialogue between newsprint and political interest, and shrugged off the accusation that they represented a narrow "party-faction" rather than "public opinion." Ye Chucang argued that a newspaper that declined to represent a "party-faction" represented nothing at all apart from "a few editors seated around a room writing under pseudonyms." The health of public opinion, he believed, was best measured by the number of party-factions competing for space in the public arena, rather than by specious claims of newspaper independence. Ye regretted that there were not a great many *more* parties and factions in existence so that every newspaper might have a faction of its own that it could claim, in fairness, to represent. The problem, to his liberal turn of mind, lay not with factionalized journalists but with a shortfall in the number of factions requiring representation. Ye concluded that "party-faction" newspapers would help stimulate the formation of "party-factions" by openly *representing* them.[134]

The party's little magazines were partisan, certainly, but rather less committed to the proliferation of party-factions. *Reconstruction* ranked alongside the independent magazines *New Youth* (*Xin qingnian*) and *New Tide* (*Xin chao*) as one of the most influential and authoritative serials of the May Fourth journals, achieving a circulation of around 13,000 copies per issue. In contrast to these other magazines, the political line of *Reconstruction* was unashamedly partisan from the inaugural issue. But in contrast to the party's *Shanghai Republican Daily*, the journal had little intention of ceding any ground to its rivals.

The choice of *Reconstruction* as title for the magazine flagged a single-minded determination to reconstruct China's psychology (*xinli*), society (*shehui*), and material economy (*wuzhi*) after the model of Sun Yatsen's revolutionary philosophy.[135] Sun insisted on the title *Reconstruction* over the alternative *Reform* (*gaizao*), favored by his colleague Hu Hanmin, because he associated reconstruction with revolution and preferred revolution to reform.[136] More to the point, Sun preferred destruction to reform. Without the saving grace of reconstruction, he argued, the more destructive aspects of the revolution made little sense. "Reconstruction is the one and only goal of revolution, and if we do not take reconstruction to heart then there is no need of destruction either, and certainly no need to talk of revolution." The two terms were harnessed uncomfortably in the charter of the Reconstruction Society, which aimed for the "reconstruction and reform of state and society." [137]

The mission of the second party magazine, *Weekly Commentary*, was to awaken the consciousness of the "mass self" (*zhong wo*) to the politics of the mass-democratic faction of the Nationalist party. Its editor, Shen Dingyi, published news and commentary on national and international politics, and on issues affecting labor, women, and youth, as well as a number of poems, short stories, pieces of literary criticism, and contributions to the debate on "new thought." [138] Shen's inaugural declaration on behalf of *Weekly Commentary*, published in June 1919, grounded the wider politics of the journal in an ethical relationship between self and community conceived as a single collective subject. He proposed to awaken and unify the "mass mind":

> I say: I am my me. All of the world is created from thoughts in the mind. This mind is in fact my own individual mind but every person has a mind and so each has a "me." And uniting the thought and consciousness of our mass mind (*wo zhong xin*) is the basis of all creation and reform of the world. Nothing is difficult under heaven when all depends on people with minds—and I ask our readers, is there a person without a mind? And are not all minds conscious?

Not all, however, appeared to be as conscious of the source of suffering as Shen himself. He echoed Kang Youwei's sympathy for the suffering about him and, like Kang, found in this suffering a foundation for ethical reflection:

> If I want to eat, nobody can sate himself for me; when I want to keep warm, nobody can warm himself on my account; and if I want shelter, nobody can find comfort for me. But while I am unlikely to go without food, clothing, and shelter myself, those who till the fields go hungry, those who weave cloth go cold, and those who build houses have nowhere to live. Is this a situation of my own making? Is it perhaps something my mind desires? If I do not think [about this], where does my mind go?

Shen was also conscious of the bestial imagery of popular ethnography, and urged his readers not to act like dogs. "If I do choose to think about [suffering]," he continued, "I should not harbour the kind of mind that is happy to bemoan slavishly, like a dog or an ox, 'such is fate' or 'this is retribution from a past life.' Were I to harbour this kind of mind then I should not even have a 'me'!" His personal self-realization supplied a foundation for collective action: "My mind should dwell upon everything that is of vital interest to the mass self," he wrote. "All that has happened in domestic or in international affairs has destroyed everything that is of vital interest to our mass self." Shen urged his editors and contributors to focus on mattters of concern to this "mass self" in subsequent issues of the journal.[139]

With its emphasis on the awakening of consciousness and on collective solidarity, *Weekly Commentary* was more closely attuned than its parent newspaper to the mood of May Fourth. The *Shanghai Republican Daily* distributed *Weekly Commentary* free to its own subscribers. With additional help from Shen Dingyi's mother, who helped to mail it out, the journal achieved a circulation of around 30,000 copies per issue. This was reputed to be the largest circulation of any May Fourth journal.[140]

The third party magazine, *Awaken*, was the most prestigious of a number of supplements to the *Republican Daily* and the only supplement issued daily with the parent paper itself.[141] As its title implied, the journal was the mainstay of the awakening enterprise launched by the Nationalist movement into the maelstrom of the May Fourth movement. Its task was to awaken the magazine's readership to the issues and the style of the new mass politics, and to lay claim to the movement on behalf of the Nationalist party. *Awaken* made a modest first appearance on 16 June 1919, as a single tabloid sheet. It expanded prodigiously over subsequent years to two tabloid sheets early in 1920, four double-tabloid sheets by mid-year, and progressively to a sixteen-sheet publication in 1925. From July 1920 it could also be purchased as a separate monthly collection. *Awaken* was written in the vernacular, unlike the general run of newspaper supplements, and published regular editorials, reports of speeches, and commissioned articles, along with translations, poems and works of fiction, and irregular columns on social issues and social research.[142]

Politically, the magazine was identified with the inclinations of its editors. At the outset it embraced the rainbow coalition of "new thought." But from the establishment of the Chinese Communist party in 1921 to the May Thirtieth movement in 1925, its editors systematically narrowed the focus of their concerns to the particular causes of the international communist movement, ranging from wholehearted support for the Soviet Russian government to unrelenting criticism of Christian "cultural imperialism" in China. Then it abruptly reversed course. In May 1925, the general editor, Shao Lizi, left the journal after falling out with the editor of the *Republican Daily*, Ye Chucang, and took with him his stable of radical contributors. The new direction of *Awaken* was announced in July with the publication of the first of a series of seminal articles on the incompatibility of communism and nationalism in China, written by the former Nationalist party propaganda chief Dai Jitao. Over the following years, the magazine consistently reserved space for Nationalist party members who were disillusioned with the radical policies of the Guangdong party headquarters, and who openly opposed the Communist presence in the party.[143]

The troubled relationship between *Awaken* and the editors of the *Shanghai Republican Daily* highlights the distinction between newspapers and magazines I have been trying to draw here. Tension between the newspaper and the magazine was as much a function of the way in which magazines were organized and produced, in contrast to the metropolitan dailies, as it was a product of the competing ideas each conveyed in print. Metropolitan newspapers and the little magazines of the May Fourth movement each conveyed an impression of standardized, pervasive, one-to-many communication of the kind Ernest Gellner has classified as the "core idea" of nationalism.[144] With their different formats, however, they conveyed subtle distinctions within this core idea and hinted at distinct styles of political organization.

When party headquarters renounced liberal parliamentary politics in favor of mass politics, it turned its back on the factional politics of newspaper journalism. There was no longer any place for competing factions within the party, nor any need for competing parties within the state. While Sun Yatsen was alive, the unity of party, state, and nation had been personified in the man himself. When he died in 1925, the party turned to the little magazines to supply the authoritative voice of the party-state.

At the moment of Sun's death, party newspapers retreated behind a line of silence. Few party members could claim to represent the party with any authority, and those who could claim some authority declined to represent it. The responsibility was an awesome one: representing the party now meant representing the nation and the state. The editor of the *Guangzhou Republican Daily* (the Central Propaganda Bureau's only serial publication at the time) announced that his paper "dare not claim to represent the party."[145] At the offices of the *Shanghai Republican Daily*, Ye Chucang's frankness in acknowledging the factional foundations of newspapers was no longer welcome. Now his well-known liberal views laid him open to the charge that his paper represented a counterrevolutionary faction within the Nationalist movement. Mao Zedong, as Nationalist director of propaganda, branded Ye a representative of the counterrevolutionary faction of the middle-of-the-roaders in the Chinese bourgeoisie. Ye Chucang's refusal to follow directions from Guangzhou party headquarters sufficed to condemn him.[146] With Sun dead, Mao Zedong was determined that the Nationalist propaganda bureau should speak with a single authoritative voice, to eliminate all factions and to make the nation one.

It was the discipline of the little magazines that now impressed party headquarters. The party's highly successful *Republican Daily* newspapers were not easily converted into instruments for trumpeting the mass politics of the Nationalist Revolution. In 1924 Ye Chucang refused to comply with central Nationalist party instructions to convert his newspaper into a propaganda sheet because he would have lost his sponsors, his readership, and his credibility.[147] Faced with a similar situation in Guangzhou, the editor of the local *Republican Daily*, Shu Feng, indicated his willingness to make the paper more compliant, but was forced to acknowledge that a newspaper was not amenable to the kind of discipline the revolutionary state required. It simply could not represent the party, in its present form, by competing with other papers in the marketplace.

In attempting to explain his dilemma as a newspaper editor, Shu Feng likened the unwieldy Nationalist Revolution of the 1920s to the turmoil of the New Culture and May Fourth movements of the past decade. The Nationalist Revolution was in dire need of discipline and unity, he conceded, just as the earlier movements had been, but a newspaper could not be expected to supply the direction required. He advised the Nationalist party to look elsewhere for a model and extolled *New Youth* for its achievement in harnessing the May Fourth movement to the narrower aims of the Communist party.

New Youth was the precursor of and the model for many of the little magazines of the May Fourth movement. It had always been a magazine with a mission. When it was launched in 1915, its mission had been to renovate Chinese culture and society. Within five or six years, the focus of the magazine narrowed to the point where its agenda was indistinguishable from the program of the Chinese Communist party. This development marked the start of a second phase in the history of the journal, which split the cultural and political reform movement generally into liberal and mass-democratic camps.[148] It was not, of course, the content of *New Youth* that the editor of the *Guangzhou Republican Daily* admired, but rather the authority and consistency with which *New Youth* proclaimed a single-minded allegiance to the principles and policies of its parent party. This distinguished *New Youth* not only from his *Republican Daily* but from every newspaper in the country.[149]

The editor's sentiments were widely shared on the Central Executive Committee and on the Political Council of the Nationalist party. Within a year they managed to produce a central magazine committed to achieving a high level of party discipline on the model of *New Youth*. The new journal, *Political Weekly* (*Zhengzhi zhoubao*), was founded and edited on the Nationalists' behalf by Mao Zedong. It was not long before Mao had mastered the principles of revolutionary discipline, urged upon him by the Nationalists, and learned to discipline the party and the nation in order to perfect the unity of both.

6

ONE PARTY, ONE VOICE
The Nationalist Propaganda Bureau

I've always been a little distrustful of the general theme of liberation. . . . When a colonial people tries to free itself of its colonizer, that
is truly an act of liberation, in the strict sense of the word. But as we
also know that in this extremely precise example this act of liberation
is not sufficient to establish the practices of liberty that later on will be
necessary for this people, this society and these individuals to decide
upon receivable and acceptable forms of their existence or political
society. That is why I insist on the practices of freedom rather than on
the processes which indeed have their place, but which by themselves
do not seem to me to be able to decide all the practical forms of liberty.

Michel Foucault, 1984[1]

"Why must we engage in revolution?" asked Mao Zedong in 1926. "In order
that the Chinese nation might attain its liberation." [2] Mao was writing as director of propaganda for the Nationalist party. Over the autumn and winter he had
spent a good part of each day turning over newspapers, surveying the latest
magazines coming off the press, and listening to reports of public speeches
brought in by loyal office boys, with an eye to purging the Nationalist movement of anyone who voiced dissent from party policy. The Nationalist party
had never seen policing on this scale before. "Previously," Mao told the Central Executive Committee in May, "inspection was just a matter of taking clippings from newspapers. But improvements have been underway from the start
of the year." In fact, the hunt for errant voices was hastened by Mao's apppoint-
ment as director of the Central Propaganda Bureau (*Zhongyang xuanchuan
bu*) and further accelerated by the creation of a special propaganda inspection
committee within his bureau.[3] Mao had become chief inspector of Nationalist
propaganda at the very moment revolutionary discipline came to be mooted as
a condition for attaining the freedom of the nation.

Sun Yatsen had often spoken of the relationship between revolutionary
discipline and national liberation. In November 1924, Sun explained that alien
European and American ideals of liberty and equality had initially inspired
the revolution in China but had long outlived their usefulness. What China

needed from a Nationalist Revolution was not personal freedom but "corporate (*tuanti*) freedom and equality." He explained further:

Political organizations such as states and political parties . . . should all enjoy freedom and equality in their dealings, whether in struggles between one country and another or in struggles between one party and another. This is not to say that in our party or our state everyone should have freedom and equality.

To the contrary, "if the revolution is to succeed then it is the institution that must have freedom and not the individual."[4] Still, it is not at all clear that Sun intended that the surrender of individual freedom to the disciplined party should serve as a paradigm for the submission of the citizen to the liberated nation. This was Mao's particular contribution to the Nationalist Revolution. He was determined to purge the revolutionary movement in anticipation of purging the nation in revolution.

The propaganda bureau was a fairly recent innovation in the history of the Nationalist movement. The idea of exercising routine discipline through a propaganda bureau was a greater novelty still. Institutional predecessors to the Nationalist party were more like gatherings of friends than committees of comrades, and nobody thought to set up a propaganda bureau until 1919, when the May Fourth movement alerted Sun Yatsen to the potential of organized mass publicity.[5] Even then it was mainly party parliamentarians who took advantage of the new facility. After Sun chastened party parliamentarians, few other party activists rushed in to replace them. In the event, the new propaganda bureau lapsed back into silence until the advent of the Nationalist Revolution.

This was a matter of little consequence while Sun Yatsen was alive, because he was a figure of national importance. What he elected to say mattered because he said it. The general run of newspapers carried his comments along with generous reports of his activities; party branches circulated his books and pamphlets; and staff attached to the various bureaus dealing with overseas Chinese, peasants, workers, youth, women, and merchants were more than happy to run their own publicity operations without anybody looking over their shoulders apart from Sun himself. As the need for revolutionary discipline played little part in the establishment of the propaganda bureau in Sun's lifetime, the bureau payed little regard to discipline. While Sun Yatsen remained in effective control of party affairs, the propaganda bureau was the least active and least productive of all central party offices.

The part of chief censor fell to Sun himself. Even after the Leninist party reorganization of 1924, when responsibility for inspecting and correcting party publications was technically vested in the propaganda bureau, Sun continued to assume responsibility for keeping party publications in line.[6] In August and September of 1924 he personally reprimanded the *Guangzhou Republican Daily*

on three separate occasions. On 1 August, he objected strongly to the placement of an article entitled "Let's Talk Less of -Isms" (*Shaotan zhuyi*) directly
above the transcript of one of his lectures on "Democratism" (*Minquan zhuyi*).
The author of the offending piece, Sun Jingya, had been writing and editing
Nationalist party propaganda for more than a decade, and had developed a
fine sense of the contradiction between Sun Yatsen's early profession of the
liberal principles of Lincoln and Jefferson and the less liberal implications of
his new revolutionary vision. But his article went to press just as Sun Yatsen
was delivering a talk on the Three Principles of the People to a packed hall in
Guangzhou. Sun Yatsen demanded his removal. A week later, Sun Yatsen instructed the same paper to cease publication of a serial entitled "The Suicide
Club" (*Zisha gonghui*), and in the following month called upon the Central Executive Committee to rebuke the paper again for misnaming his administration
the "military government" (*jun zhengfu*).[7]

At this time Sun Yatsen effectively ran the party's propaganda apparatus.
From the time of the party reorganization in the winter of 1923 and 1924 until
his death in March of the following year, Sun not only bypassed the propaganda bureau but turned the entire system of committee management of party
affairs into a "minor administrative device" for the exercise of his personal
authority.[8] While preparing to leave Guangdong on his second Northern Expedition, he bypassed the Central Executive Committee in favor of his own
Political Council, through which he initiated a number of far-reaching changes.
The propaganda bureau's key internal publication, the *Nationalist Party Weekly*,
was abolished. A few of its regular columns were transferred to the *Guangzhou
Republican Daily*, and Wang Jingwei was assigned to edit the paper to ensure
that it no longer insulted the party president.[9]

Sun's purges were not, however, bloody ones. While Sun was alive, differences within the party and the nation took on a fraternal aspect, much as
his patriarchal syle prevailed over the routine disciplinary regime written into
the new party constitution. In principle, once the party had adopted a Leninist
command structure, even minor indiscretions could have been counted violations of party discipline. Delegates to the First Nationalist Party Congress
instructed the propaganda bureau to "attain unity in propaganda and opinion"
and charged it with ensuring that all public utterances were spoken with authority and consistency irrespective of what they happened to say.[10] But at this
early stage, recognition of a need to police propaganda bore little relation to
the ideological inclinations or even factional affiliations of party functionaries.
Revolutionary discipline was invoked only to ensure that Sun Yatsen was not
personally insulted.

After Sun died on 12 March 1925, charismatic leadership gradually yielded
to bureaucratic discipline. When party leaders returned to Guangzhou from

Sun's funeral in Beijing in May, the Central Executive Committee convened a plenary session to formulate plans and procedures for the testing times ahead. Discipline was placed at the top of the agenda. It was felt that only discipline could offer assurance that the party would survive the death of the president: "While the president was with us, his character offered protection for all principles, political platforms, and policies. But with the president dead, *party discipline* is the only thing that can protect the teachings he has bequeathed us." [11] After Sun Yatsen's guiding hand had been withdrawn, the staff of the Central Propaganda Bureau began to feel more acutely the weight of its responsibility for policing the statements of everyone associated with the Nationalist movement. In time, the attainment of "unity in propaganda and opinion" became the primary function of the bureau.

In April, an editorial in the propaganda bureau's daily newspaper, the *Guangzhou Republican Daily*, pointed in alarm at the proliferation of Nationalist publications and propaganda agencies over the past few years. The party had customarily operated on the assumption that the louder its members shouted and the more publications they circulated to the world at large, the greater was the likelihood of the party making some kind of impression in the liberal polity of the Republic. But pressing the party's claims upon the public counted for little once the party had withdrawn from the liberal arena. What mattered was that the party should speak with a consistent and authoritative voice.[12]

Wang Jingwei pressed his personal claims to party leadership with a call for unity. After reflecting on the party's response to the Shamian Incident of 23 June 1925, he announced that propaganda was lacking in leadership and discipline. British and French naval officers guarding the foreign settlements on Shamian Island had shot and killed over 50 demonstrators, exposing the oppressive face of imperialism for all to see, but the Nationalists had failed to capitalize on the opportunity to press home their exclusive claims to lead the anti-imperialist movement. Party propaganda exposed a deplorable lack of unity. Wang then called on all party bureaus to abide by the propaganda guidelines issued by party headquarters. Others confessed that the commemorations surrounding Sun's death had been a propaganda disaster. The *Guangzhou Republican Daily* conceded that the mountain of declarations and obituaries issued by party members failed to uphold the dignity of the leader or to demonstrate the unity of his party.[13] By the summer of 1925 the propaganda bureau had discovered a problem of worthy of its attention. The party-state needed a single authoritative voice to eclipse and silence all others. But who was to do the talking?

Competing Voices I: Shanghai and Guangdong

With the "Father of the Nation" dead and buried, intraparty disputes lost their fraternal aspect and began to assume a fratricidal character. Ideological differences erupted in bitter factional feuds. But it is difficult to make sense of the fratricidal struggles that erupted after Sun's death without also taking account of the nonideological sources of friction within the Nationalist movement. Lingering personal differences and institutional rivalries were no less stressful than the ideological differences that divided party offices in Shanghai and Guangzhou. The Shanghai offices of the party, for example, served as headquarters for conservative Nationalists in 1925, when Dai Jitao set up his personal office in the city, and late in the following year, when the breakaway Western Hills faction (*Xishanpai*) established its headquarters there. In each case, a major source of irritation for the Shanghai old guard was Sun Yatsen's imperious attitude in transferring party headquarters from Shanghai to Guangzhou in the winter of 1923.[14]

Senior staff members of the Shanghai bureau were jealous of their autonomy for a variety of reasons. One was the status of Shanghai headquarters in the party hierarchy. Throughout the period of the Nationalist Revolution, senior officers in Shanghai continued to think of their city as the authentic site of party headquarters, and were incensed at the way in which Sun Yatsen effectively eroded their authority through a number of key decisions taken without consultation. Sun transferred party headquarters from Shanghai to Guangzhou over the winter of 1923 and 1924 without obtaining their prior agreement. It was a matter not just of personal jealousy but also of institutional procedure: under the party constitution, Shanghai was the site of the Nationalist party headquarters (known as *benbu*). In fact, the first party propagandists assigned to Guangzhou in the new year, the Communist Tan Pingshan and Nationalist party veteran Lin Yungai, were both Shanghai appointees.[15] But from March 1923, Guangzhou took the initiative in filling further positions with Sun Yatsen's own nominees, and in July, Sun added the Communists Chen Duxiu and Feng Jupo to the propaganda committee of his military government, along with the veteran Nationalist labor activist Ma Chaojun. He delegated authority over his propaganda committee to the Communist party secretary-general, Chen Duxiu.[16] In time, Sun began to make appointments in Shanghai as well.

The Guangzhou propaganda committee was technically a government body, not a party one, and so fell outside the jurisdiction of Shanghai Party Center. It also enjoyed access to funds denied to party headquarters. Total income for the Central Propaganda Bureau in Shanghai from January through March 1923 was ¥1,630, and did not exceed ¥300 in total for the remainder of the year. In July, when the Shanghai office pleaded desperately for additional funds, Sun granted his Guangzhou committee a subsidy of YI,000 and turned down a similar request from Shanghai. In August, when the Shanghai bureau could no longer afford to subsidize a party journal, the Guangzhou propaganda committee published the fourth in a series of sixteen monographs, each printed in runs of 10,000 copies and distributed free of charge.[17] Sun's generosity toward his government officers irked Shanghai party staff, but in view of the established division between party and government, they had no formal ground for complaint.

What most riled the staff of Shanghai party headquarters was Sun's determination to set up alternative party bodies in Guangzhou. On 1 August Sun created a Party Affairs Office (*dangwu chu*) within his military government. Shanghai Party Center was informed of the decision a week after the event. It responded meekly with a request for close "cooperation" with the new body in Guangzhou, "for our mutual benefit."[18] Such was not to be. The party reorganization launched toward the end of the year involved a systematic downgrading of the status of Shanghai party headquarters in the new party structure. On 10 October 1923, Sun convened a party affairs discussion meeting (*dangwu taolunhui*) in Guangzhou and telegrammed Shanghai headquarters with a direction to make preparations for a major party reorganization. He gave few details. Despite the constitutional provisions that Shanghai headquarters was responsible for "managing the affairs of the party as a whole" and that the Shanghai Cadre Council should "plan party affairs and determine policy," Sun empowered the Guangzhou party affairs discussion meeting to "discuss appropriate means for conducting the business of the party." In the event, party officers in Shanghai learned formally of the meeting only after it had wound up, when they received a letter requesting further cooperation in implementing a number of decisions taken on their behalf.[19]

Party members in Guangzhou were by no means unaware that they were encroaching on the prerogatives of Shanghai headquarters. When party propaganda came up for discussion, the Guangzhou panel considered a motion that the Guangdong provincial branch should take charge of communication with overseas branches of the party. A review committee advised that this motion was out of order because, if implemented, it would give the Guangdong branch powers in excess of its constitutional status. "The Party Headquarters established in Shanghai," the meeting was reminded, "is the peak body charged with overseeing party affairs." But supporters of the motion were not to be deterred by a procedural technicality. As overseas party members were for the most part natives of Guangdong, it was argued, they should be expected to correspond with the branch of their native province. The acting chairman of the meeting, Xie Yingbo, noted the divisive potential of the proposal. Nevertheless, the meeting accepted a motion by the head of the Guangdong provincial branch, Deng Zeru, to create an Overseas Chinese Information Office (*Huaqiao tongxun chu*) in the propaganda division of the Guangdong provincial branch. The review committee's misgivings were effectively ignored. Deng Zeru later claimed that his Guangdong branch had taken the initiative in founding the Overseas Chinese Information Office only after Shanghai party headquarters had surrendered authority over "all liaison activities with Overseas Chinese." To the contrary, the Shanghai office was presented with this and other decisions in the aftermath of a remarkable coup conducted by Sun Yatsen and ambitious non-Communist party officials in Guangzhou.[20]

Later in October, following the arrival of the Soviet adviser Mikhail Borodin, Sun appointed a provisional Central Executive Committee to press on with the reorganization. The provisional committee made further inroads into the domain of Shanghai party headquarters. First, it founded a new central party journal, the *Nationalist Party Weekly*, with editors and editorial offices drawn from Sun's military government in Guangzhou. Next, it brought all existing propaganda institutions in Guangdong under its own wing, thereby converting government agencies into party ones and placing itself in command of all party propaganda in South China. Sun clearly intended that the provisional committee was to take full responsibility for all party affairs.[21]

On hearing of the reforms under way in Guangzhou, the reaction of Shanghai party headquarters alternated between apprehension and relief, before finally settling into outright indignation. Senior party officers were not well informed. Sun Yatsen gave some indication of what was in store through a telegram directing bureau heads (*buzhang*) to change their titles to bureau directors (*bu zhuren*) and to reduce their staff by around half, to a maximum of four officers per bureau. After Shanghai queried his command, Sun replied on 17 October that these "temporary" measures would lead to "reform and expansion" in the near future. He neglected to point out that expansion was destined to take place in Guangzhou. In an earlier telegram Sun informed Shanghai headquarters that he was setting up a reorganization committee to oversee reform in Shanghai itself. The effect of these communications was to confuse party officers in Shanghai and so render them incapable of mounting an effective response.[22]

A curious and quite misguided version of the party reforms was published in the *Shanghai Republican Daily* in November 1923. The tenor of the report gives some idea of the confusion under which the Shanghai officers labored. A national congress of the party was scheduled to convene in Guangzhou, the paper announced, but the party's Executive Committee (*zhixing weiyuanhui*) was to be located at the traditional center of party affairs in Shanghai. This new peak committee was to be established immediately for the purpose of executing decisions taken by a Provisional National Committee (*Linshi quanguo weiyuanhui*). Readers were assured that the composition of the Executive Committee was to be decided by Shanghai party headquarters itself. The article ended with a ringing endorsement of the reorganization on the understanding that central party offices "should be situated in Shanghai." Between publication of the article and the convening of the Shanghai Central Cadre Council later in the same month, Shanghai party officers were told that Shanghai was not to feature quite so prominently in the reorganization after all. The prominent parliamentarian and party publicist Zhang Ji expressed the council's disappointment. "It goes without saying that Party Headquarters should be located in Shanghai," he remarked. "It should not be transferred to Guangdong." The council meeting broke up in acrimony.[23]

The Shanghai branch could make little advance preparation for its reduced role—"due to lack of detailed information"—until Sun Yatsen dispatched Liao Zhongkai as his personal envoy to Shanghai in November. Liao tried to cool things down but appears to have made things worse by misrepresenting Sun's intentions. He is reported to have said that there were to be two central organs (*zhongyang jiguan*), one in Guangzhou to handle party affairs in the three southern provinces and the other in Shanghai to cover the rest of the country. Party officers remained under this erroneous impression until they gathered for the opening of the party congress in Guangzhou in January of the following year.[24] It was only then that they learned that the Shanghai executive was to be one of five regional party executives, each responsible for a few neighboring provinces and all under the direct control of a higher party authority in Guangzhou, the Central Executive Committee. This arrangement had not been spelled out in the draft party constitution passed on to Shanghai headquarters for inspection and approval in November.[25]

Early in the new year, Sun Yatsen went a step further and reduced the salaries of all staff members in the old Shanghai headquarters. From mid-year they received no salaries at all. In December 1924, the demoralized staff of the Shanghai executive branch wrote to Party Center in Guangzhou threatening to resign en masse. "It appears that the Centre is deliberately treating the staff of this Branch in a biased and unfair manner," they complained. "What we cannot understand is how the Centre can treat our branch with such derision." The letter drew a labored comparison with the favored treatment meted out to party officers in Guangzhou, where staff members were still paid regularly by the month, and it ended with a demand for an end to the pay cuts and for full compensation for the shortfall in salaries to date. A small sum arrived by return mail to carry the branch over into the new year. But when no further assistance was forthcoming, the Shanghai branch called a general strike of party officers beginning on 19 January 1925. It appears that Nationalist and Communist executives of the Shanghai branch went out together.[26]

Some sense of the betrayal felt by Shanghai party officers was conveyed in a report to the First Nationalist Party Congress by the party's retiring director of propaganda, Ye Chucang. Ye directed a stinging rebuke at Guangzhou party officials for the devastating effects of the party reorganization on the performance of his duties. In 1923, he reported, propaganda had been "totally without success." Its only redeeming feature was the cautionary example it offered for future reference. Ye did not dispute the new concentration of authority in party affairs. Instead he complained bitterly of the way in which his own attempts to centralize authority as director of propaganda had been undermined over the preceding year. While conceding that there might be some benefit in spreading propaganda operations far and wide across the country, he pointed out that any marginal advantage was likely to be lost without clear demarcation of lines of authority. What was needed was respect for formal authority and discipline in the exercise of duties. He proposed that future propaganda operations should be centralized on the model of "the central post office with its regional branches." Otherwise, he argued, "we can neither assess the results of propaganda nor can we even discover what content is making its way into propaganda." Ye Chucang had already suggested that the site of the party's "central post office" should be located in Shanghai, China's "centre of public opinion." But public opinion was of little account to party headquarters in Guangzhou. What mattered now was the Will of the People, manifest in Sun Yatsen and his new party-state.[27]

Ye Chucang's call for greater discipline was not intended to buttress the claims of the new party-state in Guangzhou, and he refused to obey his own counsel over the following years. This was no minor indiscretion. His *Shanghai Republican Daily* was the only party newspaper with a truly national circulation and the sole party publication with a measure of influence outside of party circles. In a poll of students conducted at Beijing University in December 1923, the paper ranked second overall in popularity behind the *Beijing Morning Post* (*Chenbao*), and first among female respondents.[28] Ye Chucang was certainly jealous of the newspaper's reputation. He declined to submit to an editorial committee appointed over his paper by the new party headquarters in Guangzhou, and he followed his own instincts in editorial policy in the belief that his judgment of party and public affairs in central China was likely to be better informed and more judicious than decisions taken by party officers seated a thousand miles away in Guangzhou. Moreover, the paper was basically self-supporting and sensitive to market demands. Ye knew that his readership was a little more sophisticated than Guangzhou was prepared to concede, and, as a founding manager of the paper, he was acutely aware that Shanghai was a marketplace as well as a political center. So his editorial tone was rarely strident, and partisan pieces were usually interleaved among news items of general interest. The paper's major concession to the party reorganization was the inclusion of a margin surrounding each page of newsprint that set out party policies and principles.[29]

Institutional jealousies such as these had ideological implications. Much as he may have sympathized with the general thrust of the party's anti-imperialist, antimilitarist and mass-oriented policies, Ye's position as editor of the *Shanghai Republican Daily* obliged him to compromise them. With one eye on his established readership and the other focused on the Shanghai party offices, located in the French concession, Ye returned or significantly revised manuscripts and party documents that seemed excessive in their criticism of imperialism. He was also soft on "warlords." Like many other Shanghai residents living under a local military administration, Ye had difficulty reconciling opposition to militarism in the abstract with his practical preference for some factions over others. The Zhejiang military governor, Lu Yongxiang, earned his respect. When Lu came into conflict with a Jiangsu warlord who happened to be allied with the party's longtime enemy in North China, Cao Kun, in September 1924, Ye sided with Lu Yongxiang in the dispute. He was not alone. The party's Zhejiang provincial branch and parliamentary wing both joined the *Republican Daily* in issuing public declarations in support of the Zhejiang leader in defiance of the party principle that all warlords were enemies of the Nationalist Revolution. Ye aroused considerable hostility among Communists for his presumption. Still, his sense of party traditions and interests coincided with the feelings of Sun Yatsen, who issued a declaration in support of Lu Yongxiang the day after Ye Chucang's piece went to press.[30]

Nor could Ye Chucang afford to condone labor agitation when it was directed against his major advertising clients or threatened the party's corporate benefactors. The Nanyang Tobacco Company was a party benefactor of long standing—it had made a donation of ¥50,000 as recently as 1922—and the party customarily rewarded loyal donors with substantial political favors. Nanyang called on its credit with the party in September 1924, as it had done many times in the past, when a strike broke out at its Shanghai factories. Ye was also alarmed at the prospect of company directors withdrawing their advertising accounts if the paper should either fail to publicize the management's version of the dispute or perhaps devote excessive space to the workers' claims. The paper faced financial difficulties in the summer of 1924, not least on account of the reluctance at party headquarters in Guangzhou to subsidize party activities in Shanghai. In any event, the *Republican Daily* ended up supporting the Nanyang Tobacco Company without reservation. Ye Chucang's sympathy for local merchant houses paid off some months later, when the Wing On Company offered to pay Shanghai party officers' salaries at a time when Guangzhou party headquarters was slow in meeting branch expenses.[31]

Within a year after the Nationalist Revolution had gotten under way, Ye

Chucang and his newspaper had compromised the three most important tenets of the Nationalist Revolution: the overthrow of both imperialism and militarism, and the promotion of the mass movements. Ye published his paper in the relatively open and privileged political environment of Shanghai, and worked to a strict commercial budget, but these appeared lame excuses to radical party officers in Guangzhou, who pilloried him for his "counterrevolutionary" attitude. Nevertheless, he received the quiet endorsement of the nominal director of propaganda, Dai Jitao, who shared Ye's conviction that Shanghai was the appropriate center for national propaganda operations and who resented growing Communist control of the local labor movement.[32]

Once ideological differences crystallized around these institutional sources of friction, especially between the Shanghai and Guangzhou offices of the party, they had the effect of reinforcing the autonomist sentiments of the Shanghai party executive. Shanghai commentators accused the Guangzhou movement of "turning red" and were branded, in turn, as representing a counterrevolutionary current within the Nationalist movement. It is useful nevertheless to distinguish the later development of ideological cleavages between "left" and "right" factions from the range of earlier disagreements that divided the Shanghai and Guangzhou offices of the party and to recognize the part Sun Yatsen played in precipitating both sources of tension. Sun all but destroyed the liberal parliamentary movement within the party early in 1923, and he overrode formal constitutional procedures later in the year when he initiated his major party reorganization without consulting party headquarters in Shanghai.[33] Although Sun was personally responsible for some of the ill feeling in the party, he could never be held to account for it, or at least not in public. The fortunes of every party member and each faction in the Nationalist movement were bound up with the preservation of his good name. Some of the frustration felt on Sun's account was vented against Communists in the Nationalist movement, who were, in a sense, the chief beneficiaries of the party reforms that he instituted.

The Communists, needless to say, were not innocent bystanders in the party reorganization. Mikhail Borodin and Chen Duxiu drafted some of the most important documents of the reorganized Nationalist party and consistently manipulated factional differences in the Nationalist movement to their own advantage.[34] The Communist party was bedevilled by problems of its own and, significantly, one of its greatest lines of fracture ran between Shanghai and Guangzhou. During the Guangzhou merchant insurrection in October 1924, the Shanghai headquarters of the Communist party counseled retreat from Guangzhou against the advice of Borodin and the Guangdong provincial committee. Even family ties could not prevail against their differences. In Shanghai, Chen Duxiu called on his comrades to abandon Guangdong, while

his son, in Guangzhou, urged perseverence on behalf of the Guangdong committee of the Communist party. Disagreement arose again early in 1926, when
Communist agencies and advisers in Guangzhou decided to attack Ye Chucang, Shao Yuanchong, and other members of the "middle" faction of the
Nationalist party based in Shanghai, while Shanghai Communist party headquarters advised greater discrimination in targeting Nationalists as enemies of
the revolution. It was clear to Communists in Shanghai, at least, that there were
serious differences among conservative factions of the Nationalist party and
that their own relations with Ye and Shao in Shanghai were still quite service-
able. Their persistence on this point led to their own alienation from Guangzhou Communist party offices. Further disagreements along similar lines arose
when preparations for the Northern Expedition got under way in 1926.[35] None
of these disputes indicates particularist sentiment in Shanghai, in the sense of
sentimental attachment to a particular locality, but the eruption of a similar
range of disputes between the Shanghai and Guangzhou offices of each party
does point to the emergence of a new kind of strategic particularism within
each party. The emergence of systemic differences also raised new problems
of party discipline. Propaganda agencies needed to cope with strategic as well
as ideological differences, and to manage disagreements taking place among
party offices dispersed widely throughout the country.

When parochial disagreements overlapped with ideological cleavages, they
ranked as problems for the Nationalist party's new disciplinary apparatus. The
selection of committee members from Shanghai, Beijing, and Guangzhou to
sit on the Provisional Political Propaganda Committee (*Linshi zhengzhi xuanchuan weiyuanhui*) in June 1925 was intended to make the transprovincial propaganda network more responsive to direction from the Central Propaganda
Bureau in Guangzhou. In fact, however, it exacerbated existing tensions to the
point of rupture. In Guangzhou, the Communist Tan Pingshan lent his newly
acquired authority to the publication of an unofficial party journal, *The Revolution* (*Geming*), which enjoyed the backing of radical factions in Guangzhou.
Articles published in the magazine infuriated others on the Provisional Political Propaganda Committee based in Shanghai, notably Dai Jitao, by referring
to elements in the Nationalist party as "counterrevolutionary" (*fan geming*).
In a fit of rage, Dai invited the two other provisional committee members in
Shanghai, Shen Dingyi and Shao Yuanchong, to join him in editing another
informal party magazine entitled *The Independent* (*Duli*). The committee was
powerless to police its own members, let alone the party at large.[36]

The Independent issued from Dai Jitao's personal address in Shanghai,
with the stated aim of "explaining and researching the Three Principles of the
People." Its editors wished to remain "independent" of the sectional, class,
and vested interests that they held responsible for tainting the purity of Sun

Yatsen's principles. But they were by no means aloof from the disputes that were beginning to rend the Nationalist movement itself. The title was an unequivocal statement of their battle-front position as self-styled independents, elevated far above the politics of sectional representation. Around the same time, Dai Jitao also wrote and published his two influential tracts, "The Philosophical Foundations of Sun Yatsen-ism" and "The National Revolution and the Nationalist Party," in which he forcefully reiterated the call for a popular awakening independent of class and sectional interests. Dai Jitao's fiercely independent stance soon came to be associated with a factional alliance of party members in Shanghai, and eventually fanned anti-Communist feeling in the Nationalist party from one end of the country to the other. Hence the seats parceled out among Communists and non-Communists on the Provisional Political Propaganda Committee only confirmed the symmetry between factional differences and geographical distance, with conservatives working from Shanghai and radicals pressing on in Guangzhou, and further reduced the prospect of disciplining propaganda activities outside Guangdong from Nationalist party headquarters in South China.

Competing Voices II: The Staff of the Propaganda Bureau

Dai Jitao was the first Nationalist director of propaganda to be appointed after the party reorganization. By the time of his appointment in 1924 he had served as Sun Yatsen's private secretary for over a decade and had earned an enviable reputation in radical circles for his eloquent writings on Marxism and many passionate essays on the state of the nation. His commitment to the routine work of the propaganda bureau was, however, qualified by an erratic temperament.

Dai was a native of Zhejiang who lived in Shanghai by preference. He never felt at home in the revolutionary base of Guangdong and did not relish the prospect of joining soldiers on campaign in the hills bordering Guangxi, or shouting through loud-hailers in the provincial townships of Huizhou and Shantou, and having to make sense of difficult southern dialects in return. Just sixteen months before his appointment to the bureau, at the age of 31, he had been deeply affected by a series of personal and professional disappointments, and attempted suicide. Passing fishermen dragged him from the river. In later years he retreated frequently into pastoral solitude and religious sanctuary before finally succeeding in taking his life on 11 February 1949, just as the Communists were marshaling their forces for a final assault on South China. At one time he had been very close to the founders of the Chinese Communist party. But he never quite recovered from the angst that overcame him early in his career when Sun Yatsen began courting the favors of Russian and Chinese Communists against his advice. Dai was enervated and disillusioned by Sun's persistence. Some of his friends who opposed the admission of Communists into the Nationalist party secretly schemed to defeat them; others petitioned Sun Yatsen to throw them out. Dai, however, turned his attention to doctrinal exegesis and to pedantic questions of punctuation in revolutionary propaganda. His time in the propaganda bureau is chiefly remembered for the opportunities foregone.[37]

He certainly did very little to keep the Communists out of office while he had the chance. Dai was offered the key post of director of the politburo of the Huangpu Academy in addition to directorship of the propaganda bureau. He turned down the first offer and declined to exercise full responsibility for the second. In July he was offered a seat on the Political Council as well, soon to become the supreme organ of party and government in Guangdong. Appointments to the council were made by Sun personally, and no party member known to be hostile to the Communists ever won selection apart from Dai Jitao. Yet Dai declined that position as well.[38] Zhou Enlai accepted the job at the Huangpu Academy in his stead and within two years came to exercise unrivaled influence over the expansion of military, government, and party authority at the local level in Guangdong. In 1925, Mao Zedong took over from Dai Jitao in the propaganda bureau after an interval during which it was headed by Wang Jingwei. When Dai finally began to lodge a series of complaints about excessive Communist influence in the Nationalist party, his own responsibility for this turn of affairs was not lost on his friends.[39]

In 1924 Dai wandered back and forth between Guangzhou and Shanghai before finally locking himself away in his self-styled "Dai Jitao Office" (*Dai Jitao banshichu*) in Shanghai, to pen desultory letters to friends and try as best he could to ignore telegrams from party headquarters in Guangzhou asking him to clarify his intentions. In a letter to Chiang Kaishek, he responded that he would prefer to remain in Shanghai "to manage a publishing house or a newspaper." [40] In the intervals between Dai's unpredictable visits to Guangzhou, the day-to-day management of the propaganda bureau seems to have fallen into the hands of Peng Sumin and the bureau secretary, Liu Luyin.

Peng Sumin was an experienced party organizer and propagandist who had recently completed a term as head of the party's Central Affairs Bureau. It was probably his "Memorandum on Party Affairs," addressed to Sun Yatsen in January of the previous year, that recommended him for the post. Sun added a marginal comment to the effect that the memo was "most accurate and should be publicized to all party members." [41] It is not difficult to see why. Peng traced the party's past misfortunes to the failure of party followers to adhere to their leader's doctrines and to carry them into effect, referring in particular to the performance of party parliamentarians and government officials associated with the Guangzhou Rump Parliament, who had done little to advance the cause of party rule while they were in office. Instead of complaining of the new direction in party leadership and organization, like many of his colleagues, Peng highlighted insufficient loyalty and devotion to the leader as the source of the party's problems. The party's foremost task, he noted, was to offer instruction in party principles to party members to ensure their compliance with Sun's wishes. He suggested this might be achieved through intensive instruction in the Three Principles of the People in "party schools." Peng also detected misgivings about Sun and his principles among students, workers, and other sections of the community outside the party, and concluded that there were few people in the country who would not benefit from drilling in the teachings of Sun Yatsen. The neat symmetry between the views of Peng and Sun on the key issues of party leadership, the failings of liberal parliamentarians, and the need for mass instruction in the Three Principles would have recommended Peng for the job of leading party propaganda into the era of party rule. But his candidacy was never finally confirmed. Dai Jitao returned to Guangzhou in April and occupied his chair at the propaganda bureau until June. Peng moved sideways to direct the Central Peasant Bureau, but he died just five months later.[42]

Continuity in the management of the propaganda bureau was supplied by a minor functionary, Liu Luyin, who was secretary of the bureau from February to June 1924, and acting director from June to August. Liu was born in Yangfeng County, Jiangxi Province. At the time of joining the propaganda bureau, at the age of 33, he was already a qualified lawyer, sociologist, and publicist with considerable experience in Shanghai, the United States, and Canada behind him. He took his first degree in sociology at Fudan University, where he was active in student politics and came into contact with the Shanghai circle of Sun Yatsen's Chinese Revolutionary party. His graduate studies were undertaken at the law school of a campus of the University of California. Liu became a leading contributor to the newspaper of the U.S. party headquarters, the *Young China Morning Post* (*Shaonian zhongguo chenbao*), and in 1920 took charge of the entire U.S. Nationalist party network. In the summer of 1923 Liu moved to Vancouver, where he assumed a comparable position supervising the work of Canadian party headquarters. He was selected at the close of the year to be a U.S. party delegate to the First Nationalist Party Congress. He stayed on in Guangzhou after the congress to work as secretary to Dai Jitao in the propaganda bureau.[43]

Liu's education and experience in Shanghai and abroad shaped his understanding of the historic mission of the Nationalist party and the function of its propaganda. In particular, his years supervising the party network in North America made Liu an ardent spokesman for Sun's Three Principles. While in the United States, he commended the Three Principles as a unique and systematic "reform program" that drew upon the best of East and West and delivered the unique benefits of both without recourse to violent social revolution. Liu traced the inspiration behind the Three Principles to a marriage of the traditional Chinese virtues of universal love (*boai*) and mutual aid (*huzhu*) with the principles of liberty and equality enshrined in the Constitution of the United States of America. His emphasis on the traditional virtues anticipated the thinking of his mentor, Dai Jitao, when Dai turned to reinterpreting Sun Yatsen's Three Principles as the foundation for a traditionalist nationalism in 1925.[44]

At first Liu Luyin had much in common with Dai. He was initially one of Dai Jitao's greatest admirers, sharing his distaste for Marxism and his mistrust of Chinese Communists in the Nationalist party. After leaving the propaganda bureau, Liu accepted an offer to serve as Dai's personal assistant in Shanghai in 1925, and subsequently occupied a key position in the breakaway Western Hills faction of the Nationalist party. Like Dai, Liu placed great faith in the capacity of enlightened intellectuals to awaken the people of China from their slumber. Early in his career he had tried in vain to shift the attention of the Canadian party headquarters from the commercial hub of Vancouver's Chinese community to a small circle of local intellectuals.[45] His elevated notion of the place of intellectuals in the Chinese diaspora was somewhat out of touch with the historic role of the manual laborers, market gardeners, and shopkeepers who had kept the Nationalist movement solvent with their modest regular remittances. His conviction was nevertheless consonant with Dai Jitao's belief in the responsibility befalling scholars to awaken their countrymen back home in China. Liu shared with Dai Jitao a firm conviction that individual ethical cultivation and mass political education offered the keys to national renewal.

Liu was, however, a liberal democrat at heart and was destined to fall out of favor with Dai Jitao once Dai began to embrace a more authoritarian brand of nationalism. Neither man had any patience for the chicanery of parliamentary factions in the early Republic, but Liu, at least, was never shaken from the conviction that the Chinese polity should be modeled on the liberal democratic system he had seen at work in North America. Speaking in the United States in 1921, Liu had defined the Nationalist party as a "political school for training the citizens of a republic." [46] When he accepted the propaganda bureau appointment three years later, Liu was no less committed to ensuring that the Nationalist party remain a training college for democratic citizenship. At the First Nationalist Party Congress he rose to defend a motion to adopt an American electoral system for use within the Nationalist party, aimed at ensuring minority representation at the highest levels. On that occasion, Mao Zedong responded that a more representative system of party elections would do harm to a revolutionary party, and Xuan Zhonghua condemned the idea of proportional representation as "a device of the capitalist class for deceiving people." Liu took umbrage at both suggestions, but lost the argument. Mao's success on the floor of the congress gave fair warning of further challenges after he succeeded Dai Jitao as director of propaganda. By then, however, Liu Luyin had already discovered that respect for the institutions and practices of liberal democracy placed him in a minority even within his own party.[47]

Liu ultimately fell afoul of right-wing demagogues in the Nationalist movement after Dai Jitao had withdrawn from the center of party affairs and moved to support the military commander, Chiang Kaishek. Liu Luyin parted company to join Hu Hanmin's faction. He returned to direct the Central Propaganda Bureau early in the following decade, during Hu's brief ascendency in the Nanjing government, and before Hu was placed under house arrest by Chiang Kaishek in March of 1931. Liu subsequently grew to loathe many of the powerful members of Chiang Kaishek's inner circle of bureaucratic aides, including Chiang's chief adviser Yang Yongtai. In October 1936 Liu conspired in Yang's assassination. He was arrested and charged with Yang's murder, and languished in jail for a decade.[48]

Lang Xingshi and Zhou Fohai worked under Liu Luyin in 1924. Lang was an old friend and colleague of Liu who had cooperated in managing the affairs of the U.S. and Canadian party headquarters in San Francisco and Vancouver. Zhou Fohai was introduced to the bureau through Dai Jitao, who offered him the position in April shortly after Zhou had returned to China from studying in Japan. Zhou Fohai and Dai had much in common. Neither had time for liberal democratic politics, and both had flirted briefly with Marxism; both were involved in discussions leading to the founding of the Chinese Communist party before they returned to the fold of "Sun Yatsenism." Zhou's precocious familiarity with Marxism gave him an early taste of historical materialism. Rather than make a Communist of him, however, this only strengthened Zhou's resolve to suppress class struggle in China through mass instruction in the principles of Sun Yatsen.[49]

Dai Jitao and Zhou Fohai were far less tolerant of liberal politics than were Liu Luyin and Lang Xingshi; Liu Luyin and Lang Xingshi were rather naive about Marxism; and Peng Sumin seems to have hovered about the office talking of the need to respect and obey the party leader. For all their differences, personnel appointed to the propaganda bureau in 1924 were united by a desire to protect the Nationalist Revolution from the politics of "class struggle." They understood this to mean limiting the influence of the Chinese Communist party over the direction of the revolutionary movement. Their shared distaste for class struggle also united them in the belief that mass political indoctrination in the principles of Sun Yatsen was the only sure antidote to social revolution in China. After they left the propaganda bureau in the following year, they kept in touch with one another through their shared involvement with the breakaway Western Hills faction of the Nationalist party.[50]

Wang Jingwei's appointment as director of propaganda on 14 August 1924 ushered in a second period of propaganda bureau operation. This covered a crucial phase in the history of the party, from Sun Yatsen's second Northern Expedition to his tour of Shanghai and Japan and his death in Beijing. Within the province itself, it coincided with Chiang Kaishek's suppression of the Guangzhou merchant militia, the first expedition against Chen Jiongming in eastern Guangdong, and the outbreak of the great Guangzhou–Hong Kong strike. The bureau seems to have played a minor role in the commemorations and campaigns, strikes and rebellions erupting around it. Other party agencies were leading the revolution out of the city into the countryside and formulating and policing propaganda for the Nationalist movement as they went. Zhou Enlai was directing propaganda for the armed forces and Peng Pai for the peasant associations. Feng Jupo and other Communist organizers of the Guangzhou–Hong Kong Strike Committee were making the major decisions bearing on the labor movement. A host of other party, government, and military agencies at central, provincial, and local levels were showing little hesitation in speaking out. The propaganda bureau, at the eye of the storm, kept its counsel.

Sun's death dealt an immediate blow to the Nationalists, but its full implications did not come home with full force until 20 August, when his trusted confidante and chief troubleshooter, Liao Zhongkai, fell to a hail of bullets fired by a hired party assassin. Liao was a pivotal figure in the party after Sun's death. Sun had entrusted him with the most onerous positions in his movement, including provincial governor, provincial treasurer, director of the party's Central Labor Bureau, and director of the Central Peasant Bureau. His assassination deprived the Nationalists of a major contender for leadership and splintered the party into many competing fragments. Coincidentally, his assassination also marked the close of the second phase of propaganda bureau operation. A senior propaganda bureau officer, Chen Qiulin, happened to be accompanying Liao Zhongkai when the gunman opened fire. Liao died on the spot. Chen was grievously wounded and died in the hospital three days later, on 23 August.[51]

Wang Jingwei directed the bureau from August to November 1924 before heading for Beijing with Sun Yatsen's entourage. He bided his time over these few months. He neither came out publicly to condemn the growth of Communist influence in the Nationalist movement nor proscribed their opponents. After Wang returned to Guangdong from the scene of Sun's death, however, he began seriously courting Russian and Chinese Communists in the hope of improving his chances of gaining control of the party. Dai Jitao had already withdrawn from the propaganda bureau by this stage and had taken Liu Luyin and Zhou Fohai with him. Their replacements, Chen Fumu, Chen Yangxuan, and Chen Qiulin, did little to divert the propaganda bureau from its earlier course. Nevertheless, they showed themselves a little more willing to compromise with the "revolutionary" faction of the Nationalist movement than their predecessors had been. This meant working in close association with a revitalized Wang Jingwei.[52]

Chen Fumu entered the propaganda bureau almost by accident. He began his career in the Nationalist party in mid-1924 as an employee for the *Hong Kong News* (*Xinwen bao*), at a time when that paper was brought over from Chen Jiongming's camp by a hefty grant from the Nationalist party. After abandoning Chen Jiongming, one of the co-owners of the newspaper, Huang Jusu, threw in his lot with anti-Communist elements in the Nationalist party. He rose rapidly to the position of head of the Central Peasant Bureau in October 1924, where he faced the daunting task of ridding that bureau of Communist influence. Huang tried valiantly but in vain. His master stroke was an attempt to replace the peasant bureau's dynamic Communist secretary, Peng Pai, with one of his own employees on the *Hong Kong News*, Chen Fumu. The attempt failed. In the upshot, Huang Jusu lost his seat in the Peasant Bureau and Peng Pai strengthened his grip over the peasant movement as a whole. Chen Fumu, after failing to gain entry to the peasant bureau through the abortive coup, was offered the rather less formidable job of editing the Nationalist party newspaper, the *Guangzhou Republican Daily*, and of preventing that from turning red as well. Over the following year, Chen grew equally concerned about Communist influence in the local labor movement and founded the Association of Revolutionary Workers to rally independent labor unions into an alternative socialist organization. His own political loyalties in the internecine politics of the Nationalist movement are difficult to pin down. The labor historian Ming Chan has caught something of the nuance of Chen's position in his memorable assessment of the man as "somewhere to the left of the KMT right." [53]

Two other new figures in the propaganda bureau, Chen Qiulin and Chen Yangxuan, had similar backgrounds. Chen Qiulin had worked on the propaganda staff of Chen Jiongming in southern Fujian in 1919 and 1920, and proceeded to write for Chen's newspapers in Hong Kong before the *Hong Kong News* was bought out by the Nationalist party. On returning to Guangzhou in the spring of 1925, he was appointed to head the Central Propagandist Training Institute and commissioned to write editorials for the *Hong Kong News*, the *Guangzhou Republican Daily*, and another Guangzhou newspaper, the *Republican News* (*Guomin xinwen*). His editorials show little sympathy for Communist members of the Nationalist party. Writing for the *Hong Kong News* in April, Chen conceded that Communists should be allowed to work within the Nationalist party on the condition that they stay within the limits of the Nationalist

Revolution. Some weeks later, in the *Republican News*, he went a little further. Some Communists had infiltrated the Nationalist party for "counterrevolutionary" purposes, he argued, and should be expelled immediately. Chen Qiulin also kept company with members of the revolutionary faction of the Nationalist party and was described by one contemporary observer (apparently unaware of the byzantine factional politics of the Nationalist movement) as "one of the most radical communists." [54] Regrettably, Chen Qiulin left the propaganda bureau as haphazardly as he entered it. He was the propaganda officer killed along with Liao Zhongkai in August 1925.

The other new staff member, Chen Yangxuan, replaced Liu Luyin as bureau secretary shortly after Wang Jingwei was promoted to the position of director in August 1924. Chen represented the bureau at Central Executive Committee meetings in Wang's place from November 1924 to May of the following year.[55] Chen was not a Communist. Under his direction, the propaganda bureau cooperated in publicity campaigns with an organization known for its strident opposition to the Communist party, the Society for Commemorating the Revolution (*Geming jinian hui*), which was headed by one of the Communists' most embittered opponents in Guangzhou, Deng Zeru. Whatever their individual political inclinations, the three Chens (Chen Fumu, Chen Qiulin, and Chen Yangxuan) were only minor party functionaries, and their humble standing in the Nationalist movement was reflected in the low profile of the propaganda bureau over this phase of operation. Before the Third Plenum of May 1925, the bureau was also the only central office of the party without a single Communist on its staff.[56] This may account for its lethargy.

The third and most active phase of Nationalist propaganda operations began in October 1925, when Mao Zedong was appointed to run the bureau on Wang Jingwei's behalf. In this phase the bureau finally came into its own, although not on Mao's account alone. His appointment followed closely on a number of initiatives to bring order and discipline into party propaganda by routinizing its procedures and inviting Communists and Nationalists to work together in overseeing propaganda operations. Some months earlier, members of the Communist party had gained entry to a peak propaganda institution for the first time when Yu Shude, Zhang Guotao, and Tan Pingshan were appointed to the Provisional Political Propaganda Committee under the Central Executive Committee. Yu, Zhang, and Tan were balanced on the committee by Dai Jitao, Shao Yuanchong, and Shen Dingyi, three men hostile to Communist activities in the Nationalist movement. Wang Jingwei, as director of propaganda, straddled the division in the belief that he could play one group off against the other and reserve for himself the right to speak on behalf of the party as a whole.[57] In fact, though, only two of the seven committee members (Wang Jingwei and Tan Pingshan) remained stationed in Guangdong. The Communists Zhang Guotao and Yu Shude resumed their previous positions in Shanghai and Beijing respectively, whereas the three non-Communists, Dai Jitao, Shao Yuanchong, and Shen Dingyi, all made their way to Shanghai, where they set up an alternative party propaganda apparatus.

This provisional committee was created shortly after the Guangzhou plenum, which was called in the wake of Sun's death to discipline the party and "protect the teachings he has bequeathed us." In April and May, members of Sun's entourage returned disconsolately to Guangzhou from the scene of his death. Before leaving Beijing they had convened the Third Plenary Session of the Central Executive Committee, but in the face of mounting opposition from the northern government (which forced closure of the Nationalists' *Beijing Republican Daily*) and residual concern in Guangzhou about the merits of convening a meeting in Beijing, the delegates returned to Guangzhou to resume the plenum in mid-May. Even Dai Jitao made his way south. He was rewarded with the task of drafting the formal Declaration and Instructions issued by the plenum. Dai worked hard to attribute the success of recent party initiatives to popular instruction in the principles and platform of the Nationalist party, and exhorted comrades to greater efforts in their propaganda work to "awaken" the masses.[58]

Dai's draft of the "Instructions on Accepting the President's Will" defined the president's ideological legacy as an integral corpus of seven canons composed or authorized by Sun Yatsen. These were never to be contradicted or challenged. The Third Plenum also reaffirmed the policy of admitting Communists into the Nationalist party on the condition that they show "respect for the character of the President and acceptance of the works he has bequeathed us." These were to form the "foundation of discipline" for the party. For all its stress on discipline, there was no mistaking the significance of the plenum documents for the internecine conflicts that were beginning to surface in the Nationalist movement. The documents were immediately pressed into service by factions hostile to the presence of the Communists.[59]

Provincial branches outside Guangdong felt at liberty to attack the radicals from a safe distance. Shen Dingyi waited until he was back in Shanghai before donning his cap as Provisional Political Propaganda Committee member and mobilizing the Zhejiang provincial branch to issue "Instructions on the Attitude Toward Class Struggle Which Should Be Adopted in Propaganda Work." His instructions on class struggle became, in turn, a rallying point for members associated with Dai Jitao. Drawing on Dai's plenary documents, the Zhejiang instructions stated bluntly that the proper function of propaganda was to ameliorate rather than exacerbate differences among social classes. This principle was extended to conflict within the Nationalist movement itself, which was defined as a struggle not between social classes but between more and less enlightened party cadre: "The distinction between revolutionaries and counter-revolutionaries lies not in their class background, but in their levels of understanding and awakening." [60] The idea of awakening took out a new lease on life as an antidote to the poison of social revolution in society at large, and as an antidote to political divisions within the party itself.

The two problems started to overlap once divisions within the party were interpreted as reflections of divisions within society. The link was more symbolic than real: class origins had little direct bearing on political differences within the revolutionary camp. On the Nationalist side, Sun Yatsen felt that workers, peasants, and other underprivileged social groups stood to profit from the help and guidance of their superiors. "Even among the leaders of labor unions there are many who are not workers," he remarked in his third lecture on democracy. Among these, "there have been quite a number who have served the workers out of a genuine sense of justice." [61] Communist labor organizers shared Sun's prejudices. The leadership of organized labor in Guangdong did in fact have a significant working-class element but was not noticeably more radical on this account. Certainly the proletarian origins of local labor representatives offered little defense against the inroads of Communist organizers, who felt qualified by an enlightened sense of proletarian interest to seize control of the provincial labor movement. Communist labor organizers dismissed their working-class opponents as ignorant dupes of capitalism.[62]

In either case, it was their level of consciousness—not wealth or penury, power or impotence—that distinguished revolutionaries from counterrevolutionaries. The chief distinction separating Communist from Nationalist cadre, in their own minds, was that each had awoken to the historical necessity of mobilizing people around "class" or "national" interests to attain the unity and independence of China. Hence the target of Zhejiang Nationalists was not a particular social class, nor even self-assigned class representatives in the Communist party, but rather a new kind of political strategy touted in Communist literature as an alternative to the kind of awakening Sun Yatsen had in mind. Sun wanted to awaken the nation, by which he meant rallying as wide a coalition of social forces behind him as possible. The Communists were becoming more selective in their choice of allies and more readily inclined to target political "representatives" of privileged classes as enemies of the revolution.

As early as January 1925, the Communist party resolved to play upon factional differences within the Nationalist movement in order to isolate representatives of counterrevolutionary classes. Struggle among classes and their assigned representatives in the Nationalist movement soon came to be counted as an inevitable development, and one that needed careful nurturing to ensure that it developed as history intended. So the declaration issued at the close of the Communists' Fourth Congress called on all "workers, peasants, handicraft

workers and intellectuals" to ally against capitalism. This social alliance required an awakening under Communist guidance: "The Chinese Communist
Party will make sure that the Chinese liberation movement progresses along
its natural course to a situation of awakening." [63]

To stem the swelling tide of class "awakening," Shen Dingyi and Dai Jitao
then began to ransack the doctrines of Sun Yatsen to show, in chapter and verse,
that Sun had a different kind of awakening in mind. The works to which they
referred—those defined by the Third Plenum as the core of party doctrine—
made no mention of class struggle except to condemn it. Accordingly, they
maintained, the plenary instructions of the Nationalist party imposed a prohi-
bition on any kind of awakening other than a "national" one. [64] This difference
in strategies for mass awakening subsequently served as the basic criterion
for distinguishing friends from enemies among all factions of the Nationalist
movement.

Although Dai Jitao won the contest of words at the May plenum, his propaganda victory proved short-lived. His friends in the provinces rallied to Dai's
aid, but when it came to staffing the central propaganda apparatus and responding to the pattern of events unfolding in Guangdong, class awakening carried
the day. Tan Pingshan, we noted, was the only member of the Provisional Political Propaganda Committee apart from Wang Jingwei to stay on in Guangzhou.
Tan was also the architect of Nationalist party branch organization in Guangdong Province, and his interest in provincial affairs set the agenda for the
Propaganda Committee. Its first propaganda program was a damage-control
exercise designed to restore credibility to the Nationalist administration. Tan
tried to limit the political fallout of a recent rebellion by two allied contingents
of the Yunnan and Guangxi armies and to allay fears arising from threatening
gestures on the part of Tang Jiyao, a powerful warlord in neighboring Yunnan
Province. Tan Pingshan also managed to include in the propaganda program an
attack on landlord militia, which had begun to pose a formidable threat to the
extension of Nationalist authority in Guangdong itself. [65]

The appointment of Mao Zedong in October 1925 confirmed this new trend
toward growing Communist influence over the direction of Nationalist propaganda. Mao came to Guangzhou on the run after an unsuccessful effort to lay
the foundation for a peasant movement in Hunan Province. In fact, he barely
escaped with his life after evading a military patrol sent on orders from the
provincial governor, Zhao Hengti, to take him captive. Shortly after reaching
Guangzhou on 29 September, Mao accepted an invitation to cooperate with
Wang Jingwei and the editor of the *Guangzhou Republican Daily*, Chen Fumu,
in preparing the Nationalist party's propaganda report for the Second Nationalist Party Congress, which was scheduled to be held in Guangzhou in January of the new year. Mao was placed in effective command of the Nationalist

party Central Propaganda Bureau at the request of Wang Jingwei over the first week of October. He served as acting head until the convening of the Second Congress, and on 5 February secured Wang Jingwei's approval to continue to manage the bureau into the new year.[66]

Historians in China generally pass over this phase in Mao's development as a momentary diversion from peasant mobilization. The records of his stint in the bureau remain inaccessible.[67] His directorship of the bureau does, however, seem to have marked a critical moment in his development as a revolutionary disciplinarian. Mao's tenure in office was the longest and most stable period of leadership experienced by the bureau since the time of its founding. He ran the bureau for eight months before resigning in May 1926, in compliance with a decision of the Second Plenary Session of the Central Executive Committee to remove Communists from senior positions in central party bureaus. The propaganda bureau had undergone broken periods of directorship under Dai Jitao and possibly Peng Sumin (five months in intermittent spells), Liu Luyin (six weeks), Chen Yangxuan (six months on behalf of Wang Jingwei), and Wang Jingwei himself (eight months broken up over several periods). Mao's tenure also coincided with a marked improvement in the management of the bureau. Dai Jitao was certainly derelict in the performance of his duty, but the substitution of Wang Jingwei in August 1924 did little to improve the bureau's performance. Wang departed for Beijing with Sun Yatsen's entourage in November and left the propaganda bureau without effective leadership. Until Mao's appointment, the propaganda bureau distinguished itself as the one central party agency reluctant to speak out on behalf of the revolutionary movement.[68]

The Communist party leadership had a say in Mao's style of management. Some months before the appointment of Mao Zedong, the Communist party decided to take a more vigorous role in issuing propaganda through its own agencies, beyond the range of Nationalist supervision and discipline. From June 1925, the Communists issued a salvo of "comments on current developments, appeals made to particular social sectors or the general masses, congratulatory messages, open letters to the [Nationalist party] and general manifestos." [69] As far as the Communists were concerned, Mao's elevation in the Nationalist party was intended not to expand the range and volume of Communist propaganda but to coordinate Nationalist propaganda with its own and to discipline Nationalists who appeared to be getting out of line.

Both parties were in agreement on the need for unity and discipline—indeed, even on the means of its enforcement. The problems that divided them were the nature of the awakening to be sponsored by the propaganda bureau; who, exactly, was to speak on behalf of the party; and who was to be disciplined. The problems first surfaced in discussion surrounding proposals to found a new, authoritative party magazine. Before Mao took over, the Central Executive Committee had announced that Tan Zhitang, Gan Naiguang, and Chen Yannian (son of the Communist leader Chen Duxiu) would supply a "central journal of opinion" in the name of the Nationalist party. Their initiative was not approved by the propaganda bureau and, on 9 May, the Central Executive Committee was forced to issue a retraction. Though the propaganda bureau had discovered a problem, it had not yet found the means or the will to resolve it.[70]

Mao Zedong supplied the will. As soon as he took charge of the bureau in October, he approached the Central Executive Committee with plans for a new central publication entitled *Guangdong Magazine* (*Guangdong zazhi*). The committee reserved its judgment, referring the matter to the Political Council, which continued to assume responsibility for sensitive political decisions following the precedent set by Sun Yatsen himself. The Political Council approved publication of a new central Nationalist party magazine, although not quite along the lines Mao had envisaged. The proposed title *Guangdong Magazine* was discarded in favor of *Political Weekly* (*Zhengzhi zhoubao*), and responsibility for the journal was vested in the Political Council itself rather than in the Central Executive Committee. The Central Propaganda Bureau nevertheless retained editorial and publishing control over the magazine. Mao was appointed general editor.[71] When it finally appeared in January 1926, *Political Weekly* marked a turning point in the coordination and discipline of Nationalist propaganda, and a further shift in the ballast of political authority within the Nationalist party. The Political Council became the formal patron of the Central Propaganda Bureau, and Communists were permitted to determine the direction that discipline would take.

Coordination and Discipline of Propaganda

A number of measures had already been adopted in 1925 to coordinate and discipline party propaganda. The first was to take a new broom to the offices of the propaganda bureau to make way for Mao Zedong, Mao Dun, and others more sympathetic to the radical policies of the Political Council. Structural modifications were also introduced to integrate propaganda among party, government, and military agencies at all levels. Most common among these was the creation of joint committees on which the staffs of several bureaus worked together on specific projects. This idea was not new. The Peasant Movement Committee had been set up a year earlier to coordinate peasant movement activities with the propaganda of the peasant, labor, organization, and propaganda bureaus at central party headquarters.[72] It was not until 1925, however, that joint committees became routine in the general management of party affairs.

The departure of Sun Yatsen served as catalyst for the first joint committee of the new year when a committee for recruiting new party members was set up, to channel public sympathy for the dead president into a recruitment campaign. Publicity was orchestrated through a subsidiary propaganda committee drawn from representatives of the propaganda bureau and all other central party offices. In June, the Provisional Political Propaganda Committee was created to coordinate propaganda as issues arose. An editorial committee on party history was set up in October to bring together appropriate talent from the Central Propaganda Bureau and the Guangdong provincial propaganda bureau. Another two special-purpose propaganda committees were created in February and March 1926, to coordinate publicity drives for a National Citizens' Conference and for the first anniversary of Sun's death.[73]

The most important of these joint committees was the pioneering Peasant Movement Committee, reconstituted in March 1926 with the aim of establishing formal contact between staff of the Central Peasant Bureau, Mao Zedong in the Central Propaganda Bureau, and Gan Naiguang in the Guangdong provincial propaganda bureau. The revival of the Peasant Movement Committee followed closely on two key resolutions of the Second Nationalist Party Congress. By special provision of the congress, the peasant movement was assigned the role of vanguard of the revolutionary enterprise, and party propaganda was subordinated to the demands of the peasant movement. In one key resolution, carried among congress resolutions on propaganda, the congress ordered the propaganda bureau to help make the peasantry the party's center of gravity. A second resolution listed among resolutions on the peasant movement called for closer consultation between propaganda agencies at provincial, district, and town levels on the one hand and the Central Peasant Bureau on the other. The object in both cases was to coordinate party propaganda from the desks of the Central Peasant Bureau.[74] The revived Peasant Movement Committee tried to ensure that the Central Peasant Bureau complied with propaganda bureau guidelines, and that propaganda bureaus at all levels kept abreast of developments within the peasant bureau itself. The implications of this development were wider still. By preference, the peasant bureau directed its propaganda toward the demands of mass organization. The Peasant Movement Committee worked to familiarize the party's propaganda apparatus with the results of peasant bureau experiments in mass mobilization. Successful experiments were transferred, through this novel extension network, into standard operational procedures throughout all areas of Nationalist party activity.

Intraparty communication improved markedly in 1925. Party headquarters had customarily kept its subsidiary bureaus and branches informed of current policy and thinking by issuing public declarations (*xuanyan*) on current issues as they arose. When these carried the seal of Sun Yatsen, they generally had the desired effect. A problem arose after Sun's death, however, when the general expository tone of public declarations encouraged contradictory interpretations of central policy.[75] Little was done to resolve the problem until Mao took the helm, when a more detailed form of internal communication came into circulation. The propaganda outline (*xuanchuan dagang*), as it was called, offered ready-made analyses and prescribed slogans for adoption by all party, military, and government agencies under the jurisdiction of the issuing authority.

The earliest propaganda outline I have come across was devised by Zhou Enlai's General Political Bureau for use on the second Eastern Expedition in the autumn of 1925. Mao learned from Zhou. When the victorious regiments filed back to their barracks in November, the new technique was adapted for civilian use by the propaganda bureau. Mao presented the first of a series of propaganda outlines to the Central Executive Committee for ratification on 27 November. Its subject was the Fengtian war in North China. The outline offered an analysis of the reasons behind the war, gave instructions on appropriate preparations to be undertaken by all Nationalist party agencies, and finished with nine slogans for adoption in all related propaganda. Propaganda outlines were subsequently issued by the various joint committees set up to coordinate publicity campaigns in 1925 and 1926.[76]

Few civilian propaganda agencies could yet match the detail and precision of the propaganda outlines issued by Nationalist military authorities. The peak political authority governing propaganda in the revolutionary army, the Political Training Bureau of the National Government Military Affairs Commission, devised a system for issuing propaganda outlines on a regular basis. The prototype for a series of regular monthly outlines appeared in March 1926, to set the agenda for propaganda in the armed forces a full month in advance by specifying not only what was to be said but when it was to be said from one day to the next. Every soldier and civilian who passed within earshot of an army political bureau was to be told the same thing, at the same time, wherever they happened to be. Years were to elapse before their civilian equivalents in the Nationalist or Communist parties achieved anything comparable.[77]

The disciplinary regime adopted by the party also seems to have originated in the armed forces. Underpinning the rational efficiency of military communication and propaganda in the Nationalist armies lay an impressive system for regulating, investigating, and disciplining speech and behavior. Party and government agencies needed to establish comparable disciplinary systems in order to see similar results. In the early phase of the Nationalist Revolution, there was little prospect of achieving rigorous discipline in the general community when party authority barely extended beyond the city of Guangzhou and a few model counties. There was, nevertheless, considerable scope for exercising discipline within the party itself. Indeed, declarations, propaganda outlines, central publications, and joint-committee initiatives could only work as intended when they were enforced by regulation, supervision, and discipline within the party.

The party, then, served as a laboratory for testing disciplinary procedures that were later applied to the people of Guangdong and, eventually, to the people of all China.

Routine disciplinary procedures were gradually introduced after Sun Yatsen died in March 1925. In that month, the Central Executive Committee withdrew the financial subsidy of the party's Hong Kong daily, the *Xiangjiang Morning Post* (*Xiangjiang chenbao*), for denouncing Communist activity in the Nationalist party. The editor was dismissed. The paper managed to continue publishing for some months with assistance from the Yunnan warlord Tang Jiyao but collapsed in bankruptcy toward the end of the year. The propaganda bureau also pressed the prosecution of two anti-Communist pamphleteers in the Nationalist party, Ma Su and Jiang Weifan, who were subsequently expelled from the party.[78] When Mao Zedong came to office, the propaganda bureau began systematically scouring party publications in order to identify maverick journals that defied the policies laid down by the Second Nationalist Party Congress. Mao passed irregularities on to the Central Executive Committee for prosecution. In February 1926, the bureau indicted the Beijing Society for the Study of Sun Yatsenism, the fourth sub-branch of the Shenzhen County branch (in Guangdong), the Shanghai party magazine *Revolutionary Guide* (*Geming daobao*), and the long-standing daily of the U.S. party headquarters in San Francisco, the *Young China Morning Post*, on which former bureau secretary Liu Luyin had cut his teeth as a party publicist. Mao also issued a directive to party agencies to pass on to his bureau for inspection all *nonparty* propaganda material issued by individuals and institutions at public gatherings.[79] Finally, he took advantage of his position as editor of the new "central organ of opinion," *Political Weekly*, to reprimand writers and editors of other journals and newspapers thought to be out of step with current party thinking.

Hitherto, discipline had been the responsibility of a number of different party agencies that reported directly to Sun Yatsen. Communists were conspicuously absent from the disciplinary agencies established by the First Nationalist Party Congress in January 1924, including the Central Inspection Commission (*Zhongyang jiancha weiyuanhui*). By a curious twist of fortune, it was anarchists within the party who were asked to police and coerce compliance with party regulations.[80] The party's propaganda bureaus formed close ties with inspection commissions at every level. Central Propaganda Bureau Secretary Liu Luyin was appointed to the inaugural Party Affairs Inspection Commission in January 1924, and in April received a concurrent appointment to the Guangzhou Municipal Investigation Commission. Propaganda officer Chen Qiulin held a concurrent appointment to the National Government Inspection Commission at the time of his death. Similar contacts were established between the Central Propaganda Bureau and the Central Legal Affairs Com-

mission. The inaugural director of propaganda, Dai Jitao, chaired the Central
Legal Affairs Commission, and on retiring to Shanghai was replaced on the
commission by his secretary Liu Luyin.[81] When Communists were excluded
from these early disciplinary agencies, they made easy targets. Their chosen
means of defense was to take command of these agencies themselves.

On 18 June 1924, the Central Inspection Commission considered its first
major case of impeachment involving breaches of discipline. The target was
Communist propaganda in the Nationalist movement. Three anti-Communist
members of the commission, Zhang Ji, Xie Chi, and Deng Zeru, compiled a
list of alleged violations of party discipline drawn from the decisions and publications of the Communist party and affiliated organizations. Most of the items
cited in the indictment touched on propaganda to the extent that they affirmed
the Communists' intention to wage a publicity war on "warlords and imperialism" and to shore up the Nationalist party's resolve to do the same. In some
respects, the inspection commissioners seem to have misread Sun Yatsen's intentions in inviting the Communists to join him. Among the grounds listed for
impeachment were Communist decisions "to expand the party of the Nationalist Revolution, the Chinese Nationalist Party," "to make sure that revolutionary
elements throughout the country congregate around the Chinese Nationalist
Party," and to undertake "low-ranking practical work" in the Nationalist Revolution. Sun could hardly object to Communist participation on these grounds.
In fact, he found their revolutionary determination and enthusiasm for grass-
roots organization and propaganda a refreshing change from his followers'
general preference for comfortable and lucrative desk jobs. Sun dismissed the
charges.[82]

More serious allegations charged that the Communist party and the Socialist
Youth League planned to retain disciplinary powers over their own members
after they joined the Nationalist party, and intended to win over to their side (as
one Communist document put it) "left wing members of the Nationalist Party
who have undergone a genuine class awakening." "Class awakening" was held
to be the Communists' most potent weapon. Another Communist document
cited in the indictment predicted that "revolutionary elements with greater
class awakening will do their utmost to join our organization." In view of the
condition under which the Communists had been admitted into the party by
the First Nationalist Party Congress, these were significant charges. First, the
Communists were not supposed to form a "party within the party," and second, although both parties were committed to the politics of mass awakening,
Sun Yatsen clearly had a national awakening in mind and not a class one. The
commissioners also cited an article by Cui Wenchong that was published in
Awaken, the daily supplement sponsored by the Nationalist *Shanghai Republican Daily*, in which Cui had advocated a "proletarian revolution" on com-

pletion of the national one. Sun filed this complaint away with the others and proposed no further action. He resolved instead to tighten party discipline, to reassert Nationalist jurisdiction over Communist members of the party, and to reaffirm the fundamental goals and principles of his Nationalist Revolution.[83]

The gravity of the charges was not diminished by Sun Yatsen's casual dismissal, and his failure to act did little to dampen resentment among party veterans over the prominence of Communists in the reorganized party. The exercise was foiled when around 2,000 party members in Wuhan, Beijing, Shanghai, and Guangdong presented sixteen additional petitions seeking redress against Communist activities in the party. In August, the head of the Beijing-Hankou General Labor Union, Zhang Dehui, visited Guangzhou to submit a protest about Communist infiltration of the union. "We workers have yet to learn of a Communist Party member who could propagate our party's principles," he informed the Central Inspection Commission; "they clamour about nothing but Marx, Marx." Recent elections for Nationalist party branch officers in Beijing and Shanghai prompted further petitions charging Communists with rigging results. Others petitions were inspired by Communist publicity in North China favoring negotiations then under way between Beijing and Moscow for the normalization of diplomatic relations between Soviet Russia and the government in North China. Zou Degao and 100 signatories from "learned circles in Beijing" complained they had been misled by Communist publicity into believing that Sun Yatsen had urged Nationalists to promote the negotiations. They did so until they learned that Sun Yatsen (who was hostile to the negotiations) had never said anything of the kind.[84]

The Standing Committee of the Central Executive Committee delayed action on the petitions. Some were referred to the Central Inspection Commission, but that body was powerless to act without Sun's approval. The bulk of the petitions was held over pending a plenary session of the Central Executive Committee scheduled for mid-August, until Sun Yatsen intervened. Sun scheduled his Political Council to meet two days before the Central Executive Committee was due to consider the matter. He favored the council over the committee because it was more responsive to his personal direction.[85] On 13 August, the council treated the impeachment petitions neither as a sign of Communist perfidy nor as a consequence of Nationalist treachery but rather as the result of an unfortunate misunderstanding. Instead of dealing with each petition on its merits, Sun proposed setting up a "liaison bureau" (*Lianluo bu*) to prevent the recurrence of similar problems.

This proposal failed to satisfy the delegates, who came together two days later to attend the plenary session of the Central Executive Committee. Tan Zhen agreed to go along with the fiction that the complaints were all the result of a misunderstanding, but on the understanding that responsibility lay with the Communists. He put forward a counterproposal for an international propaganda committee (*Guoji xuanchuan weiyuanhui*) to facilitate communication among the Nationalist and Communist parties and the Third International. For Tan, the problem of communication lay not within the Nationalist movement itself but with their allies, who refused to consult or to heed the Nationalist party. In fact, Tan was proposing a new mechanism for publicizing the Three Principles of the People to the world beyond China and for establishing relations between the Nationalists, the Communists, and the Comintern on a more equal footing. The Political Council met Tan Zhen's proposal with a counterproposal of its own on 20 August by mooting an international liaison committee (*Guoji lianluo weiyuanhui*) in place of the liaison bureau proposed at its earlier session. The ascribed functions of this committee differed from Tan Zhen's committee chiefly in ignoring the suggestion that the Three Principles of the People should be more widely propagated abroad. In the event, Tan's motion failed to gain the approval of the Central Executive Committee, which adopted instead the Political Council's recommendation for resolving the disciplinary problems identified in the petitions of June, July, and August through creation of the International Liaison Committee.[86] In practice, few Communists were disciplined, the International Liaison Committee failed to materialize, and neither side felt satisfied with the outcome of the impeachment process.

The politics of disciplinary inspection swung in the other direction in 1925 and 1926, when party members who had shown themselves hostile to the Communists became targets themselves. In the absence of Sun's restraining hand, the outcomes grew increasingly harsh and divisive. When the Central Inspection Commission impeached the *Xiangjiang Morning Post* for publishing anti-Communist articles in March and April 1925, the Central Executive Committee resolved to sack its editors without seeking an explanation or apology. Three editors of the *Post*, Zhao Shilong, Li Gongci, and Xu Tianfang, requested details of the charges and compiled a formidable defense of their action in which they strenuously denied they had committed any breach of party principles, policies, or regulations. When their protests were ignored, the journalists promptly switched their allegiance from the Nationalist party. Discipline also began to be exercised over nonparty newspapers, news agencies, and journalists operating in the public arena. In June the Central Propaganda Bureau acted on a report by bureau officer Chen Fumu to the effect that the Pacific News Agency (*Taipingyang tongxunshe*) was circulating false rumors to its client newspapers in Hong Kong and elsewhere. The bureau passed on a request that the provincial government prosecute journalists working for the private news agency and prohibit offending newspapers from entering the province.[87]

Immediately following Sun's death, the party continued to rely on older methods of control, favoring the demonstration effect of exemplary punishment rather than routine inspection and discipline. Party Center made an example of the *Xiangjiang Morning Post* early in 1925 because it had little capacity to regulate propaganda through routine bureaucratic procedures. This was soon to change. By its founding charter, the Central Propaganda Bureau was empowered to "guide the propaganda bureaux of all [regional] executive committees and provincial branches for the purpose of attaining unity in propaganda and opinion." [88] In Sun's time it had done nothing of the kind. By mid-1925, however, it assumed responsibility for directing and disciplining all newspapers, magazines, leaflets and posters, schools, film production units, and performing art groups set up by the party or by any of its members around the country. By developing routine procedures for reporting and monitoring party activities, the bureau rapidly developed into one of the most powerful institutions in the Nationalist movement.

Systematic reporting from region to center was a mark of provincial and local submission to central party authority, and helped party headquarters in Guangzhou keep abreast of developments in distant municipal and provincial party offices. Failure to report thus constituted a breach of party discipline. The Communist Tan Pingshan complained of the center's neglect in enforcing this regulation in January 1926. Although director of the Nationalists' Central Organization Bureau, Tan was reluctant to accept full responsibility for the oversight in the belief that the provinces were more at fault than he was. The problem lay in the failure of local party branches to report their activities: "The Shanghai Executive Branch has not once submitted a report on party affairs to party centre over the entire period. Beijing has reported, but not often." [89] After Mao Zedong took charge of Nationalist propaganda, the propaganda bureau began to count failure to report as a serious breach of party discipline. Mao was incensed by the "counterrevolutionary" propaganda of the *Shanghai Republican Daily*, and listed the paper's failure to submit regular reports to Guangzhou near the top of his list of grievances. When reporting failed, monitoring took other forms. At the height of public controversy over the private writings of Dai Jitao, Mao persuaded the Nationalist Central Executive Committee to order Dai's return from Shanghai to Guangzhou, where he could be kept under closer supervision.[90] Reporting, monitoring, and supervision become standard procedures for exercising routine discipline within the Nationalist movement under Mao's direction.

Measures for improving bureaucratic efficiency in communication, inspection, and discipline were invariably accompanied by purges of recalcitrant party officials. When party headquarters finally succeeded in coordinating propaganda within Guangdong, for example, it was as much a political achievement as a technical one. Creation of the Guangdong provincial branch had long been delayed by acrimony between anti-Communist party officials who had staffed

the branch before the party reorganization and the Communists and "revolutionary" Nationalists who began to dominate political work from 1924. The
leader of the original provincial branch, Deng Zeru, is today remembered as
one of the first party members with the foresight to impeach the Communists
for their activities in the Nationalist party. Many other staff members in the
prereform Guangdong branch were concurrently members of the Society for
Commemorating the Revolution, an association intent on stemming Communist infiltration of the Nationalist movement. The Central Executive Committee withheld approval for a new provincial party network until Deng Zeru and
his faction had been removed from office in the province. When the provincial branch was finally reestablished in October 1925, not a single officer of the
original provincial executive secured reappointment. The provincial director
of propaganda, Gan Naiguang, was drawn from the self-styled "revolutionary"
faction of the Nationalist party.[91] As a consequence of the delay, the provincial
propaganda bureau opened in the same month that Mao Zedong took over from
Wang Jingwei in the Central Propaganda Bureau. Unity of opinion was then
reduced from a political to a technical problem within the propaganda apparatus of Guangdong Province. Not surprisingly, the combination of improved
procedures and political purges meant that the new system of surveillance and
reporting worked best where it was least required.

Routine reporting was nevertheless useful for inspecting activities below
the provincial level, where the old guard of the Nationalist party retained some
influence. Provincial party officials worked in the shadow of the central bureau
and could conceal little from Mao or from his superiors on the Political Council. Local branches were less exposed to the watchful eye of the center. It was
the task of Gan Naiguang's provincial bureau to examine and authorize materials prepared by these subordinate town and county branches.[92]

In practice, the provincial bureau worked as an agent of the central one,
relaying instructions and propaganda outlines to subsidiary town and county
branches and complying with central instructions by publishing monthly reports of the activities of the executive committee and all other bureaus at the
provincial level along with summaries of local branch activities. Before issuing
major propaganda guidelines, it sought the advice and approval of the Central
Propaganda Bureau. When confronted by difficult cases of discipline inspection, it passed them up to the central office for prosecution.[93] In organizing
particular propaganda campaigns, the provincial bureau drew on the resources
of the Central Propaganda Bureau, and in some cases invited cooperation from
other bureaus as well. By any reasonable estimate, the procedures followed in
reporting, coordinating, and disciplining propaganda in Guangdong deserved
high commendation.[94]

The provincial bureau also assisted party headquarters in disciplining town and county propaganda. Provincial officers were entitled to examine and correct party publications issued at provincial, town, and county levels in order to "ensure the uniformity" of party propaganda.[95] Although the output of its five companion bureaus taxed the provincial propaganda bureau's supervisery and disciplinary capacities, efforts were made to follow the branch charter in practice. Routine procedures introduced late in 1925 are well illustrated in the case of the provincial merchant bureau. On 16 December the merchant bureau petitioned provincial party headquarters for permission to set up a monthly magazine catering exclusively to the party's merchant movement in Guangdong. The provincial executive committee approved the plan and assigned responsibility for preparing the magazine to the merchant bureau on the condition that a draft of each issue gain executive committee (that is, propaganda bureau) approval before publication. A week later, the merchant bureau submitted an outline of contents for the magazine, which was duly passed on to the propaganda bureau for inspection. The merchant bureau then invited Gan Naiguang and his secretary, Chen Kewen, to accept positions on an in-house editorial committee to facilitate propaganda bureau inspection and correction of future merchant-movement publicity. All this was duly reported to higher levels of the party and published, from early in 1926, through the provincial newsletter.[96]

Discipline, Chaos, and "Class Struggle"

Political purges and routine discipline could only carry the party so far toward its objectives. Mao Zedong noted at his desk in the propaganda bureau that the Nationalist Revolution would not have been a revolution without its share of "chaos" as well.[97] In fact, chaos erupted as discipline tightened.

The leafleting, parading, picketing, and violence associated with the momentous Guangzhou–Hong Kong strike and boycott, which ran for a year from June 1925, was far and away the most unwieldy exercise in the entire revolutionary movement. Workers in Hong Kong set down their gunnysacks and tools on 19 June to support a set of specific demands for improvements in the working and living conditions of Chinese laborers in the colony and to protest the massacre of Chinese demonstrators in Shanghai on 30 May. Within days they began filing out of the colony in an exodus that grew to around 200,000 workers and dependents, along with a steady flow of merchants, workshop owners, and out-of-work warlords, who could no longer afford to remain in the colony as business ground to a halt.

Within Guangzhou itself, the initial reaction to the Shanghai massacre was more temperate. Two thousand Chinese employees of the Shamian foreign concessions walked out in sympathy, and steamer movements between Guangzhou and Hong Kong were suspended. Local civic and government leaders in

Guangzhou initially opposed more drastic action.[98] The movement developed a momentum of its own in Guangzhou on 23 June, when the city was shaken by British and French sharpshooters, who staged a local reenactment of the Shanghai massacre on Shamian Island in the heart of the revolutionary capital. Naval gunners on Shamian opened fire on a rowdy parade of workers, students, merchants, and cadets as they aproached the small stone bridge leading from Guangzhou to the island. Fifty-two of the demonstrators were killed in a hail of rapid fire, and over 100 more were wounded.[99] The Shamian Massacre galvanized even the most conservative government leaders in Guangzhou to declare a complete embargo on trade and commercial relations with Hong Kong, and eventually to boycott all British firms, goods, and services in South China.

The appearance of chaos in Guangzhou belied intensive organization and solid infrastructural support directed toward the strikers. This was organized chaos with organizational consequences. The extension of the boycott throughout the province gradually buttressed the authority of the Nationalist government in areas where it had previously exercised little influence. And as it extended the reach of the Nationalist state, the boycott offered new incentives and opportunities for factions in the party and the government to compete for influence within a rapidly expanding movement.[100] Chaos erupted inside the party when factions jostled to take advantage of the opportunities the movement afforded.

Some lost out rather badly. Moderate elements associated with Sun Fo, Zou Lu, and Hu Hanmin were fully aware that the aims of the strike were unassailable. Far from diminishing factional differences, however, the general agreement on the objectives of the strike seems to have added greater urgency to these disputes. Radical elements led by Liao Zhongkai, Wang Jingwei, Chen Gongbo, and Gan Naiguang strengthened their hold over party and government affairs at the expense of conservatives. Factional tensions finally erupted in violence when Liao Zhongkai was assassinated, and when the highest-ranking opponent of the Communists in the Nationalist movement, Hu Hanmin, was forced to resign for his alleged involvement in the assassination.[101]

The Guangzhou–Hong Kong strike and boycott exposed a degree of disunity within the Nationalist movement that was beyond the reach of technical adjustment by the party's disciplinary apparatus. Coordination and discipline were effective only when accompanied by general agreement on the goals of the revolution, on the nature of the awakening under way, and on the distribution of power through government and party office. The quest for "unity of opinion," then, raised important issues about the guiding ideology and objectives of the Nationalist Revolution. Most particularly, should the rancorous and at times violent disagreements emerging within the movement itself be counted as disputes among friends, or as contradictions between the revolutionaries and the forces of counterrevolution, between the people and the enemy? Did the enemy lurk, in real or symbolic ways, within the revolutionary camp itself?

Over the year of the Guangzhou–Hong Kong strike and boycott, the Nationalist party's Political Council and propaganda bureau began formulating a new definition of the friends and enemies of the revolution for the purpose of isolating and alienating more moderate elements in the Nationalist camp. The Communists had already developed an elaborate social critique of political factions in the Nationalist movement that was designed to explain the origins and outcome of the merchant crisis of October 1924. They launched a series of attacks on individuals and factions in the Nationalist party, including the Prince faction of Sun Fo and an unfortunate cohort of party veterans associated with Feng Ziyou, who was expelled for his public outbursts against the Communists.[102] The Communists' actions were prompted by reactions to two questions: first, whether there was a counterrevolutionary element within the revolutionary movement, and second, whether and how this element may have been related to counterrevolutionary forces in society at large. Mao Zedong played a leading role in bringing the Communist party's answers to these questions to the attention of the Nationalist party.

The clearest expression of Communist outrage at counterrevolutionary elements in the Nationalist movement followed a tragic incident that took place in Shanghai on the thirteenth anniversary of the founding of the Republic in 1924. Huang Ren, a young student from Shanghai University, was beaten to death by anti-Communist Nationalist party members at the site of the National Assembly building on Henan Road. Chen Duxiu penned a letter of protest to the Nationalist Central Executive Committee that was published openly in the Communist weekly *The Guide* and in the Nationalist daily *Awaken*, under the title "Is This the Behavior of the Right Faction? Or Is It Counterrevolution?" [103] In raising the possibility that sections of the Nationalist movement might be enemies of the revolution, Chen's question highlighted the new direction in Communist thinking. Communists, of course, were not the only ones outraged. The sacrifice of Huang Ren at a sacred site of the revolution could hardly be defended by veteran party members, whose sympathies might otherwise have lain with the murderers. Still, Chen Duxiu's provocative question failed to elicit a satisfactory answer from Nationalist disciplinary agencies.

Earlier complaints had met with a similar fate. Shortly before the Huang Ren incident, the Communist Yu Shude asked the Nationalist Central Executive Committee to prosecute party newspapers that refused to follow central party guidelines. At the time Yu had not yet been elevated to the Provisional Political Propaganda Committee, and his motion sank without trace.[104] Even after Yu's promotion, no further action was taken. In fact, it was not until Mao Zedong was appointed to the Nationalist propaganda bureau that the Communists succeeded in establishing their critique of left and right factions as alternately revolutionary and counterrevolutionary, and in affirming this as the basic criterion for distinguishing among friends and enemies of the Nationalist Revolution in the party and in society.

Mao is best remembered over his stay in Guangzhou for his lectures at the Peasant Movement Institute and for his pioneering writings on the role of peasants in China's national revolution. Even before his arrival in the city, he had begun to develop an interest in peasant welfare and to acquire rudimentary skills in rural political mobilization. In Guangzhou, however, he had other things on his mind. As his biographer Stuart Schram observes, Mao's role in the Second Nationalist Party Congress of January 1926 "reflected above all a strong concern for the problems of organization and discipline which were to be at the root of developments during the next few months." [105]

Mao's interest in problems of organization and discipline preceded his participation in the congress and seems to have outweighed his interest in the peasant movement over his tenure in the propaganda bureau. He understood his responsibility as director of propaganda as identifying the friends and enemies of the revolution, and alternately lauding the friends and exposing the enemies to ridicule and discipline. The zest Mao brought to this task was a good deal more spirited than the concern shown by his predecessors and subordinates in the propaganda bureau, and it rubbed off onto his writings on peasants and other social forces. If anything, his experience in the Nationalist propaganda bureau from October 1925 added a greater sense of urgency to his appreciation of the role peasants might be called upon to play in China's national revolution.

At the Second Nationalist Party Congress, Mao favored comradely solidarity over the harsher options canvassed by some of his Communist colleagues. But his actions belied his words. As director of propaganda, Mao showed a greater concern for solidarity than for comradeship. Along with other Communists in the Nationalist movement, he was under instruction from the Third International to isolate Nationalist party elements hostile to Communist and Soviet Russian activity in South China, and if necessary to drive them out of the Nationalist movement.[106] His first step in this direction was to try to split the Nationalist party in half. As editor of the "central journal of opinion" for the Nationalist movement, *Political Weekly*, Mao assumed responsibility for ensuring that Comintern instructions were carried through to the letter. His propaganda bureau succeeded in alienating the more moderate elements of the Nationalist party to the point where they moved beyond the pale of central authority and ceased to respond to its discipline. This was as intended. Technical measures for achieving unity in party propaganda could achieve only a semblance of uniformity. Real unity required a systematic purge.

Mao's purge was painfully protracted, chiefly because it required the approval of senior figures in the Nationalist party who were initially reluctant to lend their support. At the time of the First Nationalist Party Congress, any suggestion that there were "counterrevolutionary" factions in the party had met with a blanket denial. In conversation with Hu Hanmin in January 1924, the Comintern adviser Mikhail Borodin speculated that the Nationalist party possibly harbored left and right factions. Borodin stopped short of calling them revolutionary and counterrevolutionary, but Hu Hanmin was quick to recognize the implication, and just as quick to deny it. Hu's denial did not stop the Communist party from resolving in May to advertise, aggravate, and take advantage of factionalism within the Nationalist party. This decision was formally written into policy at the Fourth National Congress of the Communist party in January of the following year, when it resolved to strengthen the left faction, to contest the position of the middle faction, and to oppose the right within the Nationalist movement.[107] The Nationalists, meanwhile, went on issuing repeated denials that there was any scope for factional disagreement at all.

The matter first attracted the attention of the party's disciplinary apparatus in October 1924, when Zou Lu brought an article from the Communist magazine *The Guide* to the attention of Sun Yatsen. Sun instructed the Central Executive Committee to rebuke the magazine for writing of left, right, and center factions in the Nationalist party, and in particular for characterizing one faction as less "revolutionary" than the others.[108] Sun's judgment was reaffirmed immediately after his death in response to another round of Communist publicity on factionalism within the Nationalist party. The controversy focused on an article by "Chen Dong" published in a new magazine, *The Revolution*. The piece carried the offending statement:

At this moment we can see once again that right-wing elements in the party, representing the interests of the comprador class and working in league with militarists and imperialists, are plotting to destroy the party, and that only the worker and peasant masses led by left-wing elements are inclined to protect the party day in and day out.

The Central Propaganda Bureau promptly addressed a letter to the editors of *The Revolution* upholding the position maintained in Sun's lifetime that there were no significant factional differences within the Nationalist movement and hence that no party members could plausibly be branded counterrevolutionary.[109]

Just four months after rebuking *The Revolution*, the Central Propaganda Bureau reversed its position. Propaganda Director Wang Jingwei addressed a meeting convened to commemorate the assassination of Liao Zhongkai on 20 August 1925, urging:

Those of our comrades who wish to oppose imperialism, step to the left; those who want to live under the unequal treaties and to allow China to remain a semicolonial country in perpetuity and help imperialism last forever as a force in the world, step right.[110]

The choice of Liao's memorial ceremony as the occasion for breaking with precedent and finally acknowledging the existence of left and right factions was singularly appropriate. Liao himself had recently broached the issue in an article on revolutionary and counterrevolutionary cliques in the party. Regrettably, his assassination appeared to validate his insight. The differences of which he had spoken were now brutally fratricidal. Wang Jingwei's comments on factions were more authoritative than those of Liao Zhingkai, as they were made in his capacity as director of propaganda. He attracted the criticism that he was intent on breaking Sun Yatsen's commitment to a united party. Chiang Kaishek rose to his defense. In a formal letter to party members issued in December 1925, Chiang described Wang Jingwei's comment on party factions as "most penetrating and discerning." [111] Borodin, it seemed, had been right all along. Hu Hanmin was immediately sent into political exile.

Once the matter had been settled within the ranks of the Nationalist party, Mao Zedong felt at liberty to utilize the resources of that party's propaganda bureau to expose the right faction as the "counterrevolutionary" enemy inside the party. Before proceeding, however, he was careful to cite the precedents set by Liao Zhongkai and Wang Jingwei:

Mr. Liao put forward the slogan "Revolutionary faction, unite!" and Mr. Wang put forward the slogan "All who want revolution step to the left." Today these two slogans must be propagated to all revolutionary comrades and revolutionary masses all over the country.[112]

By merging Liao's theme of revolutionary unity with Wang's summons to separate into right and left wings, Mao married unity with division. Sun Yatsen had been reluctant to admit that there were party factions in the belief that such an admission would pose serious problems for party unity. For Mao this presented no problem. Disunity could be overcome by fomenting further disunity: party members who dissented from central policy would no longer present a problem in the revolutionary camp because they would no longer be counted in the revolutionary camp at all.

Mao took the additional step of announcing on behalf of the propaganda bureau that the division between left and right was equivalent to a conflict between the forces of revolution and counterrevolution. From January 1926 he attacked the "counterrevolutionary faction" relentlessly. In announcing new disciplinary measures applying to the *Shanghai Republican Daily*, for example, Mao counseled Nationalist party members that the choice confronting them was "either to run left and join the revolutionary faction or to run right and join the counterrevolutionary faction." [113] Those who ran to the right joined the camp of the enemy. Mao fulfilled the propaganda bureau's responsibility to achieve "unity of opinion" by disinheriting party members whose words and behavior threatened the appearance of unity.

His chief instrument for effecting unity of opinion was the new central organ, *Political Weekly*. "The responsibility of *Political Weekly*," he announced in his introduction to the magazine, "is simply to 'attack the counterrevolutionary faction through propaganda in order to destroy all counterrevolutionary propaganda.'" In practice, *Political Weekly* carried a much wider brief. Mao predicted when the first issue came off the press that "nine out of ten articles will describe actual events and only one in ten will engage in debate with the propaganda of the counterrevolutionary faction." [114] His prediction was generally borne out. The magazine carried major party declarations on current affairs as they came to hand, along with official reports on the progress of the revolution. Relatively few of the commissioned articles that appeared in the period of Mao's editorship focused on "attacking the counterrevolutionary faction through propaganda." In fact, Mao reserved this particular responsibility for himself and revived an old pen name, Ziren, for the purpose. Four of the five articles he penned under the name Ziren singled out for attack the large body of party members who were assembling in Shanghai and Beijing under the title of the "Western Hills" faction. Under another of his pen names, Run, he pilloried the behavior of particular reactionaries and "counterrevolutionaries," including party veterans Zou Lu and Feng Ziyou. [115]

Mao developed the simple exhortations of Wang Jingwei and Liao Zhongkai into an elaborate analysis of the deviant behavior of errant Nationalist party factions. Building on earlier Communist assessments of the Nationalist movement, he assigned a particular and inalienable class character to all protagonists in the revolution and concluded that struggle within the Nationalist movement was a political reflection of divisions among social classes over the goals of the revolution. [116] Though not the first to assert a correspondence between political actors and social forces in the revolution, Mao was a pioneer in presenting this claim as a Nationalist and on behalf of the Nationalist Revolution. Aware that the term "class struggle" was generally associated with proletarian socialist revolution, Mao was at pains to point out that the revolution at hand was not a communist one at all:

The counterrevolutionary party generally regards the Nationalist Revolution as a communist revolution, the Nationalist party as a communist party, the Nationalist government as a communist government, and the National Revolutionary Army as a communist army. In every case these [arguments] concede the aims of imperialism in manufacturing a few simplistic expressions and spreading them for the purpose of destroying the united front of cooperation among all classes in the Nationalist Revolution. [117]

Mao was not proposing a communist revolution at all, but a national one involving "cooperation among all classes." Class struggle had nothing to do with communism or socialism. All classes, he pointed out, were invited to join the united front under Nationalist party leadership to liberate the country from international capitalism and domestic feudalism, and it was not the fault of Communists if some rejected the invitation. Not all classes in China were prepared to concede the need for a national revolution. So the nation needed to struggle with them. "The great bourgeoisie attaches itself to imperialism," he wrote, "and becomes a force for counterrevolution while the middle bourgeoisie wavers uncertainly between revolution and counterrevolution." Mao then applied to social classes the same rational criterion that he had already developed for "counterrevolutionaries" within the Nationalist movement—although in this case it was not membership in the party that was at issue but membership in the nation itself. As the Nationalist movement was the champion of the nation, those who failed to respond to its summons surrendered their right to be counted part of the nation at all.[118]

Mao completed his case by linking dissent within the Nationalist movement with social resistance to the Nationalist Revolution. Responding to the criticism that disunity in the Nationalist movement was a simple consequence of manipulation by the "left faction," Mao replied in the winter of 1925:

At this time in semicolonial China a party of national revolution needs to have a split of this kind. It is an inevitable phenomenon. We need not rejoice at it but it is certainly no great misfortune either. To understand the reason for this one need only take a glance at the present situation and a glance at the history of the Chinese Nationalist party since the Revive China Society to understand it completely.[119]

The "history of the Chinese Nationalist party" that Mao had in mind was not, however, the history of the party as Sun Yatsen had recounted it. It was instead a moral tale of the party's historical links with counterrevolutionary social classes.

Sun had attributed the shortcomings of the Nationalist movement from the days of the Revive China Society to the time of his death to a failure on the part of party members to "awaken" to a correct understanding of his principles. In Sun's history, this explanation generally preceded an instruction for party members to read and study the Three Principles of the People more thoroughly in the future.[120] Nothing was further from Mao's mind. He stressed the social forces at work in the revolution in diagnosing the Nationalist party's historical problems: "If we wish to understand this split completely we must look at the social class character of party members since the time of the Revive China Society." In *Political Weekly* Mao offered an overview of Nationalist party history designed to show that contending class interests made past failure and present factional struggle inevitable. The Revive China Society was a loose gathering of the proletariat and "rootless people" (*youmin*). Its successor, the Revolutionary Alliance (*Tongmenghui*), was a party of the proletariat, semiproletariat, petty bourgeoisie, and middle bourgeoisie. After the 1911 revolution, representatives of the petty-landlord class split from the Revolutionary Alliance to form the Parliamentary Nationalist party (*Guomindang*), which abandoned Sun Yatsen's revolutionary program and compelled him in 1914 to found the Chinese Revolutionary party. Even then, Sun's efforts were thwarted when representatives of the middle bourgeoisie and the comprador class infiltrated the new party. Exasperated by the intransigence of his old comrades, Mao explained, Sun reorganized the Chinese Nationalist party in 1924 to mobilize alternative sources of support among workers, peasants, and activists of the Chinese Communist party. Now that the revolutionary movement was finally under way, the imperialists, the comprador class, the landlord class, and reactionary warlords "took offense" and marshaled their supporters to form a "Nationalist party of the right faction." The battles lines of the revolution were clear:

On the one side we have a counterrevolutionary united front formed between the comprador class and the big bourgeoisie, made up of large landlords, bureaucrats, warlords and others, all under the leadership and direction of imperialism. On the other we have a revolutionary united front formed between the petite bourgeoisie (owner-cultivators, small merchants, and proprietors of small handicraft enterprises), the semi-proletariat (part-owner–cultivators, tenants, handicraft workers, shop assistants, and peddlers), and the proletariat (industrial workers, coolie laborers, poor peasants, and the rootless proletariat), all under the leadership and direction of the Nationalist party.

The factional lines taking shape in the Nationalist party were a direct reflection of the battle lines forming in society at large. The party had consistently failed because it neglected to redress the internal contradictions arising from its tolerance of representatives of counterrevolutionary social forces. It followed that a purge of counterrevolutionaries in the party was imperative before victory was assured in national revolution.[121]

When Mao devised his political calculus for determining which struggles were fraternal and which were fratricidal within the Nationalist movement— and by extension which classes and their "representatives" were to be counted members of the nation—he gave priority to the state aims of the revolution itself. Though the Comintern and the Chinese Communist party certainly helped to define the state aims of China's national revolution, they never counted membership in particular social classes a sufficient criterion for distinguishing between friends and enemies of the revolution. Instead, enemies were isolated from friends by the "attitudes" (*taidu*) they adopted toward the elimination of warlords and imperialism. In practice, this usually meant that enemies were identified by the attitude shown toward the party-state itself. Party factions and social classes were at liberty to declare which sides they were taking in the revolutionary struggle by showing what they thought of the leadership of the Nationalist Revolution. Their freedom to choose came at the cost of "class struggle."

The development of Mao's thinking from party purges to the mass movement is illustrated in three articles completed over his term as director of propaganda. The first was a tentative explanation of the factional divisions currently emerging in the Nationalist movement. "The Reasons Underlying the Secession of the Nationalist Right Faction and Its Ramifications for the Future of the Revolution," completed toward the end of 1925, was Mao's first systematic attempt to tie the counterrevolutionary attitudes and behavior of the Nationalist "right faction" with the attitudes of particular social classes toward the state goals of the Nationalist Revolution.[122] It was significant that his first major analysis of classes in society should have proceeded from an analysis of political tension within the Nationalist party. His second piece, "An Analysis of the Various Classes of the Chinese Peasantry and Their Attitudes Toward Revolution," was completed early in the new year. Here Mao qualified his class analysis of the enemy with recognition of the role China's peasant farmers might play as class allies of the revolution. The third article, written in February, moved progressively to an "Analysis of All the Classes in Chinese Society." [123]

The progress in Mao's thinking from purges to organized mass movements is accentuated by the consistency of his method. In each case he offers a crude but effective analysis of the relationship between the interests ascribed to various social classes on the one hand and the interest ascribed to warlords and imperialists on the other, and attempts to link both sets of interests to emerging political divisions within the revolutionary movement. This procedure was sufficient, to Mao's satisfaction, to situate each social class and party faction along a gradient of political loyalties that identified the friends and enemies of the revolution.

Despite the Nationalist focus of Mao's writings, the salience of social class in his analysis was not easily reconciled with Sun Yatsen's principles. Sun emphatically ruled out the prospect of distinguishing between friends and enemies along class lines in his talks on the Three Principles of the People. The contradiction may not have mattered if Mao were not the Nationalist director of propaganda, or if Sun's views on the matter had been buried with him in 1925. But Sun's views were set in concrete as the official standard for identifying friends and enemies in the "Declaration on Accepting the President's Will," drawn up and ratified at the Third Plenum of the Nationalist Central Executive Committee in May 1925. This document unequivocally proclaimed loyalty to Sun's principles and programs as criteria for distinguishing comrades from enemies:

All citizens of the Republic of China who are capable of accepting the principles and political programs of our president in order to carry on the work of the Nationalist Revolution and plan for the welfare of the country and of the masses deserve respect and love as our comrades. We swear to unite with them in good faith and to work together with all our might to bring the constructive work of the revolution to fruition. Conversely, anyone who offers support for counterrevolutionary actions or is conferred office or protection by the great imperialist powers and hinders the progress of the Nationalist Revolution shall be counted as our enemy.

Party members were exhorted to "sacrifice everything" to vilify and destroy the enemies of the revolution. Mao could hardly be faulted on this account. In view of party pronouncements that there were no enemies *within* the party, however, the exhortation of the May plenum was clearly designed to rally the party against a common enemy outside of it. Indeed, the document specified a very different "responsibility" for the party from the one that Mao chose to pursue himself. In May, the party plenum declared, "Our only responsibility today is to accept without reservation the Will of our President." [124] Mao's self-assigned responsibility "to attack the counterrevolutionary faction" inside the party was inconsistent with Sun Yatsen's practice in his own lifetime, was nowhere mentioned in his will, and was quite out of keeping with the spirit of the plenary documents drawn up after his death. The problem for Mao was that he could no longer accept Sun Yatsen's will or ideology because it ruled out recourse to class analysis in intraparty and external struggle. That is, by placing unwarranted restrictions on the identification of friends and enemies, Sun's principles inhibited a thorough party purge and limited the scope for mass mobilization. Mao then set out to undermine the ideological foundations of the Nationalist party from within its own propaganda bureau.

The May plenum had supplied one further maxim to hang on the wall by the director's desk in the propaganda bureau: "The foundation of discipline is respect for the character of the President and acceptance of the teachings he has bequeathed us." [125] Mao showed little respect for either. He came to command the propaganda bureau at a time when "brothers" (*xiong*) (as Nationalists used to call one another) were giving way to "comrades" (*tongzhi*) in the leadership of the revolution, and he moved swiftly to dissolve the old bonds of fraternity. Mao was a comrade in the true sense of the Chinese term: "United in Purpose." In place of Sun's teachings, the goals and purpose of the revolution assumed paramount importance in his thinking on discipline and unity, in his assessment of the friends and enemies of the revolution, and in his appreciation of the significance of Sun and his legacy. The purpose of the revolution, Mao argued, was to overthrow warlords and imperialists and establish a Nationalist party-state. Everyone, including Sun Yatsen, had agreed to this. So Mao showed little sympathy as director of propaganda for those who claimed membership in the revolutionary brotherhood by virtue of common descent from Sun Yatsen, or who claimed to respect his principles but appeared reluctant to press the revolution to its purposeful conclusion. This conclusion, as Mao understood it, required recognition of the ways in which different class interests bore on the political movement to overthrow warlords and imperialism, and it called for the will to act on this knowledge without regard for the costs to unity or cohesion of the party or the nation.

Mao's emphasis on Sun Yatsen's revolutionary purpose at the expense of his more doctrinaire teachings surfaced frequently in his attacks on "counter-revolutionaries" in the Nationalist party. He rarely referred to Sun Yatsen's books, speeches, or casual writings except to cite with approval the president's record of granting admission to the Communists, forging a close alliance with Soviet Russia, and promoting the welfare of workers and peasants. On the sensitive issue of class struggle, Mao was obliged to ignore the letter of Sun's law and invoke what he took to be Sun's purpose instead. Mao claimed to know what Sun was "really like" and rebuked others who quoted the president with faultless accuracy to argue that class politics had no place in national revolution. Referring to Dai Jitao and other editors of the magazine *The Independent*, Mao asserted:

Members of this bourgeois "independent" revolutionary faction (most of them children of small landlords) are still masquerading in Sun Yatsen's name, claiming that his "principles" and "doctrines" in fact represent themselves. Was Sun Yatsen really like this? Sun's principles and doctrines are definitely for "relieving distress" and certainly not for "growing rich," definitely for liberating people from oppressive classes and certainly not for preparing the way for a new oppressive class. No matter how Sun's principles and doctrines may be misconstrued, this point will never change.[126]

For all Mao's assertions, Sun Yatsen's record on the politics of class struggle was quite intractable. Dai Jitao and his friends illustrated the point by citing chapter and verse from the "misconstrued" writings to which Mao referred. In order to make his arguments stick, Mao needed to show that Sun Yatsen's revolution was greater than either the man or his principles. Sun Yatsen Thought was to be distinguished clearly from what the man himself happened to think or to say.

Mao's next step was bolder still. He attempted to reduce Sun to size in the iconography of the Nationalist movement. In this he was again handicapped by the "Declaration on Accepting the President's Will," which placed respect for the person and the principles of Sun Yatsen at the center of party loyalty. There was no room for doubt: "If there are any who happen to harbor doubts about the president's proposals they must come to appreciate the correctness of the president's proposals and the error of their own doubts."[127] To ensure that party members showed due respect for their departed leader, the Third Plenum resolved that all party and government bureaus, branches, and agencies should hold a brief commemorative ceremony in Sun's honor every Monday morning.[128] The ceremony began with the assembled company bowing three times before a portrait of Sun and then listening to a reading of his last will. This was followed by three minutes of silence. It was then that presiding officers would present their reports on the recent political work of their units. The ceremony effectively established the ritual descent of the party leadership from Sun Yatsen, but at the price of ensuring that successive party leaders showed due respect for his principles and his person.

The Central Propaganda Bureau was supposed to police compliance. Before Mao came to Guangzhou, the bureau had already formulated a set of "Regulations for the Weekly Commemoration," prescribing disciplinary action for anyone who neglected to attend the ceremony or who failed to display appropriate deference while it was under way.[129] The rate of compliance had fallen away by the time Mao took charge. Mao referred to the problem in January 1926 in the minutes to the Nationalist Central Executive Committee meeting. He noted that a number of party and government units were failing to treat the ceremony with the respect it required. On the surface, he said, the ritual was dutifully enacted, but it was actually ignored "in secret." As acting head of the bureau, Mao was responsible for disciplining offenders, and in matters close to his heart he could exercise his responsibility ruthlessly. But on this occasion he motioned the Central Executive Committee to loosen regulations governing the ceremony in order to avoid having to police it too strictly. The committee consented.[130]

The propaganda bureau encountered stiffer resistance from the Central Executive Committee when it tried to reduce the status of Sun Yatsen's Three Principles in Nationalist ideology. Mao rarely mentioned the Three Principles in his own work, but when he proposed that provincial and county propaganda officers should follow his example, the ruse backfired. He was brought severely into line over his involvement in preparations for the first anniversary of Sun's death, scheduled for 12 March 1926. In keeping with recent practice, the Central Propaganda Bureau was asked to prepare a propaganda outline for the guidance of all other party bureaus as well as army and government agencies. On 16 February the bureau presented its outline to the Standing Committee of the Central Executive Committee. Members of the Standing Committee were taken aback on noting that the "Propaganda Outline for Commemorating the First Anniversary of the Death of the President" failed to mention Sun's life or the Three Principles at all. In place of Sun's principles, the outline referred to Sun Yatsen's support for the three policies of alliance with Soviet Russia, admission of Communists into the party, and advancing the interests of the workers and peasants.[131] This time the propaganda bureau had gone too far.

In a rare but significant departure from party norms, Gan Naiguang and the Guangdong provincial propaganda bureau issued two addenda to the central propaganda outline, entitled "A General Outline of the Life of the President" and "An Outline of the President's Principles." Gan listed himself in the revolutionary left faction and would normally have been counted among Mao's comrades. He was not, however, at liberty to depart from the decisions of the Third Plenum. Leftist attacks upon the "right faction" made much of its alleged departures from plenum decisions, so members of the left could hardly countenance disregard for the plenum from their own quarter. The Guangdong branch addenda were intended to serve as corrigenda to the central propaganda outline and as a rebuke to the Central Propaganda Bureau. Radical Nationalists on the Central Executive Committee were caught in the same dilemma. The Standing Committee charged Wang Jingwei with making up the central outline's deficiencies by penning another outline on the Three Principles. Meanwhile, Mao requested two weeks' leave of absence on the grounds of illness.[132]

These rebukes did little to deter Mao Zedong from his self-appointed responsibility to purge political enemies from within the party or from finding friends elsewhere in the political and mass movements to assist in eliminating the enemies of the nation. Still, Mao's thoughts no longer mattered for the internal politics of the Nationalist party. He lost his position in the propaganda bureau in the wake of Chiang Kaishek's coup of March 1926, and reverted to a position in the Communist party. There he drew extensively on his experience in the Nationalist propaganda bureau to devise principles and strategies of his own and, in time, to build a disciplined revolutionary movement responsive to his own leadership. Mao's national revolution (or national "liberation," as it came to be known) pursued essentially the same objectives as those which Sun Yatsen had had in mind, but without the handicap of Sun Yatsen's principles. What Mao devised was a strategy for national revolution that exacerbated differences among social classes where tactically appropriate, in order to displace the Nationalists' party-state with his own.

1. (*Above*) The Sun Yatsen Memorial Hall in Guangzhou, c. 1946. (From Tsao 1947)

2. Gao Qifeng, *Roaring Lion*, 1927. (From Croizier 1988: 90)

3. Student suit and Sun Yatsen suit, ca. 1927. (from Wang Bushi 1986: Items 760–61)

陳烱明　　孫文

4. Sun Yatsen and
Chen Jiongming.
(Adapted from Zai
Dongfan 1956, 33:
Inside cover)

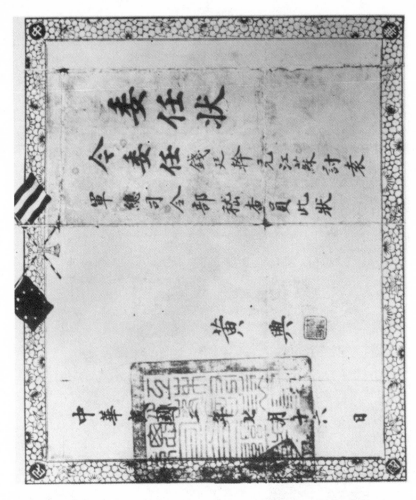

5. A nine-star flag crosses the Republican flag on a certificate of commission for the Jiangsu Anti-Yuan Army, under Huang Xing, in 1913. (From Qin Xiaoyi 1978, 1: 288)

中華革命黨

黨員證

6. Sun Yatsen's party flag and his alternative national flag, 1914, as they appeared on a membership certificate of the Chinese Revolutionary Party. (From Qin Xiaoyi 1978, 1: 301)

7. Republican flags line the route to the Ming Tombs in Nanjing, 1912, as Sun Yatsen accompanies an official party to announce the founding of the Republic of China. (From Qin Xiaoyi 1978, 1: 259)

8. Commemorative poster of the Northern Expedition, published in Shanghai. c. 1927. Flags feature in all four cameos. At the top, a portrait of deceased president Sun Yatsen is framed by Nationalist party and Nationalist government flags, and by Sun's final exhortation: "The revolution is not yet completed. Comrades must carry on striving." Below, General Chiang Kaishek addresses troops arranged under Nationalist regimental flags at the launch of the Northern Expedition in Shaoguan. The battle for Changsha, to the left, shows the "party army" charging troops arrayed under the original five-color flag of the Republic of China. To the right, the "revolutionary army" approaches the city wall of Yuezhou, where counterrevolutionary soldiers stage resistance under the Republican flag. (From Wood 1985: 59)

7

AWAKENING INC.

Government, Party, and Army Propaganda Institutions

> The native, after having tried to lose himself in the people and with
> the people, will on the contrary shake the people. Instead of according
> people's lethargy an honoured place in his esteem, he turns himself into
> an awakener of the people.
>
> Frantz Fanon[1]

Today, visitors to Guangzhou who display an interest in Mao Zedong's role in
the Nationalist Revolution are likely to be pointed in the direction of the Peasant Movement Training Institute, off Yuexiu Road, where peasant-movement
activists once took classes on the strategy and tactics of peasant mobilization.
Others might catch a ferry down the Pearl River and pull over by the site of
the Huangpu Academy, where Chiang Kaishek helped to train military officers
for the revolution.[2] It is not just their association with Mao Zedong and Chiang
Kaishek that secures for these sites a place on the tourist map. The Huangpu
Academy and the Peasant Movement Training Institute are remembered as
staging posts on the long march of the Chinese nation from the disunity of the
early Republic to the unified and centralized polities of Nationalist and Communist China. Much of the credit for this achievement goes to dashing military officers and straw-sandaled peasant cadres, and hence to the institutes that
trained them.

There were also hundreds of cadre-training institutes and propaganda agencies established in and around Guangzhou to turn out the back-room dealers,
petty officers, street orators, pen-pushers, and paper shufflers of the revolution. Some of these cadre followed along with the baggage wagons, and others
remained behind when the narrative of the Nationalist Revolution pushed on.
Today, only a handful of old-timers can still recall where these institutes once
stood. Party schools for clerks produced few heroes, academies attached to
local armies never matched the caché of the Huangpu Academy, and no one
seems to have predicted that the Merchant Movement Training Institute would
inspire a "mighty storm or hurricane."[3] These academies and propaganda agencies are omitted from the tourist route. So, too, are the schools and colleges

that were placed under Nationalist tuition, and the newspaper and magazine offices that were converted from civil institutions into party ones. In the 1920s Guangdong Province was the site of a momentous training and propaganda experiment designed to convert everyone within reach of the Nationalist state into an awakened citizen of Nationalist China.

State Institutions

On 5 August 1925, the Nationalist administration dedicated the Guangxiao temple complex in Guangzhou to a new mission.[4] Thirteen centuries before, the sixth patriarch had brought a set of sacred Buddhist scrolls to the site from India, and it developed over the centuries into a major center of the Chan (or Zen) school of Buddhism. This school was distinguished by belief in a sudden, rather than incremental, awakening to the light. The temple has been restored in recent years, and some of the old scrolls and inscriptions have been returned to their places. Over the eastern hall now hangs a Chan scroll that reads: "Five thousand words of classical learning may plumb the depths of Chan wisdom; eight hundred blows on the bell will awaken us from our foolish dreams." One morning in August 1925, the monks were awakened from their dreams and herded into the rear of the complex to make way for an institute for awakening government functionaries.

The new Institute for Bureaucrats (*Keliguan*) was dedicated to ensuring that town and county government functionaries in areas captured by the Revolutionary Army were alerted to the principles and wisdom of the Nationalist party. The aims of the institute were set out in draft regulations gazetted in July:

The purpose of the institute is to produce administrative personnel imbued with principles and knowledge for selection as county heads, through education in the principles and the political program of the Chinese Nationalist party and in the sciences of practical administration.[5]

One of the most difficult challenges facing the Nationalist party-state was to ensure that accountants in party bureaus, police officers in Guangzhou, and administrators attached to rural county governments all displayed "principles and knowledge" in the exercise of their duties. The challenge was met through political instruction.

Few of the personnel occupying government positions had been screened before their appointments. Before the founding of the Nationalist government in July 1925, responsibility for screening administrative party and government personnel fell to the secretariat of the party's Central Executive Committee. On 15 May, party headquarters tested 200 candidates on aspects of Sun Yatsen's Three Principles and his revolutionary objectives and assessed their familiarity with the Nationalist party program and the current political situation. Around the same time, the Central Executive Committee approved a motion from the party secretariat to set up an examination committee for screening local government personnel. Party leader Wang Jingwei was appointed to head an examination committee, on which he presided with administrative experts Tan Pingshan and Gan Naiguang, and two consummate propagandists, Dai Jitao and Shen Dingyi. Results of the party-sponsored examinations exposed a desperate need for party education and training among candidates for party and government office.[6]

The provincial Department of Civil Administration began screening and training government personnel. In February 1926, it opened an Accountancy Training School (*Huiji jiangxisuo*) to impart professional qualifications and knowledge of party principles and goals to public accountants.[7] On 6 May it opened a Graduate Police Academy (*Gaodeng jingguan xuexiao*) "to raise police personnel well versed in party principles and well suited to the new age." A Political Training Bureau for the constabulary had already been opened by the Guangzhou Municipal Public Security Bureau, so the Graduate Academy focused on courses in policing and party doctrine for career officers. Its program of political instruction was closely interwoven with the administration of the police force, with each course offering political training in anticipation of promotion. Graduates of the highest-level Research course were granted preference in the appointment of security-bureau and police-station chiefs; graduates of the Specialist course were given priority in the appointment of police-station and substation chiefs; and the better graduates of the lowest-ranking Police Studies program received preferential treatment in appointments of sergeants of police.[8]

There was, however, no comparable institute for training general administrative staff. Foremost on the agenda of the Department of Civil Administration in July 1925 was the training of functionaries to extend the reach of the party-state to all counties and municipalities in the Nationalist base area. The peak institution for screening and training local government officials was to be the Institute for Bureaucrats.[9] On 5 August 1925, the department began enrolling students for the new institute in the Guangxiao temple. Candidates were screened to ensure that any who were in the least likely to oppose the regime never crossed the threshold. Only Nationalist party members who had never voiced dissent from party policy were eligible for enrollment. Eligible candidates were then tested for knowledge of the principles of Sun Yatsen and the programs of the Nationalist party. With the exception of senior local officials—who qualified for admission on party membership and a minimum of one year's administrative experience alone—candidates were required to have completed university or college degrees and to undergo entrance examinations in politics, economics, finance, law, and current administrative practice. Those who made it past this second barrier were finally screened for personal failings and habitual vices, including bankruptcy, mental illness, opium smoking, and addiction to religion. On the faculty side, the provincial government budgeted for seventeen full-time administrative and other staff members at the institute, and for a number of sessional teachers. Two courses ran concurrently, one by day and one by night.[10]

Early plans for the Institute for Bureaucrats envisaged an enrollment of 100 students who would sit for 35 hours of classes each week for a year in prescribed readings of Sun Yatsen's works and of administrative sciences. The writings of Sun Yatsen on the draft curriculum included *The Three Principles of the People*, *The Five-Power Constitution*, *First Steps Toward Democracy* (also known as *Parliamentary Procedure*), *Outlines for National Reconstruction*, and *The Program for National Reconstruction*. The administrative curriculum covered handbooks on farmer, worker, merchant, education, communications, financial, and police administration, as well as household registration and issues in local self-government, social policy, international law, accountancy, and record-keeping. The curriculum was revised over the following months, partly to correct mistakes. The inclusion of *First Steps Toward Democracy* alongside *The Program for National Reconstruction* was a particular embarrassment — the one was in fact a chapter of the other. The oversight was hastily corrected in the program finally presented for approval to the provincial government in October when a few other subjects were added to the list, including military science.[11]

On 11 February 1926, the director of the institute, Xie Yingzhou, reported that rapid progress had been made over the first half-semester. Classes commenced in November. Results in the monthly examinations were gratifying, absenteeism (5 percent) was very low, and students were said to show exceptional interest in undertaking research into the practical business of revolutionary administration. In view of these achievements, Xie confidently invited Wang Jingwei to deliver an additional course of lectures on the history of the party and on recent political developments. In fact, however, his report on the institute's progress was prompted by a concern to expand the enrollment of students to cast the net more widely over incumbent local officials. Their busy schedules had reduced the first cohort of sitting county heads and clerks to around 70 students. If it were to implement Sun Yatsen's goal of party rule (*yi dang zhi guo*), Xie argued, the Nationalist administration needed to make provisions for an extra class catering to the remaining county officials. Once permission was granted, the institute enrolled a further class of 22 students in May.[12]

Xie knew that the problem was not simply one of busy county schedules, and his revised plan was meant to establish once and for all who was prepared to undergo retraining and who was not. The minister for civil administration,

Gu Yingfen, addressed the problem of incumbent local officials who refused to undertake a course of political training in submitting plans to the provincial government for a "Bureaucrat Institute Extramural Supplementary Course for County Heads." In the preamble to his submission, Gu reaffirmed the importance of offering training in party principles to achieve "constitutional government":

The reorganization of county government is the point of departure for all reform of government, and the selection of county-level officials is the very foundation for the implementation of constitutional government. Indeed, the head of a county should be an official of the new citizenry (*xinmin zhi guan*) and very close to the masses. . . . Even people with abundant learning will be incapable of fulfilling their role of caring for the people if they are not fully conversant with party principles.

Gu Yingfen reaffirmed the Nationalist government's intention to remove recalcitrant officials through institute procedures and to enroll those who met with party approval in the institute program. For a variety of "local" reasons, he explained, many county heads had not been fully screened when classes commenced at the institute. He now proposed a compulsory extramural course for incumbent county heads to be undertaken *in situ*. The only officials to be exempted from compulsory training were those who had graduated from three-year tertiary courses in politics, law, or economics and who had been faithful party members for at least two years. Few county officials met these criteria. The majority of county heads were then required to take courses over a full year by correspondence. Continued enrollment was conditional on passing monthly assessments, and graduation followed successful completion of a final examination.

Gu was well aware that a system of political training and assessment by correspondence was open to abuse. For the correspondence course he proposed a number of amendments to the institute's system of assessment. Extramural students could opt for practical rather than written assessment in all classes apart from those in Sun Yatsen's principles and in party programs. A new disciplinary provision was added to the rules governing written assessment, apparently to counter the temptation for county heads to invite local scholars or relatives to complete their examinations for them. In all, the provisions governing the extramural course bore out its designers' intentions. The institute screened incumbent county heads through initial and continuous assessment, and it offered additional political and practical instruction to those who passed the test to ensure their continued loyalty to the party.[13]

The institute devised a second and more comprehensive system for monitoring local administration in the field. Students studying on campus, at the Guangxiao temple, were required to undertake local investigations into county-level administration and report back to the institute as part of their assessment. A special program was created for the purpose. Ten student-investigators were dispatched each month for investigations lasting eight weeks, to provide the institute with details of existing local administrative practice through 60 individual case studies. The manifold aims of the exercise were set out in an early draft of the plan, which placed student education last on its list of "purposes":

The position of Local Administrative Investigator has been created for the following purposes: to clarify the circumstances surrounding local administration in all counties, to plan a program of reform, to propagate the political platform of the Chinese Nationalist party, and to give students of the Institute for Bureaucrats an opportunity for practical work.[14]

The "circumstances surrounding local administration" of greatest interest to provincial administrators lay in the fields of communications, business, police and militia, education, sanitation, and local finance. Subjects for propaganda exercises included Sun Yatsen's last will and testament and discussion of the "spirit of Sun Yatsen." The draft also laid down regulations for recording and reporting the dates, venues, sizes of audiences, and content of propaganda performances for assessment purposes. Finally, it obliged local administrative organs and "institutions of self-government" to offer all due assistance and protection for the student-investigators and propagandists as they went about their business. In his report in February, Institute Director Xie Yingzhou proposed that the results of the student investigations into local administration be compiled and edited by institute staff into a comprehensive program for the reform of local administration. He set up a Local Administration Advisory Office employing institute staff and other qualified personnel to advise the provincial government and county heads on all matters bearing on local administration.[15]

The influence of the institute extended well beyond its walls in monitoring local administration and implementing administrative reforms in the name of the Nationalist government. In this respect, it was not unlike the mass-movement institutes of the Nationalist party, whose influence extended beyond their formal courses into every aspect of the organized peasant, labor, youth, women's, and merchant movements. But the differences outweigh the similarities. The institute was concerned with the formal apparatus of state administration rather than with development of the social movement, and it had nothing whatever to do with the Chinese Communist party. Its managers, staff, and sponsors in the Department of Civil Administration maintained little contact with Communists, partly because the radicals tended to neglect government administration, but also because government administrators largely ignored the mass movement. Even within the inner circle of the Nationalist party, provincial government personnel tended to be more conservative than staff of the provincial party branch. The proportion of radicals to conservatives at the highest levels of the provincial government was the reverse of that in the provincial party headquarters. Fan Qiwu was a conservative exception in an otherwise radical party headquarters, and Chen Gongbo was the radical exception in an otherwise conservative provincial government. From the founding of the Nationalist government to the launching of the Northern Expedition, the pivotal figures in the provincial government were the leading conservatives Sun Fo in the Ministry of Reconstruction, Gu Yingfen in Civil Administration, Song Ziwen in Commerce, and Xu Chongqing in Education.[16]

The founders and directors of the Institute for Bureaucrats were well known for their anti-Communist leanings. As far as the founding director, Lin Yungai, was concerned (and his successor as director, Xie Yingzhou), the new party-state was to be a distinctly Nationalist one.[17] Lin was a native of Guangdong. He was a qualified lawyer and economist and had been at the fore of the party's intervention in the May Fourth movement. At that stage he introduced a Marxist perspective to the party magazines *Weekly Commentary* and *Reconstruction*, and prepared translations of two books on Marxism. Lin was active on the educational front of the movement as well. In the early 1920s he edited the magazine of the Guangdong Provincial Education Association. After accompanying Sun Yatsen to Guangzhou in 1920, he served as secretary to the military government before rising to the position of mayor of Guangzhou City in 1923. In February he was invited to head the propaganda section of the Guangdong provincial branch of the Nationalist party (under Deng Zeru), and in March he accepted a senior position in the treasury of Sun Yatsen's government. He subsequently served on a number of provincial and central party and government committees before accepting an appointment to the board of the Central Bank. Over this period Lin distanced himself from Marxism and aligned himself more closely with forces hostile to Communist party activity in the Nationalist movement. Three months after founding the institute, he came out in support of the anti-Communist Western Hills faction, and was offered a position as adviser to its Central Executive Committee. He declined in favor of continuing his work in the Nationalist government.[18]

Lin's successor, Xie Yingzhou, was also a native of Guangdong. In 1924 he joined Lin on the Legal Affairs Commission of Sun Yatsen's alternative national government, and over the following year earned valuable experience in political training on the faculty of Guangdong (later Sun Yatsen) University, where he conducted courses on the principles of Sun Yatsen. At the university he worked with the minister for civil administration, Gu Yingfen, who served as his patron at the Institute for Bureaucrats. Xie emerged around the same time as Lin Yungai as an active opponent of Communists in the Nationalist movement. He resigned from Guangdong University in December 1925,

in protest over left-wing interference in its administration, and was elected to
an executive position on the stridently anti-Communist Society for the Study
of Sun Yatsenism in February 1926.[19]

Guangdong University was one of many schools and colleges converted into
political training institutions. Once the Nationalist government was founded in
1925, it set out to realize a long-standing ambition of the Nationalist movement:
to implement a party education policy through the state school system. There
were precedents for this development. In 1918, Sun Yatsen's *First Steps Toward
Democracy* was used as a textbook in a number of schools sympathetic to the
aims of the Nationalist movement. In the following year, Zhu Zhixin designed
a series of school textbooks for the state school system, which was eventually
edited by Dai Jitao after Zhu was killed in the recovery of Guangzhou in 1920.
Around the same time, an education section was set up at party headquarters
in Shanghai with the aim of promoting party principles through schools. Later,
in 1925, the party's Shanghai Executive Committee announced plans for an
additional textbook series to be edited by its propaganda bureau. In the same
year, the party's Shanghai University opened a teachers' college with the aim
of training teachers to propagate party principles through the schools.[20]
    The Shanghai textbook series was never finished, and Shanghai University
was closed down by local authorities on 4 June 1925, to signify their displeasure with its involvement in the May Thirtieth movement. But the losses were
sustainable. Teachers and students could be found preaching party principles
in local school districts throughout central and southern China. From the pan-
optic perspective of the Central China Teachers' College in Wuhan, it seemed
there was barely a teacher who was not a Nationalist:

It was noticed in the frequent changes of Government school teachers in widely separated areas of China, the new-comer was always a member of the Kuo Min Tang.
When, as in the case of some missionary schools, it was not possible to introduce
members of the Kuo Min Tang as teachers, secret committees were formed amongst
the scholars to carry on the work.[21]

In Guangdong itself, however, management of education had been placed in
the hands of the Communist party by Chen Jiongming, who appointed the
Communist leader Chen Duxiu to oversee the provincial education system.
With Chen's defeat in 1923, the Nationalists recovered authority over the education system, and in February 1925 ordered the Central Propaganda Bureau to
edit a definitive series of textbooks on the history and principles of the party
for use in civics classes in schools within the Nationalist base area.[22]
    One of the first acts of the new Nationalist government was to instruct the
provincial Department of Education on 18 July to reform the school system in
Guangdong. In November, the provincial government approved a motion from

the minister of education, Xu Chongqing, to incorporate the Three Principles of the People into school courses. One hour was to be set aside each week in primary schools and two hours in secondary schools for party education. Additional special-purpose textbooks were designed for use in schools under county, city, and provincial jurisdiction. The provincial Department of Education also enforced a rigorous system of school reporting and inspection to facilitate supervision of school operations and to police compliance with central party and government directives.[23]

When the new school system was introduced in 1926, party authority was extended to embrace private as well as state schools in the province. Existing schools were to register under new guidelines within three months, and all new schools were to meet the guidelines before they could commence classes. Public and private schools were required to fly the emblem of the Nationalist movement—the Blue Sky and White Sun national flag—and were expressly forbidden to teach religion. Additional regulations were promulgated for private schools. Authority was conferred on local state authorities to dismiss any teacher who appeared unsuited to the position and to compel changes to courses and equipment (including books and insignia) considered "harmful to education." The provincial government also specified the kinds of breaches it deemed sufficient to force the closure of a private school, including disobeying the law, disturbing order, "harming customs" (*baihuai fengsu*; a term referring to the baneful effect of foreign influence generally and to the teaching of Christianity in particular), ignoring instructions from relevant state authorities, impeding the reforms, and ceasing classes without good cause for any period in excess of three months. In order to police these regulations, state authorities reserved the right to inspect private schools at their discretion and required schools to report regularly on all aspects of management and teaching practices to relevant state authorities. This was not always necessary. In some cases, school students worked closely with local party authorities to seize control of mission schools and private colleges, and forced teachers and administrators to comply with the new directives.[24]

The Nationalist administration looked upon middle-school students as a reserve force of party agitators. In February 1926, shortly after promulgating the new regulations, the provincial government distributed thousands of copies of a proclamation outlining the party's position on the national political situation to all schools. On other occasions it obliged schools and colleges to volunteer large numbers of students for specific propaganda projects. School principals and college presidents ignored these requests at their peril. The principal of Guangzhou High was reported when his school appeared to show little enthusiasm in promoting party doctrine, and private colleges were threatened with closure should they fail to cooperate.

By 1926 the profession of school principal was one of the most uncertain in the province. This was not always on account of the Nationalists. The principal of Shuibei Upper-Primary School in Wenchang County, Han Qingwu, was murdered by the local warlord, Deng Benyin, in the winter of 1924 for allegedly sympathizing with the revolutionary movement.[25] But seeking accommodation with Deng Benyin could be costly for a school principal as well. Once Deng Benyin had been routed on the Southern Expedition, the party branch of Hua County appealed to the provincial government to remove Zhang Hetu, the principal of the county state middle school, for acceding to Deng Benyin's requests. Under the new provincial regulations, nominations for principals of public and private schools required formal approval from educational authorities before final confirmation. Zhang was, in fact, appointed during Deng Benyin's tenure in the district, but his position as principal was initially confirmed by the newly installed Nationalist government authorities. It was the party branch that requested that his appointment be rescinded. Zhang Hetu was said to have connived with "local bullies and evil gentry" in impeding party activity among students of the school. After an investigation by the local county head, one of the signatories to the petition from the local party branch, Peng Yi, was appointed to replace Zhang as principal.[26]

The impact of Nationalist education policy was felt most strongly in the universities and colleges of the city. On 4 February 1924, the Nationalist authorities merged Guangdong Senior Teachers' College (*Guangdong gaodeng shifan daxue*), the Guangdong University of Law (*Guangdong fake daxue*), and the Guangdong Specialist School of Agriculture (*Guangdong nongye zhuanmen daxue*) into a new university known as National Guangdong University (*Guoli guangdong daxue*), and on 9 June appointed the widely respected party veteran Zou Lu as its foundation president. The university began advertising nationwide for prospective students the day before Zou's appointment, and he immediately set about finding sufficient funds to house, feed, and teach them. He tried without success to claim a portion of the Boxer indemnity fund earmarked for educational subsidies. Eventually the Guangzhou cement factory and North River stone quarry, two government enterprises, were required to set aside a portion of their incomes to meet the establishment and operating expenses of the university. Staff members were not particularly well paid (one observer commented that they were the lowest-paid faculty in the entire country), but the university seems to have managed happily under this arrangement over its first year of operation.[27]

In the following year, the creation of the new Nationalist government ushered in a period of crisis for the university. In April, the party decided that the institution should be renamed Zhongshan University in honor of the recently deceased leader, who was generally known in China as Sun Zhongshan. But the university was first to be "reorganized" in order to merit the honor.[28] Zou Lu favored the change of name but strongly resented the proposal for reorganization. He resigned in December 1925. Forty-two of the 60 faculty members of the university followed him out the school gate, complaining bitterly that there was far too much political interference in the management of the university and far too little funding from the new Nationalist government.

The reasons put forward for the mass resignations in December 1925 were not all well-founded. The university had, admittedly, accumulated Y200,000 in outstanding debts, and political interference in curriculum design and university management had become a feature of the institution. In fact, however, political interference had been a feature of the university from the moment of Zou Lu's appointment. The claim that the staff was compelled to "partify" the university after July 1925 was quite disingenuous. Regulations governing universities and colleges proclaimed on 13 August 1924 specified that they should "pursue the very latest theories and skills through close communication with the outside world." [29] In practice, however, Guangdong University enjoyed closer ties to the Nationalist party than to the world of international scholarship from the very start.

Zou Lu was director of the Nationalist party's Central Youth Bureau at the time of his appointment. His bureau ran an active program on campus and promoted Nationalist political instruction through the state and private school systems. Schools and colleges, in turn, supplied the party with ranks of young students who could be mobilized for mass propaganda campaigns too large for the youth bureau staff to handle unaided. In addition, general party activity was coordinated through a special branch attached to the university, whose directors frequently worked and wrote for Zou's youth bureau. The party consistently interfered in the management and curriculum of the university. In November 1924, Zou Lu passed on to the teaching staff of the university a directive from the party's Central Executive Committee requiring that all faculty be members of the Nationalist party (the same ruling applied to high-school teachers in Guangzhou municipality). The directive was carried out under Zou Lu's administration: faculty members who were not party members were faced with the option of joining the party or submitting their resignations.[30] As far as senior administrators were concerned, the ruling merely served to confirm their joint party and university status. Huang Jilu, formerly head of the U.S. party network, ran the Political Science department. The chair of the Department of Economics, Zhou Fohai, acted as secretary to the Central Youth Bureau. Course content, predictably, reflected their loyalties: by April 1925, classes on the principles of Sun Yatsen formed an integral part of accredited courses on campus, including the degree course offered in the university law school.[31]

The entrenchment of the Nationalist party in the management, faculty, curricula, and general ethos of Guangdong University compromised its autonomy as an institution of education and led eventually to its conversion into a full-fledged party school. The president and faculty all spoke indignantly of the "partification" of the campus at the time Zou Lu was replaced by Chen Gongbo in December 1925. But 38 of the 42 faculty members who resigned in protest immediately reaffirmed their party affiliation by heading en masse to Shanghai and swelling the ranks of the breakaway Western Hills faction.[32] The fight on campus, like most of the squabbles that broke out after Sun Yatsen's death, was more of a factional struggle within the Nationalist movement than a disagreement over the role of the party on campus. That is to say, the staff members who resigned in protest in the winter of 1925 directed their fury not against Nationalist party control but against the left-wing faction that had come to dominate management and funding of the university.

Immediately following Sun's death, brawling erupted among rival student gangs, including the Sun Yatsen Study Society, the Stick Society, and the Communist Youth League, each gang rallying factional allies and party patrons at higher levels to intervene on its behalf. When the conflict on campus spilled over into these other party arenas, and engaged larger factional groupings in the Nationalist movement, outside intervention was effected in the administration of the university. On 20 June, the university's Special Party Branch tried valiantly to limit feuding to within the confines of the university. The resolution of the university branch failed to satisfy the party branch of the Huangpu Academy, which lodged a formal complaint of "counterrevolutionary" activities at the university with the Central Executive Committee.[33] This signaled the start of a much greater struggle, which led ultimately to the resignation of the university president, Zou Lu.

Huangpu branch intervention in the management of Guangdong University was technically confined to party affairs, but in view of the dominant role of the party on campus, this did not amount to a significant restriction. There was little to stop the Huangpu party branch from interfering in the educational policies and teaching practices of the university because the party dominated all areas of education. As it happened, the Huangpu party branch was proposing a more rigorous model of party education for state institutions at the time factional strife erupted at Guangdong University. It boldly instructed the university's faculty and students to abandon the study of science and the humanities and to work directly for the worker and peasant masses, who were maintaining the idleness of intellectuals with their "sweat and blood." For all his efforts on behalf of the party, Zou Lu had never quite conceded that the university was simply a cadre-training academy for the party and the government. His critics at the Huangpu party branch, nevertheless, would not be satisfied until the teaching of "philosophy, literature, and science" had been eliminated from the curriculum and the university had become a "training ground for nurturing staff of the revolutionary government." [34]

In this spirit, the Huangpu party branch pressed the Central Executive Committee for a definitive statement on educational policy applying to all educational institutions under Nationalist control in the first week of July 1925.[35] By then, even the beleaguered university president felt compelled to appeal to party headquarters for instruction. At its 95th session, Zou Lu asked the Central Executive Committee to define the "educational direction" of his university. The answer satisfied nobody, least of all Zou Lu, for it reaffirmed the common ground over which all factions were fighting for preeminence: the official function of Guangdong University was to provide "training in [party] principles." [36] Factions were divided over the degree to which the party should try to impart additional instruction in the humanities and sciences *as well as* party principles, and in this respect the decision of Party headquarters favored the Huangpu model, which relegated all other educational goals to the background. Henceforth the university was to be a party school (*dangxiao*), turning out civilian cadres indoctrinated in party principles, much as the Huangpu Academy was a military school for turning out loyal party soldiers. And—as we shall see of the Huangpu Academy—Guangdong University performed the additional function of displacing existing colleges with a single, authoritative party institution.

The party's decision on Guangdong University signaled, above all, a victory for one party faction over another in the struggle to give concrete form to the ideal of party rule. Zhou Fohai left the university for Shanghai in December 1925, along with the other members of the staff. On reaching Shanghai he immediately penned a piece for the party journal *Awaken* in which he took issue with the slogan "Down with the intellectual class!" currently trumpeted by the Huangpu party branch. In the name of "enlightened intellectuals," Zhou explained why an elite cadre of revolutionaries was necessary to lead the Nationalist movement. He elaborated on an earlier article published in an independent magazine, *The Lone Sentry* (*Gujun*), in which he had argued that intellectuals needed to be enlightened in the Way (*dao*) of the Nationalist Revolution in order that workers and peasants not be misled by less enlightened party activists. The leaders of the revolution should forego a class awakening in favor of an awakening to the nation.[37] For Zhou and other critics of the Central Executive Committee, the fault lay less in the university's emphasis on party education than in its provision of the wrong kind of awakening by the wrong type of people.

The Nationalist government also targeted labor unions, social clubs, and professional societies in its comprehensive program to educate the people of Guangdong in the meaning of citizenship under a Nationalist party-state. Civic associations were obliged to register with the government. Associations with approved educational objectives secured registration without difficulty, but registration was denied those which failed to meet with approval. So, for example, provincial authorities certified the Guangdong Society for Researching International Problems (*Guangdong guoji wenti yanjiuhui*) because it set itself the task of publicizing the Nationalists' opposition to the Unequal Treaties. Among professional associations, it approved the formation of the Guangzhou Municipal Doctors Union (*Guangzhou shi yishi gonghui*), which had the declared objective of promoting public sanitation. A propaganda section attached to the Zhenguang Company Workers Club earned approval from the Peasant and Worker Department (*Nonggong ting*), and the provincial government made a substantial donation of Y12,000 toward the running costs of the Guangdong Provincial Educational Association (*Guangdong sheng jiaoyu hui*), whose aims coincided with its own.[38] Before his untimely death in August 1925, Provincial Governor Liao Zhongkai had ruled that local philanthropic societies should be tolerated if they were found to comply with specified guidelines. This tolerance did not, however, extend to associations that spread "superstition." In March 1926, a Nationalist preparatory administration in Meilu municipality set out "to reform local customs" and, in the course of its investigations, came upon a benevolent society that "spread superstitious propaganda" to "lead people astray." Its least pardonable crime was getting in the way of the new Nationalist administration in Meilu. At the request of the local party administration, the provincial government ordered the disbandment of the association.[39]

The provincial government also cooperated with other levels of government and with party bureaus in staging festive rituals and public rallies. It helped manage the annual May Day celebrations and a series of massive public welcome ceremonies for Hong Kong strikers and their families, as well as the burial and commemoration services for the "Shamian Martyrs" gunned down by colonial troops at the entrance to the Guangzhou foreign concession. It assisted in commemorations surrounding Sun Yatsen's death in March 1925, and on the anniversary of his death in 1926. Far and away the largest propaganda enterprise undertaken by the government was the mammoth training and publicity program planned for the municipal census over the summer of 1925.

The first step in converting people into citizens was to make them more accessible to state investigators by registering them on the municipal and county rolls. "Investigating the population is the basis of city government," proclaimed a memorandum from the Guangzhou municipal government in 1925. "All earlier additions to the population [registers] of the city are inaccurate and hence inadequate for effective investigation of the population."[40] Local officials complained that people had never voluntarily registered in the past and were highly suspicious of current plans for a census. Experience had taught that a census invariably heralded a new poll tax or some form of conscript labor.[41] On this occasion the mayor of Guangzhou, C. C. Wu, was determined to correct the flaws of earlier censuses and was especially keen to overcome the tendency for respondents to falsify their returns. He decided to break with precedent and, rather than employ city police as census-takers, to try instead to persuade the residents of Guangzhou that it was in their interests as citizens to comply with the census. There were, however, too few political instructors for the task. Mayor Wu then approached the principals of state and private colleges in Guangzhou to assist by releasing their senior students from class for a period of a week to ten days for intensive training and propaganda before taking the census. It was suggested that any refusal to comply with the request would not be viewed favorably.[42]

In July the city administration put forward a detailed census proposal for provincial government ratification. The plan envisaged a massive propaganda exercise mobilizing school students from all over the city for training as "propagandists" before sending them onto the streets (under police protection) to explain to householders and passersby why they should register their names and addresses with the revolutionary government. By its charter, the Ministry for Civil Administration was responsible for keeping population registers. The ministry accepted the assignment and approached provincial and municipal educational authorities to hold discussions with school principals and student representatives. On 5 September, 48 representatives from 28 state and private schools and colleges convened under the chairmanship of Wen Zhongliang, an executive of the provincial education department, to devise procedures for the door-to-door publicity campaign. Over the following fortnight, 2,000 students were given intensive briefing sessions at five strategic points around the city. They were then organized by school into propaganda teams, provided with census forms and leaflets explaining the purpose of the exercise, and dispatched around the city for three days of intensive propaganda work before the census forms were distributed.[43]

Other state demands on the students, however, competed with the census. On Saturday, 23 September, school and college students throughout the city were given the day off to participate in a state funeral for the 53 victims of the Shamian Massacre. These students joined tens of thousands in a solemn parade, the students walking immediately ahead of the wagons bearing the dead. They returned to their census work on the following Monday, when census propaganda was extended for a further day to compensate for the unscheduled loss of time. The students' efforts were duly appreciated. Those who participated in the Shamian commemorative march received no formal recognition for their attendance, but students who took part in the census-propaganda exercise were issued commemorative plaques to mark their contribution to the revolution.[44]

Party Institutions

Participation in commemorative parades, boycotts, and mass rallies offered its own rewards to those who took part. But mass rituals did not erupt spontaneously. Behind the public face of the mass movement, considerable organization, preparation, and training was coordinated through the mass organizations of the party. The First Nationalist Party Congress charged central party bureaus with responsibility for training cadre and undertaking mass propaganda in their respective fields. The Central Women's Bureau, Youth Bureau, Labor Bureau, Peasant Bureau, and, in time, the Merchant Bureau were each instructed to assist in the project of national awakening. Below each central bureau there was a corresponding provincial bureau for propaganda, women, youth, labor, peasants, and merchants, each supervising in turn the work of corresponding bureaus at the town and county level in Guangdong. These party bureaus were the institutional underpinnings of the mass revolution.

No one phrase can quite capture the range of pedagogical tasks undertaken by all party bureaus. Out of deference to the sensibility of officers of the propaganda bureau, the word "propaganda" was generally elided in the definition of responsibilities of other bureaus. The word "education" was generally inserted in its place. The peasant bureau, for example, was entrusted with the task of "rural education," the labor bureau with "workers' education," and the women's bureau with "women's education." In practice, this reference to education was rarely interpreted to mean training in literacy and numeracy. Schooling was the function of the provincial education system, which fell into the domain of the Nationalist government rather than of the party. On this point, party headquarters was careful to avoid the word "education" in its description of youth bureau responsibilities, in deference to the state educational system. Instead, the Central Youth Bureau was exhorted to "guide the political views" of students in provincial schools.[45] Irrespective of the responsibilities defined in their founding charters, all bureaus interpreted education and political guidance to mean that they were entitled to train their own political educators and produce and disseminate their own propaganda.

By design, at least, the preeminent party training and propaganda institution was the Central Propaganda Bureau. In practice, things worked out differently. From the time of the bureau's transfer to Guangzhou in February 1924 to the death of Sun Yatsen a year later, the Central Propaganda Bureau did very little to justify its title. It neither centralized party propaganda nor produced much of its own accord. The bureau published the *Nationalist Party Weekly*, a journal founded by the party's provisional Central Executive Committee in the winter of 1923 and handed over to the bureau in the new year as a fait accompli. Had it shown greater initiative, the propaganda bureau might also have adopted the *Guangzhou Republican Daily*, a newspaper founded by the provisional Central Executive Committee in 1923, but the bureau declined to accept responsibility until Sun Yatsen urged the newspaper upon it.[46] Similarly, although the bureau opened a Propaganda Training Institute (*Xuanchuan jiangxi so*, or *Xuanchuanyuan yancheng so*), the institute conducted only one four-week-long class before closing down, and fell so far short of meeting existing demand for trained propagandists that other central bureaus, and even provincial and county bureaus, took it upon themselves to set up cadre-training institutes on their own initiative.[47]

The early failings of the Central Propaganda Bureau were partly offset by the performance of the provincial propaganda bureau, or, more properly, the Propaganda Bureau of the Guangdong Provincial Executive Committee (*Guangdong sheng zhixing weiyuanhui xuanchuan bu*). The provincial bureau was empowered by its charter to supply propaganda materials to local party newspapers, to print and distribute materials in its own right, and to examine and authorize materials prepared by its subordinate town and county branches. It oversaw a large number of propaganda instruments and turned out a prodigious amount of material. In November 1925, the provincial bureau assumed management of a major daily newspaper in Guangzhou and launched a network of local party dailies throughout Guangdong. In April 1926 the bureau began issuing an official monthly magazine as well.[48] It set up a training institute for propagandists, dispatched student propaganda teams to far-flung corners of the province over school vacations, opened libraries and reading rooms, promoted the establishment of party bookshops, inspected schools, pressed for the introduction of courses on Sun's Three Principles, and in virtually every month of its operation printed and distributed thousands upon thousands of leaflets, booklets, and photographs. Even so, the provincial propaganda bureau accounted for only a small portion of the total activity and output of the provincial party headquarters. Like their counterparts at the central level, the women's, youth, merchant, labor, and peasant bureaus at the provincial level assumed responsibility for propaganda in their particular domains, and together they turned out the bulk of propaganda issued by the Guangdong branch.[49]

The propaganda bureau was nevertheless the technical center of propaganda operations within the provincial party headquarters. It established the Committee for Artistic Propaganda, which utilized the talent of the Guangzhou School of Fine Arts to improve the quality of pictures and posters pasted about the towns and hamlets of Guangdong.[50] It monitored the feedback that came in to provincial headquarters from other propaganda agencies and drew on the lessons of their experience to improve the quality and heighten the impact of propaganda in Guangdong. In November 1925, for example, the provincial propaganda bureau took note of reports from the army's political bureaus on the second Eastern Expedition that pictures were proving more effective in stimulating sympathy for the aims of the revolution among illiterate farmers than were printed leaflets. The bureau adjusted its own propaganda accordingly. In preparing materials for distribution in remote rural communities, the provincial bureau reversed its earlier propaganda ratio of written to pictorial material from about three-to-one in favor of written material to three-to-one in favor of pictures.[51]

Another major function of the provincial propaganda bureau was to train propagandists for local party work. In March 1926, it drew up plans for a propagandist training institute to address a growing demand from party headquarters and local party branches for propaganda staff to work at the town and county level. So great was this demand that local branches were moving to set up propaganda institutes on their own initiative in Zijin, Yingde, Nanxiong, and Xijiang counties. Up to this point, the bureau had consistently answered demands for trained propagandists for local work by calling on town and county branches to nominate candidates for the Central Propaganda Bureau's Propagandist Training Institute. When it had become clear, however, that the central institute had little interest in training officers for local propaganda, the provincial propaganda bureau grew alarmed at the prospect of losing control over local activities should training institutes proliferate in every county. In February it ordered that no institute be set up without its approval or participation. The bureau then set up a Propaganda Training Institute on its own initiative to satisfy local party requirements.[52]

Initial plans envisaged an intake of around twenty students, but local branches and other agencies put forward the names of 800 applicants for entry to the new provincial institute in March 1926. In view of the large number of applicants, the bureau doubled the size of the first class to 40. Successful candidates attended classes for 30 hours each week in politics, economics, social psychology, and the martial arts, and their eighteen part-time teachers were drawn from the provincial propaganda bureau, from the Central Youth Bureau, and from a number of universities and colleges in Guangzhou. The selection of teachers reflected the commitment of the institute's founder, the radical Nationalist Gan Naiguang, to progressive labor and peasant policies.[53]

The institute opened on 3 April 1926, in the midst of confusion surrounding a political coup that had taken place some weeks earlier when Chiang Kaishek ordered the arrest of the Communist commander of the gunboat *Zhongshan* for allegedly conspiring to attack his headquarters. In the early hours of 20 March, Chiang staged a brilliant coup. On the pretext of discovering a Communist plot to spirit him away on the *Zhongshan*, Chiang placed Guangzhou under martial law, and dispatched police and cadets to occupy government buildings and surround the headquarters of the Guangdong–Hong Kong Strike Committee.[54]

Radical elements were intimidated by the incident, and a number of political instructors at the Propaganda Training Institute failed to show up for classes.

Students at the institute were less cautious. They began conducting classes themselves and organized a range of extracurricular activities to compensate for the shortcomings of their formal courses. Informal activities included preparation of propaganda materials, participation in public propaganda activities, and training in work units of associated news agencies, newspapers, peasant and labor groups, educational institutes, and political training institutions. The students also set up three voluntary societies—a student society, a debating society, and a lecture society—which not only gave the students something to do in lieu of formal study but also extended the reach of the institute to many more than the 40 students who had enrolled in the first class. An extramural education unit, staffed by students of the institute, conducted additional classes for upwards of 50 party members who were not themselves enrolled at the institute. Students also toured the province to conduct campaigns on particular issues and incidents, including the anniversary of the Shamian Massacre in June 1926.[55]

The students' apprenticeship in news agencies and newspaper offices was a critical part of their training, for expanding the network of party newspapers to supplement or displace private newspapers was one of the key functions of the provincial propaganda bureau in expanding the reach of the party-state at the local level. In 1924 the party was well represented in metropolitan newspapers but enjoyed little access to newspapers and journals beyond Guangzhou and adjacent counties. Two important developments over the autumn and winter of 1925 changed this. First, Chiang Kaishek and his commanders led a number of successful military expeditions into eastern and southern Guangdong that eliminated all but a few rival military units in the province and created favorable conditions for extending party and government authority beyond the metropolitan area. Second, the provincial bureau was strongly encouraged to extend its range of operations and, with the assistance of the revitalized Central Propaganda Bureau under Mao Zedong, it was staffed and equipped for the job.

By the start of 1926, the central bureau was managing the *Guangzhou Republican Daily* and had begun production of the new authoritative magazine of "central opinion," *Political Weekly*. In November 1925, it persuaded the provincial bureau to take control of another daily newspaper in Guangzhou, the *Republican News (Guomin xinwen)*. The intention was not that the *Republican News* should compete with the central bureau's *Guangzhou Republican Daily*. To the contrary, the aim of the provincial bureau was to take out of circulation a private newspaper that was a thorn in the side of the central bureau. The *Republican News* was an embarrassing irritant, edited by a political group that passed under the title of "The Hall of Literary Splendor" (*Wenhua tang*). This group persisted in publishing veiled attacks on Communists and their sympathizers in the Nationalist party. When Gan Naiguang assumed editorship of the paper and it came under direct control of the provincial propaganda bureau, the *Republican News* abruptly changed its tone and won the approval and financial support of central party headquarters.[56]

The provincial propaganda bureau then turned its attention to local newspapers. It was empowered by section 6 of the provincial branch charter to correct, inspect, and guide all party publications at the town and county level. To discharge its responsibilities for correction and inspection, the bureau commanded all local branches to submit their publications for review immediately when they were issued, and from the start of 1926 began to examine and correct about 30 titles each month. The bureau was also expected to expand the network of party publications and sow the seeds of party doctrine on untilled and often stony fields in the furthest corners of the province. In this respect, the most ambitious enterprise of the provincial propaganda bureau was to promote the official party *Republican Daily* newspaper chain from the metropolitan capital southward to areas bordering on French Tonkin, eastward along the coast, and north to counties adjacent to Fujian Province.[57] This, too, was intended to displace existing newspapers in each region and substitute party ones.

The expansion of the *Republican Daily* network took place within guidelines laid down by the provincial propaganda bureau in a series of "Regulations on Establishing Party Newspapers" promulgated on 18 November 1925. These specified the conditions to be met before any existing or proposed local newspaper could profess to be an official organ of the Nationalist party. In effect, they invested the provincial branch with absolute discretion over which papers were to be accredited and with absolute control over those which succeeded in gaining accreditation. The regulations were vigorously effected. Papers that laid claim to the title of *Republican Daily* without fulfilling the prescribed conditions were refused accreditation. The *Qinlian Republican Daily* in southern Guangdong, for example, was denied accreditation because it was directed by an individual rather than by an approved party institution. Other accredited newspapers that failed to abide by the conditions of accreditation were severely reprimanded. The editors of the *Jiangmen Republican Daily* received a formal reprimand after failing to submit copies of the paper for regular inspection and approval by the propaganda officers of provincial party headquarters.[58]

Most of this activity took place in the interval between the completion of the provincial military expeditions and the mounting of the Northern Expedition. By June 1926, eight local editions of the *Republican Daily* had been developed to the point of seeking accreditation, and three others were in preparation. These complemented one another in a patchwork pattern corresponding to counties and regions over the territory brought under Nationalist control on completion of the provincial expeditions. Each *Republican Daily* was placed under the direct authority of a particular town or county branch but was designed to cater to the population of the wider region for which the town or county happened to form the commercial or administrative focus. The *East River Republican Daily*, for example, was based at local party headquarters in Huizhou City and was intended to circulate in the wider East River region. The editor of the *Qinlian Republican Daily* proposed supplying the area between Qinzhou, in Guangxi, and Lianzhou, in the far south of Guangdong. The circulation of the *Liangyang Republican Daily* was limited to the region between the "two Yangs," Yangjiang and Yangchun, in central-southern Guangdong. The *Qiongya Republican Daily*, based in Haikou, was designed to serve all of Hainan Island. From Shantou, the *Lingdong Republican Daily* circulated throughout the northeast. Three other town and county party branches that sought accreditation for local editions of the *Republican Daily* in Zhongshan, Jiangmen, and Dongwan also intended that their papers should complement the others in effecting comprehensive coverage by daily party newspapers of all areas occupied by the Revolutionary Army on the provincial military campaigns. No region was to be without its own party daily.[59]

Between planning and execution, the local *Republican Daily* network encountered two major obstacles. The first involved internecine factional struggles and other political differences between the local editors and the provincial party officers charged with overseeing their operations. In this respect, the expansion of the *Republican Daily* network faced difficulties similar to those which had earlier bedeviled Guangdong University when Zou Lu tried to implement party education on campus. Indeed, both cases supplied ammunition for the argument that party rule required a far stricter disciplinary regime than the party had been accustomed to maintaining under the liberal Republic. The ruling party could not be said to speak with one voice while the party itself was divided. A second range of problems arose from the severe financial constraints under which the party operated in the months preceding the Northern Expedition. The newspapers initially profited from Chiang Kaishek's success on the provincial expeditions, but soon fell victim to his ambition to reunify the country at the expense, if need be, of securing Guangdong.

The problem of partisan political disputes was seen from Guangzhou as a question of discipline to be resolved by outside party intervention. Problems of this order played havoc with the Lingdong, Jiangmen, and Qiongya newspapers. The editor of the *Lingdong Republican Daily*, Li Chuntao, was obstructed by a senior provincial party official who wielded considerable authority in Shantou, Fan Qiwu.[60] In this case, the local editor was appointed through Communist party connections (Zhou Enlai's entourage in Shantou), whereas the regional supervisor, Fan Qiwu, was one of very few anti-

Communist officials to retain a measure of authority at provincial party headquarters. In this case, Fan prevailed. It was, however, more common for local
editors to be branded "right wing" and for party agencies to intercede on behalf of the masses to correct the local deviation. Problems of this kind arose
with the both the Jiangmen and the Qiongya *Republican Daily* through the involvement of Luo Han, an evanescent Nationalist party activist who showed up
wherever radicals seemed in a position to effect control of local party affairs.
He accompanied the first Eastern Expedition as an official propagandist, but
was on that occasion reprimanded by Zhou Enlai and the Special Party Branch
of the Huangpu Academy for his vitriolic denunciations of the Communists.
On the second Eastern Expedition, Luo made his way to Jiangmen, where he
set up the *Jiangmen Republican Daily*.[61] Within a short time the paper's chief
editor, Chen Riguang, was arrested in the course of a labor dispute, and the
local party branch fell into acrimonious bickering over Chen's arrest. The labor
movement in Jiangmen was well known for initiating a series of strikes involving local employers as well as Nationalist government and party agencies, and
at the time of this particular expedition the Jiangmen General Labor Union was
agitating for a rise in workers' wages. In February of the new year, when the
Southern Expedition was under way, the union entered into dispute with the
municipal government as well. It was at this time that Chen Riguang came to
blows with an official of the local Restaurant and Tea-House Workers Union
and was "arrested" by the union. In retaliation, a number of other disputants
were "arrested" by the party's Jiangmen Town Branch Preparatory Committee, after which a number of sub-branches petitioned provincial party headquarters to condemn the actions of the town branch in return. The matter was
finally passed on to the head of the provincial labor bureau, the Communist
Liu Ersong. Chen Riguang and the township party committee were disciplined.
Luo Han and his *Jiangmen Republican Daily* disappeared.[62]

Leaving Jiangmen, the indefatigable Luo Han made his way south to
Hainan Island on the trail of the Fourth Army. In Hainan he took part in preparations for establishing the *Qiongya Republican Daily* and became embroiled in
a dispute that ultimately put an end to plans for the Hainan newspaper as well.
Responsibility for founding the *Qiongya Republican Daily* was formally vested
in the Hainan Special Committee, one of four special committees created by
provincial party headquarters to reorganize and oversee local party affairs on
its behalf. The Hainan Special Committee appointed a manager and editor for
the newspaper and arranged for its establishment costs to be met by the headquarters of the Fourth Army, then occupying Hainan. But around February or
March 1926, Luo arrived in Haikou and succeeding in persuading the editor
and manager to reject the offer of money from the Fourth Army. Apparently the
cash was tainted by association with its left-wing political bureau. Luo man-

aged to gather Y3,000 from other sources and acquired the existing regional newspaper, the *Hainan Island Daily*, for conversion into an official party organ of the *Republican Daily* network. When the Hainan Special Committee learned of this change of plan, it raised formal objections and blocked the maneuver. By June 1926, nothing had come of plans for a party newspaper on Hainan Island.[63]

The heavy drain on provincial revenues brought on by preparations for the Northern Expedition was the second constraint on the growth of the local *Republican Daily* network. The revenue base of the provincial government expanded greatly, and its income rose markedly with the conquest of the southern and eastern regions. Nevertheless, revenues could not keep pace with the expense of recruiting and equipping the massive forces required for the Northern Expedition, so there was little prospect of returning revenue to those areas of the province from which it was extracted. This was a source of immense grievance among villagers and townspeople in the areas affected. Provincial party headquarters was also starved of funds and could no longer afford to finance local party activities in the southern and eastern regions.[64] The Huiyang County branch, located in Huizhou, could afford to maintain publication of the *East River Republican Daily* for no more than a few months, and the first issue of the *Dongwan Republican Daily* was delayed for a considerable time by the financial problems of the Dongwan County branch.[65]

Once the various dailies ran into financial difficulties, neither provincial nor central party agencies could step in to assist them. In one case, however, wealthy members of the local community came to the aid of the party newspaper in the hope of diminishing Communist influence over its management. This was the Shantou-based *Lingdong Republican Daily*. The hefty establishment cost of the paper, estimated at around Y10,000, was supposed to have been met from opium-prohibition levies and the sale of bandit treasure and enemy booty collected by the Revolutionary Army en route to Shantou. But neither the army nor the opium-suppression bureau showed any inclination to meet their obligations. Even the minimum monthly subsidy of Y30, which was to have been covered by the party's Central Finance Bureau, was counted too heavy for the limited resources of central party headquarters. When the finance bureau informed the Central Executive Committee that it could not afford to maintain the new paper in Shantou, the committee referred the matter to the Guangdong provincial executive committee. But the provincial committee was in no position to meet the establishment and running costs of the paper either, and passed responsibility down to the Shantou municipal party branch. Here the buck stopped. Shantou was a large commercial and industrial city with a healthy merchant community, and the *Lingdong Republican Daily* ultimately went to press with their assistance. It seems Fan Qiwu was instrumental in securing the support of local merchants and industrialists, and that their dona-

tions offset the influence of the regional Special Committee when it attempted
to give Fan's rival, Li Chuntao, management of the paper. The regional party
committee could not match the financial resources at Fan Qiwu's disposal.[66]

Women activists in the Nationalist party believed that propaganda for
women required a different order of cadre and propaganda techniques from
those employed in other bureaus. Certainly the content of women's bureau
propaganda was consistent with the general party line; attacks on patriarchal
structures and "feudal" practices were framed in the anti-imperialist and antiwarlord rhetoric of the Nationalist Revolution. In its early stages, the political revolution imposed few restrictions on the articulation of women's issues.
Revolutionary social goals appeared to match calls for international proletarian solidarity. Vera Vladmirovna Vishnyakova-Akimova, a translator attached
to the visiting Russian delegation, recalls her reception when she dressed as
a young Chinese woman for a cameo performance at the 1926 Women's Day
celebrations in Guangzhou: "I portrayed awakened China and stretched out my
hands towards Soviet Russia. No matter how surprising it may seem, the Chinese recognized themselves in me and applauded deafeningly." [67] There was
little cause for surprise, for women *and* men recognized themselves in the
symbol of the awakening female, and both invested in her struggle to free the
suppressed hopes of a captive nation. The subordination of women's liberation
to the Nationalist movement took place in this highly charged symbolic arena,
where the figure of the oppressed woman was ultimately transformed from
one expressing gender-specific demands into a denatured symbol of collective
national suffering.[68] For the time being, women and China were supposed to
awaken together.

How they were to awaken was a different question. To many women activists, it seemed that men were unlikely agents for liberating women and that
orthodox male techniques of public assembly, pamphleteering, and magazine
publication were not always appropriate for the "mass of women." [69] The
women's bureau developed new techniques to compensate for these deficiencies. It employed an independent team of propagandists to develop appropriate
propaganda strategies, and it set up a Women's Movement Training Institute
to acquaint women activists with their use. From 1925, graduates of the institute toured factories, hospitals, nursing colleges, and other places where
women made up a majority of the employees. In addition, the bureau ran regular night schools for working women, convened public gatherings for women,
and orchestrated publicity campaigns on women's issues for festive and commemorative occasions. The bureau produced a monthly magazine, *Women's
Voice* (*Funu zhi sheng*), and published sheaths of revolutionary leaflets. Bureau
cadre also assisted in the work of affiliated organizations, including the Guang-

zhou Women's Association, with which they jointly produced *Women's Weekly* (*Funu xunkan*).[70]

Beneath the Central Women's Bureau was the Guangdong provincial women's bureau, and as many town and county women's bureaus as there were party branches. These played a key part in political training and propaganda in smaller urban centers and rural villages. The provincial bureau employed five full-time propagandists—more than the provincial *propaganda* bureau—and funded a theatrical society, known as the Popular Drama Society, that performed works charged with "revolutionary significance" in towns and hamlets up and down the province. It set up a propaganda section specifically to encourage women to join the Nationalist party, and it composed, printed, and distributed leaflets on its own account. Like its central counterpart, the provincial bureau also dispatched propagandists to schools and public places to lecture on issues of particular concern to women.[71]

In fact, the provincial women's bureau served as an effective conduit connecting the propaganda network of the party's women's bureaus from the center to the city, town, and county branches. In 1924 the powers of coordination and policing vested in the Central Women's Bureau were seldom exercised because there was little call for them. This changed once He Xiangning assumed control of the central bureau and Deng Yingchao began work as secretary of the provincial bureau. The two women headed a remarkable team.[72] The provincial bureau co-edited and distributed the magazine of the central bureau, *Women's Voice*, and circulated the publication of the Guangzhou City branch women's bureau, *New Woman* (*Xin funu*). The staff of the provincial bureau cooperated closely with the central and Guangzhou City bureaus in planning propaganda activities for the celebration of International Women's Day on 8 March 1926. Beyond the city, the provincial bureau helped establish another Women's Propaganda Training Institute in Luoding County and, following the appointment of women's propagandists to the four regional special committees that toured Guangdong over the first quarter of 1926, it extended its reach to the southernmost and easternmost points of the province. By this stage, the women's movement had grown to encompass over one and a half million women. The Central Women's Bureau then began to convene formal conferences of provincial and city propagandists with the aim of coordinating their activities, and established a joint propaganda committee to liaise with the provincial bureau.[73]

The party's Central Youth Bureau found itself immersed in cadre training and mass instruction of a different kind. The bureau was heir to a long tradition of youth activism, and it inherited all of the strife that came with it. A national youth movement had been rolling along under a variety of different institutional patrons ranging from the YMCA to the Communist Youth League for a number of years before the bureau was founded in 1924. In that year, the bureau found itself entangled in the headlong drive for a popular awakening conducted by rival and often hostile political factions through publications, demonstrations, soap-box oratory, and mass-education classes in most major cities of the country. Zou Lu, head of the Central Youth Bureau for its first eighteen months, channeled the bountiful energy of the movement away from public awakening in the general sense toward enlightening young people themselves. The youth bureau directed its attention toward youth in the universities, colleges, schools, and factories of Guangzhou and its immediate vicinity.

The youth bureau, we noted, played a key role in orchestrating party propaganda through the state and private school systems and, under its director, Zou Lu, at Guangdong University. The bureau also set up schools of its own in Guangzhou, known as "commoners schools" (*pingmin xuexiao*), and drew up a general education program for ratification by the party's Central Executive Committee.[74] The school system repaid the bureau's attentions by supplying a pool of young people to assist in propaganda campaigns too large for bureau staff to handle unaided. In addition to a copious supply of leaflets, the bureau prepared and published a number of dramatic scripts and, from 1926, two weekly party magazines, entitled *Scouts* (*Tongzi jun*) and *Youth Work* (*Qingnian gongzuo*). Finally, like other central party bureaus, the youth bureau kept a close watch on affiliated organizations with propaganda and training arms of their own, notably the All China General Union of Students and the Young Soldiers Association.[75]

At the provincial level, the Guangdong provincial youth bureau ran a staff-training institute similar to those run by other party bureaus and published its own monthly magazine, *Guangdong Youth* (*Guangdong qingnian*). The Youth Movement Training Institute opened in April 1926, in the same week that the provincial propaganda bureau's training institute commenced classes, and scheduled its first course to run for three months through to July. Admission was by way of an entrance examination that tested candidates' familiarity with the materialist conception of history. Courses on the syllabus included an introduction to the peasant and labor movements, the history of socialism, the nature of imperialism, and the background to the international anticolonial struggle. Among the lengthiest of courses was one on the provincial peasant movement conducted by Mao Zedong along similar lines to the classes then under way at the nearby Peasant Movement Institute. The only class that matched Mao's in duration was one conducted by the institute director, Li Yueting, who was an old colleague of the pioneer peasant activist Peng Pai and was in sympathy with the aims of the peasant movement. In fact, Communist party members were employed at all levels of the faculty. At the early stages of planning, around half of the anticipated teaching positions for the Provincial Youth Institute were assigned to Communists. But the Zhongshan Gunboat Incident intervened between planning and execution and, as in the case of the provincial Propagandist Institute, the strengthening of Chiang Kaishek's hand curbed radical influence in the organization of the Youth Institute. Still, when the Youth Institute finally opened its doors in April, Communists made up about one-third of the staff and accounted for roughly one-third of all classes given. The first class graduated on schedule, as the massed armies of the Northern Expedition crossed the provincial borders into Hunan and Hubei in July.[76]

Whereas most central party bureaus could trace their origins to the First National Party Congress of January 1924, or at least to the party's own initiatives in trying to mobilize sectoral mass movements, the Central Merchant Bureau came as an afterthought in the wake of a disaster that befell the merchant community of Guangzhou and jolted the Nationalist leadership from its complacency. On 25 August 1924, the merchants of Guangzhou closed their shops and markets in response to the government's refusal to return a cache of small arms seized while on consignment to the city's merchant militia and to allow the merchant militia to continue operation. The strike culminated in a skirmish on 10 October, China's National Day, when units of the militia opened fire on demonstrators who were approaching the merchant quarter. This galvanized the Nationalists into action. Before the week was out, Chiang Kaishek led a contingent of Huangpu cadets to quell the "treacherous" merchants by razing an entire section of the city. If nothing else, the tragedy appears to have taught the Nationalist administration that it could ignore the power of the merchant community only at peril to itself. Five days later, on 20 October, the party established the Central Merchant Bureau.[77]

The new bureau was designed to organize merchants under the umbrella of the Nationalist party and to mobilize them around party objectives with the aim of preventing further merchant resistance. Like other party bureaus, the merchant bureau published a range of books, leaflets, and documents, issued a regular monthly magazine, *The Merchant Movement* (*Shangmin yundong*), and distributed its propaganda through an extensive network of provincial and local bureaus.[78] The bureau founded a specialist Merchant Movement Training Institute to train party cadre. It was also among the first central party bureaus to give priority to mass organization over mass propaganda, and it set up a network of institutions for placing merchants under direct party control. These were termed "merchant associations" (*shangmin xiehui*), in contrast to independent chambers of commerce (*shanghui*). It also equipped its mass institutions with political-education and publishing units. At the provincial level, the

Guangdong merchant bureau set up a merchant movement training institute of
its own accord to train local party cadre, and it published a monthly magazine,
The New Merchant (Xin shangmin).[79]

The merchant movement eventually outgrew its inauspicious beginnings.
In January 1926, the Second Nationalist Party Congress instructed the merchant bureau to organize small merchants to combat the financiers, industrialists, and larger traders who dominated the chambers of commerce. The
simple division in party propaganda between "petty" and "big" or "national"
and "comprador" capitalists failed to capture the complexity of the tensions
within the Chinese bourgeoisie, although this does not appear to have deterred
merchants who felt ill-served by existing public associations from taking advantage of differences between the chambers of commerce and the Nationalist
merchant movement. Nationalist propaganda played upon these differences, in
turn, by promising small merchants a stronger voice in public affairs if they
joined a party-sponsored merchant association. The strategy was quite successful. When the Nationalists moved north to Shanghai in 1927, the party's
merchant organizations generated sympathy among smaller traders and some
substantial capitalists who felt aggrieved by the practices of established chambers of commerce.[80]

When delegates from the peasant bureau heard merchant bureau staff announce their preference for mass organization at the Second Nationalist Party
Congress, they nodded in knowing agreement. The peasant bureau had specialized in organizational work from its inception. Before taking on the position,
bureau secretary Peng Pai had already amassed years of experience in peasant
organization in Hailufeng, east of Guangzhou, where he had learned the value
of intensive mass organization.[81] But he did not neglect propaganda. The publishing record of the peasant bureau was far and away the most impressive of
all central party offices: it included the weekly magazine *Peasant Movement
(Nongmin yundong)* and the monthly *Chinese Peasant (Zhongguo nongmin)*, in
addition to an impressive monograph series and frequent propaganda guidelines. But its publications were not, like those of other bureaus, addressed to
readers at large. They were designed instead for the use of the bureau's own
cadre and for selected staff members of its affiliated organizations. Peasants
themselves only absorbed peasant bureau propaganda in small oral doses after
it had been predigested by a carefully selected and trained cadre of special
envoys *(tepaiyuan)*.[82]

Here the peasant bureau seems to have been listening to Soviet advisers,
who drew on Lenin's distinction between propaganda and agitation as set out
in his seminal work *What Is to Be Done?* (1902). Contrary to general Nationalist party practice, Lenin had proposed that the function of propaganda was to

present "many ideas" to a "few persons." Agitation, on the other hand, should offer "a single idea to the masses." The distinction was not an arbitrary one. It was a practical extension of Lenin's concept of the vanguard party, which was distinguished from that of his enemies in the Russian labor movement by its skepticism about the possibility of awakening any but the vanguard itself. Lenin set out his strategy to distinguish it from that of the "economists" who looked upon propaganda as a form of reasoned explanation and counted agitation a form of mobilization for action. Such, indeed, was the strategy of all but the peasant bureau in the early stages of China's Nationalist Revolution.[83] The peasant bureau distinguished its propaganda from that of other Nationalist agencies in much the same way. Cadre imbibed propaganda, but for peasants it was agitation all the way down.

The bureau employed several hundred special envoys in Guangdong Province between 1924 and 1925. Their propaganda was geared exclusively to mass organization. No sooner had the first cohort of special envoys graduated from the Peasant Movement Training Institute than they set out to convince peasants of the advantages of organizing themselves into peasant associations.[84] This linkage of propaganda and mass organization in the role of the special envoy provided propaganda with a simple test of its efficacy that few other bureaus could match. Words and pictures, speeches and meetings, promises and curses that failed to muster peasants into peasant associations were counted ineffective and abandoned on that account. Other bureaus — notably the youth, women's, and propaganda bureaus — were inclined to measure the value of their efforts by the volume of their output, rather than by their reception among readers and listeners, and they set up institutional hurdles between propagandists (*xuanchuan yuan*) and organizers (*zuzhi yuan*) that special envoys circumvented with ease. In the politics of mass awakening, other bureaus had much to learn from Lenin and Peng Pai.

The peasant bureau was an exception in another sense as well. In most cases, the work of a provincial bureau rivaled or excelled that of its parent bureau at the central level. The provincial peasant bureau, however, was little more than a cipher compared to its central counterpart. At first, Peng Pai had been placed in charge of the central and provincial peasant bureaus concurrently, but he ceded his position in the central bureau in November 1925 to his Communist colleague, Luo Qiyuan. They worked in tandem until January 1926, when Luo assumed charge of the Guangdong bureau as well.[85] In addition to sharing its senior staff with the central bureau, the Guangdong peasant bureau borrowed low-level cadre from the center. In the event, the provincial bureau had few staff of its own and very little propaganda that it could claim to its credit. This, too, was a function of Lenin's dictum on the distinction between propaganda and agitation. The central bureau supplied "many ideas" to the "few persons" who occupied official positions in subsidiary bureaus at provincial and county levels.[86]

Labor organization was as important to the progress of the revolution as the peasant movement, but the Central Labor Bureau came nowhere near matching the peasant bureau in personnel, activity, or influence. The work of the peasant bureau was enhanced by a Communist policy of conducting peasant-movement activity through Nationalist party institutions. But the Communists insisted on retaining their own institutional autonomy in the field of labor organization, preferring to penetrate and establish labor organizations beyond the purview of Nationalist discipline. These included the Chinese Labor Union Secretariat (*Zhongguo laodong zuhe shuji bu*), the All-China General Union (*Zhonghua quanguo zong gonghui*), and, in time, the Guangdong–Hong Kong Strike Committee (*Shenggang bagong weiyuanhui*). The organizational and propaganda work of these affiliated organizations rendered the Nationalist labor bureau all but redundant. It was responsible for very little in the way of labor organization and was the only mass-movement bureau without a serial publication to its name.[87] To the limited extent that the labor bureau assisted in labor organization, it showed even less interest in propaganda. All nineteen items of bureau work reported for the months of February and March 1926 involved questions of labor organization. Only one mentioned political education at all. This was not because propaganda was counted irrelevant to the progress of the labor movement; to the contrary, some of the most vocal propagandists in Guangzhou worked on behalf of the Guangdong–Hong Kong strike. Rather, responsibility for awakening the workers of China in the Nationalist Revolution rested with cadre who had undergone a "class awakening" in the Communist party.[88]

Military Institutions

The independence of peak labor organizations from Nationalist control was a particularly sensitive issue over the spring and summer of 1926, when Chiang Kaishek was regrouping Nationalist armies for a massive assault against forces arrayed against them in central and northern China. Money was one point of contention. The Nationalist government was billeting and subsidizing tens of thousands of workers who had flocked to Guangzhou since the start of the Guangdong–Hong Kong strike in June of the previous year, at a cost estimated by Finance Minister T. V. Soong at ¥10,000 per day. Chiang Kaishek hoped to divert these funds to the expedition, along with all other revenues collected in the province. In December, he anticipated that the expedition would cost between 28 and 35 million yuan over its first year, or around double the sum of all provincial revenues collected over the preceding year. Civil expenditure had to be slashed and new sources of revenue found and exploited before Chiang could hope to get the expedition under way. When it finally did set out, the expedition left the city of Guangzhou looking "like a squeezed lemon," as one observer put it. "All the juice and flavour was gone." [89]

Maintaining idle strikers, needless to say, appeared to Chiang an insupportable burden. As it happened, the expeditionary force required an army of porters to carry supplies beyond the railway terminus at Shaoguan, over the 1,000-foot incline of the Nanling ranges, and on to the plains of Hunan on the first stage of the expedition.[90] The solution to both problems lay in employing striking workers from Hong Kong, who were already on the government payroll, as porters for the expedition. This solution did not, however, appeal to the Communists who were coordinating the strike. Communist party leaders opposed mounting a national expedition before the province of Guangdong itself had been fully secured for the revolution, while Communist labor organizers feared that the subordination of workers to military authority would deprive them of the independent field of action to which they had grown accustomed.

Neither Chiang nor senior Nationalist government officials were deterred by Communist intransigence. Foreign Minister C. C. Wu commenced secret negotiations with British officials in Hong Kong, in order to avoid direct confrontation with the strike committee, over conditions for resolving the strike and boycott. Chiang Kaishek moved more directly to bring the Communists to heel. On the morning of 20 March, he placed Guangzhou under martial law and effectively silenced opposition to the Northern Expedition. On 20 May, Chiang exercised his newly acquired influence over the party's Central Executive Committee to elicit a "request" for the strike organization to release striking workers for duty as porters in the expedition. The first cohort of 2,000 striking workers boarded the train for Shaoguan on 5 July, and a further 1,500 assembled at the forward base of the expedition over the following week. More than three-quarters of the carriers who eventually lugged the heavy weapons and supplies over the Nanling range to Hunan in the steamy summer of 1926 were drawn from among striking workers from Hong Kong.[91]

Chiang Kaishek's difficulties in securing porters for the Northern Expedition highlighted a unique problem facing Nationalist military forces. The Nationalist Revolutionary Army was handicapped because, unlike the general run of warlord armies, its offices renounced the use of force in recruiting porters. The cheapest way to assemble a squad of porters had always been to request the local constabulary to make a batch of summary arrests, or to encourage a few burly officers to swoop down on able-bodied men who could be pressed into service from the river tracks, wharves, and wine shops near at hand. This was now ruled out of order. The new policy was not entirely to the Nationalists' disadvantage, for the practice of conscripting laborers gave warlord armies a fearsome reputation that frequently rebounded against them. Labor conscription was particularly counterproductive in rural areas, where healthy villagers would disappear into the hills at a call from the village watchman that an army was approaching. In time, even the great northern warlord Zhang Zuolin acknowledged the strategic advantages of voluntary recruitment, and in March 1927 renounced the use of compulsion in recruiting porters. In 1926, however, the new system of voluntary recruitment had yet to be perfected by the Nationalists.[92]

There was, they soon discovered, no such thing as a peasant volunteer. Whatever recruiters may have promised them, few peasants (or laborers) were inclined to volunteer for the back-breaking toil and occupational hazards that marked the life of the army porter. In fact, the Nationalists' recruitment policy entailed two additional ingredients. One was access to mass organizations through which to secure voluntary compliance. Chiang Kaishek, after all, finally obtained his porters by compelling mass organizations to supply teams of volunteers at the start of the expedition. And by extending the reach of mass organizations along the route of the expedition, into Hunan, peasant-movement activists managed to recruit porters at a pace to match the advancing columns.[93] The second element was the reconstruction of the army itself, from top to bottom, with the aim of ensuring that officers and men would learn to treat one another with respect; only then could they begin to respect the villagers and townspeople with whom they came into contact. This was entirely overlooked by Zhang Zuolin in 1927, but it was at least attempted by the Nationalists.

The carrier policy of the Nationalists was only one aspect of a wider strategic doctrine that counseled close and friendly relations between soldiers and civilians. The political aim of the doctrine was to mobilize popular support for the Nationalist movement generally; the strategic aim was to neutralize civilian hostility toward the demands of the Nationalist Army as it passed through their communities. Political officers instructed the soldiers in their care not only to refrain from conscripting carriers but also to forego any temptation to occupy private dwellings or to seize provisions without adequate compensation. These three prohibitions were reduced to a catchy phrase, the "Three Don'ts" (*sanbuzhuyi*), which scanned neatly alongside the Three Principles of the People (*sanminzhuyi*) in propaganda jingles. Still, implementing the policy presented challenges. The Three Don'ts were honored more often in the breach than in the example on the Guangdong provincial campaigns that preceded the Northern Expedition.

Chiang Kaishek's report on the first Eastern Expedition (31 January to 23 March 1925) offered a damning indictment of his soldiers' conduct toward civilians. Officers failed to arrange accommodation for their men in tents, or at public sites such as schools and temples, so soldiers resorted to raiding houses in search of shelter and fought one another for the right to occupy them. They grabbed and ate whatever they could lay their hands on. As a consequence, the system of "voluntary" recruitment turned out to be even more oppressive than the old system of forced conscription. Formerly it had been the practice to induct porters for the duration of a campaign. Under the new system, it was presumed that carriers would volunteer their services for a short distance and then return home once new volunteers had been recruited in their place. Things did not quite work out that way. The general behavior of the soldiers so intimidated people along the route of the campaign that when the first body of short-distance volunteers returned to their villages, all able-bodied men in the vicinity vanished into the thickets. The First Expeditionary Army was then compelled to dragoon hundreds of women and scores of infirm old men to carry their provisions. The conduct of soldiers on the second Eastern Expedition (28 September to 7 November) showed little sign of improvement. In this case, however, the carrier problem was circumvented by conscripting 3,000–4,000 striking workers with the assistance of the Guangdong–Hong Kong Strike Committee.[94] With mass organizations ready to hand, troop behavior did not matter quite so much. In this respect, Chiang's recourse to striking workers in planning his Northern Expedition marked an advance on the practices of his enemies, although it marked a defeat in his contest with his own military officers.

Chiang could not derive much comfort from his officers' treatment of their men either. He was enraged by the corruption and sadism of "most military officers," as he saw it, and tried to put a stop to the more sadistic practices. But his efforts were largely wasted. In November 1925, Chiang noted that in spite of his instruction, officers were still siphoning off pay intended for their men, "stuffing soldiers' mouths with shit, dealing out brutal lashings and cursing them mercilessly. One finds, even more often, that they could not care whether their men are starving or freezing."[95] Chiang believed that good officers made good soldiers, and so held officers to account for their men's behavior. He managed to overcome the problem of retreat or desertion on the Northern Expedition by instituting a severe disciplinary regime. "If a company of soldiers retreated in action," Hollington Tong writes, "the head of the company was summarily shot. . . . It was a drastic rule but it proved effective."[96]

For all his concern for the welfare of his soldiers and the goodwill of the people of Guangdong, Chiang was part of the problem. He consistently placed himself above civilian authority. According to current party thinking, there was little point reciting jingles about the Three Principles of the People and the Three Don'ts until top commanders respected the authority of the party, until officers saw to the welfare of their men, and until all ranks respected the lives, welfare, and property of civilians. Chiang scored only two out of three.

Improving relations between the party and the army, or between soldiers and civilians, called for institutional reforms bearing on the internal organization of the Nationalist Revolutionary Army and its relationship to the highest organs of party authority—in short, for creation of a party army.

The idea of a party army entered Sun Yatsen's thinking by a roundabout route. In the autumn of 1922, Sun learned from discussions with the visiting Comintern representative, Henk Sneevliet, that the secret of Russian success had been mass agitation among workers and peasants. In time Sun began to reproduce Sneevliet's judgments as if they were his own, to the point where the intensity of his avowed conversion to mass propaganda appeared to rule out the use of armies at all.[97] It was Sun's talent for capturing and securing territory that had commended him to the Russians in the first place; Sneevliet and the Communists then found themselves in the curious position of having to dampen Sun's enthusiasm for mass propaganda and organization.[98] Gradually, as Russian and Comintern advisers began arriving thick and fast over the coming year, Sun learned to qualify his newfound enthusiasm for mass propaganda by making allowances for the use of armed force. His Soviet advisers persuaded him to establish a party army, and offered to subsidize a new military academy at Huangpu.[99]

Military education at the Huangpu Academy was comparable to that of other academies in the country, but its political education involved close indoctrination in the principles of the Nationalist party and the rationale and objectives of the Nationalist Revolution. Problems arose in implementing this educational strategy, partly because of the novelty of the idea and partly due to the intransigence of military officers. The Huangpu Academy had its share of political disagreements over the aims of the revolution, and over the significance of Sun Yatsen's principles as well. But there was barely a party, government, or military agency that was spared political conflict in the revolution. What was most distinctive about the Huangpu Academy among Nationalist agencies was not its internecine conflicts but the way its director deliberately and systematically denied access to party training to all other military institutions in the province. Huangpu was not just a party-military academy but *the* party-military academy, and it is remembered as the paramount military training institution of the revolution because it succeeded in wiping all other training academies from the record. The history of the academy traces, in its outline, the larger history of attempts to create unique party institutions through which to enforce "uniformity of opinion" in the party-state.

It was perhaps inevitable that there should have been friction between a central party-military academy on the Russian model and alternative proposals for indoctrination of existing armies under nominal party authority. The Huangpu Academy was designed to serve as the foundation for a new army and not as a corrective for old ones.[100] Nevertheless, there were still plenty of old armies roaming about Guangdong offering embarrassing testimony to Sun Yatsen's commitment to the mercenary putsch as a revolutionary strategy. Sun was embarrassed on his own account. He constantly berated his commanders for taking a despotic hold on regions under their control and many times denied that the allied armies were in any sense "revolutionary armies." [101] Reform, he noted, was required at all levels in the forces: at the top, the structure of command needed to undergo reform to eradicate local despotism, whereas at the bottom, the rank and file required several months of intensive ideological indoctrination to overcome their political indifference.[102] On the penultimate day of the First Nationalist Party Congress in January 1924, Dai Jitao introduced an unscheduled motion to the effect that existing militarist armies should be converted into a revolutionary army by means of a party propaganda program. Curiously, there was neither a scheduled nor an unscheduled motion at the conference to establish a new and exclusive academy at Huangpu. This appears to have been an executive decision taken by the provisional Central Executive Committee before the congress opened. At the congress itself, however, a number of delegates felt that something had to be done with the armies already occupying Guangdong.[103]

Though the Huangpu unit no doubt benefited from the concentration of disciplined officers within its ranks, it was only one of many that made up the array of forces in the province. As the purpose of the Huangpu Academy was to create a new army (xinjun), all 1,052 cadets who passed out by the summer of 1925 were duly assigned to the Huangpu Corps. This corps was expanded in turn into the party army (dangjun), and eventually was accorded the title of First Army of the Nationalist Revolutionary Army. In February 1925, the Huangpu Corps totaled no more than 3,500 men. It grew to about 10,000 by July, but even then made up only a small portion of the estimated allied strength of 65,000 soldiers. The Guangdong Army had 30,000 troops, the Hunan Army 12,000, the loyal Yunnan Army 10,000, and the remnants of the second Northern Expeditionary Army some 3,000 men.[104] The proportion of First Army to allied army soldiers in the force that finally set out on the Northern Expedition shrank still further with the addition of the Fujian Army, Cheng Qian's Sixth Army, Tang Shengzhi's Hunan Army, and the Guangxi Army of Li Zongren. These armies had little prospect of converting themselves into model party-armies by the force of moral example emanating from Huangpu. Sun's dream of converting mercenary military forces into "revolutionary" ones required additional academies to service existing armies, and awaited development of a comprehensive political network that could be grafted onto the military command itself.

This conflict of purpose, between creating a new party army and fixing old ones, was partly offset by the creation of additional military academies to complement the one at Huangpu. At the time of Huangpu's founding, the Yunnan Army was already operating an officer school. Within a week of Huangpu's opening, the Guangdong Army decided to establish an academy as well. In February 1925, a fourth academy opened to service the Guangxi Army and recruited a cohort of officer cadets as large in number as the current student body at Huangpu. By April the Hunan Army had also founded a military academy in Guangdong.[105] The Hunan, Yunnan, and Guangdong army schools came to cater to the Second, Third, and Fourth armies of the Revolutionary Army respectively, once the provincial armies had been incorporated into the Nationalist Revolutionary Army. Even then, Huangpu continued to supply officers for the First Army alone. The Fifth Army was operating a client academy by the end of 1925, and the Sixth Army established an academy early in the new year. By the onset of the Northern Expedition, in fact, even the smallest of allied forces had established political-military academies.[106]

This was not, it seems, a welcome development at Nationalist party headquarters, for the new military academies operated in competition with the Huangpu Academy. Yet in the eyes of those responsible for converting existing armies into "revolutionary" ones, it was the Huangpu Academy that seemed to be the problem. It made inroads into their domains, stole their most promising recruits, hogged provincial resources, and was seen to receive favored treatment from party headquarters. Cheng Qian's military school is a case in point. In 1923, when he was director of the Army Political Department of Sun Yatsen's administrative headquarters, Cheng Qian acknowledged the need to train "genuinely revolutionary" officers for the various armies nominally under his direction. In October he enlisted a small number of officer cadets from a large body of candidates put forward by the Yunnan, Guangxi, Guangdong, and Hunan armies into a Central Army Instruction Brigade (*Zhongyang lujun jiaodaotuan*). The brigade was allotted a monthly allowance of ¥9,000 from the provincial treasury and was allocated the strategic site of Huangpu, on the Pearl River. Toward year's end, however, Cheng Qian ran into "numerous difficulties" when another academy, funded with Russian assistance, was granted priority over the Huangpu site. In April, Cheng reluctantly announced that the brigade was to be reduced in size to 300 cadets (200 of the "best" of the old brigade and 100 troops drawn from the four aforementioned armies), that it was to be renamed the Army Military School (*Lujun jiangwu xuexiao*), and that it was to be transferred to an alternative site to make way for the Huangpu Academy. The Army Military School conducted courses in politics, economics, and social sciences, in addition to the military sciences, and was staffed by teachers who "followed completely and understood implicitly" the Three Principles of Sun Yatsen.[107]

In the event, the school was disbanded in November by order of the Central

Executive Committee against the wishes of the school's commanding officer. Its trainee officers were transferred to the Huangpu Academy. On graduating with the first cohort of Huangpu cadets, they were assigned to Chiang Kaishek's School Army and, later still, to the First Army of the Nationalist Revolutionary Army. The Huangpu Academy profited considerably from Chiang Kaishek's encroachments on Cheng Qian's achievements, for the cadets recruited from the Army Military School were reckoned far more skillful than all other cohorts from Huangpu by those who fought alongside them in the Eastern Expeditions of 1925.[108]

In drawing its cadets from a variety of different armies and promising to return them after they had graduated, the Army Military School followed a different model from that of the Huangpu Academy. The advantage of creating a new army in place of renovating the old ones was, of course, that a new army would presumably be free of the personal entanglements and regional loyalties of the established provincial armies. Political indoctrination of seasoned mercenaries could only be expected to achieve so much. But even assuming that the object of the exercise was to create an army united in spirit and loyal to the party, the operation of the Huangpu Academy left much to be desired. Chiang Kaishek's dealings with the Huangpu Academy embittered veteran party commanders like Cheng Qian, who became an implacable enemy of Chiang for life. Other allied armies objected to the wealth, status, and authority of the Huangpu Academy and Corps.[109]

Their resentment came to a head in the autumn of 1924, when Chiang Kaishek refused to share a valuable cargo of modern weapons seized while on consignment to the Guangzhou merchant militia. Sun Yatsen was miffed as well. Sun cabled Chiang from the forward base of his 1924 Northern Expedition in Shaoguan, asking him to distribute the weapons equitably among the allied armies. From late August to October, Sun urged that the weapons be distributed to his own expeditionary armies, to one section of the Yunnan Army, to the Guangxi Army, and to the Henan Army and the air force, as well as to two independent military schools, the Yunnan Army Officer School and Cheng Qian's Army Military School. Chiang Kaishek refused. By the end of October, Chiang's defiance reduced Sun to pleading only for those arms surplus to Chiang's requirements to be sent on to Shaoguan. The response of the allied commanders was less polite. If the Huangpu contingent was in fact the only party army in Guangdong and uniquely fit to be entrusted with the weapons, they argued, then the Huangpu cadets should fight all of the party's wars unaided. Chiang's prima donna conduct won for the Huangpu cadets the title of "Dolls Army" and earned for Chiang the sobriquet "Dolls' Chief" in the abuse of envious commanders. The staff and cadets of Huangpu returned this contempt by refusing to acknowledge or salute the officers of allied armies.[110] Ad-

mittedly, animosity among the curious assortment of armies parading around
Guangdong was not a new phenomenon, nor was it all directed toward the
Huangpu Academy. In May 1924, quarreling between the Yunnan, Guangdong,
and Guangxi armies was held responsible for their resounding defeat at the
hands of a numerically inferior army loyal to Chen Jiongming. In September of
the following year, Xu Chongzhi's section of the Guangdong Army was called
to account for squandering resources while other allied armies were going hun-
gry. But these ancient grievances and the divided loyalties they engendered
were symptoms of the malaise that a party army was supposed to cure. Instead,
the Huangpu Academy and Corps fired old rivalries with a new range of grievances.[111]

Once the Huangpu Academy had inspired imitations all over the province,
the rise of separate military academies on the Huangpu model posed novel
problems for disciplinary officers charged with coordinating political work
throughout the Nationalist Revolutionary Army. Duplicated over six different
armies, the Huangpu model of an army with its own client academy entailed
a diffusion of authority across political courses and among commanders of the
various armies and their subordinates. Needless to say, political workers were
also handicapped by the military hierarchy itself, which, in every case, ranked
political indoctrination low on its list of priorities. The Huangpu Academy
was no exception. Richard Landis has chronicled a notable decline in political
training relative to military training in the operation of the academy through
1925. A contemporary examination of graduates of all military schools conducted in February 1926 indicated that none (including the Huangpu Academy)
had succeeded in cultivating appreciation for the goals of the party.[112] Results
from the field were hardly more encouraging. In September and October 1925,
propaganda teams for the second Eastern Expedition had to be drawn from a
mixed bag of institutions when it was found that the military schools could not
supply trained personnel in sufficient numbers. The Huangpu Academy fielded
18 cadets and the Attack Hubei Army's military school supplied 25 cadets, for
a total of 43 of the 249 propagandists employed on the expedition. Those deployed from the military schools were not only few in number but also short
on skill. It was found that propagandists from the political training class of the
Nationalist government's Political Training Bureau and from the propagandist
training schools of the Central Propaganda Bureau and its subordinate offices
outshone all other propaganda team members on the expedition. The rest, including the cadets from the Huangpu Academy, were counted more of a hin-
drance than a help.[113]

Around December 1925, the head of the Political Training Bureau, Chen
Gongbo, observed that the political education provided by each and every army
school fell far short of party expectations. He traced the source of the problem
to the party's failure to centralize and police the propaganda issued by the vari-

ous armies, to poor selection of personnel, and to a general neglect of political training on the part of school administrators. Chiang Kaishek, although personally responsible for the decline in political instruction at the Huangpu Academy, was nevertheless deeply concerned about the standard of military training in the academies as a whole. Chen Gongbo and Chiang Kaishek proposed abandoning the client-school and patron-army system pioneered by the Huangpu Academy in favor of a central academy that would cater to every contingent in the Nationalist Revolutionary Army.[114] In keeping with this advice, on 12 January 1926 the Nationalist government Military Affairs Committee resolved to dissolve all existing military academies and reconstitute them in a central institution located on the site of the Huangpu Academy. The new school was named the Central Military and Political Academy (*Zhongyang junshi zhengzhi xuexiao*) to acknowledge that it was to be a central institution, servicing all armies, and that equal emphasis was to be placed on military and political education. The third and final class of the Huangpu Academy graduated in January 1926, and the other military academies gave notice of their intention to close their doors once the current cohorts of cadets had passed out. In their place, the Central Military and Political Academy opened on 1 March 1926.[115]

Significantly, the first class of the Central Military and Political Academy has come to be remembered as the famous Fourth Class of the Huangpu Academy. This slippage in names is telling. Despite plans for the Central Academy to replace the allied military schools, it followed much the same recruiting procedures as the disbanded Huangpu Academy, enrolling cadets chiefly from among young intellectuals sent south from the provinces rather than from among candidates from the allied armies. It then failed to assign them to any but the original Huangpu army corps.[116] The amalgamation of the allied army military schools with the Central Academy then repeated the experience of Cheng Qian's Army Military School in 1924, again to the advantage of Chiang Kaishek. Chiang eliminated the rival schools without replacing them. By the time the Fourth Class graduated on 5 October 1926, the Nationalist Revolutionary Army had already mobilized for the final Northern Expedition and was on the verge of capturing the three cities comprising the strategic capital of Wuhan.[117] The failure of the new Central Academy to offer political training for officers of the allied armies was subsequently overlooked as the army marched north through central China to Nanjing. Even the goal of founding a "party army" was forgotten once it had become clear that the historical function of the Huangpu Academy was to create an officer corps loyal to the commandant, Chiang Kaishek, and to identify the party with its new military leader.

By default of the army schools, the extension of party authority over political education in the armed forces was left to a system of external political agencies attached to the military structure as it stood. The major contribution of the Huangpu Academy to the conversion of "reactionary military forces" was not the training that it offered within its walls but the pioneering of extramural political organizations and methods of political indoctrination by some of its more ambitious political staff, with the help of Soviet Russian advisers. In time, political officers of the Huangpu Academy created durable structures that found their way into units that never came within rifle shot of the academy itself. Among these, three permanent and coexisting political structures evolved under the influence of Huangpu instructors: a commissariat, or system of party representatives (*dang daibiao*), political bureaus (*zhengzhi bu*), and party branches (*dangbu*). Another kind of unit, the propaganda team (*xuanchuan dui*), was also set up on a temporary basis to service particular expeditions. It was this structure that was largely responsible for the discipline that characterized the combined forces when they marched out of Guangdong on the Northern Expedition, and carried the Nationalist government to Nanjing.

Although there was some overlap of function between the three permanent structures, each came in time to cater to different aspects of party activity in the armed forces. Party representatives were entrusted primarily with overseeing the compliance of military officers with party directives. Political bureaus were expected to train troops to maintain discipline, to conduct themselves properly in dealing with civilians, and, most importantly, to convince civilians of the advantages of cooperating with the Revolutionary Army. Party branches were set up to foster understanding and cooperation between officers and men. Though the difficulties encountered in introducing and developing each system throughout the Nationalist Revolutionary Army suggests that some units fell short of meeting party ideals, the development of the systems indicates the strength of the party's determination to compel their compliance.

Chiang Kaishek had witnessed the operation of a commissariat system in the Red Army during a visit to Soviet Russia in September of 1923. He understood from his observations that the chief function of party commissars was to keep military officers in line. Accordingly, when commissars were first introduced into Chiang's Huangpu brigades, they were given veto power over military orders issued by military officers of equivalent rank.[118] Chiang was also led to believe in Moscow that party commissars would be required only as long as the military structure remained aloof from the party one. So his support for the introduction of the system was conditional. As soon as the army was under the command of party members—or as soon as the commanders of the provincial armies were prepared to submit to central authority without haggling and bargaining—the commissariat would be dissolved. In addition to their supervisory functions, a number of other tasks came to be ascribed to party commissars at one time and another, from indoctrinating foot soldiers to keeping the rolls. These duties were shared with other political structures in

the armed forces and were neither essential to the operation of the party commissariat nor sufficient excuse for retaining the system when party control over
the armed forces no longer appeared necessary or desirable.[119] In April 1926, a
fortnight after adding another warlord army to the growing list of "revolutionary" ones, Chiang decided that military commanders were now sufficiently
responsive to his direction to warrant the abolition of the party representative
system entirely. In fact, Chiang was determined to remove Communists from
positions of influence in the army. He later reintroduced the system to assert
his personal authority over a number of armies involved in the Northern Expedition that were beginning to show the limits of their allegiance to anything
other than the recapture of their home provinces.[120]

Political bureaus were also introduced into the allied armies by way of
the Huangpu Academy, but there the resemblance to the party commissariat
ends. The first political bureau was set up within the Huangpu Academy itself,
where its functions were prescribed by the aims of the academy: to indoctri-
nate cadets, to oversee military training, and to monitor, publish, and distribute
reading material within the academy. A political bureau made its way from the
academy to a field unit in the spring of 1925, when the academy suspended the
operation of its own political bureau and created another in the party army.[121]
Once transferred from school grounds to the battlefield, the political bureau
underwent a transformation. Although it retained its general brief for political instruction, the bureau was freed from the constraints imposed by the
academy and expanded its operations to cater to enemy troops, to residents of
the areas traversed by the army, and to allied officers and men. By the advent
of the Northern Expedition, this included subverting the enemy and indoctrinating captured enemy soldiers; winning the cooperation of peasant farmers
and merchants in obtaining provisions, transporting goods, offering financial
credit, spying, scouting, and sundry other practical tasks; securing conquered
territories by establishing local party branches, provisional police forces, and
administrative committees and organizing worker, peasant, and merchant associations; and, for the allied soldiers, arranging rest and recreation, caring for
the wounded, offering political and literacy education, and establishing party
branches within the forces. Before the launching of the Northern Expedition, at
least, this transformation in the role of the political bureau was not matched by
any change of personnel between the academy's political bureau and bureaus
of the field armies. The changes all took place under the supervision of Zhou
Enlai, the head of the academy political bureau, the head of the party army
political bureau, and in due course commander of the political bureau of the
First Army and of the entire Eastern Expeditionary Army.[122]

Political bureaus fared rather better than the commissariat in the wake of
the Zhongshan Gunboat Incident. On 3 April, Chiang Kaishek requested that

all party commissars be withdrawn from service, but the system of political
bureaus was spared from censure. These were to remain in the forces to undertake general political work and "spread propaganda on the Three Principles
of the People." Though the system was left intact, many of its staff members were replaced. Zhou Enlai was relieved of command of the First Army
political bureau, which was placed in the charge of Deng Yanda on 11 April.
In May, new appointments were made at the intermediate level: in the First
Army, Feng Ti and Zhou Shimian replaced the Communists Liu Kanghou and
Jiang Xianyun in the political bureaus of the First and Third divisions.[123] Still,
the different treatment that Chiang meted out to party commissars and political
bureaus suggests that he was concerned with more than simply circumventing
Communist domination of political work in the armed forces. He could, had
he wished, have replaced Communist commissars with men of his own choice,
much as he replaced Communists in the political bureaus of his First Army. In
choosing to spare the system of political bureaus while eliminating the commissariat, Chiang showed that he was in sympathy with political work so long
as it remained limited to political indoctrination. By the spring of 1926 he was
no longer prepared to tolerate political workers, of any persuasion, holding authority comparable to that of the military hierarchy.

In light of Chiang Kaishek's conditional tolerance of political workers, it
is worth noting a significant qualitative change in the choice of personnel appointed to political work around the time of the second Eastern Expedition.
First, Chiang began to select military officers for political posts previously
filled by civilian party staff. Second, he selected wounded troops to fill lesser
political posts previously filled by nonarmy staff. At least two officers of the
First Army wounded on the second Eastern Expedition were subsequently appointed as party commissars. At the same time, political bureaus began to assemble wartime propaganda teams from troops fresh out of the hospital. Once
political instruction had fallen behind military training in the academy, a use-
less soldier was counted more reliable than a healthy civilian out in the field.[124]

Party branches formed a third tier of political organization in the Nationalist Revolutionary Army. Far and away the crudest measure for defining a
party army was the proportion of party members in its ranks. Given the ease of
entry into the Nationalist party, membership signified very little, but the prospect of entire divisions joining the party en masse appealed to military officers
who were eager to limit party interference in their affairs. Chiang himself announced that his instruction brigades were a party army on the ground that the
entire contingent had signed the party register. Other commanders protested
that their own membership in the Nationalist party should excuse them from
scrutiny by party political officers.[125] But the party held quite a different idea of

its role in the armed forces. It hoped to organize and discipline party members and to disseminate propaganda through party branches.

On 30 June 1924, within a fortnight of the academy's opening, the Central Executive Committee ratified the charter of its special district party branch. On 3 July, five sub-branches were set up within the branch, and four weeks later these were each divided into cells. Cell leaders were expected to monitor the cadets' thinking and behavior and to censor their reading material. The district branch was entrusted with responsibility for the army's "propaganda to the outside world." [126] The party branch accompanied the instruction brigades on the first Eastern Expedition and adapted to the contingencies of war in a manner very similar to Zhou Enlai's political bureau. That is, it conducted propaganda work among residents of the East River region, assisted in the establishment of local party branches, and investigated local administrative practices—most notably in the field of education—in addition to working among soldiers of the Expeditionary Army.[127] In time, the unique position of an independent party structure within the military gave party branches other, and quite distinctive, functions, which ultimately overshadowed the duties they happened to share with political bureaus.

The most conspicuous thing about a party branch in an army unit was not its propaganda, its monitoring of cadets, or its administrative work among the local people, but its provision of a setting in which all party members were nominally equal and the military hierarchy was left momentarily in abeyance. Party egalitarianism provided relief from hierarchical military authority. It also subverted military authority, at least at intermediate levels, and military officers warned that military discipline would suffer should party branches be set up for all rank and file.[128] In fact, tension between party branches and the intermediate military hierarchy converted branches into champions of foot soldiers against the overwhelming authority of their immediate superiors. This served a number of purposes. Chiang Kaishek fostered the spread of party branches throughout the armed forces to improve the lot of his men, encouraging troops to take advantage of its sanctuary to expose the officers who mistreated them. He was frequently angered by the corruption and sadism of intermediate-level officers. As one officer would never inform against another and as those targeted by complaints would invariably punish the complainers, Chiang declared that party branches should provide an outlet for the troops to "express their opinions and report their hardships with absolute freedom, without [fear of] resentment or reprisals from their superiors." [129] A second and related purpose was to establish direct lines of communication between foot soldiers and command headquarters through the party network. Through the party-branch system, Chiang managed to circumvent intermediate officers and establish a far more direct and comprehensive system of patronage and command that extended directly from his headquarters to soldiers in the field.

A third purpose behind the expansion of the army's party network was to give the armed forces a greater voice on the inner councils of the Nationalist party itself. The spread of party branches from the First Army to the other units of the Revolutionary Army was slow and uneven at first. There was a brief spurt of activity in July 1925, but by October the most rudimentary forms of party organization were still lacking in all but the First, Second, Third, and Henan armies. Even in these four cases, it is doubtful that brigade-level branches and the smaller party cells had spread beyond the First and perhaps Second divisions of the First Army. Certainly no party branch had reached brigade level in the Third Division of the First Army until January of the following year. The creation of lower-level branches in the Third Division coincided with a spurt of party-branch activities that took place between December 1925 and January 1926, just before the Second Nationalist Party Congress was due to convene. In the event, the congress was informed that in the three months since October, special district branches had been established in the Fourth, Fifth, Hubei, and Attack Hubei armies, as well as in the navy and the police force. The timing of their creation helps explain why commanders of different armies who did not happen to share Chiang Kaishek's eagerness to stop malpractice among their subordinates finally agreed to tolerate party branches in their domains. In the wake of this flurry of party activity, the armed forces between them managed to muster around 70 delegates to the Second Nationalist Party Congress and to occupy more than a quarter of all congressional seats.[130] As the military was "partified," the party was militarized.

The winter of 1925–26 also witnessed a great spurt in the creation of town and county party branches in Guangdong, following the pattern of the extension of military power. Forty-six town and county party branches were set up over the first two-and-a-half years of Nationalist occupation, but almost as many again, 40 in all, opened over the five months of the second Eastern and Southern expeditions from October to February. In the following four months, to May, party membership in Guangdong more than doubled.[131] This accelerated rate of growth applied exclusively to the eastern and southern areas of Guangdong occupied by the expeditionary armies. Party membership in Guangzhou City remained more or less static over the same period, and the only other regions that failed to register significant growth lay to the far north and west, where the expeditionary armies failed to penetrate.[132]

Political agencies attached to the Nationalist Revolutionary Army also determined the quality of party membership and the style of party activity in localities gathered under Nationalist authority on the expeditions. Army political bureaus were the vanguards of the party. They were directly responsible for organizing and accrediting local party branches. Where branches were already well established along the route of an expedition, the bureau would investigate and reorganize them. Where none existed, they set about creating them. As the expansion of the party structure into the countryside followed the direction of military expansion toward the east and south of Guangdong, local party organs and activities tended to reflect the political colors of their parent political bureaus.

Political bureaus undertook civilian political indoctrination in the interval between occupying a region and establishing local party branches. After the cessation of hostilities along the southern route in Guangdong, for example, the expeditionary armies found local people ignorant of the aims and principles of the Nationalist movement, so they convened public assemblies to announce party policy on provincial and national reunification, on the Japanese menace in North China, on the Guangdong–Hong Kong strike, and on women's liberation, and they expounded at length on the principles of Sun Yatsen. Fourth Army political bureaus jointly set up a theater troupe, the People's Star Dramatic Society (*min xing jushe*), which held its inaugural performance on 7 February 1926, before an audience of 4,000 to 5,000 citizens of the city of Haikou, on Hainan Island. The opening play on their program was a revolutionary romance, entitled "The People's Star," written by the Fourth Army political bureau for the occasion with the help of its Soviet adviser, Gorev. It portrayed a curious collection of imperialists, local militarists, corrupt local officials, and gentry bullies conspiring to harrass and oppress the common people but being foiled in the end by the arrival of the Revolutionary Army. According to eyewitness reports, the audience readily identified with the oppressed victims of the play, grew very excited when the Nationalists came to the rescue, and finally "applauded without end" when the archvillain (the despised local warlord Deng Benyin) was captured and punished. A one-act comedy rounded off the evening's entertainment. Fourth Army propaganda made its way from urban Haikou to neighboring rural communities through teams of local youths who were recruited and issued with propaganda guidelines by the Fourth Army political bureau, and then sent "from village to village" to spread the message.[133]

Placement as defensive garrisons offered armies additional opportunities for influencing civilian political activity. Garrisons frequently arbitrated in local disputes. When the Guangdong–Hong Kong Strike Committee came south to Haikou, it soon found itself embroiled in a local dispute involving the American-owned Asiatic Oil Depot. The strike committee activated its own propaganda machinery to wage a war of words with the oil company, but it ended up also confronting the local merchant community, which was inclined to sympathize with Asiatic Oil. Committee members asked the Fourth Army political bureau to lend its weight in the dispute. Once the political bureau had agreed, the dispute was rapidly settled in favor of the strike committee. Some time later, merchants closed their shops when the strike committee arrested a local merchant. Merchant militia surrounded and beat up a team of party propagandists sent to dissuade them from continuing their strike. The party's Hainan Special Committee called out the local garrison to protect the propagandists, and when the propaganda team ventured into the marketplace a second time, in the company of a cohort of seasoned soldiers, its message was far more readily understood. Merchant resistance folded again.[134]

Armies also controlled access to official war booty and recovered bandit treasure, and were at liberty to disburse money according to the whims of their military officers and the priorities of their political bureaus. In April 1926, for example, the First Army was responsible for underwriting the propaganda expenses of the Chaomei-Hailufeng Party Congress and could reasonably expect some assurance of the congress's fealty. The selective distribution of army funds affected the kind of political activity conducted in a given area. Around Huizhou, the spoils from bandit clearance were divided between the peasant, labor, and popular-education movements to the exclusion of a party-sponsored merchant movement. Merchant-movement activists were forced to appeal to the Provincial Executive Committee for redress. To the south, the Fourth Army also promoted other popular movements at the expense of the merchant movement.[135]

In fact, merchants rarely fared well in their dealings with army garrisons, political bureaus, and party branches of any kind. The merchants of Huizhou had particular cause for complaint. At the time of the second Eastern Expedition, the Huizhou branch of the Nationalist party was staffed by members of a faction claiming links with the anti-Communist party committee in Shanghai. In collusion with local government agencies and the local garrison command, the branch ran a profitable commercial protection racket. For a fee of ¥50 to ¥200 per boat, the Huizhou garrison would contract to guard merchant vessels against bandit harrassment on the journey downriver. The bandits in fact rarely attacked commercial traffic, preferring instead to levy charges on its passage through their territory. As these charges tended to be lower than the fees charged for protection, merchants generally preferred the threat of bandits to the exorbitant cost of party protection. Following a left-wing reorganization of the branch, Huizhou merchants voiced their support for the new branch in the expectation that it would put an end to the protection racket and tackle the bandit problem at its source. But the new branch was staffed by Communist sympathizers equally hostile to local merchants. In some cases, local garrisons also withheld support from peasant and labor activists or tried to suppress publicity that placed a radical interpretation upon the party's peasant and labor policies. Either way, the nature and impact of party organization, policy, and propaganda at town and county levels was heavily influenced by the local garrison, and merchants lost out whoever was in charge.[136]

Far and away the greatest source of the army political agencies' influence over the direction of mass propaganda was their authority to organize, reorganize, and discipline local party branches. On the first Eastern Expedition, Zhou Enlai was authorized to supervise Nationalist branch affairs in his capacity as director of party affairs and party organization for the East River region. Things were arranged a little differently for the second Eastern Expedition, although not to Zhou's disadvantage. Civilian party affairs directors were named for every major town and county along the route of the expedition and accompanied the army until they reached their appointed destinations, where they set up offices under army protection. Even then, party affairs directors remained on intimate terms with the General Political Bureau, continuing to use its resources and, in some cases, remaining stationed within it when their destinations happened to coincide. On the Southern Expedition, the political bureaus of each participating army and division, rather than the regional political bureau, were responsible for local party affairs. The political bureau of the Tenth Division was responsible for local party affairs on the first stage of the Southern Expedition, that of the Third Army on the second stage, and the Fourth Army political bureau handled party affairs over the final stage of the Southern Expedition.[137]

Local branches established with army assistance tended to inherit the ideological features of their parent bureaus and to take up pedagogical activities where the parents left off. The Qingxian party branch on Hainan set up army-style propaganda teams and held candlelight processions in the manner of the Fourth Army political bureau, which had sired it.[138] This particular political bureau, attached to the Fourth Army, defined the political character of all branches on Hainan Island by declining to enlist "self-seeking" notables who volunteered for party work and refusing to accredit "Nationalist party branches" and "Nationalist party branch preparatory offices," which sprang up at the initiative of local elites as Nationalist units moved into their territories. Chief among the concerns of local elites in the period succeeding the expeditions was a desire to gain and maintain control over any Nationalist party branches set up in their vicinity. Without external intervention of the kind undertaken by the Fourth Army political bureau, the shape of town or county branches tended to reflect existing local power structures. The style of intervention of the political bureau was thus crucial, in every case, to determining the character of the revolution itself.[139]

Where local power structures took the form of agnatic kinship groups, the party branch was sometimes incorporated into the local kinship system. One of the county branches along the route of the Third Column of the second Eastern Expedition, at Longchuan, fell into this pattern. Without exception, every one of the nineteen office-bearers in the First, Second, Third, and Fourth sub-branches of the Longchuan County branch bore the surname of Zhang, and the formal opening ceremony of the county branch was conducted in the Zhang family temple to cement the identity of lineage and party authority.[140] This was more the exception than the rule. In most cases, branches set up in anticipation of the Nationalists' arrival were said to have been founded by "bad gentry" (*lieshen*) of no particular family background, who wished to influence local government administrators in their favor, or to press for party and government positions for themselves. All branches created in the East River region before the arrival of the Nationalist Revolutionary Army were reported by Zhou Enlai's General Political Bureau to have been founded on this pattern. Branches in the area were set up without the authority, and in many cases without the knowledge, of party headquarters in Guangzhou. Their failure to abide by routine procedure made easy targets of such branches, as did their clumsy attempts to turn revolutionary slogans to their advantage. "Given the sorry state of party branch organization," reported the General Political Bureau, "and in view of party members' lack of political training there has of course been no achievement of any note in party propaganda." The bureau extended its own political training agencies to correct the deficiency.[141]

In other cases, however, army political units supported attempts by local elites to make a successful transition to a new state structure. On the southern peninsula, the Fourth Army's Tenth Division was far more conciliatory toward local elites. The Tenth Division was commanded by Chen Mingshu, and its political bureau was under the direction of an archenemy of Communist sympathizers in the Nationalist movement, Li Linong. As a consequence, party branches that sprung up in the trail of the Tenth Division tended to be colored more conservatively than branches set up by the political bureaus of Fourth Army headquarters or by Zhou Enlai's General Political Bureau. Li Linong suffered for his pains, earning a rebuke from Zhou Enlai on the first Eastern Expedition and the displeasure of the Guangdong Provincial Executive Committee on the Southern Expedition for his "many errors" in local party organization.[142]

The appointment of county heads (*xian zhang*) followed much the same pattern as the selection of local party personnel, with military and political commanders of the Eastern and Southern expeditions leaving distinctive trails of political sympathizers occupying civilian posts in their wake. On the second Eastern Expedition, Zhou Enlai attempted to replace "gentry bullies" occupying county magistracies with county heads more to his liking. Not many were actually replaced, however, because the authority to install new county

heads was vested exclusively in the General Political Bureau, and the scope
of its authority was effectively confined to the southern flank of the expedition. Further south, Chen Mingshu's Tenth Division was initially vested with
the authority to appoint county heads over its stage of the Southern Expedition, and, in keeping with its local party appointments, it confirmed the appointment of conservative local figures not noted for their sympathy toward
the peasant and labor movements. At a later stage of the expedition, when
authority had been transferred from Chen Mingshu and Li Linong to Gan Naiguang, the political complexion of local government appointees changed from
conservative opponents to radical supporters of the peasant and labor movements. Yet even Gan made little lasting impression on the character of local
administration in southern Guangdong. A report on provincial administration
issued in December 1926 noted that in virtually every county in the province,
there remained government officials "who conspire with reactionary forces to
crush the mass movement." [143] Generally speaking, bearing in mind the sum
of counties on the southern peninsula, on Hainan Island, and in the Huizhou,
Hailufeng, and Chaomei areas of eastern Guangdong captured by Nationalist
forces on the Eastern and Southern expeditions, it seems that no more than a
small minority of incumbent officials were displaced. Only county heads who
were well known for maintaining close personal ties with the deposed warlords
Chen Jiongming and Deng Benyin appear to have been removed from office.
The rest were confirmed in office in order to mobilize local resources for the
Northern Expedition with a minimum of disruption.[144]

The history of the mass movements themselves tells a similar story. The
regional government agency for southern Guangdong, under the supervision
of Gan Naiguang, had three aims: to transfer local power from the "gentry
class" to the "people" by reforming or disbanding existing gentry organizations and setting up representative assemblies and mass associations at the
county level; to shift the tax burden from the poor to the wealthy; and to popularize education. On Hainan, the overriding aim of local government reorganization was to rid the island of "despotic gentry." [145] There is little evidence
of success in either case. A parallel government agency in eastern Guangdong
under Zhou Enlai and First Army Commander He Yingqin resolved to disband
gentry militia groups that were subverting government authority and resisting
party policy, and actively promoted the establishment of peasant associations
and labor unions. But mass-movement organization in eastern Guangdong
stumbled over obstacles similar to those impeding the new administration in
the south, including dependence on outside political leaders and the goodwill
of local garrison commanders, elite intransigence, and a shortage of time and
personnel. Few gentry militia were disbanded, and few local magistrates were
replaced. In the event, the expedition to liberate the people and unite the coun-

try imposed heavy new demands on Guangdong and returned the province to
the local elites and regional warlords who had run the place before the Nationalists disturbed them.[146]

The tendency for local elites to seek control over party branches and government officers in their vicinity taught the revolutionaries a number of strategic lessons. One was that subordinated social groups were unlikely to find representation in local party affairs without concerted intervention on their behalf
by external military and party agencies working in concert. A second lesson
was that a political movement seeking to extend effective centralized control
over local communities would be likely to find allies in subordinated social
groups, whoever, or wherever, they happened to be. In either case, the local
party branch or government office played a critical role in advancing or retarding the party's claims against those of local elites. A third lesson was that unless
party headquarters devoted sufficient resources to organizing, reorganizing,
and disciplining party branches and yamens at the town and county level, the
party-state would never reach far into local society at all. Some higher agencies
in place, including one or two political bureaus of the Nationalist Revolutionary Army, were unwilling to undertake the kind of intervention required. Yet
even where there was a will, there was a limit to what could be achieved with
the resources available. A brief survey of one county where some effort was
made in this direction helps to highlight each of these lessons in turn.

One region in Guangdong that drew the attention of army and party headquarters was Huiyang County. At the heart of Huiyang stood the city of Huizhou, an ancient town whose stout walls had withstood attacks by marauding
armies for a thousand years and more. In more recent times it had served as
Chen Jiongming's retreat. But the walls of Huizhou were no match for the new
Russian artillery of Chiang Kaishek's expeditionary force, which demolished
the fortifications and ransacked the city in October 1925.[147] Civilian party officials followed in their trail, trekking through the rubble. The General Political
Bureau of the second Eastern Expeditionary Army set up a Huizhou Area Party
Organization Committee to reorganize party affairs in the eight counties of
Boluo, Heyuan, Zijin, Longchuan, Lianping, Heping, Xinfeng, and Huiyang.
On 8 December, the committee delivered an interim report to the provincial
headquarters detailing its activities in the region. The compilers of the report,
reflecting Zhou Enlai's influence, were unequivocally opposed to imperialism
and warlords and supported the party's peasant and labor movements.[148]

The experience of the Huizhou committee illustrates the limitations of
army-sponsored intervention in local party affairs. Of the eight counties targeted by the Huizhou Area Party Organization Committee, only one was subject to thorough investigation and intervention. Three others—Heping, Lianping, and Xinfeng—were located too far from Huizhou to make intervention

practicable. In another two counties, Longchuan and Heyuan, attempts had been made to establish contact, but after weeks had elapsed without response, their reorganization was postponed indefinitely. In the case of Heyuan, this was a cause for alarm, because a local branch had assumed the committee's compliance and proceeded with its elections and formal opening ceremony without informing the committee or inviting its scrutiny. Neither the committee nor Guangzhou party headquarters could penetrate the branch. Not much was known about a sixth county, Zijin, except that its branch organization appeared to be hampered by the reluctance of a local government official to meet its running costs. Only in the case of the seventh county branch, at Boluo, did the committee show any sign of satisfaction with the progress of local branch affairs, although even here it was in no position to intervene had it wished to do so. The committee decided to cut its losses and to concentrate upon reorganizing the county branch that encompassed the city of Huizhou, Huiyang County.

A county branch had been set up in Huizhou in July 1925, when it attracted a number of "onetime soldiers and gentry layabouts" who could see that the writing was on the wall for Chen Jiongming and his Huizhou ally, Yang Kunru. Once Huizhou fell to the Nationalist Army in mid-October, those who had not already foreseen the advantages of joining the Nationalist party rushed to take up membership before it was too late. The new garrison commander, Hu Shusen, assumed the title of director of the Huiyang party branch as soon as he took charge, and under his patronage the branch swelled to around 2,000 members. Hu Shusen was not, however, to the liking of the branch reorganization committee, which alleged that under his direction the party recruited about 90 percent of its members from among soldiers and local gentry. The Huiyang branch and its sub-branches allegedly excluded peasant and worker membership by introducing excessive entry fees, and resisted the spread of peasant and labor organizations. Hu Shusen also set the political climate for the town as a whole by outlawing some party tracts and promoting others. Prohibited were the Communist party magazines *The Guide* and *Chinese Youth*, Tan Pingshan's pamphlet *Why Must We Overthrow Chen Jiongming?* and Wang Jingwei's *The Sense of Determination Appropriate to the People of Guangdong Today*, along with other tracts issued by the radical General Political Bureau. Hu did, however, promote Dai Jitao's pamphlet *The Nationalist Revolution and the Nationalist Party* and other material supplied by the Society for the Study of Sun Yatsenism.[149] Even after Chen Jiongming had been put to flight, the Huiyang Nationalist party branch was still classified by party headquarters among the branches requiring intervention and reorganization. It was under nominal Nationalist control, but not under the control of the factions then in ascendance at Guangzhou party headquarters.

The Huizhou Area Party Organization Committee resolved to reconstitute the Huiyang branch in mid-November 1925. The committee placed its own appointees within the county branch secretariat before proceeding to reorganize its seven sub-branches. It vetted the credentials of listed party members and withdrew membership from all "onetime soldiers, gentry layabouts and traitor merchants." But the committee met with outraged opposition from incumbent branch officials, and well after the reorganization its attempts to promote more radical policy were limited by community obstruction and insufficient funds. The reformed branch established a daily newspaper in Huizhou, the *East River Republican Daily*, but the paper collapsed within a month of publication for want of financial subsidy. It was eager to distribute the mountain of propaganda material built up by various party agencies, but the local bookshops refused to stock or to sell them. The regional Financial Reform Office hindered the promotion of the peasant and labor movements by declining to allocate Y20,000 in war booty, as instructed, and it obstructed the branch's own activities by withholding its monthly allowance of Y300. The reformed branch turned to mass activities to make up for its deficiencies in other areas. It set up a club for young men and women that served eventually as a propagandist training school and organized club members to journey into the countryside on political-education missions. Girls in Christian schools were instructed in the evils of imperialist "intellectual aggression"; workers were rallied into six new labor unions; and a number of merchants were persuaded "through the influence of revolutionary propaganda" to join the party-sponsored merchant association.

At the close of this rigorous attempt at party reorganization, the Huizhou committee concluded that reorganization of local branch affairs was required throughout the province, but that success could only be achieved through a massive investment of staff, time, and resources.[150] Huiyang County alone had stretched the capacity of the eight-county committee to the limit. The experience in Huiyang was not, as party reformers had hoped, a first step along a well-ordered path leading to wholesale investigation and reorganization of local branches throughout the Huizhou area using routine procedures. Instead, the committee had little choice but to circumvent existing power structures and resort to mobilizing young students to "awaken" the people. Once again, techniques initially devised to arouse the nation were employed to purge the party that practiced them. This was typical of broader developments in the party, government, and armed forces of the new Nationalist state. The impulse to awaken the people of China, which had initially propelled a partisan movement to replace the established Republican state with a single-party one, was rapidly diverted through factional struggle to the displacement of established institutions within the party-state itself.

Factional struggle was by no means divorced from the greater project to awaken China. All political actors in the Nationalist Revolution claimed to act on behalf of social forces seeking democratic representation through new state structures, and their struggles were thought to revolve around the nature of relations between party institutions and social organizations—that is, between factional struggle and "class struggle." The experience of party reorganization in Huiyang County hinted at a deepening institutional relationship between factional struggles within state instrumentalities on the one hand, and elite resistance to state penetration on the other, or mass support for the new state expressed through worker, peasant, and student organizations. The many instances of factional strife enumerated here—whether at Guangdong University, within and between central, provincial, and local organs of party and government, or among military academies and army political agencies—raise a common question. Who was representing whom in the Nationalist Revolution?

CONCLUSION
Representing Class and Nation

A multitude of men, are made *one* person, when they are by one man,
or one person, represented; so that it be done with the consent of every
one of that multitude in particular. For it is the *unity* of the presenter,
not the *unity* of the presented, that maketh the person *one* . . . unity
cannot otherwise be understood in multitude.

Thomas Hobbes, 1651[1]

These people are so shameless and so quick of hand that at any time
they can proclaim themselves *representatives* of some group or other.
Louis XIV said "We are the State," they say "We are the Nation."

Liang Qichao, May Day, 1925[2]

In *Nations and Nationalism,* Ernest Gellner mocks the disappointment of
Marxists when faced with the overwhelming victory of nationalism this century. "The awakening message was intended for *classes,*" notes Gellner, "but
by some terrible postal error was delivered to *nations.*"[3] In the nineteenth century, the portents had been good. In the towns of Europe and America, workers
were arising from their beds each morning to the rhythms of a working day
that separated their mode of life, their interests, and their culture from those of
other classes. In semibarbarian, semicivilized villages across the globe, peasant farmers were slowly discarding their worship of nature.[4] As science overcame fate, humankind appeared set to embrace a universal destiny rather than
particularist national ones. Today much of this faith appears misplaced, but
none more than the belief that the sentimental community of the nation would
be replaced by a more rational and international community of the working
class. The "awakening message" clearly went astray somewhere between 1848
and 1949.

Nationalism has inspired a burst of scholarship over the past decade, partly
in an effort to explain its historical survival and more recent revival, and partly
to explain why Marxism so clearly failed to predict either. The two are not
unrelated. As Ben Anderson explains, nationalism presents Marxism with an
uncomfortable anomaly both in theory and in practice.[5] But this is not the issue

that concerns me here. In fact, the place of Marxism in nationalist movements presents as formidable a problem for the liberal historian as nationalism does for the Marxist one. The Chinese revolution is a case in point. In China, the postmaster seems to have delivered the awakening message to class and nation at the same address.

Neither class consciousness nor national consciousness was highly developed in early twentieth-century China, yet there were moments in the Chinese revolution when it certainly appeared that the "awakening message" was getting through to classes more effectively than to the nation. The revolutions of twentieth-century China come as close as any to endorsing Lenin's claim that "every revolution, by destroying the state apparatus, shows us the naked class struggle." [6] When gentry-scholars gave way to "evil gentry" in the late nineteenth century and magistrates were transmogrified into "local bullies," the state bureaucracy lost the capacity to mediate social conflict, and conflict was inclined to flare in the absence of mediation.[7] With the collapse of the Qing state, possession of property translated more directly into the exercise of power than it had under the imperial system. The reconstitution of state power under the Nationalists in the 1930s and subsequently under the Communists entailed intensive mass mobilization to displace the power of local elites with the authority of new, centralized, bureaucratic state structures. It was, I have argued, this conflict between the revolutionary state and entrenched local interests that raised the specter of class struggle in China's national revolution. Nevertheless, the juxtaposition of divisive class struggle and cohesive nation-building confounds attempts to theorize Chinese nationalism. In China, an alliance of revolutionary social classes "awoke" as a nation-state.

A related question is why the arrival of nationalism should be heralded by an "awakening" message at all. Anderson and Gellner each locate nationalism at the intersection of revolutionary politics, social change, and the emergence of modern mass cultures, alternately organized around the idea of an "imagined community" or an "awakening" nation. This study has been more closely concerned with the awakening message than with the address on the envelope—with the imagining, the awakening, and the representing rather than with the identity of the community in question—and in tracing the evolution of the awakening subject I have suggested that an awakening message invariably starts with the self but could in fact end up anywhere. The awakening self anticipated awakenings of youth, gender, class, nation, humankind, and even (Kang Youwei might have said) of all living creatures on Mars, in its search for an ideal ethical community. The nation took precedence in China when nationalist reformers and state functionaries began actively policing dreams of awakening communities. In China, Marxist and non-Marxist Nationalists generally believed that a community would come into being when it became conscious of itself as a community, and that a community could be rationally reconstituted as a nation in the act of being awakened to consciousness by a representative state.

The question remains, however, why an awakening revolutionary class alliance should have behaved as though it were an awakening nation. Is the awakening message that foretells a class awakening inevitably a postscript to the message of national awakening? Certainly Marx and Engels anticipated that class struggle would initially take national form. In fact, they were surprisingly off-handed about the national particularity of the "proletariat of each country":

> Though not in substance, yet in form, the struggle of the proletariat with the bourgeoisie is at first a national struggle. The proletariat of each country must, *of course*, first of all settle matters with its own bourgeoisie.[8]

There is an anomaly right here. In an earlier passage of *The Communist Manifesto*, Marx and Engels note a growing "inter-dependence of nations" and observe of their own day that "national one-sidedness and narrow-mindedness become more and more impossible."[9] Elsewhere Engels hints at the process whereby nationality is destroyed by the proletariat: "The great mass of proletarians are, by their very nature, free from national prejudices," he affirmed after walking out of the Festival of Nations in London in 1845. "Only the proletarians can destroy nationality, only the *awakening* proletariat can bring about fraternalism between the different nations."[10] When the proletariat awakens (or is awakened) to its true position in the relations of production, and to its destiny in establishing fraternalism among nations, Marx's "substance" and "form" will presumably be reconciled. It would seem to follow, as Sanjay Seth has argued, that there is no "of course" about a narrow-minded, nationalist class struggle.[11] The paradoxical "of course" makes sense only if we concede, with Engels, that the "proletariat of each country" has not yet woken up.

In conclusion, I propose to explore the place of mass awakening in attempts to bridge the gap between form and substance in Marxist *and* Nationalist thought by focusing on the idea of the representative state. The gap is one between what can be realized or made true on the one hand, and what is merely concrete on the other. When an underlying substance is presumed to be real, although unawakened and unrealized, actual form appears no more than a chimera even when it is ("of course") concrete. In the passage from Marx and Engels just cited, the nation supplies the form and international class struggle the substance. Elsewhere in the writings of Marx and Lenin, class of itself and class for itself, or the spontaneous element and its "conscious" leadership, mark the divide between form and substance.[12] Similar distinctions, we shall see, are drawn in Chinese Marxism and revolutionary nationalism between what is in fact "real" and what merely appears so. In each case, it is presumed that revolutionary truth can be *made* real through political and literary representation. Hence the practices of representative politics and the forms of representational literature can each tell us a good deal about the other.

In histories of the Chinese revolution, the distinction between form and substance is often conflated with one between theory and practice. It is tempting to approach the writings of Mao Zedong, for example, in the belief that his major contribution lay in the attempt to reconcile Marxist theory and revolutionary practice through application of "dialectics."[13] In its immediate context, however, Mao's preoccupation with the relationship between theory and practice appears to arise from a different source: literary realism. Mao aspired to reconcile actual form with real (but hidden) substance through revolution, in much the same way that heroes in realist fiction invariably awaken to the nature of the forces constraining them before they struggle to shrug them off. The task for Mao was only incidentally to develop theory through practice. More pressing was a need to devise techniques for awakening people to a certain vision of reality, or to impress upon the nation the truth of Marxism-Leninism-Mao Zedong Thought as this was represented by the revolutionary state.

Here Mao borrowed more heavily from Lenin than from Marx or Engels. From the perspective of Marx and Engels, the historical task of the proletariat was to demolish the bourgeois state and unmask the fallacy of the nation that it claimed to represent. The nation-state was, after all, but the "executive committee" of the bourgeoisie.[14] For Lenin, things were not quite as simple. In his "Theses on the National Question" and "Theses on the Colonial Question," the destruction of nationality was held over until a more propitious time, when national-democratic revolutions in Asia would lead to the downfall of metropolitan capitalism in Europe. The task at hand in the 1920s was to awaken the nations of Asia to bourgeois nationalism. Meanwhile, the revolutionary nation would be represented by the executive committee of a local Nationalist or Communist party in a far more literal sense than the "executive committee" of the bourgeoisie ever claimed to represent the nation.

Lenin's judgment confirmed Marx's view that the nation-state is the executive committee of the dominant class.[15] But the "modern representative State," as Marx and Engels called it, need no longer be the executive committee of the bourgeoisie. After Lenin, it could serve the interests of any class or group of classes it claimed to represent. In fact, it could constitute its own referent— class or nation—by representing it as though it were a class or nation that had not yet awakened to its own identity or interests. In China, the idea of the nation came wrapped in the idea of the representative state, and the nation took form and character from the state that presumed to awaken and represent it.

The executive committees of the Chinese Nationalist and Communist parties both claimed to represent a distinctively Chinese people. This was not a matter of deception: the politics of awakening encouraged belief in a particular kind of state that would represent a community until it woke up. It was not the fault of the awakened functionary if he or she was obliged to represent something that still only existed in substance, and not yet in form; nor was the revolutionary state to be counted unrepresentative simply because it was accountable to nothing but its functionaries. Indeed, it was representative to the extent that it could create its own social referent. The politics of mass awakening would climax in the self-realization of a new mass community when the community finally reflected the contours of the state that represented it. Until then, substance would be reconciled with form in the realist, representational rhetoric of the revolutionary state itself.

National Awakening and Social Interest

The actual composition of the nation was decided in social conflict, or more precisely, in conflict between social interest and interests of state. When the boundaries of a national community are staked out around the interests of a state, some sectors of society are likely to find themselves stranded beyond the pale. This is what happened in the Nationalist Revolution when leading figures in the Chinese Nationalist party first targeted "selfish" sectional interest. Given the implicit identification of the Nationalist party-state with the nation, it was difficult for Sun Yatsen or Chiang Kaishek to interpret the insurrection of the Guangzhou merchants in the autumn of 1924 as anything but the manifestation of a contradiction between a sectoral interest and the national interest.

In the first week of August 1924, Sun Yatsen ordered his military commanders in Guangzhou to intercept a shipment of arms destined for the city's merchant militia. Before the month was out, the British consul-general in Guangzhou signaled his sympathy for the merchants. On 27 August, Sir James Jamieson issued a formal warning that British naval forces in Guangzhou Harbor should rally to the aid of the city's merchants if they came to blows with Nationalist authorities. To Sun Yatsen, merchant attempts to create an independent militia appeared quite unforgivable, but the additional threat from His Majesty's representative tainted their dissent with treason. In his reply, on 1 September, Sun vowed to resist "imperialist" intervention in China's domestic affairs and showed his resolve by sanctioning war against the merchant community of Guangzhou. Chiang Kaishek carried Sun's vow into effect. In October, Chiang led cadets of the Huangpu Academy into battle against the merchant militia, decimated the merchant community, and laid waste the commercial part of the city. Fires raged out of control in the commercial quarter for two days.[16] More radical theorists in Shanghai and Guangzhou needed only to endorse the course of action pursued by Sun Yatsen and Chiang Kaishek to conclude that bourgeois "interests" made China's merchant class a reluctant ally in a national revolution against imperialism.

All the same, the fracture of the nation posed far greater problems for a party committed to a racial ideal of the nation than it did for the Chinese Communist party. To Chen Duxiu, the Guangzhou merchant incident offered the first tangible evidence of bourgeois class treachery. For other Communist theorists, it appeared to signal a turning point in the revolution, a marker separating the bourgeois (Nationalist) leadership of the past from the worker and peasant (Communist) leadership of the future.[17] Still, these were early days. The temptation to condemn members of the urban bourgeoisie as irremediably opposed to the national interest was tempered by a lingering reluctance to exclude them entirely from a national-bourgeois revolution.[18]

The May Thirtieth movement of 1925 offered a more damning indictment of the bourgeoisie. The May Thirtieth movement is chiefly remembered in Western memoirs and histories as the beginning of the end of the imperialist presence in China. Western prestige certainly never recovered from the affair, and foreigners learned to speak and to act with greater circumspection in the knowledge that their safety was no longer assured and that their privileges could not last indefinitely.[19] But this is not how Chinese activists saw the movement. For revolutionary Nationalists, the goal of the May Thirtieth movement was nothing less than the elimination of all foreign privilege and influence as proclaimed in the program of the Nationalist Revolution. The dismal outcome of the movement was both a defeat and a betrayal. The defeat was one more event to add to an already overstocked calendar of days of national humiliation. But the betrayal was a new one. For the first time, national betrayal could be traced to a significant domestic social constituency: the bourgeoisie of Shanghai.

Sun Yatsen's ideal of the nation was partly undermined by his own actions in 1924. Over the following year, this ideal was dispatched to the clouds as an absurdly romantic notion. His nation was modeled on the family, or more particularly, on the extended patriarchal lineage group, and it embraced everyone who was reputedly related by blood. But in May and June 1925, some nationalists spotted social traitors within the family — "internal foreigners" in Maurice Meisner's phrase — whose blood ties offered no defense for their treachery.[20] Organized mass discontent was then directed with equal fury against both the enemy within, in the form of the bourgeoisie (and eventually the landlord class), and the imperialists abroad. Both were targeted in a class war waged in the name of the nation.

Chen Duxiu's early faith in bourgeois support for the revolution had been shaken by the Guangzhou merchant insurrection, but it was shattered by the outcome of the May Thirtieth movement. Although a Communist, Chen was one of the most ardent proponents of an all-class revolution, and among the first to pronounce himself disappointed by the "attitude of the Chinese bourgeoisie." [21] But Chen's was a contingent judgment. His disappointment at the exposure of his "illusions" came nowhere near matching the disillusionment of Nationalists such as Dai Jitao. Chen Duxiu was at liberty, as Dai was not, to reinterpret sectional opposition to the revolution without damage to his ideology as indicating conflict between class and national interest, and to train his sights on bourgeois class interest in the name of the nation. The betrayal of the bourgeoisie was certainly disappointing, but a party of the proletariat could live with this kind of disappointment. It was a far more bitter disappointment to Dai Jitao.

"The consciousness of the Chinese people is determined by immediate interests after all," Dai confided to his deputy in the Nationalist propaganda bureau, "just as the historical materialists would have it." [22] It was a significant concession. Dai had withdrawn from active involvement in the affairs of the Central Propaganda Bureau over a year before he wrote to Liu Luyin in August 1925, but he remained one of the most active, and certainly among the most brilliant, writers on the Nationalist side. For ten years he had worked tirelessly alongside Sun Yatsen in an effort to demonstrate the ethical cohesion of the Chinese people and to resist the conclusion that they were driven by immediate interests as the "historical materialists would have it." Early in the alliance with the Nationalists, the Communist leadership had conceded that immediate social interests should remain subordinate to the more distant national interest.[23] But events in Guangzhou had already sharpened suspicions that some social interests may have been fundamentally incompatible with the national interest as it was now defined, that is, with the unimpeded expansion of the revolutionary state. By the time Mao Zedong had taken charge of the Nationalist propaganda bureau in autumn of the following year, these suspicions had hardened into convictions. The Communists began talking openly of the inevitability of *class* struggle in *national* revolution. By August 1925, even Dai Jitao was prepared to concede that they may have had a point.

Dai appreciated the implications of recent developments for the long-term leadership and direction of the revolution. From June through August he worked furiously on a rebuttal to Chen Duxiu, and the results of his efforts, two pamphlets entitled *The Nationalist Revolution and the Nationalist Party* and *The Philosophical Foundations of Sun Yatsenism*, contributed in no small measure to mounting tension within the Nationalist movement.[24] This tension erupted in violence just days before Dai wrote to his deputy, Liu Luyin. The immediate inspiration for the letter was the news, just confirmed in a telegram from Guangzhou, that his old comrade Liao Zhongkai had been assassinated by a maverick faction of Nationalist party members on 20 August. Despite his recent differences with the more radical Liao, Dai grieved sorely for his dead comrade. He grieved, too, that struggles within the Nationalist movement had spilled over into violence. Dai feared that this development bade ill for the nation as a whole: "When a man as accommodating and full of human sympathy as Liao Zhongkai, so earnest and faithful in his work, can meet such an end—there can no longer be any peaceful outcome for our China, or for our party." [25] Dai's remarks were prescient. It is significant, nevertheless, that it was the death of a political activist rather than the outbreak of "class struggle" in society that prompted Dai's bleak reassessment of the prospects of the Chinese revolution. Liao's assassination proved beyond a measure of doubt that historical materialism was not only a plausible philosophical position but also a potent weapon in the armory of the Communist party in its struggle with the Nationalists. So it was in a tone of melancholy bordering on despair that Dai wrote of his disappointment with the "consciousness" of the Chinese people. In pursuing their material interests, the people had let him down and given comfort to his enemies. China, he felt sure, would never be the same again.

It is worth noting that Dai Jitao confided his disappointment with the Chinese people in a personal letter to his deputy. His critics chose to answer him in public. Shortly after writing to Liu, Dai met with Communist Party Secretary-General Chen Duxiu to confide his misgivings about the recent turn of events. On this occasion, Dai was prepared to concede (again in private) that class struggle was inevitable, but he argued that its appearance required modification of Communist party tactics. Present Communist strategy, he warned, would intensify class struggle beyond manageable limits. Clearly perplexed by Dai's arguments, Chen Duxiu immediately published an open "Letter to Dai Jitao" in the Communist party journal, *The Guide*. Chen dispatched his letter through the press rather than through the post because he felt confident that radical opinion would support him. The "facts," as he put it, were on his side.

Chen mounted a triumphant defense of historical materialism and a scathing attack on "empty theory" and "empty ideas" in an effort to combat Dai Jitao's claim that although class struggle may be a fact of life, it had little place in a national revolution. "We are of course historical materialists," Chen rebuked Dai Jitao, "and certainly not empty idealists." Dai was the empty idealist. His ideas sounded reasonable enough, Chen conceded, but the only test of their validity was practice, and practice had already shown that the abrupt entry of the mass movement into the revolution had exposed deeper layers of contradiction and struggle than Dai Jitao was prepared to admit. Chen then compiled a list of significant events from the Guangzhou merchant militia incident to the May Thirtieth movement and the Shamian Massacre in an effort to demonstrate that "these facts all convey a clear message: class struggle is inevitable in nationalist struggle." Real nationalists forswore representing counterrevolutionary classes and shouldered instead the interests of the revolutionary classes of the workers and peasants. The worker and peasant masses themselves could only place their faith "in a political party which struggles concretely for their immediate interests. They have no faith in abstract ideals." To expect otherwise was "empty idealism." [26] Dai had already conceded some of Chen's arguments in private, and he was in no mood to answer them in public. If the facts were against him, so, too, was the voice of radical opinion. Dai could no longer represent the facts or the interests of the people with the conviction a revolution required.

Awakening and Representation

Conviction certainly mattered. On the one hand, awakening people involved teaching workers, peasants, merchants, women, and students where their "real" interests lay; on the other hand, it meant pointing out, as forcefully as possible, who it was that represented their interests in the political arena. Both required a good deal of conviction.

Learning to identify the differences between Chen Duxiu and Dai Jitao, or between Communist and non-Communist labor organizers, occupied a good part of the workers' curriculum. In April 1925 the Communist Cai Hesen warned workers not to be deceived by bourgeois advocates of mutual compromise in the labor movement, and later in the year, Chen Duxiu and Qu Qiubai launched a scathing attack upon the suitability of promoting universal love and benevolence within an organized labor movement. In every case, the reference was to Dai Jitao's curriculum for labor. Later still, after the Nationalists had purged the labor movement in April 1927, workers were taught to recognize the errors of these Communist teachings. The workers presumably learned, if nothing else, that their political representatives were those who taught them where their real interests lay with the greatest conviction and authority.[27]

A variety of rationales was put forward to explain the representative relationship between leaders and led in the politics of Chinese nationalism. Representation was rarely a matter of formal delegation.[28] Nor could it be. Representation was thought to mean standing in for a sleeping subject rather than speaking at the explicit direction of an awakened one. The assertion nevertheless needed to be justified: how was it that one could speak and act on behalf of others who had never actually offered their endorsement?

By the 1920s, revolutionaries of every persuasion had come to imagine that representation meant standing in for an unconscious or sleeping agent (the "sleeping masses" or "unawakened people") rather than speaking at the explicit direction of a conscious agent. In view of lingering regard for the forms of delegated representation, however, this assertion needed to be justified. One form of justification appealed to "sympathy," or *tongqing*, which was generally associated with the idea that revolutionary nationalists represented an unconscious people and their unarticulated interests through an ethical relationship of fellow-feeling. In 1920 the Nationalist veteran Hu Hanmin argued that student agitators inevitably represented the consciousness of repressed social classes as yet unconscious of their class character because they "sympathized" with them. Hence "before the proletariat became conscious of itself . . . the overseas students of the late Qing temporarily represented the consciousness of the proletariat." In defense of this proposition, Hu cited not the scientific socialism of Lenin but the personal circumstances of Marx himself, whose intellectual representation of the oppressed, Hu argued, was effected through "human sympathy" (*renlei de tongqing xin*). Once conscious, the proletariat would inevitably concede the students' right to speak on its behalf. In the meantime, it was the duty of the writer and the agitator to ensure that workers and peasants were adequately represented, and to alert them to the identity of those who represented them sympathetically.[29]

Hu's position was much closer to the Chinese ethical tradition than either to Marx or to Lenin. Marx posited a symbolic, or semiotic, relationship between a subordinate social class and its representatives, and Lenin, following Kautsky, grounded the intelligentsia's claim to represent the proletariat in the rational appropriation of scientific socialism—that is, in a form of knowledge.[30] Classical Confucianism, on the other hand, assumed an innate human propensity to sympathize with kin and neighbors, which in turn established an ethical framework for extending sympathy to all by cultivating the virtue of human-heartedness. The Mencian tradition stressed common ties of sympathy binding people by virtue of the human endowment itself. This classical conception of sympathy was, we have seen, revived in recent times by Kang Youwei, whose acute awareness of the violent reactions of his body to the suffering about him grounded the idea of sympathy in empirical observation and launched Kang on his journey of discovery of the universal ethic of "One World."[31] The first cohort of Marxists and revolutionary Nationalists in China subsequently embraced the idea of sympathy in appropriating the suffering of the proletariat and the people as their own, and in asserting their right to represent them in revolutionary politics.[32]

But this was not Marx's own position. Discussing the role of the bourgeoisie in *The Eighteenth Brumaire*, Marx formulated a general principle governing the relationship between social classes and their "political and literary representatives":

What makes them representatives of the petty bourgeoisie is the fact that in their minds they do not get beyond the limits which the latter do not get beyond in life, that they are consequently driven, theoretically, to the same problems and solutions to which material interest and social position drive the latter practically. This is, in general, the relationship between the *political* and *literary representatives* of a class and the class they represent.[33]

Here Marx asserted an analogous relationship between the representatives of a class and the interests of the class they represented. As with sympathy, there was neither a structural correspondence nor a relationship of identity between interests and their representation. But now there was no place for sympathy, either. Representation simply manifested social interests. On this model—in Sandy Petrey's words—ideas are representative "because they express (rather than develop from) the operations of material interests." [34] Basically, Marx's model of representation appears to have been one in which representatives represent through a simple coincidence between their patterns of thought and the underlying patterns of social relations that happen to drive a class in one direction or another. Precisely what drives a class's representatives to the same position is unclear. What is clear is that literary and political representatives arrive at the same point, fortuitously, together. If the bourgeoisie's representatives can represent by a simple act of correspondence, so, presumably, can the representatives of the proletariat. In this case, however, there is no longer an accidental correspondence between the material interests of the proletariat and the expression of its interests by its self-appointed representatives if the representatives happen to be Marxist. Social interests are ascribed according to the prescriptions of scientific socialism.

It was the arrival in China of scientific socialism, or Leninism, that first challenged the place of sympathy as the foundation for political representation in radical politics.[35] Formal authorization by the class in question or sample membership in the class itself still counted for little. Instead, Lenin's distinction between a spontaneous (or unconscious) mass movement and its conscious representatives was translated into the cognate formula of the sleeping masses and their awakened tutors.

Lenin defined the relationship between consciousness and political leadership in his seminal work *What Is to Be Done?* (1902). Polemically the problem was framed as a disagreement within the socialist movement over the proper relationship between revolutionary intellectuals and the working class.[36] Thematically, however, the argument revolved around questions of direction and spontaneity, consciousness and unconsciousness, and the advisability of "awakening the masses." Accounting for what was distinctive about Lenin's contribution to the politics of awakening and representation is not quite as simple as it might appear. As Lenin himself pointed out, his model of disciplined mass awakening was just one form of pedagogical politics among many put forward by revolutionary groups competing to "awaken" the masses. Lenin drew comfort from the observation that all socialists were committed to the same end. There was barely an agitator alive, he said, who "doubted that the strength of the present-day movement lies in the awakening of the masses." More particularly, " 'Everyone agrees' that it is necessary to develop the political consciousness of the working class." The question Lenin posed in his pamphlet was "*how* that is to be done and what is required to do it." [37] Lenin's distinctive contribution to the politics of awakening lay not in suggesting what was to be done, as the English title of his pamphlet would seem to suggest, but rather in establishing a new rationale and procedure for "awakening the masses."

Lenin was quite frank about the implications of his pedagogical style for political action and leadership. His selective application of the term "consciousness" to the vanguard party removed the criterion of ethical and political judgments from the realm of conscious intention to that of *effects*. The unconscious element, as Lenin called his enemies, was noted chiefly for the unintended effects of its actions rather than for its intentions. Even well-intended revolutionary action was of little value if its effect was to undermine the truly conscious element: "*All* worship of the spontaneity of the working-class movement, all belittling of the role of the 'conscious element,' of the role of social democracy, *means, quite independently of whether the belittler desires it or not, a strengthening of the influence of bourgeois ideology upon the workers.*" Those who opposed his program, intentionally or otherwise, were agents of the bourgeoisie: "To belittle socialist ideology, in any way, to turn aside from it in the slightest degree means to strengthen bourgeois ideology." The political effects of social consciousness, not its material causes, were to be the criteria for effective political representation, and effects were evaluated chiefly by the advantages they conferred upon a particular political faction. By severing the connection between consciousness (in the ordinary sense) and social interest, Lenin reduced the conflict among the revolutionary factions that were competing to "awaken the masses" to the old adage: If you are not with us, you are against us. "The only choice is," he wrote, "either bourgeois or socialist ideology. There is no middle course." [38]

Ascribing interests to an unconscious (or "forgetful") people was a Marxist strategy as well as a Leninist one.[39] To Lenin, however, proletarian consciousness was a completely blank sheet on which class representatives were at liberty to ascribe material interests according to the prescripts of "scientific socialism." In *What Is to Be Done?* Lenin argued that workers' perceptions of their interests were not only wrong, in the sense of not reflecting the objective situation of their class, but were positively injurious to the pursuit of their real interests. He proposed that the pursuit of workers' interests as workers themselves understood them could never lead beyond "trade-union consciousness," a defective form of consciousness that effectively confined workers' demands to the pursuit of temporary economic advantage. This was a shortcoming to be overcome through propaganda and agitation by a "conscious" leadership, which would compensate for the incapacity of the working class to "elaborate . . . an independent ideology for itself." [40] An awakening to scientific socialism conferred an awakening to real working-class interests. So "spontaneous" (cognate with sleeping) elements of the working class were condemned to lead their lives in an ignorant stupor until awakened elements located outside the class itself intervened to alert them to their real class interests. Lenin's achievement, Tony Polan has remarked, was not so much to inject "consciousness" into the proletariat as to argue the need "for a revolutionary party to combat the consciousness of the people." [41] *What Is to Be Done?* is the foundational text for a pedagogical system designed to awaken subjects to the hidden knowledge of who they really are, where their true interests lie, and what it is that really makes them think, and for establishing a rigorous disciplinary regime to ensure that people "awaken" accordingly.

In the 1920s, when Leninism made its way into the Chinese Nationalist and Communist parties, an awakening to specific forms of consciousness came to substitute for sympathy in conferring the right to represent the people. Now the awakened few represented the sleeping masses not by sympathizing with them but by ascribing to them real, material interests of which the masses themselves were but dimly aware. Lenin's disciplinary regime was imported as well. The first journal of the Chinese Communists, *The Communist Party* (*Gongchandang*), introduced Lenin's writings to the Chinese socialist movement in November 1920, and employed Lenin's tactical maneuver in an attempt to seize control of the revolutionary movement from its inaugural issue. The lead editorial warned that other social revolutionaries would be counted enemies if they failed to join the Communist faction. Whatever their intentions, the failure of revolutionaries to concede Bolshevik leadership of the revolution would serve the interest of the bourgeoisie. They would, in effect, represent the capitalist class and deserve whatever punishment should fall the way of an intractable class enemy.[42]

In China, however, Lenin's strategic distinction between the conscious few and the unconscious many required modification to accommodate a lingering respect for sympathetic representation. China's conscious proletarians were prompted by feelings of sympathy to awaken their unconscious brothers and sisters to a degree Lenin had never even imagined. In his own pedagogy, Lenin drew a sharp distinction between propaganda and agitation: revolutionary propaganda was reserved for members of the revolutionary party, whereas agitation was directed at the masses. This distinction derived from the belief that only the members of the leading party needed to be fully conscious of the details of scientific socialism and that the unconscious masses were to be "agitated" only as far as the goals of the conscious party required. The masses need not become conscious themselves.[43] The idea of sympathy would not allow so inegalitarian a distinction to be drawn in China.

Sympathy demanded that a Chinese Marxist should awaken as many people as made up the nation. As they understood him, Marx had said that relations of production determine social consciousness. What, then, was a young Chinese revolutionary to make of his duty to awaken the sleeping people to consciousness of their oppression? This question perplexed many awakened youths, including Mao Zedong's close friend Cai Hesen in February 1921:

The revolutionary doctrine of Marx is entirely based on the theory of objective necessity. Since the revolution is inevitable, why must we conscious proletarians also go and rouse the consciousness of other members of the same class? 1.) Because, having become conscious ourselves of the origins of our sufferings . . . our existence becomes even more intolerable to us. 2.) Because we have a feeling of *sympathy* for the members of our class who suffer in the same way as we do.[44]

Cai Hesen worked only briefly as a factory hand, but his sympathy for the "members of our class" earned him life membership in the proletariat. His sympathetic membership obliged him, in turn, to awaken his unconscious comrades. Cai had moved beyond Hu Hanmin's representation-by-sympathy to something approaching Lenin's representation-by-consciousness, albeit with a difference. Neither sympathy nor consciousness alone conferred the right to represent. Sympathy made a proletarian of Cai Hesen, and it prompted him to share his proletarian consciousness by awakening others. But it was a specialized knowledge of the real source of suffering that gave him the confidence to act. That is to say, he was a conscious member of the proletariat because he had fathomed the "origins of our sufferings" and felt certain that if he made the workers feel as he did, then they, too, would become fully conscious proletarians like himself.

Mao Zedong mastered the Leninist purge intuitively, yet shared the hope of his friends and teachers that one day everyone would wake up. It was this curious combination of violence and sympathy that was to baffle his critics and confound his supporters: in his later career, Mao's politics had the flavor of a Stalinist show trial set in a YMCA summer camp. He first developed this style in Guangzhou in 1925 and 1926, when he drafted speeches and articles explaining the categorical differences between revolutionary and counterrevolutionary social alliances and urging as many as possible to wake up to the urgency of the task at hand. There was to be no place for revolutionaries who failed to ally with the revolutionary faction within the Nationalist party. Yet almost everyone was to be given a chance to join the alliance. "China has already reached the time of fixing bayonets for close combat," Mao wrote in the closing months of 1925.

In times as urgent as these, not only is there no hope in delay, but it is also certain that this urgency will not subside. We can predict that in the near future the intermediate faction will have but two routes between which to choose: either to step right, into the counterrevolutionary faction, or to step left, into the revolutionary faction (which remains a possibility for its left wing). There is no third route.

"Gentlemen standing in the middle!" he challenged at another point, "What are you going to do? Go left? or go right?" [45]

Although Mao held out the choice of redemption to all but a tiny proportion of die-hard counterrevolutionaries, the choice was available to only the tiniest fraction of the Chinese people. By Mao's calculation, 99 percent of the population had no choice in the matter at all: 98.75 percent were irrevocably on side (if not yet fully awakened), 0.25 percent were die-hard enemies, and the wavering bourgeoisie was calculated at 1 percent.[46] For most, the decision was made for them, one way or the other, by their inalienable class interests, even if they were unaware of where their interests lay. The sympathetic majority would be awakened to the identity of its political representatives in the leadership of the revolution when it was shown, in simple logical sequence, how the manifest world of *political* struggle related to the hidden but conflicting class interests immanent within it. The irredeemable 0.25 percent was to be eliminated rather than awakened. Mao was more deeply concerned with the wavering 1 percent, to whom he directed his most forceful arguments as director of propaganda. This 1 percent, the only group offered a real choice in the matter, was not a social category at all. Its size and membership indicated a political category embracing all of the writers, artists, journalists, and activists of various parties, factions, and coterie that the propaganda bureau had singled out for attack. The only category given a chance to wake up was basically a residual category for all of the *political* enemies of the revolution: a group of self-appointed representatives, like Mao's own, that had yet to decide whom it was going to "represent."

Once political cooperation entered service as an indicator of class status, confusion arose as to who was representing whom in the leadership of the revolution. There had always been some confusion. Given that there was little structural correspondence between the consciousness doing the representing and the "unconscious" interests represented, assigning political representatives to social constituencies was a slippery task. The Communist party claimed exclusive rights to represent the proletariat and to lead the peasantry, and assigned the bourgeoisie to the Nationalist party. Its arguments failed to persuade Nationalist labor activists to relinquish their claims to organized labor, or to convince Sun Yatsen that the bourgeoisie was in dialogue with the workers when he took tea with Chen Duxiu. The Nationalists believed that they represented the nation as a whole and were most reluctant to settle for anything less. As the revolution progressed, there emerged a pressing need for someone in authority to compile a definitive handbook of symbolic correspondences.

To be sure, Nationalists, Communists, and members of other partisan movements embraced the idea of representation by formal delegation as well. The Communist mass movement upheld the principle of delegated representation through elite committees and mass organizations, a principle duly elaborated in organized representation for the labor, peasant, youth, and women's movements. This formal system of representation was not open to external verification, nor was it accountable to those it claimed to represent outside of the framework of scientific socialism. A mill-worker, for example, who challenged the party's right to represent her interests by joining a chapter of the YMCA women's league, inevitably betrayed by her choice either her lack of "class awakening" (to be remedied by education) or her counterrevolutionary intention (to be remedied by re-education). On the Nationalist side, Sun Yatsen paid due deference to democratic electoral procedure in his Five Power Constitution and three-stage constitutional program. By the 1920s, however, he faced an insurmountable obstacle. Sun ran a party that was keen to represent the nation, but he could no longer find a nation willing to be represented by Sun or his party alone. Sun concluded that the nation was asleep. In the last years of his life, Sun Yatsen applied the idea of majority rule to a new program for mass conversion to the principles of his party. Rather than risk exposing the party to ridicule in free and open elections, he chose to secure a mandate in the Nationalist Revolution by "awakening" the nation and ensuring that "our party's principles should become universal among the people of the entire country." If Nationalist ideology eventually became universal, the Chinese people would concede the party's right to represent them. Formal delegation would follow as a matter of course when the people awoke to the fact that they were already *being* represented by the Nationalist party.[47] There was of course plenty of room for negotiating the correspondence between the behavior of the actor representing and the interests ascribed to the thing represented. What mattered, however, was that there should be a definitive relation between the one and the other. Defining this relationship was one of the tasks Mao Zedong took upon himself in the Nationalist propaganda bureau. As the workers, and the nation, were not consulted directly on the matter, it was important that somebody in a position of authority should determine, once and for all, who represented whom.

Mao encoded political struggle in the analogic terms of class struggle. He was directing the Nationalist propaganda bureau when he first tried his hand at social analysis, penning vitriolic essays on political divisions within the revolutionary movement one day and turning to a class analysis of society the next. In fact, these were two sides to the one coin. Mao wished to show how potential social cleavages overlapped with political fractures within the Nationalist movement, and hence to highlight a need to purge the revolutionary movement of hostile elements whose interests appeared to overlap, symbolically, with the social ones he had targeted through his research. Political struggle was intensified by a procedure of realist reduction whereby political actors were reduced to unwitting representatives of deeper forces, embedded in society, and social struggle was intensified to the same degree by its political ramifications.

Having assigned symbols to referents, the next task for the propagandist was to make the one match the other. The Nationalists represented a national interest of which the sleeping nation remained unaware, and the Communists represented the interests of subordinated social classes at a time when workers and peasants had yet to acknowledge that they required distinctive party representation. In each case, the respective party propagandist was asked to make the symbol match the referent by transforming the masses so that they more closely approximated the characteristics ascribed to them in each ideological system. Mass representation was then effected through mass propaganda and mass organization, the one designed to illustrate the affinity between ascribed interests and the interests of the parties acting to represent them, and the other to exclude from the represented sample all who declined to acknowledge their appointed representatives. Propaganda and organization were, in other words, both representational *and* disciplinary procedures.

The model of a conscious vanguard representing an unconscious constituency, to which both parties subscribed, was grounded in a conception of mass representation that arrived quite independently of either party. It was grounded in the realist aesthetic of the age. This is not to deny the significance of Lenin's intervention through the Comintern nor the salience of institutional politics generally. There was an intimate relation between the imperatives of representation, awakening, and institutional organization. Social consciousness was felt to be situated in social institutions, and its progress was measured by the growth of organized participation in political struggle. When Dai Jitao reflected back on his first sighting of "class consciousness" in China, he identified its emergence with the mass mobilization of the May Fourth movement with its "organization of labor in new forms" and with the organized response of capital to the emergence of militant labor.[48] Literary realism also had its origins in the emergence of the mass movement. Writers sought to awaken social consciousness through literary representation of the masses just as political activists sought to penetrate the institutional sites of labor and capital. The struggle to awaken and to represent the interests of particular social groups then took the form of competition within and between rival unions, associations, party committees, and organized literary factions. Workers, peasants, and the nation were represented on party councils and in literary journals by the arguments mobilized on their behalf, and they demonstrated their affinity with their representatives by their willingness to respond to calls to mobilize on the streets. The winners in this contest to represent the masses were those who could mobilize their arguments with the greatest *conviction* and mobilize the masses with the greatest *effect*.[49] It was here, in the contest to represent the Real, that Dai Jitao and the Nationalists showed signs of faltering in 1925.

Representing the Real

The realist conception of representation found a secure home in Chinese revolutionary politics around the same time that it settled comfortably into literature and art. This was not the result of a conspiracy. Sun Yatsen and Chen Duxiu aspired to awaken the masses not because they kept company with avante-garde literary circles in Shanghai but because writers and revolutionaries all aspired to represent a people who were not yet aware that they needed to be represented in quite the way artists and activists aspired to do so. As Theodore Huters notes of the relationship between literature and politics in twentieth-century China, "It would appear better not to say that one dictates to the other, but rather that both share an ideal of the powers of representation to bring imagined worlds into existence." The realist conception of representation brought them together of its own accord, ensuring "a perpetual series of encounters and mutual interventions between the two spheres." [50]

Here it is worth recalling the literary background to Marx's own writing. In its origins, its concern for politics, and its unbounded faith in the powers of representation, the realist movement of nineteenth-century France anticipated the forms that realism assumed in the literature, polemic, and politics of China's Nationalist Revolution. Realism was born in revolutionary politics. "The conscience that awoke to find itself called realism," notes Damian Grant, in a style sensitive to the rhetoric of the occasion, "was stirred from the dreams of the romantics by a group of artists in mid-nineteenth-century France." The revolutionaries of 1848 announced the dawn of realism by trumpeting their commitment to the "people," to "truth," and to "awakening." When the painter Gustave Courbet hung the words "Du Réalisme" over the entrance to his exhibition in 1855, he declared himself a "supporter of the whole revolution, and above all realist, that is to say sincere friend of the whole truth." [51] In art and in revolution, these claims were set out in a language that explicitly counterpointed the dreams of romantics and the awakening of the realist, and that contrasted the melancholy of the artist to the practice of the revolutionary. Realism was born in revolution, and refused to be confined to art.

By practice, realists understood mass action in contrast to the solitary striving of romantics. In Europe, the victory of realism over romanticism was celebrated as a "triumph of the group over the individual, the crowd over the hero." [52] Realists drew confidence from the crowd in proclaiming their commitment to self-awareness, truth, sincerity, and action, but in their sincere adulation of the common people they strove to represent a world far more real than the actual one. Only in the artistic imagination and in revolutionary politics, they believed, could the truth of the crowd be captured in all sincerity. Revolutionaries repaid the compliment. Engels once announced that he learned more about French society from the novels of Balzac than from "all of the historians, economists and statisticians of the period together." [53] The writings of Karl Marx bear characteristic traces of the realist school. Marx's classic account of the revolution of 1848, *The Eighteenth Brumaire of Louis Bonaparte*, pillories the failure of the state to represent a social referent (the dominant class) in a rhetorical style that mirrors, in its frenzied repetition, the aberrant dissociation of words from things in the politics of France. In this case, the purpose of Marx's scathing indictment of the state was not to undermine the possibility of representation (as modernists would have it) but to reassert the possibility of more ideal forms of political representation against the misrepresentations perpetrated by the regime.[54]

In China, literary realism complemented historical materialism in forging a style of literature and politics that restored a direct correspondence between the flow of words and the movement of history that, it seemed, the corruption of literary and political representation had conspired to put awry. China was not at one with its own dreams of itself. Realists and materialists assumed responsibility for restoring this correspondence by representing, and realizing, the dreams. An important contribution of realist literature to politics lay in the scope it offered for radical dreaming. At a time when the old social imaginary of empire had ceased to make sense, the new literature brought promise of a world beyond the immanent one that classical literature did not imagine.[55]

The language and forms of traditional narrative conveyed an impression that they existed within the world, or as an extension of the world, rather than beyond it. Of course, the language of the classical narrative referred to something beyond itself, which it stood for or represented, but in this case something intimately belonging to the world that the readers and the texts themselves inhabited. In the words of Andrew Plaks, each "element of the [traditional] Chinese allegory, by virtue of the existential process of ebb and flow in which it is caught up, 'stands for,' or 'partakes of,' the sum total of all existence that remains invisible only in its extent, and not in essence." [56] Realist literature, by contrast, spoke of a real world outside the actual one awaiting realization. Realism posited an absent essence and was not content to recount another episode in life's long story. In dreams of what the world might yet become, it found a world of substance more real than the actual world itself.

Realism was an appropriate adjunct to the many other innovations that flowed from the May Fourth movement. The audience for realist literature was coextensive with the nation imagined in its pages: compulsory school education for children and work-place literacy classes for their elders were intended to enable everyone to read the uplifting tracts being prepared for them at a furious pace. Together, innovations in language reform, literary education, and politics harnessed faith in the power of representation to national campaigns for popular literacy and to mass movements for political enlightenment. Each innovation was enacted in the name of representing a reality that was still over the horizon, for the movement was built on a denial of the relationship between language and actuality. It affirmed instead the responsibility befalling artists and revolutionaries to represent a social reality as yet unrealized in history.[57] "What strikes one as most evident about the post–May Fourth era in China," remarks Huters, "is precisely the extent to which the New Culture Movement centered itself around extravagant hopes for literary representation—in other words that something literally absent could be made present to the reader and, by extension, to the largest possible community of readers, society itself." [58] Extravagant hopes were matched by the equally extravagant expectation that awakening people to this absent world would bring it into being—that the world, once awakened, would no longer be "absent."

China's realists yearned to make things correspond with words by extending their faith in representation to the domain of social and political action. Paris had moved on; European realism fell with the revolutionary aspirations that had inspired it. But when they discovered realism in the 1920s, Chinese writers were not afflicted by the "crisis of representation" then facing European modernism. The realist conception of representation struck Chinese politics under the momentum of a mass revolution in the mid-twenties with the same compelling force that had awakened Paris in 1848. It was not a crisis of representation but a crisis of *misrepresentation*. In China, realists shrugged off all of the debilitating doubts of modernism and heartily embraced all that was "modern," in the belief that by clinging to dreams of the future they were embracing a more real world than the discordant one in which they found themselves. In encountering realism and Marxism at much the same time, China's artists and revolutionaries discovered the forms of mass representational art and the imperatives of mass representative politics together. They encountered the "deep common cultural assumption" that, in the words of Raymond Williams, underpins both the literary and the political usages of the term "representation" in modern Europe.[59]

An early sign of the convergence of the political and literary senses of representation was the use of shared vocabulary in political conflict and literary controversy. That is to say, conflict among Nationalists between materialists and idealists had its counterpart in a literary controversy between realism and romanticism. The romantic posture had affected a perspective on the nation looking down, as it were, from the mountaintop. This was a literal as well as a literary posture; many felt the call of the mountains and found there the inspiration for their writings.[60] For less-intrepid romantics, it was enough to look down from a window over the passing crowd below, going about its business, or over a sea of pupils asleep at their desks, and note the fate that lay in store for China if they did not wake up. The country's borders were threatened, its sovereignty was compromised, and its society was everywhere in disarray. Few seemed to know, and even fewer to care. For those who did know, their awakened consciousness conferred authority and responsibility: authority to impart their vision, and responsibility to ensure that the nation awoke to their instruction.

The romantic posture was common to Nationalist party propaganda as well as to creative literature at the time of the New Culture movement, which accounts to some degree for the party's early success in politicizing the movement. Day in and day out from 1919 to 1922, the Nationalist journal *Awaken* published poetry and short stories alongside political, social, and cultural commentary composed from the perspective of the elevated observer. This was Sun Yatsen's point of observation as well. To the moment of his death, Sun felt that his terrible knowledge of what lay in store for China and his fantastic vision of what China might yet become isolated him from his fellow countrymen in equal measure. He sincerely believed that the nation was destined to "die in a dream" unless it awoke to his vision, and that only when it awoke would he and the nation be reconciled.

Sun died, unreconciled, in March 1925. "In point of actual achievement," recalled a contemporary, "Sun did very little during this period. His efforts were largely frustrated. But he held fast to his great revolutionary spirit and vision." [61] His death reminded people of the gap between the dream and the fact of a unified China. Yet Sun had long shown by personal example that hard and sharp facts should never be allowed to puncture a good dream. While the romantic posture remained in vogue, Sun Yatsen and Dai Jitao could reasonably expect that their authority would command respect even if it did not always command obedience. But it was not in vogue for long. "Romantic used to be a good term," recalled Zhu Ziqing in 1928; "now its meaning is reduced to slander and a curse." [62] Sun's failures now counted against him, and Dai Jitao's enemies called Dai a romantic dreamer spouting "empty ideas." Chen Duxiu, we noted, felt at liberty to state publicly what Dai would only concede in private, because by 1925 the public mood favored realists over romantics, facts over dreams.[63]

This judgment was rather unfair to Sun and his party. Though certainly a dreamer, Sun dreamed in an age when dreaming was a way of life. The terms "dreamer" and "romantic" become terms of abuse only when some dreams began competing more successfully than others in the race to give *effect* to dreams. If we trace the substantive content of the term "romantic," we find that it varied along with the direction of historical experience and with the course of political debate. For the Communists, any critique of political action that failed to take account of social struggle was prone to romantic delusion. Sun and Dai Jitao were counted romantics because they failed to concede that there should be any correspondence between political and social struggle. Materialists were counted realists to the extent that they related material interests to social constituencies. And yet even materialists could be counted romantics if they appeared to make the wrong connections. Communists frequently branded one another "realist" or "romantic," depending upon where they stood on the question of which social forces favored or opposed the revolution. In April 1923, Chen Duxiu branded all those who disagreed with him as "romantics," but by 1925 his assessment of the social foundations of warlord power exposed him to the charge that he, too, was a hopeless romantic.[64]

The turning point came in 1925. Before the May Thirtieth movement, there had been an air of fantasy about historical materialism and its calls for social revolution. There were, of course, exceptions. Arif Dirlik observes that the political philosopher Li Dazhao "waxed poetic" in 1920 over his discovery of historical materialism. But historical materialism did not appeal to poets until May 1925.[65] "The May Fourth Movement stimulated the awakening of individuality among youths and individuals," Tao Xisheng recalls of his experiences in 1919. It was not until 1925 that mass politics finally

entered the realm of actuality from the realm of fantasy. The Labor problem was the link between society and politics, and the May Thirtieth Movement the key to this link. The May Thirtieth Incident . . . led from the awakening of youth and intellectuals to the awakening of the urban laboring masses.[66]

Writers who no longer wished to be counted romantic had to master a style of expression and techniques of research, exposé, and *practice* suited to the "awakening of the urban laboring masses."

Marston Anderson has shown how the crowd was turned into a discursive effect in his seminal study of Chinese fiction, *The Limits of Realism*. At its most elementary, the contest between romanticism and realism in the literature of the 1920s was "a battle of pronouns, . . . a contest between the romanticist *wo/women* (I/we) and the realist *ta/tamen* (he/they)."[67] The movement from romanticism to realism was a flight from the first-person pronoun to the crowd in a literary and a literal sense. As Li Dazhao once waxed poetic, poets now started to wax political. Novelists turned to grounding their stories in "real life," and critics read Ibsen's *The Doll's House*, once again, in an effort to uncover the deeper social significance of Nora's captivity and emancipation. Mass politics became a fashionable literary subject. The appeal of political revolution came to match the appeal of sexual attraction in Mao Dun's trilogy, *Eclipse*, and Ba Jin's trilogy, *Love*.[68] And the May Thirtieth movement of 1925 entered fiction as a literary device for jolting heroes and heroines from their romantic complacency. In Ye Shaojun's acclaimed novel *Ni Huanzhi*, the protagonist abandons a life of contemplation and teaching for political agitation after the May Thirtieth Incident. Even when not cited directly, the May Thirtieth movement was invoked in anonymous crowd scenes and left its mark in literary bloodshed, horror, poverty, and other surface effects of "deeper" contradictions at the social level.

Representation in politics and letters then converged around the idea of uncovering the occult sources of oppression and social consciousness within society itself. Realists approached the actual world as though it were no more than a superficial manifestation of deeper forces hidden beneath layers of surface appearance, which they duly stripped away to expose revolutionary possibilities for the edification of the people. The approved method (in literature and polemic) was not unlike that which Lenin recommended for political activists intent on instilling "consciousness" in the masses: the worker was to be taught to "grasp the meaning of catchwords and all manner of sophisms, by which each class and each stratum *camouflages* its selfish strivings and its *real* 'inner workings'; he must understand what interests are reflected by certain institutions and certain laws and how they are reflected." [69] Chinese fiction writers conceived of their own responsibility in much the same way. "Realism analyses through all social problems," commented the novelist Mao Dun shortly after taking leave from the Nationalist propaganda bureau, "and endeavours with all its force to lay open their darker aspects." [70] Metaphors of surface and depth applied to authors and activists as well. Like Lenin's scientific socialists, few Chinese Nationalists spoke on behalf of themselves alone. The contest to plumb the depths and arrive at a comprehensive understanding of the forces shaping nature, society, and history was at the same time a competition among authors for the right to represent the hapless victims of the forces they identified. Authors and ideologues were part of the story. Correct identification of the source of oppression signified an awakening to reality, and an awakening conveyed the right to represent what was real.

A posture privileging the awakened author is by no means unique to Chinese writing on self and community. It has been a persistent feature of European philosophy from Socrates to Heidegger. Nevertheless, in European philosophy, the authoritarian implications of this idea for the production of knowledge and for forms of politics have long been challenged.[71] There is little evidence of comparable critical appraisal of the privileged stance of the awakened "knower" in China in the period of the Nationalist Revolution. Perhaps this is merely symptomatic of a more general failure to think critically about the nature of political authority at all in New Culture thought. Helen Siu has observed that the patriotic momentum of the New Culture movement foreclosed "deeper examination of the authoritarian assumptions of the state" that were embedded within it, and she traces the failure to explore these authoritarian assumptions to cultural expectations that "permeated the heart and rigidified the mind." [72] To this explanation we might add the authoritarian assumptions of the romantic and realist postures of literary production. The function of the awakening trope in both cases was to locate the author above the sleeping nation as the awakened, all-knowing, and alienated observer, and to compel the author to bridge the gap opened by this posture through the act of writing, speaking, and arousing the nation.

Realism and Practice

The line dividing the romantic from the realist was drawn along a gradient of "practice." Practice did not simply mean action, or participation in public affairs; nor was realism mistaken for grudging acceptance of actuality, of the way things stood. Practice meant engagement with the actual world in an effort to transform it, and realism was the art of exposing the forces that worked for and against its transformation. Hence practice helped to distinguish the realist from the romantic and the materialist from the idealist by measuring how far revolutionary ideals could be implemented with good *effect*. The test was a Leninist one. A realist grasped the inner workings of a social contradiction and resolved it through action. Romantics, on the other hand, were doomed to failure because they failed to comprehend the laws governing action. They were ineffectual activists.

It was practical effect, not fidelity to the facts, that identified the realist. The poet and essayist Zhu Ziqing ended his comment that romanticism had become a "slander and a curse" with the observation: " 'Romanticism' was to release to the utmost one's animated emotions, thereby expanding oneself. But now what is needed is work, and the animated emotions, undisciplined, cannot produce *practical effect*." [73] The realism of modern Chinese literature, Marston Anderson has noted, was never associated with the "simple desire to capture the real world in language." This was reserved for the empirical sciences and was roundly condemned as "naturalism" whenever it made an appearance in literature.[74] Realism referred to dreams that were practical, and romanticism to dreams beyond hope of realization. Though both portrayed emotions, realism tamed emotions and harnessed them to "practical effect." These, at least, were the terms in which the rhetorical opposition between realism and romanticism found its way into the polemics of the Nationalist Revolution.

Still, realism required awakening the people. The counterpointing of romanticism and realism developed from an earlier distinction between "empty talk" (*kongyan*) and "real action" (*shixing*) in revolutionary thought. In this case, the motif of awakening linked theory with practice on the assumption that theory was made real by awakening others to its reality. As early as 1896, Tan Sitong mounted a defense of "empty talk" along these lines:

All religious followers and founders leave to posterity "empty talk," even though they may not be able to practise the wisdom of their words and risk being cursed and humiliated by posterity ... they sacrificed their own lives in order to apply the understanding they first attained to awaken those who were slow to understand, and [to apply] the awakening they first acquired to enlighten those who were slow to awaken.[75]

From the turn of the century, revolutionary thinkers steeled themselves against "evil men [who] consider the revolution 'empty talk.' " The first line of defense was to argue, following Tan Sitong, that the dissemination of words was a practical exercise insofar as it was directed toward a popular awakening. Wu Zhihui mounted a defense of anarchist ideals and methods in which he roundly condemned all those who complained that anarchist theory and educational philosophy were impractical: "When the empty talk of anarchism becomes more and more widespread," he wrote, "this is precisely like establishing countless schools to nourish the sense of civic virtue and schools to nourish the revolution as well." Similarly, Li Shizeng argued that propaganda was a form of practice. And after mounting a spirited defense of anarchist ideals in 1914, Liu Sifu (Shifu) appended the conclusion, "It is mistaken to say that anarchism is idealistic and impossible." [76] Long before 1925, anarchists wanted to be thought realistic and derived comfort from the belief that they would realize their ideal society by awakening the people of China to the truths they espoused. Coaxing the masses out of their stupor was a task for realists, and propaganda the sign of the practical activist.

This early distinction between empty talk and real action took a dialectical turn in the 1920s.[77] Sun Yatsen was not content to die a dreamer, and those who followed in his trail wished to be remembered as effective activists.[78] Yet few of them were completely disheartened when the world let them down. To Sun, the world of appearance was a thin veneer overlaying a more vital world awaiting its own awakening and self-discovery. Cynics alleged that he had little patience for "unpleasant facts," but he could always console himself that, however unpleasant they may have been, facts were still only *facts*.[79] The world of facts could be transformed when it awoke to the ideas that he espoused.

Ideas mattered, in other words, in a material sense. Sun Yatsen posited a Hegelian relation between thought and action when he attempted to link the two in his single most important philosophical statement: "Doing is easy, knowing is difficult" (*xingyi zhinan*).[81] Here he inverted received wisdom handed down from the days of Emperor Wu Ding of the Yin dynasty (1324–1265 B.C.), which counseled that "Knowing is not difficult, only doing presents difficulties" (*zhi zhi fei nan, xing zhi wei nan*). Sun felt that so long as this saying was entrenched in common sense, it would encourage ignorance, fatalism, and indolence in the modern nation. He wanted it rooted out.

The Hegelian dialectic arises from a similar attempt to resolve, philosophically, a range of contradictions that present themselves in politics between the universal and the particular, and between unity and division. Specifically, Hegel wished to conceptualize in a universal language the fracture of the German polity at the time he put pen to paper. In Herbert Marcuse's words, the "universal contradictions that, according to Hegel, animate philosophy concretely exist in the antagonisms and disunity among the numerous German states and estates and between each of these and the Reich." [80] China's Nationalists faced similar circumstances in the fracture of the Chinese state. Their search for a unified-field theory that might resolve contradictions in the separate domains of philosophy, art, literature, science, ethnography, history, and politics was inspired by a craving for historical and semantic order in the midst of political chaos similar to the one that drove Hegel in Germany. The common point of departure in this search for discursive unity in China and in Germany suggests a common destination: this was the point at which a unified system of meaning would declare itself through the establishment of a unified state-system. In each case, the rhetorical linkage between a unified system of philosophy (an awakening to the Idea) and a unified state (the awakening of the nation) conceded to politics a leading role in effecting unification in thought and art as well as in institutions of state. The resolution of contradictions in the realm of ideas was part and parcel of the social and political reintegration of the nation-state.

Sun's intention in pronouncing action easier than knowledge was informed by two related designs. In illustrating his counterstatement, Sun scolded Republican politicians who had abandoned the revolutionary program in 1911 on the pretext that it was too "utopian." He concluded that if they had shown greater daring, China would not have reached its present state of crisis.[82] Their temerity was not the only fault Sun hoped to correct. He wished secondly to elevate knowledge above the banal realm of facts and to affirm its intrinsic relation to action. In the second part of the epigram, "knowing is difficult," Sun came out in support of dreamers to show that dreaming was an integral part of acting. He sought to rescue "idealists" (*lixiangjia*), as he called them, from the disparagement of doubters and skeptics. The knowledge of the idealist was not something acquired by empirical observation but a rare and precious gift acquired by foresight (*xianzhi xianjue*) into the nature of historical progress itself. Sun's target, like that of Hegel, was the complacency of liberal empiricism, and he implemented his philosophy in an illiberal brand of politics. China's liberals, recognizing the challenge for what it was, struck back after their own fashion. "Putting it bluntly," complained Hu Shi, "this is dream talk." It was, however, a dream with teeth. On 30 September 1929, the Nanjing branch of the Nationalist party submitted a recommendation to the state council that Hu Shi "be duly punished" for his irreverent commentaries on Sun Yatsen's cryptic dreams.[83]

In the arguments supporting his double aphorism, Sun linked thought, action, and political leadership in two important but distinct ways. First he revived the traditional rationale for rule by an enlightened elite with the qualification that a grasp of the principles of science and democracy established the legitimacy of rulers in a Republican democracy. Nevertheless, the wise still led and the ignorant still followed. Second, he established a relationship between knowledge and action that was only revealed over time or, in Hegelian terms, in history. The knowing few, among whom Sun counted himself, were not just people of knowledge but people of "fore-knowledge and fore-awakening" who knew what was real before it was actually realized. The dreams of idealists embraced truths that had yet to manifest themselves through action. Foreknowledge, in other words, was knowledge that would be *made true* in practice.

Sun's epigram offered a compelling justification for political leadership of the kind he institutionalized in the Nationalist party-state. In 1925, Propaganda Bureau Secretary Zhou Fohai offered a simple and uncontested explanation of Sun Yatsen's division of the Chinese people into three. First came the "first awakened" (*xianjuezhe*), or the "discoverer" (*famingzhe*) of the truth, who led by virtue of his discovery. This was Sun himself. The "next awakened" (*houjuezhe*) were his propagandists (*xuanchuanzhe*). The third category of the "unawakened" (*wujuezhe*) were the "practitioners" (*shixingzhe*), who did as they were told even if they did not quite know why they were doing so.[84] Sun foreknew, his party disseminated his knowledge, and the sleeping masses acted upon it and, in acting, realized the truth of his knowledge.[85] The truth of the leader's foreknowledge was ultimately demonstrated, dialectically, in the mobilization of the mass of his followers.

Sun's concern with the relationship between thinking and acting was matched by an emphasis on the connection between theory and practice among China's Marxists. Mao Zedong cut his teeth as a Marxist theorist on the problem of theory and practice. Yet the subtitle of *On Practice* also defers to the native tradition within which Sun Yatsen had been writing. It reads: "On the Relation Between Knowledge and Practice, Knowing and Doing." In a personal sense, the two men came at the problem from different ends. In the decade following the Republican Revolution, Sun Yatsen was widely regarded as a loud-mouthed talker rather than a practical leader, in a popular prejudice that found expression in the sobriquet "Cannon-mouth Sun." He bridled at the implication: "Some members of our party say, 'So and so is a thinker!' 'So and so is a man of action!' What a great mistake they make . . . our people respect the practical men more than the thinkers and inventors.[86] Thinkers were activists, Sun consoled himself, to the extent that they realized their foreknowledge in practice.[87] Mao, on the other hand, was rapidly developing a reputation as an untheorized pragmatist when he set out to establish his credentials as a thinker. The answer, for each of them, was to argue that theory and practice were both dissolved in the one revolutionary solution, and hence that neither theory nor practice could be separated out quite as discretely as their critics implied.

Philosophically Sun and Mao also worked to a similar purpose. Sun's notion of "anticipated knowledge" (*xianzhi*) was not far removed from Mao Zedong's proposition that knowledge is verified in practice. "What actually happens," Mao remarked in 1937, "is that knowledge is verified only when people achieve the anticipated results in the process of social practice."[88] Sun and Mao also maintained that knowledge is acquired not just by anticipating what is true but by intervening in history to ensure that it comes true. The efforts of the foreknower confirm the initial hypothesis by remaking the world after its own propositions.[89] "If you want knowledge," Mao remarked bluntly, "you must take part in the practice of changing reality."[90]

Mao's idea of practice was not far removed from Sun's idea of "doing." For Sun, doing meant implementing prearranged plans in mechanical fashion. His favorite metaphors for describing relations between knowing and doing, in political practice, generally involved mechanics, chauffeurs, and engineers, and referred to their achievement of specific targets through application of specialist training and mechanical dexterity. "The nation is a great automobile," Sun explained in March 1924, "and its government officers are great chauffeurs." In a talk the following month, he extended his mechanical model to the issue of sovereignty: "Where is sovereignty? The engineer in control of the machine possesses the sovereignty." Hence the achievement of sovereign government objectives ("the movement of the great steam vessel forward and backward, to the right and left") depended "upon the control of a good engineer."[91] "Doing," in short, meant the mechanical achievement of goals that had been specified in the act of "knowing."

Werner Meissner argues with some justification that the word "practice" in Chinese Marxist usage should also be translated as "the method for realising a goal."[92] Mao's idea of practice was perhaps a little more experimental than this translation would suggest, but it was certainly associated with goals, plans, and strategies. The connection is clearest in a passage of "On Practice" that echoes Sun Yatsen's reference to the engineer as a master of practice. Sun had imagined that engineers follow their blueprints to "act" on their "knowledge." Mao begged to differ slightly. Although conceding that "the fulfilment of an engineering plan" was a good illustration of the link between theory and practice, Mao asserted that the engineer inevitably changes the blueprint in the process of construction, in order to make allowance for "unforeseen circumstances in the course of practice." [93] Mao's practitioner was a *flexible* engineer, or an adaptable chauffeur, prepared to learn on the job.

This admission of the need for flexibility and training marked a critical distinction between Mao and Sun. That is, Mao's difference with Sun lay more in pedagogy than in epistemology. For Sun, there was little prospect that Nationalist cadre (the "engineers" of political practice) would learn anything from their reform of political society (the engineering project). For Mao, on the other hand, practice always entailed a pedagogical element. For the leadership, it meant learning from experience; for middle management, it meant cadre training; and for the masses, it entailed consciousness-raising or "waking up." Practice supplied leaders, cadres, and the masses with a basic knowledge of the transformative power of organized class struggle that only direct experience of mass movements could provide.

Insofar as Sun and Mao were both Hegelians, it could be said that one was an idealist and the other a materialist—that Mao stood Sun on his head, so to speak. In terms of their pedagogy, however, it makes more sense to say Mao was a *realist* of a kind Sun Yatsen could never be. Mao believed that awakening the people entailed stripping away layers of surface appearance to uncover fundamental social truths that were always and everywhere disguised by willful misrepresentation on the part of certain sections of society. Such truths could only be revealed in class struggle.[94] This class struggle was always most intense and most bitter at the level of its political and literary representations, that is, within the party and among journalists and writers who persisted in expressing views that undermined the claims of the conscious faction to fathom what was real and to lead the revolution. Mao was a realist in the sense in which Corbet and Zola, Mao Dun and Guo Moruo were realists—a sense that made a romantic of Sun Yatsen.

With his emphasis on social practice and political effect, Mao had more in common with the realist writers of his day than with his "idealist" comrades in the Nationalist party. By the mid-1920s, a commitment to practice no longer distinguished revolutionaries from literati, as it had earlier in the century. Now practice helped distinguish between realists and romantics *among* revolutionaries and writers alike. The boundaries between writing and action collapsed: revolutionaries began branding their political enemies romantic just as serious fiction writers began boasting of their realism. Historians joined in the rout.

From 1925, the New History began to shift its focus from the individual to the crowd, and at the same time to turn attention to the question of practice. Some young historians followed the example of their literary colleagues and left their desks for a spell in the streets. Gu Jiegang, who had long championed the separation of scholarship from politics, finally joined the masses on 30 May 1925, in Shanghai, where he drew on his unrivaled knowledge of popular folksong to compose anti-imperialist songs for the edification of the folk. In choosing the life of the propagandist, Gu rejected romantic isolation in favor of merging with the real life of the masses.[95]

Political romantics could no longer merge with the masses even if they wished to. Romantics and idealists were now said to represent (unwittingly) the subterranean forces that conspired to keep the masses in a state of sleep. There was no escaping the iron grip of the realist paradigm. Try as they might to take to the streets or organize mass protests, romantics could not possibly represent the masses because, like Lenin's "unconscious" elements, they were blind to their own limitations and hence behaved as representatives of counter-revolutionary social forces. In fact, they constituted these counterrevolutionary forces themselves: a symbolic correspondence between the course of action proposed by romantic political actors and the behavior that scientific socialism would predict of counterrevolutionary social classes made counterrevolutionaries of all but the realists. So one realist critic of "romantic" revolutionaries in the peasant movement complained:

Such people may call themselves social-movement activists, but they have in fact become new evil gentry and local bullies themselves and certainly cannot plan anything beneficial for the poor peasants . . . activists must, then, persevere in throwing off their thoughts of romantic heroism.

If romantics could "become new evil gentry" by symbolic correspondence, realist revolutionaries could equally become the peasants or workers whose interests they represented. In fact, they were likely to be even more peasant-like than actual peasants, because they had "undergone a true self-awakening" to the occult forces governing social life that peasants themselves had yet to undergo following a course of party instruction. Neither local grandees nor peasant elders needed to be consulted on the question of who the gentry and the peasants really were. It was far more important to establish who was the realist and who the romantic among the revolutionaries, and hence to sort out the symbolic correspondence between words and things in ways that might have the desired effect.[96]

The one tangible measure of effectiveness in this kind of representative politics was mass mobilization. In time, a capacity to mobilize people became a commonly agreed test for distinguishing the materialist from the idealist, the realist from the romantic. On this score, the Communists were far more successful than the Nationalists. Already in Guangdong and Hunan, Communist peasant organizers had begun to develop a rudimentary "mass line" that oriented party propaganda and agitation to mass organization and mobilization.

After a couple of years working among tenant farmers and small landholders, Peasant Bureau Director Luo Qiyuan observed that individuals, families, and in some cases whole villages felt sorely aggrieved over local issues but failed to relate their grievances to comparable ones outside their communities. By 1925 he was convinced that, for all their limitations, these local grievances provided useful points of entry for revolutionary propagandists attempting to foster a sense of class consciousness among peasant householders. "Propaganda about class," Luo asserted "must start from problems which the masses face constantly themselves." Peasant-movement cadre were instructed to investigate local conditions in detail, to isolate local grievances, and to formulate systematic programs for resolving them with the aim of getting peasants on their side. "Through rural investigation we can find out exactly what these difficulties and needs of the masses may be and then set out through propaganda the methods for resolving their difficulties and supplying their needs and so draw them closer to us." The final step in Luo's program involved peasant-movement cadre pointing out that peasant problems could be resolved only through cooperation with the leadership of the revolutionary movement.[97] Out in the field, graduates of the Peasant Movement Institute married local grievances with revolutionary goals to good effect in mobilizing peasants to join peasant associations and respond to party direction.[98]

Luo's strategy contained many of the rudimentary elements of the mass line, which was to come to prominence in a later phase of the revolution: a determination to research and reveal "the ideas of the masses" in the form of local grievances and expressed wishes, an assertion of potential differences between peasant consciousness of grievance and revolutionary consciousness of class "needs," and an affirmation of the role of revolutionary cadre in converting a sense of local grievance into higher-order class consciousness (translating "wishes" into "needs") through mass propaganda and mass organization.[99] In Mao Zedong's later formulation, the distinction between perceived wishes and actual needs was attenuated further, to the point at which both needs and wishes were aspects of party thinking. "In working for the masses," Mao advised in 1944, "we must start from their needs, not from our wishes." The distinction was a deceptive one, however, for "their needs" were not easily distinguished from "our wishes":

It sometimes happens that the masses *objectively need* some reform but are not yet *subjectively awakened* to it and willing or determined to bring it into effect. In that case, we should wait patiently and introduce the reform only when, through our work, the great majority of the masses have become awakened to the need and are willing and determined to start it.

Mao's advice was eminently sensible. A party-directed movement mobilized by it own willfulness was preferable to an unwilling one, and nothing short of an "awakened" mass movement was likely to be willing. Mass awakening was a sound prescription for effective action: "We absolutely must not proceed by orders or constraints. Unless the masses are awakened and willing, all work that needs their participation will turn out to be an empty formality and end in failure." [100] Again the emphasis was on practical effect. Mao drew implicitly upon the experience of Luo Qiyuan and the peasant-movement activists of the Nationalist Revolution: Luo, like Mao, valued peasant consciousness in its un-tutored state only as far as this was strategically useful, first as a point of entry into local communities, then as point of departure for fostering class awaken-ing, and finally for securing peasant compliance with their own re-education and mobilization. But in proclaiming the possibility that needs and wishes, as defined by the party, would eventually be embraced enthusiastically by the masses once they had been "awakened," Mao was drawing on a still wider legacy in the pedagogical politics of the Nationalist Revolution.

Theory was linked to practice through intensive local research. Research-ing local conditions entailed researching the "real" cleavages thought to be lying beneath the surface of local society with an eye to evaluating how they could be turned to advantage in the organized mass-movement. During his apprenticeship in the propaganda bureau, Mao Zedong began to see the clas-sification of different strata within society and the identification of cleavages among them as his most urgent task, and to imagine that awakening the people to the real sources of their suffering would provide the key to success in China's national revolution. He wanted to share his insights into the subliminal forces in society with the people he proposed to awaken and, by awakening them, to reshape society in turn.[101]

Awakening Class *and* Nation

In time, the realist emphasis on hidden social cleavages transformed the nationalist quest by introducing the idea of class struggle into nationalist thought itself. The point at issue here is not the existence of social classes in early twentieth-century China, nor even the salience of class analysis in social revolution. It is, rather, the manner in which the idea of class took root in a state-oriented politics of national awakening. Class first entered the vocabu-lary of radical activists around the turn of the century, along with all that was modern and cosmopolitan. Talk of a revolution among social classes was commonplace among anarchists, who were not in the least concerned about the reunification of the state and who were only marginally interested in the attainment of national "wealth and power." [102] It was the ethical community of the nation, not of social class, that required the clearest elaboration and closest justification in early revolutionary thought.

Around the turn of the century, social classes were imagined as existing in the natural order of things, whereas nations appeared irrational and artificial contrivances born of the international state system. They were curious by-products of a Western way of organizing the world. "Now, in this multitudinous universe, the earth is but a small grain of rice," wrote the Nationalist Zhang Binglin. "Yet today we who live on it have divided it up into territories, we protect what is ours and call it a 'nation.' Then we established institutions, divided ourselves into various classes, and called it 'government.' " [103] Nations had no rationale other than as functional categories for organizing the affairs of people. For reasons we have noted, nationalism and Leninism converged in the 1920s. Many socialists moderated their commitment to class struggle, and some nationalists conceded the inevitability of social struggle. This development culminated in the Nationalist Revolution with the introduction of class struggle into nationalist thought, broadly conceived.

If we overstate the appeal of Marxism-Leninism among early nationalists, we can easily miss the point of the Nationalist Revolution. There was, initially, an immense reluctance to embrace the idea of class division or class struggle within nationalist thought. Indeed, there was little incentive for either Nationalist or Communist party theorists to relinquish the modern ideal of the unified nation or to abandon the inherited Confucian ideal of social harmony until both ideals had been rendered untenable within nationalist thought itself. Marxism-Leninism could only became a plausible option within nationalist thought when obstacles to the reception of class struggle had been eliminated.

The removal of these obstacles took place over three early phases of the revolution. At first, class struggle was conceived as analogous to the struggle among nations, specifically between wealthier and stronger states and the territories they sought to bring into their colonial empires. In this phase, China was imagined as a single class struggling against international capital, that is, a proletarian nation. From around 1922, however, struggle against "feudal" military forces within the country came to be conceived as a form of domestic class struggle. The antifeudal struggle was intended to hasten the historical evolution of a national mode of production. Finally, from 1925 and throughout the period of the civil war, the reluctance of certain powerful and well-organized groups in society to follow the directives of the revolutionaries singled them out for class struggle waged in the name of the nation itself. In this phase, advocacy of class struggle against the bourgeoisie and the landlord classes served the further function of destroying the only social formations that held any prospect of staging effective local resistance to an expanding party-state.

The institution of the party-state was crucial to the development of these last two phases. The Communist and Nationalist parties saw themselves as institutions for representing the people until they had awakened to realization of their own unity. Those who persisted in displaying indifference to imperialist influence, or disregard for political partition under warlord rule, betrayed in their behavior their counterrevolutionary class status. The idea of class struggle then ceased to be an unpalatable option in nationalist thought and came to appear, instead, a palatable necessity. It came to appear unavoidable.[104] If the people themselves were divided over the fundamental issues of who should rule them and how they should be ruled, then only *some* of them deserved to be included among the people of the nation. A Marxist emphasis on class struggle offered a rational principle for exclusion from the nation of those class interests which could not be represented (with the desired effect) by the state.

Nevertheless, the appearance of class struggle in the revolution did not signal its departure from nationalism, nor did it transform the revolution into a socialist enterprise. The dispute associated with class struggle took place within nationalist thought itself, testing the limits of an established consensus on the composition of the nation and forcing a massive rupture in nationalist thought between a continuing commitment to Sun Yatsen's vision of the nation as a race and an alternative vision of the nation as a constellation of social classes. The question at issue was how to essentialize the national self, which was to be represented by the state and awakened as a mass community.

The division between the Nationalists and Communists in the Chinese revolution is best characterized not as a struggle between Marxism-Leninism and nationalism but as a struggle between two phases of nationalism. Ideologically, it was a conflict over membership in the nation at a time when the nation was still under negotiation. Institutionally, it was a struggle between two highly competitive state-building parties, competing not only with one another but with rival political movements and organized society as well. It was also a clash of dreams. When Sun Yatsen and Chen Jiongming, Dai Jitao and Mao Zedong, asked what the future held in store for their country, each felt certain that his answer would assist in awakening the people. In fact, however, it was their efforts at dreaming and awakening that decided what the future held in store. The politics of mass awakening decided which dream came true.

REFERENCE MATTER

NOTES

Complete author's names, titles, and publication data are given in the Bibliography, pages 403-37. The following abbreviations are used in the Notes and Bibliography:

GFQJ   *Guofu quanji* (The complete works of the father of the country)
GMR   *Guangzhou minguo ribao* (Guangzhou republican daily)
GMWX   *Geming wenxian* (Documents on the revolution)
GSGB   *Guangdong shengzhengfu gongbao* (Guangdong provincial government gazette)
JSYK   *Junshi zhengzhi yuekan* (Military and political affairs monthly)
LYLC   *Liuda yiqian: dang de lishi cailiao* (Before the Sixth Congress: Party historical materials)
SMR   *Shanghai minguo ribao* (Shanghai republican daily)
ZGGY   *Zhongguo guomindang guangdongsheng dangbu dangwu yuebao* (Party affairs monthly of the Guangdong provincial branch of the Chinese Nationalist party)
ZGHS   *Zhongguo guomindang diyi, erci quanguo daibiao dahui huiyi shiliao* (Historical materials on the first and second national congresses of the Chinese Nationalist party)
ZGZK   *Zhongguo guomindang zhoukan* (Chinese Nationalist party weekly)
ZGZY   *Zhongguo guomindang zhongyang zhixing weiyuanhui dangwu yuebao* (Party affairs monthly of the Chinese Nationalist party Central Executive Committee)
ZZZB   *Zhengzhi zhoubao* (Political weekly)

Preface

1. An exception may be made for the work of Lucian Pye, which is particularly sensitive to the rhetoric of Chinese politics. See Pye 1968. The present work is not, however, a study of political culture in the sense that Pye has made his own. My interest lies in the study of politics *and* culture; that is, in tracing the political appropriation of culture in the discourse of modern Chinese nationalism.

2. See Introduction below, note 10.

3. I use the word "reflective" here after the style of Greg Dening. See Dening 1993: 83, 88–89.

Introduction

1. Sun [31]: 102, 113. Sun Yatsen's 1924 speeches on the Three Principles of the People are cited from the English translation by Frank W. Price published in Chunking in 1943. For a Chinese-language version, see Sun [33].

2. Mao [11]: 318. 3. Croizier 1988; Li Jianer 1941: 12.

4. Sun [31]: 133. 5. Vogel 1989: 24.

6. On He Xiangning and the Nationalist women's movement, see Gilmartin 1994: 206–17.

7. B. Anderson 1991: 114, 163.

8. Tao 1964: 77; Dirlik 1978: 47.

9. Lü 1989: 69–70.

10. I have been unable to locate the source of this quotation, which seems to be cited nowhere but in accounts of the collapse of the Chinese empire, and there almost without exception. Napoleon read the account of Macartney's mission while in exile on the isle of St. Helena, where he also entertained Lord Amherst on his voyage back from China in July 1817. On that occasion Napoleon lectured the English "on their inability to speak effectively to the Orient." Peyrefitte 1993: 512–18.

11. Pye 1972: Preface.

12. See Chapters 1 and 8 below.

13. Arendt 1951.

14. The complete couplet reads, "When the Doctrine Prevails, All Under Heaven Is for the Common Good" (*Da dao zhi xing ye, tian xiawei gong*). William Rowe notes that the identification of the phrase "common good" with government occurred much later, in Tang and Song times. Rowe 1990: 316–17. Even in its original form, the expression was not entirely divorced from the political. In the Age of Great Unity (when presumably "All Under Heaven Belongs to All"), the Book of Rites records that "the worthy and able were selected for office." See Ch'ing 1972–73: 4–5.

15. Bao 1964: 42–43. The emergence of the modern museum is discussed in Chapter 1 below. On the evolving relationship between state and "public" institutions in the late empire and early Republic, see Rowe 1989 and Rankin 1986.

16. Adapted from Sun [31]: 169–70. 17. Foucault 1984: 2–3.

18. Zou 1929, I: 331–41. 19. Sun [31]: Author's Preface.

20. Ibid.: 33, 86, 102. 21. Ibid.: 139. Emphasis added.

22. Ibid.: 136–37. 23. Cranmer-Byng [1902] 1962: 225.

24. Barrow 1806: 77. Fifty years later, an English gentleman apologized to the French for the anti-French prejudice of English polite society over the preceding century. His purpose was to distinguish the civilized French from the heathen Chinese of his own day. De Quincey [1857] 1897: 351–52.

25. Zarrow 1990: 170.

26. Sun [31]: 137–38.

27. See Chapter 3.

28. Sun [31]: 138–39. The origins of Chiang Kaishek's New Life movement can also be traced to a belief on Chiang's part that foreigners failed to respect China because the Chinese people were not respectable. Thomson 1969: 156–57.

29. Sun [31]: 135.

30. P. Brown 1988.

31. Vogel 1969: 31. The nationalist preoccupation with toilets was also subject to ridicule. Lin Yutang offers a characteristically insightful and acerbic response to preoccupations with hygiene and toiletry among modern nationalists: "Since the invention of the flush toilet and the vacuum carpet cleaner, the modern man seems to judge a man's moral standards by his cleanliness." Lin Yutang 1939: 22. Toilet humor also features in a novel by Zhang Tianyi, *Guitu riji* (Diary of the land of ghosts; 1931), a parody of Chinese nationalism in the 1920s. In the world of the novel, "there are only two political parties: one advocating squatting toilets; the other advocating sitting toilets." On coming to office the "sitting" party converts all ditch-style public toilets to upright sitting toilets and a political crisis ensues. Dolezelova-Velingerova 1988: 218–19.

32. The Nanjing monument was also subject to ridicule for its grandiose pretensions. See Lin Yutang [1931] 1969a.

33. De Francis 1950. On the noninstrumental function of language and literature in revolutionary France, see Hunt 1984: 24.

34. Taylor 1948: 32.

35. Chow Tse-tsung lists the titles and publishing details of 587 of 700 new journals issued between 1915 and 1923. Circulation of the most popular journals did not exceed 30,000. Chow Tse-tsung 1963: 1.

36. Taylor 1948: 33.

37. Shimada 1990: 19.

38. Sun [31]: 75.

39. De Francis 1950: Ch. 2.

40. F. Lee 1926: 20.

41. De Francis 1950: 19.

42. Schurmann 1968.

43. Kuo 1956: 21.

44. Analysts who note Sun's propensity for idle dreaming are sometimes tempted to deny that China existed in any real sense in the 1920s: the want of political unity is identified with the absence of a "real" China. See Iriye 1965: 160.

45. Sun [11]: 731–32.

46. Sun [31]: 345.

47. T'ang 1936: 168.

48. Sun [31]: 345.

49. *San Tzu Ching* 1964: 2–4.

50. *The Four Books* 1973: 2.

51. Watson 1993: 80–103.

52. Dai 1925b: 23; Sansom 1988: 170.

53. Mao [1]: 352.

54. *The Independent* (*Duli zhoukan*). See Chapter 6 below.

55. Sun [17]: 593–604.

56. G. Yu 1966: 126.

57. Bhaba 1990: 3.

58. Gluck 1985: 11, 15.

59. Mao [3]: 371–72.

Chapter 1

1. Mao [13]: 94.

2. Ayscough 1938: 127.

3. B. Anderson 1991: 114.

4. O'Brien 1988: 48ff.

5. "Sheping" 1924.

6. In August 1924, comrades in Shanghai informed Sun Yatsen that they did not trust the Central Executive Committee. Li Yunhan 1966, 1: 322–23.

7. Foster 1928: 68.   8. Wilbur 1976: Conclusion.

9. Bland 1932: 57–58.   10. Foster 1928: 66–67.

11. Ayscough 1938: 65.   12. Foster 1928: 217.

13. Sun [31]: 124.   14. *SMR*, 6 November 1923.

15. Ye was not the only party member to reflect critically on the motif of the awakened lion. In 1920, the forthright Nationalist propagandist Zhu Zhixin published an article entitled "Shuideren xingla" (Sleepers awaken) in which he argued that "nations and individuals should love and help each other instead of being aggressive and causing fear. They should be humans, not lions." Lü 1992: 10.

16. *SMR*, 6 November 1923. See also Cai Hesen 1922f.

17. On propaganda bureau appointments and animosity between Shanghai and Guangzhou party headquarters (which underlay much of the tension between Sun and Ye Chucang), see Chapter 6.

18. Croizier 1988: 70–71.

19. Tan Sitong 1984: 217.

20. The *Awakened Lion* was edited by Zeng Qi and other leaders of the Youth Party on behalf of the Statism (*Guojia zhuyi*) movement. *Chinese Youth* was founded in October 1923 as an official organ of the Communist Youth League and was edited successively by Deng Zhongxia, Xiao Chunü, and Yun Daiying. Zhang Jinglu 1954–56, 1: 63.

21. T. Chow 1960: 283–84.

22. Ayscough 1938: 164–65.

23. In 1923, two awakening societies—the Cock Crow Society (*Jiming she*) and the Dawn Society (*Weiming she*)—competed for space within the same supplement to the Beijing *National Currents Daily News* (*Guofeng ribao*). T. Chow 1963: 125–26.

24. T. Chow 1963: 70, 81, 123.

25. See Chapter 5.

26. T. Chow 1963: 74–75, 127–28. The Tianjin *Awaken* is to be distinguished from the more influential Shanghai Nationalist party journal of the same title.

27. The British used the lion to represent their own role in China. A fierce British lion holds down a folio of "Bolshevist Propaganda" with its claws, while the wispy figure of an evil Oriental is caught by the watchful gaze of Austen Chamberlain in a cartoon that appeared in the *North China Herald*, 27 June 1925.

28. Gellner 1983: 6.   29. Chiang [1943] 1947: 114.

30. B. Anderson 1991: 114.   31. *GMR*, 18 and 24 April 1925.

32. Bland 1932: 57–58.

33. Peter Gregory translates the term *zhi* as "awareness." Gregory 1985: 29–69.

34. Kang Youwei 1967: 31; Liang [1902] 1967, 1977.

35. Ma 1974: 67; Dirlik 1989: 84.

36. See Chapter 2. Old religious terminology (and demonology) retained its hold over the imaginations of those who awakened to the new moral communities of class and nation. Hsia 1968: 23–24.

37. Wakeman 1973: 110–12.
38. H. Chang 1987: 18–20; 1971.
39. H. Chang 1987: 10–20.
40. Zarrow 1990: Chap. 1.
41. H. Chang 1987: 54; *The Four Books* 1973: 2.
42. Sun [42]: 460–63.
43. See Conclusion.
44. H. Chang 1987: 15.
45. H. Chang 1987.
46. G. Yu 1966: 126.
47. Sun [47]: 701.

48. Sun [31]: 120. Health was a matter of some concern to early Chinese Nationalists. See Dikötter 1992; Croizier 1968; Mao [18].

49. *China Medical Journal* 1915: 340–41.

50. Nathan 1985: 134.

51. In Spring 1924, the Presbyterian *Hainan Newsletter* published an apposite anecdote: "It is said that Dr. Stewart, who lately died in Africa, was asked, 'Why don't you civilize your people first and then make them Christians?' He answered, 'We don't do work twice over; when we have made them Christians we have made them civilized.' " *Hainan Newsletter* 1924: 17.

52. Heimert 1966.
53. Nathan 1985: 134–44.
54. Yip 1980; Lutz 1988.
55. Sun [8]: 575; [17]: 594.
56. Sun [46]: 559.
57. Sun [17]: 601.

58. Ibid.: 594. The sentiment was a common one. John Foster cites a passage from an unnamed Chinese Christian journal of the 1920s: "Jesus . . . considered it his meat to spread the Gospel. As His followers . . . we should try our utmost to broadcast the principles of the revolutionary movement." Foster 1928: 76–77. See also Liang 1953.

59. When he reached the borders of Guangdong Province (in his calculations), Sun turned from the ideal of *universal* conversion to a kind of liberal formalism: when converts made up an absolute majority of the population of the country, "this would truly mark a great victory for our party." Sun [46]: 563. See also Sun [6].

60. Sun [8]: 575.

61. Sun [46]: 559.

62. Gellner 1964: 169. Emphasis added.

63. On the earlier search for native roots, see Wakeman 1973: 82–86.

64. Min 1989.
65. Hobson [1902] 1965: 310–11.
66. Sun [31]: 95.
67. *SMR*, 6 November 1923.

68. Wolfe 1991: 204–5. For Darwin's reception in China, see Pusey 1983.

69. De Certeau 1988: xxv–xxvii; Montrose 1991.

70. Hegel 1944: 140–41. Emphasis in original.

71. Connerton 1980: 116.

72. Marx [1853] 1969a; [1853] 1969b.

73. Hegel 1944.

74. Marx observed that the state substituted for "voluntary association" in Oriental empires that were organized for hydraulic purposes, such as China and India, where "civilisation was too low and the territorial extent too vast to call into life voluntary association." Marx [1853] 1969a: 115.

75. Sun [31]: 301.
76. See Chapter 7; Fewsmith 1985.
77. Sun [31]: 306.
78. Ibid.: 314–15.
79. Ibid.: 297.
80. Ibid.: 94.

81. O'Brien 1988: 48; P. Johnson 1991: Chap. 8.

82. Fargusson 1972; Gillespie 1983: 43, 52.

83. Peyrefitte 1993: 423. By the time Macartney returned to London, hot-air balloons and the Enlightenment had both lost their innocence. Surviving engravings of scientific fantasies of the Napoleonic era depict balloons transporting troops for an invasion of England, and English defenders arising in armed kites to protect their homeland. The first actual use of balloons in combat was in 1794, when they were employed by the French army at Maubeuge. Gibbs-Smith 1985: 20.

84. Barrow 1806: 13, 69, 117.   85. Barrow 1806.

86. Desmond and Moore 1991.   87. P. Johnson 1991: 343–55.

88. Barrow 1806: 85.

89. Cohen 1984. "China-centered" historians who start their narratives well before the advent of Western contact, or alternately make a point of studying events, issues, and people not notably affected by that contact, prefer nevertheless to chart the emergence of an incipient *indigenous* nationalism rather than question the metanarrative of nationalism embedded in the historiography of East-West contact. See Naquin and Rawski 1987; Johnson, Nathan, and Rawski 1985.

90. See Fairbank 1971, 1986. Like all dominant historical paradigms, this "Harvard School" of historiography has come in for its share of criticism. Some critics regard it as unsympathetic to Mao's China (Peck 1971), and others as too sympathetic to Maoism (Mosher 1990).

91. Liang [1922] 1979.

92. Ibid. Liang's idealist historiography of the reform and revolutionary movements is reproduced in histories of these movements written from very different perspectives. See Fairbank 1971, 1986; Dirlik 1978: 37.

93. Liang [1922] 1979.

94. Dirlik 1978: 38. See also Chapters 4 and 7 below.

95. Sun [31]: 33.

96. B. Anderson 1991: 37.

97. Mote 1977: 116–17; Mumford 1938: 4.

98. Graham Peck records the distinction nicely. See Peck 1967: 7.

99. R. Johnson 1991: 79.

100. Bao 1964: 12–13. As early as the Warring States period, King Wen of Zhou built a garden of 70 square *li* and is said to "have shared it with the people" (*yu min gong zhi*). Ibid.: 6. Similarly, the halls that formed the centerpoint of many celebrated private gardens of wealthy merchants and gentry in late imperial Hangzhou, Suzhou, and Yangzhou were "built to receive and entertain guests." R. Johnson 1991: 76.

101. A. Smith 1894: Chap. 5 ("The Disregard for Time").

102. Vogel 1989: 74.

103. B. Anderson 1991: 28.

104. Bao 1964: 15–16.

105. Whitewright 1893: 234–35. I am grateful to Antonia Finnane for bringing this source to my attention.

106. Ibid.: 235, 239–41.

107. Ibid.: 239–41.

108. Ibid.: 242.

109. Sir Auriel Stein seized 24 boxes of manuscripts from the Dunhuang Caves for the British Museum, and five boxes of embroideries and banners for a museum in New Delhi. Paul Peliot took away 2,000 volumes of classical texts. Bao 1964: 8-9.

110. Ibid.: 24.

111. Ibid.: 24-26, 31, 37.

112. The museum was proposed by the Nationalist Ministry of Education in April 1933, and opened in Nanjing a few years later. Fu Sinian was at first appointed chairman of its preparatory committee, but the heavy demand of his work at the Academia Sinica forced Fu to resign in favor of Li Ji in July of the following year. The committee also included Hu Shi, Zhu Jiahua, Cai Yuanpei, and Wang Shijie. Tang Dantong 1960: 1-7.

113. Ibid.: 9.

114. Bao 1964: 31; Levenson 1971b: 57.

115. Schneider 1971: 27. Fu was inaugural head of the preparatory committee for the National Central Museum. Bao 1964: 52.

116. Schneider 1971: 8-11. Gu's new history was not always welcomed among Nationalist party leaders, who resented his attacks on the historical veracity of the Golden Age. Schneider 1971: 189-91.

117. Ibid.: 60-61.

118. Levenson 1971a.

119. Cited in March 1974: 16.

120. Lu Xun writes: "Queues were cut off in Beijing by order of Yuan Shih-kai; but this was no simple order, it must have been backed by swords. If not, the city would probably still be filled with queues today." Lu Xun [1927] 1980: 353-55.

121. Three studies published in 1989 indicate increasing market integration in the late empire and early Republic: Brandt 1989; Faure 1989; T. Rawski 1989. See also Myers 1991: 604-28. The social and cultural implications of the expanding marketing network are discussed in Johnson, Nathan and Rawski 1985; Naquin and Rawski 1987. See E. Rawski 1991: 84-111.

122. Mao [13]: 65.

123. Ibid.: 93-94.

124. Ibid.: 103-4.

125. "The True Story of Ah Q," a novella, was completed in 1921 and published in Lu Xun's earliest volume of short stories, Na han (Call to arms), in 1923. See Lu Xun [1923] 1980a: 102-54.

126. Mao [13]: 94, 103.

127. V. S. Naipaul describes the fountain pen as "the badge of the rural literate." Theroux 1972: 12.

128. Josipovici 1982: 22.

129. Kwok 1965: 56.

130. Zarrow 1990: 78.

131. In addition to the works of Mercier and Bellamy discussed here, those of William Morris and H. G. Wells also employ the awakened-sleeper device in projecting their ideal worlds into the future. Kumar 1987: 39.

132. In an unintended parody of its own utopian rationalism, the work was translated into English under the more rational title *Memoirs of the Year 2500* "for the sake of a round number." See Mercier 1795: "Advertisement."

133. Mercier placed an epigraph from Leibnitz on the cover of the book: "The present is pregnant with the future" ("Le Temps present est gros de l'avenir"). I. F. Clarke counts the book the "first influential story of the future in world history." Kumar 1987: 38.

134. Bellamy 1888. It was claimed at the time of Bellamy's death in 1898 that his writing exerted a greater influence on society than the works of Karl Marx in his lifetime. Many decades later, in 1935, John Dewey ranked *Looking Backward* as the most influential international work of the nineteenth century after Marx's *Das Kapital*. Kumar 1987: 136.

135. By 1891, the movement inspired by Bellamy's book had established 165 "Nationalist Clubs" and two specialist journals in the U.S. alone. Kumar 1987: 133–34. In 1889 one of Bellamy's followers claimed that 50 newspapers and journals could be counted supporters of the movement. Between 1891 and 1896 the movement participated directly in U.S. party politics through the People's party (or Populists). Bowman 1962: Chap. 5 passim.

136. Wagar 1988: 106–25.

137. *Wanguo gongbao* commenced publication in 1875 as successor publication to the earlier missionary journal *Jiaohui xinbao* (Church news). Its initial English title was *The Globe Magazine*. In 1889, after a six-year suspension of publication, it reappeared under the new English title *Review of the Times*. Cohen 1974: 293; Bernal 1976: Chap. 2. The translation was published under the title "Huitou kan jilüe" (Outline of *Looking Backward*). Ma Ruiran 1991: 13–14.

138. Whitewright 1893: 240.

139. Ma Ruiran 1991: 13–14; Bernal 1976. Kang Youwei first listed his subscription to *Review of the Times* in his autobiography alongside the year 1883. See Kang Youwei 1967: 38.

140. Hirai 1903; Sakai 1904. For the French connection, see Zarrow 1990: 78.

141. Kang Youwei began his attempt to recast the three ages (chaos—*juluan*; rising peace—*shengping*; and universal peace—*taiping*) from a regressive sequence into a progressive one around the time that *Looking Backward* appeared in translation. H. Chang 1987: 50–55.

142. Tan Sitong 1984: 215–16. The translator attributes the reference to Rip Van Winkle in Washington Irving's *The Sketch Book* (1819), but Arif Dirlik correctly traces the reference to Bellamy's *Looking Backward*. Dirlik 1991: 56.

143. Knechtges 1973: 101–19; R. Hegel 1988: 1–10.

144. Jin Shengtan's 70-chapter edition was translated by Pearl Buck under the title *All Men Are Brothers*. See Buck 1958. J. Wong 1972; R. Hegel 1988: 4.

145. Even deceptive femme fatales, ghosts, and fox fairies come to the aid of the nation in the popular fiction of dream awakenings. The hero of Xu Xu's *Guilian* (In love with a ghost; 1937) awakens to a terrible revelation that the spectral beauty who has captured his heart has been transformed into a ghost by the failure of the Nationalist Revolution. In a less romantic vein, Zhang Tianyi deployed the old device of

ghosts to expose the hypocrisy and irrelevance of republican parliamentary politics in *Guitu riji* (Ghostland diary; 1931). In this case the reader is awakened, through allegorical inversion, to a world that is not quite as it should be. Dolezelova-Velingerova 1988: 122–23, 188–89, 211–14, 218–20.

146. Cited in Dirlik 1991: 66–69. Eight years later Cai Yuanpei was offered the opportunity to put his dream into effect when he was appointed minister of education in the national government.

147. H. Chang 1987.

148. Kauffman 1965: 315; cited in Fogel 1989: 183.

149. Guerard [1924] 1968: 146.

150. Sun [36]. Translation based on Sun [27]: 262. Sun's difficulty securing his leadership is discussed in Chapter 5 below.

151. Mao [2]: 365.

152. On Kang, see Croizier 1968: 62; Kang Youwei 1935: 428; 1958: 256. On Liang, see H. Chang 1971: 243–45. On Sun, see Schiffrin 1970: 15. On Chiang, see Vishnyakova-Akimova 1971: 166; Widmer 1977: 118; Lary 1975: 79; Vorontsov 1989. On Mao, see Schram 1967: 25. The most curious aspect of Napoleon's place in the Chinese revolution is the part he now plays among self-reflective biographers of Mao. See Leys 1991.

153. H. Chang 1987: 20.   154. Cantlie and Jones n.d.: 167.

155. Liang 1953: 226–38; 1978: 22–29.   156. Liang 1953: 226–38.

157. Sun [11]: 733.   158. Lu Xun [1934] 1980: 138.

Chapter 2

1. Mao [9]: 132.

2. Lukács 1971: 29.

3. Frederic Wakeman notes that "Kang Yu-wei's perception announced the birth of ideology for modern China." Wakeman 1973: 122.

4. Nipperday 1983: 4, 9–10.

5. Hsia 1968: 26.

6. Other terms are also used in preference to "rational" to describe the instrumentalist strain in nationalist thought, and there are forms of nationalism that cannot usefully be described as rational at all. See Brass 1976. The focus here is on the instrumentalist strain of Chinese Nationalist thought.

7. Kang 1967: 32–42. Kang had been raised by his grandfather following the death of his father. *One World Philosophy* was begun in 1884, largely completed by 1902, but only partly published before the founding of the Republic in 1912. The complete (and revised) edition appeared in 1935.

8. The Treaty of Shimonoseki was signed on 17 April 1895. In addition to the cession of the three territories, the treaty also provided for recognition of Korean independence, an indemnity of two hundred million taels, the opening of the ports of Chongqing, Suzhou, Hangzhou, and Shashi to Japanese interests, and the right of Japanese nationals to open industrial and manufacturing enterprises in China generally. Hsü 1990: 341–43; Jansen 1975.

9. Spence 1982.

10. H. Chang 1987: 21–26.

11. Ibid.: 29–30, 46–48. The five "constant" relationships refer to those of ruler-subject, father-son, brother-brother, husband-wife, and friend-friend; the three bonds, as set out by Dong Zhongshu, are the relations of ruler-subject, father-son, and husband-wife; the four Mencian virtues are human-heartedness (*ren*), righteousness (*yi*), propriety (*li*), and wisdom (*zhih*).

12. Dirlik 1978: 38.

13. Dennerline 1988: 9.

14. Sun prepared his major treatise on this subject in English while in political retirement in Shanghai in 1918 and 1919. He envisioned around a million miles of paved roads, 100,000 miles of railway track, and three new harbors. His plans included a blueprint for the development of the Pudong region (the east bank of the Huangpu River in Shanghai) that was retrieved and consulted in the 1990s in planning for the Pudong Special Development Zone. Author's interview with Pudong planners, Shanghai, July 1992. Sun [20]: 127–360.

15. Prominent exponents of this localist reaction included Sha Ting, Ai Wu, Wu Zuxiang, Xiao Hong, Duanmu Hongliang, and Shen Congwen. M. Anderson 1990: 190–91; Kinkley 1987.

16. M. Anderson 1990: 190.   17. Kang 1967: 41.

18. Gu Jiegang 1931: Introduction.   19. Kang 1958: 63.

20. Ibid.: 63. Kang was drawing here on the philosophical writings of Dong Zhongshu. See H. Chang 1987: 32–37. Ye Shaojun dealt with a comparable problematic of affective sympathy and of delimiting boundaries in his fiction. See M. Anderson 1990: 93–118.

21. On the risks attached to this rationalist procedure, see Heller 1988: Introduction; and Benhabib 1986: 8.

22. Kang 1958: 80.

23. An apparent contradiction between the thought and the behavior of Kang, as Frederic Wakeman notes, "has puzzled many historians." Wakeman finds a satisfactory resolution to this contradiction in Kang's discovery and application of the theories of relativity and evolution, which established an irreducible connection between utopia and praxis. Wakeman 1973: 115–36.

24. China's anarchists were exceptional. See Dirlik 1991.

25. Seyla Benhabib discusses this question in relation to Marx and Hegel. Benhabib 1986: Chap. 2.

26. Wagar 1988: 107; 1979.   27. H. Chang 1987: 18–20.

28. Wagar 1988: 116–17.   29. H. Chang 1987: 61, 178–79.

30. Cited in Dirlik 1991: 68. See also above, Chapter 1. Cai's story appeared twenty years before Zamyatin's better-known novel, *We*, in which all characters are identified by number. Zamyatin 1972.

31. Chan and Dirlik 1992: 83.   32. Zarrow 1990: 17.

33. Chan and Dirlik 1992: 41, 51.   34. Schurmann 1968.

35. Polan 1984: 21–23.

36. Althusser went a step further in justifying Lenin's conception of the state by

trying to accomplish theoretically for the bourgeois state what Lenin had effectively accomplished for the revolutionary socialist one: absorbing civil society into the state. Althusser's definition of the "ideological apparatus of the state" was sufficiently inclusive to embrace all of the major institutions hitherto associated with bourgeois civil society, including the family, the church, the educational system, the press, the law, all forms of organized political activity, and culture. Althusser 1971; Polan 1984: 33–35.

37. Heller 1988.

38. Zarrow 1990: 122.

39. Ibid.: 120.

40. Nathan 1985: 133.

41. H. Chang 1971: 279–82.

42. See Chapter 8.

43. Marx [1852] 1968: 172.

44. On the concept of class, see Thompson 1963: 10 and his Chap. 16. The concept of false consciousness never gained great credence among liberal sociologists and is presently in bad odor among Western Marxists as well. See Polsby 1959; Bottomore 1983: 220.

45. G. Hegel 1953: 134.

46. This kind of prescriptive reduction of Marxist thought has been criticized for failing to acknowledge the subtleties of Marx's own writing and for ignoring evidence of the emergence of class consciousness in civil society quite independently of the efforts of outside agitators to foment it. I am not disputing this. I am more concerned with the activists' understanding of what was required to build national and class consciousness. See Thompson 1963: Introduction.

47. Hegel presented the problem of proper and "defective" identity in a pedagogical context: "It is part of education, of thinking as the consciousness of the single in the form of the universal, that the ego comes to be apprehended as a universal person in which all are identical." G. Hegel 1953: 134.

48. The significance of the term "mass" in late Qing thought is noted in H. Chang 1987: 6, 109–11. See also H. Chang 1971: 155–56. Kang had argued in conversation with Emperor Guangxu in 1898 that the task of politics was to preserve the territory and people who made up the "nation." Dirlik 1991: 53.

49. Kang 1958: 66, 80, 157.

50. Zarrow 1990: 51–52.

51. A later generation of anarchists arrived at similar compromises with a different kind of nationalism in the 1920s. Dirlik 1991: 259.

52. Zarrow 1990: 51–52.

53. Kang 1958: 69–74, 84.

54. Ibid.: 84.

55. Ibid.: 69–74.

56. Dirlik offers a fine analysis of ways in which "consciousness of the globe" informed early Chinese nationalism. Dirlik 1991: Chap. 2.

57. H. Chang 1971: 155.

58. Min 1989: 121.

59. Sun [31]: 5.

60. Ibid.: 113–15.

61. Ibid.: 67–68.

62. Ibid.: 89.

63. Ibid.: 74–75.

64. Ibid.: 99–100.

65. Ibid.: 159.

66. Ibid.: 164–66.

67. Ibid.: 260–61.

68. H. Chang 1971: 260.

69. See Chapter 3 below.

70. Sun [31]: 115. See Chapter 7 below.

71. New Culture writers saw Western literature less as a different "national" tra-

dition than as a universal or "human" one. This idea they encountered in Western learning itself. Bonnie McDougall cautions that such a perspective is more properly described as international than cosmopolitan. McDougall 1977: 44-45, 60. The nation had to compete with Chinese universal values as well: a number of prominent revolutionaries retreated to scriptures and to the monastery for reacquaintance with a "big me" far greater than any nation. These included two leaders of the Chinese Communist party: Li Dazhao, who flirted briefly with the Buddhist "Pure Land" sect in 1913, and Qu Qiubai in later years. See Meisner 1974: 14; Hsia 1968: 14-15, 23. Disillusioned government functionaries also turned to the traditional contemplative life: Hutchinson 1924.

72. See Chapter 5 below; Sun [31]: 67-68, 74-75.

73. Emphasis added. Liang [1922] 1979: 272. I have replaced the word "conscious" in the translation with the word "awaken" for the sake of consistency in the present study.

74. Kang 1958: 84. Hao Chang presents a brilliant exposition of Liang's understanding of the principle of Reason of State. H. Chang 1971: 255-59. See also Friedrich 1957.

75. Within seven years Chen and Li would overcome their differences and arrive at sufficient agreement to cofound the Chinese Communist party. Chen Duxiu [1914] 1969; Li Dazhao [1915] 1969.

76. Chen Duxiu [1914] 1969: 204-6.   77. Li Dazhao [1915] 1969: 208.

78. Sun [31]: 38.   79. Ibid.: 12.

80. Ibid.: 75.   81. Meisner 1974: 19.

82. Li Dazhao [1915] 1969: 207.

83. Meisner notes that Li's stress at this point "on the ability of conscious, active men to shape events" was a departure for Li, marking the source of an original and indigenous strain of Marxism that was to develop under his tutelage. Chen Duxiu's rather different emphasis on the limitations imposed by "objective" conditions also had its adherents among Chinese Marxists. Meisner 1974: 21-26.

84. Sun [31]: 75-76.

85. Dolezelova-Velingerova 1977; L. Lee 1973; M. Anderson 1990.

86. Ba Jin [1935] 1970: 71.

87. See, for example, Yu Dafu 1921; Bing Xin 1982: vol. 1.

88. M. Anderson 1990: 38-44.

89. L. Lee 1973: 263.

90. C. Cheng 1977: 81.

91. L. Lee 1973: 262-63; Dolezelova-Velingerova 1988. One novel told in the form of a collection of love letters is Guo Moruo 1926; a novel told in the form of a single letter is Jiang Guangci 1926; a novel told in the form of a diary is Mao Dun 1958a.

92. McDougall 1977: 44-45.

93. The novel in general traces "the movement of a solitary hero through a sociological landscape of a fixity that fuses the world inside the novel with the world outside. The picaresque *tour d'horizon*—hospitals, prisons, remote villages, monasteries, Indians, Negroes—is nonetheless not a *tour de monde*." B. Anderson 1991: 35.

94. Liang [1902] 1979. Sun described the movement as "a great movement in-

deed, unprecedented in intellectual circles in our time." He traced the achievements of the movement to "the exhortations of just one or two enlightened publishers." Sun [39]: 670–72.

95. This statement was subsequently elided from Mao's published works, apparently because it overstated the role of intellectuals. Schram 1989: 4.

96. Schram 1992: xxxi–xxxiii. Mao [9]: 208.

97. T. Chow 1960.

98. Patterson 1991.

99. L. Lee 1973: 273.

100. Jiang Guangci 1930; Dolezelova-Velingerova 1988: 98–99.

101. Dolezelova-Velingerova 1988: 132–33; Mao Dun 1958c. *The Canker*, a trilogy, was published serially in *Xiaoshuo yuebao* (Short story monthly), 18: 9–10; 19: 1–3, 6–9 (1927–28).

102. Mao Dun 1958b: 43. See Berninghausen 1977; Rickards 1990.

103. Mao Dun 1928. Rickards 1990: 37.

104. L. Lee 1973: 274.

105. Yu Dafu 1984b: 10.

106. Yu Dafu 1984a: 124. This horrific story is cited as evidence of Yu Dafu's faithfulness to the revolution in the comments on the back cover of this edition.

107. Pye 1968: 70.

108. In contrasting rationality to passion—rather than to irrationality—Pye assimilates rationality with a gradual and technocratic approach to national development (which can in fact be cruelly dispassionate), and irrationality with revolution. Pye 1968: Chap. 5.

109. M. Anderson 1990: 26.   110. See Chapter 1.

111. Schneider 1971: 86.   112. Ibid.: 108.

113. Ibid.: 7.   114. Ibid.: 8, 67–68, 183.

115. The phrase *chulu* (lit. "a way out") has a far greater currency in Chinese than any comparable phrase in English. I would speculate that this is linked to the similar currency of the term "awakening," which invariably anticipates an escape of some kind: an awakening that does not presage a "way out" is thus a nightmare. As Lu Xun remarked, "The most painful thing in life is to wake up from a dream and find no way out." Lu Xun [1923] 1980b: 87.

116. Liang [1922] 1979: 270. Qu Yuan (343–290 B.C.) was the preeminent ethical and literary figure of his age, remembered for his long prose poem, the "Li Sao," and for committing suicide rather than serve a court that had fallen into disrepute.

117. In Lu Xun's brief summary, "Nora originally lives contentedly in a 'happy home' but then awakens to the fact that she is simply a puppet of her husband and that her children are puppets of her own. So she leaves home—as the door is heard closing, the curtain falls." Lu Xun [1923] 1980b: 85.

118. I have profited from a number of excellent studies that trace the significance and reception of the play. See Schwarcz 1975: 3–6; Eide 1985: 193–222; Eide 1987; Brown 1993: 74–75. Brown notes that the title is more properly translated *A Doll House*.

119. Hu Shi 1918; M. Anderson 1990: 32.

Notes to Pages 100–106

120. Eide 1985: 216.

121. Ibid.: 203.

122. The group of intellectuals associated with *New Tide* (*Xin chao*) magazine, including Luo Jialun, Fu Sinian, and Gu Jiegang, dealt closely with this problem. Schneider 1971: 28.

123. Eide 1985: 199.

124. Grieder 1970.

125. Ding Ling's fate is traced sensitively and with appropriate irony in Spence 1982: 288–335.

126. Spence 1982: 327–35. Around this time—in May of 1942—Mao Zedong pronounced on the function of writers and artists in revolutionary war: "It is very good that since the outbreak of the War of Resistance Against Japan, more and more revolutionary writers and artists have been coming to Yenan and our other anti-Japanese base areas. But it does not necessarily follow that, having come to the base areas, they have already integrated themselves completely with the masses of the people here. The two must be completely integrated if we are to push ahead with our revolutionary work." Mao [19]: 70. McDougall 1980.

127. Lu Xun [1925] 1980: 263.

128. Lu Xun [1923] 1980b: 87. The same point was conveyed in Lu Xun's famous metaphor of China as a claustrophobic "iron house," in which the inhabitants should be allowed to die of suffocation in their sleep rather than awaken to discover that there is no way out. This suggests to me that his comments on Nora's awakening were not confined to women but extended to the awakening metaphor *as such*. See Lu Xun [1922] 1980: 37; L. Lee 1987.

129. Liang [1922] 1979.

Chapter 3

1. Lao She [1929] 1980: 35–36.

2. See Chapter 4 below.

3. Chatterjee 1986: 38. See also Said 1978.

4. On foreign economic interests in Republican China, see Feuerwerker 1968 and Hou 1965; on the foreign community, see Feuerwerker 1976; on Christianity and nationalism, see Lutz 1988 and Yip 1980.

5. Sun [31]: 33, 135–39.

6. Thomson 1969: 156–57; Dirlik 1975.

7. Interest in etiquette also has its origins in the emergence of bourgeois civil society. See Rowe 1993: 139–57.

8. Zhang Jingsheng, cited in L. Lee 1973: 270. Others advocated the total "Westernization" of Chinese literature. See Luo Jialun 1919; Schneider 1971: 154–60.

9. Sun [31]: 70.

10. The Unequal Treaties refer to nineteenth-century treaties and settlements forced upon the Chinese empire following successive defeats in war. See Morse 1910–18; Willoughby 1920; Fairbank 1953; Hsü 1990. For an authoritative Chinese view of the treaties, see Chien, Shao, and Hu 1964.

11. Spence 1988.

12. *The Oxford English Dictionary* (Oxford, 1893). Western studies of Chinese ethnography are largely confined to the folkloric movement of the 1920s and 1930s. See Hung 1985 and Schneider 1971. Informal commentary on the "characteristics" of the Chinese and other peoples, however, extended far more widely through literary and political discourse.

13. Barrow 1806: 4.

14. Liang 1900: 18.

15. Liang 1902. Translation adapted from Teng and Fairbank 1979: 222.

16. The contrast between Chinese self-flagellation and Japanese self-congratulation in their respective nationalist movements is worth noting in this regard. Generally speaking, Japanese nationalists were content to discard the less progressive aspects of their traditional culture as alien importations, inherited long ago from China, and to embrace modernity with a style, enthusiasm, and flair for adaptation that they believed unique to the culture of Japan. By the 1920s, the question for Japanese nationalism was not what was wrong with the Japanese but rather what it was about them that enabled them get everything so very right. This question was answered then (as now) by celebrating unique "characteristics" of the Japanese people. Nationalists who took exception to this judgment of Japan's achievement generally took exception to modernity itself. See Najita and Harootunian 1988: 712.

17. Maugham 1955: 94. De Francis 1950: 245. Reference to the Chinese as a "yellow" race or people (*huangzu, huangmin*) was commonplace in Chinese nationalist writing. Zhang Binglin, the "father of racial consciousness," employed the term, although he was less inclined than some of his contemporaries to deride the character of the Chinese people. See Shimada 1990: 37.

18. Edwardes 1971: 104.

19. Said 1978: 80–92.

20. P. Johnson 1991: 350– 51.

21. It was only toward the end of the classical period of "imperialism," early in the twentieth century, that social theorists such as J. A. Hobson thought to reduce imperialism to economic fundamentals. Hobson [1902] 1965; Lenin 1916.

22. W. Taylor 1835: 9.

23. Ibid.: 7.

24. Ibid.: 9. Taylor cited this commonplace aphorism in the conviction that the acquisition of knowledge was an integral part of all relationships of power, not least in the colonial mission in Asia. Contrast Foucault 1972; Said 1978.

25. W. Taylor 1835: 8.

26. Lao She [1929] 1980: 204. The novel *Ma and Son* was written over the course of Lao She's stay in London, beginning in 1924, and was completed around the time of his departure in June 1929.

27. Barrow 1839: 35. Anson's visit to Guangzhou was not quite as accidental as is generally assumed. It is true that his ship was in a bad way when he hove to on the China coast, but he was acting under explicit orders from the king.

28. Ibid.: 58.

29. Anson had laid waste the Spanish settlement of Paita. Ibid.: 55–61.

30. Clendinnen 1991: 65.

31. Edwardes 1971: 107.

32. Barrow 1839: 72.

33. Anson's memoirs were written by another hand. They first appeared under the name of "Mr Walter," the ship's chaplain, but were more probably the work of the ship's engineer, Mr. Robins. See John Barrow's "Preface," in Barrow 1839.

34. Rule 1988: 5.

35. Barrow 1839: 72.

36. This episode falls in the less widely circulated second volume of *The Life and Strange Adventures of Robinson Crusoe*. Zhang Longxi 1988: 122.

37. Cranmer-Byng [1902] 1962; Barrow 1806. On the Amherst mission, see Ellis 1817.

38. See, for example, de Quincey [1857] 1897: 345-67; for a general survey, see Dawson 1967.

39. De Quincey [1857] 1897: 350-53.

40. Rule 1988: 6.

41. Gilbert 1926: 13. Gilbert's jaundiced view of missionaries echoes earlier sentiments in Barrow 1806: 28-31.

42. Dukes 1885: 77-78 and Chap. 8 ("The Habits and Manners of John Chinaman").

43. Bird 1899: 12-13.

44. Edwardes 1971: 108.

45. Rodney Gilbert urged the foreign powers to intervene not only in the political life of China but in a biological program to correct the inherited flaws of the people. Gilbert 1926: 18-19.

46. *North China Herald*, 26 May 1923.

47. Chatterjee 1990: 623.

48. Liang 1900: 5.15; Liang 1903: 14.1-27; Liang 1901: 6.3.

49. Liang 1900: 5.15. Before the modern period, the term *zhongguo* designated neither the nation nor the territorial state but the place of the emperor at the center of the world. Its first appearance in the formal designation of state was in the attenuated form of *Zhonghua minguo* (Republic of China) in 1912, although it was frequently used to refer both to the state and to the nation in the Republic. Even then, however, the usage was not universal. Not far from the capital, in the 1930s, locals still referred to their country as The Great State (*Daguo*). See R. Johnstone 1934: 115.

50. Liang 1900: 5.14.

51. Liang 1900; 1953: 226-38. An abridged translation of "On China's Weakness" appears under the apposite title "What Is Wrong with the Chinese?" in D. Li 1978: 22-29.

52. Liang 1900: 5.18-23.

53. Wu Zhihui 1908: 312.

54. Liang 1900: 5.24-27. Liang contrasted European virtues with each of the Chinese vices listed here, but described the characteristics of the "European race" in more fulsome detail in Liang 1953.

55. Liang 1953: 234-35.

56. Liang ended this essay with an inspirational song composed in *English*, a token of his hope that China would survive despite the faults of its people. Ibid.: 237–38.

57. Lin Yutang 1939: 8. For further comments on Chinese "bandits," see Lin Yutang [1931] 1969b.

58. Conrad 1980: 46. See also C. P. FitzGerald's astute remarks on the curious phobias of the expatriate community of Shanghai: FitzGerald 1985: Chap. 3.

59. See below, this chapter.

60. Ye Xiaoqing 1992: 33–52.

61. Bickers and Wasserstrom 1995; Ye Xiaoqing 1992.

62. Teng and Fairbank 1979: 263. Sun [36]: 419–506. Sun repeated this claim in his lectures on the Three Principles of the People in 1924: "Our past oppression can be attributed to the ignorance of the masses, who 'live in a stupor and die dreaming.' " Sun [31]: 120.

63. Sun [31]: 113–14. The alternative was national extinction: "If we do not earnestly promote nationalism and weld together our four hundred millions into a strong nation we face tragedy." Ibid.: 12.

64. Dikötter 1992: 4, 122.

65. Zarrow 1990: 297.

66. Ch'ing 1972–73: 23.

67. Racial nationalists frequently lamented the absence of racial consciousness. Zou Rong, Zhang Binglin, Sun Yatsen, and many now-forgotten young nationalists worked consciously to create a new kind of racial consciousness through propaganda. This point is made forcefully in Gasster 1980: 497. Although he notes the celebrated case of Zou Rong (who "regretted the absence of a strong 'racial consciousness' [*zhongxing*] in China capable of uniting the people in their struggle against the oppressors"), Dikötter devalues this self-consciously constructed aspect of nationalist racial consciousness. Dikötter 1992: 114–15, 117.

68. Shimada 1990: 62.

69. Sun [31]: Lecture 1.

70. Chiang [1943] 1947: 13. Emphasis added.

71. Sun [20]: 131; Chiang [1943] 1947: 10. Two of Chiang's closest associates, the Chen brothers, implemented this vision in a language-reform program in the 1930s and 1940s. De Francis 1950: 83.

72. Dikötter 1992: 4.

73. Yu Dafu 1921; R. Chow 1991: 144.

74. Ye Xiaoqing 1992: 51; Li Weiqing [1907] 1989: 72.

75. Ba Jin [1931] 1980: 114–16. In "The Dog's Retort" (1927), Lu Xun draws a similar parable involving a beggar and a dog. See Lu Xun [1927] 1974. In fact, references to dogs were commonplace in fiction. See Fu Sinian [1919] 1967: 355–58; Yu Dafu 1921.

76. R. Chow 1991: 143–44.   77. Ba Jin [1931] 1980: 114–16.

78. Lao She [1929] 1980: 15.   79. Ibid.

80. Lu Xun advised in 1931 (responding to an earlier call from Xiang Peilang for New China activists to "show their teeth like wolves") that an awakened dog craves a master and invariably turns its fangs on others at its master's bidding: "We should

be careful, because wolves are the ancestors of dogs, and once tamed by men they become dogs themselves." Lu Xun [1931] 1980: 135.

81. Deng Zhongxia [1924] 1980: 93–96.

82. See Gu Jiagang's comments on the "natural genius," spontaneity, anonymity, freshness, and imagination of the villagers he discovered in his folkloric research. Schneider 1971: 164–67. Li Dazhao's exhortation to youth to return to their villages in 1919 conveys a similar sense of excitement. Li Dazhao [1919] 1959: 146–50.

83. See Liang 1953. Sun Yatsen compared his attempts to find a route to national development more than favorably with Columbus's attempts to find a route to the New World, on the understanding that China would profit from the errors of earlier Western pioneers. Sun [20]: 334; Schiffrin 1980: 198–99. The association between discovery and awakening in Amerigo Vespucci's "rediscovery of America" is discussed above, in Chapter 1.

84. Todorov 1984.   85. Seth 1992.

86. Nehru [1945] 1956: 51.   87. Cantlie and Jones n.d.: 19.

88. The first geographical survey of the empire on modern cartographic principles was undertaken over the decade from 1707 by a team of Jesuits and Chinese apprentices. Some of the resulting maps were not printed, and those that were printed were not widely circulated. The art of map-making was soon lost, and was not recovered for another century. Teng and Fairbank 1979: 16–17, 41–46.

89. Spence 1982: 43.

90. Sun [31]: 480. Sun Yatsen's "Railway Plan of China" (1921) embraced all of continental China with a spider's web of red lines that made little sense from the perspective of transport economics but lent greater geographical integrity to the old empire. See the illustration in Sun [20]: 127–360, following map 16. On the actual state of railway development on the eve of the Republican Revolution, see G. Anderson 1911. On the economic history of rail in China, see Heunemann 1984.

91. Teng and Fairbank 1979: 263. Scholars of popular folklore displayed a similar determination to employ local song and legend to tutor the people in their responsibilities as Chinese citizens. Schneider 1971: 143–48. See also Holm 1990.

92. See Pearl Buck's "Introduction" to Lin Yutang 1939: vii.

93. Lin Yutang wrote *My Country and My People* specifically to counter the "misunderstandings" fostered by Gilbert's *What's Wrong with China?* Some foreigners, such as Robert Hart and Bertrand Russell, showed due sympathy, he noted, but "for one Sir Robert Hart there are ten thousand Rodney Gilberts, and for one Bertrand Russell there are ten thousand H. G. W. Woodheads. The result is a constant, unintelligent elaboration of the Chinaman as a stage fiction, which is as childish as it is untrue and with which the West is so familiar." Lin Yutang 1939: 11. Lin appears to have had in mind two books published successively in 1925 and 1926, H. G. W. Woodhead's *The Truth About the Chinese Republic* and Rodney Gilbert's *What's Wrong with China?* See Woodhead 1925; Gilbert 1926; also Mackerras 1989: 72.

94. Smith 1894; Doolittle [1865] 1966. Neither book, to my knowledge, was available in translation over the period under study, although the existence of the books was well known. See Lu Xun [1936] 1980: 302. Among Chinese newspapers, the *Beiyang Pictorial (Beiyang huabao)* ran a column entitled "Customs of Beijing" (*Beijing*

fengsu) in 1926. The text and pictures were published separately in book form. See *Beijing fengsu tu* 1986.

95. Hu Pu'an [1922] 1990. Hu Pu'an is listed among the editors of the Nationalist newspaper *Shanghai minguo ribao* in Huang Jilu 1969-, 7: 101-2.

96. Zhang Shizhang [1922] 1990: 1-2.

97. Hu Pu'an, Postcript to Hu Pu'an [1922] 1990: new pagination 1.

98. Edwardes 1971: 110; H. Ch'ien 1944: Chap. 5.

99. Li's chief literary influences were Chinese. See Hu Shi 1934: 121-27; Ropp 1981: 150; Eberhard 1964: 118-19.

100. Zeng Pu 1905.

101. Lao She [1929] 1980: Preface.

102. Shirley Hazzard makes a comparable point when contrasting her heroine's responses to the landscapes of Australia and Europe. Hazzard 1980.

103. Shen Congwen [1928] 1982. See also H. Ch'ien 1944: xv; Kinkley 1987. Shen Congwen's *Alice* inspired Chinese imitators in its turn, including Zhang Tianyi's *Guitu riji* (Ghostland diary) of 1931. See Dolezelova-Velingerova 1988: 218-20.

104. De Quincey [1857] 1897: 357.

105. Samuel Johnson began: "In former times the pen, like the sword, was considered as consigned by nature to the hands of men; the ladies contented themselves with private virtues and domestic excellence, and a female writer, like a female warrior, was considered as a kind of excentric [*sic*]." S. Johnson 1969: 283-84. See also Turner 1992.

106. P. Johnson 1991: 538.

107. Andolsen 1988: 31. Lucy Vaughan brought this reference to my attention.

108. Barrow 1806: 138

109. Denby 1906, 1: 163.

110. Gilbert 1926: 179.

111. Chatterjee 1990: 623. See also Chatterjee 1993: 116-34.

112. Gender roles are reversed in Li Ruzhen's clever parody of contempory mores, *Jinghuayuan* (Flowers in the mirror; 1825), which offers a highly sympathetic perspective on the injustices endured by women in "civilized" society. Li Ruzhen 1965.

113. Liang 1897: 37-44.

114. Even among anarchists, the feminist argument ultimately rested "not on justice or on self-evident rights, but on China's need to liberate her women in order to save the nation." Zarrow 1990: 151. See also Ono 1989; Witke 1967: 128-47.

115. Liang 1900: 18.

116. Gilbert 1926: 117.

117. Ibid.: 170.

118. Schneider 1971: 165-68. Gu also tried to revive the suppressed philosophical traditions of Mozi and Zou Yan, which he held to be models of egalitarian political philosophy suited to the modern age, in contrast to the hierarchical ethics of orthodox Confucianism. Ibid.: 15.

119. Ibid.: 143-48. Only a thin line of optimism separated nationalism from colonial racism. When his own optimism faltered, Gu's admiration for barbarian vitality and his positive judgments on the historical role of foreigners as resuscitators of a

moribund Chinese culture led him to concede that China should welcome barbarian salvation once again in the twentieth century—precisely Gilbert's point. Ibid.: 14.

120. Keyte 1925: 282.
121. Gilbert 1926: 170, 105.
122. Li Dazhao [1919] 1959: 149–50.
123. Tian Nong 1923; Qing Song 1923. See Hung 1985: 12, 187.
124. Mao [14]: 28–37.
125. Pearl Buck, "Introduction," in Lin Yutang 1939: x.
126. Shen Congwen [1928] 1982: 208.
127. Luo Qiyuan 1926b: 21–28. See Chapters 7 and 8 below.
128. Mao [12]: 289.
129. Pearl Buck, "Introduction," in Lin Yutang 1939: x.
130. Lin Yutang 1939: 8.
131. For a comprehensive survey of bandits in twentieth-century China, see Billingsley 1988.
132. Gilbert unwittingly endorsed many aspects of Liang's diagnosis of the faults of the Chinese, including docility, blind obedience, fear of humiliation, timidity, and an incapacity to sire heroes. Gilbert 1926: 27, 63, 155, 158–59. Liang's comments to this effect are noted above.

133. Gilbert 1926: 45.   134. Ibid.: 18–19.
135. Liang 1953.   136. Gilbert 1926: 169.

137. Lin included bandits within the orbit of "my country and my people" and went on to extend Gilbert's favorable judgment of bandits to all Chinese, noting that apparent indifference to public affairs was no more than a mask of self-defense, disguising a universal chivalry and public spirit among the people of China generally. Lin Yutang 1939: 47.

138. North China Herald, 26 May 1923.
139. Weekly Review, 6 January 1923.   140. Gilbert 1926: 281.
141. Powell 1945: 92–93.   142. Gilbert 1926: 170.
143. North China Herald, 26 May 1923. The Daily News response is cited in this source.
144. Weekly Review, 12 May 1923.
145. Weekly Review, 19 May 1923.
146. Cited in Weekly Review, 19 May 1923.
147. North China Herald, 19 May 1923.
148. Cited in North China Herald, 26 May 1923. In the time-honored tradition of bandit legend, Cao Kun offered a pardon and amnesty to the bandits in return for the captives, and then executed their leaders once the captives had been returned to safety.
149. Gilbert 1926: 284–87.
150. Ibid.: 289.
151. Rigby 1980; Clifford 1979. See also below, Chapters 6 and 8.
152. Gilbert 1926: 18. Gilbert's apocalyptic vision recalls de Quincey's prediction of 1857 regarding the "fierce necessity of conflict, past and yet to come, through which we British, standing alone—but henceforth, we may hope, energetically supported by the United States, if not by France—have, on behalf of the whole West-

ern Nations, victoriously resisted the arrogant pretensions of the East." De Quincey [1857] 1897: 359.

153. This lesson was not lost on the Japanese Imperial Army, which regularly paraded Western captives before assembled crowds of jeering Chinese in its attempts to present itself as a force for national liberation in occupied China in the early 1940s. Those on parade recognized that their humiliation signaled the end of "the era of Western dominance in Asia." Langdon Gilkey recalled of his forced march to Beijing Railway Station in February 1943: "We knew that the Japanese intended that these marches, which took place throughout the cities and ports of China, be the symbol of the final destruction of Western prestige in the Orient. For that reason, we tried our best to walk erect and to present a dignified mien. But that is hard enough for a young man carrying four or five heavy bags. It was hopeless for the elderly. . . . It is plain that the Japanese had guessed correctly: the era of Western dominance in Asia ended with that burdened crawl to the station." Gilkey 1966: 4.

154. See Chapter 8.

155. Lu Xun [1936] 1980: 302. Emphasis added.

156. The Paramount film *Shanghai Express* hastened conflation of the terms "bandit" and "revolutionary" in Western accounts of contemporary China, starting with the Nationalist Revolution and ending with Communist victory two decades later. The next great revolutionary movement to engulf China inspired a sequel (at the height of the McCarthy era) that was released in 1952. *Peking Express* was directed by William Dieterle and starred William Cotton and Corinne Calvert. In this version, the bandits make the transition to Communist thugs. Leyda 1972: 82; Sadoul 1972: 337–38. I should like to thank Antonia Finnane for this reference.

157. Lu Xun [1936] 1980: 297–302.

158. M. Anderson 1990: 53; 59–60.

Chapter 4

1. Sun [31]: 186.

2. Magruder 1921; L. Chen 1988: 8.J3A. I wish to thank Leslie Chen for making this source available.

3. Magruder 1921.	4. Tuchman 1970: 251.
5. Magruder 1921.	6. Cantlie and Jones n.d.: Chap. 2.
7. Ibid.: Foreword.	8. Ibid.: 69, 64.
9. Chang and Gordon 1991: 148.	10. Li Ao 1987: 185.

11. In recent years, dissident writers on Taiwan have begun to reassess Chen Jiongming's role in the revolution. See Li Ao 1987. Chen Jiongming's son, Chen Dingyan (Leslie Chen), has dutifully combed the press and archives for neglected materials on his father's role in the revolutionary movement, and has undertaken personal research in an effort to restore balance to evaluations of his father. See L. Chen 1991

12. Cai 1922e: 78.

13. Sun's personal integrity is often cited in support of his political authority. See, for example, Chang and Gordon 1991: 148.

14. See Abend 1944.

15. Sun [31]: 185–86.
16. Sun [35]: 411.
17. L. Chen 1991: 21–37.
18. *Huazi ribao*, 2 August 1921. Myers 1921; L. Chen 1988: 8.J201. Governor Chen had appointed only 68 county heads on schedule in November, and the outcomes were contested by law in around one-third of the counties. *Huazi ribao*, 11 November 1921.
19. Swatow 1921; L. Chen 1988: 8.J9.
20. *Huazi ribao*, 24 December 1921; L. Chen 1988: 8.J202.
21. *Hong Kong Times*, 17 November 1921; L. Chen 1988: 8.J9.
22. Swatow 1921.
23. Hsieh 1962: 209.
24. *Huazi ribao*, 28, 30, and 31 July 1921; L. Chen 1988: 8.J5B.
25. *SMR*, 22 January 1922. Tochigi 1974: 68.
26. Hsieh 1962: 217. Here Winston Hsieh refers to the election of district magistrates.
27. Sun allegedly told Chen that he would not interfere with Guangdong provincial affairs if the Northern Expedition proved successful. By Sun's own account, Chen Jiongming was not persuaded. Sun [31]: 185–86.
28. Luk 1990: 82–83.
29. Chen Duxiu 1922: 2.
30. Cai Hesen 1922d: 15.
31. Chen Duxiu 1922: 2.
32. Cai Hesen 1922d: 14.
33. Rorty 1989: 12–13.
34. De Francis 1950: 83. Chen Lifu took his brother Guofu at his word, and as minister of culture in 1942 ordered compulsory instruction in the Chinese script beyond the confines of the Han community to all minority nationalities in the border regions.
35. On this model, intellectuals were to mediate between local communities and the nation: "Items of nation-wide interest can be translated and given wide distribution by intellectuals. . . . This will aid the unity of China." Declaration of the Shanghai Society to Study the Latinization of Chinese Writing (1935), cited in de Francis 1950: 118–19.
36. De Francis 1950: 251.
37. Kang 1958: 97–99.
38. Liang n.d.: 46–48.
39. De Francis 1950: 238–39.
40. Sun [31]: 89.
41. Fishman 1972: 66–72.
42. Western-style punctuation was first used in New Culture magazines in the fourth volume of *New Youth* in 1918, and was adopted by the Nationalist publications *Reconstruction* and *Weekly Commentary* in the following year. Lü Fangshang 1989: 63. Dai Jitao claimed that he was following Sun Yatsen's advice in presenting his motion on punctuation; it was certainly approved in Sun's presence. *ZGZK*, 11 May 1924: 5. Dai finally put his system of punctuation into effect when he was appointed director of the Examination Yuan in 1929. Chen Tianxi 1971: 100–101.
43. Benedict Anderson proposes that the state is experienced by its functionaries through a common language of state. B. Anderson 1991: 105.
44. De Francis 1950: 225, 231. The rather loose use of the term "official" to embrace the state and public spheres reflected a common slippage in discussion of civil

society and the state in the late Qing and early Republican periods. See Rowe 1990: 316–17; 1993: 139–57.

45. Fitzgerald 1990a.

46. Kuhn 1970; Lamley 1977: 1–39. *Late Imperial China* devotes a special issue to the question of ethnicity in early modern China: *Late Imperial China* 11, 1 (June 1990).

47. *Huazi ribao*, 2 December 1920; L. Chen 1988: 8.J6.

48. Kong 1933: 1.

49. Here Dong was following the lead of an earlier scholar, Yang Ziyun. Dong 1943: 1.

50. See Min 1989.

51. Foster 1928: 80.

52. Chen Duxiu 1923f: 162; Qu Qiubai 1923: 170–71. See also Luk 1990: 148.

53. Min 1989.   54. Li Dazhao [1923] 1978: 416–17.

55. Chen Duxiu 1922: 2.   56. Cai Hesen 1922d: 14.

57. Chen Duxiu 1922: 2.

58. Ou Qujia presented the most radical proposals for provincial autonomy in the late empire, yet declined to mount a case for Guangdong nationalism. He promoted the ideals of self-government, self-management of resources, and "independence" for Guangdong on the understanding that "the people of Guangdong are truly the masters of Guangdong" and that China as a whole stood to profit from greater competition among relatively independent provinces. Duara 1990: 4.

59. Ibid.: 7–9.

60. Yiping 1924: 7; Liu Renjing 1924: 3–5

61. Liu Zhih-po 1921; L. Chen 1988: 8.J203.

62. L. Chen 1991: 21–37.

63. Sun [31]: 202–4, 214. The weakness of the Nationalist state on the mainland should not be mistaken for weak aspirations. See Eastman 1974: 43; Amsden 1985: 85–86.

64. Chen Dingyan 1990.

65. The confederal model of self-government was termed *liansheng zizhi*; federal "state union" was termed *lianbang*. Duara 1990: 5–8. Duara notes that Zhang Binglin first devised the term *liansheng zizhi* in August 1920.

66. Li Dajia 1986: 145; Duara 1990: 11.

67. Tochigi 1978: 95–116.

68. So, for example, Kang's 1884 memorial to the emperor anticipating locally elected parliaments was presented to court under the heading "reforms to local administration." Min 1989: 114.

69. Min 1989: 126.

70. Kang 1967: 79–80, 85.

71. Fincher 1968: 201–2, 220, 224. Others have taken exception to the linear conception of a "transition" to nationalism, arguing in favor of the fluidity (and fixity) of provincial and national loyalties. I do not believe that Fincher's use of the term "transition" either entails or implies the abandonment of one set of loyalties for another. To the extent that there is a hierarchical relationship among loyalties, it might best

be described as a hierarchical relationship among urban places, or more particularly among elites situated at different positions in the spatial geography of early twentieth-century China. See Schoppa 1982; Rankin 1986.

72. "Zhongguo guomindang diyici quanguo daibiao dahui xuanyan" [1924] 1930; Li Chien-nung 1956: 452.

73. *Zhonguo guomindang diyi, er ci quanguo daibiao dahui huiyi shiliao* 1986, 1: 88, 443. I quote from the original Chinese document in this case because the translation in Li Chien-nung's book fails to make the distinction sufficiently clearly. See Li Chien-nung 1956: 450–58. In fact, there were several competing texts of the First Congress declaration. See Hazama 1992.

74. Similarly, "spontaneous" peasant agitation was directed against state agencies and functionaries outside the revolutionary base area. Bianco 1986. See also McDonald 1978. On the state orientation of the Nationalist peasant movement in Guangdong, see Fitzgerald 1990b.

75. Duara 1990: 7.

76. The two institutions were the *Guangdong difang xingzheng renyuan jiangxi suo* and the *Zizhi renyuan yanchengsuo*. *Minguo shiqi guangdong sheng zhengfu dangan shiliao xuanbian* 1987, 1: 77, 135, 139–40. The Self-Government Institute was possibly a creation of the self-government preparatory committee established by the Political Council on 9 September 1924. Luo Jialun and Huang Jilu 1969, 2: 1131–32.

77. Luk 1990: 71. At the close of the revolution, the Communists abandoned use of the term "Nationalist Revolution" in favor of "Great Revolution" (*dageming*), severing the connection between the Nationalist Revolution and the Nationalist party implied by the former. The first history of the period employing this new term is Hua Gang [1931] 1982. Only in recent years have mainland historians returned to employing the term "Nationalist Revolution." See Li Xin 1991. I wish to thank Professor Xu Youwei for bringing this recent historiographical development to my attention.

78. "Zhongguo gongchandang dierci quanguo dahui xuanyan" 1922: 41.

79. Chen Duxiu 1924b: 3–4.

80. "Guangdong zhibu tanhe gongchandang wen" 1923: 917; Huang Jilu 1964a: 16; 1964b.

81. Leong 1976.

82. Luk 1990: 71–72.

83. Mast 1970; Mast and Saywell 1974; Sansom 1988.

84. Ungar 1989: 94–106.

85. "Guangdong zhibu tanhe gongchandang wen" 1923: 916–19. The impeachment followed a party meeting attended by 53 representatives of party branches abroad.

86. Huang Jilu 1964a: 10–14; 1964b.

87. Sun [5]: 539; Sun [16]: 624.

88. From 1920 to early 1923, party membership grew from around 100,000 to 238,000 members. Most were recruited abroad. In 1924 the party attracted fewer than 5,000 new members abroad, and 6,000 of 15,000 current members failed to reregister at the U.S. party headquarters in San Francisco. Remittances to the party from overseas Chinese communities fell over the same period: U.S. branches remitted

US$800,000 over the last six months of 1922, but only a few hundred dollars in 1924 and 1925. See *ZGZK* 9 (24 February 1924): 6; 12 (16 March 1924): 7; and 23 (1 June 1924): 7. *ZZZB* 6–7 (10 April 1926): 81.

89. Sun wrote a major work on the subject in English—*The International Development of China*—which he dispatched around the world in the hope of garnering international support. Sun [20]: 127–360; [21]: 419–666. The book's lukewarm reception is noted in Schiffrin 1980: 199–201.

90. Sun's long-established opposition to "antiforeignism" was upheld again in 1924, in the face of revisionist Communist historiography that cast the Boxer Uprising in a favorable light. *ZGZK* 32 (3 August 1924): 7; Cai Hesen 1924c. See also Mast 1970: 235–42.

91. Sun [44]: 526.

92. Wilbur 1976: 133–48; F. Chan 1979.

93. Stremski 1979: 17. In 1921 *The New York Times* made a similar claim on Sun's behalf in negotiations leading to the convening of the Washington Conference, arguing that Sun's government had a higher claim to de iure status than did the Beijing government. Schiffrin 1980: 217.

94. Stremski 1979: 15–16.

95. Zou Lu 1929, 1: 331–41. On Borodin's role, see "Guangdong zhibu tanhe gongchandang wen" 1923: 916–19.

96. As late as 1923, the Communists "continued to regard the division of political power and regional rule as the chief criteria of a feudal system." Luk 1990: 144–49.

97. "Theses on the Colonial Question" 1971: 138–44; "Theses on the Agrarian Question" 1971: 155–61.

98. "Directives on the Application of the 1920 Agrarian Theses" [1920] 1971: 394–98.

99. "Theses on the Eastern Question" 1971: 382–93.

100. Luk 1990: 147.

101. Brandt, Schwartz, and Fairbank 1952: 54–63.

102. D. Li 1978: 198–200; Degras 1971, 2: 25–26.

103. Li Chien-nung 1956: 454.

104. Ye Chucang 1920.

105. Li Hanwei 1922. Comparable complaints were directed against the student movement: "Tongxin" 1922.

106. Ye focused on "massification" and "partification" as the most significant developments in the recent history of the party. Ye Chucang 1923.

107. *Minxin rikan*, 23 January 1923. *The People's Trust*, a party journal, was edited by Zhao Pixie and published daily from February 1920 to January 1923. For discussion of "corporatist" strategies in the Nationalist Revolution, see Fewsmith 1985.

108. The modern Chinese concept of citizenship embraced an ideal of harmony of interests between state and people that sat uneasily with the idea of political mobilization for particular individual or sectional interests that were not identical to those of the state. Nathan 1985.

109. Sun [23]: 638–39.

110. The foremost Nationalist theorist Dai Jitao believed that Sun Yatsen's Three

376 Notes to Pages 175–84

Principles were challenged by the emergence of sectoral opposition to the revolution and urged social classes to "discard their class character and take on a national character." Dai Jitao 1925b: 37.

111. Sun [5]: 537–43; [17]: 598; [44]: 524–31; [46]: 558–67.

112. Sun [8]: 575; [17]: 598; [31]: 3–27.

113. Sun [15]: 719–23; [17]: 602; [26]: 713–18; [48]: 679–85. Li Chien-nung 1956: 453; Chiang [1943] 1947: 114.

114. Fewsmith 1985: 183–95; T. Wright 1989: 135. Sun [15]: 719–23; [17]: 602.

115. Meisner 1974: Chap. 10.   116. Chen Duxiu 1923d.

117. Yun Daiying 1924.   118. Li Chien-nung 1956: 454.

119. Luk 1990: 149.   120. Wilbur 1976: Chap. 7.

121. Tan Pingshan and Feng Jupo 1923; Chen Duxiu 1923c.

122. Yiping 1924; Liu Renjing 1924.

123. Peng Pai 1924.

124. Ruan Xiaoxian 1926.

125. "Qiaogang Qiongyai gongmin weichihui" 1924.

126. Huang Ao 1926; Miao Xiangchu 1926; Luo Yangqing 1926.

127. Sun [46]: 559.

128. Lin Yizhong 1926.

Chapter 5

1. Cited in Schorske 1980: 165. Herzl liked designing flags for a nonexistent nation, "for with a flag one can do anything, even lead the people into the promised land." Cited in Mosse 1973: 49.

2. Sun [31]: 277.

3. *North China Herald*, 3 and 10 January 1925.

4. Cantlie and Jones n.d.: 170.

5. *Zhongguo jinbainian lishi tuji* 1976: 193.

6. Qin Xiaoyi 1978, 1: 288. Hsüeh 1961.

7. *Zhongguo jinbainian lishi tuji* 1976: 193; Qin Xiaoyi 1978, 1: 364.

8. Galbiati 1985: 41.

9. See, for example, the curious combination of two *national* flags at a Shanghai Nationalist party function in 1921. Qin Xiaoyi 1978, 1: 363.

10. Sun [32]: 155–56.

11. Qin Xiaoyi 1978, 1: 232–33, 259, 288, 311–15, 346, 351, 355; *Zhongguo jinbainian lishi tuji* 1976: 237, 240.

12. Qin Xiaoyi 1978, 1: 362.   13. *GMWX* 1973, 51: 327–29.

14. Kataoka 1984.   15. Sun [1]: 165–66.

16. Sun [34]: 461.

17. Sun [32]: 155. Contrast Li Dazhao's favorable assessment of the Republican flag in 1923 made on the very ground that irritated Sun Yatsen: the assertion of "unity in difference" among the peoples of China. Li Dazhao [1923] 1978: 407–27.

18. *North China Herald*, 28 February 1925.

19. *North China Herald*, 21 March 1925.

20. An English translation of the "Song of the Republic" appears in Cantlie and Jones n.d.: 167.

21. Sun [44]: 527.

22. The first person in poetry circles to pay attention to this omission was Huang Gongdu, who composed 24 martial songs to "unite the hearts of soldiers" (*tuanjie junxin*), and a further 19 songs for schoolchildren—"all full of nationalist (*minzu*) spirit but not suited for general dissemination." Chen Jingwen 1961: 18–19.

23. Sun [44]: 533.

24. *ZGHS* 1986, 1: 42.

25. Translation based on the standard English version by Tu Ting-hsiu. Significantly, the word "party" (*dang*) is elided from the standard translation, which reads "San Min Chu Yi, Our Aim Shall Be." Qin Xiaoyi 1978: 1. Both the flag and the anthem remain to this day national symbols of the Republic of China on Taiwan.

26. The insignia of the Chinese Revolutionary party was a Blue Sky and White Sun party flag on one side, crossing a national flag bearing the Blue Sky and White Sun on its canon. Qin Xiaoyi 1978, 1: 301.

27. Shao Yuanchong 1973–: 99.   28. Sun [4]: 509–11.

29. Nathan 1976.   30. Sun [17]: 593–604.

31. The word *zhi* can mean both "to govern" and "to prepare or to make," but the old expression *zhi guo you chang* referred to the constancy of rules for *governing* a state. Sun's use of the term *jian* ("to build/construct") made his meaning unmistakable.

32. *ZGHS* 1986, 1: 5.   33. Tochigi 1974: 67–68.

34. *ZGHS* 1986, 1: 15.   35. Ibid.: 15–18.

36. Ibid.: 6–7. See also Huang Jilu 1964a, 1964b.

37. *ZGHS* 1986, 1: 6–7. Tochigi 1974: 67; Nozawa 1971.

38. *ZGHS* 1986, 1: 58–60.

39. *Minguo renwu da cidian* 1991: 1308.

40. Minutes of the 18th session of the Central Executive Committee (31 March 1924). *ZGZK*, 18 (27 April 1924): 4.

41. The Nationalist peasant association flag was adopted late in 1925 or early 1926. See pictorial cover of *Zhongguo nongmin* 2 (1 February 1926).

42. Mao [20]: 13.

43. Dai Jitao [1925] 1959a: 980; Chen Tianxi 1958: 28; "Ben dangbu dangwu baogao" 1924: 6–7.

44. Sun [39]: 669–73.

45. Cited in Hsia 1968: 15–16.

46. Schneider 1971: 26; T. Chow 1960: 49. Hung 1985.

47. Boorman and Howard 1967–71, 1: 477–78.

48. Wu Tingfang 1920.   49. "Benzhi qishi yi" 1920.

50. Lin Sen 1920.   51. Wu Jinglian and Chu Fucheng 1920.

52. Zhang Qiubai 1920: 78–98.

53. Wu Jinglian and Chu Fucheng 1920.

54. "Xingqi pinglun kan xing zhongzhi de xuanyan" 1920; Lü 1989: 59.

55. Shu Sheng 1920.

56. Zhong Jiu 1920: 1.

57. Sun [37]: 401-2.

58. Sun [39]: 669-73. The press was known in English-language documents of the time as "Intelligence Press," but in Chinese as *Minzhi shuju* (Popular wisdom press). My estimate of the U.S. proportion of remittances is based on figures for the six months from July 1922 when all funds were channeled through the Shanghai party office. Before and after this period Sun was resident in Guangzhou and party finances were divided between the cities (listed in *yuan* and calculated at US$100 = Y180): U.S. — Y405,000; Canada — Y78,000; Australia and New Zealand — Y40,000; Philippines — Y38,000; Hawaii — Y17,000; South Africa — Y11,000; and others — Y81,000. "Zhongguo guomindang benbu caizhengbu tongbao" 1923. The press came into its own only after 1928, when the resources of the Nationalist state were added to those of the party.

59. Sun [3]: 399-400.

60. The 1919 party reforms generally ignored organization and propaganda *within* China except to the degree required for coordinating overseas party work. Zou Lu 1929, 1: 287-98.

61. G. Yu 1966: 56; Hsüeh 1961: 52-54; Friedman 1974: Chap. 4.

62. Both documents appear in Zou Lu 1929, 1: 298-302. Of the six party members listed as proposing motions in the minutes, four were parliamentarians: Tian Tong, Lu Zhiyi (*zi* Tianmin), Tan Zhen, and Ju Zheng. "Shiyiyue jiuri wuhou sanshi benbu kaihui jishi" 1921: 22-23.

63. Emphasis added. Zou Lu 1929, 1: 299-300. In 1918, Sun had effectively conceded that recruits could join his party without swearing the oath of personal loyalty: Sun [40]: 557-58.

64. Clauses 4 to 14 of the Constitution of the Chinese Revolutionary Party, in Zou Lu 1929, 1: 161-62.

65. The Revolutionary Alliance proposed a three-stage revolutionary program of military government, government by treaty (*yuefa*, limited to six years), and constitutional government. Zou Lu 1929, 1: 53-5; G. Yu 1966: 116.

66. Ju Zheng 1973-b: 84-86.

67. Sun [45]: 398-99.

68. "Shiyiyue jiuri wuhou sanshi benbu kaihui jishi" 1921: 22. George Yu suggests Sun disguised his three-stage proposal in the form of two stages. G. Yu 1966: 156. See also Tochigi 1974; Nozawa 1971, 1974.

69. Zou Lu 1929, 1: 300-302.

70. Sun [43]: 394-98. Sun had not yet developed his thesis that the state itself had to be founded on a party and hence, in his case, on an individual.

71. Emphasis added. Zou Lu 1929, 1: 299-300.

72. Sun [35]: 403.

73. Luo Jialun and Huang Jilu 1969, 2: 817-18.

74. Sun [35]: 411.

75. Staff numbers in other divisions were: General Affairs, 17; Party Affairs, 26; Financial Affairs, 3. "Zhongguo guomindang benbu teshe banshichu zhiyuan biao" 1922.

76. Huang Jilu 1969–, 12: 492–96.

77. "Liu hu guohui yiyuan Lin Sen deng zhu feichang guohui yanqi gaizu dian" [1918] 1973–: 91.

78. Zhang Ji 1951b: 243.

79. Sun [35]: 411.

80. Luo Jialun and Huang Jilu 1969, 2: 838, 849; Clubb 1978: 104.

81. Luo Jialun and Huang Jilu 1969, 2: 858; Sun [25]: 961–64.

82. Huang Jilu 1969–, 1: 264.   83. Sun [7]: 451–55.

84. Sun [25]: 963–64.   85. Sun [24]: 477–506.

86. Sun [38]: 850.

87. As early as 28 September, Zhangi Ji signed a document in his capacity as head of the Party Center's propaganda bureau in Shanghai: "Ren Chen Dongping wei yangguang zhibu buzhang zhuang" 1921. Yet Guangdong records indicate that he left Guangdong in October. "Zhongguo guomindang benbu teshe banshichu zhiyuan biao" 1922.

88. Luo Jialun and Huang Jilu 1969, 2: 839.

89. "Zhongguo guomindang gesheng zhiyuan biao xiuzheng gao" 1922; "Zhongguo guomindang benbu teshe banshichu zhiyuan biao" 1922.

90. Parliamentarians on the committee included Chen Baixu, Ding Weifen, Fang Qian, Guan Peng, Hang Xinzhai, He Leshan, Li Xieyang, Ling Yi, Liu Rongtang, Mao Zuquan, Peng Jieshi, Tan Zhen, Wan Hongtu, Wang Leping, and Zhang Ji: "Xuanchuan bu gongwen digao" 1922–23. Xu Ruilin and Huang Zhanyun were administrators: "Minguo liu zhi qi nian dayuanshuai fu jianren renyuan zhiwu xingming lu" [1918] 1973: 286.

91. Chen Baixu, Guan Peng, Hang Xinzhai, Mao Zuquan, Tan Zhen, Wang Leping, and Zhang Ji could claim experience as journalists; Wan Hongtu had worked in the propaganda division of the Special Office. Ye Chucang, Shao Lizi, and Sun Jingya were drawn from the party's *Shanghai Republican Daily*. "Xuanchuan bu gongwen digao" 1922–23.

92. T. Chow 1963: 125–26; Huang Jilu 1969–, 4: 14; 7: 250–53; 9: 278–81; Sun [30]: 827.

93. Huang Jilu 1969–, 7: 250–53.

94. Li Chien-nung 1956: 409–21. Sun came out in support of the Constitution Protection movement in 1916: Sun [19]: 359–60.

95. Li Chien-nung 1956: 421.

96. Nathan 1976: 178–81.

97. Luo Jialun and Huang Jilu 1969, 2: 877.

98. Ju Zheng 1973–a: 32–35. National parliamentarians included Chen Baixu, Ding Weifen, Fang Qian, Hang Xinzhai, Huang Fusheng, Jiao Yitang, Li Xilian, Liu Rongtang, Liu Jixue, Lu Zhiyi, Ma Junwu, Mao Zuquan, Song Yuanyuan, Sun Hongyi, Tan Zhen, Tian Tong, Wang Faqin, Wang Leping, Wang Yongbin, Xie Chi, Yang Shukan, Zhang Fengjiu, Zhang Ji, Zhang Qiubai, and Zhou Zhenlin. Huang Zhanyun had served on Zhang Ji's constitutionally oriented propaganda committee in 1922. Wang Boqun had served on the Constitutional Council (*yuefa huiyi*) prior to the establishment of the Constitution-Protection Parliament in Guangzhou in 1917,

whereupon he followed Sun to Guangdong; Guan Peng was a member of the Anhui Provincial Assembly. "Xuanchuan bu gongwen digao" 1922–23; Huang Jilu 1969, 3: 11–13; 7: 250–53.

99. Parliamentarians from the 1922 reorganization conference who joined the Western Hills faction in 1925 and 1926 included Guan Peng, Huang Fusheng, Liu Jixue, Mao Zuquan, Tan Zhen, Tian Tong, Xie Chi, and Zhang Ji. Li Yunhan 1966, 1: 448–49.

100. Zou Lu 1976: 121–27; Ju Zheng 1973-a: 32; Nathan 1976: 182–86.

101. Cai Hesen 1922c: 4–6; Zhang Ji 1951a: 49.

102. Wang Jianmin 1965, 1: 60–61.

103. Zhang Guotao 1971: 234–35; Nathan 1976: 178–95; Zou Lu 1976, 1: 129, 194; Cai Hesen 1922b: 4–5.

104. Meisner 1974: 220; Zhang Guotao 1971: 250, 283; Wang Jingwei 1926b: 12.

105. It was Sun Yatsen's responsibility to appoint cadres. Zou Lu 1929, 1: 309–11.

106. Parliamentarians included Hang Xinzhai, Huang Fusheng, Ju Zheng, Liu Jixue, Lu Zhiyi, Sun Hongyi, Tan Zhen, Tian Tong, Wang Yongbin, Xie Chi, Yang Shukan, Zhan Dabei, Zhang Ji, and Zhou Zhenlin. "Zhongguo guomindang benbu xian ren zhiyuan yilan biao" 1923: 8–9.

107. Mao Zuquan, a representative from Jiangsu Province on the National Assembly, was appointed deputy head of Party Center's propaganda bureau on 26 January 1923. *Zhongguo guomindang benbu gongbao* 3 (30 January 1923): 51.

108. There were theoretically 31 members of the council (21 advisers, 5 bureau heads, and 5 committee heads). In fact, few of the proposed committees were set up. If the five "committee heads" either failed to take their seats or were appointed from among current councillors, then parliamentarians formed a majority. Zou Lu 1929, 1: 310–11.

109. *SMR*, 11, 18, 20 November 1923.

110. Luo Jialun and Huang Jilu 1969, 2: 931. The Beijing liaison office published a book on Sun's Three Principles entitled *Sun Zhongshan xiansheng sanmin zhuyi yanshuo* (Speeches by Sun Yatsen on the Three Principles of the People).

111. Li Jui [1957] 1977: 270.   112. Chun Mu 1923a: 2–3.

113. See Chapter 6.   114. Zhang Guotao 1971: 235–36.

115. Sneevliet wrote under the Chinese pseudonym Sun Duo. Bing 1973: 22–30. Sun Duo 1922: 4–6.

116. Zhang Guotao 1922: 1.

117. Chen Duxiu 1923e: 1–2.

118. Sun Duo 1923b: 7.

119. The "able men" cabinet, which included Nationalist sympathizers, was brought down late in November by an enemy of Sun's party, Wu Jinglian. See Li Chien-nung 1956: 430; Sun [10]: 813; [28]: 863. Sun's chief criticism of the "political" route to power was that it was unreliable: Sun [4]: 509.

120. Sun [4]: 509–10. In the last months of his life Sun revived his hopes for a constitutional settlement: Sun [2]: 735–38; [41]: 907. But the Communists remained adamantly opposed: Peng Shuzhi 1924a.

121. Chen Duxiu 1923a: 1–2; and 1923b: 2–3; Chun Mu 1923b: 1–2; Cai Hesen 1923: 8–9.

122. Sun Duo 1923a: 5–6. Note the similar argument in Sun Duo 1923b.

123. Habermas 1989. William Rowe argues that there was indeed a "public sphere" in late imperial China, although not perhaps a "civil society" — for which there is still no agreed term in Chinese. Rowe 1993: 139–57.

124. Rowe 1993.   125. Cited in Fogel 1983: 69–70.

126. Ibid.: 68–70.   127. See Hua Zhou 1920.

128. Cited in Nathan 1976: 133.   129. Nathan 1976: 140.

130. The paper was funded by Chen Qimei and edited from its foundation by Ye Chucang. Huang Jilu 1969, 7: 101–2. Nathan 1976: 131. Chen Baixu was editor of a supplement to *China News* and a member of Sun's party. Wang Xinming 1957: 131.

131. Nathan 1976: 132, 253–57; Wang Xinming 1957: 140–45.

132. Wang Xinming 1957: 163–66. One instance of collaboration by members of the national union was their joint response to news of the Karakhan Declaration in April 1920. See *Juewu*, 14 April 1920.

133. Lin Yutang 1939: 47.

134. Ye Chucang 1922.

135. Sun entitled his major writings of this period "Psychological Reconstruction" (*Xinli jianshe*), "Material Reconstruction" (*Wuzhi jianshe*), and "Social Reconstruction" (*Shehui jianshe*). Sun [21]: 419–750.

136. Lü 1989: 61.   137. Sun [22].

138. Lü 1989: 56–57.   139. Shen Dingyi 1919; Lü 1989: 53.

140. In its editors' estimation, the readership of *Weekly Commentary* outstripped all other publications of the May Fourth period. "Xingqi pinglun bannian lai de nuli" 1919: 4. Lü Fangshang estimates 30,000 copies per issue. Lü 1989: 59.

141. The *Shanghai Republican Daily* published weekly supplements on a variety of themes and on behalf of a number of different organizations. Lü 1989: 85–86.

142. Ibid.: 84–85.

143. *Awaken* published Dai Jitao 1925b and Zhou Fohai 1925a.

144. Gellner 1983: 127; Deutsch 1966.

145. The comment by the editor of the *Guangzhou Republican Daily*, Shu Feng, appeared in a two-part assessment of the problems of party propaganda published in *GMR*, 18 and 24 April 1925. In fact, journals claiming to be authoritative sprung up in profusion, but none carried the imprimatur of the propaganda bureau until the advent of *Political Weekly*. See Chapter 6.

146. Mao [17]: 4–5.   147. See Chapter 6.

148. T. Chow 1960.   149. *GMR*, 18 and 24 April 1925.

Chapter 6

1. Foucault 1984: 2–3.   2. Mao [22]: 1.

3. Mao [21].   4. Sun [11]: 731–32.

5. Sun [39]: 669–73.   6. *ZGZK* 11 (9 March 1924): 5–7.

7. Luo Jialun and Huang Jilu 1969, 2: 1108.

8. Shirley 1965: 71–74.

9. "Zhongyang zhi Guangzhou minguo ribao jin kan zisha gonghui xiaoshuo han" 1924; *ZGZK* 24 (8 June 1924): 4; Luo Jialun and Huang Jilu 1969, 2: 1133.

10. "Zhongguo guomindang zhongyang zhixing weiyuanhui xuanchuan bu ban-shi zhangcheng" 1924: 4.

11. "Zhongguo guomindang diyi qu zhongzhihui disanci quanti huiyi tongguo guanyu jieshou Sun Zhongshan yishu zhi xunling jueyian" [1925] 1986: 116–17. Emphasis added.

12. *GMR*, 18 and 24 April 1925.

13. *GMR*, 18 and 24 April, 21 July 1925.

14. Communist leaders and advisers shared this concern over the move to Guangzhou. See Li Dazhao [T.C.L] 1923: 154–55; Chen Duxiu 1924a: 687–88; Sun Duo [Sneevliet] 1923b: 2–9; Isaacs 1971: 102–9.

15. *Zhongguo guomindang benbu gongbao* 8 (20 March 1923): 6. Tan was appointed Guangdong labor propagandist by the propaganda bureau of Party Center in Shanghai in January 1923; Lin was appointed in February to head the propaganda division of the Guangdong provincial branch of the party. *Zhongguo guomindang benbu gongbao* 4 (10 February 1923): 3; and 7 (10 March 1923): 6.

16. *GFQJ* 4: 577, 644, and 969. Ma Chaojun was associated with the Guangdong Mechanics Union and helped to establish the Guangdong Labor Federation. Li Yunhan 1966, 1: 312. Sun also nominated his personal secretary, Huang Changgu, to the committee. *GFQJ* 4: 474. Samples of its propaganda include Tan Pingshan and Feng Jupo 1923, and Feng Jupo 1923.

17. *GFQJ* 4: 742; *Zhongguo guomindang benbu gongbao* 21 (30 July 1923): 10–11; 23 (20 August 1923): 7; "Zhongguo guomindang xuanchuanbu shouzhipu" 1923.

18. *Zhongguo guomindang benbu gongbao* 23 (20 August 1923): 7–9.

19. *GFQJ* 2: 534–36; *Zhonguo guomindang dangwu taolunhui jishilu* n.d.: "Gong-wen" (Letters) 2–3.

20. *Zhongguo guomindang dangwu taolunhui jishilu* n.d.: "Yishi lu" (Records) 5–6, "Yijue yuanan" (Decisions) 3–4, "Shenchayuan baogaoshu" (Reviewers' reports) 3. *ZGZK* 9 (24 February 1924): 12.

21. The first issue of the *Nationalist Party Weekly* (*Guomindang zhoukan*) was dated 25 November 1923. From issue no. 9, the title changed to *Chinese Nationalist Party Weekly* (*Zhongguo guomindang zhoukan*). Xu Suzhong and Tan Pingshan were co-opted from the military government propaganda committee to edit the journal, which was housed at the same site as the propaganda committee — Sun's government headquarters on Yonghan North Road. See Luo Jialun and Huang Jilu 1969, 2: 1018–22; *Xin minguo* 1, no. 2 (12 December 1923): 17; Feng Jupo 1923. *ZGZK* 4 (16 December 1924).

22. Sun appointed five members to the reorganization committee: Wang Jingwei, Dai Jitao, Liao Zhongkai, Zhang Ji, and Li Dazhao. *GFQJ* 3: 931–32. Previous staff levels ranged from five officers in the finance bureau to ten in the general affairs bureau. *Zhongguo guomindang benbu gongbao* 4 (10 February 1923): 9.

23. *SMR*, 9 November 1923; Li Yunhan 1966, 1: 227.

24. "Shanghai zhixingbu de chengli ji qi gongzuo baogao" 1924; Luo Jialun and Huang Jilu 1969, 2: 1020, 1042–43. A Shanghai bureau report to Guangzhou dated 8 January reveals plans for a propaganda program for all provinces apart from the three southern ones presumed to be under Guangzhou's jurisdiction. "Shanghai zhixingbu dui linshi zhongyang zhixing weiyuanhui gongzuo baogao" 1924.

25. The five regional executive committees were to be based in Beijing, Shanghai, Hankou, Harbin, and an unspecified site in Sichuan. Luo Jialun and Huang Jilu 1969, 2: 1070; *Zhongguo guomindang benbu gongbao* 31 (20 November 1923): 7–14.

26. At least seven of these wage-strikers were Communists: Zhang Tinghao, Shen Zemin, Shao Lizi, Shi Cuntong, Yang Zhihua, Yun Daiying, and Han Juemin. "Shanghai zhixingbu suoxin huiyi jilu" 1924–25. An undated telegram from Guangzhou to Shanghai suggests that funds were cut off because of the "foul odour" of political infighting in Shanghai and the state of provincial finances in Guangzhou. "Liao Zhongkai zhi Chucang dian" n.d.

27. *Zhongguo guomindang quanguo daibiao dahui huiyi lu* 1929: 24; *SMR*, 9 November 1923.

28. Zhu Wushan 1924: 8.

29. *ZGZK* 9 (24 February 1924): 5–6; 13 (23 March 1924): 4; "Shanghai zhixingbu dui linshi zhongyang zhixing weiyuanhui gongzuo baogao" 1924; *GMR*, 4 December 1924; Li Yunhan 1966, 1: 334–36.

30. Yu Shude 1924: 4; Mao [17]: 4–5; Peng Shuzhi 1924b: 680–82; Sun [41]: 907. On the attribution of this and other "Ziren" articles to Mao Zedong, see Fitzgerald 1983: 1–16.

31. "Shanghai zhixingbu suoxin huiyi jilu" 1924–25. Nanyang presented ¥20,000 to Shanghai party headquarters in September and December 1922, and loaned it ¥10,000 in November. "Zhongguo guomindang benbu caizhengbu gongbao" 1923: 25, 34, and 36; Sun [19]: 359–60; Wang Xinming 1957: 164; Peng Shuzhi 1924c: 685; Mao [17]: 4–5.

32. Yu Shude 1924: 4; Mao [17]: 4–5; Li Yunhan 1966, 1: 334–35; Dai Jitao [1925] 1959a: 980–81.

33. As early as 1912 the Revolutionary Alliance (*Tongmenghui*) developed factions in Shanghai and Guangdong delineated by their advocacy of constitutional or military routes to power. G. Yu 1966: 67–70, 79–80.

34. Wilbur 1976.

35. Chen Duxiu 1924a; Luk 1990: 85–86, 107, 123; Brandt 1966: 91–113; Jordan 1976: 190–93.

36. The first issue of *The Revolution (Geming)* was dated 1 May 1925. Dai's response to the journal is set out in the foreword to Dai Jitao 1925a. The first issue of *The Independent (Duli)* was dated 1 November 1925. In the same year, Dai published Dai Jitao 1925a and 1925b. Another committee member, Shao Yuanchong, lent public support to Dai's controversial writings. See Shao Yuanchong 1954, 2: 919–30.

37. *ZGZK* 20 (11 May 1924): 5. Dai Jitao's first suicide attempt followed a futile mission on which Sun Yatsen had dispatched him in August 1922, shortly after Chen Jiongming's "betrayal" in Guangzhou. Boorman and Howard 1967–71, 3: 201; Mast 1970.

38. Zhou Fohai 1925a; Luo Jialun and Huang Jilu 1969, 2: 1103. The full title of the Political Council was *Zhongguo guomindang zhongyang zhixing weiyuanhui zhengzhi weiyuanhui*. Party members could do little about the council's unconstitutional status while Sun was in charge, but after his death, in July 1925, the Central Executive Committee ordered that the Political Council cease issuing directives in the name of the CEC except in emergencies. Nevertheless, it remained the de facto decision-making body. GMR, 29 July 1925; Mast 1970: 256, 280–81; Shirley 1965: 69–84; Li Yunhan 1966, 1: 324.

39. Zhou Fohai 1925a.

40. Dai Jitao [1925] 1959a: 981.

41. Fang Gang 1924; Luo Jialun and Huang Jilu 1969, 2: 1101, 1115; Li Yunhan 1966, 1: 270; "Peng Sumin guanyu dangwu tiaochen" 1923: 5–7. In 1921 Peng edited the *Zhongguo guomindang benbu tongxin* ("Weekly of the Chinese Nationalist party" [*sic*]), and he contributed regularly to the party's *Minxin rikan* (People's trust daily) in 1922.

42. "Peng Sumin guanyu dangwu tiaochen" 1923; SMR, 24 June 1924; Mast 1970: 228; Luo Jialun and Huang Jilu 1969, 1: 1085, 1113.

43. Woodhead 1912–39 (1929–30), 2: 964; Dai Jitao [1925] 1959b: 971; Cheng Tianfang 1962: 25; Huang Jilu 1969–, 10: 263; Luo Jialun and Huang Jilu 1969, 1: 1092, 1101; 2: 813; *Zhongguo guomindang benbu gongbao* 3 (30 January 1923): 4; and 19 (10 July 1923): 7; Zou Lu 1929, 1: 318.

44. *Zhongguo guomindang quan meizhou tongzhi dier ci kenqin dahui shimoji* 1921: 90–100; Mast and Saywell 1974: 73–98.

45. Dai Jitao [1925] 1959a: 984. Liu was appointed head of the Organization Bureau of the breakaway ("Western Hills") Central Executive Committee in January 1926. Li Yunhan 1966, 1: 449; *Zhongguo guomindang benbu gongbao* 25 (10 September 1923): 5.

46. *Zhongguo guomindang quan meizhou tongzhi dier ci kenqin dahui shimoji* 1921: Preface; Mast and Saywell 1974.

47. ZGHS 1: 58–60. This episode is discussed above in Chapter 5.

48. Boorman and Howard 1967–71, 1: 290; 2: 165; 4: 19.

49. Luo Jialun and Huang Jilu 1969, 2: 1092. *Qingshidun zhongguo guomindang jiu nian jingguo dangwu* 1925; Zhou Fohai 1967a: 132–33; 1967b: 138, 152–53; and 1925b: 1–9; "Minguo renwu xiaozhuan" 1979: 144.

50. Li Yunhan 1966, 1: 438–39.

51. *North China Herald*, 5 September 1925.

52. Luo Jialun and Huang Jilu 1969, 2: 1154. On Wang's misgivings, see Wang Jianmin 1965, 1: 108. Dai and Liu moved to Shanghai, whereas Zhou remained in Guangzhou until late 1925 as a member of the faculty of Guangdong University.

53. Chan 1975: 257; ZGZK 31 (27 July 1924): 4; 33 (10 August 1924): 7; 34 (17 August 1924): 6. See also *Xinwen bao*, 1 April, 3 April, 14 April, and 16 May 1925; Zhang Jinglu 1957: 179; Luo Jialun and Huang Jilu 1969, 2: 1149–50; Li Yunhan 1966, 1: 275. Chen Fumu's editorials appeared in the *Guangzhou Republican Daily* by February 1925. He was referred to as "general editor" in GMR, 13 July 1925.

54. *North China Herald*, 29 August and 5 September 1925; Li Yunhan 1966, 1: 376; *Xinwen bao*, 1 March and 3 April 1925; *Guomin xinwen*, 14 May 1925, in "Dangbu shelun tiecun pu" n.d.

55. ZGZK 42 (26 October 1924): 1. Chen was referred to as "acting head" in a document dated 6 April 1925. GMR, 1 December 1924, 9 April and 16 May 1925.

56. Zou Lu 1929, 1: 358; GMR, 11 April 1925; GFQJ 4: 865; Li Yunhan 1966, 1: 383; Mast 1970: 228.

57. The Provisional Political Propaganda Committee was formally renamed the Propaganda Committee at Wang Jingwei's request and placed under the direction of his Central Propaganda Bureau late in July. GMR, 21 June, 2 July, and 18 July 1925.

58. Li Yunhan 1966, 1: 364; Luo Dunwei 1963: 19; Dai Jitao [1925] 1959a: 983; "Di san ci quanti huiyi zhongyao jueyi an" [1925] 1973–: 25–29; "Zhongguo guomindang jieshou zongli yishu xuanyan" [1925] 1973–: 130–34.

59. The works listed were (1) *Jianguo fanglue* (Strategy for national reconstruction), (2) *Jianguo dagang* (Outline for national reconstruction), (3) *Sanmin zhuyi* (The three principles of the people), (4) the declaration and platform of the First Nationalist Party Congress, (5) the declarations of 13 September and (6) 10 November 1924, and (7) Sun's last will and testament. "Di san ci quanti huiyi zhongyao jueyi an" [1925] 1973–: 23. Compare ZGHS 1: 117.

60. Li Yunhan 1966, 1: 411–12.

61. Adapted from Sun [31]: 241.

62. M. Chan 1975.

63. "Zhongguo gongchandang disici dahui xuanyan" 1924: 67; Luk 1990: 96.

64. Sun [31]: 408–44.

65. Li Yunhan 1966, 1: 270–71; Luo Jialun and Huang Jilu 1969, 2: 149; Zou Lu 1929, 1: 355–56; "Linshi zhengzhi xuanchuan weiyuanhui diyi qi xuanchuan jihua gao" 1925.

66. Mao was appointed acting head of the Central Propaganda Bureau at Wang Jingwei's request at the 111th session of the Nationalist Central Executive Committee on or about 2 October 1925. GMR, 9 and 14 October 1925. Mao's deputy in the propaganda bureau in 1926 was another Communist, the renowned novelist Shen Yanbing [Mao Dun]. Shen replaced Mao for a brief spell in February. *Zhengzhi gongzuo rikan*, 22 February 1926. See also Schram 1967: 81–97; Li Yunhan 1966, 2: 474.

67. Interview with Li Rui, 7 April 1992. Stuart Schram has consistently noted Mao's concern with discipline over this period. Schram 1967. Curiously, even the public report of Nationalist propaganda bureau activities in 1924 and 1925 that was prepared by Mao Zedong and tabled at the Second Nationalist Party Congress in January 1926 cannot be traced in university or public libraries. I wish to thank Eugene Wu of the Harvard-Yenching Library for assistance in attempting to trace this document.

68. "Dier ci quanti huiyi zhongyao jueyi an" [1926] 1973–: 46–53, esp. 49. Mao was replaced by Gu Mengyu. Li Yunhan 1966, 2: 507, 512–13.

69. Luk 1990: 98.

70. GMR, 18 April, 24 April, 27 April, and 9 May 1925.

71. GMR, 3 November 1925; Wang Zhong 1957: 50–51. Wang's essay is misleading

on points bearing on Mao Zedong's role in Nationalist propaganda, but as Mao's stature is neither enhanced nor damaged by the recorded connection between *Zhengzhi zhoubao* and the Political Council I take his claim as accurate in this case.

72. *ZGZK* 22 (25 May 1924): 5.

73. *GMR*, 15–18 April, 22 April, 25 April, 31 October 1925; "Guomin huiyi shijian ziliao jianbao tiecunpu" 1926; "Xuanchuan bu gongzuo baogao" 1926: 11.

74. "Zhongyang dangbu zhongyao wenjian" 1926: 7; Olenik 1973: 91–92; "Guanyu xuanchuan jueyi an" 1926: 77; "Nongmin yundong jueyi an" 1926: 60–61.

75. *GMR*, 24 April 1925.

76. "Zhongguo guomindang zhi fanfeng zhanzheng xuanchuan dagang" 1925: 8–11. One example is the propaganda outline of the February Seventh Commemoration Coordination Agency in *Zhengzhi gongzuo rikan*, 1 February 1926. The coordination of this campaign is set out in "Erqi jinian yundong" 1926: 63–65.

77. "Zhengzhi xunlian bu shishi xuanchuan dagang huibian" 1926: 38–52.

78. The paper had been subsidized in the amount of ¥2,000 per month. Zou Lu 1929, 1: 399; *GMR*, 7 April, 9 April, 11 April, and 26 November 1925; *Zhongguo xinwen bao*, 27 May 1925.

79. Mao [21]: 10–11.

80. At the founding of the commission in January 1924, the anarchists Wu Zhihui, Li Shizeng, and Zhang Ji made up a majority of its five full members; another anarchist, Cai Yuanpei, was enlisted as a provisional member. There were no Communists. The commission was expanded to twelve full members in January 1926, including two Communists (Shao Lizi and Gao Yihan), two Communist sympathizers (Liu Yazi and Chen Bijun), and four anarchists (Wu Zhihui, Li Shizeng, Cai Yuanpei, and Zhang Jingjiang). Li Yunhan 1966, 1: 270, 472–73; Zou Lu 1929, 1: 382–87; Zarrow 1990: 202–4.

81. Luo Jialun and Huang Jilu 1969, 2: 1056, 1082–83, 1089; Li Yunhan 1966, 1: 376; *ZGZK* 23 (1 June 1924): 5.

82. Zou Lu 1929, 1: 361–67; Li Yunhan 1966, 1: 291–305; Sun [5]: 537–43; [6]: 870; [13]: 640–53; [29]: 916.

83. Zou Lu 1929, 1: 362–68; Li Yunhan 1966, 1: 311. The offending article in fact favored nationalism over "so-called" socialism: "Open propaganda and movements for so-called socialism, intended to make the majority of people in the community acquire a thorough understanding of socialism, is in the realm of a dream." Cui Wenchong 1924.

84. Li Yunhan 1966, 1: 317–22.

85. Mast 1970: 256, 280–81; Shirley 1965: 69–84.

86. Li Yunhan 1966, 1: 324–30.

87. *Xiangjiang chenbao*, 11 April 1925, in "Dangbu shelun tiecun pu" n.d.; *GMR*, 11 April 1925; "Qing zhengfu yanjin Huazi, Zhihuan dengbao rukou an" n.d.

88. "Zhongguo guomindang zhongyang zhixing weihuanhui xuanchuan bu banshi zhangcheng" 1924: 4, clauses 1, 3.

89. Tan Pingshan [1926] 1986: 205–15. Tan's key role is confirmed in *GMR*, 20 November 1925.

90. Mao [17]. "Ge shengqu dangwu baogao jueyian" 1926: 50– 51; *GMR*, 5 November 1925.

91. Staff members of the branch in 1923 who belonged to the Society for Commemorating the Revolution include Huang Longsheng, Deng Muhan, Zhao Shijin, and Deng Zeru. Luo Jialun and Huang Jilu 1969, 2: 964. Li Yunhan 1966, 1: 383; *GFQJ* 4: 865; "Guangdong zhibu tanhe gongchandang wen" 1923: 916–19. Bureau heads of the reformed branch in 1925 were Gan Naiguang (propaganda), Fan Qiwu (merchant), Chen Fumu (youth), He Xiangning (women), and the Communists Yang Paoan (organization), Peng Pai (peasant), and Liu Ersong (labor). "Zhixing weiyuanhui jiancha weihuanhui huiyilu" 1926: 1–2. On Gan, see Sansom 1988: Chap. 5.

92. *GMR*, 5 November 1925. In some cases staff members of the central and provincial bureaus served concurrently or in succession: Yang Paoan in both organization bureaus, Peng Pai in both peasant bureaus, Gan Naiguang in the provincial propaganda and central merchant bureaus, and He Xiangning in women's bureaus at both levels.

93. Guangdong provincial branch orders nos. 17 and 23, for example, conveyed and executed central headquarters' orders nos. 263 and 273. *ZGGY* 1 (February 1926): 4; 2 (March 1926): 7; 3 (April/May 1926): 7; 4 (June 1926): 30–32. The same monthly magazine regularly carried reports of party agencies within the province: 1 (February 1926): 19; and 3 (April/May 1926): 77.

94. "Zai ben dang zhidao xia zhi ge zhong minzhong yundong baogao" 1926: 34–66. Specific instances of central-provincial cooperation in propaganda ventures for the labor, youth, merchant, and women's movements are listed in *ZGGY* 1 (February 1926): 15–16; 2 (March 1926): 63–65; 3 (April/May 1926): 25–27. See also *ZGZY* 1: 21, 24, 39.

95. *GMR*, 5 November 1925.

96. *ZGGY* 1 (February 1926): 27, 30, 41.

97. Mao [20]: 13.

98. The Guangzhou chief of police, Wu Tiecheng, Mayor C. C. Wu, and the leader of the Prince faction, Sun Fo, joined merchant leaders and some labor organizers in opposing more drastic action. They were preoccupied with quelling a rebellion of mercenaries around Guangzhou. See M. Chan 1975: 311. My understanding of the composition of the refugees draws on interviews conducted in 1990 with a resident of Hong Kong who had joined the exodus.

99. *North China Herald*, 27 June 1925; Fung 1991: 39.

100. Propaganda included a weekly magazine, *The Route for Guangdong Labor* (*Guangdong gongren zhi lu*), a "workers' college" for labor organizers, eight schools for adult workers, and another eight schools for their children. M. Chan 1975: 309–45; Chesneaux 1968: 292; Li Yunhan 1966, 1: 63.

101. Reuters reported that Liao had survived an attempt on his life at a labor rally ten days before he was assassinated, and noted rumors circulating in Guangzhou and Hong Kong that acrimonious labor disputes in Guangdong had led to his death. *North China Herald*, 29 August 1925. Hu Hanmin was implicated in Liao's death when his cousin Hu Yisheng, an avowed enemy of Liao Zhongkai, fled the city after the assassination for fear of recrimination.

102. Li Yunhan 1966, 1: 355; Luk 1990: 94–97.

103. Chen Duxiu 1924c; Li Yunhan 1966, 1: 243, 331, 336–37.

104. Yu's proposal was passed on for implementation, but I have found no reference to action flowing from it. Li Yunhan 1966, 1: 335–36.

105. Schram 1967: 86.

106. Zhang Guotao 1971: 329; Wilbur and How 1956.

107. Hu Hanmin 1973–: 59–60; Zhang Guotao 1971: 329; Luk 1990: 96.

108. The article appears to have been Cai Hesen 1924a. The Nationalist Central Executive Committee responded on 23 October 1924. Luo Jialun and Huang Jilu 1969, 2: 1143. The Communist party responded in turn in November. Jizhe 1924: 5–8. According to a letter from the CEC published in May 1925, the point at issue in this exchange was whether it could be said that the Nationalist party harbored left, right, and center factions. GMR, 13 May 1925.

109. Chen Dong 1925; GMR, 13 May 1925.

110. Wang Jingwei n.d.

111. Li Yunhan 1966, 1: 381; Mao Sicheng 1965: 569.

112. Mao [4]: 5.

113. Mao [17]: 4.

114. Mao [22]: 1–2.

115. Mao [15]: 11; [23]: 12. In an early publication I suggested that the name Ziren was a homonym for the word "responsibility" (zeren). Fitzgerald 1983. This seems unlikely in light of the fact that Mao first employed the name Ziren in 1910 while still a student at the Tongshan Primary School. He adopted the name in honor of Liang Qichao, whose honorific was Rengong (Ziren implies "Son of Ren"). See Schram 1989: 38. Mao's secretary and biographer, Li Rui, confirmed Schram's argument with me in an interview on 7 April 1993. Brief synopses of three of the Ziren articles and a translation of the fourth are presented in Fitzgerald 1983. The fifth dealt with the dispatch of students to Sun Yatsen University in Moscow.

116. Chen Tanqiu, a founding member of the Communist party in 1921, presented a systematic analysis of Nationalist factions, their attitudes toward the Nationalist Revolution, and their purported socioeconomic foundations a year before Mao did. Chen divided the Nationalists into three groups, each with its own distinctive class basis in society. The Left represented industrial workers, handicraft workers, peasants, and small merchants; the Center represented intellectuals, owners of industrial and commercial houses, and part of the petty bourgeoisie ("As their economic position is indeterminate so their class character is uncertain and they are most prone to compromise"); the Right was the faction of big merchants who preserved links with imperialism, landlords, soldiers, politicians, and compradors. This last group was counterrevolutionary. Chen Tanqiu 1924.

117. Mao [5]: 12.

118. Mao [6]: 10. An English translation is appended in Fitzgerald 1983.

119. Ibid.

120. See, for example, Sun [36].

121. Mao [6]: 11–12.

122. Mao [6]. An internal reference to the First Nationalist Party Congress of

January 1924 as taking place "in January last year" indicates that this article was written in 1925.

123. Schram 1969: 241–46, 210–14.

124. "Zhongguo guomindang jieshou zongli yishu xuanyan" [1925] 1973–: 130–34.

125. "Zhongguo guomindang diyi qu zhongzhihui disanci quanti huiyi tongguo guanyu jieshou Sun Zhongshan yishu zhi xunling jueyian" [1925] 1986: 117.

126. Mao [6]: 14.

127. "Zhongguo guomindang jieshou zongli yishu xuanyan" [1925] 1973–: 130–34.

128. "Di san ci quanti huiyi zhongyao jueyi an" [1925] 1973–: 23.

129. "Zhongyang zhixing weiyuanhui wei banfa jinian zhou tiaoli tonggao di erbai shiliu" 1925.

130. "Zhongyang dangbu zhongyao wenjian" 1926: 4; GMR, 26 November 1925.

131. Zhengzhi gongzuo rikan, 18 and 19 February 1926.

132. "Xuanchuan bu gongzuo gaiyao" 1926, 2: 9–10; "Guangdong sheng dangbu jiqi" 1925: 6; Zhengzhi gongzuo rikan, 22 and 24 February 1926. ZGZY 1 (May 1926): 51–55. Mao may have been ill, but at this stage of his career it was not unknown for him to excuse himself from duties that he found irksome on the pretext of illness. He withdrew from the Fifth Communist Party Congress in April 1927 on this pretext. Schram 1967: 110.

Chapter 7

1. Fanon 1967: 179.

2. Galbiati 1985; Gillespie 1971; Hofheinz 1977; Landis 1964, 1969; Price 1976.

3. Cf. Mao [14]: 23.   4. GSGB 8 (29 August 1925): 35.

5. GSGB 3 (25 July 1925): 15.   6. GMR, 16 and 19 May 1925.

7. GSGB 34 (10 February 1926): 33–35.

8. The basic Police Studies course was intended for primary-school graduates and police officers with one year's experience; the Specialist course was offered to middle-school graduates with a year's experience as an officer in the force, and to graduates of military academies and lower-ranking police schools; and a Research course was offered to higher-level graduates of specified feeder schools, including the Police Inspectors Academy (*Jingjian xuexiao*), the Land Army Police Academy (*Lujun jingcha xuexiao*), and the Police Training Institute (*Jingyuan jiangxi suo*). In the higher courses, around one-third of classroom hours were devoted to party principles and doctrine. GSGB 27 (30 November 1925): 35–39; 43 (10 May 1926): 13–24.

9. A local institute was already operating in Yingde. GSGB 28 (10 December 1925): 51–53.

10. GSGB 3 (25 July 1925): 15–17; 22 (10 October 1925): 16–19; and 14 (12 September 1925): 62.

11. GSGB 22 (10 October 1925): 16–19.

12. GSGB 45 (30 May 1926): 154; 35 (20 February 1926): 123–25.

13. *GSGB* 34 (10 February 1926): 64–67.

14. *GSGB* 30 (31 December 1925): 36–38.

15. Ibid.; *GSGB* 33 (31 January 1926): 62–68; and 35 (20 February 1926): 123–25.

16. Fan Qiwu aside, bureau heads of the provincial party branch in 1925 were the radical Nationalists Gan Naiguang (propaganda), Chen Fumu (youth), and He Xiangning (women), and the Communists Yang Paoan (organization), Peng Pai (peasant), and Liu Ersong (labor). See Chapter 6.

17. *GSGB* 28 (10 December 1925): 35, 40.

18. Liu Shaotang 1977–, 2: 78; Luo Jialun and Huang Jilu 1969, 2: 960, 1083; *Zhonghua minguo shishi jiyao* 1975, 2: 33; *Zhongguo guomindang benbu gongbao* 7 (10 March 1923): 3; *ZGZK* 35 (24 August 1924): 3–4; Li Yunhan 1966, 1: 439.

19. *GSGB* 28 (10 December 1925): 40; Luo Jialun and Huang Jilu 1969, 2: 1103; Wang Zhangling 1973: 328; *Qishier hang shangbao*, 24 April 1925; *GMR*, 3 March 1926. Neither Lin nor Xie was close to Chiang Kaishek. Both were chiefly committed to their native province and, like many other staff members and students of the institute, continued to serve in Guangdong when the Nationalist government moved north to Nanjing in 1928. Liu Shaotang 1977, 2: 78; *Guangdong minzheng* 1941: 3; *Minguo shiqi guangdong sheng zhengfu dangan shiliao xuanbian* 1987, 11: 269–70.

20. *GFQJ* 5: 417; Chen Tianxi 1959: 29; Mast 1970: 131; "Xuanchuan bu gongwen digao" 1922–23: 19–20; "Jiaoyu yundong weiyuanhui yishilu" 1925; *GMR*, 15 July, 5 November 1925.

21. Chapman 1928: 13.

22. *GMR*, 10 February 1925.

23. *GSGB* 2 (18 July 1925): 18; 26 (20 November 1925): 63–64, 71–73.

24. *GSGB* 30 (31 December 1925): 30, 46–53. The Reverend Murdo C. Mackenzie filed a colorful report on the seizure of schools by students in the Shantou area in *North China Herald*, 5 September 1925. Similar events occurred on Hainan Island in 1926: "Rumblings Before the Storm" 1926: 18–22; and "The Educational Situation in Hainan" 1926: 27–28. For Guangzhou, see Foster 1928 and Swisher 1977.

25. *GSGB* 27 (30 November 1925): 31; 37 (10 March 1926): 31–33; and 45 (30 May 1926): 124. Swisher 1977: 14–15.

26. *GSGB* 30 (31 December 1925): 30, 46–53; 36 (28 February 1926): 105.

27. Luo Jialun and Huang Jilu 1969, 2: 1073, 1092, 1105; *SMR*, 10 June 1924; *ZGZK* 30 (20 July 1924): 6; Si Dun 1925: 2–3.

28. *GMR*, 24 April 1925.

29. "Daxue tiaoli" 1924: 986. Zou Lu's connection is set out in *GFQJ* 4: 226; Li Yunhan 1966, 1: 437–38. "Dai Jitao xiansheng yanjiang" 1926: 20–21.

30. *GMR*, 11 November 1924, 22 April 1925. *Qishier hang shangbao*, 24 April 1925; Chen Gongbo 1926c: 63.

31. Interview with Huang Jilu, Taibei, 27 August 1979; *GMR*, 15 July 1925; *Qishier hang shangbao*, 24 April 1925.

32. *GMR*, 15 July 1925; Si Dun 1925: 2–3; Li Yunhan 1966, 1: 434–35.

33. Li Yunhan 1966, 2: 528–30; Mast 1970: 350; *GMR*, 30 June 1925.

34. Hu Chenghan 1925; *GMR*, 30 June 1925.

35. *GMR*, 15 July 1925.

36. *GMR*, 28 July 1925.

37. Zhou Fohai 1925b: 1–9; *Juewu*, 16 December 1925.

38. *GSGB* 26 (20 November 1925): 54–56; 27 (30 November 1925): 44–49; 32 (11 January 1926): 17–21; 36 (28 February 1926): 83.

39. *GSGB* 45 (30 May 1926): 29–30.

40. *GSGB* 4 (1 August 1925): 9–11.

41. "Nanlu geshu xianzhang huiyi yijue an" 1926: 15.

42. Swisher 1977: 14–15.

43. *GSGB* 4 (1 August 1925): 9–11; 6 (15 August 1925): 2.

44. Swisher 1977: 17–18. *GSGB* 16 (17 September 1925): 25–29.

45. *GMR*, 5 November 1925.

46. Luo Jialun and Huang Jilu 1969, 2: 1133. The *Guangzhou Republican Daily* was managed until September 1924 by the rightist Guangzhou City party branch. Interview with Huang Jilu, Taibei, 27 August 1979. Sun Yatsen possibly transferred the paper to the Central Propaganda Bureau to signify his disapproval of the Guangzhou branch.

47. The institute was first mooted in October 1923, and finally opened on 29 June 1924 with 360 students. Luo Jialun and Huang Jilu 1969, 2: 1032, 1100. See also "Zhongguo guomindang jiangxi so zuzhi jueyi an" 1924: 4; "Zhongguo guomindang jiangxi so kai xue ji" 1924: 6.

48. *GMR*, 5 November 1925. The monthly was entitled *Zhongguo guomindang guangdongsheng dangbu dangwu yuebao* (Party affairs monthly of the Guangdong provincial branch of the Chinese Nationalist party).

49. "Xuanchuan bu gongzuo gaiyao" 1926, 1: 8–11; 2: 9–10; 3: 12–14; 4: 5–6.

50. *ZGGY* 4 (June 1926): 5–6.

51. *ZGGY* 1 (February 1926): 15. Compare Zhang Qixiong 1926: 27. The output of the provincial propaganda bureau in November 1925 totaled 70,000 photographs and 20,000 books and leaflets. "Xuanchuan bu gongzuo gaiyao" 1926, 1: 9.

52. "Ge xianshi dangbu ji choubei chu gongzuo baogao" 1926: 23; *ZGGY* 1 (February 1926): 13, 30, 36–37, 42. "Guangdong sheng zhixing weiyuanhui xuanyan ji tonggao" 1926: 8; "Xuanchuan bu gongzuo gaiyao" 1926, 2: 10.

53. "Xuanchuan bu gongzuo gaiyao" 1926, 2: 10. Gan Naiguang was an independent member of the Nationalist left wing who had come to believe in the efficacy and inevitability of class struggle in the Nationalist Revolution. See Sansom 1988: Chap. 5. The universities that supplied teachers included Guangdong, Lingnan, and Nationalist (*guomin*) universities: "Xuanchuan bu gongzuo gaiyao" 1926, 3: 12–13.

54. Chiang Kaishek 1968: 39–40; Jordan 1976: 39; M. Chan 1975: 31.

55. Graduates had not yet been stationed at town and county branches when the Northern Expeditionary Armies marched out of Guangdong. "Xuanchuan bu gongzuo gaiyao" 1926, 3: 12–13; 4: 5–6.

56. "Xuanchuan bu gongzuo gaiyao" 1926, 1: 8; Li Yunhan 1966, 1: 384. In Gan's absence from Guangzhou from November 1925 to February 1926, the paper was edited by Chen Fumu. The Political Council allocated it a subsidy of ¥1000 per month from November 1925. *ZGGY* 1 (February 1926): 14; *GMR*, 20 November 1925.

57. *GMR*, 5 November 1925; "Xuanchuan bu gongzuo gaiyao" 1926, 2: 9–10; 3: 12–14. The *Republican Daily* was a uniform title for official party newspapers before

the advent of the *Central Daily (Zhongyang ribao)* in 1928. The only two editions of the *Republican Daily* in publication at the time of the Guangdong branch's expansion of the network were from Shanghai and Guangzhou. A Beijing edition was published around the time of Sun Yatsen's visit to the city in the spring of 1925 and closed down on instruction from the Beijing government. Luo Dunwei 1963: 19.

58. *ZGGY* 1 (February 1926): 10–11, 28; "Guangdong gedi dangbao xiaoxi huizhi" 1926: 41.

59. "Guangdong gedi dangbao xiaoxi huizhi" 1926: 41; "Yangjiang xian dangbu" 1926, 3: 49; 4: 32–35; "Qiongya tebie weiyuanhui gongzuo baogao" 1926: 25–26; *ZGGY* 3 (April/May 1926): 77; "Zhongshan xian dangbu xuanchuan bu gongzuo jingguo qingxing" 1926: 39.

60. Li Chuntao was appointed by the Central Propaganda Bureau under Mao Zedong's direction. *ZGGY* 3 (April/May 1926): 77, 84.

61. "Ben dangbu dongzheng riji zheyao" 1925: 13; "Qiongya tebie weiyuanhui gongzuo baogao" 1926: 25–26.

62. *ZGGY* 1 (February 1926): 23, 34–35. On labor organization in Jiangmen, see Lin Yizhong 1926: 21; on labor disputes, see Li Linong 1926: 18–33; also "Gongren bu gongzuo baogao" 1926: 24. The *Jiangmen Republican Daily* was not listed among current publications in June 1926. See "Guangdong gedi dangbao xiaoxi huizhi" 1926: 41.

63. "Guangdong gedi dangbao xiaoxi huizhi" 1926: 41; "Qiongya tebie weiyuanhui gongzuo baogao" 1926: 25–26.

64. Fitzgerald 1990a.

65. "Guangdong gedi dangbao xiaoxi huizhi" 1926: 41

66. *ZGGY* 3 (April/May 1926): 77, 84; 4: 56. Shantou's national industrial enterprises included electric-power generation, oil mills, canneries, breweries, and distilleries. Chesnaux 1968: 415–19.

67. Vishnyakova-Akimova 1971: 209, cited in Gilmartin 1994: 203. Christina Gilmartin offers a comprehensive survey of the organized women's movement in Guangdong.

68. See Chapter 2. For a fine analysis of this reductionist procedure in the literature of the People's Republic, see Meng Yue 1993: 118–36.

69. "Funu yundong jueyi an" 1926: 70; He Xiangning 1926: 69; Yihong 1924.

70. Women's bureau propagandists included Feng Mingguang, Wang Guoying, and Li Shanqin. Bureau officers who engaged in propaganda work included Wu Xiali, Zhao Xuru, Feng Jingyun, and Gao Tianpo. "Funu bu gongzuo baogao [central]" 1 (May 1926): 22–24. (Note that the central and provincial women's bureaus published reports bearing identical titles; they are distinguished here as [central] or [provincial].) He Xiangning 1926: 70; "Zhongyang dangbu funu bu minguo shisan nian san yue zhi shiwu nian san yue gongzuo zheyao" 1926: 26. Over 10,000 leaflets were distributed at International Women's Day celebrations in Guangzhou in 1924. "Funu ri da yundong jingguo qingxing" 1924: 5. *Women's Voice* was co-edited by the Central Women's Bureau and the Guangdong provincial women's bureau.

71. *ZGGY* 1 (February 1926): 5, 20; "Funu bu gongzuo baogao [provincial]" 1926, 1: 19; 2: 13–14; 3: 19–21.

72. Gilmartin 1994.

73. "Funu bu gongzuo baogao [provincial]" 1926, 1: 14, 19–20; "Funu bu gong-zuo baogao [central]" 1926: 22. Criticism of the coordination of women's movement propaganda was aired at the Second Nationalist Party Congress. He Xiangning 1926: 69; "Funu bu xuanchuan huiyi an" 1926. Gilmartin 1994: 208.

74. GMR, 15 July 1925; *Guangdong qingnian* 3 (1926): 14; ZGZK 26 (22 June 1924): 4.

75. Students were involved in the Eastern and Southern expeditions and in the Guangdong–Hong Kong strike and boycott. The student union published *Zhong-guo xuesheng* (Chinese student) and a series of anti-Christian monographs. *Juewu*, 22 December 1925; "Quanguo xuesheng zonghui zhi xuanchuan jihua" 1924: 5–6. The Young Soldiers Association produced *Zhongguo junren* (Chinese soldier), edited by Wang Yifei. It had a circulation of 5,000–10,000 copies each issue. In 1926 the asso-ciation passed from youth bureau supervision to the armed forces' Political Training Bureau. Chen Gongbo 1926c: 61–63; "Qingnian bu gongzuo baogao" 1926: 14.

76. *Guangdong Youth* was planned to circulate as a monthly when it appeared in August 1926, but from the second issue it appeared fortnightly. The fifteen staff mem-bers listed in early plans included seven Communists: Yun Daiying, Shen Yanbing, Xiao Chunu, Zhang Tailai, Deng Zhongxia, Huang Ping, and Mao Zedong. Yun and Mao joined Guo Moruo among the ten staff members who actually taught at the in-stitute. Mao took 61 hours of classes, Yun 16, and Guo 13, of a total of 291 classroom hours. "Zhixing weiyuanhui gebu gongzuo gaiyao" 1926: 1–13; ZGGY 1 (February 1926): 42; 4 (June 1926): 66–67. On Li Yueting's early association with Peng Pai, see Peng Pai 1924: 5.

77. Bergère 1989. For two mutually contrasting positions, see Luo Jialun and Huang Jilu 1969, 2: 1119–20, 1140–41; and L. Chen 1989.

78. "Shangmin bu gongzuo baogao [central]" 1926: 19. Publication of the maga-zine was delayed by the onset of the Northern Expedition. The first issue appeared not (as initially planned) in Guangzhou but in Hankou, in September 1926.

79. The institute commenced classes on 1 October 1925 and ran for three months. Gan Naiguang 1926a: 65–68. The magazine was launched in Guangzhou in January 1926. The provincial merchant movement training institute is reported in "Shangmin bu gongzuo baogao [provincial]" 1926, 1: 23–26; 3: 31–36; 4: 17. See also ZGGY 1 (February 1926): 20–21, 24, 27, 41, 44; 3 (May 1926): 89.

80. "Shangmin yundong jueyi an" 1926: 68–69; Fewsmith 1985.

81. The secretary of the peasant bureau, Peng Pai, was replaced in November 1924 by fellow Communist Luo Qiyuan. Luo Jialun and Huang Jilu 1969, 2: 1149–50. Peng went on to head the Guangdong provincial branch peasant bureau. GMR, 5 November 1925. For varying interpretations of Peng's activities in Haifeng and their significance for the Chinese revolution, see Galbiati 1985; Marks 1984; Hofheinz 1977.

82. "Benbu tepaiyuan dahui zhi jueyi an" 1926: 2. *Nongmin yundong* (Peasant movement) first issued from Guangzhou, in August 1926, and later from Hankou. *Zhongguo nongmin* (Chinese peasant) first appeared in Guangzhou in January 1926. The bureau was initially asked to edit a monographic series on rural reform in May 1924. By October 1926, 31 titles had been issued in three separate monograph series. Luo Qiyuan 1926a: 3; "Benbu gongzuo baogao" 1926: 3–4. The latter report also

notes that a "propaganda outline" was drafted by the bureau on the first anniversary of Liao Zhongkai's assassination.

83. Lenin [1902] 1988: 131-33. See also Kenez 1985. Lenin's distinction between propaganda and agitation was conceived in relation to his distinction between revolutionary "consciousness" and mass "spontaneity" (or "unconsciousness"). See Chapter 8 below.

84. Chen Gongbo 1926b: 59; Luo Qiyuan 1926a: 5.

85. GMR, 5 November 1925; Li Yunhan 1966, 1: 270; Luo Jialun and Huang Jilu 1969, 2: 1149-50.

86. ZGGY, 1: 6. Peasant-movement materials distributed at the town and county levels appear to have been produced by affiliated organizations as well as by the bureau itself. The Zhongshan County branch of the Nationalist party, for example, reported receiving copies of the Central Peasant Bureau publication *Zhongguo nongmin*, and materials from the peasant association headquarters. "Nongmin gongzuo baogao" 1926: 30-32.

87. Zou Lu 1929, 1: 391-92; Li Yunhan 1966, 1: 101, 362-63; Chesnaux 1968: 178-80, 292; Zhang Jinglu 1954-56, 1: 19. Publications issued by non-Nationalist labor agencies include *Gongren zhoukan* (Workers' weekly), issued by the Beijing Communist party branch; *Zhongguo gongren* (Chinese worker) and *Laodong zhoubao* (Labor weekly), both published by the Labor Union Secretariat; and *Guangdong gongren zhi lu* (The route for Guangdong labor), issued by the Guangdong–Hong Kong Strike Committee.

88. "Gongren bu gongzuo baogao" 1926: 24-25.

89. Abend 1944: 33. Jordan 1976: 184. In July 1925, Chiang estimated military expediture at between 18 and 20 million yuan; his December estimates of between 28 and 35 million yuan took into account his plans for launching the Northern Expedition. In fact, income and expenditure both exceeded Chiang's estimates. Revenues exceeded 80 million yuan and military expenditure 50 million yuan over the year to the autumn of 1926. Fitzgerald 1990a: 751-52.

90. Jordan 1976: 190-91.   91. Ibid.: 39, 183-93.
92. Ibid.: 212-13.   93. Ibid.: 193ff.

94. Mao Sicheng 1965: 513-14; Zhang Qiuren 1926: 17. Circumvention of the carrier problem on the second Eastern Expedition is borne out in Chiang Kaishek's analysis of the first and second Eastern expeditions: whereas the first dwells on the carrier problem, the second overlooks it. Mao Sicheng 1965: 513-14 and 530-32.

95. Mao Sicheng 1965: 429, 440, 513-15, 541-42.

96. Tong 1953: 63.

97. Isaacs 1971: 107. There is a striking resemblance between a speech given by Sun in January 1923 and an article published by Sneevliet two months beforehand. Compare Sun [4] and Sun Duo 1922: 4-6. See also Sun [9]: 512. Sun dismissed those among his troops who were old, infirm, or lacked weapons. Luo Jialun and Huang Jilu 1969, 2: 961.

98. Cai Hesen 1922f: 1-2; Chen Duxiu 1923c: 4-6; Sun Duo 1922.

99. Wilbur 1976: 209; Li Yunhan 1966, 2: 487; MacFarquhar 1953: 151. A Communist cadre then working in Guangzhou recalls that it was generally believed in

Communist party circles that the Russians were providing Y400,000 per month for the Huangpu Academy. Interview with Hu Yungong, Nanjing, March 1980.

100. Sun often used the expression *xinjun* (new army) to describe the armed forces of the Huangpu Academy. See Mao Sicheng 1965: 326, 334. The academy had a number of branch schools: see Li Yunhan 1966, 2: 481; Vishnyakova-Akimova 1971: 162.

101. Sun [8]: 571–72; [12]: 605; and [14]: 693.

102. Sun [8]: 571, 576; [13]: 640–52.

103. Luo Jialun and Huang Jilu 1969, 2: 1034–35, 1041–42; *Zhongguo guomindang quanguo daibiao dahui huiyi lu* 1929: 49. Some studies claim that Sun presented to the First Nationalist Party Congress a motion to establish a party military academy. See MacFarquhar 1953: 151; and Landis 1969: 22. I can find no record of such a motion. Though Sun certainly supported its establishment at the time of the congress, he possibly harbored doubts about the direction the academy was taking later in the year. In a valedictory speech to students and staff delivered at the academy on 3 November 1924, he passed up a golden opportunity to celebrate the new party-army and chose instead to speak on the need for dedication and obedience among members of a revolutionary party. See Sun [11]; Landis 1969: 107–8 and 128.

104. Vishnyakova-Akimova 1971: 161–62, 183; Landis 1964: 150; Du Congrong 1975: 31–37; Mao Sicheng 1965: 459. Some sources claim Chiang tended to exaggerate the strength of forces under his personal command. See Vishnyakova-Akimova 1971: 167. The loss of further rebellious contingents of the Yunnan and Guangxi armies under generals Yang Ximin and Liu Zhenhuan pared the allied force down considerably from the number credited to Nationalist forces in 1924.

105. Mao Sicheng 1965: 276, 302. There were around 1,000 cadets at the Guangxi Army School: *GMR*, 19 February 1925; "Guangdong geming shili de tuanjie" 1926: 10; Mao Sicheng 1965: 449. On the Hunan Army School, see *GMR*, 15 July 1925; and "Qingnian junren lianhe hui disici daibiao dahui huiyu lu" 1925: 40–44.

106. "Junshi weiyuanhui junshi zhengzhi yuekan jianzheng" 1926: 9–12; *Zhengzhi gongzuo rikan*, 26 February 1926. Even the small Attack Hubei Army opened an academy. See Zhang Qixiong 1926: 25. A general report on the state of army military schools is presented in Wilbur and How 1956: 194–96.

107. The order of 24 April 1924 is published in *GFQJ*, 4: 1118–19; another, of 21 October 1923, is in *GFQJ*, 4: 865. Fewer students are listed in Deng Wenyi 1976: 145.

108. Du Congrong 1975: 30, 57; Mao Sicheng 1965: 321; Deng Wenyi 1976: 145; Vishnyakova-Akimova 1971: 161–62.

109. Vishnyakova-Akimova 1971: 185.

110. Mao Sicheng 1965: 299–303, 312, 326–27, 347, 366; Du Congrong 1975: 44.

111. Mao Sicheng 1965: 260–61, 506.

112. Landis 1969: 105–13. Cadre from the Huangpu Academy offered political-education classes for a number of officers from other academies, although very few attended their classes. Mao Sicheng 1965: 305, 455; Fang Dingying 1927: section 2.6; *Zhengzhi gongzuo rikan*, 16 February 1926.

113. Zhang Qixiong 1926: 25, 35.

114. Chen Gongbo 1926a: 1–15; Mao Sicheng 1965: 559–60.

115. Fang Dingying 1927: section 1.60; *Zhengzhi gongzuo rikan*, 26 February 1926.

116. Fang Dingying 1927: sections 1.60, 2.58; Landis 1969: 39–40; Chen Guofu 1973–: 27–36; Wilbur and How 1956: 203–4. Candidates from among the cadets of the other military schools did not perform well in entrance exams. *Zhengzhi gongzuo rikan,* 16 and 26 February 1926.

117. Fang Dingying 1927: sections 1.60, 2.58; *Huangpu jianjun sanshi nian gaishu* 1954: 15.

118. Mao Sicheng 1965: 206, 541, 643; Chen Xunzheng 1973–: 7; "Guoming gemingjun dang daibiao tiaoli" 1926: 8.

119. Mao Sicheng 1965: 343–44, 642–45; Chen Xunzheng 1973–: 6–8; "Guoming gemingjun dang daibiao tiaoli" 1926: 7. The commissariat system was shelved immediately after the Zhongshan Gunboat Incident in March 1926 but reinstated in the course of the Northern Expedition. Vishnyakova-Akimova 1971: 240–41.

120. On 8 April (a fortnight after Li Zongren's Guangxi Army joined the Nationalist Revolutionary Army) Chiang stated his reasons for abolishing the system. He sacked party representatives of every persuasion after the Zhongshan Gunboat Incident in March 1926. Landis 1969: 112; Mao Sicheng 1965: 631, 642–45; Vishnyakova-Akimova 1971: 240–41.

121. Qian Dajun 1973–: 37–38. Mao Sicheng 1965: 370; Li Linong 1926: 33. The Huangpu Political Bureau was placed in the care of a skeleton staff and transferred to a branch school on 4 January 1925, in preparation for the first Eastern Expedition. Mao Sicheng 1965: 363.

122. Mao Sicheng 1965: 508; Qian Dajun 1973–: 42; Li Yunhan 1966, 1: 390; Xie Cilin 1926: 45–57; Chun Tao 1925: 12–19. Zhou was also secretary of the Guangdong Provincial Committee of the Chinese Communist party and a member of the Nationalist party.

123. Mao Sicheng 1965: 639, 645, 663.

124. Landis 1969: 110–13; Du Congrong and Leng Xin were both wounded shortly before being appointed party representatives. Du Congrong 1975: 60–61; Mao Sicheng 1965: 447, 548, 574.

125. Mao Sicheng 1965: 432, 644.

126. ZGZK 29 (13 July 1924): 3–4; Mao Sicheng 1965: 281, 290–91, 370.

127. "Ben dangbu dongzheng riji zheyao" 1925: 5–21.

128. Mao Sicheng 1965: 287–88.

129. Ibid.: 429, 440, 513–15, 541–42.

130. Reports of branch activity begin to appear regularly in the GMR from July 1925. See also Tan Pingshan 1925: 5–9; and 1926: 42–49; Wang Erzhuo 1926: 15–16; Wu Yuzhang 1926: 22–26.

131. Tan Pingshan 1925: 2–3. Party membership in Guangdong rose by 60,828 (to 108,831) between January and May 1926. "Zhongguo guomindang zuijin dangbu zuzhi gaikuang" 1926: 14–16.

132. Tochigi 1978: 95–116.

133. Miao Xiangchu 1926, 4: 16; 5: 4; Luo Yangqing 1926: 1–18; *Zhengzhi gongzuo rikan,* 19 and 26 February 1926.

134. Luo Yangqing 1926: 14–15; "Qiongya tebie weiyuanhui gongzuo gaishu" 1926: 37.

135. *ZGGY* 2 (March 1926): 39; 3: 84. Political bureaus in the Fourth Army launched a number of peasant associations and labor unions during the Southern Expedition but neglected to set up merchant associations. Miao Xiangchu 1926, 5: 5-7.

136. "Ge xianshi dangbu ji choubei chu gongzuo baogao" 1926: 1-27; "Huishu tebie weiyuanhui gongzuo baogao" 1926: 26-27.

137. *GMR*, 21 February 1925. The party affairs directors for Huiyang and surrounding counties were stationed in the General Political Bureau. "Ge xianshi dangbu ji choubei chu gongzuo baogao" 1926: 1; *ZGGY* 1 (February 1926): 5-7; Miao Xiangchu 1926, 5: 3-4.

138. "Ge xianshi dangbu ji choubei chu gongzuo baogao" 1926: 31.

139. Miao Xiangchu 1926, 5: 3-4; Luo Yangqing 1926: 7-8.

140. "Ge xianshi dangbu ji choubei chu gongzuo baogao" 1926: 18.

141. Zhang Qixiong 1926: 32.

142. *GMR*, 16 May 1925; *ZGGY* 1 (February 1926): 5-7.

143. "Guangdong dierci quansheng daibiao dahui xuanyan" 1926: 1-9, esp. 5; He Chi 1926: 3; Zhang Qixiong 1926: 31. County heads appointed by Chen Mingshu for the counties of Yangjiang, Lianjiang, and Suixi were considered unsatisfactory by mass-movement sympathizers. Of the eight magistrates appointed by Gan's committee on whom information is available, two (for Wenchang and Lesha) were considered unsatisfactory by mass-movement activists. Miao Xiangchu 1926, 5: 12-13. The southern route administrative committee was made up of Gan, the Fourth Army commander Li Jishen, and a Fourth Army political bureau representative, Zhang Shanming. Luo Yangqing 1926: 17.

144. Fitzgerald 1990a. A similar pattern of appointments unfolded on the Northern Expedition itself. Tochigi Toshio 1978: 97-99.

145. *Zhengzhi gongzuo rikan*, 20 February 1926; "Nanlu geshu xianzheng huiyi yijue an" 1926: 13-18.

146. "Dongjiang geshu xingzheng huiyi jilue" 1926: 17-20; Fitzgerald 1990a.

147. Mao Sicheng 1965: 515-23. For a compelling criticism of the Huizhou affair, see Li Ao 1987: 214-16.

148. The following account is based on "Ge xianshi dangbu ji choubei chu gongzuo baogao" 1926: 1-7; "Huishu tebie weiyuanhui gongzuo baogao" 1926: 26-27.

149. Tan Pingshan, *Wei shenma yao dadao Chen Jiongming?* and Wang Jingwei, *Guangdong renmin jinri yingyou zhi juexin.* "Ge xianshi dangbu ji choubei chu gongzuo baogao" 1926: 6. The significance of Dai Jitao's work is discussed in Chapter 8. The Society for the Study of Sun Yatsenism was under gentry control in Puning County. Marks 1977: 65-99, esp. 94.

150. "Huishu tebie weiyuanhui gongzuo baogao" 1926: 26-27; "Ge xianshi dangbu ji choubei chu gongzuo baogao" 1926: 4.

Conclusion

1. Hobbes [1651] 1946: 107. Emphasis in original.
2. Liang Qichao 1984: 853. Emphasis added.
3. Gellner 1983: 129. Emphasis in original.

4. Marx [1852] 1968: 172. See also Marx [1853] 1969a; [1853] 1969b.

5. B. Anderson 1991: 3. See also Munck 1986; Laroui 1976; and Chatterjee 1986.

6. Lenin [1917] 1965.

7. Kuhn 1970.

8. Marx and Engels [1848] 1976: 495. Emphasis added.

9. Ibid.: 488.

10. Engels 1976: 6; Munck 1986: 6. Emphasis added.

11. Seth 1989: 4.

12. Marx and Engels distinguish between the "incoherent mass" of workers and the historical "organisation of the proletariat into a class." Marx and Engels [1848] 1976: 492–93. Lenin proposes an operational distinction between the "spontaneous element" and its "conscious leadership." Lenin [1902] 1988: Chap. 2.

13. See Knight 1990; Mao [10].

14. Marx and Engels [1848] 1976: 486.

15. Ibid.: 486. This view of the state—one of several to be found in the writings of Marx—was favored by Lenin in *The State and Revolution* when he purported to reestablish the "real" teaching of Marx on the state. Lenin [1917] 1965: Chap. 1. For a broader reading of Marx on the state, see McLellan 1983: 143–88.

16. L. Chen 1989; Bergere 1989.

17. Chen Duxiu 1924a. The emergence of this new line of thought is closely traced through the writings of Peng Shuzhi, Zhang Tailei, and Qu Qiubai in Luk 1990: 91–93.

18. Zhou Enlai [Wu Hao] 1924; Cai Hesen 1924b.

19. Rigby 1980.

20. Meisner 1982: 55.

21. Chen Duxiu 1923d; 1925b.

22. Dai Jitao [1925] 1959b: 971. Dai uses a word—*liangxin*—that is generally translated as "conscience" rather than "consciousness." It was nevertheless in common use at the time to refer to ethical "consciousness." Dai also wrote on the need for groups to subordinate sectoral interests to the national good: Dai Jitao [1926] 1969.

23. Chen Duxiu 1923d.   24. Dai Jitao 1925a and 1925b.

25. Dai Jitao [1925] 1959b: 971.   26. Chen Duxiu 1925a.

27. Cai Hesen 1925; Chen Duxiu 1925a; Qu Qiubai 1925a, 1925b; Luk 1990: 95; Chesneaux 1968.

28. On forms of representation, see Birch 1971; Pitkin 1967.

29. Hu Hanmin 1920: 3.

30. Petrey 1988a and 1988b; Lenin [1902] 1988: 105–7.

31. Shun 1991: 25–35. See above, Chapter 2.

32. Shen Dingyi's opening preface to the Nationalists' *Weekly Commentary*, in 1919, was a plea for sympathetic representation. Shen Dingyi 1919; Lü Fangshang 1989: 53.

33. Marx [1852] 1968: 121. Emphasis in original.

34. Petrey 1988b: 458.

35. Munro 1977: 18–19.

36. Chapter 2 of *What Is to Be Done?* is aptly titled "The Spontaneity of the Masses and the Consciousness of Social Democracy." The targets of Lenin's attack

were the "economists" who favored a relatively confined and (he believed) passive role for intellectuals at the rear of the mass movement. "Social democrats" favored a vanguard model of leadership. Lenin [1902] 1988.

37. Ibid.: 96, 143.

38. Ibid.: 105–7. Emphasis in original.

39. Lenin's habit of ascribing interests to the workers can be traced to Marx, who asked (in his discussion of the events of 1848) why the masses' perception of their interests failed to match their "revolutionary interests." Marx wrote of the proletariat as "forgetful." Marx [1852] 1968: 155.

40. Lenin wrote, "There could not have been social democratic consciousness among the workers. It could only have been brought to them from without. The history of all countries shows that the working class exclusively by its own effort is able to develop only trade-union consciousness. . . . The teachings of socialism, however, grew out of the philosophical, historical and economic theories elaborated by educated representatives of the propertied classes, by the intelligentsia." He characterized as a profound mistake the belief that "the labour movement pure and simple can and will elaborate an independent ideology for itself." Lenin [1902] 1988: 98, 105, and his Chap. 2.

41. Polan 1984: 9. Lenin cites with approval Karl Kautsky's draft program of the Austrian Social Democratic Party (1901): "Socialist consciousness is something introduced into the proletarian struggle from without and not something that arose within it spontaneously. . . . The task of social democracy is to imbue the proletariat with the consciousness of its position and the consciousness of its task." Lenin [1902] 1988: 106–7.

42. Dirlik 1991: 209.

43. Lenin [1902] 1988: Chap. 2.

44. Cai Hesen [1921] 1969: 212. I have substituted "inevitable" for the translators' "necessary." Emphasis added.

45. Mao [6]: 10–12; [20]: 12–13. Mao's first request to the wavering "middle" faction was possibly made in October 1925 in an address to the congress of the Guandong provincial branch of the Nationalist party. GMR, 28 October 1925.

46. Mao [6]: 10–12. Stuart Schram notes that Mao consistently placed the overwhelming majority of the Chinese people in the revolutionary camp, estimated the enemy as a small fraction, and counted the "wavering people" a tiny fraction of the total population. Schram 1989: 38–39.

47. Sun [46]: 559, 563. Sun's notion of democratic procedure was quite different from the procedures developed and practiced in Europe and America. See Nozawa 1971.

48. Cited in Dirlik 1989: 122.   49. Compare Taylor 1948: 33.

50. Huters 1991: 18.   51. Grant 1970: 20–21.

52. Émile de Vogüé (1886), cited in Grant 1970: 32.

53. Cited in Petrey 1988b: 448–68.

54. The place of Marx's work in the realist movement of the mid-nineteenth century has been widely debated by literary theorists. See Mehlman 1977; Eagleton 1981; and Petrey 1988a and 1988b. My point here is also the conclusion to Sandy Petrey's

challenge to Mehlman's interpretation of *The Eighteenth Brumaire*. See Petrey 1988b: 468.

55. Huters 1991: 12.

56. Plaks 1976: 14. The significance of Plaks's arguments for discussion of May Fourth realism was brought to my attention by Theodore Huters. See Huters 1991.

57. Petrey 1988a: Chap. 2.

58. Huters 1991: 12.

59. Williams 1983: 269.

60. Kang Youwei's earliest epiphany took place in the Xiqiao hills, near Guangzou, where he discovered his calling to save the world. On a visit to Beijing in 1888 he found in the surrounding mountains the inspiration to save his country: "In the ninth month I visited the Western Hills. Since I had been studying China's domestic problems and foreign relations, I felt, as I looked down from a height, a vast concern for China and her people." Kang Youwei 1967: 45.

61. Kuo 1956: 18.   62. Cited in L. Lee 1973: 273.

63. Chen Duxiu 1925a.   64. Chen Duxiu 1923c.

65. Dirlik 1978: 25, 39; L. Lee 1973: 247–53.

66. Tao Xisheng 1964: 123–24. Adapted from Dirlik 1978: 47.

67. M. Anderson 1990: 26.

68. Ba Jin 1931–35. See also Ba Jin 1929.

69. Lenin [1902] 1988: 135. Emphasis added.

70. M. Anderson 1990: 42.

71. See Stanley 1982. Hannah Arendt's critique of the philosophical personae of Hegel and Heidegger is noted in Bruehl 1982: 302–5, 322–24.

72. H. Siu 1990: 10.

73. Cited in L. Lee 1973: 273. Emphasis added. Zhu was writing in 1928.

74. M. Anderson 1990: 37.

75. Tan Sitong 1984: 218.

76. Zarrow 1990: 119, 121, 124, 214.

77. On Chinese acquaintance with Hegelian thought and resonances within Chinese philosophy, specifically in relation to the principle of negation and the dialectic, see Feng Yu-lan 1966: 278; Wakeman 1973: 185–86, 286–87. China also appealed to Hegel: Spence 1990: 132–36.

78. See Wang Jingwei 1926a.

79. Compare Bland 1932: 178; Cantlie and Jones n.d.: Preface.

80. Marcuse 1960: 50. Marcuse's historical reading is challenged by others who would picture Hegel's practical philosophy emerging "immanently" from the philosophy of Immanuel Kant. See Ritter 1982: 7.

81. Sun [36]: 457–63. For a translated excerpt, see Sun [27]. Joseph Fewsmith was the first among recent historians to note the significance of this cryptic epigram. Fewsmith 1985: 96–97.

82. Sun [36]: 458, 463–74.

83. Grieder 1970: 124; Hu Shi [1931] 1969; T'ang Leang-li [1931] 1969: vii.

84. Zhou Fohai 1925a.

85. Sun [36]: 460–63; Fewsmith 1985: 97.

86. Cited in Hu Shi [1931] 1969: 52–53.

87. Sun [31].   88. Mao [10]: 295–309, esp. 300.

89. Sun [36].   90. Mao [10]: 296.

91. Sun [31]: 314, 332, 342; and Chapter 6, passim.

92. Meissner 1990: 92.

93. Mao [10]: 305–6.

94. The appeal of the idea of "false consciousness" to practically oriented Marxists in the mold of Mao Zedong is noted in Wakeman 1973: 68–73.

95. Schneider 1971: 281. The transition from romanticism to realism in historical scholarship over this period is discussed above. A similar pattern can be traced in the evolution of sociology and social theory in the late 1920s. See Dirlik 1978.

96. Zeng Rong [1925] 1980: 238–39. By 1925, the target of attacks on "romantic" supporters of the local militia was just as likely to have been anarchist strategists as Chen Duxiu. See Dirlik 1991: 239–40.

97. Luo Qiyuan 1926b: 21–28, esp. 26–27.

98. "Nong so" 1926: 21; Luo Qiyuan 1926a: 16, 26; Zhou Qijian 1926: 1–11; Chen Gongbo 1926b: 59–60; Hofheinz 1977: 21, 93.

99. Note Mao's classic statement of the "mass line": "In all the practical work of our Party, all correct leadership is necessarily from the masses, to the masses. This means: take the ideas of the masses (scattered and unsystematic ideas) and concentrate them (through study turn them into concentrated and systematic ideas), then go to the masses and propogate and explain these ideas until the masses embrace them as their own, hold fast to them, and translate them into action, and test the correctness of these ideas in such action. Then once again concentrate ideas from the masses and once again take them to the masses so that the ideas are persevered in and carried through. And so on, over and over again in an endless spiral, with the ideas becoming more correct, more vital and richer each time. Such is the Marxist-Leninist theory of knowledge." Mao [11]: 316–17.

100. Emphasis added. Mao [7]: 318.

101. Schram 1984: 31–32.

102. Bernal 1976; Zarrow 1990; Chan and Dirlik 1992; Dirlik 1991.

103. Cited in Zarrow 1990: 51–52.

104. Slogans and posters advocating "class struggle" in Guangzhou in the 1920s declared not that class struggle was glorious but that "class struggle is inevitable." See Swisher 1977: 32.

BIBLIOGRAPHY

Abend, Hallett. 1944. *My Years in China*. London.

Althusser, Louis. 1971. *Lenin and Philosophy*. London.

Amsden, Alice H. 1985. "The State and Taiwan's Economic Development." In Theda Skocpol, Peter B. Evans, and Dietrich Rueschemeyer, eds., *Bringing the State Back In*. Cambridge.

Anderson, Benedict. 1991. *Imagined Communities: Reflections on the Origins and Spread of Nationalism*. London.

Anderson, George E. 1911. *Railway Situation—China*. Washington, D.C.

Anderson, Marston. 1990. *The Limits of Realism: Chinese Fiction in the Revolutionary Period*. Berkeley, Calif.

Andolsen, Barbara. 1988. *Daughters of Jefferson*. Macon, Ga.

Arendt, Hannah. 1951. *The Origins of Totalitarianism*. New York.

Ayscough, Florence. 1938. *Chinese Women Yesterday and Today*. London.

Ba Jin. 1929. *Miewang* (Destruction). Shanghai.

——. [1931] 1980. "Gou" (The dog). In *Ba Jin xuanji* (Selected works of Ba Jin), 2 vols., vol. 1. Beijing.

——. 1931–35. *Aiqing* (Love). A trilogy published in installments: *Wu* (Fog), 1931; *Yu* (Rain), 1933; *Dian* (Lightning), 1935. Shanghai.

——. [1935] 1970. "Juexing yu huodong" (Awakening and action). In *Ba Jin wenji* (Collected writings of Ba Jin), 14 vols., vol. 10. Hong Kong.

Bao Zunpeng. 1964. *Zhongguo bowuguan shi* (A history of Chinese museums). Taipei.

Barrow, John. 1806. *Travels in China*. London.

——. 1839. *The Life of George Lord Anson*. London.

Beijing fengsu tu (Portrait of the customs of Beijing). 1986. Beijing.

Bellamy, Edward. 1888. *Looking Backward: 2000–1887*. Boston.

"Ben dangbu dangwu baogao" (Party center report on party affairs). 1924. *ZGZK* 9.

"Ben dangbu dongzheng riji zheyao" (A summary diary of the [Huangpu Special] party branch on the eastern expeditions). 1925. *Geming jun* 6/7.

"Benbu gongzuo baogao" (Report on the work of the [central peasant] bureau). 1926. *Zhongguo nongmin* 9.

"Benbu tepaiyuan dahui zhi jueyi an" (Resolutions of the [peasant] bureau special envoy conference). 1926. *Zhongguo nongmin* 1.

Benbu tongxin (Party center gazette). Shanghai.

Benhabib, Seyla. 1986. *Critique, Norm and Utopia: A Study of the Foundations of Critical Theory*. New York.

"Benzhi qishi yi" (First public announcement by this magazine). 1920. *Minjue* 1, no. 1.

Bergère, Marie-Claire. 1989. *The Golden Age of the Chinese Bourgeoisie, 1911–1937*. Translated by Janet Lloyd. Cambridge.

Bernal, Martin. 1967. "The Tzu-yu Tang and Tai Chi-T'ao, 1912–1913." *Modern Asian Studies* 1, no. 2.

————. 1976. *Chinese Socialism to 1907*. Ithaca, N.Y.

Berninghausen, John. 1977. "The Central Contradiction in Mao Dun's Earliest Fiction." In Merle S. Goldman, ed., *Modern Chinese Literature in the May Fourth Era*. Cambridge, Mass.

Bhaba, Homi K., ed. 1990. *Nation and Narration*. London.

Bianco, Lucien. 1986. "Peasant Movements." In John K. Fairbank and Albert Feuerwerker, eds., *The Cambridge History of China*, vol. 13, pt. 2. Cambridge.

Bickers, Robert A., and Jeffrey N. Wasserstrom. 1995. "Shanghai's 'Dogs and Chinese Not Admitted' Sign: Legend, History and Contemporary Symbol." *China Quarterly* 142.

Billingsley, Phil. 1988. *Bandits in Republican China*. Stanford, Calif.

Bing, Dov. 1973. "Ma-lin's Activities in China from the Beginning of June till December 10, 1921." *Issues and Studies* 9, no. 5.

Bing Xin. 1982. *Bing Xin quanji* (The complete works of Bing Xin). 5 vols. Shanghai.

Birch, A. H. 1971. *Representation*. London.

Bird, Isabella. 1899. *The Yangtze Valley and Beyond: An Account of Journeys in China, Chiefly in the Province of Sze Chuan and Among the Man-Tze of the Somo Territory*. London.

Bland, J. O. P. 1932. *China: The Pity of It*. London.

Boorman, Howard L., and Richard C. Howard, eds. 1967–71. *Biographical Dictionary of Republican China*. 4 vols. New York.

Bottomore, Tom, ed. 1983. *A Dictionary of Marxist Thought*. Oxford.

Bowman, Sylvia E., ed. 1962. *Edward Bellamy Abroad: An American Prophet's Influence*. New York.

Brandt, Conrad. 1966. *Stalin's Failure in China, 1924–1927*. New York.

Brandt, Conrad, Benjamin Schwartz, and John K. Fairbank. 1952. *A Documentary History of Chinese Communism*. Cambridge, Mass.

Brandt, Loren. 1989. *Commercialization and Agricultural Development in East-Central China, 1870–1937*. Cambridge.

Brass, Paul R. 1976. "Ethnicity and Nationality Formation." *Ethnicity* 3, no. 3.

Brown, Carolyn T. 1993. "Woman as Trope: Gender and Power in Lu Xun's 'Soap.' " In Tani E. Barlow, ed., *Gender Politics in Modern China*. Durham, N.C.

Brown, Peter. 1988. *The Body and Society: Men, Women and Sexual Renunciation in Early Christianity*. New York.

Bruehl, Elisabeth Young. 1982. *Hannah Arendt: For Love of the World*. New Haven, Conn.

Buck, Pearl. 1939. "Introduction." In Lin Yutang 1939.

———. 1958. *All Men Are Brothers*. London.

Cai Hesen. [1921] 1969. "Ts'ai He-sen on Proletarian Revolution in China." In Hélène Carrère d'Encausse and Stuart R. Schram, eds. and trans., *Marxism and Asia: An Introduction with Readings*. London.

———. 1922a. "Shishi duanping" (Brief comment on current affairs). *Xiangdao* 7.

———. 1922b. "Sun Wu ke zai yizhong shenma jichu shang lianhe ne?" (On what basis can Sun Yatsen and Wu Peifu come together?). *Xiangdao* 4.

———. 1922c. "Tongyi, jiezhai yu guomindang" (Unification, loans, and the Nationalist party). *Xiangdao* 1.

———. 1922d. "Wuli tongyi yu liansheng zizhi: junfa zhuanzheng yu junfa geju" (Military reunification and federalism: Warlord dictatorship and warlord separatism). *Xiangdao* 2.

———. 1922e. "Zhao Hengti yu Hunan sheng zizhi" (Zhao Hengti and provincial self-government in Hunan). *Xiangdao* 10.

———. 1922f. "Zhongshan xiansheng de binggong zhengce shi junfa shuofa de ma?" (Is Mr. Sun Yatsen's soldier-worker policy a warlord proposition?). *Xiangdao* 7.

———. 1923. "Beijing zhengbian yu ge zhengxi" (The Beijing coup and various political factions). *Xiangdao* 31/32.

———. 1924a. "Jinggao guomindang zhongpai zhu lingxiu" (A respectful message to leaders of the center faction of the Chinese Nationalist party). *Xiangdao* 85.

———. 1924b. "Shangtuan shijian de jiaoxun" (The lessons of the merchant militia incident). *Xiangdao* 82.

———. 1924c. "Yihetuan yu guomin geming" (The Boxers and the Nationalist Revolution). *Xiangdao* 81.

———. 1925. "Jinnian wuyi zhi zhongguo zhengzhi zhuangkuang yu gongnong jieji de zeren" (The political situation of China and the responsibility befalling the worker and peasant classes this May Day). *Xiangdao* 112.

Cantlie, James, and C. Sheridan Jones. N.d. *Sun Yatsen and the Awakening of China*. London.

Chan, F. Gilbert. 1979. "An Alternative to Kuomintang-Communist Collaboration: Sun Yat-sen and Hong Kong, January–June 1923." *Modern Asian Studies* 13, no. 1.

Chan, Ming Kou. 1975. "Labour and Empire: The Chinese Labor Movement in the Canton Delta, 1895–1927." Ph.D. diss., Stanford University.

Chan, Ming K., and Arif Dirlik. 1992. *Schools into Fields and Factories: Anarchists, the Guomindang, and the National Labor University in Shanghai, 1927–1932*. Durham, N.C.

Chang, Hao. 1971. *Liang Ch'i-ch'ao and Intellectual Transition in China, 1890–1907*. Cambridge, Mass.

———. 1987. *Chinese Intellectuals in Crisis: Search for Order and Meaning, 1890–1911*. Berkeley, Calif.

Chang, Sidney H., and Leonard H. D. Gordon. 1991. *All Under Heaven: Sun Yat-sen and His Revolutionary Thought*. Stanford, Calif.

Chapman, H. Owen. 1928. *The Chinese Revolution, 1926–1927*. London.

Chatterjee, Partha. 1986. *Nationalist Thought and the Colonial World: A Derivative Discourse*. London.

———. 1990. "Colonialism, Nationalism and Colonialized Women: The Contest in India." *American Ethnologist* 17, no. 1.

———. 1993. *The Nation and Its Fragments*. Princeton.

Chen, Leslie H. [Chen Dingyan]. 1988. "A Collection of Historiographic Materials for a Biography of Chen Chiung-ming (1878–1933)." 21 vols. Unpublished manuscript deposited in Columbia University Library.

———. 1989. "Federalism and the Unification of China—An Historical Perspective." Unpublished paper.

———. 1991. "Chen Jiongming (1878–1933) and the Chinese Federalist Movement." *Republican China* 17, no. 1.

Chen Dingyan [Leslie H. Chen]. 1990. "Chen Jiongming yu liansheng zizhi yundong" (Chen Jiongming and the federal self-government movement). Unpublished paper.

Chen Dong. 1925. "Minzu geming you nonggong wenti" (National revolution and the worker-peasant problem). *Geming* 1.

Chen Duxiu. [1914] 1969. "Patriotism and Consciousness of Self." In Hélène Carrère d'Encausse and Stuart R. Schram, ed. and trans., *Marxism and Asia: An Introduction with Readings*. London.

———. 1922. "Liansheng zizhi yu zhongguo zhengxiang" (Federalism and China's political situation). *Xiangdao* 1.

———. 1923a. "Dui deng huiyi yu Sun Cao xieshou" (The meeting of equals and the Sun-Cao alliance). *Xiangdao* 22.

———. 1923b. "Guomindang yu jiaotong anfu" (The Nationalist party and the Communications and Anfu cliques). *Xiangdao* 25.

———. 1923c. "Zenyang dadao junfa?" (How are we to overthrow warlords?). *Xiangdao* 21.

———. 1923d. "Zhongguo guomin geming yu shehui ge jieji" (The Chinese Nationalist Revolution and all classes in society). *Qianfeng* 2.

———. 1923e. "Zhongguo zhi da huan—zhiye bing yu zhiye yiyuan" (The great problems in China—professional soldiers and professional politicans). *Xiangdao* 19.

———. 1923f. "Zichan jieji de geming yu geming de zichan jieji" (Bourgeois revolution and the revolutionary bourgeoisie). *Xiangdao* 22.

———. 1924a. "Guomindang de yige genben wenti" (A basic problem with the Nationalist party). *Xiangdao* 85.

———. 1924b. "Guomindang zuoyou pai zhi zhen yiyi" (The true significance of left and right factions in the Nationalist party). *Xiangdao* 62.

———. 1924c. "Zhe shi youpai de xingdong ma? Haishi fan geming?" (Is this the behavior of the right faction? Or is it counterrevolution?). *Xiangdao* 87.

———. 1925a. "Gei Dai Jitao de yifeng xin" (A letter to Dai Jitao). *Xiangdao* 129.

———. 1925b. "Zhongguo minzu yundong zhong zhi zichan jieji" (The proletariat in China's nationalist movement). *Xiangdao* 136.

Chen Gongbo. 1926a. "Dang daibiao tiaoli he zhengzhi xunlian bu de jieshi" (Explanation of regulations governing party representatives and the political training bureau). *JSYK* 2.

———. 1926b. "Nongmin yundong baogao" (Report on the peasant movement). *ZZZB* 6/7.

———. 1926c. "Qingnian yundong baogao" (Report on the youth movement). *ZZZB* 6/7.

Chen Guofu. 1973–. "Jianjun shi zhi yi ye" (One page in the history of creating the army). *GMWX* 10.

Chen Jingwen. 1961. *Zhonghua mingguo guoge shi* (A history of national anthems in the Republic of China). Taipei.

Chen Tanqiu. 1924. "Guomindang de fenxi" (An analysis of the Nationalist party). *Zhongguo qingnian* 59.

Chen Tianxi. 1958. *Dai Jitao xiansheng biannian zhuanji* (Chronological biography of Dai Jitao). Taipei.

———, ed. 1959. *Dai Jitao xiansheng wencun* (Collected writings of Mr. Dai Jitao). 5 vols. Taipei.

———, ed. 1967. *Dai Jitao xiansheng wencun xu bian* (Collected writings of Mr. Dai Jitao: Supplement). Taipei.

———, ed. 1969. *Dai Jitao xiansheng wencun zai xubian* (Collected writings of Mr. Dai Jitao: Further supplement). Taipei.

———, ed. 1971. *Dai Jitao xiansheng wencun san xu bian* (Collected writings of Mr. Dai Jitao: Third supplement). Taipei.

Chen Xunzheng. 1973–. "Dangjun zhi zhaoji" (Laying the foundations of the party-army). *GMWX* 10.

Cheng Ching-mao. 1977. "The Impact of Japanese Literary Trends on Modern Chinese Writers." In Merle S. Goldman, ed., *Modern Chinese Literature in the May Fourth Era*. Cambridge, Mass.

Cheng Tianfang. 1962. "Li gongci sinian" (Four years in the Li temple). *Zhuanji wenxue* 1, no. 7.

Chesneaux, Jean. 1968. *The Chinese Labor Movement, 1919–1927*. Translated by H. M. Wright. Stanford, Calif.

Chiang Kaishek. [1943] 1947. *China's Destiny*. Translated by Wang Chung-hui. New York.

———. 1968. *Soviet Russia in China: A Summing Up at Seventy*. Rev. ed. New York.

Ch'ien, Hsiao, comp. 1944. *A Harp with a Thousand Strings*. London.

Chien Po-tsan, Shao Hsun-cheng, and Hu Hua. 1964. *Concise History of China*. Beijing.

Ch'ing, Julia. 1972–73. "Neo-Confucian Utopian Theories and Political Ethics." *Monumenta Serica: Journal of Oriental Studies* 30.

Chow, Rey. 1991. *Woman and Chinese Modernity: The Politics of Reading Between East and West.* Minneapolis, Minn.

Chow Tse-tsung. 1960. *The May Fourth Movement: Intellectual Revolution in Modern China.* Stanford, Calif.

———. 1963. *Research Guide to the May Fourth Movement.* Cambridge, Mass.

Chun Mu. 1923a. "Guomindang muqian zhi liangzhong zeren" (Two responsibilities currently facing the Nationalist party). *Xiangdao* 30.

———. 1923b. "Xiu jian guomin de zhongguo guomindang" (The Chinese Nationalist party slights the nation). *Xiangdao* 29.

Chun Tao. 1925. "Dong zheng jilue" (Outline of the Eastern Expedition). *ZZZB* 3.

Clendinnen, Inga. 1991. " 'Fierce and Unnatural Cruelty: Cortés and the Conquest of Mexico." *Representations* 33.

Clifford, Nicholas R. 1979. *Shanghai, 1925: Urban Nationalism and Defense of Foreign Privilege.* Ann Arbor.

Clubb, O. Edmund. 1978. *Twentieth-Century China.* 3d rev. ed. New York.

Coble, Parks M., Jr. 1980. *The Shanghai Capitalists and the Nationalist Government, 1927–1937.* Cambridge, Mass.

Cohen, Paul A. 1974. *Between Tradition and Modernity: Wang T'ao and Reform in Late Ch'ing China.* Cambridge, Mass.

———. 1984. *Discovering History in China.* New York.

Connerton, Paul. 1980. *The Tragedy of Enlightenment: An Essay on the Frankfurt School.* Cambridge.

Conrad, Joseph. 1980. *Heart of Darkness.* Harmondsworth.

Cranmer-Byng, J. L., ed. [1902] 1962. *An Embassy to China: Being the Journal Kept by Lord Macartney During His Embassy to the Emperor Ch'ien-lung, 1793–1794.* London.

Croizier, Ralph. 1968. *Traditional Medicine in Modern China: Science, Nationalism and the Tensions of Cultural Change.* Cambridge, Mass.

———. 1988. *Art and Revolution in Modern China: The Lingnan (Cantonese) School of Painting, 1906–1951.* Berkeley, Calif.

Cui Wenchong. 1924. "Zhongguo guomin geming yu wuchan jieji" (China's Nationalist Revolution and the proletariat). *Juewu,* 23 April.

Dai Jitao. 1925a. *Guomin geming yu zhongguo guomindang* (The Nationalist Revolution and the Chinese Nationalist party). Shanghai.

———. 1925b. *Sunwen zhuyi zhi zhexue de jichu* (The philosophical foundations of Sun Yatsenism). Shanghai.

———. [1925] 1959a. "Zhi Jiang jieshi xiansheng shu" (Letter to Mr. Chiang Kaishek). In Chen Tianxi, ed., *Dai Jitao xiansheng wencun,* vol. 3. Taipei.

———. [1925] 1959b. "Zhi Liu Luyin xiansheng shu" (Letter to Mr. Liu Luyin). In Chen Tianxi, ed., *Dai Jitao xiansheng wencun,* vol. 3. Taipei.

———. [1926] 1969. "Quanti de liyi yu bufen de liyi ji dangtuan de yiyi" (The interests of the whole, the interests of the part, and the significance of partisan institutions). In Chen Tianxi, ed., *Dai Jitao xiansheng wencun zai xubian.* Taipei.

"Dai Jitao xiansheng yanjiang" (Speech by Mr. Dai Jitao). 1926. *Guoli Zhongshan daxue xiaobao* 2.

"Dangbu shelun tiecun pu" (Scrapbook of editorials from party newspapers). N.d. Historical Archives Commission of the Kuomintang 436.117. Taipei.

Dawson, Raymond. 1967. *The Chinese Chameleon: An Analysis of European Conceptions of Chinese Civilization.* Oxford.

"Daxue tiaoli" (University regulations). 1924. In *GFQJ* 2.

de Certeau, Michel. 1988. *The Writing of History.* Translated by Tom Conley. New York.

De Francis, John. 1950. *Nationalism and Language Reform in China.* Princeton.

Degras, Jane, sel. and ed. 1971. *The Communist International, 1919–1943, Documents.* 3 vols. London.

Denby, Charles. 1906. *China and Her People: Being the Observations, Reminiscences and Conclusions of an American Diplomat.* 2 vols. Boston.

d'Encausse, Hélène Carrère, and Stuart R. Schram, ed. and trans. 1969. *Marxism and Asia: An Introduction with Readings.* London.

Deng Muhan. [1919] 1973-a. "Deng Muhan baogao zai yue lianluo qingxing yimou zai wo zhengquan shang zongli han" (Letter from Deng Muhan to the president detailing liaison work undertaken to plot a return to power in Guangdong). *GMWX* 48.

———. [1919] 1973-b. "Deng Muhan chenshu lianluo baoguan ji guangdong zhengqing shang zongli han" (Letter from Deng Muhan to the president detailing his liaison with newspaper houses, and the political situation in Guangdong). *GMWX* 48.

Deng Wenyi. 1976. *Huangpu jingshen* (The spirit of Huangpu). Taipei.

Deng Zhongxia. [1923] 1980. "Lun nongmin yundong" (On the peasant movement). *Zhongguo qingnian* 11. Reprinted in *LYLC*.

———. [1924] 1980. "Zhongguo nongmin zhuangkuang ji women yundong de fangzhen" (The general situation of China's peasants and the direction of our agitation). *Zhongguo qingnian* 13. Reprinted in *LYLC*.

Dening, Greg. 1993. "The Theatricality of History Making and the Paradoxes of Acting." *Cultural Anthropology* 8, no. 1.

Dennerline, Jerry. 1988. *Qian Mu and the World of Seven Mansions.* New Haven, Conn.

de Quincey, Thomas. [1857] 1897. "The Chinese Question in 1857." In Masson 1897: vol. 14.

Desmond, Adrian, and James Moore, 1991. *Darwin.* Harmondsworth.

Deutsch, K. W. 1966. *Nationalism and Social Communication.* New York.

"Dier ci quanti huiyi zhongyao jueyi an" (Important resolutions of the second plenum). [1926] 1973–. *GMWX* 79.

Dikötter, Frank. 1992. *The Discourse of Race in Modern China.* Stanford, Calif.

"Directives on the Application of the 1920 Agrarian Theses." [1920] 1971. In Degras 1971: vol. 1.

Dirlik, Arif. 1975. "The Ideological Foundations of the New Life Movement: A Study in Counter-Revolution." *Journal of Asian Studies* 34, no. 4.

————. 1978. *Revolution and History: Origins of Marxist Historiography in China, 1919–1937*. Berkeley, Calif.

————. 1989. *The Origins of Chinese Communism*. Hong Kong.

————. 1991. *Anarchism in the Chinese Revolution*. Berkeley, Calif.

"Di san ci quanti huiyi zhongyao jueyi an" (Important resolutions of the third plenum). [1925] 1973–. *GMWX* 79.

Dolezelova-Velingerova, Milena. 1977. "The Origins of Modern Chinese Literature." In Merle S. Goldman, ed., *Modern Chinese Literature in the May Fourth Era*. Cambridge, Mass.

————, ed. 1988. *A Selective Guide to Chinese Literature 1900–1949*. Vol. 1, *The Novel*. Leiden.

"Dongjiang geshu xingzheng huiyi jilue" (Record of the conference on administration in the East River region). 1926. *ZZZB* 9.

Dong Ziguang. 1943. *Chaoxian fangyan* (The local language of Chaoxian). Shanghai.

Doolittle, Rev. Justus. [1865] 1966. *Social Life of the Chinese*. Taipei.

Duara, Prasenjit. 1988. *Culture, Power and the State: Rural North China, 1900–1942*. Stanford, Calif.

————. 1990. "Nationalism as the Politics of Culture: Centralism and Federalism in Early Republican China." Washington, D.C.

Du Congrong. 1975. *Huangpu junxiao zhi chuangjian ji dongzheng beifa zhi huiyi* (Recollections of the founding of the Huangpu Academy and the Eastern and Northern expeditions). Taipei.

Dukes, Edwin Joshua. 1885. *Everyday Life in China*. London.

Eade, J. C., ed. 1983. *Romantic Nationalism in Europe*. Canberra.

Eagleton, Terry. 1981. *Walter Benjamin, or, Towards a Revolutionary Criticism*. London.

Eastman, Lloyd E. 1974. *The Abortive Revolution: China Under Nationalist Rule*. Cambridge, Mass.

Eberhard, Wolfram. 1964. "Ideas About Social Reform in the Novel *Ching-hua yüan* ('Insubstantial Connections')." In Eike Heberland, Meinhard Schuster, and Helmet Straube, eds., *Festschrift für Ad. E. Jensen*. Munich.

"The Educational Situation in Hainan." 1926. *Hainan Newsletter*, Fall.

Edwardes, Michael. 1971. *East-West Passage: The Travel of Idea, Arts and Inventions Between Asia and the Western World*. London.

Eide, Elisabeth. 1985. "Optimistic and Disillusioned Noras on the Chinese Literary Scene, 1919–1940." In Anna Gertslacher, Ruth Keen, Wolfgang Kubin, Margit Miosga, and Jenny Schon, eds., *Women and Literature in China*. Bochum.

————. 1987. *China's Ibsen: From Ibsen to Ibsenism*. London.

Ellis, Henry. 1817. *Journal of the Proceedings of the Late Embassy to China*. London.

Engels, Frederick. 1976. "The Festival of Nations in London." In Karl Marx and Frederick Engels, *Collected Works*, 46 vols., vol. 6. London.

"Erqi jinian yundong" (February seventh commemorative movement). 1926. *ZGZY* 1.

Fairbank, John K. 1953. *Trade and Diplomacy on the China Coast*. Cambridge.

————. 1971. *The United States and China*. 3d ed. Cambridge, Mass.

————. 1986. *The Great Chinese Revolution, 1800–1985.* New York.

Fang Dingying. 1927. *Fang jiaoyu zhang Dingying yanlun ji* (Collected speeches of the officer in charge of education, Fang Dingying). Guangzhou.

Fang Gang. 1924. "Guomindang gaizu hou de guangdong" (Guangdong after the Nationalist party reorganization). *Xin Minguo* 1.

Fanon, Frantz. 1967. *The Wretched of the Earth.* Harmondsworth.

Fargusson, Sir James of Kilkerran. 1972. *Balloon Tytler.* London.

Faure, David. 1989. *The Rural Economy of Pre-Liberation China.* Hong Kong.

Feng Jupo. 1923. *Guomin geming yu gongren* (The Nationalist Revolution and the workers). Guangzhou.

Feng Yu-lan. 1966. In Derk Bodde, ed., *A Short History of Chinese Philosophy.* New York.

Feuerwerker, Albert. 1968. *The Chinese Economy, 1912–1949.* Ann Arbor.

————. 1976. *The Foreign Establishment in China in the Early Twentieth Century.* Ann Arbor.

Fewsmith, Joseph. 1985. *Party, State and Local Elites in Republican China: Merchant Organization and Politics in Shanghai, 1890–1930.* Honolulu.

Fincher, John. 1968. "Political Provincialism and National Revolution." In Mary C. Wright, ed., *China in Revolution: The First Phase, 1900–1913.* New Haven, Conn.

Fishman, Joshua A. 1972. *Language and Nationalism: Two Integrative Essays.* Rowley, Mass.

FitzGerald, C. P. 1985. *Why China? Recollections of China 1923–1950.* Melbourne.

Fitzgerald, John. 1983. "Mao in Mufti: Newly Identified Works by Mao Zedong." *The Australian Journal of Chinese Affairs* 9.

————. 1988. "Did the National Revolution Succeed or Fail: A Point of Difference in Chinese and Western Perspectives on Republican Chinese History." *Republican China* 14.

————, ed. 1989. *The Nationalists and Chinese Society, 1923–1937: A Symposium.* Melbourne.

————. 1990a. "A Greater Disunity: The Politics and Finance of Guangdong Separatism, 1926–1936." *Modern Asian Studies* 24.

————. 1990b. "The Misconceived Revolution: State and Society in China's Nationalist Revolution, 1923–26." *Journal of Asian Studies* 49, no. 2.

Fogel, Joshua A., ed. and trans. 1983. "Naitō Konan and the Development of the Conception of Modernity in Chinese History." *Chinese Studies in History* 17.

————. 1989. *Nakae Ushikichi in China.* Cambridge, Mass.

Foster, John. 1928. *Chinese Realities.* London.

Foucault, Michel. 1972. *The Archaeology of Knowledge.* Translated by A. M. Sheridan. London.

————. 1984. *The Ethic of Care for the Self as a Practice of Freedom: An Interview with Michel Foucault on January 20, 1984.* Conducted by Raul Fornet Betancourt, et al., translated by J. D. Gauthier, S. J. Paris.

The Four Books. 1973. Translated by James Legge. Taipei.

Friedman, Edward. 1974. *Backward Toward Revolution: The Chinese Revolutionary Party*. Berkeley, Calif.

Friedrich, J. C. 1957. *Constitutional Reason of State*. Providence, R.I.

Fung, Edmund S. K. 1991. *The Diplomacy of Imperial Retreat: Britain's South China Policy, 1924–1931*. Hong Kong.

"Funu bu gongzuo baogao" ([Central] women's bureau work report). 1926. *ZGZY* 1.

"Funu bu gongzuo baogao" ([Provincial] women's bureau work report). 1926. *ZGGY* 1–4 (February–June).

"Funu bu xuanchuan huiyi an" (Documents on the propaganda meetings of the [Central] Women's Bureau). 1926. Historical Archives Commission of the Kuomintang, 436/302. Taipei.

"Funu ri da yundong jingguo qingxing" (Events surrounding the great movement on women's day). 1924. *ZGZK* 12.

"Funu yundong jueyi an" (Resolutions on the women's movement). 1926. *ZZZB* 6/7.

Funu zhi sheng huikan (Collection from *Women's Voice*). 1926. Guangzhou.

Fu Sinian. [1919] 1967. "Zhongguo gou yu zhongguo ren" (Chinese dogs and Chinese men). In *Fu Sinian xuanji* (Selected works of Fu Sinian), 7 vols., vol. 3. Taipei.

Galbiati, Fernando. 1985. *P'eng P'ai and the Hai-Lu-Feng Soviet*. Stanford, Calif.

Gan Naiguang. 1926a. "Shangmin yundong zhi jingguo" (The progress of the merchant movement). *ZZZB* 6/7.

———. 1926b. "Shenshi mintuan xianzhang heyi fandui nonghui?" (Why do the gentry, the local militia, and county heads oppose peasant associations?). *Zhongguo nongmin* 10.

Gasster, Michael. 1980. "The Republican Revolutionary Movement." In D. Twitchett and J. K. Fairbank, eds., *The Cambridge History of China*, vol. 11, pt. 2. Cambridge.

Gellner, Ernest. 1964. *Thought and Change*. London.

———. 1983. *Nations and Nationalism*. Ithaca, N.Y.

Geming wenxian (Documents on the revolution). 1973–. Edited by Luo Jialun. Unfinished multivolume series. Taipei. [Abbreviated as *GMWX*.]

"Ge shengqu dangwu baogao jueyian" (Decision regarding reports on party affairs from all provinces and regions). 1926. *ZZZB* 6/7.

"Ge xianshi dangbu ji choubei chu gongzuo baogao" (Report on the work of all party branches and preparatory offices at town and county levels). 1926. *ZGGY* 1 (February).

Gibbs-Smith, Charles H. 1985. *Aviation: An Historical Survey from Its Origins to the End of World War II*. London.

Gilbert, Rodney. 1926. *What's Wrong with China?* London.

Gilkey, Langdon. 1966. *Shantung Compound: The Story of Men and Women Under Pressure*. New York.

Gillespie, Charles Coulston. 1983. *The Montgolfier Brothers and the Invention of Aviation, 1783–1784*. New York.

Gillespie, Richard Eugene. 1971. "Whampoa and the Nanking Decade, 1924–1936." Ph.D. diss., American University, Washington D.C.

Gilmartin, Christina A. 1994. "Gender, Political Culture, and Women's Mobilization in the Chinese Nationalist Revolution." In Christina A. Gilmartin, Gail Hershatter, Lisa Rofel, and Tyrene White, eds., *Engendering China: Women, Culture and the State*. Cambridge, Mass.

Gluck, Carol. 1985. *Japan's Modern Myths: Ideology in the Late Meiji Period*. Princeton.

Goldman, Merle S., ed. 1977. *Modern Chinese Literature in the May Fourth Era*. Cambridge, Mass.

"Gongren bu gongzuo baogao" (Labor bureau work report). 1926. *ZGZY* 1.

"Gongzuo baogao" (Work report). 1926. *ZGGY* 4 (June).

Grant, Damian. 1970. *Realism*. London.

Gregory, Peter N. 1985. "Tsung-Mi and the Single Word 'Awareness.'" *Philosophy East and West* 35, no. 3.

Grieder, Jerome. 1970. *Hu Shih and the Chinese Renaissance: Liberalism in the Chinese Revolution, 1917–1937*. Cambridge, Mass.

"Guangdong dierci quansheng daibiao dahui xuanyan" (Declaration of the second Guangdong provincial assembly). 1926. *JSYK* 8.

"Guangdong gedi dangbao xiaoxi huizhi" (News of party papers in various localities in Guangdong). 1926. *ZGGY* 4 (June).

"Guangdong geming shili de tuanjie" (The unity of revolutionary forces in Guangdong). 1926. *ZZZB* 10.

Guangdong minzheng (Civil administration in Guangdong). 1941. Edited by Guangdong sheng zhengfu mishu chu. Qujiang.

Guangdong qingnian (Guangdong youth). 1926. Guangzhou.

"Guangdong sheng dangbu jiqi" (The Guangdong provincial party branch follows suit). 1925. *ZZZB* 2.

Guangdong shengzhengfu gongbao (Guangdong provincial government gazette). [Abbreviated as *GSGB*.]

"Guangdong sheng zhixing weiyuanhui xuanyan ji tonggao" (Declarations and announcements of the Guangdong provincial executive committee). 1926. *ZGGY* 1 (February).

"Guangdong zhibu tanhe gongchandang wen" (Letter from the Guangdong branch impeaching the Communist party). 1923. In *GFQJ*, vol. 4.

"Guangdong zhixing weiyuanhui zhangcheng caoan" (Draft constitution of the Guangdong provincial executive committee). 1925. *GMR*, 5 November.

Guangzhou minguo ribao (Guangzhou republican daily). [Abbreviated as *GMR*.]

"Guanyu xuanchuan jueyi an" (Resolutions on propaganda). 1926. *ZZZB* 6/7.

Guerard, Albert L. [1924] 1968. "Hero of the Will." In Harold Lubin, ed., *Heroes and Anti-Heroes: A Reader in Depth*. San Francisco.

Gu Jiegang. 1931. *The Autobiography of a Chinese Historian*. Translated by Arthur Hummel. Leiden.

Guofu quanji (The complete works of the father of the country). 1973. Edited by Dangshi shiliao bianzuan weiyuanhui. 6 vols. Taipei. [Abbreviated as *GFQJ*.]

"Guoming gemingjun dang daibiao tiaoli" (Regulations concerning party representatives in the Nationalist Revolutionary Army). 1926. *JSYK* 1.

"Guomin huiyi shijian ziliao jianbao tiecunpu" (Collection of newspaper clippings of materials on the National Citizens Conference). 1926. Historical Archives Commission of the Kuomintang, 472/9. Taipei.

Guo Moruo. 1926. *Luoye* (Fallen leaves). Shanghai.

Habermas, Jurgen. 1989. *The Structural Transformation of the Public Sphere: An Enquiry into a Category of Bourgeois Society*. Cambridge, Mass.

Hainan Newsletter. 1924. Haikou.

Hazama Naoki. 1992. " 'Chūgoku kokumintō daiichiji zenkoku daihyō daikai sengen' ni tsuite no kosatsu" (Resarch into the declarations of the first national congress of the Chinese Nationalist party). In Hazama Naoki, ed., *Chūgoku kokumin kakumei no kenkyū* (Research into China's Nationalist Revolution). Kyoto.

Hazzard, Shirley. 1980. *The Transit of Venus*. London.

He Chi. 1926. "Dongzheng zhanshi" (History of the eastern expeditionary war). *JSYK* 4.

Hegel, Georg. 1944. *The Philosophy of History*. Translated by J. Sibree. New York.

———. 1953. *Hegel's Philosophy of Right*. Translated by T. M. Knox. Oxford.

Hegel, Robert E. 1988. "Heavens and Hells in Chinese Fictional Dramas." In Carolyn T. Brown, ed., *Psyco-Sinology: The Universe of Dreams in Chinese Culture*. Washington, D.C.

Heimert, Alan. 1966. *Religion and the American Mind: From the Great Awakening to the Revolution*. Cambridge, Mass.

Heller, Agnes. 1988. *General Ethics*. London.

Heunemann, Ralph W. 1984. *The Dragon and the Iron Horse: The Economics of Railroads in China, 1876–1937*. Cambridge, Mass.

He Xiangning. 1926. "Funu yundong baogao" (Report on the women's movement). *ZZZB* 6/7.

Hirai, Kogoro. 1903. *Hyakunengo no Shakai* (Society one hundred years from now). Tokyo.

Hobbes, Thomas. [1651] 1946. In Michael Oakeshott, ed., *Leviathan: Or the Matter, Forme and Power of a Commonwealth Ecclesiasticall and Civil*. Oxford.

Hobson, J. A. [1902] 1965. *Imperialism: A Study*. Introduction by Philip Siegelman. Ann Arbor.

Hofheinz, Roy, Jr. 1977. *The Broken Wave: The Chinese Communist Peasant Movement, 1922–1928*. Cambridge.

Holm, David. 1990. *Art and Ideology in Revolutionary China*. Oxford.

Hou Chi-ming. 1965. *Foreign Investment and Economic Development in China, 1849–1937*. Cambridge, Mass.

Hsia, Tsi-an. 1968. *The Gate of Darkness: Studies on the Leftist Literary Movement in China*. Seattle.

Hsieh, Winston. 1962. "The Ideas and Ideals of a Warlord: Ch'en Chiung-ming (1878–1933)." *Papers on China* 16.

Hsü, Immanuel C. Y. 1990. *The Rise of Modern China*. 4th ed. New York.

Hsüeh Chun-tu. 1961. *Huang Hsing and the Chinese Revolution*. Stanford, Calif.

Hua Gang. [1931] 1982. *Zhongguo dageming shi* (The history of China's Great Revolution). Beijing.

Huang Ao. 1926. "Nanzheng de jingguo he ganxiang" (Processes and impressions of the Southern Expedition). *JSYK* 4.

Huang Jilu. 1964a. "Chusheng zhi du bu wei hu" (A newborn calf has no fear of a tiger). *Zhuanji wenxue* 4, no. 4.

———. 1964b. "Jin sishi nian lishi de xin ye" (A new page in the history of the past forty years). *Zhuanji wenxue* 4, no. 5.

———, ed. 1969. *Geming renwu zhi* (Records of revolutionaries). Taipei.

Huangpu jianjun sanshi nian gaishu (General outline of the creation of the army at Huangpu over thirty years). 1954. Edited by Dangshi shiliao bianzuan weihuanhui. Taipei.

Hua Zhou. 1920. "Pinglun" (Commentary). *Juewu*, 9 September.

Hu Chenghan. 1925. "Bu geming de guangdong daxue" (Nonrevolutionary Guangdong University). *Geming jun* 6/7.

Hu Hanmin. 1919. "Zhongguo zhexue shi zhi weiwu de yanjiu" (Materialist research into the history of Chinese philosophy). *Jianshe* 1, no. 3.

———. 1920. "Jieji yu daode xueshuo" (The theory of class and ethics). *Jianshe* 1, no. 6.

———. 1973–. "Zhongguo guomindang piping zhi piping" (Criticism of criticisms of the Chinese Nationalist party). *GMWX* 9.

"Huishu tebie weiyuanhui gongzuo baogao" (Report on the work of the special committee for the Huizhou region). 1926. *ZGGY* 2 (March).

Hung Chang-tai. 1985. *Going to the People: Chinese Intellectuals and Folk Literature, 1918–1937*. Cambridge, Mass.

Hunt, Lynn. 1984. *Politics, Culture, and Class in the French Revolution*. Berkeley, Calif.

Hu Pu'an. [1922] 1990. *Zhonghua quanguo fengsu zhi* (Gazetteer of local customs throughout China). Zhengzhou.

Hu Shi. 1918. "Yibusheng zhuyi" (Ibsenism). *Xin qingnian* 4, no. 6.

———. [1931] 1969. "On knowledge and action." In T'ang Leang-li, ed., *China's Own Critics: A Selection of Essays*. With commentaries by Wang Ching-wei. New York.

———. 1934. "A Chinese 'Gulliver' on Women's Rights." *People's Tribune* 7.

Hutchinson, Paul. 1924. *China's Real Revolution*. New York.

Huters, Theodore. 1991. "Mirages of Representation: May Fourth and the Anxiety of the Real." In Theodore Huters and Xiaobing Tang, *Chinese Literature and the West: The Trauma of Realism; the Challenge of the (Post) Modern*. Durham, N.C.

Iriye, Akira. 1965. *After Imperialism: The Search for a New Order in the Far East 1921–1931*. Cambridge, Mass.

Isaacs, Harold. 1961. *The Tragedy of the Chinese Revolution*. 2d rev. ed. Stanford, Calif.

———. 1971. "Notes on a Conversation with H. Sneevliet." *China Quarterly* 34.

Jansen, Marius B. 1975. *Japan and China: From War to Peace, 1894–1972*. Chicago.

Jiang Guangci. 1926. *Shaonian piaobozhe* (The young wanderer). Shanghai.

———. 1930. *Chongchu yunwei de yueliang* (The moon breaking out from behind the clouds). Shanghai.

"Jiaoyu yundong weiyuanhui yishilu" (Minutes of the meetings of the education movement committee). 1925. Historical Archives Commission of the Kuomintang, 446/7. Taipei.

"Jieshao hainei zui you jiazhi baozhi" (Introducing the most valuable newspapers in the country). 1912. *Minyi* 1.

Jizhe. 1924. "Da Guomindang zhongyang zhixing weiyuanhui" (Reply to the Nationalist Central Executive Committee). *Xiangdao* 92.

Johnson, David, Andrew Nathan, and Evelyn Rawski, eds. 1985. *Popular Culture in Late Imperial China.* Berkeley, Calif.

Johnson, Paul. 1991. *The Birth of the Modern.* London.

Johnson, R. Stewart. 1991. *Scholar Gardens of China: A Study and Analysis of the Spatial Design of the Chinese Private Garden.* Cambridge.

Johnson, Samuel. 1969. "Selections from *The Adventurer,* Number 115." In Mona Wilson, ed., *Johnson: Prose and Poetry.* London.

Johnstone, Reginald F. 1934. *Twilight in the Forbidden City.* New York.

Jordan, Donald. 1976. *The Northern Expedition: China's National Revolution of 1926–1928.* Honolulu.

Josipovici, Gabriel. 1982. *Writing and the Body.* Brighton.

"Junshi weiyuanhui junshi zhengzhi yuekan jianzheng" (Constitution of the *Military and Political Affairs Monthly* of the Military Affairs Committee). 1926. *JSYK* 1.

Junshi zhengzhi yuekan (Military and political affairs monthly). 1926. [Abbreviated as *JSYK.*]

Ju Zheng. 1973–a. "Bendang gaijin dafan" (Outline of the party reforms). *GMWX* 8.

———. 1973–b. "Zhonghua gemingdang shidai de huiyi" (Recollections of the Chinese Revolutionary party period). *GMWX* 5.

Kang Youwei. 1935. *Datong Shu* (One world philosophy). Shanghai.

———. 1958. *Ta T'ung Shu: The One-World Philosophy of K'ang Yu-wei.* Translated by Laurence G. Thompson. London.

———. 1967. "Chronological Biography of K'ang Yu-wei." In Jung-pang Lo, ed., *K'ang Yu-wei: A Biography and a Symposium.* Tucson.

Kataoka Kazutada. 1984. "Shingai kakumei ki no go zoku kyowa ron o megutte" (On the origins of the theory of five races in the 1911 revolution period). In *Chūgoku kindai shi no shomondai: Tanaka Masayoshi sensei taikan kinen ronshū* (Problems of modern Chinese history: Festschrift in honor of the retirement of Professor Tanaka Masayoshi). Tokyo.

Kauffman, Walter. 1965. *Hegel: Reinterpretation, Texts and Commentary.* Garden City, N.Y.

Kenez, Peter. 1985. *The Birth of the Propaganda State: Soviet Methods of Mass Mobilization, 1917–1929.* Cambridge.

Keyte, J. C. 1925. *The Passing of the Dragon.* 2d ed. London.

Kinkley, Jeffrey C. 1987. *The Odyssey of Shen Congwen.* Stanford, Calif.

Knechtges, David. 1973. "Dream Adventure Stories in Europe and T'ang China." *Tamkang Review* 4, no. 2.

Knight, Nick. ed. 1990. *Mao Zedong on Dialectics: Writings on Philosophy, 1937.* Armonk, N.Y.

Kong Zhongnan. 1933. *Guangdongyu suyu kao* (An investigation into common sayings in the Guangdong language). Guangzhou.

Kuhn, Philip A. 1970. *Rebellion and Its Enemies in Late Imperial China: Militarization and Social Structure, 1796–1864.* Cambridge, Mass.

Kumar, Krishan. 1987. *Utopia and Anti-Utopia in Modern Times.* Oxford.

Kuo, Ping-chia. 1956. *China: New Age and Outlook.* London.

Kwok, D. W. Y. 1965. *Scientism in Chinese Thought 1900–1950.* New Haven, Conn.

Lamley, H. J. 1977. "Hsieh-tou: The Pathology of Violence in South-eastern China." *Ch'ing-shih Went'i* 3, no. 7.

Landis, Richard B. 1964. "The Origins of Whampoa Cadets Who Served in the Northern Expedition." *Studies in Asia* 5.

———. 1969. "Institutional Trends at the Whampoa Military School, 1924–1926." Ph.D. diss., University of Washington, Seattle.

Lao She. [1929] 1980. *Ma and Son.* Translated by Jean M. James. San Francisco.

Laroui, Abdallah. 1976. *The Crisis of the Arab Intellectual.* Berkeley, Calif.

Lary, Diana. 1975. *Region and Nation.* Cambridge.

Lee, Frederick. 1926. *Travel Talks on China.* Washington, D.C.

Lee, Leo Ou-fan. 1973. *The Romantic Generation of Modern Chinese Writers.* Cambridge, Mass.

———. 1987. *Voices from the Iron House: A Study of Lu Xun.* Bloomington, Ind.

Lenin, V. I. [1902] 1988. *What Is to Be Done?* Translated by Joe Fineberg and George Hanna. Revised with an introduction by Robert Service. Harmondsworth.

———. 1916. *Imperialism: The Highest Stage of Capitalism.* Moscow.

———. [1917] 1965. *The State and Revolution.* Moscow.

Leong, S. T. 1976. *Sino-Soviet Diplomatic Relations, 1917–1926.* Canberra.

Levenson, Joseph. 1971a. *Revolution and Cosmopolitanism: The Western Stage and the Chinese Sages.* Berkeley, Calif.

———. 1971b. "The Province, the Nation and the World: The Problem of Chinese Identity." In Joseph Levenson, ed., *Modern China: An Interpretive Anthology.* New York.

Leyda, Jan. 1972. *Dianying: Electric Shadows.* Cambridge, Mass.

Leys, Simon. 1991. *The Death of Napoleon.* London.

Li, Dun J., trans. and ed. 1978. *Modern China: From Mandarin to Commissar.* New York.

Liang Qichao. 1897. "Lun nü xue" (On the education of women). In Liang Qichao 1928: vol. 1.

———. 1900. "Zhongguo jiruo suyuan lun" (On the source of China's weakness). In Liang Qichao 1928: vol. 2.

———. 1901. "Zhongguo shi xulun" (Preface to a history of China). In Liang Qichao 1927: vol. 3.

———. 1902. "Xin min shu" (The renovation of the people). *Xinmin congbao* (The new people). Tokyo.

———. [1902] 1967. "Sanshi zi shu" (An autobiography at thirty). In *Yinbingshi quanji* (Complete works from the ice-drinker's studio). Taipei.

———. [1902] 1979. "The Renovation of the People." In Teng and Fairbank 1979.

———. 1903. "Lun zhongguo guomin zhi xingge" (On the character of the Chinese citizenry). In Liang Qichao 1927: vol. 5.

————. [1922] 1979. "A General Survey of China's Progress over the Past Fifty Years." In S. Y. Teng and J. K. Fairbank, eds., *China's Response to the West: A Documentary Survey, 1839–1923*. 2d ed. Cambridge, Mass.

————. 1927. *Yinbingshi heji* (Collected works from the Ice-Drinker's Studio). 21 vols. Shanghai.

————. 1928. *Yinbingshi wenji* (Collected essays from the Ice-Drinker's Studio). 30 vols. Shanghai.

————. 1953. "Lun jinqu maoxian" (On adventure). In Liu Yanling and Hu Lunqing, eds., *Ming Qing sanwenxuan*. Taipei.

————. 1977. "An Autobiographical Account at Thirty." Translated by Li Yu-ning. *Chinese Studies in History* 10, no. 3.

————. 1978. "What Is Wrong with the Chinese?" In Dun J. Li, ed., *Modern China: From Mandarin to Commissar*. New York.

————. 1984. "Wuchan jieji yu wuye jieji" (The class with no property [proletariat] and the class with nothing to do). In Li Xinghua, ed., *Liang Qichao xuanji*. Shanghai.

————. N.d. "Shenshi yinshu xu" (Preface to Master Shen's phonetics). In Liang Qichao 1928: vol. 3.

Li Ao. 1987. *Li Ao lun Sun Zhongshan* (Li Ao on Sun Yatsen). Tainan.

"Liao Zhongkai zhi Chucang dian" (Telegram from Liao Zhongkai to [Ye] Chucang). N.d. Historical Archives Commission of the Kuomintang, 413/5. Taipei.

Li Chien-nung. 1956. *The Political History of China, 1840–1928*. Edited and translated by Teng Ssu-yü and Jeremy Ingalls. Stanford, Calif.

Li Dajia. 1986. *Minguo chunian de liansheng zizhi yundong* (The provincial self-government movement in the early Republic). Taipei.

Li Dazhao. [1915] 1969. "Pessimism and Consciousness of Self." In Hélène Carrère d'Encausse and Stuart R. Schram, ed. and trans., *Marxism and Asia: An Introduction with Readings*. London.

————. [1919] 1959. "Qingnian yu nongcun" (Youth and the countryside). In *Li Dazhao xuanji* (Selected works of Li Dazhao). Beijing.

————. [T.C.L.] 1923. "Pubian quanguo de guomindang" (The Nationalist party [should be] everywhere throughout the whole country). *Xiangdao* 21.

————. [1923] 1978. "Pingmin zhuyi" ("Democracy" [sic]). In *Li Dazhao xuanji* (Selected works of Li Dazhao). Beijing.

Li Hanwei. 1922. "Zhongguoren weishenma quefa zuzhi nengli?" *Juewu*, 1 January.

Li Jianer. 1941. *Guangdong xiandai huaren zhuan* (Biographies of contemporary Guangdong painters). Guangzhou.

Li Jui. [1957] 1977. *The Early Revolutionary Activities of Comrade Mao Tse-tung*. Translated by Anthony W. Sariti. Edited by James C. Hsiung. Introduction by Stuart Schram. White Plains, N.Y.

Li Linong. 1926. "Guomin gemingjun dishi shuai zhengzhibu nanlu zhanshi zhengzhi xuanchuan gongzuo" (Political propaganda work of the political bureau of the Tenth Division of the Nationalist Revolutionary Army during the war on the southern route). *JSKY* 6.

Lin Sen. 1920. "Zhuci si" (Fourth congratulatory preface). *Minjue* 1, no. 1.

"Linshi zhengzhi xuanchuan weiyuanhui diyi qi xuanchuan jihua gao" (Draft of the propaganda program for the first period of provisional political propaganda committee [operations]). 1925. Historical Archives Commission of the Kuomintang, 436/2. Taipei.

Lin Yizhong. 1926. "Nanzheng ji" (Diary of the Southern Expedition). *JSYK* 5.

Lin Yutang. [1931] 1969a. "The Metropolitan Village of Nanking." In T'ang Leang-li, ed., *China's Own Critics: A Selection of Essays*. With commentaries by Wang Ching-wei. New York.

———. [1931] 1969b. "The Model Bandit." In T'ang Leang-li, ed., *China's Own Critics: A Selection of Essays*. With commentaries by Wang Ching-wei. New York.

———. 1939. *My Country and My People*. Rev. ed. London.

Li Ruzhen. 1965. *Flowers in the Mirror*. Translated by Lin Tai-yi. Berkeley, Calif.

Liuda yiqian: dang de lishi cailiao (Before the sixth congress: Party historical materials). 1980. Edited by Zhonggong zhongyang shujichu. Beijing. [Abbreviated as *LYLC*.]

"Liu hu guohui yiyuan Lin Sen deng zhu feichang guohui yanqi gaizu dian" (Telegram from Lin Sen and other parliamentarians in Shanghai proposing that the extraordinary parliament be postponed and reorganized). [1918] 1973-. *GMWX* 7.

Liu Renjing. 1924. "Henan lushi xian renmin dui junfa zhi fankang" (Resistance against a warlord by the people of Lushi County in Henan). *Xiangdao* 69.

Liu Shaotang, ed. 1977-. *Minguo renwu xiaozhuan* (Brief biographies of Republican figures). 19 vols. to date. Taipei.

Liu Zhih-po to [Hong Kong Postmaster General] Ross. 1921. Foreign Office 371-6649 (44-9).

Li Weiqing. [1907] 1989. *Shanghai xiangtu shi* (Shanghai local history). Shanghai.

Li Xin, ed. 1991. *Guomin geming de xingqi* (The rise of the Nationalist Revolution). Shanghai.

Li Yunhan. 1966. *Cong ronggong dao qingdang* (From the admission of the Communists to the purification of the party). 2 vols. Taipei.

Lü Fangshang. 1989. *Geming zhi zaiqi: Zhongguo guomindang gaizu qian dui xin sichao de huiying, 1914-1924* ("Rekindle the Revolution: The Kuomintang's response to new thought before the reorganization, 1914-1924." [sic]). Taipei.

———. 1992. "The Intellectual Origins of Guomindang Radicalization in the Early 1920s." *Chinese Studies in History* 26, no. 1.

Luk, Michael. 1990. *The Origins of Chinese Bolshevism: An Ideology in the Making, 1920-1928*. Hong Kong.

Lukács, Gyorgy. 1962. *The Meaning of Contemporary Realism*. Translated by John and Necke Mander. London.

———. 1971. *The Theory of the Novel: A Historico-Philosophical Essay on the Forms of Great Epic Literature*. Translated by Anna Bostock. Cambridge, Mass.

Luo Dunwei. 1963. "Laoyu zhi zai" (An unfortunate jailing). *Zhuanji wenxue* 2, no. 3.

Luo Jialun. 1919. "Shenma shi wenxue?" (What is literature?). *Xin qingnian* 1, no. 2.

Luo Jialun and Huang Jilu, eds. 1969. *Guofu nianpu zengding ben* (Revised chronology of the father of the country). 2 vols. Taipei.

Luo Qiyuan. 1926a. "Benbu yinian lai gongzuo baogao gaiyao" (Outline report on [peasant] bureau work over the past year). *Zhongguo nongmin* 2.

———. 1926b. "Guomin geming yu nongmin yundong zhi guanxi" (The relationship between the Nationalist Revolution and the peasant movement). *Zhongguo nongmin* 1.

Luo Yangqing. 1926. "Disi jun zhengzhibu nanzheng gonzuo jingguo gailue" (General outline of the progress of work of the Fourth Army political bureau on the Southern Expedition). *JSKY* 6.

Lutz, Jessie Gregory. 1988. *Chinese Politics and Christian Missions: The Anti-Christian Movements of 1920–1928*. Notre Dame, Ind.

Lu Xun. [1922] 1980. "Preface to *Call to Arms*." In Lu Xun 1980: vol. 1.

———. [1923] 1980a. "The True Story of Ah Q." In Lu Xun 1980: vol. 1.

———. [1923] 1980b. "What Happens After Nora Leaves Home?—Talk at the Beijing Normal Women's College, 26 December 1923." In Lu Xun 1980: vol. 2.

———. [1925] 1980. "Regret for the Past." In Lu Xun 1980: vol. 1.

———. [1927] 1974. "The Dog's Retort." In Lu Hsun [Lu Xun], *Wild Grass*. Beijing.

———. [1927] 1980. "Anxious Thoughts on 'Natural Breasts.' " In Lu Xun 1980: vol. 2.

———. [1931] 1980. "A Glance at Shanghai Literature: A Talk Given to the Social Science Study Group on August 12, 1931." In Lu Xun 1980: vol. 3.

———. [1934] 1980. "Napoleon and Jenner." In Lu Xun 1980: vol. 4.

———. [1936] 1980. "For Future Reference (3)." In Lu Xun 1980: vol. 4.

———. 1980. *Selected Works*. Translated by Yang Xianyi and Gladys Yang. 3d ed. 4 vols. Beijing.

McDonald, Angus W., Jr. 1978. *The Urban Origins of Rural Revolution: Elites and the Masses in Hunan Province, China, 1911–1927*. Berkeley, Calif.

McDougall, Bonnie S. 1977. "The Impact of Western Literary Trends." In Merle S. Goldman, ed., *Modern Chinese Literature in the May Fourth Era*. Cambridge, Mass.

———. 1980. *Mao Zedong's "Talks at the Yan'an Conference on Literature and Art": A Translation of the 1943 Text with Commentary*. Ann Arbor.

MacFarquhar, Rodney. 1953. "The Whampoa Military Academy." *Papers on China* 9.

Mackerras, Colin. 1989. *Western Images of China*. Hong Kong.

McLellan, David. 1983. "Politics." In David McLellan, ed., *Marx: The First Hundred Years*. Oxford.

Magruder. 1921. Letter from Major Magruder, assistant military attaché to the Peking legation, Hong Kong, to the military attaché, Peking. United States Department of State, 3338, Enclosure 4. 27 January.

Ma King-Sheuk. 1974. "A Study of *Hsin Ch'ing-nien* (New Youth) Magazine, 1915–1926." Ph.D. diss., London University.

Ma Ruiran [N. G. D. Malmquist]. 1991. "Cong 'Datongshu' kan zhongxi wutuobang de chayi" (Differences in Chinese and Western utopianism seen from a reading of Datongshu). *Ershiyi shiji shuangyuekan* 5.

Mao Dun. 1928. "Cong Guling dao Dongjing" (From Guling to Tokyo). *Xiaoshuo yuebao* 19.

———. 1958a. *Fushi* (Decay). In *Mao Dun wenji* (Collected works of Mao Dun), 10 vols., vol. 5. Beijing.

———. 1958b. "Huanmie" (Disillusion). In *Shi* (The canker), in *Mao Dun wenji* (Collected works of Mao Dun), 10 vols., vol. 1. Beijing.

———. 1958c. *Shi* (The canker). In *Mao Dun wenji* (Collected works of Mao Dun), 10 vols., vol. 1. Beijing.

Mao Sicheng, ed. 1965. *Shiwu nian yiqian zhi Jiang Jieshi xiansheng* ([The diary of] Mr. Chiang Kaishek to 1926). Hong Kong.

Mao Zedong:

[1] "China Is Poor and Blank." [1958] 1969. In Schram 1969.

[2] "For the Germans, the Painful Signing of the Treaty." [1919] 1992. In Schram 1992.

[3] "The Founding and Progress of the 'Strengthen Learning Society.' " [1919] 1992. In Schram 1992.

[4] "Geming pai dangyuan qunqi fandui Beijing youpai huiyi" (Party members of the revolutionary faction rise together to oppose the meeting of the Beijing right faction). [Written as Ziren.] 1925. *ZZZB* 2.

[5] "Gongchan zhangcheng yu shifei gongchan" (The Communist platform and whether or not it is communist). [Written as Run.] 1925. *ZZZB* 1.

[6] "Guomindang youpai fenli de yuanyin ji qi duiyu geming qiantu de yingxiang" (The reasons underlying the secession of the Nationalist right-faction and its ramifications for the future of the revolution). [Written as Ziren.] 1925. *ZZZB* 4.

[7] "Let Us Transform the Consciousness of the Masses." [1958] 1969. In Schram 1969.

[8] "Letter to Li Jinxi." [1917] 1992. In Schram 1992.

[9] *Mao's Road to Power: Revolutionary Writings, 1912–1949.* Vol. 1: *The Pre-Marxist Period, 1912–1920.* 1992. Edited by Stuart R. Schram. Armonk.

[10] "On Practice." [1937] 1967. In Mao [16]: vol. 1. Beijing.

[11] "On the Mass Line." [1944] 1969. In Schram 1969.

[12] "On the New Stage." [1938] 1969. In Schram 1969.

[13] *Report from Xunwu.* [1930] 1990. Translated with an introduction by Roger R. Thompson. Stanford, Calif.

[14] "Report on an Investigation of the Peasant Movement in Hunan." [1927] 1967. In Mao [16]: vol. 1. Beijing.

[15] "San san san yi zhi" (The system of 3:3:3:1). [Written as Run.] 1925. *ZZZB* 1.

[16] *Selected Works of Mao Tse-tung.* 1967. 4 vols. Beijing.

[17] "Shanghai minguo ribao fandong de yuanyin ji guomindang zhongyang dui gaibao de chuzhi" (The reasons underlying the reaction of the *Shanghai Republican Daily* and the punitive measures adopted by the Nationalist Party Center). [Written as Ziren.] 1925. *ZZZB* 3.

[18] "A Study of Physical Education." [1917] 1969. In Schram 1969.

[19] "Talks at the Yenan Forum on Literature and Art." [1942] 1967. In Mao [16]: vol. 3.

[20] "Xiang zuo haishi xiang you?" (To the left or to the right). [Written as Run.] 1925. *ZZZB* 2.

[21] "Xuanchuan bu gongzuo baogao" (Propaganda bureau work report). 19 May 1926. Historical Archives Commission of the Kuomintang. Taipei.

[22] "Zhengzhi zhoubao fakan liyou" (The reasons for publishing *Political Weekly*). 1925. *ZZZB* I.

[23] "Zou Lu yu geming" (Zou Lu and revolution). [Written as Run.] 1925. *ZZZB* I.

March, Andrew L. 1974. *The Idea of China: Myth and Theory in Geographic Thought.* Melbourne.

Marcuse, Herbert. 1960. *Reason and Revolution: Hegel and the Rise of Social Theory.* 2d ed. New York.

Marks, Robert B. 1977. "The World Can Change." *Modern China* 3, no. I.

——. 1984. *Rural Revolution in South China: Peasants and the Making of History in Haifeng County, 1570–1930.* Madison, Wis.

Marx, Karl. [1852] 1968. "The Eighteenth Brumaire of Louis Bonaparte." In *Karl Marx and Frederick Engels: Selected Works.* Moscow.

Marx, Karl. [1853] 1969a. "The British Rule in India." In d'Encausse and Schram 1969.

Marx, Karl. [1853] 1969b. "The Future Results of the British Rule in India." In d'Encausse and Schram 1969.

Marx, Karl, and Frederick Engels. [1848] 1976. "Manifesto of the Communist Party." In Karl Marx and Frederick Engels, *Collected Works*, 46 vols., vol. 6. London.

Masson, David, ed. 1897. *The Collected Writings of Thomas De Quincey.* 14 vols. London.

Mast, Herman, III. 1970. "An Intellectual Biography of Tai Chi-t'ao from 1891 to 1928." Ph.D. diss., University of Illinois at Urbana-Champaign.

Mast, Herman, III, and William G. Saywell. 1974. "Revolution out of Tradition: The Political Ideology of Tai Chi-t'ao." *Journal of Asian Studies* 24, no. I.

Maugham, W. Somerset. 1955. "The Philosopher." In W. Somerset Maugham, *The Travel Books of W. Somerset Maugham.* Melbourne.

Mehlman, Jeffrey. 1977. *Revolution and Repetition: Marx/Hugo/Balzac.* Berkeley, Calif.

Meisner, Maurice. 1974. *Li Ta-Chao and the Origins of Chinese Marxism.* New York.

——. 1982. *Marxism, Maoism and Utopianism: Eight Essays.* Madison, Wis.

Meissner, Werner. 1990. *Philosophy and Politics in China.* Stanford, Calif.

Meng Yue. 1993. "Female Images and National Myth." In Tani E. Barlow, ed., *Gender Politics in Modern China.* Durham, N.C.

Mercier, Louis-Sebastien. 1795. *Memoirs of the Year 2500.* Translated by W. Hooper. Philadelphia

Miao Xiangchu. 1926. "Nanzheng zhengzhi xuanchuan gongzuo zong baogao" (General report of political propaganda work on the Southern Expedition). *JSYK* 4 and 5.

"Minguo liu zhi qi nian dayuanshuai fu jianren renyuan zhiwu xingming lu" (List of names of staff appointed by the grand marshal's office, and of the nature of their appointments, from 1917 to 1918). [1918] 1973. *GFQJ*: vol. 4.

Minguo renwu da cidian (Greater dictionary of Republican personalities). 1991. Shijiazhuang.

"Minguo renwu xiaozhuan" (Microbiographies of personalities of the Republic). 1979. *Zhuanji wenxue* 34, no. 2.

Minguo shiqi guangdong sheng zhengfu dangan shiliao xuanbian (Selected materials from the historical archives of the Guangdong provincial government in the Republican period). 1987. Edited by Guangdong sheng danganguan. 11 vols. Guangzhou.

Minguo zhuren. 1912. "Fakan ci" (Foreword to the first issue). *Minyi* 1.

Min Tu-ki. 1989. *National Polity and Local Power: The Transformation of Late Imperial China*. Edited and translated by Philip A. Kuhn and Timothy Brook. Cambridge, Mass.

"Minyi zazhi chushi songci" (Elegy on the launching of *Minyi*). 1912. *Minyi* 1.

Montrose, Louise. 1991. "The Work of Gender in the Discourse of Discovery." *Representations* 33.

Morse, Hosea Ballou. 1910–1918. *The International Relations of the Chinese Empire*. 3 vols. London.

Mosher, Steven W. 1990. *China Misperceived: American Illusions and Chinese Reality*. New York.

Mosse, George L. 1973. "Mass Politics and the Political Liturgy of Nationalism." In Eugene Kamenka, ed., *Nationalism: The Nature and Evolution of an Idea*. Canberra.

Mote, F. W. 1977. "The Transformation of Nanking, 1350–1400." In G. William Skinner, ed., *The City in Late Imperial China*. Stanford, Calif.

Mumford, Lewis. 1938. *The Culture of Cities*. New York.

Munck, Ronaldo. 1986. *The Difficult Dialogue: Marxism and Nationalism*. London.

Munro, Donald J. 1977. *The Concept of Man in Contemporary China*. Berkeley, Calif.

Myers. 1921. Consul Myers (Swatow) to Washington. United States Department of State, 4079. 1 September.

Myers, Ramon H. 1991. "How Did the Modern Chinese Economy Develop?" *Journal of Asian Studies* 50, no. 3.

Najita, Tetsuo, and H. D. Harootunian. 1988. "Japanese Revolt Against the West: Political and Cultural Criticism in the Twentieth Century." In Peter Duus, ed., *The Cambridge History of Japan*, vol. 6. Cambridge.

"Nanlu geshu xianzheng huiyi yijue an" (Resolutions of the conference of all county heads in the southern route region). 1926. *zzzb* 11.

Naquin, Susan, and Evelyn Rawski. 1987. *Chinese Society in the Eighteenth Century*. New Haven, Conn.

Narramore, Terry. 1989. "The Nationalists and the Daily Press: The Case of *Shenbao*, 1927–1934." In Fitzgerald 1989.

Nathan, Andrew J. 1976. *Peking Politics, 1918–1923: Factionalism and the Failure of Constitutionalism*. New York.

———. 1985. *Chinese Democracy*. New York.

Nehru, Jawaharlal. [1945] 1956. *The Discovery of India*. Calcutta.

Nipperday, Thomas. 1983. "In Search of Identity: Romantic Nationalism, Its Intellectual, Political and Social Background." In J. C. Eade, ed., *Romantic Nationalism
in Europe*. Canberra.

"Nongmin gongzuo baogao" (Peasant work report). 1926. *ZGGY* 4 (June).

"Nongmin yundong jueyi an" (Resolutions on the peasant movement). 1926. *ZZZB* 6/7.

"Nong so" (The Peasant [Movement Training] Institute). 1926. *Zhongguo nongmin* 1.

Nozawa Yutaka. 1971. *Son Bun to Chūgoku kakumei* (Sun Yatsen and the Chinese
revolution). Tokyo.

————, ed. 1974. *Chūgoku kokumin kakumei shi no kenkyū* (A study of the history of
the Chinese Nationalist Revolution). Tokyo.

Nozawa Yutaka and Tanaka Masatoshi, eds. 1978. *Kōza chūgoku kin gen dai shi* (A
series of studies in modern and contemporary Chinese history). 7 vols. Tokyo.

O'Brien, Connor Cruise. 1988. *God Land: Reflections on Religion and Nationalism*.
Cambridge, Mass.

Olenik, John Kenneth. 1973. "Left Wing Radicalism in the Kuomintang: Teng Yen-ta
and the Genesis of the Third Party Movement in China, 1924–1931." Ph.D. diss.,
Cornell University.

Ono, Kazuko. 1989. *Chinese Women in a Century of Revolution*. Translated by Joshua
Fogel and others. Stanford, Calif.

Patai, Daphne, ed. 1988. *Looking Backward, 1988–1888: Essays on Edward Bellamy*.
Amherst.

Patterson, Orlando. 1991. *Freedom*. Vol. 1: *Freedom in the Making of Western Culture*.
New York.

Peck, Graham. 1967. *Two Kinds of Time*. 2d ed. Boston.

Peck, James. 1971. "The Roots of Rhetoric: The Professional Ideology of America's
China Watchers." In Edward Friedman and Mark Selden, eds., *America's Asia:
Dissenting Essays on Asian–American Relations*. New York.

Peng Pai. 1924. "Guanyu Haifeng nongmin yundong de yi feng xin" (A letter on the
Haifeng peasant movement). *Xiangdao* 70.

Peng Shuzhi. 1924a. "Beijing zhengbian yu touji wuchi de gongtuan zhi qingqiu"
(The Beijing coup and the demands of the opportunistic and shameless public
associations). *Xiangdao* 89.

————. 1924b. "Jiangsu zhanzheng yu guomindang" (The Jiangsu war and the
Nationalist party). *Xiangdao* 84.

————. 1924c. "Nanyang yanchang bagong zhong Shanghai baojie zhi yuanxing"
(The real face of the Shanghai newspaper world in light of the strike at the Nanyang Tobacco Company). *Xiangdao* 84.

"Peng Sumin guanyu dangwu tiaochen" (Memorandum from Peng Sumin on party
affairs). 1923. *Zhongguo guomindang benbu gongbao* 3.

Petrey, Sandy. 1988a. *Realism and Revolution*. Ithaca, N.Y.

————. 1988b. "The Reality of Representation." *Critical Inquiry* 14.

Peyrefitte, Alain. 1993. *The Collision of Two Civilisations: The British Expedition to
China in 1792–4*. London.

Pitkin, Hanna Fenichel. 1967. *The Concept of Representation*. Berkeley, Calif.

Plaks, Andrew. 1976. *Allegory and Archetype in the Dream of the Red Chamber*. Princeton.

Polan, A. J. 1984. *Lenin and the End of Politics*. London.

Polsby, Nelson W. 1959. "The Sociology of Community Power: A Reassessment." *Social Forces* 37.

Powell, John B. 1945. *My Twenty-Five Years in China*. New York.

Price, Jane L. 1976. *Cadres, Commanders and Commissars: The Training of the Chinese Communist Leadership, 1920–1945*. Boulder, Colo.

Pusey, James. 1983. *China and Charles Darwin*. Cambridge, Mass.

Pye, Lucian W. 1968. *The Spirit of Chinese Politics: A Psychocultural Study of the Authority Crisis in Political Development*. Cambridge, Mass.

————. 1972. *China: An Introduction*. Boston.

Qian Dajun. 1973–. "Huangpu junxiao kaichuang shiqi zhi zuzhi" (The organization of the Huangpu Academy at the time of its founding). *GMWX* 10.

"Qiaogang Qiongya gongmin weichihui" (Citizens protection committee of Hong Kong and Hainan). 1924. Second Historical Archives of China, Nanjing.

"Qingnian bu gongzuo baogao" (Report on the work of the [Central] Youth Bureau). 1926. *ZGZY* 1.

"Qingnian junren lianhe hui disici daibiao dahui huiyu lu" (Minutes of the Fourth Congress of the Young Soldiers Association). 1925. *Zhongguo junren* 5.

Qing Song. 1923. "Dao neidi qu" (Go inland!). *Nuli zhoubao* 66, no. 4.

"Qing zhengfu yanjin Huazi, Zhihuan dengbao rukou an" (Request to the government to prohibit importation of the *Huazi* and *Zhihuan* dailies). N.d. Historical Archives Commission of the Kuomintang, 433/182. Taipei.

Qingshidun zhongguo guomindang jiu nian jingguo dangwu (Nine years of party affairs at the Kingston branch of the Chinese Nationalist party). 1925. Kingston.

Qin Xiaoyi, ed. 1978. *Zhonghua minguo shihua* (Pictorial history of the Republic of China). 3 vols. Taipei.

"Qiongya tebie weiyuanhui gongzuo baogao" (Work report of the Hainan special committee). 1926. *ZGGY* 2 (March).

"Qiongya tebie weiyuanhui gongzuo gaishu" (Outline work report of the Hainan special committee). 1926. *ZGGY* 3 (April/May).

Qishier hang shangbao (Commercial news of the Seventy-Two Hongs). Guangzhou.

"Quanguo xuesheng zonghui zhi xuanchuan jihua" (Propaganda plan of the All China General Union of Students). 1924. *ZGZK* 13.

Qu Qiubai. 1923. "Zhongguo zhi difang zhengzhi yu fengjian zhidu" (Chinese local politics and the feudal system). *Xiangdao* 23.

————. 1925a. "Wusa yundong zhong de guomin geming yu jieji douzheng" (Nationalist Revolution and class struggle in the May Thirtieth movement). *Xiangdao* 129.

————. 1925b. "Yihetuan yundong zhi yiyi yu wusa yundong zhi qiantu" (The significance of the Boxer movement and the future of the May Thirtieth movement). *Xiangdao* 128.

Rankin, Mary. 1986. *Elite Activism and Political Transformation in China: Zhejiang Province, 1865–1911*. Stanford, Calif.

Rawski, Evelyn S. 1991. "Research Themes in Ming-Qing Socioeconomic History— The State of the Field." *Journal of Asian Studies* 50, no. 1.

Rawski, Thomas G. 1989. *Economic Growth in Prewar China*. Berkeley, Calif.

"Ren Chen Dongping wei yangguang zhibu buzhang zhuang" (Notice of appointment of Ren Dongping as head of the Yangguang party branch). 1921. In *GFQJ*, 4: 399.

Rickards, Jane. 1990. "Mao Dun's 'Disillusionment.' " Honors diss., University of Melbourne.

Rigby, Richard. 1980. *The May 30 Movement: Events and Themes*. Canberra.

Ritter, Joachim. 1982. *Hegel and the French Revolution*. Translated with an introduction by Richard Dien Winfield. Cambridge, Mass.

Ropp, Paul S. 1981. *Dissent in Early Modern China: Ju-lin wai-shi and Ch'ing Social Criticism*. Ann Arbor.

Rorty, Richard. 1989. *Contingency, Irony and Solidarity*. Cambridge.

Rowe, William T. 1989. *Hankow: Conflict and Community in a Chinese City*. Stanford, Calif.

———. 1990. "The Public Sphere in Modern China." *Modern China* 16, no. 3.

———. 1993. "The Problem of 'Civil Society' in Late Imperial China." *Modern China* 19, no. 2.

Ruan Xiaoxian. 1926. "Huiyang xian nongmin xiehui chengli zhi jingguo" (The process of establishing a peasant association in Huiyang County). *Zhongguo nongmin* 3.

Rule, Paul. 1988. "China: The Gilding and Tarnishing of the Image." Unpublished paper, Asian Studies Association of Australia Biennial Conference. Canberra.

"Rumblings Before the Storm." 1926. *Hainan Newsletter*, Fall.

Sadoul, Georges. 1972. *Dictionary of Films*. Translated by Peter Morris. Berkeley, Calif.

Said, Edward. 1978. *Orientalism*. New York.

Sakai, Kosen. 1904. *Hyakunengo no Shakai* (Society one hundred years from now). Tokyo.

Sansom, Brenda. 1988. "*Minsheng* and National Liberation: Socialist Theory in the Guomindang, 1919–1931." Ph.D. diss., University of Wisconsin-Madison.

San Tzu Ching (Elementary Chinese). 1964. Translated by Herbert A. Giles. Taipei.

Schiffrin, Harold Z. 1970. *Sun Yatsen and the Origins of the Chinese Revolution*. Berkeley, Calif.

———. 1980. *Sun Yatsen: Reluctant Revolutionary*. Boston.

Schneider, Laurence A. 1971. *Ku Chieh-kang and China's New History: Nationalism and the Quest for Alternative Traditions*. Berkeley, Calif.

Schoppa, R. Keith. 1982. *Chinese Elites and Political Change: Zhejiang Province in the Early Twentieth Century*. Cambridge, Mass.

Schorske, Carl E. 1980. *Fin-de-Siècle Vienna: Politics and Culture*. New York.

Schram, Stuart. R. 1967. *Mao Tse-tung*. Rev. ed. Harmondsworth.

———, ed. 1969. *The Political Thought of Mao Tse-tung*. Rev. and enlarged ed. New York.

———. 1984. "Classes Old and New in Mao Zedong's Thought, 1949–1976." In

James L. Watson, ed., *Class and Social Stratification in Post-Revolutionary China*. Cambridge.

———. 1989. *The Thought of Mao Tse-tung*. Cambridge.

———, ed., 1992. *Mao's Road to Power: Revolutionary Writings, 1912–1949*. Vol. 1: *The Pre-Marxist Period, 1912–1920*. Armonk.

Schurmann, H. Franz. 1968. *Ideology and Organization in Communist China*. Rev. ed. Berkeley, Calif.

Schwarcz, Vera. 1975. "Ibsen's Nora: The Promise and the Trap." *Bulletin of Concerned Asian Scholars* 7, no. 1.

Seth, Sanjay. 1989. "Marxism and the Question of Nationalism in a Colonial Context: The Case of British India." Ph.D. diss., Australian National University, Canberra.

———. 1992. "Nationalism, National Identity and 'History': Nehru's Search for India." Unpublished paper. La Trobe University, Melbourne.

Shanghai minguo ribao (Shanghai Republican Daily). [Abbreviated as *SMR*.]

"Shanghai zhixingbu de chengli ji qi gongzuo baogao" (The creation of the Shanghai Executive Bureau and its work report). 1924. Historical Archives Commission of the Kuomintang, 439.2/1. Taipei.

"Shanghai zhixingbu dui linshi zhongyang zhixing weiyuanhui gongzuo baogao" (Work report of the Shanghai Executive Bureau to the Provisional Executive Committee). 1924. Historical Archives Commission of the Kuomintang, 415/223. Taipei.

"Shanghai zhixingbu suoxin huiyi jilu" (Meeting to reclaim salaries of the Shanghai Executive Branch). 1924–25. Historical Archives Commission of the Kuomintang, 433/24. Taipei.

"Shangmin bu gongzuo baogao" ([Central] merchant bureau work report). 1926. *ZGZY* 1.

"Shangmin bu gongzuo baogao" ([Provincial] merchant bureau work report). 1926. *ZGGY* 1 (February), 3 (April/May), and 4 (June).

"Shangmin yundong jueyi an" (Resolutions on the merchant movement). 1926. *ZZZB* 6/7.

"Shangmin yundong zhi jingguo" (The progress of the merchant movement). 1926. *ZZZB* 6/7.

Shao Yuanchong. 1954. *Xuanpu yishu* (The works of Xuanpu [Shao Yuanchong]). 2 vols. Taipei.

———. 1973–. "Zhonghua gemingdang lueshi" (Outline history of the Chinese Revolutionary party). *GMWX* 5.

Shen Congwen. [1928] 1982. *Alisi zhongguo youji* (Alice in China). In *Shen Congwen wenji* (The collected writings of Shen Congwen), vol. 1. Hong Kong.

Shen Dingyi. 1919. "Xingqi pinglun fakanci" (Inaugural statement on the launching of *Weekly Commentary*). *Xingqi pinglun* 1.

"Sheping" (Social commentary). 1924. *Jiaoyu zhoubao* (Education weekly) supplement to *Shanghai minguo ribao*. 29 May.

Shimada, Kenji. 1990. *Pioneer of the Chinese Revolution: Zhang Binglin and Confucianism*. Translated by Joshua Fogel. Stanford, Calif.

Shirley, James. 1965. "Control of the Kuomintang After Sun Yatsen's Death." *Journal of Asian Studies* 25, no. 1.

"Shiyiyue jiuri wuhou sanshi benbu kaihui jishi" (Minutes of the meeting of party headquarters held at 3 p.m. on 9 November). 1921. *Benbu tongxin* (Party center gazette) 60.

Shun, Kwong-loi. 1991. "The Self in Confucian Ethics." *Journal of Chinese Philosophy* 18.

Shu Sheng. 1920. "Duiyu 'Xingqi pinglun,' 'Jianshe' tingkan de ganxiang he xiwang" (Feelings and hopes on the closure of *Weekly Critic* and *Reconstruction*). *Juewu*, 7 June.

Si Dun. 1925. "Jiaoshou cizhi" (Professors resign). *Guangda xuesheng hui zhoukan* 5.

Siu, Helen F. 1990. *Furrows: Peasants, Intellectuals and the State*. Stanford, Calif.

Smith, Arthur H. 1894. *Chinese Characteristics*. 15th ed. New York.

Sneevliet, Henk. See Sun Duo.

Spence, Jonathan D. 1982. *The Gate of Heavenly Peace: The Chinese and Their Revolution, 1895–1980*. Harmondsworth.

———. 1988. *The Question of Hu*. New York.

———. 1990. *The Search for Modern China*. New York.

Stanley, John. 1982. *Sociology of Virtue: The Political and Social Theories of Georges Sorrel*. Berkeley, Calif.

Stremski, Richard. 1979. *The Shaping of British Policy During the Nationalist Revolution in China*. Taipei.

Sun Duo [Henk Sneevliet]. 1922. "Guomin yundong geming jun he geming xuanchuan" (The Nationalist movement, revolutionary armies, and revolutionary propaganda). *Xiangdao* 9.

———. 1923a. "Wu Peifu yu guomindang." *Xiangdao* 24.

———. 1923b. "Zhongguo guomin geming yundong de guoqu ji jianglai" (The past and future of the Chinese national revolutionary movement). *Qianfeng* 1.

Sun Yatsen:

[1]. "Banian shiyue shihao" (10 October [national day] 1919). 1919. In *GFQJ*, 2: 165–66.

[2]. "Beishang zhi yiyi yu xiwang" (The significance and prospects of the trip north). 1924. In *GFQJ*, 2: 735–38.

[3]. "Chengli zhengshi zhengfu gonggu minguo jichu" (Establish a formal government and consolidate the foundations of the Republic). 1921. In *GFQJ*, 2: 399–400.

[4]. "Dangwu jinxing dang yi xuanchuan wei zhong" (In the conduct of party affairs we should stress propaganda). 1923. In *GFQJ*, 2: 509–11.

[5]. "Dangyuan bu ke cunxin zuoguan" (Party members must not set their hearts on becoming officials). 1923. In *GFQJ*, 2: 537–43.

[6]. "Dangyuan xu duoliang jieshao tongzhi rudang" (Party members should introduce more comrades into the party). 1924. In *GFQJ*, 2: 870.

[7]. "Dangyuan xu xuanchuan geming zhuyi" (Party members must spread propaganda on the principles of revolution). 1921. In *GFQJ*, 2: 451–55.

[8]. "Dapo jiu sixiang yao yong sanmin zhuyi" (To smash old ways of thinking we must use the Three Principles of the People). 1923. In *GFQJ*, 2: 567–77.

[9]. "Fahui bimo zhi weiquan yi yu junfa bozhan" (Develop the power of the pen to wage war upon warlords). 1923. In *GFQJ*, 2: 512–14.

[10]. "Fu Jiao Yitang gao jiejue guohui jiufen banfa han" (Letter in reply to Jiao Yitang outlining a method for resolving the dispute in the national assembly). 1922. In *GFQJ*, 3: 813.

[11]. "Geming chenggong geren bu neng you ziyou tuanti yao you ziyou" (In successful revolution, institutions must have freedom but individuals may not). 1924. In *GFQJ*, 2: 727–35.

[12]. "Geming jun bixu yi yi dang bai" (One member of the Revolutionary Army must be a match for one hundred soldiers). 1924. In *GFQJ*, 2: 605–12.

[13]. "Geming jun bu ke xiang shengguan facai" (The Revolutionary Army cannot think of winning promotion and growing rich). 1924. In *GFQJ*, 2: 640– 53.

[14]. "Geming jun de jichu zai gaoshen de xuewen" (The foundation of a revolutionary army lies in profound learning). 1924. In *GFQJ*, 2: 691–700.

[15]. "Gengzhe yao you qi tian" (Land to the tiller!). 1924. In *GFQJ*, 2: 719–23.

[16]. "Guanyu minsheng zhuyi zhi shuoming" (Explanation of the Principle of People's Livelihood). 1924. In *GFQJ*, 2: 624.

[17]. "Guomindang fendou zhi fa yi jian zhuzhong xuanchuan bu yi zhuan zhu-zhong junshi" (The best method of struggle for the Nationalist party is one that lays equal stress upon propaganda and does not emphasize military affairs exclusively). 1923. In *GFQJ*, 2: 593–604.

[18]. "Guoqu dangwu shibai zhi yuanyin" (The reasons for past failures in party affairs). 1923. In *GFQJ*, 2: 534–37.

[19]. "Hufa zhi jichu" (The foundations of constitution protection). 1916. In *GFQJ*, 2: 359–60.

[20]. *The International Development of China*. 1921. In *GFQJ*, 5: 127–360.

[21]. *Jianguo fanglüe* (Strategy for national reconstruction). Comprising "Psychological Reconstruction" (*Xinli jianshe*), "Material Reconstruction" (*Wuzhi jianshe*), and "Social Reconstruction" (*Shehui jianshe*). In *GFQJ*, 1: 419–750.

[22]. "Jianshe zazhi fakanci" (Inaugural statement on the launching of *Reconstruction Magazine*). 1919. *Jianshe* 1, no. 1.

[23]. "Jiuguo jiumin zhi zeren zai geming jun" (Responsibility for saving the country and saving the people rests with the Revolutionary Army). 1924. In *GFQJ*, 2: 633–40.

[24]. "Junren jingshen jiaoyu" (Spiritual education of soldiers). 1921. In *GFQJ*, 2: 477–506.

[25]. "Luhaijun dayuanshuai dabenying tiaoli" (Regulations for the headquarters of the grand marshal of land and naval forces). 1922. In *GFQJ*, 2: 961–64.

[26]. "Nongmin da lianhe" (The great union of the peasants). 1924. In *GFQJ*, 2: 713–19.

[27]. "Philosophy of Sun Yatsen. Doc. 64: Sun Yat-sen's Theory of Knowledge and Action, 1919." In Teng and Fairbank 1979.

[28]. "Pi Beijing hufa yiyuan lun hufa shi han" (Letter in reply to constitution-protecting parliamentarians in Beijing discussing the protection of the constitution). 1922. In *GFQJ*, 3: 863.

[29]. "Pi Guangdong zhibu Deng Zeru deng tanhe gongchandang wen (Document commenting on the impeachment of the Communist party by Deng Zeru and others of the Guangdong branch). 1923. In *GFQJ*, 4: 916.

[30]. "Pixiu tielu ji jiquan fenquan zhi jieshi" (Explanation of the parceling out of railroad construction and the centralization and dispersal of political authority). 1912. In *GFQJ*, 2: 827.

[31]. *San Min Chu I, The Three Principles of the People*. [1924] 1943. Translated by Frank W. Price. Edited by L. T. Chen. Chungking.

[32]. "Sanmin zhuyi" (The three principles of the people). 1919. In *GFQJ*, 2: 154–65.

[33]. *Sanmin zhuyi* (The three principles of the people). 1924. In *GFQJ*, 1: 1–284.

[34]. "Sanmin zhuyi wei zaocheng xin shijie de gongju" (The Three Principles of the People are instruments for building a new world). 1921. In *GFQJ*, 2: 459–66.

[35]. "Sanmin zhuyi zhi juti banfa" (A concrete method for the Three Principles of the People). 1921. In *GFQJ*, 2: 401–12.

[36]. "Sun Wen xueshuo" (The philosophy of Sun Yatsen). 1918. In *GFQJ*, 1: 419–506.

[37]. "Tongyi zhongguo xu kao xuanchuan wenhua" (We must rely on cultural propaganda to unify China). 1921. In *GFQJ*, 2: 401–2.

[38]. "Tuifan diguozhuyi shixian Zhongguo zhenzheng minzhi zhengfu" (Overthrow imperialism and bring a truly democratic government to China). [Interview with a correspondent for the *Washington Post*.] 1922. In *GFQJ*, 2: 850–51.

[39]. "Wei chuangshe yingwen zazhi yinshua jiguan zhi haiwai tongzhi shu" (Letter to overseas comrades regarding the establishment of an English-language magazine and a printing press). 1920. In *GFQJ*, 3: 669–73.

[40]. "Wei jian ji zhaichuan ji xishou dangyuan shi fu Zeng Yunming Huang Deyuan Rao Qianchuan han" (Letter in reply to Zeng Yunming, Huang Deyuan, and Rao Qianchuan on the subject of ceasing the transfer of bonds and admitting people into the party). 1918. In *GFQJ*, 3: 557–58.

[41]. "Wei taofa Cao Wu gao jun min wen" (Letter to the army and the people on punishing Cao [Kun] and Wu [Peifu]). 1924. In *GFQJ*, 1: 907.

[42]. "Xinli jianshe" (Psychological reconstruction). 1918. In *GFQJ*, 1: 419–506.

[43]. "Xiugai zhancheng zhi shuoming" (Explanation on revising the constitution). 1920. In *GFQJ*, 2: 394–98.

[44]. "Xuesheng yao nuli xuanchuan dandang geming de zeren" (Students must exert themselves at propaganda and shoulder the burden of the revolution). 1923. In *GFQJ*, 2: 524–34.

[45]. "Xunzheng zhi jieshi" (Explanation of tutelary gòvernment). 1920. In *GFQJ*, 2: 398–99.

[46]. "Yao kao dangyuan chenggong bu zhuan kao jundui chenggong" (Success depends on party members and not on armies alone). 1923. In *GFQJ*, 2: 558–67.

[47]. "Yuyan wenzi de fendou" (The struggle in language and writing). 1924. In *GFQJ*, 2: 701.

[48]. "Zhongguo gongren suo shou bupingdeng tiaoyue zhi hai" (The harm brought upon Chinese workers by the unequal treaties). 1924. In *GFQJ*, 2: 679–85.

Sun Zhongshan xiansheng sanmin zhuyi yanshuo (Speeches by Sun Yatsen on the

Three Principles of the People). N.d. Beijing. Historical Archives Commission of the Kuomintang, 046/34. Taipei.

Swatow. 1921. Swatow to Washington. United States Department of State, 4211. 20 December.

Swisher, Earl. 1977. *Canton in Revolution: The Collected Papers of Earl Swisher, 1925-1928*. Edited by Kenneth W. Rea. Boulder, Colo.

Tang Dantong. 1960. *Zhongyang bowuyuan ershiwu nian zhi jingguo* (Twenty-five years of progress in the central museum). Taipei.

T'ang Leang-li, ed. [1931] 1969. *China's Own Critics: A Selection of Essays.* With commentaries by Wang Ching-wei. New York.

———. 1936. *The New Social Order in China.* Shanghai.

Tan Pingshan. 1925. "Zhongguo guomindang quanguo dangwu gaikuang" (The general situation regarding Nationalist party work throughout the country). *ZZZB* 3.

———. 1926. "Tan Pingshan xiansheng dangwu zong baogoa" (Tan Pingshan's general report on party affairs). *ZZZB* 6/7.

———. [1926] 1986. "Dangwu zong baogao" (General report on party affairs). In *ZGHS*: vol. 2. Nanjing.

Tan Pingshan and Feng Jupo. 1923. *Guomin geming zhong zhi mintuan wenti* (The issue of popular militia in the Nationalist Revolution). Guangzhou.

Tan Sitong. 1984. *An Exposition of Benevolence: The Jen-Hsüeh of Tan Ssu-t'ung.* Translated by Chan Sin-wai. Hong Kong.

Tao Xisheng. 1964. *Chaoliu yu diandi* (A drop in the flowing tide). Taipei.

"Tao Yuan zhi yulun ji xuanchuan" (Public opinion and propaganda in the struggle against Yuan [Shikai]). 1973-. *GMWX* 46.

Taylor, A. J. P. 1948. *The Hapsburg Monarchy 1809-1918.* London.

Taylor, W. C. 1835. "On the Present State and Future Prospects of Oriental Literature, Viewed in Connexion with the Royal Asiatic Society: Read 6th December, 1834." *Journal of the Royal Asiatic Society of Great Britain and Ireland* 2.

Teng Ssu-yü, and John K. Fairbank. 1979. *China's Response to the West: A Documentary Survey, 1839-1923.* 2d ed. Cambridge, Mass.

Theroux, Paul. 1972. *V. S. Naipaul: An Introduction to His Work.* New York.

"Theses on the Agrarian Question." 1971. In Degras 1971: vol. 1.

"Theses on the Colonial Question." 1971. In Degras 1971: vol. 1.

"Theses on the Eastern Question." 1971. In Degras 1971: vol. 1.

Thompson, E. P. 1963. *The Making of the English Working Class.* London.

Thomson, James C., Jr. 1969. *While China Faced West: American Reformers in Nationalist China, 1928-1937.* Cambridge, Mass.

Tian Nong. 1923. "Dao minjian qu!" (To the people!). *Nuli zhoubao* 40, no. 2.

Tochigi Toshio. 1974. "Kokumin kakumei ki no kanton seifu" (The Guangdong government in the period of the Nationalist Revolution). In Nozawa Yutaka 1974.

———. 1978. "Kanton kokumin seifu to mindan" (The Guangdong Nationalist government and the rural militia). In Nozawa Yutaka and Tanaka Masatoshi 1978: vol. 5.

Todorov, Tzevtan. 1984. *The Conquest of America.* New York.

Tong, Hollington K. 1953. *Chiang Kai-shek*. Taipei.

"Tongxin" (Correspondence). 1922. *Juewu*, 22 January.

Tsao, W. Y. 1947. *The Constitutional Structure of Modern China*. Melbourne.

Tuchman, Barbara W. 1970. *Stilwell and the American Experience in China, 1911–1945*. New York.

Turner, Cheryl. 1992. *Living by the Pen: Women Writers of the Eighteenth Century*. London.

Ungar, Esta. 1989. "The Nationalists and an Overseas Chinese Community: Vietnam, 1927." In Fitzgerald 1989.

Vishnyakova-Akimova, Vera. 1971. *Two Years in Revolutionary China, 1925–1927*. Translated by Steven I. Levine. Cambridge.

Vogel, Ezra. 1969. *Canton Under Communism: Programs and Politics in a Provincial Capital, 1949–1968*. New York.

——. 1989. *One Step Ahead in China: Guangdong under Reform*. Cambridge, Mass.

Vorontsov, V. B. 1989. *Sudba kitaiskogo Bonaparta* (The fate of a Chinese Bonaparte). Moscow.

Wagar, W. Warren. 1979. "The Steel-Gray Saviour: Technocracy as Utopia and Ideology." *Alternative Futures: The Journal of Utopian Studies* 2, no. 2.

——. 1988. "Dreams of Reason: Bellamy, Wells and the Positive Utopia." In Patai 1988.

Wakeman, Frederic. 1973. *History and Will: Philosophical Perspectives on Mao Tsetung's Thought*. Berkeley, Calif.

Wang Bushi, ed. 1986. *Zhongguo minzu fushi* (Clothing styles of the peoples of China). Hong Kong.

Wang Erzhuo. 1926. "Geji dangbu zuzhi jingguo baoguo" (Report on the process of organizing party branches at all levels). *Zhongguo guomindanq guomin geming jun diyi jun tebie dangbu disan shuai shuai danqbu dangkan* 1.

Wang Jianmin. 1965. *Zhongguo gongchandang shigao* (Draft history of the Chinese Communist party). 2 vols. Taipei.

Wang Jingwei. 1926a. "Women gemingdang ren zuida de tongku jiu shi xuanchuan yu shishi bu neng yizi" (The failure of propaganda to match the facts has been the greatest source of suffering to members of the revolutionary party). *ZZZB* 6/7.

——. 1926b. "Zhongguo guomindang dierci quanguo daibiao dahui zhengzhi baogao" (Political report to the Second National Congress of the Chinese Nationalist party). *ZZZB* 5.

——. N.d. "Dai Liao Zhongkai tongzhi shu zhu tongzhi" (Advice to all comrades on mourning Comrade Liao Zhongkai). In *Liao Zhongkai xiansheng aisi lu*, n.d., n.p.

Wang Xinming. 1957. *Xinwen quan li sishi nian* (Forty years in the world of journalism). Taipei.

Wang Zhangling. 1973. "Sun Wen zhuyi xuehui chengli zhi jingguo ji qi yingxiang" (The founding and impact of the Society for the Study of Sun Yatsenism). In *Zhongguo xiandaishi zhuanti yanjiu baogao* (Report of monographic research in contemporary Chinese history) 3.

Wang Zhong. 1957. "Diyici guonei geming zhanzheng shiqi zhongyao de geming bao-zhi yu qikan" (Important revolutionary papers and periodicals of the first revolutionary civil war period). In Lai Xinxia and Wei Hongyun, eds., *Diyici guonei geming zhanzhengshi lun ji* (Collected essays on the history of the first revolutionary civil war). Wuhan.

Watson, James L. 1993. "Rites or Beliefs? The Construction of a Unified Culture in Late Imperial China." In Lowell Dittmer and Samuel S. Kim, eds., *China's Quest for National Identity*. Ithaca, N.Y.

Whitewright, Rev. J. S. 1893. "Museums." In *Records of the Triennial Meeting of the Educational Association of China*. Shanghai.

Widmer, Ellen. 1977. "Qu Qiubai and Russian Literature." In Goldman 1977.

Wilbur, C. Martin. 1976. *Sun Yat-sen: Frustrated Patriot*. New York.

———. 1983. "The Nationalist Revolution: From Canton to Nanking, 1923–28." In *The Cambridge History of China*, edited by John K. Fairbank, vol. 12, pt. 1. Cambridge.

Wilbur, C. Martin, and Julie Lien-ying How, eds. 1956. *Documents on Communism, Nationalism and Soviet Advisers in China*. New York.

Williams, Raymond. 1983. *Keywords*. London.

Willoughby, W. W. 1920. *Foreign Rights and Interests in China*. 2 vols. Baltimore.

Witke, Roxane. 1967. "Mao Tse-tung, Women and Suicide in the May Fourth Era." *China Quarterly* 31.

Wolfe, Patrick. 1991. "On Being Woken Up: The Dreamtime in Anthropology and in Australian Settler Culture." *Comparative Studies in Society and History* 33, no. 2.

Wong, John C. Y. 1972. *Chin Sheng-t'an*. New York.

Wood, Frances. 1985. *Chinese Illustration*. London.

Woodhead, H. G. W. 1925. *The Truth About the Chinese Republic*. London.

———, ed. 1912–39. *The China Yearbook*. Tianjin.

Wright, Mary C., ed. 1968. *China in Revolution: The First Phase, 1900–1913*. New Haven, Conn.

Wright, Tim. 1989. "Coping with the World Depression: The Nationalist Government's Relations with Industry and Commerce, 1932–1936." In Fitzgerald 1989.

Wu Jinglian and Chu Fucheng. 1920. "Zhuci wu" (Fifth congratulatory preface). *Minjue* 1, no. 1.

Wu Tingfang. 1920. "Zhuci yi" (First congratulatory preface). *Minjue* 1, no. 1.

Wu Yuzhang. 1926. "Zhongguo guomindang dierci quanguo daibiao dahui jingguo gailue" (Outline of the convening of the second national congress of the Chinese Nationalist party). *ZZZB* 5.

Wu Zhihui. 1908. "Zhongguoren zhi fubaibing" (The corruption of the Chinese people). *Xin shiji* 59.

Xiangdao zhoubao (The guide weekly [*sic*]). 1963. 5 vols. Tokyo.

Xie Cilin. 1926. "Dongzheng jingguo qingxing" (The passage of the Eastern Expedition). *JSYK* 2.

"Xingqi pinglun bannian lai de nuli" (Our efforts on *Weekly Critic* over the past half-year). 1919. *Xingqi pinglun* 26.

"Xingqi pinglun kan xing zhongzhi de xuanyan" (Announcing the closure of *Weekly Critic*). 1920. *Xingqi pinglun* 53.

Xuan. 1919. "Juewu de diyi bu" (The first step toward an awakening). *Juewu*, 29 and 30 September, 1 October.

"Xuanchuan bu gongwen digao" (Draft correspondence of the propaganda bureau). 1922–23. Historical Archives Commission of the Kuomintang, 415/91. Taipei.

"Xuanchuan bu gongzuo baogao" ([Central] propaganda bureau work report). 1926. *ZGZY* 1.

"Xuanchuan bu gongzuo gaiyao" ([Provincial] propaganda bureau work outline). 1926. *ZGGY* 1–4 (January–June).

Yamada Tatsuo. 1980. *Chūgoku kokumin to saha no kenkyū* (Research into the left wing of the Chinese Nationalist party). Tokyo.

"Yangjiang xian dangbu" (Yangjiang county party branch). 1926. *ZGGY* 3 (April/May) and 4 (June).

Ye Chucang. 1920. "Pinglun" (Commentary). *Juewu*, 8 February.

———. 1922. "Pinglun" (Commentary). *Juewu*, 24 July.

———. 1923. "Guomindang de minzhonghua yu minzhong de guomindanghua" (The massification of the Nationalist party and the Nationalist partification of the masses). *Juewu*, 6 May.

Ye Xiaoqing. 1992. "Shanghai Before Nationalism." *East Asian History* 3.

Yihong. 1924. "Zhide zhuyi de ji jian guomindang gongzuo" (Some Nationalist party work worthy of attention). *Xin minguo* 1, no. 5.

Yiping. 1924. "Chongbai junfa de zuie" (Worshiping the crimes of a warlord). *Xiangdao* 68.

Yip Ka-che. 1980. *Religion, Nationalism and Chinese Students: The Anti-Christian Movement of 1922–1927*. Bellingham.

Yu, George T. 1966. *Party Politics in Republican China: The Kuomintang, 1912–1924*. Berkeley, Calif.

Yu Dafu. 1921. "Chenlun" (Sinking). Shanghai.

———. 1984a. "Flight." In Yu Dafu, *Nights of Spring Fever and Other Writings*. Translated by Gladys Yang et al. Beijing.

———. 1984b. *Nights of Spring Fever and Other Writings*. Translated by Gladys Yang et al. Beijing.

Yun Daiying [Dan Yi]. 1924. "He wei guomin geming?" (What is a Nationalist Revolution?). *Zhongguo qingnian* 20.

Yu Shude. 1924. "Zhongshen bendang jilu jueyi an" (Motion for a resolution to strengthen party discipline). *ZGZK* 39.

"Zai ben dang zhidao xia zhi ge zhong minzhong yundong baogao" (Report on all variety of popular movements under the guidance of the party). 1926. *ZGZY* 1.

Zai Dongfan. 1956. *Lichao tongsu yanyi* (Simplified history of the ages). 44 vols. Reprint. Shanghai.

Zamyatin, Yevgeny. [1924] 1972. *We*. Translated by Bernard Guerney. Harmondsworth.

Zarrow, Peter. 1990. *Anarchism and Chinese Political Culture*. New York.

Zeng Pu. 1905. *Niehai hua* (Flower in the Ocean of Sin). Shanghai.

Zeng Rong. [1925] 1980. "Mintuan yu geming" (Popular militia and the revolution). *Zhongguo qingnian* 68. Reprinted in *LYLC*.

Zhang Guotao. 1922. "Gemingdang de fouren bing" (The negative malaise of the revolutionary party). *Xiangdao* 15.

————. 1971. *Wo de huiyi* (My recollections). Hong Kong.

Zhang Ji. 1951a. "Geming da shiji" (Record of great events of the revolution). In Zhang Ji 1951c: vol. 1.

————. 1951b. "Huiyi lu" (Recollections). In Zhang Ji 1951c: vol. 1.

————. 1951c. *Zhang Puquan xiansheng quanji* (The complete works of Zhang Puquan). Edited by Dangshi shiliao bianzuan weihuanhui. 5 vols. Taipei.

Zhang Jinglu. 1954–56. *Zhongguo xiandai chuban shiliao* (Documents on the history of contemporary Chinese publishing). 5 vols. Shanghai.

————. 1957. *Zhongguo chuban shiliao bubian* (Documents on the history of Chinese publishing: Supplement). Shanghai.

Zhang Longxi. 1988. "The Myth of the Other: China in the Eyes of the West." *Critical Inquiry* 15.

Zhang Qiubai. 1920. "Ziji geming yu shehui geming de guanxi" (The linkage between the revolution of the self and revolution in society). *Minjue* 1, no. 1.

Zhang Qiuren. 1926. "Shenggang bagong de guoqu he xianzai" (The Hong Kong–Guangdong strike, past and present). *ZZZB* 9.

Zhang Qixiong. 1926. "Dongzheng shiqi zhi zhengzhi gongzuo gailue" (General outline of political work during the Eastern Expedition). *JSYK* 2.

Zhang Shizhang. [1922] 1990. "Xu" (Preface). In Hu Pu'an [1922] 1990.

Zhengzhi gongzuo rikan (Political work daily). 1926.

"Zhengzhi xunlian bu shishi xuanchuan dagang huibian" (Collection of topical propaganda outlines by the Political Training Bureau). 1926. *JSYK*, 2.

Zhengzhi zhoubao (Political weekly). 1925–26. [Abbreviated as *ZZZB*.]

"Zhixing weiyuanhui gebu gongzuo gaiyao" (Outlines of work of all bureaus under the [provincial] executive committee). 1926. *ZGGY* 1 (February).

"Zhixing weiyuanhui jiancha weihuanhui huiyilu" (Minutes of [provincial] executive and inspection committee meetings). 1926. *ZGGY* 1 (February).

Zhonggong dangshi jiaocai cankao ziliao (Reference materials for teaching the history of the Chinese Communist party). N.d. 2 vols. Nanjing.

"Zhongguo gongchandang dierci quanguo dahui xuanyan" (Declaration of the Second National Congress of the Chinese Communist party). 1922. In *Zhonggong dangshi jiaocai cankao ziliao* n.d.: vol. 1.

"Zhongguo gongchandang disici dahui xuanyan" (Declaration of the Fourth Congress of the Chinese Communist party). 1924. In *Zhonggong dangshi jiaocai cankao ziliao* n.d.: vol. 1.

"Zhongguo guomindang benbu caizhengbu tongbao" (Report of the finance bureau of Chinese Nationalist party headquarters). 1923. Historical Archives Commission of the Kuomintang, 415/25. Taipei.

Zhongguo guomindang benbu gongbao (Chinese Nationalist party gazette). 1923.

"Zhongguo guomindang benbu teshe banshichu zhiyuan biao" (List of personnel of the special office of the Nationalist party center). 1922. Historical Archives Commission of the Kuomintang, 415/28. Taipei.

"Zhongguo guomindang benbu xian ren zhiyuan yilan biao" (A table of current personnel of party center of the Chinese Nationalist party). 1923. *Zhongguo guomindang benbu gongbao* 14.

Zhongguo guomindang dangwu taolunhui jishilu (Minutes of the party affairs discussion meeting of the Chinese Nationalist party). N.d. Guangzhou.

Zhongguo guomindang diyi, erci quanguo daibiao dahui huiyi shiliao (Historical materials on the first and second national congresses of the Chinese Nationalist party). 1986. Edited by Zhongguo dier lishi danganguan. 2 vols. Nanjing. [Abbreviated as *ZGHS*.]

"Zhongguo guomindang diyici quanguo daibiao dahui xuanyan" (Declaration of the First National Congress of the Chinese Nationalist party). [1924] 1930. In Li Jiannong, *Zuijin sanshinian zhongguo zhengzhi shi* (Political history of China over the past thirty years). Shanghai. Also translated in Li Chien-nung 1956.

"Zhongguo guomindang diyi qu zhongzhihui disanci quanti huiyi tongguo guanyu jieshou Sun Zhongshan yishu zhi xunling jueyian" (Resolution on accepting the instructions of Sun Yatsen's last testament passed by the Third Plenum of the First Central Executive Committee of the Chinese Nationalist party). [1925] 1986. In *ZGHS*: vol. 1.

"Zhongguo guomindang gesheng zhiyuan biao xiuzheng gao" (Revised draft of party staff members in all provinces). 1922. Historical Archives Commission of the Kuomintang, 415/29. Taipei.

Zhongguo guomindang guangdongsheng dangbu dangwu yuebao (Party affairs monthly of the Guangdong provincial branch of the Chinese Nationalist party). 1926. Guangzhou. [Abbreviated as *ZGGY*.]

"Zhongguo guomindang jiangxi so kai xue ji" (Record of the opening of the Propaganda Training Institute of the Chinese Nationalist party). 1924. *ZGZK* 28.

"Zhongguo guomindang jiangxi so zuzhi jueyi an" (Resolution on the organization of the Propaganda Training Institute of the Chinese Nationalist party). 1924. *ZGZK* 13.

"Zhongguo guomindang jieshou zongli yishu xuanyan" (Chinese Nationalist party declaration on accepting the last testament of the president). [1925] 1973–. *GMWX* 69.

Zhongguo guomindang quanguo daibiao dahui huiyi lu (Minutes of the [first] national congress of the Chinese Nationalist party). 1929. Nanjing.

Zhongguo guomindang quan meizhou tongzhi dier ci kenqin dahui shimoji (Complete record of the second fraternal congress of Nationalist party comrades in America). 1921. San Francisco. Historical Archives Commission of the Kuomintang, 429/1. Taipei.

"Zhongguo guomindang xuanchuanbu shouzhipu" (Income and expenditure records of the propaganda bureau of the Chinese Nationalist party). 1923. Historical Archives Commission of the Kuomintang, 415/75. Taipei.

"Zhongguo guomindang zhi fanfeng zhanzheng xuanchuan dagang" (Chinese Nationalist party propaganda outline for the anti-Fengtian war). 1925. *ZZZB* 1.

Zhongguo guomindang zhongyang zhixing weiyuanhui dangwu yuebao (Party affairs monthly of the Chinese Nationalist party Central Executive Committee). 1926. [Abbreviated as ZGZY.]

"Zhongguo guomindang zhongyang zhixing weiyuanhui xuanchuan bu banshi zhangcheng" (Regulations governing the operation of the propaganda bureau of the Chinese Nationalist party Central Executive Committee). 1924. *ZGZK* 22.

Zhongguo guomindang zhoukan (Chinese Nationalist party weekly). 1924. [Abbreviated as ZGZK.]

"Zhongguo guomindang zuijin dangbu zuzhi gaikuang" (The general situation of recent Chinese Nationalist party branch organization). 1926. *ZZZB* 14.

Zhongguo jinbainian lishi tuji, 1840–1975 (Pictorial history of China over the past century, 1840–1975). 1976. Hong Kong.

Zhonghua minguo shishi jiyao: chugao minguo shisinian (Outline of historical events of the Chinese Republic: First draft 1925). 1975. 2 vols. Taipei.

Zhong Jiu. 1920. "Zhuyi de yanjiu yu xuanchuan" (Research and propaganda of principles). *Xingqi pinglun* 40.

"Zhongshan xian dangbu xuanchuan bu gongzuo jingguo qingxing" (The work situation of the Zhongshan county branch propaganda bureau). 1926. *ZGGY* 3 (April/May).

"Zhongyang dangbu funu bu minguo shisan nian san yue zhi shiwu nian san yue gongzuo zheyao" (Outline of the work of the Central Women's Bureau from March 1924 to March 1925). 1926. In *Funu zhi sheng huikan* 1926.

"Zhongyang dangbu zhongyao wenjian" (Important documents from central party headquarters). 1926. *ZGZY* 1.

"Zhongyang zhi Guangzhou minguo ribao jin kan zisha gonghui xiaoshuo han" (Letter from [party] center to the *Guangzhou Republican Daily* prohibiting publication of "The suicide club"). 1924. Historical Archives Commission of the Kuomintang, 436/182. Taipei.

"Zhongyang zhixing weihuanhui shunling ji zhongyao tonggao" (Orders and important notices from the Central Executive Committee). 1926. *ZGGY* 1.

"Zhongyang zhixing weihuanhui wei banfa jinian zhou tiaoli tonggao di erbai shiliu" (Notice no. 216: Proclamation by the Central Executive Committee of the regulations for the weekly commemoration). 1925. Historical Archives Commission of the Kuomintang, 458/25. Taipei.

Zhou Enlai [Wu Hao]. 1924. "Zuijin er yue Guangzhou zhengxiang zhi gaiguan" (An overview of the political situation in Guangzhou over the past two months). *Xiangdao* 92.

———. [1926] 1980a. "Guomin geming ji guomin geming shili de tuanjie" (The union of the Nationalist Revolution with the forces for Nationalist Revolution). Reprinted in *LYLC*.

———. [1926] 1980b. "Xianshi zhengzhi douzheng zhong zhi women" (Our position in the present political struggle). Reprinted in *LYLC*.

Zhou Fohai. 1925a. "Guomin geming zhong de jige wenti" (Some basic problems in the Nationalist Revolution). *Juewu*, 16 December.

———. 1925b. "Guomin geming zhong zhi jieji wenti" (The class problem in the Nationalist Revolution). *Gujun* 3, no. 2.

———. 1967a. "Fusang ji ying su dangnian" (Looking back on those years in Japan). In Zhou Fohai and Chen Gongbo, *Huiyi lu hebian* (Co-authored reminiscences). Hong Kong.

———. 1967b. "Wo taochu le chidu wuhan" (I fled the red capital, Wuhan). In Zhou Fohai and Chen Gongbo, *Huiyi lu hebian* (Co-authored reminiscences). Hong Kong.

Zhou Qijian. 1926. "Xijiang banshichu huiwu baogao" (Report on [peasant] association affairs by the West River office). *Zhongguo nongmin* 6/7.

Zhu Wushan. 1924. "Beijing daxue ershiwu zhounian jinian liangyi ceyan zhi fenxi" (Analysis of the opinion poll conducted in celebration of the twenty-fifth anniversary of Beijing University). *Xin minguo* 1, no. 5.

Zhu Zhixin. 1925a. "Bing de gaizao yu qi xinli" (Psychology in military reform). In Zhu Zhixin 1925c: vol. 2.

———. 1925b. "Geming yu xinli" (Revolution and psychology). In Zhu Zhixin 1925c: vol. 1.

———. 1925c. *Zhu Zhixin ji* (The collected works of Zhu Zhixin). 2 vols. Shanghai.

Zou Lu. 1929. *Zhongguo guomindang shigao* (Draft history of the Chinese Nationalist party). 4 vols. Shanghai.

———. 1976. *Huigu lu* (Reminiscences). In *Zou Lu quanji* (Complete works of Zou Lu), 10 vols., vol. 1. Taipei.

INDEX

In this index an "f" after a number indicates a separate reference on the next page, and an "ff" indicates separate references on the next two pages. A continuous discussion over two or more pages is indicated by a span of page numbers, e.g., "57–59." *Passim* is used for a cluster of references in close but not consecutive sequence.

Guangzhou–Hong Kong strike and boycott

Boycotts, nationalist, of other countries, 154

Britain, 31, 41–48 *passim*, 86, 106, 109–15, 119, 131–32, 154, 170, 319, 354n27. *See also* Colonialism; Imperialism; Navy

British East India Company, 110

British Empire, 110–11. *See also* Britain; Colonialism; Imperialism; Navy

Bruce, Brigadier-general C. D., 143

Buck, Pearl, 128, 137, 145, 358

Buddhism, 60, 69, 262

Buffon, George-Louis, 41f

Bureaucrat class, 166

Bureaucrats, imperial scholar-, 109

Burping, *see* Etiquette; Hygiene

C.C.P., *see* Communist party

Cai Hesen, 149, 153, 161–62, 323, 328

Cai Yuanpei, 61, 75, 357n112, 359

Campbell, A. J., 143

Canker, The (*Shi*) (Mao Dun), 96

Cantlie, Dr. James, 127, 147ff

Cao Kun, President, 142–43, 223

Captivity, 107, 139–45. *See also* Bandits

Carpenter, Edward, 58

Carr, E. H., 170

Carroll, Lewis, 131–32

Cartoons, 29f

Censorship, 215

Census, Guangzhou, 274–75

Central Affairs Bureau, 227

Central Army Instruction Brigade, *see* Army Military School

Central Bank, 267

Central Cadre Council, Shanghai, 221

Central China Teachers' College, 268

Central Daily (*Zhongyang ribao*), 392n57

Central Executive Committee of Nationalist party, 189, 213–20 *passim*, 233–38 *passim*, 241–45 *passim*, 249, 256–63 *passim*, 271, 283, 286, 291, 296f, 303, 384

Central Inspection Commission, 241–43, 386

Central Legal Affairs Commission, 241–42

Central Military and Political Academy, *see under* Huangpu Military Academy

Central Propaganda Training Institute, 232. *See also* Propaganda; Propaganda Bureau, Central; Propaganda bureau, Provincial

Centralist movement, 164–67

Centurion, H.M.S. (vessel of G. Anson), 112

Chamberlain, Austen, 354n27

Changchow (Changzhou), 151

Changsha, 56, 201, 204–5

Chaomei, 158–59, 306, 309

Chaos (*luan*), 70, 247–48

Chatterjee, Partha, 103, 133

Chen, Captain, 144

Chen Baixu, 204

Chen Biguang, 181

Chen Dong, 251

Chen Duxiu, 89ff, 152–53, 160–62, 189, 205, 218, 224, 268, 320–23, 332–36 *passim*, 362. *See also* Communist party; Communists in Nationalist party

Chen Fumu, 232, 236, 244

Chen Gongbo, 248, 267, 298–99

Chen Jiongming, 147–52, 158, 163, 178–82 *passim*, 198–202 *passim*, 231f, 268, 309–11, 348, 371n11; attacks Sun Yatsen, 148, 182, 202; military campaigns against, 149, 178, 231, 310f. *See also* Federalist movement; Liberalism; Local self-government; Warlords

Chen Jitang, 15, 149, 158

Chen Kewen, 247

Chen Mingshu, 308f

Chen Qimei, 381

Chen Qiulin, 231–33, 241

Chen Riguang, 282

Chen Tanqiu, 388n116

Chen Yangxuan, 232–33

Lang Xingshi, 230
Language reform, 13–14, 153–59, 334
Lao She, 112, 125–26, 130f, 138, 365n26
Lee, Reverend Frederick, 14
Lee, Leo, 95
Legal Affairs Commission, 267
Leibniz, Gottfried Wilhelm, 109
Lenin, V. I., 65, 76, 171, 175, 317–18,
 324–26. *See also* Leninism
Leninism, 40, 137, 154, 171f, 216, 288–89,
 327, 338. *See also* Lenin, V. I.
Leninists, 76f
Li, Private, 143
Liang Qichao, 34, 37, 48f, 63–65, 78–88
 passim, 105–8 *passim*, 117–23 *passim*,
 134, 156, 207; on Chinese people, 64,
 81, 117–19, 138
Liangyang Republican Daily, 281
Lianping County, 310
Lianzhou, *Republican Daily* circulated in,
 281
Liao Zhongkai, 88, 186, 231, 248, 251–53,
 274; assassination of, 231, 248, 321–22,
 387n101
Liaodong Peninsular, 68
Liberal democrats, *see* Liberalism
Liberal politics, 206. *See also* Liberalism
Liberalism, 154–55, 187–93 *passim*, 198–
 99, 206, 229–30; and Sun Yatsen,
 185–86, 189–90, 195, 203, 214
Liberation Daily (*Jiefang ribao*), 101
Li Chuntao, 281
Li Dazhao, 89ff, 136, 160–61, 175–76,
 204–5, 336, 362
Li Gongci, 244
Li Hanwei, 174
Li Ji, 357n112
Li Linong, 308f
Li Ruzhen, 130
Li Shezeng, 339
Limits of Realism, The (Anderson), 336
Lin Sen, 192f
Lin Yungai, 218, 267, 390n19
Lin Yutang, 119, 128, 140–41, 208,
 353n31, 368

Lincheng Outrage, 120, 141–46, 371. *See
 also* Bandits
Lincoln, Abraham, 119
Lingdong Republican Daily, 281, 283
Lion, British, 31, 354n27
Lions, 2–3, 28, 30–32; awakened, 2–3,
 20, 22, 28, 32f, 70, 354n15; sleeping,
 29, 41
Literacy movement, 13, 155, 158, 334
Literary revolution, 92, 98
Literati, 68, 133, 135. *See also* Intellectu-
 als; Writers
Literature, 57–62 *passim*, 68, 72, 93f,
 145, 140, 333; realist, 332–33, 338;
 romantic, 94, 338–39; traditional, 57f,
 60, 145, 333. *See also* Awakening;
 Fiction; Representation
Liu E, 61, 65
Liu Ersong, 282
Liu Kanghou, 302
Liu Luyin, 227–31, 241–42, 321
Liu Shipei, 75
Liu Sifu (Shifu), 339
Liu Shifu (Sifu), 339
Li Weiqing, 123, 125
Li Yueting, 286
Li Zirong, 186
Li Zongren, 295
Local Administration Advisory Office,
 266. *See also* Local officials
Local administrators, *see* Local officials
Local customs (*fengsu*), 71, 129f
Local government, 151–52, 162, 166, 199,
 308–10. *See also* Local officials; Local
 self-government
Local officials, 265–66, 308–9, 397.
 See also Local government; Local
 self-government
Local party branches, 307. *See also
 individual entries*
Local self-government, 148, 150, 162–67
 passim, 179. *See also* Elections; Feder-
 alist movement; Local government
Localism, in Guangdong, 15
London, Chinese students in, 58

Lone Sentry (Gujun), 273
Longchuan County, 307, 310–11
Looking Backward (Bellamy), 58–61, 358
Love (Ba Jin), 337
Lu Haodong, 181
Lu Liuyin, 188
Lu Rongting, General, 162–63, 199
Lu Xun, 57, 65–66, 101–3, 145–46, 357n123, 363n117–64
Lu Yongxiang (Governor of Zhejiang), 223
Luo Han, 281
Luo Qiyuan (peasant bureau head), 139, 289, 345–46, 393n81
Luther, Martin, 119
Lü Yanzhi, 1–2, 12, 27

Ma and Son (Er Ma) (Lao), 125, 365n26
Ma Chaojun, 218
Macartney, George, first Earl, 10–12, 40, 46–47, 51, 114, 133, 356
Magazines, 30–31, 59, 194, 208f, 277, 286ff, 311, 375, 381; of Nationalist party, 209; of women's movement, 284–85. *See also individual titles*
Magistrates, *see* Local government; Local self-government
Magruder, Major John, 147, 149
Mahayana Buddhism, *see* Buddhism
Man (ethnic group), 121
Manchu dynasty, *see* Manchurian people; Qing dynasty
Manchuria, 122
Manchurian people, 2, 180, 183–84
Mandarin language, 158. *See also* Dialects; Language reform
Manners, *see* Etiquette; Hygiene
Mao Dun (Shen Yanbing), 95–96, 238, 337, 343
Mao jacket, 23, 25. *See also* Sun Yatsen suit
Mao Zedong, 21, 23, 56, 63f, 136, 139, 186, 189–90, 229–41 *passim*, 245–49 *passim*, 255f, 321, 328–29, 337, 348, 364, 388n115–89n132; heads propaganda bureau, 7, 95, 213–14, 227, 233,

236–41, 252, 256, 285–86; promotes class struggle, 16, 254; and peasant movement, 19, 137, 250, 286; on awakening, 93; undermines opponents, 188, 212, 250, 252–54, 257–58; on mass line, 215, 345–46, 401n99; theoretical work, 318, 330–31, 341–43. *See also* Communists in Nationalist party; Factionalism; Propaganda Bureau, Central
Mao Zuquan, 204
Maps, 127, 368
Marcuse, Herbert, 340
Maritime Customs Service, 170
Market, as agent of revolutionary ideas, 56–57. *See also* Fashion
Marriage customs, 94, 160
Marx, Karl, 44, 79f, 90, 317, 324, 355. *See also* Marxism
Marxism, 5, 171, 229–30, 315–16, 325, 332, 341, 348, 361f. *See also* Marx, Karl; Marxism-Leninism
Marxism-Leninism, of early nationalists, 318, 347
Marxists, 171, 315, 341
Mass campaigns, 36–37
Mass organization, 287–89
Mass politics, 77, 174–75
Mass power (*qunli*), 175
Mass mobilization, and representation, 344–46
Mass-movements, 309
"Massification of the Nationalist Party and the Nationalist Partification of the Masses, The" (Ye), 174
Maugham, W. Somerset, 108
May Fourth movement, 13, 31, 48, 87, 92–94, 153–54, 191–96, 207–15 *passim*, 267, 331, 336; publications of, 96, 193, 195, 208–11, 381
May Thirtieth movement, 96, 144, 211, 268, 320–22, 336–37, 344
Meilu municipality, 274
Meisner, Maurice, 320
Meissner, Werner, 342

San Francisco, 241

Scholar-bureaucrats, 108-9. *See also* Bureaucrat class

Schools, 268-69, 286, 312, 390n24

Schram, Stuart, 250

Science, 52, 58

Scouts (Tongzi jun), 286

Script, 155, 157-58. *See also* Language reform

Second Army of the Nationalist Revolutionary Army, 296, 304

Second Revolution (1913), 181

Second National Congress of the Communist Party, 204

Second Nationalist Party Congress, 236f, 259, 288, 304

Second Northern Expeditionary Army, 295

Seeyup *(Siyi)* dialect, 158

Self, collective, 100

Self, revolution of the, 193

Self-Awakening Monthly (Zijue yuekan), 31

Self-awareness *(zijue)*, 193

Self-determination, 192f. *See also* Liberalism

Self-enlightenment, 192. *See also* Liberalism

Self-government *(zizhi)*, 192. *See also* Liberalism

Self-Government Personnel Training Institute (Guangdong), 167, 374

Sense of Determination Appropriate to the People of Guangdong Today, The (Wang), 311

Seth, Sanjay, 317

Sexual passion, 96-97

Shaanxi Province, 178

Shamian Island, foreign settlements on, 217, 247. *See also* Guangzhou–Hong Kong strike and boycott; Shamian massacre

Shamian massacre, 274-75, 248, 279, 322

Shandong, 4, 141, 191, 201

Shanghai, 19, 27, 52, 56, 194-97 *passim*, 218-23 *passim*, 249; and sign equating dogs and Chinese, 119-20, 123

Shanghai Central Cadre Council, 221

Shanghai Express (motion picture), 371

Shanghai Journalists Club, 208

Shanghai party branch, officers' strike in, 383

Shanghai party bureau, 219

Shanghai Republican Daily (Shanghai minguo ribao), 129, 174, 194, 201, 208-11, 220-24 *passim*, 242, 255, 369, 381

Shanghai Times (Shishi xinbao), 190

Shanghai University, 268

Shantou, 56, 151, 281

Shao Lizi, 211

Shao Yuanchong, 174, 225-26, 233-34

Shaoguan, 291

Sharanpur botanical gardens, 110

Shen Congwen, 131-32, 138, 369

Shen Dingyi, 209-10, 233-36, 263

Shen Yanbing, *see* Mao Dun

Shenbao, 208

Shenzen County branch, 241

Shimonoseki, Treaty of, 68, 359

Shu Feng, 212

Shuibei Upper-Primary School murder, 270

"Shuideren xingla" (Sleepers awaken) (Zhu), 354n15

Sibpur botanical gardens, 110

Singapore, 110

Sino-Japanese War, 48

Siu, Helen, 338

Sixth Army of the Nationalist Revolutionary Army, 295-96

Sketch Book, The (Irving), 58

Sleeper Wakes, The (Wells), 59

Sleeping, 41-44, 58, 94, 323-24, 327

Smith, Arthur, 129, 145-46

Sneevliet, Henk, 167, 176, 189, 206, 294, 380

Social conflict, 319

Zhou Enlai, 31, 227–32 *passim*, 240, 271, 273, 281–82, 301–2, 307–10
Zhou Fohai, 230–32, 241, 271, 273
Zhou Shimian, 302
Zhu Ciqi, 34, 69
Zhu Jiahua, 357n112
Zhu Zhixin, 268

Zhu Ziqing, 335, 338
Zijin County, 310–11
Ziren, pen name of Mao Zedong, 253, 388n115
Zola, Émile, 343
Zou Degao, 243
Zou Lu, 248–53 *passim*, 270–73, 281, 286

Library of Congress Cataloging-in-Publication Data

Fitzgerald, John, 1951–
    Awakening China : politics, culture, and class in the Nationalist
Revolution / John Fitzgerald.
        p.   cm.
    Includes bibliographical references and index.
    ISBN 0-8047-2659-0 (cl.)   :   ISBN 0-8047-3337-6 (pbk.)
    1. China—History—Republic, 1912–1928.   2. China—History—
Republic, 1928–1937.   3. Nationalism—China—History—20th century.
4. Intellectuals—China—History—20th century.   I. Title.
DS776.6.F58   1996
951.04—dc20
                                                                                96-565
                                                                                    CIP

⊚ This book is printed on acid-free, recycled paper.
Original printing 1996
Last figure below indicates year of this printing:
05   04   03   02   01   00   99   98